# The Bicentennial Guide to Greater Cincinnati:
## *A Portrait of Two Hundred Years*

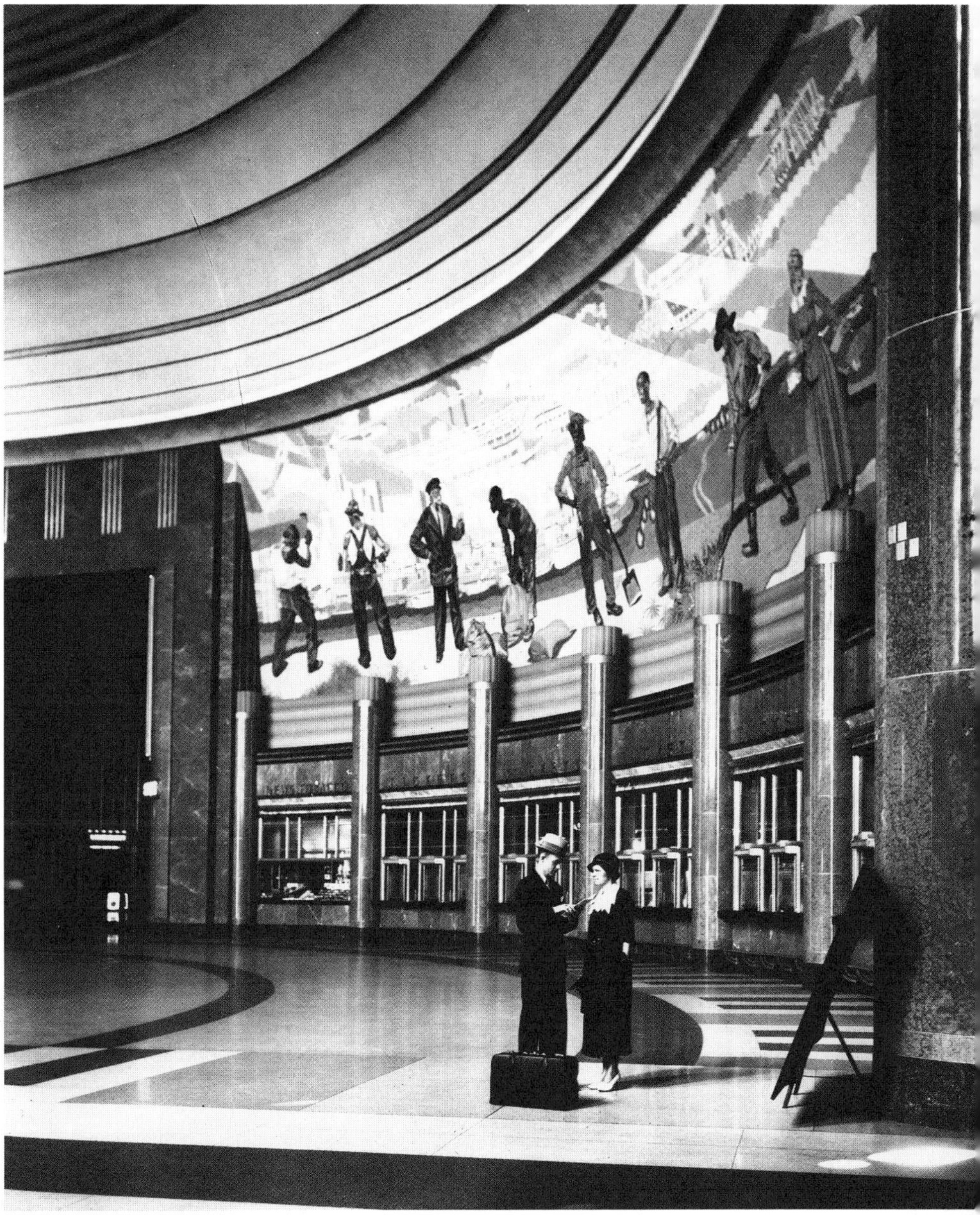

Researched and Published with the Support of:
Scripps Howard and
The National Endowment for the Humanities

A Project of the Greater Cincinnati Bicentennial Commission

*Steamboats and century-old commercial
buildings were still a familiar part of
Cincinnati's riverfront in the 1930s when
modern skyscrapers were creating a new
skyline for the city.*

# The Bicentennial Guide to Greater Cincinnati:
## *A Portrait of Two Hundred Years*

Geoffrey J. Giglierano

Deborah A. Overmyer

with Frederic L. Propas

The Cincinnati Historical Society
Cincinnati, Ohio 1988

*The Bicentennial Guide to Greater Cincinnati: A Portrait of Two Hundred Years* constitutes The Cincinnati Historical Society's principal contribution to the observance of the community's bicentennial. The Society gratefully acknowledges the support of The National Endowment for the Humanities, Scripps Howard, and The Greater Cincinnati Bicentennial Commission in making this publication possible.

Library of Congress Catalog Card
Number 88-72369

ISBN 0-911497-08-0
ISBN 0-911497-12-9 pbk.

**SCRIPPS
HOWARD**

Dear Friends,

Many Cincinnati companies have participated in the celebration of Cincinnati's 200th birthday. The Bicentennial Celebration has been not only a time to look back and recall our heritage, but also one to look forward to an even better place to live and work, learn and play. For us at Scripps Howard it seemed appropriate that we make a contribution in our chosen field, communications.

Scripps Howard, with interests in publishing, broadcasting, cable and sydication services, can trace its Cincinnati connections back a century. Its oldest local components are The Cincinnati Post, acquired in 1883, and The Kentucky Post, started in 1890. The company also is represented in this area by WCPO-TV and its own corporate headquarters.

Gale E. Peterson, director of the Cincinnati Historical Society, called to our attention The WPA Guide to Cincinnati, a book written during the depression years by the Federal Writers' Project of the Works Progress Administration. The last volume of the American Guide Series, Cincinnati: A Guide to the Queen City and Its Neighbors proved to be of great lasting value to those interested in Cincinnati history.

Published in 1943, The WPA Guide to Cincinnati has long been out of date and out of print but still is widely used as the best reference work of its kind. Mr. Peterson suggested that a reprint of the 1943 Guide would be an excellent contribution to the bicentennial year activities, and we agreed to fund it.

This still left a 45-year gap between 1943 and Cincinnati's 200th birthday, so Scripps Howard provided major funding to allow the Historical Society to begin work on a new guidebook, The Bicentennial Guide to Greater Cincinnati. Funds also were provided by the National Endowment for the Humanities.

We take pride in the work of the staff of the Cincinnati Historical Society. Several years and many hours of research, writing and editing have produced a book that will continue to serve the citizens of our metropolitan area for many, many years. We are happy to offer this gift to the citizens of Greater Cincinnati and Northern Kentucky and friends, wherever they are.

Use it and enjoy it.

*Charles E. Scripps*

Charles E. Scripps
Chairman of the Board
Scripps Howard

# Contents

► Staff

Geoffrey J. Giglierano, *Co-director, writer, photo editor*
Judith M. Daniels, *Editorial consultant*

Deborah A. Overmyer, *Co-director, writer, editor*

Frederic L. Propas, *Principal associate writer*

► Associate Writers

Robert A. Burnham
Gregory L. Rhodes

Bronwen M. Howells
Steven E. Siry

Anne Leonard

► Special Advisors

Jayne Merkel, *The Cincinnati Enquirer*

Thomas J. Schlereth, *University of Notre Dame*

► Advisory Board

Roger Daniels, *University of Cincinnati*
Zane L. Miller, *University of Cincinnati*

Raymond G. Hebert, *Thomas More College*
Abraham J. Peck, *American Jewish Archives*

Paul F. Knue, *The Cincinnati Post*
Henry D. Shapiro, *University of Cincinnati*

► The Greater Cincinnati Bicentennial Guide Project

Gale E. Peterson, *Executive Director, The Cincinnati Historical Society*
John E. Wolfzorn, *Treasurer, Scripps Howard*

Joseph S. Stern, Jr., *Chairman, The Greater Cincinnati Bicentennial Commission, Inc.*

William R. Burleigh, *Vice-president, Scripps Howard*

► Technical Assistance

Linda J. Bailey
Barbara J. Dawson
May Y. Hart
Mary Jane Neely
Jack Scally

Janine J. Bujak
Gail Finke
M. Eileen Lutz
The Reverend Christopher F. Neely

Laura L. Chace
Frances M. Forman
Judith L. Madsen
Sue Brunsman Painter

► Special Thanks To

Gail Arbino
John E. Burns
Betty M. Daniels
Joseph F. Gastright
Robert Jahnigen
Walter E. Langsam
Frederick J. Runk
Gregory Thorp
Margo Warminski

Michael R. Averdick
Christopher Cain
Bruce Ferguson
Robert C. Hahn
Charles D. King
Philip W. Overmyer
Richard Scamyhorn
Joseph Timmons
J. Miles Wolf

Christopher Burns
Judith G. Clabes
Ruth E. Fishback
Father Jerry Hiland
Leah Konicki
Genevieve H. Ray
Paul A. Tenkotte
Howard Todd
Raymond J. Zwick

► Design

Eberhard + Eberhard

Printing

Metropolitan Printing Company

Maps

Page Saver Studios

► Typesetting

Media Services, Cincinnati Milacron

# Introduction

When we began researching our community for *The Bicentennial Guide to Cincinnati: A Portrait of Two Hundred Years*, we often found people who would ask, "Why are you studying my neighborhood? It doesn't have any history!"

Their response was, in a way, understandable as we often regard the familiar places where we live, work, shop, learn, and worship as unremarkable or insignificant: "just old boarded up buildings", "an ordinary shopping center", "another run-down neighborhood", or "my poor old house with leaky plumbing."

But these pieces of our everyday environment all have some kind of story behind them. Often these stories are fascinating and are populated with characters who sometimes seem unusual and in other instances, familiar, even though these people lived long ago in the places we now live. Frequently, the stories behind different communities, institutions, businesses, or even individual homes are interwoven, so that understanding the background of one place gives insights into the development of another.

In the course of working on this book, we were frequently surprised and excited by the places and institutions we explored and studied. We hope that *The Bicentennial Guide to Greater Cincinnati* will aid its readers in making similar discoveries and that it will provide an informative, enjoyable, and practical means for better understanding how metropolitan Cincinnati has grown and changed over the past two hundred years.

*The Bicentennial Guide* was initially conceived of as an update of a book that has been a standard reference work on the city for more than forty years: *Cincinnati, A Guide to the Queen City and Its Neighbors*, published in 1943 and created by the Federal Writers' Project of the Works Projects Administration. This new guidebook, however, gradually evolved into a very different work.

*Evidence of the previous history of a building often survives on the upper stories. A garage in Brighton is crowned by this sheet metal sign that shows the structure was originally a meatpacking company's stable.*

While the old guide was essentially a portrait of Cincinnati and Northern Kentucky as the FWP writers saw it in the late 1930s and a catalogue of the significant and historic sites and buildings still existing at that time, *The Bicentennial Guide* takes a broader historical perspective, focusing on how the city and its component suburbs have developed and changed through time.

No attempt was made to rewrite the wonderful introductory essay that editor Harry Graff wrote for the 1943 guidebook. There was no reason to redo something that had been done so well and which is available in a 1987 reprint of the work by the Cincinnati Historical Society. And those who want a general overview of the city's entire history can find it in *Cincinnati: The Queen City*, which the Historical Society published in 1982. Consequently, there is no general introductory essay in the new guide at all.

Instead, this guidebook considers the metropolitan area—the city of Cincinnati and neighboring communities in Ohio and Northern Kentucky as far out as the I-275 circle freeway—in four sections. Different communities were placed in a particular section based upon geographical location as well as the time period and manner in which each developed. The first half of the book is made up of the basin—the downtown and the adjacent communities—and the older environs and suburbs. The second half is comprised of the streetcar, railroad, and automobile suburbs and the outlying communities.

Each of the two parts of the book begins with a portfolio of color photographs and a short introduction to explain how the communities described in that part of the book are related. These essays are followed by a series of chapters or tours, each of which covers a community or related group of communities in varying degrees of detail.

An overview essay at the beginning of each chapter lays out the basic story of the history and development of the area covered in that tour. This history is then illustrated and explained by essays about actual physical sites there — subdivisions, shopping centers, businesses, highways, railyards, villages, and institutions. These site essays are arranged in the form of a tour—one idea from the old guidebook that was retained—with maps and directions, so that readers can locate and visit them.

*The Bicentennial Guide to Greater Cincinnati* may not be what many readers expect. Some may be disappointed not to find certain well-known Cincinnati legends—the tunnels of the Underground Railroad, the first bathtub, washerwoman Ida Martin in her hollow tree, and others. Such tales have been told and retold elsewhere so there was no need to repeat them. In addition, while these stories do have their place in local folklore, they must be recognized as, at best, embroidered truths, and at worst, pure flights of fancy. On the other hand, this guidebook does include less well-known but documentable information about real Cincinnatians who are often more interesting than well-worn legends.

*Progress does not always require the destruction of remnants of the past. Although it has undergone considerable expansion and modernization in recent years, the Cincinnati Zoo has retained and renovated some its older facilities, including the 1905 Elephant House.*

*The Bicentennial Guide to Greater Cincinnati* is not an architectural guide to the city. Though architects and building styles are often mentioned, they are not the primary focus of the book. The Cincinnati chapter of the American Institute of Architects has begun a series of architectural guidebooks to the city and there is no reason to produce another.

Nor is the new guide an exhaustive inventory of every historic home, storefront, lamp post, and fire hydrant in the metropolitan area. Demands of space and time, and the desire to avoid too much repetition made it impossible to write about every interesting structure or each site where something significant once stood. And the tour format forced some sites to be dropped simply because there was no easy, practical, or safe way to get readers there.

An effort was made to include a representative and equitable number of sites in each tour. But the primary purpose of the site essays was to provide further details in the larger story of the community or to explain the site as a concrete example of the themes and concepts put forth in the overview that precedes it.

This volume is emphatically not merely a Baedeker's guide to Cincinnati with a historical twist. An inexpensive, short guidebook of that sort has already been produced for the bicentennial. Again, there seemed little value in duplicating another publication. Furthermore, a work focused only on Greater Cincinnati as it was in 1988 would soon become outdated. During the New Deal, the organizers of the Federal Writers' Project consciously rejected the Baedeker model—short entries, voluminous directions, and a focus on the present—in large part because they did not want their work quickly becoming obsolete. And just as the WPA's *Cincinnati Guide* has long been a standard reference tool on the history of Cincinnati and Northern Kentucky, *The Bicentennial Guide* is intended to serve on local history shelves for many years, even though the face of our city will quickly change as buildings disappear, streets are rerouted, and new structures are built.

There are a number of ways to use this book besides driving the tours. Reading an entire section or even the whole book would provide a sense of how the metropolitan area developed. The reader who takes on the book this way will discover patterns of population and industrial migration, and connections and relationships between various neighborhoods and municpalities.

But the tours, and even the individual overview and site essays, are written to stand on their own. Reading a single tour of a particular community or group of communities will provide a basic understanding of the history of those areas. Information on a certain building, business, individual, ethnic group, or institution can be located with the index. The index is the best means of cross-referencing a given subject through several tours: to track a certain church or company as it moved over time from one community to another.

The writers working on this project made extensive use of materials in the Cincinnati Historical Society's collections of maps, atlases, photographs, newspaper clipping files, insurance maps, developers' promotional pamphlets, municipal reports, census data, city planning documents, manuscripts, and church, community and business histories. Other valuable resources included the notes and drafts of the FWP

Cincinnati guidebook in the collections of the Ohio Historical Society, the Archives of the Roman Catholic Archdiocese of Cincinnati, current data from the Cincinnati Board of Education, and the historic preservation records of the City of Cincinnati and the City of Covington. Considerable time was also spent talking with local government officials, clergy, school officials, business people, and area residents.

Nonetheless, it is certain that there are omissions in *The Bicentennial Guide* and that some mistakes were not caught. Some readers may not agree with all the facts and dates as they are presented here, but a concerted effort went into making this work as accurate as possible. One of the greatest hopes for *The Bicentennial Guide to Greater Cincinnati* is that it will encourage those who read it to look more closely at their own neighborhoods and the buildings there. Anyone can learn to "read" the city and its artifacts—to find and decipher the physical clues to the stories behind our community and to understand more fully how those stories fit together.

Those who accept the notion that they and the communities where they live have no history hold a sadly mistaken view of their own communities—and of themselves. Perhaps *The Bicentennial Guide to Greater Cincinnati*, with its histories of well-known figures and "everyday" men and women can begin to demonstrate that *every* place is an historic site, *every* person is a unique and historic figure.

—Geoffrey J. Giglierano

*As neighborhoods change, new groups take over existing structures: the Southern Baptist Church in Avondale was once a synagogue.*

# The Basin and Older Suburbs

*Before the public transportation revolution of the midnineteenth century, Cincinnati—shown here in the 1840s—could not expand much beyond the basin.*

Topography has had a great impact on the development of Cincinnati. The city began in the basin—the level area between the Ohio River and a ring of hills. The flat ground here, most of which lay above flood level, invited settlement and was one of the advantages that allowed Cincinnati to grow faster than the nearby villages of Columbia and North Bend.

The surrounding hillsides initially discouraged further growth. But once cable cars, inclines, and streetcars facilitated travel up and down the slopes, many Cincinnatians moved out of the basin to a circle of hilltop suburbs including Price Hill, Fairview, and Mt. Adams which offered a cleaner, less crowded living environment. Starting in the midnineteenth century, institutions and industries also migrated out of the basin, the businesses seeking larger building sites and better transportation connections.

Cincinnati officials reclaimed the city's migrating population and industry through annexation. First, the city expanded to claim the basin and the surrounding hillsides, and then the nearby suburbs.

A similar process took place in Northern Kentucky communities on the opposite bank of the Ohio River. Newport and Covington developed on level ground by the Ohio, and subsequently spread up the hills and valies, in great part, to avoid the periodic flooding that afflicted the riverfront.

Although the metropolis continued to expand outwards, by the midtwentieth century, interest in the basin communites and the older suburbs began to revive. Government became concerned about the vitality and attractiveness of downtown areas and how that affected the entire metropolitan community. Individuals and developers gained a growing appreciation for the convenience, unique buildings, and special environments afforded by the older neighborhoods.

*The Ohio River bridges that join Cincinnati and Northern Kentucky vary widely in design, age, and appearance.*

*Although bulk cargoes requiring special terminal facilities were gradually becoming more common in the early twentieth century, the old Public Landing still accommodated numerous steamboats with passengers and freight.*

In recent years, the construction of sports facilities and the Bicentennial Commons at Sawyer Point have transformed the riverfront from an industrial and warehousing district into a recreational area.

In Covington, just a few miles away from Cincinnati's central business district, hundreds of historic nineteenth and early twentieth-century buildings have been preserved.

*In the downtown's eastern periphery are a number of historic older structures including the Taft Museum—a remnant of the wealthy residential neighborhood that once surrounded Lytle Park—and industrial buildings that were part of the manufacturing district that formerly extended to the foot of Mt. Adams.*

Plum Street North from 8th St., Cincinnati.

In the nineteenth and early twentieth centuries, the population of the downtown periphery supported numerous social and religious institutions such as these churches on the east side of Plum Street, which have since been torn down or converted to other uses.

Many Cincinnatians watched the Bicentennial parade from in front of Procter & Gamble's international headquarters complex, which covers several blocks on the eastern edge of downtown.

The architects of the telephone company building at Seventh and Elm Streets embellished their design with decorations that left no question as to who occupied the structure.

5

*Many Over-the-Rhine buildings, such as the first offices of Heinrich Rattermann's insurance company, still bear evidence of the German American culture that existed in that neighborhood.*

*One of the largest concentrations of nineteenth-century buildings to have survived in Cincinnati is in Over-the-Rhine.*

*Perhaps the most architecturally significant building in Greater Cincinnati is the Union Terminal—now the home of the Museum Center.*

*Rail passengers once waited to board trains at gates along the imposing Union Terminal concourse, which was demolished in the 1970s.*

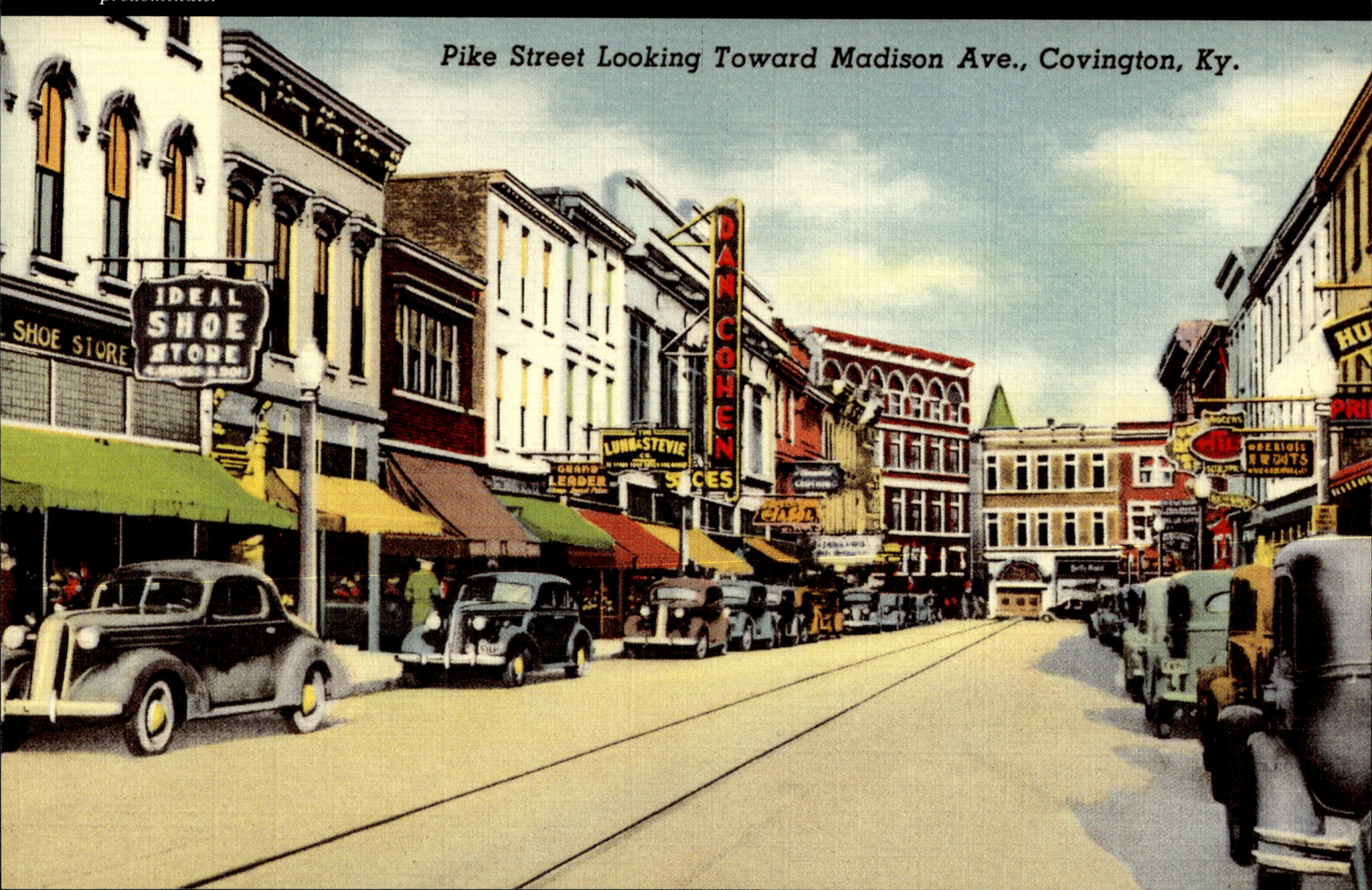

Downtown Covington was one of Greater Cincinnati's main retail districts before suburban shopping centers came to predominate.

Pike Street Looking Toward Madison Ave., Covington, Ky.

*The military post at Ft. Thomas in Northern Kentucky (shown here around the turn of the century) was the home of various regular army infantry units until World War II.*

*In the late nineteenth century, many well-to-do Newport residents built new homes like these on high ground less prone to flooding.*

9

*The view from Mt. Adams is one of the factors that has encouraged both new construction and renovation of the nineteenth-century working-class homes that cover the hillside.*

*The Gorham Worth house in Mt. Auburn is one of the city's oldest surviving "suburban" residences.*

*Many elegant old structures in Walnut Hills, particularly those near Eden Park, have been renovated in recent years for middle and upper-income homebuyers or tenants.*

*The demolition of the buildings that once covered the southern face of Mt. Adams and the construction of new roadways at its base caused sliding of the unstable hillside and necessitated construction of a massive, 60-foot high retaining wall.*

*The construction of Hughes High School on Clifton Avenue near U. C. was a part of the Cincinnati Public School system's expansion and modernization program in the early twentieth century.*

*Wealthy Clifton residents such as Henry Probasco engaged prominent local architects and artisans to design and decorate their opulent homes.*

*Despite the limited amount of available space, the University of Cincinnati has continued to expand and update its facilities.*

The Queensgate railyards spread over a large portion of the Mill Creek Valley to the west of Mohawk, Brighton, and Camp Washington.

Breweries, like the Sohn brewery in Mohawk, were often embellished with symbols of the trade.

*Northside residents of Irish descent were principally responsible for organizing the parish of St. Patrick and building this Gothic Revival style church on Blue Rock Street.*

*Camp Washington school children once attended classes at the Washington School, now scheduled for demolition to make way for road improvements.*

No. 766.  Fairmount Valley, Cincinnati, Ohio.

*In the early twentieth century, South Fairmount was a bustling industrial district, with factories and stores spread through the valley and workers' homes clustered on the hillsides.*

*St. Michael's in lower Price Hill, built in 1848, is one of the oldest churches in the basin still used for religious services.*

# The Basin

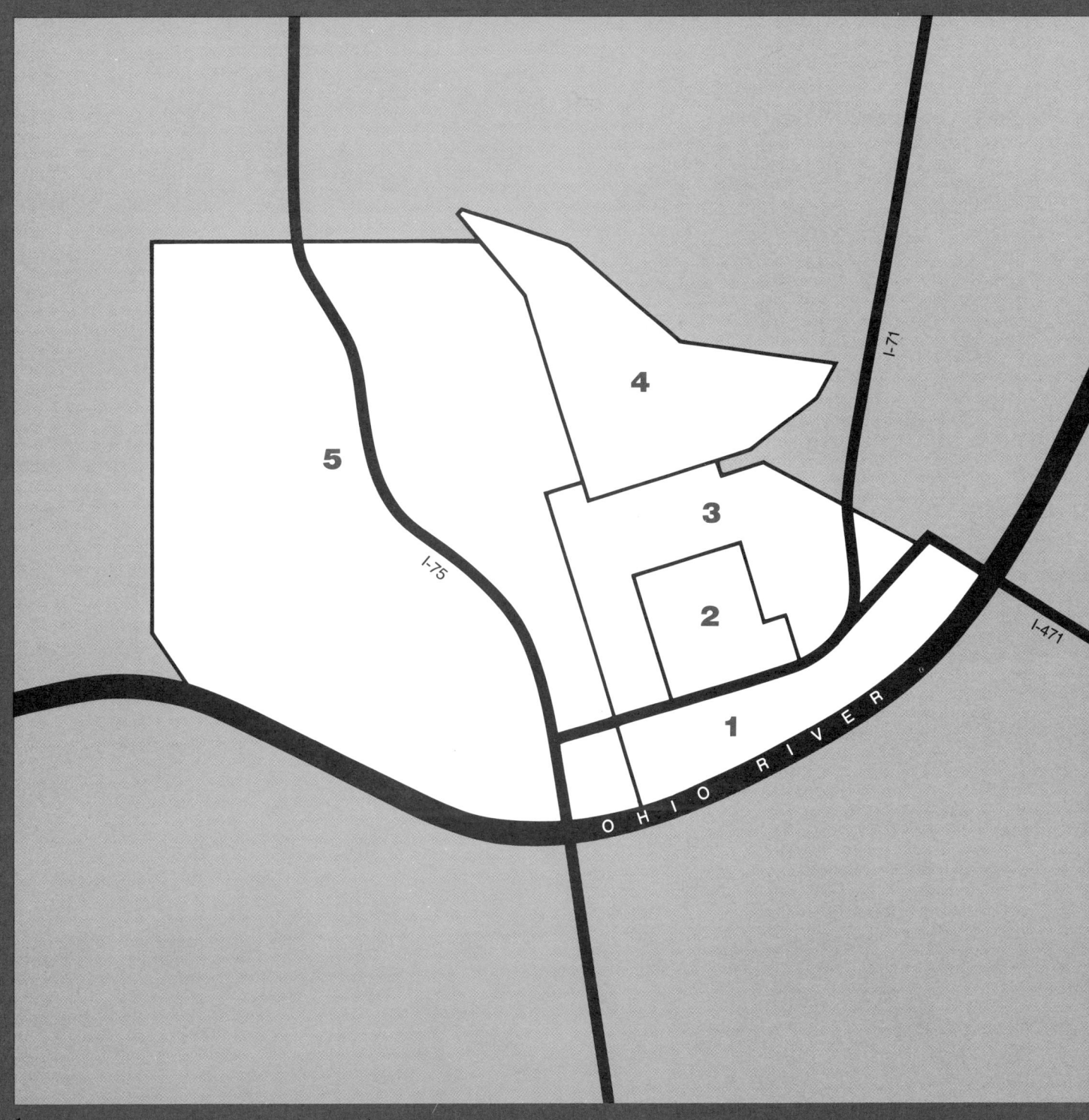

1
**Riverfront**

2
**Central Business District Core**

3
**Central Business District Frame**

4
**Over-the-Rhine**

5
**West End**

# Tour 1

# Riverfront

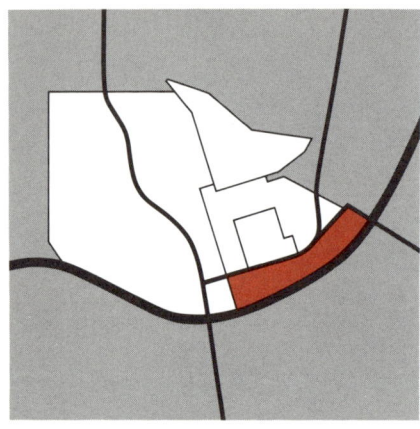

Although Cincinnati is now a regional metropolis dominating southeastern Ohio and the surrounding area, it began as a small Ohio River settlement. The riverfront, extending from the river's edge to Third Street between Central and Eggleston Avenues, defined the early community.

In September 1788, a party headed by Matthias Denman, John Filson, Israel Ludlow, Robert Patterson, and John Cleves Symmes sailed down the Ohio River. These men, mostly from New Jersey and Virginia, were land speculators, explorers, and adventurers. Three months later, on a date commonly accepted as December 28, 1788, Ludlow and a small group landed at the foot of what would later be Sycamore Street and established a permanent settlement that Filson named Losantiville.

Within a month, Ludlow surveyed the area from the river to Northern Row (Seventh Street) and from Western Row (Central Avenue) to Eastern Row (Broadway). The federal government erected Fort Washington at Losantiville in late 1789. On January 2, 1790, Arthur St. Clair, governor of the Northwest Territory, came to inspect the military post. St. Clair rechristened the town Cincinnati to honor the Society of the Cincinnati, an association of Revolutionary War officers, of which he was a founding member, that had taken its name from a Roman farmer-soldier.

After the Treaty of Greenville ended Indian warfare in 1795, Cincinnati, no longer a garrison town, became a thriving commercial village whose growth was tied to the Ohio River. The original proprietors of the town had laid out a large public landing on the river from Main Street to Broadway, and houses, stores, and taverns soon dotted the

*A series of 1848 daguerrotypes of Cincinnati's bustling riverfront shows a mix of homes, workshops, hotels, commission houses, boat outfitters, and warehouses.*

landing. In 1797, Griffin Yeatman built a tavern at Front and Sycamore Streets that, for the next several years, served the community as a city hall, courthouse, and registry.

By 1802, Cincinnati had 1,000 inhabitants and was incorporated as a town. A year later, the town's first commercial bank, the Miami Exporting Company, was organized to promote river trade with New Orleans. Fort Washington was dismantled in 1808, and the federally owned lands on which it stood were auctioned. By the second decade of the nineteenth century, Cincinnati was no longer an outpost but had become a regional center. The town's population reached 2,320 in 1810, and for the next several years would increase by 700 to 1,000 annually.

According to Daniel Drake, pioneer physician and the city's first chronicler, the town had a population of 6,000 in 1815 and had grown beyond Third Street. There were several churches along Fifth and Sixth Streets, a number of large homes, and a new courthouse at Court and Main Streets. In 1819, Cincinnati was incorporated as a city.

Increased prosperity came with the development of the steamboat and manufacturing; visionaries foresaw a network of roads, canals, and bridges with Cincinnati at its hub. In 1811, the *New Orleans* became the first steamboat to navigate the Ohio River, and by 1818, eighty steamboats, one quarter of which had been built in Cincinnati, were on the western rivers. While the banking crisis of 1819 shook the city's four banks and its infant industries—a foundry, woolen factory, glassworks, grist mill, and sugar refinery—it barely slowed the growth of what was emerging as the premier city on the Ohio River and in

the West.

By 1829, the Miami & Erie Canal linked Cincinnati to sources of raw materials and agricultural goods to the north and the west. Cholera epidemics in 1832 and 1833 took a terrible toll, and severe floods wiped out the area below Pearl Street (which was south of present-day Third Street), but the city quickly rebuilt. By 1840, Cincinnati's population had burgeoned to more than 46,000.

Despite this growth, Cincinnati's commerce and manufacturing were still centered along the riverfront. The city's major banks, including its largest, the Ohio Life Insurance & Trust Company Bank headed by Jacob Burnet, were clustered around Third Street, and its six insurance companies were all located close to the river, as were dozens of small taverns and boarding houses. Cincinnati's most prestigious hotels, including the Burnet House, were nearby.

In late 1841, the Little Miami Railroad began operating between Milford and Cincinnati. The railroads first served the river trade as the canals had earlier, and their terminals were located near the riverfront. But over the next two decades, railroads began to challenge rivers and canals as the primary means of commercial transportation. Cincinnati's rapid growth slowed as the river trade leveled off.

At mid-century, Cincinnati's riverfront was a substantial, active, and largely respectable area that was vital to the city's economy. On either side of the central riverfront and its busy offices and stores were factories and warehouses. To the west were coal and lumberyards, the gasworks, and the many small wood frame houses of black roustabouts who worked along the riverfront. To the east were numerous hotels, the waterworks, and the infamous Bucktown, an area of poverty and vice.

After the Civil War, as settlement pushed the western frontier beyond the Mississippi, the Ohio River ceased to be the most vital commercial link, and railroad networks tied the frontier to the East. Still, the regional river trade continued to grow, although the canal system did not. In 1863, the Miami & Erie Canal was filled in. As the riverfront assumed a more limited commercial role, many businesses and manufacturing firms moved from the flood zone to Fourth Street and beyond. The riverfront became a district of commission merchants, small manufacturers, wholesalers, warehouses, mills, and foundries, most of which were still tied to river transportation.

As early as the late 1830s, there had been talk of a bridge over the Ohio River, but rivermen, who feared that it would harm their trade, blocked plans to construct one. After years of delay, the Ohio legislature finally chartered the Covington & Cincinnati Bridge Company in 1849. Seven years later, work began on a suspension bridge designed by John A. Roebling.

The Panic of 1857 and the Civil War delayed completion of the span for another decade, however. Roebling's suspension bridge increased activity on the Cincinnati riverfront by linking it to the agricultural and manufacturing economy of Northern Kentucky, and contributed to the emergence of the riverfront as an area of transportation and warehousing.

As the riverfront ceased to be a prime commercial area, many factories and small shops were drawn to the area by available space and low rents. Above the businesses were cheap apartments that were home to the families of cigarmakers, rag pickers, ironmongers, manufacturing chemists, and rivermen.

On Pearl Street were the shops of many small manufacturers of ready-to-wear clothing, then Cincinnati's second largest industry. Only along Pearl and Third Streets between Sycamore and Main were there still substantial retail shops, banks, brokers, and insurance companies that recalled the era when the river was central to Cincinnati's growth.

Reflecting the slow deterioration of the riverfront, many shops and buildings throughout the area stood vacant. As the city expanded beyond the basin, those who could do so—both individuals and businesses—left the riverfront with its aging structures so often battered by floods. But for all the area's notoriety as a slum, only 6,000 people lived here at the turn of the century, a fraction of the number then living in the West End.

During the first third of the twentieth century, most of Cincinnati's major banks moved from Third Street to skyscrapers on Fourth Street. As a result of railroad bottlenecks during World War I, river trade picked up in the 1920s. At the same time, a few older buildings on the riverfront were cleared to make way for sturdier, fire resistant structures, including several produce warehouses and the offices of the Cincinnati Gas & Electric Company.

In the late 1920s, as more downtown office workers began driving to their jobs, owners of old riverfront buildings found that they could make more money from parking lots than from half-vacant factories, stores, or tenements. Gas stations and repair shops also opened around these lots. Between 1900 and 1920, with new construction and the demolition of older buildings, the riverfront's population declined by 1,700. By 1940, the area had barely half the number of people who lived here at the beginning of the century.

In the late 1930s, city planners noted the decline of riverfront property values, the large amount of undeveloped land, the high rate of vacancy in old buildings, and traffic congestion. City officials feared that the blight of the waterfront would drive commerce away from the central business district. The 1939 *Redevelopment Plan for the Central Riverfront* was the result of these concerns. World War II delayed renewal efforts, but the 1948 *Metropolitan Master Plan* presented a program to transform the riverfront into a recreational area. Although twenty years would pass before these plans were realized, the riverfront today is, to a great extent, the product of mid-century planning.

To solve traffic problems, planners proposed rebuilding the Suspension Bridge and the approaches to the Central and C&O bridges, filling in and widening the area between Second and Third Streets, and constructing a roadway that would collect and distribute downtown traffic.

The major concern, however, was redevelopment of potentially valuable land along the river that was convenient to downtown but subject to flooding. The city did not wish to encourage riverfront industry, nor did officials want the grocery and produce warehouses to remain. Instead, they looked to the riverfront in terms of recreation, luxury housing, and tourism. Through the 1950s, City Hall and several advisory boards debated a series of plans for riverfront redevelopment. Work finally got under way in 1962 when voters approved a $6.6 million bond

*Around 1960, a considerable portion of the old riverfront district was demolished to make way for road improvements, particularly Fort Washington Way.*

issue, matched by a $14.5 million federal grant.

A major element of renewal was a baseball stadium intended to replace Crosley Field in the West End. After attendance at the new stadium proved that people would come to the riverfront for recreation, plans were made for shops and promenades linked to a convention center and to hotels, apartments, and parks. A series of disguised terraces and levees, such as the Serpentine Wall, were to protect these facilities from flooding. Some buildings were to be constructed on stilts with parking underneath, while the stadium's floodgates were designed to withstand all but the highest waters.

Because of opposition to the relocation of the produce markets, almost all planning for the riverfront centered on the eastern portion of the area. Riverfront Coliseum and a luxury high-rise apartment building were constructed here, as were parks at Yeatman's Cove and Sawyer Point. More extensive plans for museums and a convention center were not realized.

Instead, in the 1980s, the City of Cincinnati and the Bicentennial Commission began work on the Bicentennial Commons at Sawyer Point, a "premier" park to be dedicated for the city's two hundredth birthday celebration. The $15 million park includes a plaza featuring a statue of Lucius Quintus Cincinnatus, a dining plaza, a promenade, the Procter & Gamble Performance Pavilion, a geological riverwalk, and three river overlooks. East of the I-471 bridge, the park features an exercise area, a children's play area, tennis and volleyball courts, a fishing pier, an amphitheater built around the foundations of the city's first waterworks, and the first outdoor, year-round plastic ice skating rink in the United States.

The park also features several sculptures, including "Law and Society" and another work representing various aspects of Cincinnati's history. One portion with four winged pigs emerging from riverboat smokestacks—a reminder of the importance of porkpacking and river trade—aroused the opposition of many who felt that it presented and undignified image of the city. The park was also designed to connect with the Sawyer Place high-rise apartment complex to be developed at the foot of Mt. Adams.

West of the Suspension Bridge, the produce warehouses, empty railroad freight depots, coalyards, and utilities are reminders of earlier years when the riverfront was a center for transportation and warehousing.

North

Start

End

**Riverfront**

Tour Length
3.5 miles

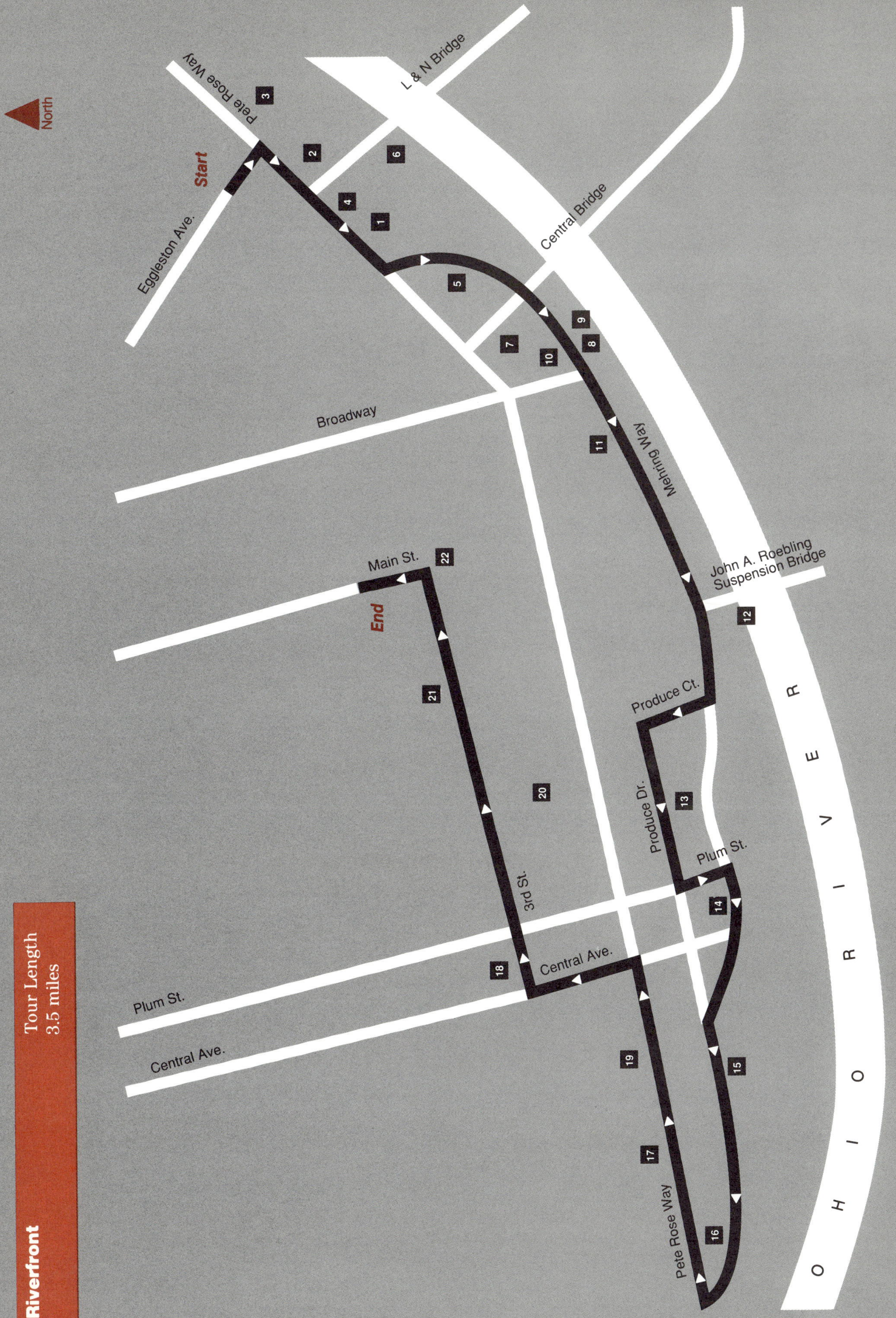

Pete Rose Way

Eggleston Ave.

L & N Bridge

Central Bridge

Broadway

Mehring Way

John A. Roebling
Suspension Bridge

Main St.

3rd St.

Produce Ct.

Produce Dr.

Plum St.

Central Ave.

Plum St.

Central Ave.

Pete Rose Way

O  H  I  O     R  I  V  E  R

1
2
3
4
5
6
7
8
9
10
11
12
13
14
15
16
17
18
19
20
21
22

23

# Riverfront

▶ ▶ ▶ ▶ ▶

*Tour begins at the foot of Eggleston Avenue. Park to look at the parks and waterworks ruins.*

The parks at **1 Yeatman's Cove** and **2 Sawyer Point** provide a perspective of the riverfront, present and past. From here, a few remaining nineteenth-century buildings and the old waterworks are visible, as are newer recreational areas.

Across Pete Rose Way (Second Street, renamed in 1986 to honor the Cincinnati Reds manager), George's Tavern, a simple brick structure, dates from the mid-1850s when the rear portion of the building was constructed. The part facing the street, added in the 1870s, is the last mid-nineteenth-century building remaining in the vicinity.

Close to the river, the ruins uncovered by park excavations are all that remain of the old **3 Front Street Pumping Station of the Cincinnati Water Works**. This building and another housed a series of steam pumps. Although other pumping stations were built upstream after 1865, the Front Street station remained in service into the first decade of the twentieth century.

In 1817, the City of Cincinnati granted the Cincinnati Manufacturing Company an exclusive franchise to replace a number of private water systems. Three years later, the company defaulted on its commitments, and its charter was sold to Samuel W. Davies. By the following July, Davies was delivering water as far as Pearl Street, but he never made much money at it.

In 1824, a cylinder taken from the steamboat *Vesta* was used to pump water, but its purchase and installation to replace an animal-turned pump ruined Davies financially. His proposal that the city purchase the waterworks was overwhelmingly rejected by Cincinnati voters. Only in 1839 did citizens finally approve city purchase of the waterworks.

In the mid-nineteenth century, the passenger and freight depots of the Little Miami Railroad were located near here. Later, the area was used for scrap metal yards and parking.

In 1960, the city acquired two and one-quarter acres on Front Street between Broadway and Sycamore,

once the site of Griffin Yeatman's tavern, for the first Yeatman's Cove park. It was built in 1962 with the aid of the Cincinnatus Association, but in the late 1960s, the park was cleared to make way for Riverfront Stadium.

Work began on a new Yeatman's Cove park east of the first location in 1971, and the present park, designed by Zion & Breen, opened five years later. The park includes the stepped Serpentine Wall at the river's edge and a concrete pool and fountain that leads up to a green. During floods, this area serves as a levee and retaining wall.

While the second Yeatman's Cove park was under construction, riverfront planners sought funds for a larger recreational development to the east that would include a stage, a fishing pier, play areas, and a show and exhibit arcade. These plans were slow to materialize until a gift of one million dollars from Cincinnati philanthropist Charles Sawyer allowed initial development of the park, jogging trails, and a parcourse. Completion of the park, aided by contributions from the city's business community, became a major part of Cincinnati's bicentennial celebration.

Plans to develop a commercial and residential complex east of Sawyer Point have been opposed by residents of Mt. Adams who fear the buildings will undermine the hill and that high-rise development will block their view of the river and the city.

*Return to Eggleston Avenue. Turn left on Pete Rose Way.*

The offices of **4 The Midland Company,** 537 Pete Rose Way East, have served a number of riverfront businesses. The structure was designed by Rendigs, Panzer & Martin and constructed in 1928 for Cincinnati Wholesale Grocery Company, a marketing cooperative formed thirty years earlier by local independent grocers. The top story was added in 1938. This building continued as headquarters for the company, which became White Villa, until 1964 when the firm moved to Dayton.

The next occupant was Atkins & Pearce, which lost its headquarters at Fifth and Eggleston where it had been since 1846 to the construction of the I-471 bridge. The company was

founded in 1817 and now manufactures fiberglass electrical insulation. In early 1986, Atkins & Pearce moved to a larger, more modern Northern Kentucky facility that offered better access to transportation.

The building was then sold to the Midland Company, founded in 1938, which finances and insures manufactured housing. In 1968, Midland founded MG Transport. The company operates ten diesel-powered tow boats and 366 barges along the Ohio and Mississippi rivers. It is the tenth largest river transporter in the United States, although a fraction of the size of the industry leader, the Ohio River Company.

Midland purchased the 60-year-old White Villa building because, even after remodeling and exterior improvements, costs were half of what new downtown construction would have entailed.

*Turn left on Mehring Way.*

With approximately 375 occupants, **5 One Lytle Place,** 621 Mehring Way, has more than tripled the residential population of the riverfront.

Ever since the 1948 *Metropolitan Master Plan*, the city has wanted to encourage residential development downtown, feeling that it would maintain the vitality of the central business district after working hours. Lytle Place was built with federal assistance and opened in July 1980.

For the first few years, the building was partially vacant and lost money. Beginning in 1983, however, the concept of downtown high-rise living seemed to gain acceptance, and several large downtown businesses bought units to house executives in Cincinnati here on short-term assignments. Most of the building's residents are upper-income professionals who value easy access to downtown via shuttle and the building's amenities, including exercise facilities. About 15% of the tenants are retired.

The lower floors of Lytle Place include 27,000 square feet of commercial space, but typical "neighborhood" services, such as banks, beauty and barber shops, convenience stores, and dry cleaners, have not located here, largely because the number of possible customers is too small.

The **6 L&N Bridge** and the **7 Central Bridge,** completed in 1872 and 1891, respectively, illustrate the history of transportation across the Ohio River. Initially, the only means of crossing the river was by ferry, but the growth of Cincinnati and Northern Kentucky communities made a more efficient and direct connection necessary. This need was first met by the opening of the Roebling Suspension Bridge to vehicular traffic in 1867.

A year later, the Louisville & Nashville Railroad, seeking a link to eastern markets, began planning a railroad bridge at Cincinnati, only the fourth to span the Ohio. Jacob Linville (1825-1907), chief engineer of the L&N, designed a truss-type bridge which carried a single set of tracks, a walkway, and a road. Although riverboat interests delayed the bridge's opening, by the 1880s, the L&N connected Cincinnati directly to the Gulf of Mexico.

By 1895, the volume of rail and wagon traffic made reconstruction of the bridge necessary, and a new rail line, a pedestrian thoroughfare, and a roadway were added. The 1897 bridge, a 4-truss structure designed by M.J. Becker, also carried two streetcar tracks—marking the spread of the city's suburbs into Northern Kentucky. In 1904, the L&N bought the bridge from its operators, the Newport & Cincinnati Bridge Company, and in 1935, the Kentucky State Highway Commission bought the roadway.

Cincinnati's third bridge, the Central Bridge, named for its location between the Roebling and the L&N, was opened with much local fanfare on August 29, 1891. Designed and built by the King Iron & Bridge Company of Cleveland, the Central Bridge has two 254-foot spans, a 520-foot central span, and trusses and girders for 555 feet. It originally carried two roadways with two streetcar tracks below them. Like the earlier bridges, the Central Bridge aided regional commerce by efficiently carrying goods and people across the river.

In 1947, the Kentucky Highway Commission bought the bridge from the Broadway & Newport Bridge Company, paying $950,000 for the structure which in 1891 had cost $1.3 million. The bond issue that allowed the purchase included $50,000 for repairs. The Commonwealth retired those bonds in 1953 when the bridge's toll booths were removed.

Over the years, engineers have expressed concern about the structural integrity of the Central Bridge, and Ohio and Kentucky have quarreled over its maintenance. In 1970, its weight limit was reduced because of deterioration. Federal funds have been allocated to replace the Central Bridge, and a new bridge is scheduled for completion in 1992.

Only a few hundred feet of the **8 Public Landing,** which once stretched from Main Street to Broadway and north to Front Street, remain. And only the **9 Showboat Majestic,** docked here, recalls the riverboats which once were the city's economic lifeblood.

Recognizing that the river was central to the development of Cincinnati, the city's founders set aside a public landing, and the city later maintained wharves here. The landing became increasingly important to the city's commerce with the development of steamboats in the first part of the nineteenth century. Between 1826 and 1834, wharfage fees collected by the city more than tripled, from $2,200 to $6,900.

The growth of Cincinnati's riverport, as measured by revenues, was much slower through the early 1840s, but fees jumped from $10,000 to $14,000 just before the Mexican War of 1846-1848. They went from about $15,000 to $19,000 in the mid-1850s, when nearly a third of revenues was being paid out for salaries, services, and supplies connected to wharf operations.

As Cincinnati's river trade leveled off in the late 1850s and began to decline, some members of city government contemplated expanding the wharves to attract commerce. Instead, the city began to rent private wharves, rather than maintaining public ones. By the 1870s, wharf revenues barely exceeded expenditures. A decade later, income from wharfage was below what it had been half a century earlier and was exceeded by costs. The municipal wharves and landing had become an economic liability.

Although the public landing has not been central to Cincinnati's economy since after the Civil War, it has been important for recreation. Through the early twentieth century, a number of private interests, including the Greene Line excursion boats, operators of the *Delta Queen*, and Billy Bryant's showboat, relied on the landing and urged the city to maintain it.

The 1948 *Master Plan* retained the landing as well as a "boat harbor and esplanade," but in the 1960s, when riverfront redevelopment got underway, the city began whittling away at the landing. By the end of the decade, only the *Delta Queen*, a floating restaurant, and the *Showboat Majestic* remained. Today, only the *Majestic* is moored at the landing.

Built in 1923 by Captain Thomas Jefferson Reynolds, the *Majestic* came after the days of the great showboats. Still, for fifteen years it toured the Ohio, Kentucky, Tennessee, and Green rivers. From 1939 to 1948, the boat was unused, but from then until 1967, it was operated by a series of colleges and universities. Since 1967, the City of Cincinnati, which bought the *Showboat Majestic* for $13,500, has leased it to the University of Cincinnati for summer theater. The boat has been at the landing since 1969.

Another part of the redevelopment of the riverfront for recreation has been the location of two sports facilities here. Conceived of in 1973 and opened two years later, the **10 Cincinnati Riverfront Coliseum** was built as an indoor concert hall and sports arena. The building has not had a steady tenant, particularly since Cincinnati has failed to attract a National Basketball Association franchise.

Professional hockey and soccer teams have played here occasionally, but the main draw has been college basketball games and tournaments, popular music concerts, and traveling shows. The Coliseum's history is marred by the 1979 Who concert, when eleven people were trampled in a rush for seats. The tragedy ended so-called festival seating at the facility.

The idea for a riverfront sports facilities was born with the 1948 *Master Plan*. But, like so much of the plan, **11 Riverfront Stadium,** 201 Pete Rose Way East, was slow to develop, and when it finally materialized, was somewhat different than originally envisioned.

The greatest obstacle to building the stadium was disagreement between the city and the Cincinnati Reds, its major tenant. Reds management feared that a downtown stadium, as opposed to one in the suburbs, would have the same problems that the club already faced with Crosley Field in the West End: unfavorable location and inadequate parking.

In the late 1960s, a change in management and the prospect of a new football franchise convinced Reds officials and city government to agree on a new stadium. It was designed by Heery & Heery of Atlanta and cost about $52 million; much of the money was raised by county revenue bonds after private efforts got the project started.

Opened in the middle of the 1970 baseball season, Riverfront Stadium seats approximately 55,000. It is home to the Reds, whose "Big Red Machine" won the 1970 and 1972 National League pennants and the 1975 and 1976 World Championships, and the Cincinnati Bengals, who won a divisional title in 1970, made the National Football League play-offs in 1973 and 1975, and lost the 1981 Super Bowl to the San Francisco 49ers.

Riverfront Stadium is also site for concerts and a popular summer jazz festival. Because of its size and architecture, Riverfront Stadium dominates the new riverfront both physically and economically—an apt replacement for the public landing in an era when sports and entertainment hold almost the same importance in the city's economy as the river trade once did.

"It broke upon us all at once, the stateliest and most splendid evidence of genius, enterprise, and skill it has ever been my lot to see." Thus wrote Thomas Kinsella, editor of the *Brooklyn Eagle*, in 1869 when John A. Roebling brought a group of New Yorkers, considering a bridge for New York City, to see the Covington & Cincinnati Suspension Bridge. Officially renamed the **12 John A. Roebling Suspension Bridge** in 1983, this span, begun in late 1856 and completed in 1867, is more than an architectural or historic landmark. Its curves and cables stir local pride and affection as later, more utilitarian truss bridges never could.

As early as 1815, Daniel Drake discussed the possibility of a bridge across the Ohio in his *Picture of Cincinnati*. In February 1846, the Kentucky General Assembly granted

*John Roebling's suspension bridge contributed to closer economic and social ties between Cincinnati and Northern Kentucky.*

a charter to the Covington & Cincinnati Bridge Company, and in September, the company accepted a set of plans for a suspension bridge submitted by Roebling.

While Kentuckians eagerly sought such a bridge, Ohio River interests fought it. Such a structure, they argued, would impede navigation, cause ice jams and floods, draw Cincinnati's business to the south, and aid escaping slaves. After rejecting several bridge projects, the Ohio legislature finally granted the bridge company a charter on March 29, 1849, but the next year, a rider was attached that did not allow the bridge to be built in line with any existing Cincinnati street.

Undeterred, the bridge company began to raise money for the project, and in August 1856, Roebling signed a contract. For the foundation, thirteen layers of oak beams were bolted together, covered with concrete, and sunk into the limestone river bed. On this base, limestone towers were built before work halted first for the winter and then because of the Panic of 1857.

Work began again in 1863, spurred by the need to build a pontoon bridge to transport Union troops defending Kentucky. Wartime shortages forced Roebling to import wire for the bridge's cables from England, and inflation forced him to pay workers in gold. Despite strike threats,

construction proceeded, and on September 4, 1865, a small footbridge to be used by workers stringing cable was completed.

On December 1, 1866, the Suspension Bridge was opened to pedestrians, and on the first two days, more than 120,000 people paid the three cent toll to cross the bridge. On New Year's Day 1867, Roebling and Amos Shinkle (1818-1892), a Covington coal baron who had tirelessly promoted the project, linked arms and led a parade across the Suspension Bridge, officially opening it to vehicles.

The Covington & Cincinnati Suspension Bridge cost nearly $1.8 million. It used one million pounds of wire for the cables and 600,000 feet of oak plank for the floor. The bridge measured 1,057 feet between the 230-foot high towers, and 1,619 feet between the shore anchors. In 1896, Roebling's bridge was given a second set of cables, new trusses and anchors, a wider roadway, streetcar rails, direct approaches, and electric lights.

During the Flood of 1937, the Suspension Bridge, its approaches protected by sandbags, was the only crossing over the Ohio River for more than 800 miles from Steubenville, Ohio to Cairo, Illinois.

In 1955, the Commonwealth of Kentucky bought the bridge and replaced the wood floor with a metal grating that gives off a distinctive hum when tires roll over it. Toll booths were removed in December 1963.

In 1968, the Kentucky Department of Highways declared the Suspension Bridge "functionally obsolete" and "subject to closing." If correct in terms of modern efficiency, this assessment underestimated local attachment to a landmark.

The bridge was placed on the National Register of Historic Places in 1975, and the following year was painted blue for the nation's bicentennial. The Roebling Bridge was illuminated with a string of sodium vapor lights on September 3, 1984, to honor the memory of Julia Langsam (1905-1984), president of the Covington and Cincinnati Bridge Committee.

**Turn right on Produce Court, one block west of Stadium Drive, and left on Produce Drive.**

In the first quarter of the twentieth century, a marketplace for fruits and vegetables developed along Front Street between Plum and Vine Streets. Although some wholesalers have since moved away, the **13 Produce Drive Warehouses** still represent Cincinnati's produce market as it existed through much of the past century. Many of these firms, today run by third generation family members, were founded by Italian immigrants who had been farmers and in this country became fruit peddlers, then shopkeepers, and finally wholesalers.

Though the riverfront developed as a wholesale district in the nineteenth century, the produce trade did not center here until the 1920s. Construction of a new United Fruit Auction building, now used by Sanzone-Palmisano, drew fruit and vegetable wholesalers from the Sixth Street market and from the area around Broadway and Second Street. Seeking ample space, access to railroads, and low property values, a great many of Cincinnati's produce jobbers moved to the river bottoms and took over grain warehouses with enclosed railroad sidings where perishable cargoes could be protected. Cincinnati quickly became a regional produce market, serving the area for 500 miles around.

After World War II, despite the economic importance of the produce market, city planners tried to move it to make way for commercial and recreational redevelopment. They ran into fierce opposition from the produce merchants and the railroads

that served them. Within a few years, however, refrigerated trucks and interstate highways replaced the railroads.

Today, trucks transport 95% of the nation's fruits and vegetables, and the produce industry is no longer linked to the river bottoms and the railroads. Many of the largest firms, such as Castellini and Crosset, are increasingly involved in preparing fruits and vegetables for food service institutions and have large warehouses outside the city.

**Turn left on Plum Street, right on Mehring Way.**

The riverfront emerged as a center for wholesale trade and warehousing largely because of its proximity to the river and later the railroad yards. By the early twentieth century, trucks had also become an important means of transportation. In 1924, the Taft family built the Cincinnati Terminal Warehouse, now the **14 Cincinnati Commercial Warehouse,** 49 Central Avenue at Mehring Way, as a truck warehouse.

The brick building was constructed with a reinforced concrete frame and roof. Its support pillars were sunk ninety feet into the ground, and the entire structure, including a 9-story central office block, was designed to survive periodic flooding.

At the time of its construction, the buff brick 7-story warehouse with 750,000 square feet of floor space was the largest public warehouse east of the Mississippi. It included freezer storage, refrigerated and dry space, as well as display and office areas.

Taft interests continued to operate the warehouse until 1972. In 1980, the Castellini and Squeri produce companies bought the warehouse and now operate it as a public warehouse where anyone may rent space. The warehouse serves approximately 4,000 customers who store items ranging from luncheon meats to light bulbs.

The riverfront was also a site for the city's early utilities, not only the waterworks, but a plant where electricity was generated and gas was produced from coal brought downriver from Pennsylvania and West Virginia. The **15 Cincinnati Gas &**

**Electric West End Power Station,** 649 Mehring Way West, stands on the 3½-acre site near where that company's first gas holding and distribution tank was built in the 1840s.

In 1837, a group of investors headed by Warner Hatch obtained a charter from the Ohio legislature to provide gas service to Cincinnati. Already, several other cities such as Baltimore, New Orleans, and Louisville had gas for lighting and industrial use, but another four years were to pass before James F. Conover and James H. Caldwell formed the Cincinnati Gas-Light & Coke Company and were granted an exclusive franchise to provide gas to the city for the next twenty-five years.

By the early 1840s, Conover and Caldwell were distilling gas from coal near Front and Rose Streets. In 1843, the city's first gaslights were installed, and by 1850, when the prestigious Burnet House at Third and Vine Streets was gas lit, the company served more than 2,500 customers. By 1870, the gas company was serving one Cincinnati family in four.

In 1883, the Cincinnati Electric Light Company began generating electricity for lighting. By the end of the decade, the Gas-Light Company had taken over the electric light company and built an electrical generating plant at Front and Rose Streets. After a decade of nearly ruinous competition with the Edison Company, the Cincinnati Gas & Electric Company (CG&E) was formed in 1901 when the rivals merged.

The Front and Rose site was used for the manufacture, storage, and distribution of gas until after World War I. In 1907, CG&E bought its first natural gas, piped in from West Virginia, and two years later stopped manufacturing gas except in emergencies.

After 1918, a new electrical plant was built on this site, and slowly the company began to dismantle the old gasworks. In 1959, the last two gas holders, including tank Number One, dating back to the 1840s, were torn down. The electrical facility continued to generate power until 1976. In 1983, the company took down the last generator at this site.

According to popular belief, the great era of river transportation passed with the steamboats. In fact, the Ohio River has remained a major

*The Cincinnati Gas-Light & Coke Company began operating this coal-gas production and storage facility on Front Street in the western riverfront during the early 1840s.*

industrial artery, and the Ohio River Company, headquartered in Cincinnati, is the largest shipper on United States inland waterways. Founded in 1925 as a wholly-owned subsidiary of West Virginia Coal & Coke Corporation, the company hauls coal for utilities and industries along the river. One of its largest customers has been CG&E. Shipments of coal to CG&E's Front and Rose plant and to smaller local customers were delivered to the **16 Loading and Unloading Facility of the Ohio River Company,** 725 Mehring Way West, now used only for storage.

During World War I when the railroads could not meet the demands for transporting goods, the federal government promoted river shipping, which had all but died out. It contrast to the colorful steamboats of the nineteenth century, the new river traffic consisted of barges under tow.

After the war, electrical generating and heavy industrial plants discovered that coal could be shipped more cheaply along the river than over land. Between 1931 and 1950, river traffic, measured in ton-mileage, increased almost fivefold. During this period, the Ohio River Company increased its tonnage from 400,000 to nearly 6 million. By 1986, the Ohio River Company carried more than 42 million tons of commodities a year; 70% of the tonnage was coal.

In the 1980s, however, river traffic stopped growing. Many old "smokestack" industries that used to burn coal shut down, and environmental regulations forced many utilities to use low-sulfur coal shipped from the west by rail or truck. According to Ohio River Company officials, river trade now grows only 2% per year.

**Make a hard right onto Pete Rose Way where it intersects Gest Street.**

Because the Ohio River continued

to be a vital link in the nation's transportation system, Cincinnati's railroads have generally built their terminals near the river. By the turn of the century, most passenger rail service went through Central Union Depot on Third Street between John and Smith, the Big Four Terminal at Third and Central, or the L&N station at Pearl and Butler. Most of the railroads had their freight depots near the river as well.

The riverfront continued to serve rail passengers until 1933, when Cincinnati Union Terminal replaced Central Union Depot. By then, too, the railroads began to abandon the riverfront, and the old freight depots were adapted to other uses or torn down. The largest remaining freight terminal in the area is the **17 Baltimore & Ohio Southwestern Railway Freight Depot,** now called Longworth Hall, 700 Pete Rose Way West.

As early as 1873, the Marietta & Cincinnati Railroad built a freight office at Second and Smith Streets. By the 1880s, the railroad, reorganized as the Cincinnati, Washington & Baltimore, was under the control of the B&O which built a large terminal on Second, stretching from Park to Rose Streets. Around 1904, the B&O set out to become the largest freight handler in the tri-state area and replaced its first terminal with one that was almost a quarter of a mile long, five stories high, and forty-eight feet wide.

For much of its history, the building was a private railroad freight terminal, but as early as 1927 a portion of the building was rented out, and during the Great Depression, falling revenues forced the railway to lease out more space. The building became the property of the Chessie System after the 1963 merger of the B&O and the Chesapeake & Ohio Railroads. Until 1981, the railroad

continued to use the building along with other tenants. After that, the depot was leased to a merchandise distributor.

In 1985, faced with the need to undertake extensive renovations, Chessie sold the building to a local partnership that renamed it Longworth Hall. The renovated warehouse opened in 1987 as a design center where manufacturers display furniture and interior design products to architects and designers. There is also meeting and exhibition space, a restaurant, offices, and warehousing.

The much smaller **18 Big Four Building** on Third Street has a similar history as a railroad building adapted to commercial use. From the time it was built in 1891 until the 1960s, it was used for offices by Central Union Depot, the Big Four, and the New York Central Railroad, successor to the Big Four. Beginning in the 1960s, the Big Four Building became a location for small service businesses, and then for artists and art-related enterprises. In early 1987, the building caught fire, and the owners, who had planned to rehabilitate it, were faced with the choice of rebuilding or demolition.

The Old Spaghetti Factory, 417 Pete Rose Way West, is a link to Cincinnati's early years as a manufacturing center, for the building was constructed as the **19 Showroom and Warehouse of the Mitchell & Rammelsberg Furniture Company**.

In 1847, two young immigrants, Robert Mitchell (1811-1899), from Ireland, and German-born Frederick Rammelsberg (1814-1863), became partners in a furniture making firm. The two cabinetmakers had arrived in Cincinnati around 1830, boarded together, apprenticed at the same time, and had been in earlier partnerships with other woodworkers.

The men complimented each other well. Mitchell was an active member of Cincinnati's business community, later an officer of the Chamber of Commerce and a developer of Avondale. Rammelsberg was an innovative craftsman and is credited with being the first Cincinnati cabinetmaker to use machinery to make furniture. When the men established their partnership, Cincinnati was the furniture making center in the West, and Cincinnati's cabinetmakers were centered around Second Street, close to the lumberyards and river and rail transportation.

In late December 1848, Mitchell & Rammelsberg's factory at the southwest corner of Second and John Streets burned down. Within a few months, the firm rebuilt, constructing one of Cincinnati's largest mechanized factories for producing furniture.

By the late 1860s, Mitchell and Rammelsberg had acquired property on the southeast corner of Second and John Streets and put up this building, an 80′ x 150′, 6-story "wareroom," where wholesale customers could view the firm's products and from which these goods could be shipped. By then, Mitchell & Rammelsberg had branches in St. Louis, Memphis, and New Orleans, and was one of the most important furniture makers in the Midwest. The company's furniture was distributed throughout the United States, and Mitchell & Rammelsburg became known for its moderately priced home furnishings and elaborately decorated, fine quality furniture.

In 1873, the company commissioned a new retail store on Fourth Street. In addition, it had two factory buildings located across from the warerooms, several lumberyards in the area, and even residence halls for its workers. In 1881, the company changed its name to the Robert Mitchell Furniture Company and under the direction of Mitchell's sons continued making furniture until 1939. After that, the Second Street wareroom was occupied briefly by a sash and door manufacturer, wholesale grocers, and a carpet outlet. Since 1975, two restaurants have been located here. The upper stories are used for storage.

**Turn left on Central Avenue, right on Third Street.**

As early as 1925, the *Official Plan of the City of Cincinnati* acknowledged a downtown traffic problem, but not until after World War II did the city attempt to collect and distribute downtown traffic by constructing **20 Fort Washington Way,** which runs between Pete Rose Way and Third Street and connects I-71 and I-75.

Despite the need to route through traffic around the central business district and to distribute inbound and outgoing downtown traffic, work on the Third Street Distributor, as it was then called, did not get started until passage of the Federal Aid Highway Act of 1956. With the promise of federal funds, voters approved a $45 million bond issue, to be matched by $140 million in federal funds. Construction of an expressway system for Cincinnati became possible.

In 1957, the city acquired land for the project at a cost of $12 million and began demolishing buildings on Pearl Street and the south side of Third. The Distributor and the Third Street Viaduct cost $21 million, making it the most expensive stretch of expressway built in Ohio up to that time. The road, renamed Fort Washington Way, opened at the end of June 1961.

The roadway was dedicated in a burst of fireworks and civic enthusiasm, although the link to the Millcreek Expressway (I-75) was not complete, and the Northeast Expressway (I-71) had not yet been built. Since then, Fort Washington Way has directed traffic going into, out of, and around Cincinnati, despite its tangle of off-ramps, on-ramps, signs, and warnings.

Since the construction of Fort Washington Way, much of **21 Third Street** has been demolished. But in the nineteenth century, it was an area of transition between the riverfront and the city.

Over the past hundred years, Third Street has passed from being the center for banking, insurance, and rail transport to little more than an annex of the downtown business district. In 1892, Third Street from Sycamore to Walnut was home to no fewer than fifteen banks, twice that number of insurance companies, and eight major brokerages. In addition, a sprinkling of realtors, real estate lenders, and a large number of wholesalers made the street an important part of the city's financial and commercial life.

Within a few years, the large banking houses moved to new skyscrapers built on Fourth Street, then downtown's most prestigious location, leaving Third Street to small and medium-sized manufacturers and businesses. To the west, Third continued to serve travelers, but to the east, the street was an area of small commercial buildings and poor tenements.

The Depression and construction of Union Terminal in the West End undercut what remained of Third Street's economic viability. By 1954, most of the buildings on the south side of the street stood vacant, awaiting demolition. By then, too, many of the older buildings on the north side of the street had fallen to make way for parking structures. Those that remained housed an assortment of small concerns ranging from saloons to barber shops to charities.

Most of Third Street's old buildings were gone by the late 1980s, and the few that remained were seriously dilapidated. The businesses along the street were marginal. Aside from a few shops and bars, Third Street's major economic role was to provide parking for downtown office workers and for sports fans going to the coliseum or the stadium.

**Turn left on Main Street.**

The **22 Third and Main Street Historic Cluster** consists of five buildings erected between 1862 and 1893. Constructed mainly of brick and stone and with common design elements, this group of buildings conveys the scale and harmony of Cincinnati's nineteenth-century cityscape.

The oldest, 300-302 Third Street, was designed by Cincinnati architect William Walter and housed the McMicken School of Design, later the University of Cincinnati School of Design, Art, Architecture and Planning. Salmon P. Chase, Lincoln's Secretary of the Treasury and later Chief Justice of the United States Supreme Court, had a law office here.

Next door, the Anderson Building, 304-306, was an early office building. Heister's Restaurant operated at 308-310 from 1875, when the building was constructed, to the turn of the century. The present tenant, E.C. Shaw Company, has been here for more than fifty years. In 1880, the C.E. Brockman Pottery put up the building at 312-314. Erected for the Clark-Sorgo Company, a nationally known maker of sugar processing machinery, the building at 316-18 dates from 1865.

**Tour ends.**

# Tour 2

# Central Business District Core

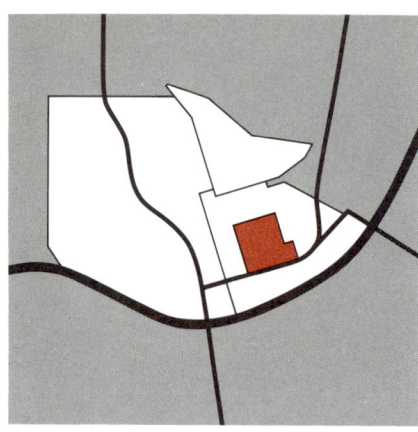

Although Cincinnati's first settlers lived between the riverfront and Third Street, the city's founders envisioned further growth. The first town plat, drawn in 1789, included the area from the river to Northern Row (Seventh Street) and from Western Row (Central Avenue) to Eastern Row (Broadway). Much of the original town is now in the part of the Central Business District (CBD) known as the Core, which extends along Fourth between Sycamore and Elm Streets, and from Fifth to Seventh Streets between Main and Race.

In 1957, city planners divided the downtown CBD into two parts, a "Core," where the major hotels, offices, and retail stores were located, and a "Frame," where there were large corporate headquarters, a few major retailers, government offices, some residences, smaller stores, service companies, and a variety of institutions.

The eleven square blocks of the Core began as a residential area, then added commerce, and finally emerged as the city's business center. Cincinnati's past and present come together in the Core of the Central Business District.

As early as 1791, James Kemper's Presbyterian congregation met in a clearing at Fourth and Main Streets. The next year, it put up a 30'x 40' frame meeting house with a floor made of boat planks and seats hewn from logs. Nearby were several cabins and the burial ground for Fort Washington. Most of the area, however, was pastureland and vulnerable to Indian raids; worshippers at Kemper's church carried their rifles to services.

When the Treaty of Greenville ended the threat of Indian attack, Cincinnati began to spread beyond Third Street. Prosperous merchants, lawyers, investors, and physicians soon built homes between Fourth

*Before the center of Cincinnati's business district shifted northward away from the riverfront, streets such as Fifth—shown here in the 1840s—were densely built up with a variety of relatively small residential, commercial, and industrial structures.*

and Seventh Streets, away from the noise and congestion of the waterfront. Here, too, a homeowner could build a larger house on a larger lot, for while riverfront property was selling at $200 a front-foot, property above Fourth Street went for half that.

By the third decade of the nineteenth century, the district north of the riverfront was built up with houses, churches, and shops. In addition to the Presbyterian congregation, there were Baptist and Methodist churches here, and those who did not trade with the area's several grocers could take advantage of the marketplace on Fifth Street between Walnut and Vine, where fresh produce, meat, and dairy products were sold two afternoons a week. The district was also a center for schools and benevolent societies, and by the 1840s, there were nearly two dozen churches ranging from Roman Catholic to Restorationist between Fourth and Seventh Streets.

Because it was centrally located, Fourth Street became increasingly important to the city's cultural and economic life. Shops that first located on Fourth to serve affluent residents of the district remained to serve a broader clientele.

In the years before the Civil War, much of the available space in downtown Cincinnati was filled by the construction of substantial multi-use structures. Investors erected buildings that combined several functions such as housing, offices, shops, and theaters. Among these was the Melodeon Building, at the northwest corner of Fourth and Walnut, which had a concert hall where well-known performers including Jenny Lind appeared. But a daguerreotype artist, a dentist, an apothecary, a music publisher, and a commercial college also rented space here. Nearby were the Hill Building on Main Street and Johnston's Row at Walnut and Fifth Streets. The upper floors of these smaller office buildings often included modest residential rooms and apartments.

The city's leading hotels were likewise concentrated along Fourth Street, close to the public landing and rail depots. Cincinnati's most prestigious hotel, the Burnet House, at the northwest corner of Third and Vine Streets, was convenient to the riverfront. Its chief competitor, the Gibson House, on Walnut between Fourth and Fifth, sometimes served as Cincinnati's City Hall.

D. J. Kenney, writing in the 1875 *Illustrated Cincinnati*, identified Fourth Street as "the principal street of the city." It served businessmen, shoppers, and travelers and continued to be a cultural center in the second half of the nineteenth century. Pike's Opera House at Fourth between Walnut and Vine, built in 1859 by Samuel N. Pike (c.1820-1872), was called by historian Charles T. Greve "Cincinnati's handsomest building."

But other cultural and entertainment facilities were established farther to the north, particularly along Vine Street. The Grand Opera was at the northwest corner of Vine and Longworth Streets, and the public library was on the west side of Vine between Sixth and Seventh Streets.

At the same time, the business district began to expand into the downtown residential quarter north of Fourth Street. In 1877, John Shillito's dry goods store moved to Seventh Street. The post office also moved from crowded quarters on Fourth to the block of Fifth Street between Walnut and Main.

The places of those who left Fourth Street were quickly taken by others, such as the growing wholesale dry goods business of George Washington McAlpin. In 1873, the furniture manufacturing firm of Mitchell & Rammelsberg built a new retail store on Fourth. The street also boasted the offices and workshops of several nationally-known businesses, including the John Holland Gold Pen Company, music publisher John Church & Company, the Strobridge Lithograph Company, and the Deuber Watch Case Company.

In the 1890s, the central part of the city's business district included the residences of some of Cincinnati's wealthiest and poorest citizens, although many people between those extremes had left. Still, throughout the area, a variety of small businesses, modest homes, apartments, and tenements were mixed with groceries, saloons, and secondhand stores.

During that decade, Fourth and Fifth remained the two major streets where Cincinnati's most prominent merchants were located. Then, as now, Fourth Street's commerce included small shops and businesses, anchored by the large dry goods stores, as the forerunners of modern department stores were then known.

Fifth Street differed little from Fourth. The Emery Hotel's block-long arcade from Vine to Race between Fourth and Fifth Streets housed much of the city's jewelry industry. Mabley & Carew, Rollman & Sons, and Fechheimer's were the great dry goods houses on Fifth, and Oskamp-Nolting sold jewelry. Barbers, druggists, hardware merchants, tailors, and an A&P grocery store near Walnut filled out the street.

At the turn of the century, East Sixth Street marked the boundary between that portion of the city which was heavily commercial and that which was mostly residential. West Sixth Street near the outdoor market between Plum and Central had already become devoted mostly to business. Aside from Shillito's store, Seventh Street west of Vine was still residential with homes, boarding houses, and the offices of dentists and physicians. East of Walnut, Seventh Street was occupied by stables, farriers, and harnessmakers.

During the next thirty years, a wave of construction by commercial and financial institutions radically altered the area between Fourth and Seventh Streets. Ever since Cincinnati became a commercial city in the 1820s, its banks, brokerages, and insurance companies had been located primarily between Second and Third Streets along Main, Walnut, and Vine. But by the 1890s, time and repeated floodings had taken their toll on the buildings there. Cincinnati bankers and businessmen looked to higher ground.

At the same time, a new generation of innovative architects working in Chicago and New York began to design large-scale commercial buildings. Between 1880 and 1910, Cincinnati businessmen and bankers commissioned nationally-known architects such as H. H. Richardson, Daniel H. Burnham, and John Russell Pope. Often in partnership with Cincinnati architects such as A. O. Elzner, Garber & Woodward, and Samuel Hannaford, these men designed new structures for Fourth and Fifth Streets. In the process, they extended the commercial district northward, creating the Central Business District of today.

This process began in the late 1890s when Jacob Schmidlapp, president of the Union Savings Bank & Trust Company, saw the work of Daniel Burnham (1846-1912). Burnham was one of the Chicago School

*By the early twentieth century, Fourth Street was Cincinnati's "main street" with the largest office buildings and most prominent retailers located there.*

of architects who had first developed "skyscrapers" in the late 1880s, creating a distinctively American style of commercial architecture. Schmidlapp, a banker and philanthropist, brought Burnham and his revolutionary ideas about the scale and design of tall buildings to Cincinnati. The Union Savings Bank Building that Burnham designed for Schmidlapp opened in 1901 at the northwest corner of Fourth and Walnut.

Burnham's architectural firm drew plans for three other skyscrapers on Fourth and Fifth Streets around Vine and Walnut: the Traction Company and the First National Bank buildings in 1902, and the Fourth National Bank in 1905.

In the first two decades of the twentieth century, more than a dozen major commercial and banking buildings were constructed downtown. The most notable of these were the Ingalls Building, the world's first concrete-reinforced skyscraper, built in 1902-1903, and the Union Central Life Insurance Building (later the Central Trust Tower), which opened in 1913. At twenty-nine stories, the Union Central Building was then the tallest building outside New York City. It was the work of Cass Gilbert (1860-1934), a New York architect who designed the New York Customs House and later the Woolworth Building.

After slowing during World War I, downtown construction resumed in the 1920s. In 1921, Garber & Woodward, who had worked with Gilbert on the Union Central Building, completed the Dixie Terminal. The firm also collaborated with nationally-known architect John Russell Pope (1874-1937) on the Cincinnati Gas & Electric Building, which opened in 1930. The last of Cincinnati's early twentieth century skyscrapers was the Carew Tower. Also opened in 1930, the Carew Tower completed the city's mid-century skyline.

Over the next three decades—an era of economic depression, war, and suburban growth—the only major construction between Fourth and Seventh Streets was the Terrace Plaza Hotel and parking garages. But as interest in the the centers of cities began to revive in the late 1960s, Cincinnati's downtown Core became both the site of new construction and the subject of controversy.

As early as the mid-1950s, city planners noted the deterioration of downtown. It was then, too, that they observed that the CBD could be divided into two areas, a central Core and a peripheral Frame, and that there were contradictory trends at work in both. Retailing had declined throughout the CBD as a whole because suburban shopping centers were drawing customers away from downtown. Retail activity had increased within the Core, but most of that growth was in marginal, low-rent, low-profit enterprises. At the same time, the number of businesses and services in the CBD had grown, while the actual amount of office space in the Core was shrinking. In the early postwar years, planners began to talk of "stagnation" and signs of "incipient decline" in Cincinnati's downtown.

The City Planning Commission responded to this concern in late 1957 and early 1958 by preparing an ambitious plan to rehabilitate, reshape, and redevelop what it regarded as the outmoded and blighted areas of downtown. The 1957-1958 *Central Business District Plan* called for a new, enlarged Fountain Square Plaza that would extend over Fifth Street, underground garages, pedestrian malls, moving elevated sidewalks, and the block-by-block redevelopment of the Core.

Not all city officials agreed with the recommendations, and some downtown businessmen, who were not consulted during the creation of the plan, brought pressure on City Council to reject it. In 1961, a less comprehensive plan for the riverfront and the Central Business District also failed to achieve broad support.

Two years later, the City Planning Commission hired Rogers, Taliaferro, Kostritsky & Lamb (RTKL) of Baltimore to put together a new plan for downtown redevelopment. The director of city planning, Herbert W. Stevens, invited a wide range of civic committees and organizations to participate in creating the plan.

The consultants observed that aging downtown buildings were increasingly unattractive and that the CBD lacked easy access for both vehicles and pedestrians. The 1964 *Plan for Downtown Cincinnati* sought to redevelop the district in order to slow the rate at which business and retail commerce were leaving. The plan called for tearing down older buildings and replacing them with new office blocks, redesigning Fountain Square, and creating a system of second-story skywalks to link downtown stores, hotels, and offices.

The 1964 plan also marked a major shift in Cincinnati city planning. The Planning Commission instituted a process of community consultation that would be used to insure the economic, social, and political acceptability of planning. City Council responded to this new strategy and approved the 1964 document.

By the mid-1970s, the first downtown skywalks had opened around Fountain Square. Three major buildings, the Provident Tower (1967) and the Fifth-Third Center/DuBois Tower (1968) and the Formica Building (1970) were up, and Fountain Square had been redesigned. New structures, including Fountain Square South, the 580 Building, the Central Trust Center, the Federated Building, and Atrium One, were planned and built in the late 1970s. By the early 1980s, there was a temporary glut in downtown office space for the first time in the city's history.

A decade of new construction not only revitalized the downtown Core but also touched off controversy. Despite the efforts of some architects to set back the upper stories of tall buildings to allow sunlight to reach street level and to prevent newer, larger structures from overpowering older ones, criticism arose. A number of local architects, planners, and writers charged that the new massive office blocks, many of which were built in the slab-like International Style, had obliterated the distinctive look of Cincinnati's downtown.

Many preservationists feared, too, that the city's distinguished older buildings would share the fate of the historic Sinton Hotel on Fourth Street and the Albee Theater and Gibson Hotel on Fifth, razed in 1977 to make way for Fountain Square South. They also worried that smaller nineteenth-century commercial buildings along Fourth, Main, and Vine Streets would be demolished to provide new office space and parking. In the mid-1980s, City Council designated portions of these three streets as local historic districts, often against the will of property owners and developers who felt that construction of new high-rises would be more profitable than adapting older buildings for more modest reuse.

Despite these difficulties, a number of early twentieth-century

*While many architecturally fine buildings in the downtown Core were lost to new construction during the 1960s through the 1980s, some—including the Dixie Terminal with its elegantly decorated arcade—were saved and renovated.*

*Downtown redevelopment has radically changed the face of Cincinnati's Central Business District in the last two decades, yet a few of its older features still stand side by side with the new.*

buildings have benefited from downtown growth. The Dixie Terminal, the Cincinnati Enquirer Building, the Cincinnatian Hotel, and the Netherland Plaza Hotel have all been restored and redeveloped rather than demolished.

In large part because of the efforts of downtown planners and developers, the Core of Cincinnati's Central Business District has remained the commercial and economic heart of the city. By the late 1980s, the downtown included more than a dozen major office buildings with more than 4.5 million square feet of space that had been built since 1969, as well as numerous older buildings that had been preserved. The new Fountain Square had become a symbol for the city and functioned admirably as a downtown gathering place.

City planners projected in 1983 that by the end of the century, another six to seven million square feet of office space would be completed. This anticipated growth—and the fact that by 1988, half a dozen major construction projects had been announced for the downtown—touched off some anxiety that the Core of the CBD would become devoted solely to business and commerce. Even so, most observers agreed that downtown planning and redevelopment in Cincinnati had successfully fostered a vital city center.

Tour Length
2 miles

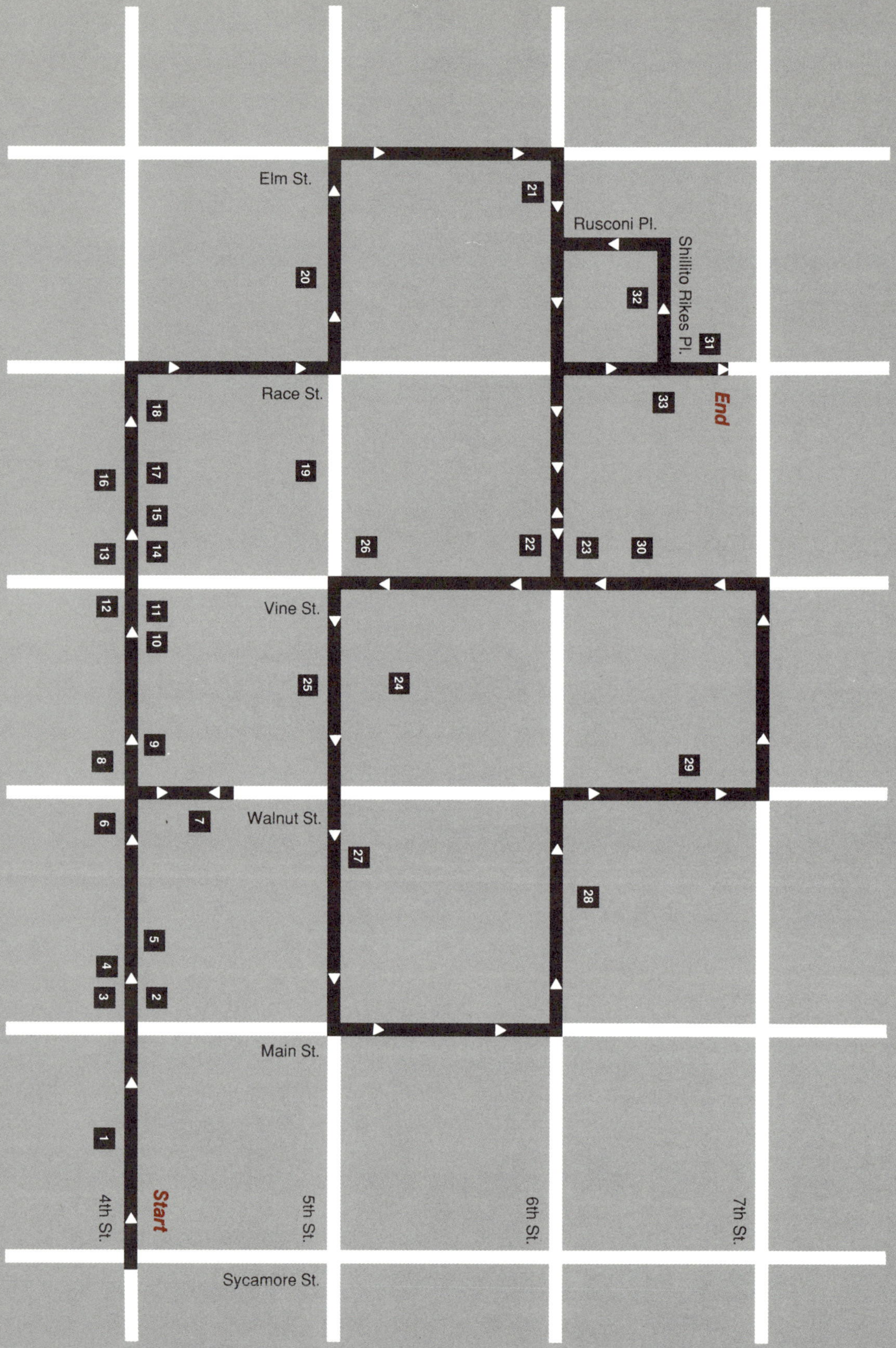

Elm St.

21

Rusconi Pl.

20

32

Shillito Rikes Pl.

31

Race St.

33

**End**

18

19

17

26

22

23

30

16

15

14

13

Vine St.

12

25

24

11

10

29

8

9

6

Walnut St.

7

27

28

5

4

3

2

Main St.

1

**Start**

4th St.

5th St.

6th St.

7th St.

Sycamore St.

North

*The walking tour of the Core of Cincinnati's Central Business District begins at the corner of Fourth and Sycamore Streets. Proceed west on Fourth Street. (Note: This is a WALKING tour. The route does not follow established vehicular traffic patterns.)*

The Core of Cincinnati's Central Business District (CBD) extends east along East Fourth Street to Sycamore Street. Although city planners originally considered this area to be part of the Frame, the recent construction of high-rise office buildings has virtually annexed the block to the Fourth Street business district.

As late as the 1970s, this block still contained older buildings with street-level storefronts, occupied by marginal businesses such as antiques and furniture dealers, and apartments on the floors above. Today, East Fourth Street includes a mix of older and newer commercial structures. New construction has not, for the most part, overpowered the smaller structures, but several old buildings have been given newer storefronts and facades that detract from their appearance.

The buildings along East Fourth Street are principally offices. Some are speculative properties, built as investments and rented out by their owners; others are occupied, often as headquarters, by the companies that own them.

The **1 Atrium One** and **Atrium Two** office buildings, 201 and 221 East Fourth Street, erected in 1981 and 1984, respectively, are large speculative office blocks. The Atriums were designed by the Chicago branch of Skidmore, Owings & Merrell, one of the nation's largest corporate architects and designers of the Sears Tower and John Hancock Building in Chicago.

Atrium Two, a large, rounded tower with set-back upper stories, features a 5-story atrium with a ceramic tile fountain made locally by the Spring Street Pottery. The work is one of a growing number of pieces of public art in downtown buildings. Atrium One's stack of four, 4-story atriums are tiered so that all of the offices overlook a high, dramatic, central space. Behind the two buildings is a covered pedestrian walkway that enables office workers to move from parking lots in the riverfront stadium area to the center of the city.

Together, the Atrium buildings contain nearly one million square feet of office space tenanted by a variety of businesses including stock brokerage houses and divisions of large corporations.

Harry Hake & Partners, a well-known local firm, designed the massive, 6-story marble-faced building that is the Cincinnati branch of the **2 Federal Reserve Bank of Cleveland,** 150 East Fourth Street.

This facility, which opened in 1972, furnishes coins and currency to member banks and holds their reserve balances, receives and sorts deposits of money, clears checks, sells treasury bills, and acts as fiscal agent, custodian, and depository for the United States government. In the 1980s, damaged bills were burned here at the rate of nearly $50 million each month.

The **3 Cincinnati Gas & Electric Company Building,** 139 East Fourth Street, is both owned and occupied by the utility company. It stands on the site of W. H. Harrison's drugstore, which in 1843 became the first commercial customer of James F. Conover's Cincinnati Gas-Light & Coke Company.

In 1841, Conover, a lawyer and newspaperman, put up $100,000, along with the city's investment of $500,000, and established a business to "manufacture and sell . . . inflammable gas." The company's headquarters were located in the basement of Conover's Fourth Street home until 1872, when the firm erected a building at Fourth and Plum Streets. In 1901, the Cincinnati Gas & Electric Company was formed with the consolidation of the Gas-Light & Coke and Cincinnati Edison Electric companies.

Completed in 1930, the CG&E building was designed by Cincinnati architects Frederick W. Garber (1877-1950) and Clifford B. Woodward (1878-1954), who won an American Institute of Architects award for it the next year. John Russell Pope, who had drawn the plans for the Jefferson Memorial and the National Gallery of Art in Washington, D.C., was a consultant on this project, designing the facade.

This Classical Revival office building stands in contrast to the plain lines of earlier skyscrapers to the west on Fourth Street. Its massive 3-story base features a row of Doric columns and bronze-trimmed windows and is topped with urns at the corners. Out of the base rises a 16-story tower also ornamented by large urns, stylized eagles, relief figures, and a detailed frieze. A 1954 addition wraps around the building to the south.

Since 1946, CG&E has been the sole supplier of gas and electricity to the Greater Cincinnati area. It ventured into nuclear power in the late 1960s with construction of the problem-plagued William H. Zimmer Power Plant, named for a former company president. After the Nuclear Regulatory Commission denied the Moscow, Ohio, facility an operating permit, it was converted to burn coal.

Just west of the CG&E headquarters are three **4 Nineteenth-Century Commercial Buildings,** 123-135 East Fourth Street, located on land that CG&E intended to use for expansion. When the utility changed its plans, these structures, which reflect the character and scale of Fourth Street before the skyscrapers, were saved.

The center store, at 127, was long the home of the John Holland Gold Pen Company, established in 1842 and a nationally-known maker of quality dip and fountain pens until the 1950s. For another thirty years, the company sold greeting cards and pens made by other firms. After John Holland closed in 1981, the building remained vacant for four years. In 1985, new owners commissioned Cincinnati architect Bruce Goetzman to plan the renovation of these three buildings for use as offices.

The 14-story **5 Formica Building,** 120 East Fourth Street, which opened in 1970, was designed by Harry Weese & Associates of Chicago and contains office space contiguous with the Mercantile Library Building. The lobby at the Fourth Street end of the glass-roofed arcade features a fountain sculpture by local artists. Composed of seven 9-foot copper panels, the work presents a photo-etched topographical plan of the city and a montage of well-known Cincinnati scenes.

Connected to this structure is the **Contemporary Arts Center (CAC),**

*The Formica Building is one of several new downtown structures which incorporates attractive public spaces that facilitate the flow of pedestrian traffic.*

115 East Fifth Street. This organization, begun in 1939 as the Modern Art Society, was located first at the Art Museum, in loft space on West Fourth Street, and then at the Taft Museum before moving to these quarters. CAC is an important regional exhibitor of avant garde works.

The Clopay Building, 105 East Fourth Street, is the largest Burnham office building in Cincinnati and most clearly reflects his style. It was completed in 1902 as the **6 First National Bank Building,** headquarters for the twenty-fourth of the first fifty banks chartered under the National Banking Act of 1863 and now the oldest bank operating under its original charter. First National Bank of Cincinnati was one of the earliest of the city's banks to move to Fourth Street.

After growing through a series of twentieth-century mergers, the bank moved to new headquarters on Fifth Street in the Fountain Square South development in 1981. In 1988, having acquired seventeen banks with seven different names, the institution became Star Bank.

This structure reflects the competition among the Cincinnati's Fourth Street banks to erect the finest headquarters. For a decade after its completion, the First National Bank Building was, at nineteen stories, Cincinnati's tallest office tower. Burnham's largely unornamented design consists of a tall first floor marked by large granite piers, a middle section of plain brick with shallow curved bays, three top floors, and a terra cotta cornice.

Since 1982, the building has been the headquarters of the Clopay Corporation, founded in 1859 as paper jobbers. Clopay later became a manufacturer of fiber and paper products, including window shades, and adopted its current name—a combination of the words "cloth" and "paper." Recently, the company has moved into the manufacture of garage and storm doors, garage door openers, and polyethylene film for packing. Clopay restored the building in 1984.

**Turn right (north) on Walnut Street.**

Not all of the speculative office buildings on or immediately adjacent to East Fourth Street are named for a commercial tenant or owner. The **7 Mercantile Library Building,** 414 Walnut Street, carries the name of a cultural institution even though

*The Mercantile Library continues to use many of the furnishings that were on hand when it occupied its present space in 1908.*

most of its space is rented to professionals and service businesses.

On April 18, 1835, forty-five young businessmen founded the Young Men's Mercantile Library Association to promote learning and to provide themselves with a downtown library and reading room. In 1840, the organization's 700 books were moved to the second floor of the Cincinnati College building, which occupied the site where the present structure stands.

The college was destroyed by fire on January 19, 1845, but the library's collection was saved. After the Mercantile Library Association raised $10,000 to help rebuild the college, Judge Alphonso Taft (1810-1891) wrote an agreement that gave the association a 10,000-year lease on the second floor of the college, rent-free. And the contract was renewable forever.

The increasing value of the city's downtown commercial property led Thomas J. Emery's Sons to acquire the old Cincinnati College building in 1902 and to strike a deal with the Mercantile Library Association. In exchange for its perpetual leasehold in the college, the library received new quarters on the eleventh and twelfth floors of a new building and a special elevator for its members. The new structure, designed by Joseph G. Steinkamp Brothers of Cincinnati, was completed in 1908. Above the 2-story granite arch over the main entrance are floral patterns, a scroll, and a book.

The Mercantile Library, one of the few remaining subscription libraries in the country, owns more than 200,000 volumes and offers members lectures, trips, and a quiet corner

downtown where they can read.

Cross Walnut at the crosswalk in mid-block and return to Fourth Street. Continue west.

As the number of offices on Fourth Street grew in the early twentieth century, so did the number of people employed downtown. Very few of these workers lived in the basin; most commuted to their jobs from the suburbs and, therefore, needed easy access to transportation. Property in the heart of the central business district, however, was too valuable to use for a transit terminal, just as it is now too valuable to be used solely for parking lots. A group of investors decided to combine a commuter facility and a retail and office building on the same site. The result was the **8 Dixie Terminal,** 49 East Fourth Street.

The idea for a streetcar terminal for Northern Kentucky commuters came from Jack Linch, an attorney for the Covington & Cincinnati Bridge Company, who suggested that the Suspension Bridge be linked directly to a downtown station. The project was supported by local investors, including the Taft family. The Dixie Terminal Company commissioned Garber & Woodward to plan a Renaissance Revival style building.

The design was highly ornate. The terminal's most notable feature was its 3-story, 35' x 225' arcade, trimmed in marble and glass and lined with shops. The vaulted ceiling, painted in pale blue and gold, was decorated with cherubs and garlands in relief. A lower concourse led to ticketing areas and boarding ramps.

When the Dixie Terminal opened on October 21, 1921, it had more square footage than any other office block in the city. The *Cincinnati Enquirer* praised it as a "great gateway between North and South" and a "splendid structure in which utility and beauty are combined. The power of public-spirited wealth and the dignity of labor have united to meet a public need, to render a public service, to bestow a civic adornment and thus to furnish a happy augury of a new era in Cincinnati's progress."

Although the streetcars stopped running in the 1950s, Kentucky public transit lines still use the lower level of the 9-story building as a bus terminal. Specialty shops and small businesses continue to rent its stores and offices. Though the Dixie Terminal has been rumored to be in danger of demolition several times, pressure from preservationists has helped protect it.

Nationally-renowned architectural firms were responsible for many of East Fourth Street's commercial buildings, even in the early twentieth century. Across from Dixie Terminal are two of four structures that Daniel Burnham & Company of Chicago designed for clients in Cincinnati.

The **9 Fourth and Walnut Building,** 36 East Fourth Street, opened on January 1, 1901 and, at eighteen stories, was then the city's tallest structure. It was built for the Union Savings Bank, founded in 1890 by Jacob Schmidlapp. The new bank building was ornamented with marble and bronze and was promoted as completely fireproof.

The Union Savings Bank later became Union Trust, and in 1927 merged with the Fifth-Third Bank, itself a product of the merger of the Fifth and Third National banks. Four years later, the central offices of the new bank were moved here, where they remained until 1971. The building has twice been expanded along Fourth Street and was restored in 1986.

Completed in 1905, the 11-story **10 Fourth National Bank Building,** 18 East Fourth Street, was the smallest and the last of the downtown "skyscrapers" designed by Daniel Burnham's firm. After the Fourth National Bank merged with Central Trust in 1923, this office was closed and the building was sold, although the bank's name remains engraved on the entablature.

From 1924 to 1947, Shaffer Rubber Company occupied the first floor, and a number of insurance companies had offices in the upper stories. In the 1950s, a steakhouse rented the ground floor, and part of the granite base of the building was altered to create a new storefront. Yet Burnham's original design—the 2-part gray granite base, the brick-faced middle portion, and a top of tan terra cotta surmounted by a projecting cornice—can still be seen above the false front.

Even before Jacob Schmidlapp brought Daniel Burnham to Cincinnati, Melville E. Ingalls (1842-1916), president of the Merchant's National Bank, as well as the Big Four and Chesapeake & Ohio railroads, decided to move his bank to Fourth Street.

The **11 Ingalls Building,** 6 East Fourth Street, was the work of local architects Alfred O. Elzner (1862-1933) and George M. Anderson (1969-1916). The idea for using steel-reinforced concrete rather than the traditional supporting girders or masonry for the skyscraper originated with Elzner, who had attended MIT and trained in the offices of H. H. Richardson.

At sixteen stories, the Ingalls Building was to be more than twice as tall as any reinforced concrete structure then built. Most engineers insisted it would not stand, and for two years, the city denied Ingalls a construction permit. After the building opened in 1903, a disappointed crowd waited all night for it to collapse. Instead, the Ingalls Building made its designers and the Cincinnati builder, Ferro-Concrete (later Turner) Construction Company, famous, and, as a plaque on the Fourth Street side of the structure records, "revolutionized the building industry."

When it opened in 1967, the **12 Provident Tower,** 1 East Fourth Street, was the first downtown office high-rise to be constructed in over thirty years. Salmon P. Wallace, a Dallas architect, designed the conventional, rectangular 19-story steel and glass structure. The Provident Bank had made arrangements to be the primary tenant, giving the building its name. In 1968, the structure was acquired by American Financial Corporation (AFC), a financial holding company that Cincinnatian Carl Lindner, Jr., founded and directs. AFC bought the tower both as an investment and an opportunity to consolidate some of its various offices.

Carl Lindner began working in his family's retail dairy business at the age of eleven, built a convenience store empire before he was forty, and ultimately became involved in banking, insurance, communications, food processing, and energy-related businesses. By the mid-1980s, *Forbes* magazine included Lindner on its list of the four hundred wealthiest people in the United States, and AFC, through

*The Ferro-Concrete Construction Company was justifiably proud of its role in the creation of the Ingalls Building and promoted the structure as an example of what was possible with the use of new concrete building methods.*

a series of acquisitions, was significantly increasing Cincinnati's importance as a commercial center.

The Lindners, including Carl's brothers, Robert and Richard, and sister, Dorothy, began their careers by establishing United Dairy Farmers, a chain of ice cream and convenience stores. In the late 1940s and 1950s, the family expanded UDF and moved into real estate, developing small shopping strips around their store sites. In the late 1950s, the Lindners started building up the Thriftway grocery chain.

Carl Lindner also entered banking, taking a seat on the board of directors of the Central Trust Company and in 1955, formed the American Financial Corporation. In 1959, AFC acquired three small savings and loans that were combined as the Hunter Savings Association. From that point on, AFC developed into a notable financial holding company.

American Financial was the vehicle by which the Lindners became involved in an even greater variety of enterprises. The company entered the insurance business in 1962, and four years later, it gained control of Provident Bank, a venerable Cincinnati institution that grocery chain founder Barney Kroger had started around the turn of the century. Communications was added to the mix when AFC bought a controlling interest in the *Cincinnati Enquirer*, the city's morning newspaper, in 1971.

AFC also invested in downtown real estate. Within a decade of the purchase of the Provident Tower, the company owned the entire block on the south side of Fourth Street between Walnut and Vine.

Through American Financial Corporation, which became a private company in a 1981 merger, and its subsidiary companies, the Lindner family gained significant interests in other firms including Penn Central, United Brands, Great American Communications, Circle K Corporation, and American General Corporation.

In some cases, the Lindners exercised overall control.

The expansion of AFC's holdings was frequently the result of transactions that converted control of one firm into an interest in another, larger corporation, as in the 1975 sale of the *Enquirer* to a communications conglomerate for cash and stock in that company. In other instances, ownership of a company was realigned. For example, when changes in federal banking laws required that AFC divest itself of Provident Bank, the company distributed ownership of the bank among its shareholders so that direction of the institution remained with the Lindner family and associates.

Over the years, family members focused on directing different businesses—Richard on Thriftway, Robert on United Dairy Farmers, and Carl on AFC—though all three men remained members of AFC's board of directors. As chairman and president of AFC, Carl Lindner played a significant role in the company's investment decisions, many of which were motivated by his desire to take action that would be good for his city as well as his business.

AFC's acquisition of the troubled Home State Savings in 1985 was intended, in part, to prevent major losses by depositors and to foster a positive image of the Cincinnati business community and its ability to solve its own problems. Investments in such operations as the *Enquirer*, the Cincinnati Reds, Taft Broadcasting, and King's Island aumsement park kept jobs and, in some cases, the businesses themselves, in the area.

When Lindner gained control of major firms through AFC, he often moved their headquarters to Cincinnati—a policy that brought both jobs and prestige to the city. The Los Angeles-based Great American Insurance Company was relocated to the Queen City following its acquisition by AFC in the mid-1970s. In the next decade, the home offices of Penn Central and United Brands, including its John Morrell meatpacking and Chiquita Brands subsidiaries, were likewise brought here.

While most of Cincinnati's downtown financial institutions have clustered on East Fourth, there are some notable banks west of Vine Street. The **13 Union Central Life Insurance Building,** now the **Central Trust**

**Tower,** 1 West Fourth Street, was the last of the great turn-of-the-century skyscrapers built on this street.

The corner was previously occupied by the old United States Post Office and Customs House, built in 1857, and later by the Chamber of Commerce Building, designed by H. H. Richardson in his famous Romanesque Revival style. Union Central Life Insurance Company, founded in 1867 by the Methodist Church, purchased the site in 1911 after fire destroyed the Chamber of Commerce Building and commissioned Cass Gilbert of New York, who worked with Garber & Woodward of Cincinnati, to create the 29-story structure.

When it opened on May 1, 1913, Union Central's tower was the fifth largest building in the world and the tallest building outside New York City. The *Cincinnati Enquirer* marveled at the huge sum spent for the project—some $3 million—and the technological "triumph" that had been achieved in the construction of the "mammoth tower." Rising from a 4-story marble-clad base, the building was faced with terra cotta and topped by a hipped roof. Above the twenty-third floor was a 4-story Classical temple capped by a pyramid roof and a smaller temple, creating one of the most distinctive elements of the Cincinnati skyline.

Union Central remained the primary occupant until 1964. The current owner is Central Trust Bank, also founded in 1867. Central Trust moved to Fourth Street in 1871 and in 1919, took part of this building for its headquarters. The bank moved its main office following the construction of the Central Trust Tower on Fifth Street in 1979, but it continues to operate a branch here, and the building still bears the Central Trust name in red neon lights on each face of the pyramidal roof.

An annex, to the south, is on the site of the Burnet House (1850-1926), one of Cincinnati's most prestigious hotels and a major landmark where Abraham Lincoln, Hungarian patriot Louis Kossuth, Sarah Bernhardt, and Jenny Lind stayed.

Most of the older bank buildings along Fourth Street have changed ownership, and many no longer serve their original purpose, but a few continue to function as banking institutions.

The AmeriTrust Savings Association Building, 2 West Fourth Street, was established as the **14 German National Bank,** which changed its name to the Lincoln National Bank during World War I. The bank was founded in 1873, and in 1903, its officers commissioned the Cincinnati firm of Rapp, Zettel & Rapp to draw plans for new offices. Unlike most of the banks built on Fourth Street at the turn of the century, this 4-story Beaux Arts style building is reminiscent of the nineteenth century in both scale and design.

In 1955, Lincoln Bank merged with Fifth-Third. The building was subsequently acquired by Eagle Savings and in the late 1980s, became a branch of AmeriTrust, with company offices upstairs.

An 1859 architectural journal described Fourth Street as the "Broadway of Cincinnati" because of the many small, fashionable shops lining

*A large section of what is now McAlpin's department store on Fourth Street was once the showrooms of the Robert Mitchell Furniture Company.*

the street. Today, office towers have replaced most of these buildings, particularly east of Vine, but to the west, many remain, serving the same type of clientele they did more than a century ago.

Dating from before the Civil War, the **15 Herschede Building,** 4 West Fourth Street, is one of the oldest structures still standing on West Fourth Street, although construction of the German National Bank cut off its eastern-most portion and ground-level alterations have changed the appearance of this early Renaissance Revival style building.

Frank Herschede founded his jewelry business on Vine Street in 1877, several decades before he began manufacturing hall clocks in a Walnut Hills plant. Since the mid-1890s, the jewelry store has occupied three Fourth Street locations and has been in this building since 1939.

Another of the older surviving retail buildings on the street is the eastern-most portion of **16 The McAlpin Company** department

store, 13 West Fourth Street, designed by James W. McLaughlin (1834-1923) and erected for the John Shillito Company in 1857. McLaughlin, a local architect who designed the original Art Museum in Eden Park, had trained with Cincinnati architect James Keyes Wilson and was the son of Shillito's first business partner. When Shillito's moved to Seventh and Race in 1877, the wholesale dry goods firm of McAlpin, Polk & Company took over the building. George Washington McAlpin (1827-1890) had been employed by the business since he was sixteen. In 1885, it became the George W. McAlpin Company.

Shortly after McAlpin's death, his younger brother, William, moved the company into retailing, and in 1900, the store expanded west into the adjacent space that had been the salesrooms of the Robert Mitchell Furniture Company. The 6-story Mitchell Company building, now the central portion of McAlpin's, was designed in 1873 by James Keyes Wilson (1828-1894), architect for Plum Street Temple and the entrance gate to Spring Grove Cemetery. In 1938, McAlpin's expanded into a third structure erected in the early 1900s and occupied by a number of tenants including the Aeolian Company, manufacturers of conventional and player pianos.

Those parts of the McAlpin's store building designed by McLaughlin and Wilson compliment each other, while the newest portion appears to have cut off Wilson's design. The original architectural character of the structures' lower levels is obscured by the modern post-World War II facade that the store's owners used to tie the three units together and by the skywalk entryway.

McAlpin's was operated by family members until 1916, when financial difficulties brought about a sale of the business to Mercantile Stores of New York.

Next to Herschede's is another Fourth Street retailer of long-standing, **17** **Gidding-Jenny,** 18 West Fourth Street. The firm was founded in 1907 as J. M. Gidding & Company, a clothing store owned by four brothers who moved to Cincinnati from Duluth, Minnesota.

The building, in Commercial Queen Anne style, was probably erected sometime in the 1880s. Its most notable feature is the Rookwood tile front executed in 1907 by architect Frank Andrews and Rookwood artist John D. Wareham. Gidding & Company aimed to be an exclusive shop, offering "Correct Dress for Women," and its owners felt that the unique storefront would help the business stand out from its competitors.

Since 1923, the business has had several owners. It was acquired in 1961 by a conglomerate, and two years later, it merged with Jenny, Inc., another women's clothing shop that had been founded next door in 1921. In 1969, the facades of both stores were remodeled and unified by an arcaded storefront.

Across from McAlpin's at 410 Race Street is the site of another major downtown retailer. **18** **The H. & S. Pogue Company** operated a store here for more than a century.

Brothers Henry (1829-1903) and Samuel (1832-1912) Pogue migrated from Ireland shortly after the potato famine of 1845-1847. They first worked in their uncle's dry goods store and then bought him out, establishing the H. & S. Pogue Dry Goods Company in 1863.

The Pogue brothers, by then five in all, moved to a 5-story building of their own on Fourth Street in 1878 and a decade later erected an addition designed by James Griffith & Sons, to the east of their original store. Pogue's expanded twice more, hiring Samuel Hannaford & Sons to design the western-most portion of the building in 1902. In 1916, Hannaford's firm remodeled the entire structure, facing the lower levels in stone with panels topped by carved lions' heads. Above, however, the name "Pogue" could still be seen near the roofline of the original store. Pogue's eventually expanded into Carew Tower.

The company was family owned until 1961, when it became a part of Associated Dry Goods Corporation. In order to attract shoppers to downtown, Pogue's built a massive parking garage across Race on Fourth in 1966. In 1984, Associated merged Pogue's with L. S. Ayres of Indianapolis, but only four years later closed its Cincinnati stores. Almost at once, plans were announced to raze the Fourth Street part of the old Pogue's store and erect Tower Place, a $47 million structure with three floors of space for specialty shops topped by a 500-car garage.

**Turn right (north) on Race Street.**

Since the nineteenth century, downtown hotels have moved northward away from the riverfront, first to Fourth Street, and then to Fifth and Sixth Streets, the current location of the Omni Netherland Plaza, Clarion, Hyatt Regency, Westin, and Terrace Hilton hotels. The latter four hotels, with 2,795 rooms, were all built after World War II. Only the Netherland, in the Carew Tower complex, survives from an earlier generation of major downtown hotels.

On August 24, 1929, Thomas Emery's Sons announced a $30 million real estate deal to erect what would be the largest building complex of its kind in the United States. The Emery Hotel on Vine and the Carew Building, a 9-story office structure at the southwest corner of Fifth and Vine, were among the properties cleared for the building site. Excavations began on November 11, 1929, and construction of the **19** **Carew Tower,** 441 Vine Street, got underway on January 8, 1930. The tower, named for John Carew (1848-1914), founder of the Mabley & Carew department store chain, was to include a 49-story office block, a hotel, garage, department store, arcade, and restaurants.

The Carew Tower was born of the booming 1920s, when architects around the world sought to design massive building complexes that would function as cities within cities. As the leading downtown developer, Emery wanted to create such a center for Cincinnati. The decision to carry out the project during the Depression was a vote of confidence in the future of the city.

Walter W. Ahlschlager, a Chicago architect with the New York City firm of Delano & Aldrich, designed the Carew Tower. The Starrett Investing Company constructed and briefly managed the building, but in November 1932, turned the Carew Tower over to Emery, which has held it since.

The building was an unusual Art Deco design, featuring exotic woods, an ornate arcade decorated with Rookwood tile, and specially designed brass and copper fittings and window settings. The black marble doorway on

Vine Street had a bronze arch set with twenty-two medallions depicting a favored theme of the Art Deco movement, industrial progress, represented here by the development of transportation from the horse and rider to the airplane.

The Carew Tower was dedicated on July 10, 1930, and its first tenant moved in October 1. The primary retail tenant was Mabley & Carew, and small specialty shops lined the 2-story arcade. (When that department store moved to a new site in 1962, Pogue's expanded into the vacated space.) During the early years, Emery struggled to fill the tower's hundreds of offices that are now occupied by lawyers, physicians, travel agents, a radio station, insurance companies, a racquet club, and the building's owner, Emery Realty, Inc. Atop the forty-eighth floor of the tower is a public observation deck that offers a sweeping view of the Ohio River, Cincinnati basin, and Northern Kentucky.

On the west side of the Carew Tower was the **Netherland Plaza**

*The Carew Tower featured an Art Deco style arcade that originally ran between the H. & S. Pogue's and Mabley & Carew department stores.*

**Hotel,** 35 West Fifth Street. Starrett planned to name it for the old St. Nicholas Hotel (1865-1911) at Fourth and Race but discovered that the Sinton Hotel owned the rights to that name. Therefore, the new hotel opened on January 28, 1931, without a name. However, the silverware had already been engraved "St. N.P.," and a month later, the owners decided to call the establishment Starrett's Netherland Plaza.

The *Times-Star* rhapsodized that the 28-story, 800 room hotel challenged the "splendors of Solomon's Temple." Its main dining room was paneled with marble and Brazilian rosewood; the 3-story entry had marble walls and fluted columns, as well as ceiling murals. There were seven restaurants, twenty-six private dining rooms, and a wedding chapel adjacent to one of the ballrooms. And the Netherland's Pavilion Caprice nightclub later featured many of the big bands of the era.

For more than fifty years, the Netherland Plaza was host to notables including Eleanor Roosevelt, who refused to leave unless the hotel allowed her to pay her bill; Presidents Truman and Eisenhower, and Queen Juliana of the Netherlands. Crooner Bing Crosby almost caused a riot when he stayed here, and Winston Churchill requested plans for the yellow-tiled bathroom in his suite, hoping to reproduce it in one of his homes.

In 1956, the Hilton hotel chain assumed management and carried out a remodeling that included necessary maintenance as well as the installation of vinyl wallpaper on the terra cotta walls and carpeting over the terrazzo floors. By the end of the 1970s, however, the hotel had, in the words of one observer, "gone to seed." There was one reservation for Christmas 1981. After Hilton's lease expired, Emery turned management over to Dunfey Hotels, a company that specialized in historic hotel renovation.

For twenty-two months during 1982 and 1983, Dunfey closed the hotel for a $28 million renovation. The rosewood paneling was refinished; moldings, columns and accents were stripped and repainted; flocked wallpaper was removed. The Omni Netherland Plaza that reopened in October 1983 had fewer but more spacious rooms, exceeded current fire standards, and had regained its former glory.

**Turn left (west) on Fifth Street.**

The newest downtown hotel is in the **20 Hyatt-Regency Hotel/ Saks Fifth Avenue** complex, 151 West Fifth Street, which opened in March 1984. Twenty years earlier, city planners had designated this site for a luxury hotel, but it was not until 1973 that Hyatt made a concrete proposal to establish a hotel here. The plans died a year later for lack of financing, but in 1981, the city revived the project by raising $21 million in local funds and winning a $6 million federal Urban Development Action Grant.

The 22-story building was designed by RTKL, the firm that put together the 1964 downtown redevelopment plan. The architects created a red brick building with a rounded side toward the river, an angular wedge facing the city, and a solarium tucked between the wings.

The hotel has 484 rooms, two restaurants, two lounges, a pool, a sauna, and numerous banquet and meeting rooms. A Saks Fifth Avenue department store is also part of the complex. Second-floor level skywalks link the store and hotel to other downtown facilities.

When city planners began to consider urban renewal in the 1950s, one of their major goals was to clear out a dilapidated area around Fifth and Elm Streets and build a convention center. For this plan to succeed, a group of new and renovated hotels was essential.

Stouffer's Cincinnati Inn, now the **21 Clarion Hotel,** 141 West Sixth Street, was the first new downtown hotel built since the Terrace Plaza had opened in 1948. The first Stouffer's tower, across the street from the convention center, opened in 1968. Seven years later, Stouffer's erected a second tower on Sixth Street.

**Turn right (north) on Elm Street, right (east) on Sixth Street.**

The **22 Terrace Hilton Hotel,** 15 West Sixth Street, originally the Terrace Plaza, is the oldest of Cincinnati's post-World War II hotels and a rare example of classic modern architecture. It was built by Emery Realty, which commissioned Skidmore, Owings & Merrill to design the International style building. Like Emery's Carew Tower, the structure was planned for mixed use, including seven floors of office and retail space, an eighth floor with a combination meeting and dining area, ten floors of hotel rooms, and a roof garden and restaurant on the eighteenth floor.

When the Terrace Plaza opened in July 1948, it featured modern artworks by Alexander Calder, Joan Miro, and Saul Steinberg. When Emery sold the hotel to the Hilton chain in 1956, company president John J. Emery donated the Calder mobile and the Steinberg mural to the Cincinnati Art Museum.

The **23 Cincinnatian Hotel,** 601 Vine Street, though not as large as its competitors, is notable as one of Cincinnati's few remaining nineteenth-century hotels. Designed for the Emery family by Samuel Hannaford in the French Second Empire style, the hotel opened in 1882 as the Palace. It had 160 rooms for $3 to $4 a night and soon added such modern conveniences as incandescent lights and hydraulic elevators.

A 1948 modernization added safety improvements and a plain stone facade that covered the lower levels. By then, the hotel had 300 rooms and was the Palace Hotel Cincinnatian. In November 1951, the name was shortened to the Cincinnatian Hotel.

Over the next three decades, the Cincinnatian became an increasingly dilapidated residential and transient hotel. In 1983, it was sold to a local partnership. After a $23 million renovation, the hotel reopened in February 1987 with 149 luxury rooms, a restaurant, and a lounge.

The redevelopment of the Cincinnatian Hotel was not without controversy. By the 1980s, the downtown market for hotel rooms was glutted. The managements of other hotels opposed the creation of more rooms, claiming that the project was receiving special treatment from the city, and initiated an unsuccessful court action to block tax credits and a $3.5 million UDAG grant.

**Turn right (south) on Vine Street.**

In late 1986, the city signed an agreement with JMB-Federated, a part of Federated Department Stores, and Emery Realty to develop **24 Fountain Square West,** with a $250 million, 50-story complex that would stretch along the north side of Fifth Street between Vine and Race. The tower was to be built on the site of the former Rollman's Department Store, which had incorporated the old Hotel Havlin. In 1962, that building was occupied by another major Cincinnati retail concern, **Mabley & Carew**—a branch of Dayton-based Elder-Beerman since 1978.

The first Mabley's store opened in 1877 on Fifth Street between Walnut and Vine. Christopher R. Mabley, a British immigrant who had come from Canada to develop a chain of clothing stores in the United States, was passing through Cincinnati and missed his train to Memphis. Mabley and his employee, Joseph T. Carew (1848-1914), stayed the night and decided that Cincinnati would be a good location for a C. R. Mabley & Company store.

A 6-story building at the northeast corner of Fifth and Vine Streets replaced the original store in 1881. After the Carew Tower was built, the store moved into retail space there. In 1962, Mabley & Carew moved its downtown operation to the former Rollman's building. Mabley's closed this downtown store in 1985 to make way for the Fountain Square West development.

When the JMB/Emery partnership backed out of the project in September 1988, the future of what was considered the prime site for new development in the Core was again uncertain.

**25 Fountain Square,** facing Fifth Street between Walnut and Main, is the central gathering place in downtown. Its centerpiece is the **Tyler Davidson Fountain,** a symbol of the city for many Cincinnatians.

The fountain was donated by Henry Probasco, a leading Cincinnati hardware merchant, to honor the memory of his business partner and brother-in-law, Tyler Davidson. Probasco and Davidson had frequently discussed the idea of giving their adopted city a monument that was both useful and attractive.

The city accepted Probasco's gift in 1867, agreeing to provide perpetual

*After completion in 1871, the Tyler Davidson Fountain esplanade quickly became a popular gathering place.*

maintenance and that the fountain should be used only for providing drinking water and as an ornament—except in cases of fire. The city also decided to construct an esplanade for the fountain, seizing an opportunity to clear the unsightly butchers' market on Fifth Street between Vine and Walnut Streets.

Since 1829, the market had been a center for the sale of meat, with fifty-four butchers located there. By 1870, however, Cincinnati residents were becoming aware that this part of the downtown was experiencing a growing volume of cultural and commercial activity. Many people were offended by the noise, congestion, and smells of the market. The butchers considered the market to be theirs by law, right, and tradition, but after consid-erable litigation, at 3 p.m. on Friday, February 4, 1870, City Council voted to tear down the market. That same afternoon, city workers moved in to demolish it, with police standing by to protect them. Within three hours, the market was rubble.

Over the next few months, a tree-lined, 60' x 400' esplanade designed by William Tinsley was constructed as a setting for the fountain. In July, Probasco laid the cornerstone, and on October 6, 1871, the fountain was dedicated.

The 43-foot high bronze and stone piece was the work of August von Kreling of Nuremberg. The Royal Bronze Foundry of Munich cast the fountain using metal from obsolete cannons purchased in Denmark.

The central figure is the the Genius of Water, a gently smiling woman from whose fingertips flow streams of water. Below her are four groups of figures depicting the impor-tance of water: a farmer and his panting dog waiting for rain, a young woman accompanying her ill father to a mineral spring, a mother leading her son to bathe, and a workman standing on the roof of his burning house, holding an empty bucket and search-ing the skies for rain.

Four bas reliefs on the base of the pedestal present the industrial uses of water for fisheries, navigation, water power, and steam power. In niches on each corner are figures of children enjoying water: a girl admires her reflection, a boy holds a lobster, another girl puts a shell to her ear, and a second boy dons ice skates.

Around the basin of the fountain, figures of four boys taming water animals served as drinking fountains, with water—cooled by a special appa-ratus beneath the fountain—spouting from the animals' mouths. Probasco hoped that the fountain and cold drinking water would attract young people to the Square and away from coffeehouses and other questionable entertainments.

For almost a century, the Tyler Davidson Fountain stood in the mid-dle of Fifth Street with traffic running on either side. By the late 1950s, the fountain and its esplanade not only obstructed traffic, but also seemed "old fashioned."

In 1961, developers proposed a landscaped boulevard-type mall for the fountain. The 1964 *Plan for Downtown Cincinnati* called for a square. In 1969, after three years of construction, the new Fountain Square was completed, and the Tyler Davidson Fountain was moved about thirty feet east and turned 180 degrees to face west.

After the move, engineers found that the fountain itself needed resto-ration, and philanthropist Frederick A. Hauck (b. 1894) donated $70,000 for the project. The new Square was dedicated on October 16, 1971, almost one hundred years to the day after the original ceremony, with several of Probasco's descendents attending.

Fountain Square has been called "the most successful public square in America," and two years after its completion, the Square's designers, RTKL, received a National Honor Award for it from the American Institute of Architects.

Fountain Square is centrally located in relation to major hotels, offices, and stores and serves as a public gathering place. Many downtown workers meet at the fountain for lunch, and summer concerts are given here from the permanent stage constructed in the mid-1980s. Artists and designers have often used the image of the Tyler Davidson Fountain to represent Cincinnati.

It has also served as a focus for new downtown development. The Fifth-Third Center/DuBois Tower was built here just before the fountain was moved, and the Fifth-Third Bank Building is to the north.

**Turn left (east) on Fifth Street.**

Completed in 1981, **26** **Fountain Square South** filled the south side of Fifth Street between Vine and Walnut. At the Walnut Street corner is the 29-story headquarters of Star Bank (formerly First National Bank of Cincinnati), 425 Walnut Street, designed by Poor, Swanke, Hayden & Cornell of New York City with the upper stories set back so that sunlight can reach the street below. The 17-story Westin Hotel comprises the eastern portion of the development. The 460-room $38 million Westin has several restaurants and lounges, retail space at street level, a pool, health club, and a large glassed-in area that was to function as a space for public events.

Fountain Square South occupies the site of the 6-story **Albee Theater**, Cincinnati's most spectacular movie palace. The $4 million Albee was designed by Charles Lamb, considered by many critics to be the world's finest theater architect.

The Albee's 3-story grand lobby had white marble walls, brass and crystal chandeliers, double marble staircases leading to the mezzanine, mahogany paneled ladies' and men's lounges, ornate brass railings, and ceilings with elaborate plaster work. The 5-story auditorium could seat 3,300. Behind the scenes were five floors of dressing rooms, each named after a different city. There were even rooms for animal performers and a tub for trained seals.

During the Depression, Cincinnatians could see a movie, several vaudeville acts, and a big band for thirty-five cents admission. The Albee also featured such big names as Eddie

Cantor, Nat "King" Cole, the Marx Brothers, Red Skelton, W. C. Fields, and Benny Goodman. But by the 1960s, most people preferred to go to movie theaters in their own neighborhoods, and the Albee, then owned by RKO Stanley-Warner, was showing "B" movies to dwindling audiences.

Cincinnati's 1964 downtown redevelopment plan proposed that a luxury hotel-office-retail complex be built on the Albee site. Efforts to preserve the old "movie cathedral" failed. The Albee closed on September 17, 1974, the contents were sold, and the theater was demolished in 1977. The marble arch from the facade, however, was removed, stored, and later incorporated into the Fifth Street side of Cincinnati's convention center.

The Star Bank Center occupies the corner where a **Gibson Hotel** had stood since February 14, 1849, when Peter Gibson opened the 5-story Gibson House. Later that year, a notice in the *Daily Atlas* announced that, "due to the fact that the Gibson House is located so far out in the country and away from the river, it necessitates a temporary cessation of services."

Gibson's hotel reopened the next year and prospered as the city grew north from the riverfront. The 5-story structure was torn down in 1873 to be replaced by a larger one. A fire destroyed the hotel in 1912, and two years later, a new 12-story Classical style Gibson Hotel was completed.

A 1922 addition made the Gibson the "largest hostelry in the Middle West" with 1,000 rooms, a bar sixty feet long, and a roof garden restaurant where Doris Day later sang. Diners in the Florentine Room heard the bands of Tommy Dorsey, Guy Lombardo, and Wayne King.

The Sheraton Corporation bought the Gibson in 1950, but by the 1970s, the aging hotel attracted few guests. The Gibson Hotel was closed on July 1974 and, like the Albee, its contents were sold before it was demolished three years later.

While most city and county government agencies are located in the periphery of downtown, the Cincinnati offices of the federal government are in the heart of the CBD. Government Square is the location of the **27** **Federal Building,** 100 East Fifth Street, and the **John Weld Peck**

**Federal Building,** 550 Main Street, as well as the principal downtown transfer point for Cincinnati's bus system.

The location of government offices and the main post office changed at the whim of each new postmaster until 1857, when the first United States Post Office and Customs House was built on Fourth Street. By 1874, that building was too small, and excavations for a new Federal Building were begun on the north side of Fifth Street between Walnut and Main. A number of businessmen objected that this site was too far from the riverfront, then the center of commerce, but they were ignored.

The ornate, 5-story Second Empire style building was designed by architects A. B. Mullel, W. A. Potter, and James C. Hill of Washington, D.C., under the supervision of Samuel Hannaford of Cincinnati. Completed in 1885 at a cost $5 million, it took eleven years to build and housed twenty-seven government agencies.

By the late 1920s, federal agencies had outgrown the structure, and plans were made for a new Post Office and Federal Building. After several years of delay, caused mainly by controversy over the site, the government decided to rebuild on the foundations of the 1885 building. Demolition of the post office began in November 1936, and the superstructure of the new 9-story building was in place by August 1937. Although the new building, completed in 1939, was smaller in overall dimensions than the old one, its usable space was more than double.

During World War II, the creation of new federal agencies led to yet another space shortage. Several proposals were made for a new federal office building, but only in 1958 did plans center on the northeast corner of Main and Fifth Streets. Construction began on a new 10-story office building in May 1962 and was completed in August 1964. In 1984, this structure was named to honor John Weld Peck, who had served for many years as a state and federal judge.

Although the main office of the postal service was subsequently moved to the West End, there is still a large post office branch here. In addition, the two federal buildings house federal courts, the Internal Revenue Service, and a range of government administrative offices including those of the FBI, CIA, armed forces recruiting, United States senators and congressmen, and field offices of the Departments of Agriculture, Commerce, Defense, Interior, and Justice.

**Turn left (north) on Main Street, left (west) on Sixth Street.**

Downtown Cincinnati restaurants range from coffee shops and fast food outlets to the finest dining rooms. **28 The Maisonette,** 114 East Sixth Street, is one of only eleven restaurants in the United States and Canada to be awarded five stars by the *Mobil Travel Guide.*

The Masionette is run by the family of Nathan L. Comisar (1901-1949), who arrived in the United States from Russia in 1914. In 1928, Comisar took over La Normandie, a restaurant he and his younger brother, Ben (1903-1966), operated in the Fountain Square Building at Fifth and Walnut.

Two years later, Comisar opened a dining room named The Maisonette, adding French items to the menu. After a 1949 renovation, the restaurant was renamed La Normandie Maisonette. Two months after the reopening, Nathan died, and his two sons, Michael J. and N. Lee Comisar, took charge of the business.

There are now two Comisar restaurants at this Sixth Street address, La Normandie, an English style chop house, and The Maisonette, serving classic French cuisine.

**Turn right (north) on Walnut Street.**

The cluster of five buildings at 625-641 Walnut Street represents the kinds of commercial structures that made up much of downtown in the nineteenth century. The most notable of the group is the Renaissance Revival style **29 Teasdale Dye House,** 625 Walnut Street (now a quick-print shop),which has been declared a historic building by the city's Historic Conservation Board.

In 1835, English-born William Teasdale opened his shop, sometimes advertised as the New York Dye House, on the east side of Walnut

Street. With success came construction of a building of his own in 1840; the present 4-story structure may be that early building, altered by later remodeling, though more likely it dates from the 1850s.

Before dry cleaning became common, the life of clothing was extended by dying faded or stained items in a darker shade. In the late nineteenth century, Teasdale's firm also began to clean dresses or suits at prices ranging from $1.50 to $2.50. The company moved to more modern headquarters in Avondale in 1929.

*The former Teasdale Dye House building is one of the few mid-nineteenth-century structures that remains in the downtown Core.*

The other building of note in this group, 635-637, belonged to the Thomas Gibson Company, a plumbing supply house founded in 1832, which moved here in 1884. Taking over three buildings, Gibson tied them together with a French Second Empire facade with the initials "TG" in the fifth-story gables. By the early twentieth century, half of this structure was used by a merchant tailoring company while the remainder had been divided up for furnished rooms and was known as the Gibson Flats.

The Gibson Apartments had tenants well into mid-century, though recently, only the street-level commercial space of these buildings has been used.

**Turn left (west) on Seventh Street, left (south) on Vine Street.**

In the nineteenth century, light industries such as printing plants were scattered throughout the CBD. Although most of these firms moved away as downtown land became increasingly valuable, others, including the *Cincinnati Enquirer,* remained. Between 1926 and 1928, the newspaper erected the present **30 Cincinnati Enquirer Building,** 617 Vine Street, on a site that it had occupied since 1866.

The paper, which can trace its roots to several early Cincinnati periodicals, began publishing on a daily basis, except Sundays, on April 10, 1841. The publishers vowed to "sustain the principles and policy of the great Democratic party of the country" and on page two of the first issue, noted the death, six days earlier, of Whig President William Henry Harrison a "dispensation of Providence."

Seven years later on April 20, 1848, the *Enquirer* published its first Sunday edition, one of the first American newspapers to do so. The editors assured those readers opposed to labor on the Sabbath that most of the work for this issue had been done on Saturday, and the Monday edition, most of which was produced on Sunday, would be suspended. The publishers also promised to return to the old arrangement if the public protested. But Cincinnatians accepted the idea of a Sunday paper, and in 1866, the Monday issue was resumed.

Between 1841 and 1866, the *Enquirer* had four different offices, its last on Vine between Third and Fourth, next to Pike's Opera House. When that famous theater burned, so did the paper, its ink and rolls of newsprint feeding the flames. The paper missed only one edition as it moved further north on Vine Street, taking over the former quarters of the Wesleyan Female College.

The old college building was enlarged several times, but by the early 1920s, the newspaper had outgrown its offices and had nowhere else to expand. Plans were made for a magnificent new 14-story headquarters and office building. Lockwood, Greene

& Company, architects for the New York Herald Tribune and Baldwin Piano Company buildings, was commissioned for the job.

Over the next two years, the new plant was constructed around the old one so that the paper's operations would be only minimally disrupted. The new building was an elaborate mixture of early twentieth-century styles including elements of Romanesque Revival, Neo-Classical, and Gothic. Its exotic interior decorations included marble walls, etched bronze elevator doors, and a bronze grille at the entry featuring figures and inventions from the history of printing. The newspaper's operations occupied the first three floors while various businesses and professionals rented the offices on the upper stories.

Two of the *Enquirer's* early writers have passed into local legend. Lafcadio Hearn (1850-1904) was renowned for his graphic descriptions of life along the riverfront and in Cincinnati's tenements; Marion Devereux (1873-1948) succeeded her mother as social editor and arbiter of high society in the Queen City.

Through the turn of the century, the paper's major owners were members of the McLean family, but when John McLean died in 1916, the paper passed from their control. In 1952, executors of the McLean estate were blocked from selling the *Enquirer* to Cincinnati's afternoon paper, The *Cincinnati Times-Star*, by a storm of public protest. Instead, ownership passed to an employee group. Between 1952 and 1979, the paper went through the hands of five owners. In 1979, it became part of an expanded Gannett chain.

The following decade, an agreement approved by the U.S. Justice Department permitted the *Enquirer* and the *Cincinnati Post*, a Scripps-Howard paper, to set up joint business, printing, circulation, and advertising operations to reduce costs, though separate newsrooms and editorial departments were maintained.

In 1981, the Enquirer Building was sold to the New York- based William Kaufman Organization, which began a careful renovation and restoration. With a variety of tenants renting the modernized commercial and office space, the Cincinnati Enquirer Building has been made economically successful while retaining its character.

**Turn right (west) on Sixth Street, right (north) on Race Street.**

Retailing is one of the most important activities in the Core, not only along Fourth Street but extending almost to the Frame. One of the largest retail operations on the edge of the Core is the Lazarus department store. Located at the corner of Seventh and Race Streets, the building was originally the **31** **Headquarters of the John Shillito Company**.

Shillito (1808-1879) entered into the first of several partnerships that led to the creation of the John Shillito Company in 1830. Seeking a prestigious location, he moved to Fourth Street later that decade, erecting what was then considered "the most commodious dry goods store west of the Alleghenies." In 1842, Shillito became sole proprietor of the business. A new store went up in 1857 but was outgrown within twenty years, and Shillito decided to leave crowded Fourth Street, choosing a tract at Seventh and Race.

Many questioned the decision that placed his store several blocks north of the city's principal retail district, but it allowed Shillito to obtain a larger piece of land than he could find on Fourth or Fifth Street. The new 6-story emporium, in which all floors overlooked a domed central atrium, was designed by James McLaughlin. Opened in 1878, Shillito's store quickly became one of Cincinnati's major attractions. Other businessmen gradually followed Shillito's lead, and by the 1920s, the area around Seventh and Race was an integral part of the downtown retail district.

By then, however, Shillito's sales had begun to decline. In 1928, the firm had slipped from being Cincinnati's largest department store to fourth, and the F. & R. Lazarus Company, a Columbus department store and holding company, bought out Shillito's sons. A year later, Lazarus, Filene's of Boston, and Abraham & Strauss in Brooklyn joined to create Federated Department Stores, headquartered in Cincinnati by 1945.

As part of the revitalization of Shillito's, Federated built an 8-story addition to the west of McLaughlin's original structure in 1936-1937. The firm of Potter, Tyler & Martin designed the new portion of the store in the Art Moderne style with rounded corners and flowing horizontal lines, and the old red brick structure was resurfaced to match the addition. The interior of the store was completely modernized and the atrium floored over. In 1946, a new garage and service building was added. The headquarters for Federated Department Stores, a triangular-shaped building at 7 West Seventh Street, was erected in 1980.

Along with McAlpin's and Pogue's, Shillito's shared the area dry goods market through the 1970s. But the 1980s brought rapid changes. Faced with declining profits and increased competition, Federated merged Shillito's and Rikes of Dayton in 1982. Four years later, the company combined Shillito-Rikes with the Lazarus chain of Columbus, and the Shillito name was dropped. In 1988, Canada's Campeau Corporation took over the business.

**Turn left (west) on Shillito Rikes Place.**

Like the Mercantile Library on Walnut Street, the **32** **Cincinnati Athletic Club,** 111 Shillito-Rikes Place, recalls an earlier age when Cincinnati's downtown was not only a business district, but the center of a city where people lived, worked, and played.

In 1853, a group of leading citizens including Thomas and Joseph Emery, Charles P. and William Howard Taft, sculptor Hiram Powers, Jr., grocer Joseph R. Peebles, and Rutherford B. Hayes founded the Young Men's Gymnastic Association. Hayes, a young lawyer, served as president of the Cincinnati Gymnastic and Athletic Club before resigning to serve in the Union Army, finally later as governor of Ohio, and President of the United States.

An 1887 booklet about the club depicts members of the Cincinnati Gymnasium, then located on the third floor of the Grand Opera House on Vine Street, pursuing physical fitness through boxing, fencing, wrestling, trapeze work, calisthenics, and gymnastics. Later generations of businessmen, local government officials, and judges were more likely to come to "The Gym" to relax and talk politics.

The Athletic Club's membership

declined sharply after World War II, and members began to liquidate club assets in the early 1960s. In 1963, membership, which early in the century had exceeded 1,500, was down to 370. At this point, a group of members decided to save the club and raised enough money to renovate its facilities.

The fitness boom of the 1980s boosted membership and allowed the athletic club to renovate its running track, install a new hardwood gym floor, and acquire modern fitness and weight training equipment. The club also has handball courts, three heat rooms, a solarium, and a swimming pool.

Club membership is exclusively male, limited to 290, and open by invitation only.

**Turn left (south) on Rusconi Place, left (east) on Sixth Street, and right (north) on Race Street.**

In the post-World War II era, Cincinnati city planners have worked to keep the CBD Core concentrated and manageable for pedestrians. An important element in their efforts to enhance the attractiveness and convenience of working and shopping in the Central Business District is the **33 Skywalk System,** which facilitates pedestrian traffic between major office buildings, stores, hotels, and public places throughout the downtown.

The idea for the city's elevated walkway network developed in the late 1950s and early 1960s as city planners sought a way to revitalize downtown. One of the most important aspects of their proposals was the desire to create a more comfortable environment for people, the crucial link in redevelopment.

In late 1957, Herbert W. Stevens, director of the City Planning Commission, set before City Council a number of plans to ease the conflict between vehicular and pedestrian traffic. One of these was a network of second-story elevated sidewalks that would connect major buildings and protect pedestrians from both traffic and inclement weather. The plan also called for downtown pedestrian malls, arcades, and subterranean walkways. But City Council rejected this and similar plans in 1958 and 1961.

Federal funds for urban renewal became available in the early 1960s. The old plans of the previous decade were revived; outside consultants were called in, and public groups were consulted. During the planning process, one element of the 1957-1958 plan gained the support of several advisory committees—the elevated sidewalks, or skywalks, as they came to be called.

The first sections of the skywalk opened in August 1971, three years after construction had begun, with spans connecting Convention Center and Fountain Square. Over the next decade and a half, the network grew to include walkways from Elm to Main Street and from Fourth to Seventh Streets, with links to Lytle Place and the riverfront sports arenas—and continued expansion seemed probable. With twenty-one sections by 1987, the skywalk system was 1.3 miles long and had cost the city $16 million.

The skywalks were a European concept developed before World War I, and no American city has adopted

*In the early 1960s, Cincinnati architect Robert Springer, working with the City Planning Commission, helped develop the downtown Skywalk system.*

them as wholeheartedly as Cincinnati. Nevertheless, the skywalks have had their problems. At times, special police patrols have been necessary to curb minor crime, and in bad weather, the early, open-sided skywalks provided little protection. Several older buildings have also been obscured or defaced by second-level skywalk entrances.

However, as their proponents predicted in the early 1960s, Cincinnati skywalks have aided the flow of downtown traffic and have been a convenience to downtown workers and shoppers. Newer bridges are more elaborate than the original ones, and a second level of retailing and specialty shops has developed along the skywalks. The skywalk system had become so integral a part of pedestrians that downtown business was noticeably disrupted when, in 1988, the L. S. Ayres' store closed, and the interior connections that the store had provided across Race, Vine, Fourth, and Fifth Streets were no longer available.

**Tour ends.**

# Tour 3

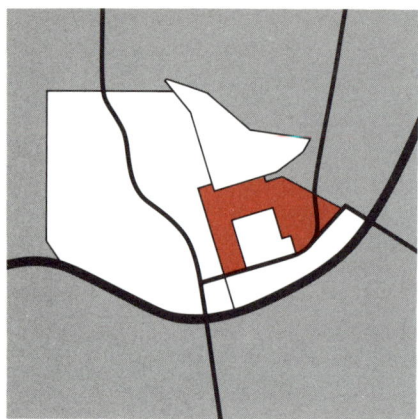

# Central Business District Frame

When city planners studied Cincinnati in the 1950s, they decided that the downtown was essentially two regions—the "Core" and an area of approximately 330 acres of land on the periphery of the Central Business District (CBD) that the planners called the "Frame."

The Frame surrounded the downtown Core on three sides, extending from Seventh Street to Twelfth Street on the north, from Main Street to Eggleston Avenue on the east, and from Elm Street to Central Avenue on the west. Land use in this subdistrict was similar to that of the Core, except that stores, offices, and banks were less densely concentrated. However, light manufacturing facilities, warehouses, religious and social institutions, city and county government offices, the main library, parking lots, and most downtown housing were also located in this part of the CBD.

Differences between the Core and its periphery have existed since the basin was first settled in the late eighteenth century. After the area that is now known as the Frame was first cleared in the 1790s, it was used as pasture by the people living in the town closer to the river.

In the early decades of the nineteenth century, Cincinnatians began erecting homes, some of them quite elegant and expensive, at the eastern and western ends of Third and Fourth Streets. These areas appealed to the wealthy because of their proximity to the city's central banking and business district. During this period, a few scattered houses were also built above Fifth Street, and by 1819, a number of Cincinnatians had homes on Seventh Street; a few had even located on Main Street north of Ninth, but demand for housing in this area was low. In the "walking city" that existed before public transportation was widely available, people tried to live close to where they shopped, worked, worshipped, and relaxed.

The large, inexpensive building sites available in the outer part of the periphery attracted entreprenuers who set up factories on the northern edge of the city. The completion of the Miami & Erie Canal along the present-day routes of Central Parkway and Eggleston Avenue in 1829 also encouraged industrial development, and soon the canal was lined with factories and warehouses.

But the growth of manufacturing did not prevent other kinds of development from taking place nearby. Houses, schools, factories, markets, stores, saloons, and churches stood side by side in the areas around the center of town.

At first, most of those living in the northern periphery were people of modest means who worked at the foundries, mills, and workshops also located on the edge of the city. Gradually, however, more well-to-do families chose to live in other parts of the periphery than the "silk-stocking district" around East Third and Fourth Streets. Some simply wished to escape the increasingly congested city center, but for the growing number of Cincinnati businessmen engaged in manufacturing, it was a question of convenience. In the early 1850s, it still made sense for a merchant or banker to live near the riverfront and the Third Street commercial district. But it was logical for ironworks owner Miles Greenwood to build a house at the corner of Ninth and Race Streets, only a few blocks from his factory at Walnut and Canal.

By mid-century, there were desirable residential properties on Seventh, Eighth, Ninth, and Main Streets, and Western Row (Central

*Not all major retailers were located in the heart of the Central Business District: the huge Alms & Doepke store was on the northern edge of the downtown periphery by the Miami & Erie Canal.*

Avenue). Mixed in with these homes were shops, churches, and civic buildings, including the city offices built in 1853 at Plum and Ninth Streets and the Hamilton County Courthouse at Main and Court Streets, and some smaller manufacturing establishments. Larger factories and warehouses, along with most of the area's less expensive housing, were generally located on the outer edges of the periphery.

The mixed character of these areas prevailed for several decades. But in the 1870s and 1880s, an increasing number of the periphery's affluent residents began migrating to hilltop suburbs such as Clifton and Avondale, motivated by concerns about disease and crime in the increasingly dirty, crowded, and noisy basin. The vicinity of East Third and Fourth Streets remained fashionable, but other once-desirable locations in the downtown periphery were abandoned by their wealthy residents. Their places were taken by middle-income Cincinnatians, and many of the large homes were divided into apartments or converted to other uses.

At the same time, many of the area's industries also began to move to larger sites or those with better access to the railroads. In addition, taxes were often lower in suburban communities than in the city. Factories and most of the area's meatpackers shifted their operations to the Mill Creek Valley. The vacated industrial sites were quickly taken over by other manufacturers or shifted to other uses.

As these changes took place, parts of the area surrounding the city center became more distinctly divided into subdistricts. The Lytle Park vicinity was a clearly identifiable cluster of upper-income housing and institutions. East of Broadway on Sixth Street was the center of the small black ghetto known as Bucktown. Sycamore above Seventh was a manufacturing area, while Main Street had become a commercial strip.

During the 1890s and early 1900s, the area from Walnut west to Plum Street still contained a diverse mix of housing, light industry, wholesalers, offices, churches, theaters, and stores. Vine Street south of the canal, however, appeared to be an extension of Over-the-Rhine's Vine Street entertainment district with shooting galleries, the Chicago Chop House, and the Muenchener Bier Garten. West of Plum were small businesses that served the densely populated West End.

The eastern fringe of the basin remained a significant manufacturing district where firms such as the Heekin Can Company and the American Tool Company had plants. Warehouses, wholesalers, and light industrial workshops were also scattered throughout the area. And many people continued to live there, even though much of the housing was in poor condition.

With notable exceptions, such as properties around Lytle Park, most of the residential structures on the streets surrounding the central city became increasingly less desirable than newer suburban housing. Low rents made these often deteriorating homes and apartments attractive to many lower-income families. The 1910 census listed more than 10,000 residents in the area roughly bounded by Seventh Street, Central Avenue, Twelfth Street and Eggleston Avenue; most were people of limited means, often living in very crowded conditions, without adequate water, sanitation, or ventilation.

City officials became increasingly aware of a need' to improve the physical environment of the basin. During 1911-1912, the administration of Mayor Henry Hunt upgraded sanitation services throughout the city. But officials also hoped to enable basin residents to move out of those areas immediately around the central city.

A rapid transit committee formed in 1912 initiated planning for a public transportation project that led to the draining of the canal in 1919 and the attempted conversion of the former waterway into a subway covered by Central Parkway. The polluted canal had become an embarrassment to many Cincinnatians; its elimination was desirable for both aesthetic and public health reasons. Further, others argued that the improvement of the city's transportation network would allow more workers to live in healthier, less crowded circumstances outside the basin.

Private citizens also attempted to address concerns about urban conditions, the city's appearance, and its future. The United City Planning Committee, for example, raised the funds to pay for the development of a city plan that ultimately was adopted by the City Planning Commission in 1925.

The 1925 *Official Plan of the City of Cincinnati* called for the beautification of downtown streets and the replacement of crowded older structures in the periphery with a rapid transit terminus and a cluster of new civic buildings and parks. This proposed group of public structures included a new main post office, municipal auditorium, City Hall annex, main library, and Board of Education office arranged on or near Central Parkway between City Hall and Music Hall. The planners said nothing about maintaining or improving the downtown as a

*Printing plants and offices—including those of "The Cincinnati Times-Star," built in 1933—were scattered throughout the fringes of downtown.*

residential district, emphasizing instead the need to encourage the "decentralization" of housing in the city.

City planners of the 1920s believed that industrial and commercial activity would gradually push residential land use out of the basin. To an extent, this did take place, as many former homes and apartment buildings in the downtown and its periphery were converted into stores, workshops, or offices. By the late 1940s when a new master plan was formulated, there were fewer than fifty apartment buildings or apartment hotels left in the area immediately surrounding the Central Business District. These buildings were generally occupied by low-income elderly people.

The authors of the *Cincinnati Metropolitan Master Plan*, adopted in 1948, believed residential land use was inappropriate in the downtown. Although the planners were beginning to perceive a difference in function and character between the heart or "high-rent" section of the Central Business District and its periphery, the new plan proposed no new housing construction in or near the downtown except for a few apartment towers on the riverfront.

Views on what were acceptable land uses in the Central Business District had changed by the time a new plan for downtown redevelopment was issued in 1957. That document specifically divided the CBD into "Core" and "Frame". The planners' view of the Frame included not only warehousing, wholesaling, parking, and offices, but residential activity as well. The authors of the 1957 plan argued that although the low-cost residential units still existed in the Frame were a "residual" land use that would disappear as demand for commercial and office space grew, there were a number of appropriate sites for new high-rent housing development in the downtown periphery.

Cincinnati officials were coming to accept the growing perception among urban planners that a healthy central business district needed a combination of commercial activity, housing, and entertainment facilities. Further, some planners also suggested that a number of people would prefer a home in the heart of the city to one in the suburbs.

The fact that there were Cincinnatians who liked city living became more evident in the late 1950s and early 1960s. Mt. Adams, a neighborhood adjacent to downtown, saw both new residential construction and the renovation of older structures as middle and upper-income housing. By 1961, this trend was manifesting itself in the frame of the CBD as two structures on East Fourth Street were renovated to include apartments.

City planners of the early 1960s increasingly supported the concept that residential projects involving both new and old buildings, with units for different income levels, were appropriate land-uses in the CBD, particularly in the Frame. An ambitious new CBD plan published in 1964 called for the development of "a broad band of downtown housing"

*The designation of local historic districts, among them the Main Street Historic District, has encouraged the preservation of older buildings in the Frame.*

*Growing demand for office space in the Frame has fostered the conversion of industrial structures like the former French-Bauer dairy plant.*

that would include the areas around Lytle Park, Garfield Park, and West Fourth Street.

The 1965 conversion of the Broadway Hotel at Fourth and Broadway into the Lytle Tower Apartments, the construction of new high-rise apartment buildings on Garfield Place in 1969 and 1982, and the opening of the former Gibson Greeting Card and Gas-Light & Coke Company buildings on West Fourth Street as housing in 1980 brought new residents to the downtown.

While housing remained an important element in the Frame during the post-World War II era, many of the area's warehousing or light industrial operations, along with some retail/wholesale outlets, gradually moved away. Office space and parking facilities occupied a greater proportion of properties within the Frame, where larger sites were available at lower cost than in the Core.

In some cases, such as the expansion of Procter & Gamble's corporate headquarters, older buildings that included factory, warehouse, and retail space were simply torn down to make room for new office structures and parking lots. In other instances, light industrial facilities, like the former French Bauer dairy at the corner of Central Parkway and Plum Street, were completely renovated for use as office buildings.

Although property in the Frame became increasingly desirable for offices, housing, or parking during the 1970s and 1980s, there was enough space available and land values were relatively low enough to allow a variety of activities and types of buildings to remain. Unlike in the Core, where the extremely high land values encouraged the demolition of small older buildings for the construction of larger new towers that could utilize the available space more profitably, a greater number of historic structures survived in the Frame, and by the late 1980s, many were being renovated and reused.

Non-commercial buildings, including churches, clubs, local government offices, social service agencies, and museums had a place in the Frame. Housing that was affordable for middle and even lower-income people could be found scattered through the downtown periphery in the late 1980s. And many businesses that could not afford space in the Core, like restaurants, art galleries, office supply outlets, antiques shops, and barbers, found suitable locations in the Frame.

The Frame has remained more varied than the Core as city planners have increasingly seen the mix of activities and building types there as necessary to support and enhance the vitality of the entire Central Business District.

The *Cincinnati 2000 Plan*, adopted by City Council in 1981, slightly expanded the boundaries of the CBD Core and divided the Frame area into several subdistricts: Oldtown (the West Fourth Street vicinity), Lytle Park, Main Street, and Garfield Place. The city hoped to see 6,000 new residential units in the CBD by the year 2000, with a significant portion of them in these districts and on the riverfront. Planned expansion of retail and office functions in these areas likely would involve the preservation and rehabilitation of existing older structures. It was principally in the Frame subdistricts that the authors of the *Cincinnati 2000 Plan* saw the greatest opportunity to "retain a sense of the City's past and a human scale" within the downtown.

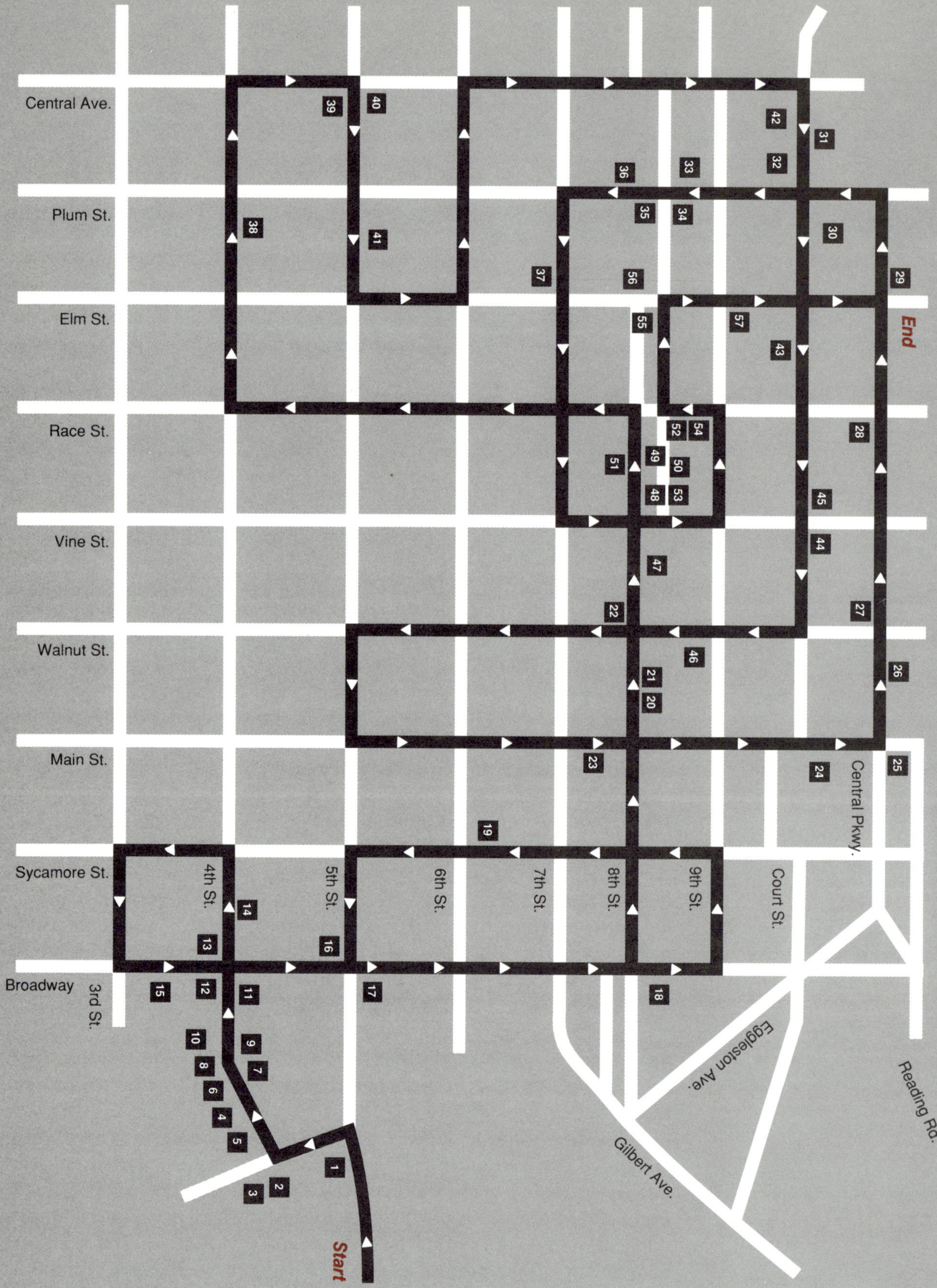

Tour Length
6 miles

End

Start

Central Ave.

Plum St.

Elm St.

Race St.

Vine St.

Walnut St.

Main St.

Sycamore St.

Broadway

3rd St.

4th St.

5th St.

6th St.

7th St.

8th St.

9th St.

Court St.

Central Pkwy.

Eggleston Ave.

Gilbert Ave.

Reading Rd.

North

56

# Tour 3

# Central Business District Frame

**Tour begins on Columbia Parkway heading west. Turn left (south) on Pike Street, right (west) on Fourth Street.**

Though the Frame has long been an area of mixed use, manufacturing activity did not come to the immediate vicinity of Lytle Park until the early twentieth century when two large homes on Fourth Street and a number of smaller residences to the east were torn down to make way for commercial structures.

The 10-story **1 Pugh Building** (now the Polk Building), 400 Pike Street, was completed around 1905 and was occupied by the A. H. Pugh Printing Company and a number of clothing firms that made pants, caps, shirts, neckwear, and uniforms. The A. H. Pugh Company had been started around 1830 by Achilles Pugh (1805-1876), a Pennsylvania-born Quaker. In April 1836, Pugh began printing *The Philanthropist*, for the Ohio Anti-Slavery Society.

Many Cincinnatians were tied to the South by sympathy and economic interests, and mobs twice vandalized Pugh's Main Street print shop. On July 30, as a contemporary newspaper recounted, a "concourse of citizens" broke into Pugh's business, scattering type into the street and tearing down the presses. Parts of the press were dragged down the street and thrown into the river.

Pugh continued publishing *The Philanthropist* in Springboro, Ohio, but later returned to the city where he became one of the city's largest job printers. His descendents headed the company until it went out of business in the early 1980s.

The R. L. Polk Company, a Detroit-based directory publishing firm whose Cincinnati division had been a tenant here since the 1940s, purchased the building in 1980.

The Lytle Park district is the only part of the Frame that has remained a desirable residential area throughout its history, despite the tenement districts that developed along the riverfront and in the Deer Creek Valley. There were fine houses in this vicinity as early as 1809 when William Haines Lytle (1770-1831) erected a mansion on Pike Street.

One of the district's historically significant mansions survives as the **2 Taft Museum,** 316 Pike Street. It was built around 1820 for Martin Baum (1765-1831), an early entrepreneur and local booster. Baum and his representatives met German immigrants arriving at Boston, Philadelphia, and New Orleans to tell them of the opportunities that awaited skilled workmen in Cincinnati.

*Although the main rooms in the Taft Museum are now used as exhibit galleries, they still have the look and feel of the elegant residence that the mansion once was.*

In 1826, financial reverses forced Baum to sell the property. The Belmont School, a female seminary, operated here for a few years before Nicholas Longworth (1782-1863), the city's first millionaire, bought the mansion in 1830.

Pennsylvania iron magnate David Sinton (1808-1900) purchased the residence in 1871. Two years later, Sinton's daughter, Anna (1852-1931), married the promising young lawyer, Charles Phelps Taft (1843-1929).

Charles and Anna Sinton Taft were dedicated to preserving the residential character of their neighborhood. On June 2, 1927, the Tafts announced that they would give their home, their personal art collection, and a one million dollar endowment for its maintenance if $2.5 million could be raised from the public. This and other conditions were met, and the Taft Museum opened to the public in 1932.

On exhibit is a varied collection of Chinese porcelain, antique furniture, Italian majolicas, French enamels, miniature portraits, and oil paintings by Turner, Gainsborough, Constable, Millet, Rembrandt, Sargent, Duveneck, Goya, Hals, and Farny.

In the 1840s, Robert Duncanson (1821-1872), noted black American artist and Longworth's protege, painted the landscape murals that decorate the entry hall of the house.

Elzner & Anderson designed the 5-story Italian Renaissance style **3 American Book Company Building,** 300 Pike Street, which the Ferro-Concrete Construction Company completed around 1904. The building housed the business that Winthrop Smith had begun in 1834 with the publication of *Ray's Eclectic Reader*.

From 1836 until 1901, Smith's firm issued William Holmes McGuffey's *Eclectic Reader* series; an estimated 122 million copies of the books rolled off the company's presses.

The American Book Company was incorporated in 1890 after a merger with three major New York City textbook houses. Two connected warehouse and shipping buildings were added to this complex in 1936.

The American Book Company closed its Cincinnati plant in 1972. A private developer attempted to convert the building into luxury condominiums—Longworth Hall—then the Fine Arts Fund Committee purchased the plant, intending to create additional gardens and parking for the Taft Museum. In 1980, the Netherlands-based SHV Holding Company bought and restored the complex to house the offices of its North American subsidiaries.

The Tafts contributed half the necessary funds for the **4 Anna Louise Inn,** 300 Lytle Street, which was named after their youngest daughter and opened in 1909 with 130 furnished rooms for working women.

Few rooming houses in the downtown area would accept single working women, claiming they were too much trouble; the Inn offered respectable lodgings. It was the project of Reverend James O. White, welfare director of the Cincinnati Union Bethel (1839), the city's oldest private social service agency and one that the Tafts supported.

A 150-room addition was completed in 1920, and the Lytle Park Child Development Center, sponsored by Procter & Gamble and opened in 1985, cares for children whose parents work nearby.

Male visitors to the Anna Louise Inn are still allowed only in the parlors on the first floor, and residents may not have visitors after 11 p.m. No longer solely a "working girls' hotel," the Anna Louise Inn now also provides safe, inexpensive housing and meals for elderly, divorced, and battered women.

Anna Sinton Taft, more than her husband, was actively involved in construction projects in the Lytle Park neighborhood. In 1919, she erected the English Tudor style **5 Earls Building,** 311 Pike Street, a 2-family residence to be occupied by the rector of Christ Church and by the director and founder of the Anna Louise Inn. The structure was remodeled for offices in 1953-1954.

**Continue west on Fourth Street.**

The Taft family opposed the creation of **6 Lytle Park,** dedicated on July 6, 1907. The park was named for Brigadier General William Haines Lytle (1826-1863), whose family home still stood on the property at that time.

At the turn of the century, the City of Cincinnati moved to develop playgrounds and parks for the poor who lived in the crowded tenements of the basin. In 1905, the city acquired the land bounded by Lytle, Third, Lawrence, and Fourth Streets and cleared a number of dwellings to construct its "first real public playground" for the children of the Eighth Ward.

This ward included the well-to-do residential district on Fourth Street and the densely-built, frequently flooded riverfront area where factories and warehouses surrounded tenements and apartments over storefronts.

Mike Mullen (1857-1921), a resident of East Fourth Street, represented the Eighth Ward on City Council for thirty-four years and was one of the politicians loyal to the Republican machine of "Boss" George Cox. Mullen was one of the prime movers in creating the park.

The playground was built on the southern half of the property and the city soon decided to expand the park and tear down the Lytle home to make way for wading pools.

Philanthropist Mary Emery offered funds to preserve the house, and attorney Gustav Tafel spoke for many fellow Civil War veterans and Cincinnatians when he wrote a local newspaper: *"Our city council, which for years has been the property of the member from the 8th ward . . . has spurned the [Emery] gift, and is determined . . . to level the Lytle Mansion to the earth . . . trampling underfoot all the associations inter-*

*Originally, Lytle Park was intended to serve principally as a playground for neighborhood children.*

*woven with its history."*

In the late 1940s, planners anticipated running the Northeast Expressway (I-71) through the area. City Councilman Charles P. Taft II headed the defense of Lytle Park, and on July 2, 1964, the city accepted the offer of the Western-Southern Life Insurance Company to pay for a concrete slab over the "ditch" that was to be cut for the roadway. The insurance company received the rights to erect an apartment building at 550 East Fourth Street over the tunnel.

Five nineteenth-century houses were torn down, including one that had been the clubhouse of the Woman's City Club and Mike Mullen's home, which had been the headquarters of the Catholic Women's Club and the Cincinnati Catholic Women's Association. But the Lytle Park area survived and retained a part of its nineteenth-century character.

Anna Sinton Taft's efforts were also responsible for the 12-story **7 Phelps Townhouse,** 506 East Fourth Street, Cincinnati's finest high-rise apartment building when it opened in 1926. She intended it for "families having large country places but who seek a town home in a restricted [solely residential] block." The Phelps Townhouse remained popular and contributed to city planners' decision more than two decades later to designate the Lytle Park vicinity as one of the focal points for downtown residential development.

Another gift to the city from the Tafts, the **8 Statue of Abraham Lincoln,** stands at the west end of

the park. The 11-foot bronze figure of a somber, weary Lincoln, executed by American sculptor George Grey Bernard (1863-1938), was unveiled in 1917. Barnard's statue was restored and rededicated in 1972.

On the curved brick wall to the right of the statue are several signs that explain and illustrate the history of this area. Also there are two bronze plaques, one with a bas-relief profile of Mike Mullen, that were moved here from the bandstand dedicated in Lytle Park in Mullen's honor in 1935.

The **9 Literary Club of Cincinnati,** 500 East Fourth Street, was founded October 29, 1849, and claims to be the oldest literary club in the country still in existence. It moved to this 2-story, early nineteenth-century Greek Revival style house in 1875, and became one of the first arrivals in what was later the Fourth Street "club district."

Members read papers on literary or historic topics, and in days gone by, anyone who talked, snored, or groaned during these after dinner presentations was automatically fined twenty-five cents per offense. Ralph Waldo Emerson, Oscar Wilde, Booker T. Washington, Mark Twain, Israel Zangwill, and Robert Frost have made informal presentations and addresses to the Literary Club.

The club's membership, limited to one hundred and exclusively male, has included manufacturer and real estate developer Thomas J. Emery, Nicholas and Joseph Longworth, artist Frank Duveneck, historian Charles T. Greve, pharmaceutical manufacturer and author John Uri Lloyd, photographer Paul Briol, University of Cincinnati presidents Walter Langsam and Henry Winkler, and Presidents Rutherford B. Hayes and William Howard Taft.

The club officially opened its doors to women but twice in its history, and then once again in 1974 for the celebration of its one hundred twenty-fifth anniversary.

In the late nineteenth and early twentieth century, many of the children of the hundreds of the families still living in the downtown periphery attended **10 Guilford School,** 421 East Fourth Street.

The present building, completed in 1913, was designed by the Cincinnati architectural firm of Garber &

Woodward and replaced "Old Guilford," built on Sycamore in 1872. The school was named to honor Nathaniel Guilford (1786-1854) who, in 1825, had introduced state legislation that provided for a property tax to support Ohio's Free Common Schools.

Open-air classes for "anemic and underweight" youngsters were held on the roof of this modern Italian Villa style structure. Guilford School served penny lunches and opened at 6:30 a.m. so that parents could leave their children here before work. The school was also a community center, open for club meetings and adult education classes.

In 1915, 698 boys and girls, K-8, were enrolled at Guilford; that number fell in the 1930s. Guilford became an elementary school, and the Retail Selling High School was established here in 1940. In 1965, the Board of Education closed the school and used building for offices until 1973, when classes for developmentally handicapped students were moved here.

The Guilford Special Education Center enrolls an average of 125 disabled youngsters, grades 7-12, each year. It serves that small percentage of youngsters who cannot be "mainstreamed" into regular schools for all or part of their junior high and high school careers. The Guilford curriculum aims to give graduates skills for employment in sheltered workshops or low-level competitive jobs and to enable them to be independent, contributing members of society.

Two bronze plaques on the school building mark the site's historic associations. One near the former Boys' Entrance commemorates Stephen Foster's stay in a house on this site during 1846-1850. The other records that this land was part of the Ft. Washington Military Reservation.

At the end of the nineteenth century, many of the large, elegant homes in the basin that wealthy families left behind were taken over by social organizations or commercial enterprises. The **11 Western-Southern Life Insurance Company,** 400 Broadway, has been located at this corner since 1901 when it moved into the 3-story mansion that was the former home of Edmund Dexter. Dexter had made his fortune as an "importer of liquors and rectifier of whiskey."

The residence was razed in 1916

to make way for a massive Greek Revival style structure designed by the Cincinnati architectural firm of Hake and Hake.

Brothers William J. (1858-1930) and Charles F. (1873-1952) Williams incorporated Western-Southern in 1888. The Williams' company was among the first insurer to offer policies with premiums collected on a weekly basis so that workingmen could afford life insurance.

*The Frame has provided large building sites for the headquarters of many Cincinnati companies, including Western-Southern Life Insurance.*

During the 1950s and 1960s, Western-Southern was the downtown's largest builder, financing the construction of two downtown parking garages, the 580 Building at Sixth and Walnut Streets, and the luxury apartments at 550 East Fourth Street.

Also in that same period, the company expanded its operating territory from fifteen states to forty-four. By 1847, with corporate assets approaching $4 billion and insurance in force going well over $16 billion, Western-Southern was Ohio's largest life insurance company and ranked among the top twenty-five in the nation. The following year, the company annouced plans for a 1.8 million square foot speculative office complex at Fourth and Sycamore.

The identity of the area of East Fourth Street and Broadway as a club district was reinforced in 1907 when the former home of Dr. William W. Seely (1838-1903), 401 East Fourth Street, was occupied by the **12 University Club**. Seely, a professor and dean of the Ohio College of Medicine, erected the imposing 4-story red brick Second Empire style structure around 1880.

The first University Club in Cincinnati was founded in 1879 but disbanded. The present University Club was established around 1905 by alumni of Yale, Harvard, and Princeton to promote "the furtherance of genuine friendship and true congeniality among college men."

Originally, club membership was exclusively male; the building had a special dining room for mixed groups and a ladies' entrance on Broadway. The first floor men's dining room is still restricted to men only during lunch. The University Club, like other downtown clubs and enterprises in the Frame, serves the Core of the Central Business District. It provides downtown businessmen with a place to dine and conduct meetings near their offices.

The all-male **13 Queen City Club,** 331 East Fourth Street, was founded in 1874 by Joseph Longworth (1813-1883), son of Nicholas, who brought members together in the "gentlemen's parlor" of the Grand Hotel on Fourth Street near Central Avenue for "literary purposes and for mutual improvement."

In December of that year, the Evangelical Ministerial Alliance, then meeting in Cincinnati, condemned Longworth's group because "*. . . liquor would be freely bought and sold at the club; games of chance would be allowed there at all times, and the ungovernable passion of the gambler would be engendered . . . . It was a place calculated to draw men away from their homes and families. It would not accomplish one worthy object; it was too heterogeneous, made up . . . of Jews, infidels, Presbyterians, Methodists, and sporting men.*"

The first clubhouse, designed by the Cincinnati firm Hannaford & Procter, opened in July 1876 at Seventh and Elm Streets, a "beautiful residential district." During February and March 1921, Sinclair Lewis stayed at the Queen City Club while doing research for his novel *Babbitt.* Lewis wrote his publisher: "Bully time, met lots of people, really getting the feeling of life here. Fine for *Babbitt.*"

By that time, however, the Queen City Club's West End neighborhood was crowded and largely lower-income. One account speaks of a nearby livery stable; another claims that a brothel operated next door. Harry Hake (1871-1955) drew plans for the present 4-story limestone structure with stylized symbols of art,

agriculture, commerce, and industry in bas relief medallions. The clubhouse opened in 1927 with separate lounges and entrances for female guests, meeting and dining rooms, a bar, overnight rooms, and a men's dining room that is still maintained.

**14 Christ Church (Episcopal),** 318 East Fourth Street, is one of several religious institutions that have remained in the Frame, despite the area's changing character. The Parish of Christ Church was formed May 18, 1817, at a meeting at Daniel Drake's Third Street home. General William Henry Harrison, Arthur St. Clair, Jr., Griffin Yeatman, and James Taylor, the founder of Newport, were among the original members. The congregation met in a number of temporary locations until the first Christ Church was dedicated on this site in 1835.

*Unlike the present building which opens on to Sycamore Street, the original Christ Church faced Fourth Street.*

The present red brick Gothic style parish house, dedicated January 30, 1909, was erected with funds donated by Mary M. Emery (1844-1927) in memory of her husband, manufacturer and developer Thomas J. Emery (1830-1906). She envisioned the facility as a nonsectarian community center and settlement house that would serve not only church members but the poor and working-class people who lived in the basin.

The parish house had an auditorium, club rooms, children's play-

rooms, cooking school classrooms, billiard room, bowling alley, and a library. In 1917, approximately 3,000 persons were involved in the thirty-five social groups that met here.

Though membership declined in the mid-twentieth century as Cincinnatians moved to newer and more distant suburbs, Christ Church chose to keep its downtown location. In 1955, the contents of the original church were sold at auction and the old building torn down. The present modern style Christ Church was dedicated on the same lot—though facing Sycamore and the center of the city—on April 14, 1957.

Christ Church, with some 450 member families in 1988, has continued its service to the community. It is the site of the annual Boar's Head Festival and offers musical programs and public talks.

Here, too, is a prenatal clinic operated by the Children's & Babies Milk Fund. Founded by the women of the church in 1882 as the Maternity Society, this was the first privately-maintained well-baby clinic in the country. It distributed thousands of gallons of milk and provided needy mothers with medical care and advice about keeping their children healthy.

**Turn left (south) on Sycamore, left (east) on Third Street, left (north) on Broadway.**

Another former residence in this

vicinity that was saved and utilized by an organization is the former home of Captain C. G. Pearce, president of a steamboat line. In 1960, it became the **15 Academy of Medicine Building** (officially the Medical Foundations Building), 320-322 Broadway.

The Italianate style house, erected around 1850, had served as the Veterans' Memorial Quarters since 1923, with an employment bureau, a restaurant, offices of several American Legion posts, and a social service agency for former service men and their widows, children, and other dependents.

The Academy of Medicine was organized in 1857 by Cincinnati physicians committed to maintaining high standards in medical training and practice, improving their own medical knowledge, and solving local health problems. Today, the Academy also operates an information service, a speakers bureau, and a physician referral service.

Two local medical associations, a medical placement service, a private club for doctors, the Academy's women's auxiliary, the offices of the *Cincinnati Journal of Medicine*, and the Daniel Drake Auditorium—named to honor the early Cincinnati physician, educator, and civic booster—are all located here.

Dedicated January 23, 1928, the limestone Neo-Classical style **16 Cincinnati Masonic Temple,** 317 East Fifth Street, is the most recent addition to the West Fourth Street "club district" and serves as headquarters for the city's Masonic groups. The imposing structure was designed by Harry Hake and Charles H. Kruck, and built by the Cincinnati Masonic Temple Company, a corporation created in 1917 by eighteen Masonic groups.

The oldest of these organizations and Cincinnati's first Masonic lodge is the Nova Caesarea Harmony Lodge No. 2 F&AM, which received its original warrant in 1791. Members first met in each others' homes until William McMillan (1760-1804) left the lodge Town Lot No. 135 at the northeast corner of Walnut and Third Streets.

The first temple, a 2-story brick structure completed there in 1825, had a post office and the U.S. district attorney's office on the first floor, and on the second, a meeting hall. A larger building erected on the same lot in

*The old and new sections of Procter & Gamble's headquarters complex are tied together visually by extensive formal gardens.*

1846 was itself replaced in 1865 by a 4-story stone-faced temple.

In the early twentieth century, the city's eighteen Masonic groups organized to erect a new, larger structure of three connected units. The eastern section, facing Broadway, contains the 1,100-seat Scottish Rite amphitheater; the central unit includes the Commandery Asylum, the Shrine Kaaba, and the main auditorium. The western wing is the 2,500-seat Taft Auditorium, named in honor of Councilman Charles P. Taft II, a Mason and general chairman of the building committee.

The theater's financial health was never robust. In the 1960s, there were proposals to convert the Taft into a garage or demolish it. But as the downtown revived, the Taft Auditorium survived, offering a number of traveling theatrical and musical shows each season.

Because large building sites in the Frame cost less than land in the Core, some Cincinnati companies selected locations in this part of downtown to build major office buildings to serve as their own corporate headquarters. The most notable of these structures, in terms of size and the company's impact on the community, is the **17 Procter & Gamble Company Headquarters,** 1 and 2 Procter & Gamble Plaza. The nation's largest produce of household consumer products, this international giant occupies a headquarters complex spreading over two and one-half city blocks between Fifth and Sixth Streets from Sycamore to Sentinel Street.

Procter & Gamble began on October 31, 1837, when brothers-in-law

William Procter (1801-1884) and James Gamble (1801-1891) joined forces to make and sell candles and soap. The new company started operations in a small shop on the northeast corner of Sixth and Main Streets. Over time, soap surpassed candles as the firm's major product. After a larger plant erected on Central Avenue and Second Street in 1853-1854 was destroyed by fire in 1885, the company then began construction of what has become the huge Ivorydale factory complex in St. Bernard.

Company headquarters were located in various downtown buildings; in 1956, an 11-story, $5 million headquarters building was completed on Sixth Street. New York architects Voorhees, Walker, Foley & Smith created a structure with a modern interior—space was available for computers when they became available—but a conventional exterior.

Locating downtown rather than in the suburbs meant that employees could easily commute to their jobs, and the site also provided easy access to the hotels for P&G's many business visitors. The new building also represented an expression of P&G's faith in the future of Cincinnati and in the downtown business district.

Between 1955 and 1980, P&G's sales rose from $966 million to over $10 billion. The firm's overseas market grew from $238 million to over $1.3 billion by the late 1970s. Today, it is estimated least one of Procter & Gamble's products can be found in over 97% of American homes. As of 1987, P&G ranked as one of the fifty largest corporations in the world.

Such growth has required constant expansion of headquarters staff. In 1971, P&G extended its original building and constructed a 5-story office and parking facility on Sixth Street. Eleven years later, P&G unveiled plans for its new international headquarters, designed by the New York City firm of Kohn Pederson Fox. Completed in 1985, the Post-Modernist style building had twin 17-story towers with pyramidal tops; a glassed-in bridge connected stories seven through ten.

The towers, designed to reflect the Art Deco shapes of the Times-Star and Cincinnati Gas & Electric Company buildings and the Classical style crown of the Central Trust Tower, effectively tie together Cincinnati's old and new commercial structures.

The company's building program has generated some criticism as it necessitated the demoliton of historic landmarks, including Wesley Chapel (1831), the oldest religious building in Cincinnati; Allen Temple (1852); the Fenwick Club (1918), and the Chapel of the Holy Spirit (1927).

In 1988, only three years after the new $10 million-plus international headquarters was completed, P&G announced plans for expansion to the north.

One of the most attractive light industrial structures in the Frame is the **18 Times-Star Building,** 800 Broadway. The offices and printing plant of *The Cincinnati Times-Star*, a daily afternoon newspaper, were located here from January 1, 1933, until 1979.

The *Times-Star* was officially born on June 15, 1880, with the merger of two Cincinnati afternoon dailies, the *Spirit of the Times* (1840) and the *Cincinnati Daily Star* (1872). Charles Phelps Taft I (1843-1929) bought the *Star* in partnership with his father-in-law, David Sinton. Hulbert Taft (1877-1959) succeeded his uncle as publisher, and was followed by David Ingalls (1899-1985), grandson of Charles P. Taft I and grandnephew of President William Howard Taft.

In the late 1920s, the Tafts decided to build a new home for their newspaper. Samuel Hannaford & Sons designed a 16-story building of reinforced concrete faced with limestone that was remarkable for its Art Deco detailing both inside and out.

Above the bronze doors and grilles of the main entrance are a carved eagle—an eagle was once on the paper's masthead—and stars. Some of the aluminum spandrels between the windows bear the letters "TS" for *Times-Star*. Atop the first set-offs are relief figures of pioneers of printing including William Caxton, Johann Gutenberg, and Benjamin Franklin. On the corner pylons are carved figures symbolizing the four essential qualities of a newspaper—Truth, Speed, Patriotism, and Progress. A special newsboys' entrance is designated by a figure of a knicker-clad youngster selling papers. Crowning the tower is an urn-shaped airplane beacon that symbolizes the flame of truth.

Newspapers across the country ran into financial trouble during the 1950s. Cincinnati had three papers, and realizing that the city could support only two, the Tafts tried to buy the morning paper, the *Enquirer*. Instead, the other afternoon paper, the *Post*, bought the *Times-Star* on July 20, 1958, and moved to the Times-Star Building. The paper operated as *The Cincinnati Post and Times-Star* until January 1, 1974, when "Times-Star" vanished from the masthead.

The *Post*, a part of the Cincinnati-based Scripps Howard chain, was first published on January 3, 1881, by Frank and Walter Wellman. It was called *The Penny Paper* and sold for one cent. James Scripps joined the paper within a few months. Two years later, he and his brother, Edward (1854-1926), took over, renamed the paper *The Evening Post*, and moved operations to Longworth Street (between Fifth and Sixth Streets) and Elm.

E.W. Scripps also became involved in news service companies in 1907 with the purchase of three small regional news services. These were combined to create United Press, later United Press International, an international service, which was controlled by the Scripps Company until 1982.

The E. W. Scripps Company eventually established three other news and feature services and held controlling stock in Scripps Howard companies that operated in broadcasting and publishing. The "Howard" in the name is Ron Howard, an assistant managing editor of the *Post* and president of UPI, and his son, Jack, who became president of the E. W. Scripps Company in 1953 when Cincinnatian Charles E. Scripps, a grandson of the founder, became chairman of the board.

When afternoon papers faced growing financial problems in the 1970s, Scripps Howard received permission from the United States Justice Department to enter into an agreement with the Gannett-owned *Cincinnati Enquirer*. The two papers would maintain joint business, printing, circulation, and advertising operations, but the papers' newsrooms and editorial departments were to remain completely separate. The *Post* subsequently moved to its present offices on East Court Street.

In 1984, the Times-Star Building was sold to Burke Marketing Services, the world's largest customer research firm, which Alberta Burke had founded in Cincinnati in 1931. Burke Marketing carried out a restoration and renovation of the building.

**Turn left (west) on Ninth Street, left (south) on Sycamore.**

Downtown residents were once served by churches and synagogues throughout the Frame and Core, but by the 1980s, many of Cincinnati's historic churches had been lost to the expansion of office facilities or were converted to other uses. **19 St. Francis Xavier Roman Catholic Church,** 607 Sycamore Street, is one of the few that has survived and still serves its original purpose.

The church stands on a site that has been occupied by a Catholic church since December 17, 1826, when Bishop Edward Fenwick dedicated St. Peter the Apostle Church as the diocesan cathedral.

Christ Church, Cincinnati's first Catholic church, was moved from Vine and Liberty Streets and set beside St. Peter's to serve as St. Francis Seminary; classes began on May 11, 1829. A new 3-story frame building was erected where the College of the Athenaeum of Cincinnati, a day and boarding school for young men, opened on October 17, 1831. On October 22, the first issue of *The Catholic Telegraph*, a newspaper that Bishop Fenwick had founded to combat attacks on Catholicism, was produced by the Xavieran Press from a space at the rear of the church.

Bishop John B. Purcell (1800-1883) had trouble staffing the Athenaeum and offered it and the church to the Society of Jesus. In 1840, eight Jesuit priests arrived and rededicated the Athenaeum and the church to their patron saint.

Both the parish and the school grew under the Jesuits' leadership. The old church was razed, and the present St. Xavier Church, a Gothic style brick and limestone structure designed by Louis Pickett (c.1838-1910) was dedicated January 20, 1860. Fire gutted the building on Good Friday 1882; Pickett directed the restoration.

Large classroom and residence buildings were erected north of the church in 1867, 1885, and 1890 when the old Athenaeum was torn down. St. Xavier parish had become one of the largest and most prosperous in Cincinnati, enjoying the support of many well-to-do families throughout the area.

In the twentieth century, many families moved to homes in hilltop suburbs. The Jesuits opened St. Xavier Branch Academy, a boys' high school, in Walnut Hills, then moved it to Avondale. In 1920, the Academy returned downtown, and the college moved to the suburban Avondale campus. Forty years later, the high school moved to Finneytown, and the old classroom buildings were demolished.

Although the schools were gone, many area Catholics continued to worship at the historic church; in the 1980s, about 1,500 still attended Masses here each week.

*Samuel Hannaford's design for the Eighth Street Salvation Army Citadel used elements that evoked the appearance of a castle or an armory.*

**Turn left (east) on Fifth Street, left (north) on Broadway, and left (west) on Eighth Street.**

As the demand for office space in downtown Cincinnati increased during the 1970s and 1980s, older structures in the Core were demolished to make room for towering new buildings. In the Frame, however, many were renovated or converted for use as offices, including several buildings along the north side of East Eighth Street between Walnut and Bowen Alley including the Citadel Building and the former headquarters of the Underwriters Salvage Corps of Cincinnati.

Evangeline Booth (1865-1950), national commander of the Salvation Army in the United States and daughter of the Army's founder, William Booth (1829-1912), laid the corner-

stone of the **20 Salvation Army Citadel Building,** 114 East Eighth Street, on July 18, 1905.

The Salvation Army, a religious/charitable organization founded in England, arrived in Cincinnati in 1885. One of its officers noted, "Many prophets of evil had foretold that the Army would experience such a repulse as had not yet fallen to them on American soil, as Cincinnati has a notoriety for drunkenness and bravado surpassed by few cities." Army members received police protection because of the hecklers, harassment, and the threats of physical abuse that they encountered.

By 1890, the Salvation Army had a "barracks" or residence hall on Plum Street, and four years later, a headquarters building, two missions, and two training "garrisons" in the basin. In the early twentieth century, the Army commissioned Samuel Hannaford to design this 4-story brick and stone building which served as its "divisional" headquarters.

In 1967, the Salvation Army moved to a new Central Parkway headquarters building that houses the Citadel Youth Corps, a youth center, and the Women's and Children's Emergency Home. Among the Army's activities in the area are the Catherine Booth Home in Avondale for unmarried pregnant women; adult centers; Booth Residence, a low-cost housing complex for adults; Booth Memorial Hospital in Covington; community and family service programs, and thrift stores.

From 1889 until 1923, the narrow brick building at 110 East Eighth Street served as the **21 Headquarters of the Underwriters Salvage Corps of Cincinnati.** The Cincinnati Insurance Underwriters' Association created the Corps to reduce fire loss claims by protecting the contents of burning buildings.

Organized in 1886, the Salvage Corps was first housed in a stable on Bowen Alley south of Eighth Street. Three years later, it moved to Eighth Street into a new one-story brick stationhouse. In 1897, the Corps added two stories for a dormitory and storage space and placed a stone tablet with the inscription "Underwriters' Salvage Corps 1897" over the second floor.

At the scene of a fire, the Corps covered goods to prevent water dam-

age, shut off sprinklers that were still working after the fire was out, tried to drain water out of the building, and, if possible, removed items threatened by flames.

In 1923, the Salvage Corps moved to larger quarters on Elm Street (now a city maintenance shop) that could accommodate its growing number of trucks. When the Underwriters' Association decided in 1959 that the Fire Department could carry out salvage work more effectively, the Salvage Corps was disbanded and its property was sold or turned over to the city.

By this time, the Salvation Army was using the Eighth Street station as a dormitory. From the 1950s to the 1980s, the building was put to a variety of uses until local architects Jones & Speer renovated the old stationhouse for modern office space.

Changes in the functions of **22 St. Louis Roman Catholic Church,** 29 East Eighth Street, relfect both changes in the area and in the administration of the Archdiocese of Cincinnati.

The first Roman Catholic church on this site was St. Ludwig, a former Campbellite chapel that was purchased and rededicated in 1870 to serve German Catholics living in this part of the downtown periphery. St. Ludwig was a small and relatively poor parish. The congregation gradually decreased as German Catholics joined the migration out of downtown neighborhoods. By the turn of the century, St. Ludwig recorded only about one hundred member families.

In the early twentieth century, the parish changed from a "national" church serving an ethnic population into a church for downtown workers and transients and became one of the archdiocese's administrative facilties. Masses in German were discontinued in 1914, except for one each week, and the church became known as St. Louis. Services were rescheduled for the convenience of employees of nearby businesses. The Printers' Mass was a 2 a.m. service instituted in 1918 for the printers and typesetters who worked the night and early morning shifts.

In 1928, St. Louis temporarily moved to another former Protestant church several doors to the south while the old church was demolished and replaced. The present St. Louis Church, completed in 1929, was

designed by the Boston firm of McGinnis & Walsh. Its five floors included two chapels, residential rooms, and office space for archdiocesan officials.

St. Louis remained a popular and convenient house of worship for downtown workers, although by the late 1960s, attendance was declining. The Printers' Mass was discontinued in 1970, and the number of other services was reduced. That same decade, St. Louis's role as an archdiocesan facility was expanded when Archbishop Joseph Bernadin decided to make the church his official residence. Later, the archdiocese consolidated its growing administrative operations, including those at St. Louis Church, at an office building at 100 East Eighth Street.

> **Turn left (south) on Walnut, left (east) on Fifth Street, and left (north) on Main Street.**

South of the corner of Sixth and Main Streets is the face of modern Cincinnati: tall office buildings, skywalks, and sports stadiums. But north of this intersection, Main Street resembles downtown Cincinnati at the turn of the century: narrow 3, 4, and 5-story buildings with cast-iron storefronts intermixed with early twentieth-century skyscrapers.

The four blocks between Sixth and Court Street make up the **23 Main Street Historic District,** a group of buildings that, with few exceptions, date from 1870 to 1920.

Development along this section of Main Street began in the 1820s after the construction of a new Hamilton County Courthouse and the opening of the Miami & Erie Canal. By the 1850s, the area had attracted lawyers and wholesalers of cigars, groceries, liquors, and wine. Retailers soon followed, and by 1860, Main Street commerce included furriers, hardware stores, clothing stores, hotels, restaurants, insurance companies, and some light manufacturing.

This mix of businesses established a pattern for Main Street: service, wholesale, and retail firms that served the larger financial and retail interests in the Core. Many of the 1840-1860 era buildings had retail shops on the first floor, stockrooms or light manufacturing equipment above, and flats on the upper floors.

*The former Hamilton County Republican headquarters on Ninth Street near Main is embellished with the symbols of its original occupant.*

At least three Greek Revival style buildings date from the pre-1860 period: 627 and 802 Main, and Arnold's Bar and Grill at 210 East Eighth, where Simon Arnold opened a restuarant and tavern in 1861.

In the last quarter of the nineteenth century, wholesale businesses and office buildings came to dominate Main Street. Two prominent examples of the taller, more ornate Italianate style structures from this period are 625 Main, the location of Henry Korf's jewelry, clock and watchmaking business, and 923-925, the shop of John Grossius, a manufacturer of stoves and furnaces, and dealer in household furnishings and metalware.

Two prominent Queen Anne style office buildings are also in this group. The Bodman Building, 621 Main, (now the Fort Washington Hotel) dates from around 1897 and was the first office of the Western-Southern Life Insurance Company. The 5-story structure at 654 Main, now a fruit market, originally housed the offices of a moulding and frame manufacturer.

Prominent Cincinnati corporations and banks settled on Main Street between Sixth and Ninth Streets in the first decades of the twentieth century. The first major bank building here was the 12-story Neo-Classical style Second National Bank at 830-832 Main, erected in 1908 and designed by the local firm of Werner & Adkins. In 1911, the Neo-Classical style Court House Savings Bank (now Fifth-Third) was constructed at 916 Main.

The most elegant of Main Street's early twentieth century buildings, the Beaux Arts style Gwynne Building at Sixth and Main, was designed by nationally-renowned architect Ernest Flagg and was erected in 1914.

For many years, this location was connected with the firm of Procter and Gamble. In the mid-1830s, William Procter rented a vacant storeroom at this Sixth and Main Street site from a Virginia investor, David Gwynne. Procter and his brother-in-law, James Gamble, set up offices in the storeroom and manufactured soap and candles in the yard behind it. In 1913, Alice Gwynne Vanderbilt commissioned Flagg to design a building for this site. She named it after her father, Abraham Gwynne, a prominent lawyer and son of the man who had rented the lot to young William Procter. The Gwynne Building served as Procter & Gamble headquarters from 1935 to 1956.

A 4-story addition designed by local architects Hake & Hake was dedicated in 1939. It featured a bas relief of Pegasus by Cincinnati artist Ernest Bruce Haswell, who also designed P&G's Lava and Camay soap bars.

Today, the Gwynne Building houses a variety of offices, from attorneys and video studios to politicians and a Christian broadcasting station.

Another Cincinnati business giant, the Kroger Company, had its headquarters at 813-817 Main Street from 1918 to 1930. This building was erected about 1913 for a retailer of furniture, carpets, rugs, and upholstery.

*The present Hamilton County Courthouse—the fourth courthouse building on this site—was completed in 1919.*

Some of the buildings in this district have detailing that reflects their original owners or ocupants. Two University of Cincinnati properties at 648 and 726 Main were constructed for investment and display the university emblem. Carved limestone elephant heads and a stone eagle surround the doorway at 125 East Ninth Street, the headquarters of the Cincinnati and Hamilton County Republican Party from 1928 to 1965.

One of the few structures on Main Street not originally designed for office space is the Aurora apartment building, 203 Eighth Street, erected in 1910. The hotels at 621 and 716 Main were converted from office and retail use in the 1920s.

Main Street above Sixth has experienced little major construction since the early twentieth century. The most significant alterations in the past forty years have involved the demolition of several buildings for parking lots. But the 1984 designation of these four blocks of Main as a local historic district was intended to make such demolition more difficult and to aid renovation efforts with tax and other incentives.

Since the mid-nineteenth century, county government has been a major presence in the Frame. Today, its legal apparatus is located in the **24** **Hamilton County Courthouse** and **Justice Center** complex that extends from Ninth Street to Central Parkway and from Main Street to Eggleston Avenue.

The city's first courthouse, a small log structure, was built about 1795 on Fifth Street and was replacaced by a brick courthouse seven years later. A

courthouse erected at this site in 1819 served for thirty years before it burned down when flames jumped from a fire at an adjacent slaughterhouse. Cincinnati's most famous courthouse, an imposing 5-story brick and stone structure designed by Isaiah Rogers, was erected in 1853, but at the end of March 1884, a mob of over 10,000 attacked and burned it.

The immediate cause of this event was the March 28 verdict of manslaughter, rather than murder, brought against William Berner for killing his employer. For several years, the community had witnessed widespread political corruption and jury tampering. To many Cincinnatians, the Berner case seemed the most outrageous miscarriage of justice yet, and a protest meeting called by several of the community's leading citizens turned into a riot. After three nights of disorder and the arrival of hundreds of National Guard troops with Gatling guns, more than fifty people lay dead, about 200 were injured, and the courthouse lay in ruins.

The new courthouse designed by James McLaughlin and completed two years later was fireproof. This court building served the community until 1914; by then both the courthouse and the jail, built in 1861, were overcrowded and outmoded.

In 1915, former President William Howard Taft (1857-1930) laid the cornerstone, and the present courthouse was dedicated four years later. The new building, designed by John H. Rankin, was celebrated as the most modern facility of its type. But by the 1930s, more room was again needed. An annex was completed in 1952, and in 1968, county administrative offices were moved out of the courthouse to create additonal space.

In the early 1970s, legal actions against the overcrowded the courthouse jail and the old Workhouse moved Hamilton County Commissioners to consider a new jail facility adjacent to the courthouse. The $55 million Hamilton County Justice Center opened in 1985. The two buildings, designed by New York City and local architects, could house 848 inmates. The new jail, however, became overcrowded soon after it opened, and county officials have continued to seek alternatives to using it for minor offenders.

One structure represents an extension of the CBD Frame's retailing and governmental functions to the north side of Central Parkway. Now housing various government and private offices, the 7-story **25 Alms & Doepke Building,** 222 East Central Parkway, was formerly the headquarters of one of the largest wholesale and retail dry goods businesses in Ohio.

The Alms & Doepke Company was founded by brothers William (d.1920) and Frederick H. Alms (1839-1898) and William D. Doepke (1838-1908), who met while serving in the Union Army. After the Civil War, the three men pooled their money to start their venture on the banks of the Miami & Erie Canal at Main Street.

Older businessmen predicted that a store located so far from the heart of the downtown shopping district would fail. But in 1878, the successful venture moved across the canal and expanded to cover an entire block from Main to Hunt Street. By the turn of the century, Alms & Doepke was the second largest mercantile establishment west of New York City.

With the decline of Over-the-Rhine, the major source of customers for the store, Alms & Doepke's profits fell, and the store closed on April 3, 1954.

The old store building was then partially rented for office space by federal agencies until the offices were moved to new federal buildings. In

*The Ohio Mechanics' Institute was erected on property near the canal where Miles Greenwood's ironworks once stood.*

1970, arrangements were made for the structure to house local government and court system offices, yet the building is still commonly referred to as the Alms & Doepke Building.

**Turn left (west) on Central Parkway.**

The Miami & Erie Canal attracted a number of factories, foundries, and breweries to the northern edge of the downtown periphery. One of the largest of these concerns was Miles Greenwood's Eagle Iron Works, established in 1832. The property occupied by Greenwood's foundry is the present site of the **26 OMI College of Applied Science,** 100 East Central Parkway. New owners relocated the Eagle Iron Works around 1890s, and the property was subdivided.

On November 20, 1828, four Cincinnatians formed a non-profit corporation "for advancing the best interests of the mechanics, manufacturers, and artisans, for the more general diffusion of useful knowledge in those important classes of the community." On January 29, 1829, the Ohio legislature granted a charter to the Ohio Mechanics' Institute (OMI), making it now one of the oldest technical schools in the nation and the oldest west of the Allegheny mountains.

One became a member of the Mechanics Institute corporation by paying three dollars or by donating a product that could be sold for that

amount. For fifty cents, minors or members' apprentices could use the Institute's library and attend evening lectures which ranged over a variety of topics including electromagnetism, law, temperance, anatomy, and optimism.

The Institute lacked permanent quarters and regularly faced financial difficulties. In 1838, the Grand Mechanics and Citizens Ball and Exhibit—a forerunner of the annual Cincinnati Industrial Expositions that began in 1870—improved OMI's financial security. In 1839, OMI trustees bought the ill-fated bazaar that Frances Trollope (author of *Domestic Manners of Americans*, 1839) had built on Third Street and moved the institution there.

After the bazaar was lost to foreclosure eight years later, the Mechanics Institute bought a lot at Sixth and Vine where Greenwood Hall, OMI's first permanent home, opened in 1848. Miles Greenwood, a loyal supporter, served as the Institute's president from 1847 to 1854.

In 1906, the Institute bought the property on the north bank of the Miami & Erie Canal, and two years later, Mary M. Emery (1845-1927) gave $500,000 for the construction of a classroom building and an assembly hall, which was to be named in memory of her husband. (Thomas Emery had refused to make such a contribution unless the school admitted black students on the same basis as whites.) The new 6-story brick and limestone building designed in the English Tudor style by Samuel Hannaford & Sons opened in 1911. The following year, a junior college-level program was set up, and the Cincinnati Symphony moved out of Music Hall and into Emery Auditorium, staying until 1936.

OMI's curriculum kept pace with technology. During the 1920s, it offered 2-year and 4-year intensive and co-operative programs, and began moving toward a college-level program in the 1950s. In 1951, the school began admitting students regardless of race. In November 1958, the day division became the Ohio College of Applied Science (OCAS), and the night program the OMI Evening College. The University of Cincinnati acquired the school—OCAS/OMI—in 1969.

The complex had deteriorated badly by 1980, and the estimated renovation cost of $12 million was one reason that UC gave for deciding to move the OMI College of Applied Science. Local preservationists organized to save the elaborately decorated, 2,200-seat Emery Theater where Nijinsky and Pavlova had performed. Early in 1988, the Ohio legislature approved funding to convert the building into an arts center.

Although city planners now regard the property just north of Central Parkway as part of the CBD, the **27 Miami & Erie Canal,** which followed the path now taken by the parkway, historically marked the division between downtown and Over-the-Rhine.

In the 1820s, city boosters dreamed of a system of canals that would link Cincinnati and the Great Lakes. State legislation passed in 1825 authorized the building of the Miami Canal from Cincinnati to Dayton. Groundbreaking ceremonies were held that July, and the canal opened in January 1829. A Dayton-to-Toledo connection was approved in 1831, and the north-south Miami & Erie Canal intersected with the northeast-southwest Wabash & Erie Canal near Toledo.

The canal entered Cincinnati along what is today I-75, went along Central Parkway from Ludlow Avenue, then turned south following the route of Eggleston Avenue to the river.

According to reminiscences, the canal was a picturesque spot to boat, fish, or swim in the summer and to skate in the winter. However, the slowly moving water became stagnant during the hot Cincinnati summers, and dead animals and wastes from the hundreds of buildings that lined the canal polluted its waters. In the late 1800s, the Miami & Erie Canal was becoming an eyesore and a menace to public health, but it was still a relatively inexpensive and effective means for short distance transportation of bulk cargoes such as gravel, ice, lumber, and agricultural products.

By the early twentieth century, however, the canal was obsolete as a means of transportation, and the electric interurban railway network had grown in importance for carrying freight and passengers. Ohio had more miles of interurban track than any state in the nation, and lines connected Cincinnati to Dayton, Lima, and Toledo.

But many of the interurbans that ran to Cincinnati's suburbs were prohibited from entering the city by the Cincinnati Street Railway Company, which held a monopoly on streetcar service and use of the tracks. Commuters and goods had to complete the trip on other cars. A 1912 report declared that no part of the streetcar system's equipment was adequate, and the movement of goods, people, and vehicles was becoming slower and slower.

Progressive city officials concluded that a **Rapid Transit Railway** would increase commerce, ease traffic congestion, and solve housing problems by providing a cheap, quick way for those who worked in the basin to get to new homes in a more healthful suburban environment.

During 1912 and 1914, City Council considered plans for transit systems with lines that would run both underground and in the open canal bed. The city finally agreed on a loop—including a subway tunnel to be built along a portion of the former canal route—that would cost about $6 million. In 1916, Cincinnati voters approved the transit bond issue 6-to-1.

Although the United States' entry into World War I doubled the costs of materials and construction, the project went ahead. The canal was drained in 1919, and construction began the following year. When funds were exhausted in February 1927, approximately 2.2 miles of subway construction and 7.7 miles of open cut construction had been completed. That year, a report noted: "... *nothing has been done in the way of track construction . . . . Nothing has been done in the way of providing rolling stock, or shop and storage facilities. Other minor items, such as lighting, ventilating, fire protection, and fencing the right of way will have to be taken care of before the line can be operated.*"

The report recommended completion at a cost of $10.6 million, but the failure of the interurban lines and the growing popularity of the automobile had practically eliminated the need or desire for mass rail transit. Construction was halted, and Central Parkway was built on the canal right-of-way.

**Central Parkway** had been planned as part of a citywide system of parks, public squares, playgrounds, and connecting roadways put forth in the 1907 *Report of the Park Commis-*

*Central Parkway's median strip marks the former path of the Miami & Erie Canal, while the traffic lanes follow the* routes of North Canal and South Canal Streets.

*sioners*, a document widely known as the "Kessler Plan" after George Kessler, the Kansas City landscape architect who developed it.

The report called for a wide road along the route of the canal that would aid development by providing "a wide passage into the very heart of the business district" and a thoroughfare to serve the entire Mill Creek Valley and the communities on the surrounding hills. Central Parkway was to be a "grand boulevard" 150 feet wide with a road "on each side of a continuous central park space" that would be embellished with fountains, gardens, walks, and benches.

A more modest Central Parkway was dedicated with parades and speeches on October 1, 1928. It still serves as a route into the downtown business district, though expressways have superseded it as the main artery.

In 1966, the city made the final payments on the transit bonds. The $13 million spent on the project did produce some benefits. A Civil Defense shelter was set up in one of the tubes in the 1950s; another tube carries a water main, and I-75 uses approximately five and one-half miles of the city-owned right-of-way property.

The Cincinnati Automobile Club, now owns the 3-story brick and stone building at 15 West Central Parkway that was erected in 1904 as the **28** **Canal Telephone Exchange Building**. The Canal Exchange was among the approximately fifty neighborhood switching offices that the Cincinnati & Suburban Bell Telephone Company placed in service between 1900 and 1930.

Telephones were available in Cincinnati by 1878, only two years after their invention, but the cost of phone service was prohibitive. As better equipment came into use, costs decreased, and the number of customers grew. The telephone company needed new exchanges, like the Canal Street Exchange, to link customers into its network.

Cincinnati & Suburban Bell introduced dial service in 1930, and during the next two decades, exchanges were altered to handle dial calls. Some old buildings were retained and updated; others were phased out. The Cincinnati Automobile Club moved into the Canal Exchange Building in 1940.

The Cincinnati Automobile Club had been organized on March 18, 1901.

The club had twelve members, and there were two gasoline-fueled cars and a dozen or so steam-powered runabouts in the city. The club's first goal was to "promote sportsmanship," and it staged "club runs" to distant regions like Mt. Healthy—when dry weather assured passable roads. The club also provided a number of services to members including road maps, warnings of bad roads, bail bonding, and twenty-four hour emergency road service.

When the American Automobile Association was founded in 1902, approximately thirty cars were in operation in Cincinnati and city ordinances set speed limits of seven miles per hour downtown and fifteen in outlying areas. The Cincinnati Automobile Club affiliated with the national organization in 1906 and prospered as automobile ownership became more common.

By the early 1980s, the Cincinnati club had approximately 235,000 members and needed larger quarters. The Auto Club retained the telephone exchange building and added the adjoining modern but architecturally compatible parking garage and office building in 1984.

When a downtown institution needed to expand its facilities, it often had to move to the Frame to find a suitable site. This was the case with the **29** **Young Men's Christian Association (YMCA) Building,** 1105 Elm Street, which stands in the extreme northwestern corner of the downtown periphery.

The international YMCA organization was founded in London in 1844. Four years later, seven young men concerned about community welfare, set up the Young Men's Society of Religious Inquiry at the Central Presbyterian Church in Cincinnati. This group became affiliated with the national YMCA movement in 1857. The local YMCA broadened its work and moved to its third building, a stone and brick structure at Seventh and Walnut Streets that later became the Shubert Theater, now demolished.

In the early twentieth century, the YMCA perceived a need to aid young men who came to work in downtown Cincinnati offices and shops but did not have suitable, permanent places to live. Yet another building was proposed where each resident would have a room with a bed, chair, and

desk, and share bathroom and dining facilities.

On April 7, 1917, former President William Howard Taft (1857-1930) laid the cornerstone for this YMCA building; World War I and an influenza epidemic delayed the dedication until December 8, 1918. The Central Parkway Y opened with recreational facilities, a cafeteria, and rooms for 427 men. A chapel was added in 1938.

Changes in living, working, and recreation habits and the conditions of the Central Parkway Y's finances and membership combined to end the tradition of offering inexpensive lodging. On May 31, 1980, the residential floors were closed, and the predominantly elderly residents who remained here moved their belongings.

In 1988, the YMCA Building contained the administrative offices of the YMCA of Cincinnati and Hamilton County, and as the Central Parkway branch, offered fitness programs for men and women. Ironically, by the mid-1980s, the City of Cincinnati, looking to create single-room occupancy housing and efficiency apartments downtown, was considering a renovation of the YMCA Building for this purpose.

The patterned, multi-colored reflective glass windows and plum-colored exterior of the Court Street Center, 250 West Court Street, give little clue that this office building was originally one of the Frame's industrial plants—the **30** **French-Bauer Dairy**. Constructed in 1917-1918, the factory took the site previously occupied by the Gerke brewery.

Breweries were attracted to sites along the canal because the waterway provided transportation for raw materials and their finished product. In 1857, the Eagle Brewery (1854) moved from West Fourth Street to the canal at Plum Street. John Gerke joined the business, and his sons later headed the concern—renamed the Gerke Brewing Company—until it closed around 1912.

Five years later, the French-Bauer Dairy Company—a firm created by a turn-of-the-century merger of the French Brothers Dairy and the Bauer Ice Cream & Baking Company—began construction of a new plant at this location. The building had four stories above ground and three below. A 5-story brick barn that housed the company's 140 delivery wagons and over 200 horses stood at Seventh and Smith Streets.

In 1980, after the business had been bought by H. Meyer & Sons Dairy Company, which consolidated operations at its Arlington Heights facility, the old plant was purchased by Chavez Properties, a private developer. It was gutted and transformed into a dramatic Post-Modern style office building with a 4-story central atrium surrounded by glass-sided offices.

**Turn left (south) on Plum Street.**

The 3 and 4-story buildings at 310 West Court Street, including the former Gerke brewery stable, are now occupied by the **31 Hennegan Company,** a nationally-recognized printing and lithography firm.

James Hennegan, his brother John, and Charles Bechter founded Hennegan & Company on Race Street in 1885. A third brother, Joseph Hennegan, later joined the business. The Hennegan company first printed advertising materials—labels for Cincinnati beers, letterheads, bills, and postcards. In 1894, James Hennegan and William Donaldson began a monthly newspaper, *Billboard Advertising,* that was devoted to the interests of advertisers and which eventually evolved into today's *Billboard,* a show business standard.

When Edison Studios brought out *The Great Train Robbery* in 1903, Hennegan & Company did the promotional work for this 12-minute moving picture. By 1910, the company was shipping to theaters all over North America and had moved into these buildings. Hennegan erected the adjoining plant and office at 311 Genesee Street in 1915.

The Hennegan Company has printed materials for movie companies literally from A to Z, including Allied Artists, Columbia, Fox, D.W. Griffith, MGM, Paramount, United Artists, Warner Brothers, and Ziv Productions. Among the films for which it has produced promotional material are *Gone With the Wind, King Kong, Meet Me in St. Louis, The Caine Mutiny, Cabin in the Sky,* and *Snow White and the Seven Dwarfs.*

James Hennegan's grandson, Robert Ott, currently heads the com-

*A portion of the Hennegan printing company complex that faces Court Street was built as the stables of the Gerke Brewing Company.*

pany which produces catalogs, travel brochures, posters, magazine inserts, displays, and calendars, in addition to movie items.

The downtown periphery offers sites suitable for small, highly specialized institutions, as well as large ones. Though probably unknown to most Cincinnatians, the **32 Lloyd Library,** 917 Plum Street, is internationally renowned for its collections of materials on the pharmaceutical sciences. Its holdings include a 1493 volume that was the first pharmaceutical book ever set in type.

John Uri Lloyd (1849-1936), scientist, professor, and author, started the library in 1864. Lloyd also produced more than 5,000 scientific papers and a number of novels, including the popular *Stringtown on the Pike, A Tale of Northern-Most Kentucky* (1900).

Lloyd founded a pharmaceutical manufacturing company in 1870 and was later joined by his brothers, Nelson Ashley (1851-1925) and Curtis Gates (1859-1928). Lloyd Brothers Pharmaceuticals first manufactured drugs for the "eclectics," physicians who advocated the use of plant extracts for the treatment of illnesses.

The Lloyd brothers' collection of books was shelved in a room of their business at Ninth and Elm Streets, then in a quarters on West Court Street near the pharmaceuticals plant. The present Lloyd Library building opened on June 9, 1971.

When Cincinnati city government

expanded its functions and was restructured with a series of "departments" in the early 1850s, local officials chose a location on the periphery of the Central Business District for the building that would house this new bureaucracy. Today, that site is still occupied by the primary municipal office building, **33 Cincinnati City Hall,** 801 Plum Street.

The first city hall erected at this location was built in 1852. The 2-story building soon proved too small for a burgeoning city government. After much debate, the old structure was torn down and the remainder of the block from Eighth to Ninth and Central to Plum was acquired for a new, larger city hall. The cornerstone for the present building was laid in 1888, but construction was not finished until nearly five years later.

The new Cincinnati City Hall, dedicated on May 13, 1893, was designed by Samuel Hannaford (1835-1911) in the massive arched and gabled, highly ornamented style that came to be known as "Richardsonian Romanesque." The 3-story City Hall was appointed with marble columns and stairways. Stained glass windows depicting allegorical and historical scenes were provided by Pottier & Stymus of New York; frescoes by Charles Pedretti adorned the City Council chambers, and the mosaic floors were designed and executed by the New York firm of Herter Brothers.

The city commissioned this building primarily to combine as many municipal offices and support facilities under one roof as possible. There were rooms for the mayor, waterworks administration, police chief, city clerk, corporation counsel, various city engineers, inspectors, and administrative boards, as well as the police court and jail cells, dormitory, library, drill room, gymnasium, and phone exchange.

But the municipal bureaucracy continued to grow and change. During the first half of the twentieth century, safety department communications and many of the separate departmental administrative offices were moved to other locations, and the police drill room and gym were converted for use as office space.

By mid-century, the structure again seemed hopelessly inadequate, and new components of the municipal bureaucracy had to occupy space some distance from 801 Plum Street or use space that had never been intended for use as offices. Many Planning Department employees, for example, worked at desks lined up in a large hallway.

City Hall was also in need of major repairs by the 1950s, and many city officials argued that the building should be replaced with something more efficient and modern. Instead, city administrators chose to clean and renovate the structure.

In 1965, City Council again con-

*Since the late nineteenth century, structures housing a variety of civic and religious institutions have formed a remarkable architectural cluster at the instrsection of Plum and Eighth Streets.*

sidered abandoning this building and buying or leasing the Kroger Building on Court Street to house the city government. But this and other proposals put forward in the late 1960s were rejected because of the cost. As architectural tastes changed, the idea that the city needed a more modern home for its public offices was counter-balanced by the belief that the old building was a unique landmark and preferable to a featureless office block.

Significant repairs to the old City Hall were carried out in the early 1970s, particularly on the roof and its structural supports. The stained glass was restored in 1976, and the building was placed on the National Register

of Historic Places.

A Protestant church, the **34 First Congregational Church-Unitarian,** occupied the lot at the northeast corner of Plum and Eighth Streets where an auto repair shop now stands. The congregation had built its first church in 1830 at Fourth and Race Streets. From 1838 to 1841, William Henry Channing (1810-1884), nephew of famed Unitarian clergyman William Ellery Channing, served as minister. On November 6, 1870, a new, 2-story brick church with a sixty-foot high metal-clad dome was dedicated on Plum Street.

On Sunday, March 3, 1867, Rabbi Max Lilienthal (1815-1882) spoke to

worshippers at First Unitarian, apparently the first recorded instance in the United States of a rabbi occupying a Christian pulpit.

Members of this congregation, too, moved away from the basin to the suburbs, and in 1887, built a new church in Avondale. Two years later, their old building was sold and remodeled for offices—the Temple Court Building. The dome was removed in 1939, and the structure was torn down in 1945.

On August 23, 1866, K.K. B'nai Yeshurun, the first Reform Jewish congregation west of the Alleghenies,

*Unlike other surviving downtown churches, Plum Street Temple has been kept intact, and the interior looks much as it did in the nineteenth century.*

dedicated **35 Plum Street Temple,** Plum between Seventh and Eighth Streets. The congregation, led since 1854 by Rabbi Isaac Mayer Wise (1819-1900), who founded Reform Judaism in America, had been organized in 1838 by German American Jews unhappy with the ritual and the patronizing attitude of the English-born Jews of Bene Israel (Rockdale Temple).

B'nai Yeshurun first met for services conducted by laymen in rented rooms on Third Street, then in a temporary synagogue on Fourth. In 1846, the congregation completed a temple of its own on a narrow street between Vine and Walnut, and founded the first private Jewish parochial school in the city three years later.

B'nai Yeshurun hired its first rabbi in 1851, but opposition to reforms that he urged forced him to resign after two years. The congregation then wrote to Rabbi Wise. Wise, who had fled Europe in 1847 during a time of suppression of liberal thought, had been denounced by members of his Albany, New York, congregation, which eventually split.

Wise arrived in the city on January 14, 1854. Under his leadership, B'nai Yeshurun adopted a series of innovations that included a new prayer book and English language services. In the 1860s, plans were made for construction of a new temple at Eighth and Plum Streets.

The day before its dedication, Plum Street Temple was opened to the public, and a contemporary newspaper account declared that "at no time had Cincinnati seen so much grandeur compressed in so small a space." The interior walls had been stenciled with Hebrew inscriptions in color and gilt, under the supervision of well-known mural artist Francis Pedretti (1829-1899).

The 1,400 seat, red brick temple, called by Wise his "Alhambra" temple, is considered one of the finest examples of Moorish Byzantine Victorian style architecture in the Western world. Some have suggested that Wise chose this style to recall the Golden Age in Spain when, for 500 years before the Inquisition, Jews lived in peace and their culture flourished. Cincinnati architect James Keyes Wilson's (1828-1894) blending of Byzantine, Gothic, and Islamic elements was the first American attempt to create a "Jewish architecture"—a mix of styles symbolizing the intellectual and cultural currents that had influenced Jewish culture.

Wise also served as president of Hebrew Union College, which he founded in 1875 to train Reform rabbis. Hebrew Union College-Jewish Institute of Religion, now in Clifton Heights, has made Cincinnati a worldwide center of Reform Judaism.

Increasing numbers of members moved to the suburbs, and B'nai Yeshurun completed the Isaac M. Wise Center, a religious school and social center, in Avondale in 1902. The congregation dedicated a new temple there in 1927.

Though Plum Street Temple is no longer used for weekly services, special events and High Holy Days are celebrated here. B'nai Yeshurun's current home is the Isaac Wise Center (1976) in Amberley Village.

Bishop John Purcell began planning for the earliest of the institutions at this intersection, **36** **St. Peter in Chains Cathedral,** Eighth and Plum Street, shortly after he arrived in Cincinnati in 1838. At that time, the cathedral church for the diocese—then the entire state of Ohio—was St. Peter the Apostle Church on Sycamore. In 1840, Purcell purchased a lot bounded by Eighth and Plum Streets, and Central Avenue from Judge Jacob Burnet. *The Catholic Telegraph* opined that the $24,000 price was "a terrible sum which . . . will keep us all a long time very busy to pay."

Every Catholic in Ohio was a member of the cathedral building society and was expected to pay at least twelve and one-half cents each month to support the project. With additional funds raised in Europe and from the sale of an old cemetery in the West End, and a generous loan from the ill-fated bank run by his brother, Father Edward Purcell, Bishop Purcell was able to lay the cornerstone for his new, larger cathedral in 1841.

St. Peter's Cathedral, the second permanent cathedral in the United States (the one in Baltimore was first), was consecrated November 2, 1845, and cost around $120,000. Henry Walter designed the imposing Neo-Classical style structure that had 4-foot thick walls of marble quarried near Dayton and transported to the city on the Miami & Erie Canal.

Reuben R. Springer (1800-1884) donated the bells and clock in the 221-foot steeple. Inside, two angels carved by Hiram Powers (1805-1873) knelt on either side of the main altar. Murillo's painting, "St. Peter in Chains," hung above the altar.

There was an adjacent bishop's residence, and in 1887, a school for the deaf, called the Springer Institute, was completed at the south side of the church. By the end of the century, the parish registered over 700 families.

As the basin became more commercial and the crowded neighborhoods to the west of the Cathedral aged and deteriorated, St. Peter's had fewer and fewer worshippers. In 1938, Archbishop John T. McNicholas (1877-1950) transferred the location of the archdiocesan cathedral to St.

Monica's Church in Fairview. Many feared that St. Peter's Church, as the cathedral was now called, would become neglected and eventually be razed.

But in 1951, Archbishop Karl J. Alter (1885-1977) announced that the cathedral location would be returned to St. Peter's, which would undergo a $3 million expansion and renovation. St. Peter's would be preserved, he explained, because of its historic associations, architectural merits, and its accessibility when new expressways were completed.

During 1952-1953, the Springer Institute and the residence were demolished, and the rear wall of the church was torn out. Services were held in a garage on West Seventh Street that had been converted into a chapel while well-known Cincinnati church architect Edward J. Schulte (c.1890-1975) directed the renovation and redecoration of the cathedral.

St. Peter in Chains was rededicated as the seat of the Roman Catholic Archdiocese of Cincinnati on November 3, 1957. It had a new chapel, baptistry, and residential and administrative wing, as well as new interior features including a specially designed organ, a stained glass mosaic mural assembled and installed by artisans from Germany, and Stations of the Cross by local artist Karl Zimmerman.

St. Peter in Chains Cathedral now hosts all liturgical functions of the archdiocese, special ceremonies like weddings and funerals, and regular Masses that, in 1987, drew about 1,000 each week. At that time, there were 249 member families registered. The Springer Institute relocated to Walnut Hills.

**Turn left (east) on Seventh Street.**

An entire block of the downtown periphery is occupied by a structure that houses both offices and technical operations of two communications companies. AT&T and Cincinnati Bell share the **37** **Cincinnati & Suburban Bell Telephone Company Building,** 209 West Seventh Street.

Cincinnati's telecommunications network, of which this facility is a vital part, was begun by streetcar magnate and real estate developer Charles Kilgour (1833-1906). On July 5, 1873,

Kilgour was granted a state charter incorporating the City & Suburban Telegraphic Association, which used telegraphs and ticker tape to link city businesses.

Kilgour's company became the City & Suburban Telegraph and Telephonic Exchange, the first telephone company in the state and the tenth in the nation. For the first exchange at Fourth and Walnut, Thomas Watson, Alexander Graham Bell's colleague, built the switchboard and supervised its installation in September 1877. John Kilgour (1834-1914), Charles' brother, had the first working telephone line, which ran from his Mt. Lookout home to his office at Third and Walnut. Within seven weeks, the company had over one hundred subscribers paying the thirty-six dollar annual subscription fee.

The 1879 telephone directory, the system's first, warned against the use of "profane, indecent, or rude language" or the use of the telephone for anything other than "bona fide business or social messages." The penalty for violations was termination of the contract and removal of the telephone. One year later, pay phones were installed in public buildings; five minutes of conversation cost fifteen cents. In 1884, City & Suburban hired its first women switchboard operators. Customers had complained that the boys who had originally been hired for the job were rude.

A perpetual contract was signed with the American Bell Telephone Company (later AT&T) in 1882, and by 1885, City & Suburban had lines to 425 surrounding cities—one of the most extensive operations in the nation. Exchange names were put into use in 1900 to facilitate quicker routing of the increasing number of calls. The company became Cincinnati & Suburban Bell Telephone in 1903.

Cincinnati Bell continued to grow, and in 1930, the cornerstone was laid for this 12-story building, designed by local architect Harry Hake. Carved stone reliefs of telephones and headsets alternated in a border above the second floor.

Cincinnati & Suburban Bell completed the conversion to dial phones in 1952 and replaced the two-letter exchange, five numeral telephone numbers with seven-digit ones ten years afterwards.

With the addition of a 20-story long-distance switching center at 229

West Seventh Street in 1975, the telecommunications facility filled the block between Elm and Plum. Cincinnati Bell is headquartered in the Atrium I building on Fourth Street.

> **Turn right (south) on Race Street, right (west) on Fourth Street.**

The three blocks of West Fourth Street between Race Street and Central Avenue constitute the **38** **West Fourth Street Historic District,** which is comprised mostly of late nineteenth and early twentieth-century buildings that exemplify the variety of structures that were prominent in the city eighty to one hundred years ago.

Prior to 1870, these blocks contained a mix of retail stores, entertainment spots, office buildings, and residences. West Fourth Street was an elegant address; a home from this period survives as Pigall's, 127 West Fourth Street, one of Cincinnati's most honored restaurants. The Greek Revival style building has, however, been extensively remodeled.

By the 1870s, the downtown business area was expanding to West Fourth. Older structures, including most dwellings, were replaced by taller office buildings, light manufacturing concerns, and a few apartments. One of the earliest buildings here from that era is the Cincinnati Gas-Light & Coke Company, 305 West Fourth, erected in 1870 and designed by a prominent local architect, James W. McLaughlin. Around the same time, new buildings were constructed at 311, 315, and 323 West Fourth. Tenants included railway and electrical suppliers, coal offices, saloons, laundries, millineries, and pharmacies.

Commercial buildings from this era include two in the Italianate style: the Meader Building at 113-119, originally the home of the Meader Furniture Company, and the Pappenheimer Building at 221. From a somewhat later period are the Queen Anne style Hooper Building, 139, and the Commercial style Textile Building, 205. The Hooper Building originally housed the John Church Company, the world's leading publisher of sacred music at the turn of the century. The Textile Building, erected in 1906, was part of a trend toward centralizing an

industry within one building. Several firms, including manufacturers of shirts, suspenders, cloaks, and neckwear were located here.

Elegant apartment buildings also soon appeared, including the Lombardy, 318-326, built by Thomas Emery's Sons and designed by Samuel Hannaford. Unlike other Cincinnati apartments of the time, the 5-room units in the Lombardy each had private baths and kitchens. William Howard Taft lived here in his bachelor days.

The building boom along West Fourth was generally over by World War I, but two significant buildings were completed in the 1920s. The Gibson Art Company manufactured greeting cards at 231 until the 1950s when it moved to Amberley Village. At 105 West Fourth is the Insight Tower, the tallest building in the district. Designed by the firm of Tietig & Lee, the Insight Tower opened in 1927 as the home of the Cincinnati Chamber of Commerce.

Since the 1920s, the most notable new construction on West Fourth has been the parking garage erected in the mid-1960s. Architecturally incompatible with the historic buildings of the area, the garage served as a rallying point for preservationists, and in the mid-1970s, West Fourth Street was added to the National Register of Historic Places. In 1986, the Cincinnati City Council designated the area a local historic district.

Recent remodeling efforts in the district have been directed toward creating additional housing along West Fourth. In 1980, the Gibson Art and Gas-Light & Coke buildings were converted to apartments. This development, combined with the addition of several art galleries in the 300 block of West Fourth, helped draw some residents back to the downtown area.

> **Turn right (north) on Central Avenue, right (east) on Fifth Street.**

From the time the city established a paid municipal fire department in 1853, the central headquarters of that organization has occupied a number of locations. For much of the twentieth century, those offices have been in the Frame. Since 1962, the **39** **Headquarters of the Cincinnati Fire**

*By the late 1980s, some of the buildings in the West Fourth Historic District had been beautifully renovated, though others continued to stand vacant and deteriorating.*

**Division,** including the chief's office, has shared the modern firehouse at 430 Central Avenue with Engine Company No. 14, Squad 52 (heavy rescue), and the Fire Department's bomb, arson investigation, and fire prevention units.

The first volunteer fire companies in Cincinnati, organized in 1808, did not have a "fire chief" until 1819 when the new city government combined them into a volunteer fire department. Initially, the "Chief Engineer" was responsible for overseeing maintenance of the fire hydrants and city-owned fire apparatus.

As the city expanded, municipal government created additional companies, all manned by volunteers equipped with hand-drawn, hand-powered engines. The volunteer companies, once composed of men from all walks of life, gradually divided along socio-economic and ethnic lines. There was, for example, an all-German company in Over-the-Rhine; well-to-do businessmen belonged to certain companies, although most served as officers or trustees. In the 1840s and 1850s, when conflict became common between different social and ethnic groups in Cincinnati, it also appeared among the firefighters.

These antagonisms between companies induced some volunteer fire officers, led by iron manufacturer Miles Greenwood (1807-1885), to recommend the creation of a new firefighting system based on the use of paid personnel, like that of Boston. They also suggested using horses to pull the fire apparatus, as was done in New Orleans, and using steam-powered pumpers, which local inventors were then perfecting.

When the city instituted the new system in 1853, Cincinnati's fire department became the first fire force in the United States to combine the use of horses, paid men, and steam pumpers. For the next several decades, it was an example followed by municipal fire departments throughout the United States. The new department was headquartered in City Hall until the 1860s when the fire chief moved to a new building near the corner of Sixth and Vine Streets.

This new structure housed the chief's office, Engine Company No. 3, Ladder Company No. 1, and the control center of the fire alarm telegraph system, the department's primary means of dispatching units to fires. The Threes' house served as fire headquarters until around 1911 when both the administration and communications components were transferred to City Hall. While the dispatchers were moved to Eden Park in the 1930s, fire division administration remained at Eighth and Plum until the present building was completed.

Today, the Cincinnati Fire Department consists of twenty-six engine companies, thirteen ladder companies, and five rescue squads.

While the other television studio in the downtown periphery—that of WLWT-TV—utilized a converted, older structure, **40 WCPO-TV** dedicated new broadcast studios at 500 Central Avenue on June 23, 1967. The station's owners, the Scripps Howard Broadcasting Company, had entered the market in 1938 with the purchase of radio station WFBE, renamed WCPO to signify its relation to *The Cincinnati Post*, a Scripps Howard newspaper.

WCPO-TV began broadcasting from studios in Walnut Hills on June 26, 1949, with seventy-five to eighty hours of weekly programing. Television personalities Ruth Lyons, Paul Dixon, and Bob Braun began their careers at WCPO before moving to WLWT where they became local institutions, hosting live programs that developed a strong regional following. The longest-running live children's program, WCPO's *Uncle Al Show*, aired daily from July 1950 through 1982 and then as a weekly show until July 1985.

In the 1960s, when FCC regulations prohibited one company from owning both a radio and television station in the same city, the company elected to retain WCPO-TV and sold its radio station in 1965.

Since the mid-nineteenth century, Cincinnati's civic leaders have regarded events such as conventions or industrial expositions as a good way to boost the city's image and economy. Starting in 1878, these types of functions were held in Music Hall. More recently, city officials chose to relocate the municipal exhibition and convention hall closer to the stores, hotels, and offices of the Core, and in 1967, the first section of **41 Dr. Albert B. Sabin Cincinnati Convention and Exposition Center,** 525 Elm Street, opened.

The city first considered replacing Music Hall in the early twentieth century, and in the 1913, voters approved a $250,000 bond for the project. The Municipal Auditorium Commission hired Cincinnati architect Harry Hake to draw up plans. The proposed site was the block once occupied by the Cincinnati Commercial Hospital on Twelfth Street between Central Avenue and the Miami & Erie Canal.

Hake proposed a 2-story stuccoed structure with an 85,000-square foot, 5,000 to 7,000-seat main Auditorium Arena "sufficiently large to stage the largest three ring circus now on the road." A 58' x 96' swimming pool in the center would "give ample space for all kinds of indoor swimming contests and . . . to demonstrate motor boats." When the pool was covered with a temporary floor, "a regular football field will be laid off and enable football enthusiasts to view the game in a safe and sane manner." The plans included a 2,500-seat restaurant, a rooftop bandstand, and numerous meeting halls.

After a Republican victory in the next election, this plan was abandoned. The 1925 *City Plan* reiterated the need, and in the 1930s and 1940s, several attempts were made to erect a municipal hall downtown. The 1948 *Metropolitan Master Plan* envisioned a riverfront development that would include an exposition hall, an auditorium, city administration buildings, a bus terminal, stadium, and heliport.

Both the funds and the determination to build a convention hall finally came together in the late 1950s as Cincinnati began urban renewal. A Hake & Hake plan for the structure offered a large meeting hall and three parking garages. Wrecking crews began clearing the block bounded by Fifth, Sixth, Elm, and Plum Streets in early 1965.

Dedicated August 4, 1967, the Cincinnati Convention Center had 95,000 square feet of exhibition space. University of Cincinnati architecture students picketed the ceremonies, insisting that the box-like structure with its facade of pre-cast concrete panels was ugly and had "no spirit." Nonetheless, the center did draw convention business.

However, the building soon came to be regarded as outdated and too small to handle many of the events Cincinnati wished to attract. An expansion and remodeling began in 1984. Though plagued by disagreements between the city and county over funding, labor and contractor disputes, and overruns that pushed the cost of the project to $61.9 million, the effort produced an elegant facility with 162,000 square feet of exhibition space, a 30,000-square foot ballroom, forty-three meeting rooms, walls clad with rose and black granite, patterned terazzo floors, and the arch from the old Albee Theater installed over the Fifth Street entrance.

On June 9, 1986, the Sabin Convention Center was dedicated in honor of Dr. Albert Sabin (b.1906), who had developed a live virus oral polio vaccine in the 1950s while working at Children's Hospital and the University of Cincinnati. The first United States test of the vaccine had taken place in Hamilton County on April 24, 1960—"Sabin Sunday."

Turn left (north) on Elm Street, left (west) on Sixth Street, right (north) on Central Avenue, and right (east) on Court Street.

Another significant older building in the Frame that has been preserved and converted to a new purpose is the **42 Cincinnati Fire Museum,** 315 West Court Street. It occupies the former Court Street Firehouse, which was built in 1906-1907 to house Engine Company 45 and Water Tower No. 1.

The Italian Renaissance Revival style building designed by Harry Hake is unusual in that it has doors both in the front and rear. The bays on Court Street were for the firefighting equipment, while those facing Genesee Alley were for the district tool and fuel wagons, which repaired and fired the boilers of the steam fire engine companies.

In 1913, a "flying squad" that provided extra men to help fight serious fires was organized as Company No. 52 and located at the Court Street house. Reorganized and re-equipped in 1918 as Cincinnati's first rescue squad, Company 52 operated out of this firehouse until it was closed.

The units in the Court Street Firehouse saw more activity than any other in Cincinnati. They were among the first to respond to fires both in the downtown and in the West End where thousands of houses, tenements, and commercial and industrial buildings were packed together.

These crowded conditions changed in the 1950s when much of the West End was torn down for urban renewal. By 1962, the Court Street Firehouse was superfluous. Its companies were moved, and the city used this building for storage.

In the 1970s, the badly deteriorated structure was turned over to the Cincinnati Fire Museum Association for renovation as a museum, one way the city manager saw of preserving the historic firehouse and making the area in the vicinity of City Hall more attractive. Cincinnati architect Bruce Goetzman drew up plans for the renovation, and the Cincinnati Fire Museum opened here in December 1980.

The Fire Museum, open to the public, offers exhibits that place Cincinnati firefighting in the context of the city's history. Exhibits of equipment, uniforms, tools, and memorabilia from 1808 to the present are combined with "hands-on" displays oriented towards children.

The **43 Court Street Historic District,** a 6-block area stretching from the Hamilton County Courthouse on the east to Plum Street on the west, contains a mix of residences and commercial and service-related businesses that reflects the economic growth and development of the city in the nineteenth century.

Court Street acquired its name in 1819 when a new Hamilton County Courthouse was erected between Main and Sycamore. This building, the Miami & Erie Canal one block to the north, and the construction of Cincinnati's fourth municipal market between Vine and Walnut made Court Street a busy commercial district in the 1830s.

Several buildings remain on Court from this canal boom era. At the southeast corner of Vine and Court Streets, 1-3 East Court and 912 Vine are Greek Revival structures typical of the type that dominated in Cincinnati before the Civil War. The stone-faced buildings at 124-130 West Court date from 1864 and were originally occupied by canal-related businesses including commission merchants and wholesale grocers.

The opening of the Canal Street Market in 1829 provided an outlet for the tons of produce and livestock sent down the canal each week. Court Street was widened to make room for the open air markethouse, curbside stalls, and stands.

The growth of Court Street as a commercial center prompted many businessmen and their families to build homes in this area. Two early houses survive, 229 and 239 West Court. The former is the oldest structure in the Court Street Historic District and was built about 1847. Its first tenant was steamboat captain William F. Mix.

After the Civil War, a second construction boom on Court Street brought the replacement of the original markethouse and the demolition of many 2 and 3-story buildings to make way for taller structures including the two of ornate Italianate style at 15 and 54 East Court. The older Greek Revival style building at 21-23 East Court was modernized with decorative elements added above windows and along the roofline.

On the south side of the street is a prominent block of Italianate buildings, constructed between 1870 and 1885, many of which housed produce firms. B. H. Kroger opened his seventeenth store at 37 East Court in 1893.

As the railroad eclipsed the river and canal trade in the second half of the nineteenth century, Court Street attracted different kinds of tenants. Numbers 21-23, 31, 33-35, 41, and 54 East Court all housed saloons between 1875 and 1890. Barber shops, cigar-stores, Chinese hand laundries, and food shops filled storefronts.

The automobile brought other changes in the first decades of the twentieth century. The Cincinnati Automobile Club was first located at 112 West Court; several auto-related businesses occupied older buildings, and a garage and "auto laundry" were built on the north side of Court between Race and Vine.

Despite new technologies and the arrival of a new century, Court Street retained its traditions. The markethouse was torn down around 1915, but a curbside market has persisted, and many small businesses have remained on Court Street for decades, often headed by several generations of the same family.

The most significant changes to come to Court Street in the twentieth century have occurred since 1950. Several structures were demolished for parking lots, and the Kroger Company relocated its corporate headquarters to Vine between Central Parkway and Court. Many feared that the street would continue to lose historic structures and that new buildings would disrupt the architectural cohesiveness of the area. The *Cincinnati 2000 Plan* recommended that Court Street be designated a local historic district in order to protect older buildings and provide tax incentives for renovation.

A restoration of Court Street between Vine and Walnut began in 1988. The rejuvenated area is to feature brick sidewalks, portable sidewalk stalls, and a bell tower with a replica of the old Court Street Market bell that will ring at the start of market days every Tuesday and Thursday. The second phase of the project is to include the block between Walnut and Main.

*Market days on Court Street were held under the shelter of this wooden markethouse from the mid-1860s until its demolition around 1915.*

Although the CBD Frame is generally not characterized by modern glass and metal office towers, one early exception—the **44 Kroger Building,** 1014 Vine Street—was erected in the late 1950s.

In 1957, as Cincinnati was undertaking several major renewal projects in the CBD, plans were announced for a new speculative office building at the southeast corner of Central Parkway and Vine Street. According to a *Times-Star* report, "blight and decay" were "deeply entrenched" in much of this area, and the 3- and 4-story commercial and residential structures there seemed to have little value for a modern city.

The Kroger Building, opened in 1960, was the city's third-tallest skyscraper—after the 48-story Carew Tower and the 43-story Union Central/Central Trust Building. It had a parking garage, street-level commercial space, and twenty-four floors of offices. The blue and white enameled interlocking steel panels that covered the exterior gave rise to the witticism that the best view of downtown Cincinnati could be had from anywhere *inside* the building.

The tower became the corporate headquarters of the Kroger Company, which had grown from a single store that Bernard H. Kroger (1860-1938) opened on Pearl Street on July 1, 1883, to one of the largest and most profitable supermarket chains in the country.

Kroger's parents immigrated from Germany and operated a dry goods store that failed during the Panic of 1873. Barney Kroger began making sales and deliveries for a succession of groceries and became store manager for the Imperial Tea Company in 1883. When his offer to buy one-third interest in the store was rejected, Kroger resigned and, with a friend, opened the Great Western Tea Company.

Seventeen years later, in 1902, the Kroger Grocery & Baking Company operated thirty stores in Cincinnati. By the end of the decade, the Kroger chain also served Hamilton, Dayton, and Columbus, Ohio. During the 1940s, the Kroger Company extended its grocery selections and added non-food items. Today's "superstores," with a minimum of 30,000 square feet of floor space, offer flower shops, pharmacies, video rentals, delis, health foods, and even financial services.

A 1982 merger with the Dillon Company, a Western grocery and convenience store chain, made Kroger the largest and most profitable supermarket chain in the United States. The following year, Kroger was Cincinnati's third-largest employer with a workforce of approximately 12,000.

When the Kroger Building was first completed, the grocery chain utilized only five floors but soon expanded to fill nine. The Kroger

Company purchased the building in 1981 and bought the adjacent **45 Brotherhood of Railway Clerks Building,** 1015 Vine Street, for an office annex. Built in 1923, the 7-story red brick structure with attractive bas relief decoration housed the offices of the Brotherhood of Railway and Steamship Clerks, Freight Handlers, Express and Station Employees and of their monthly publication, *Railway Clerk*, on the top floor. The later installation of stainless steel panels and brown brick facing on the lower levels of the modern Kroger tower made it more architecturally compatible with this older building.

Kroger rededicated the annex and its refurbished headquarters on July 1, 1983, the company's one hundredth anniversary. The annex was renamed the Cincinnatus Building for the spectacular *trompe l'oeil* mural by New York City artist Richard Haas on the Central Parkway wall that pays tribute to Cincinnatus, the Roman farmer-soldier for whom the Society of Cincinnati and, then, the city were named.

> **Turn right (south) on Walnut Street.**

As the quality of downtown housing deteriorated in the early twentieth century, various organizations sought to provide suitable accommodations, activities, and eating facilities for people with limited budgets. Completed in 1929, the stone and brick **46 Walnut Towers/YWCA Building,** 898 Walnut Street, contained a cafeteria and 285 residence rooms for single working women, as well as the offices of a social service organization that had been established in Cincinnati in 1868.

The Cincinnati Women's Christian Association (WCA), as it was originally called, aimed to provide for the "temporal, moral, and religious welfare" of young women who were threatened by poverty because of poor wages, lack of occupational training, or the intemperance, illness, or death of male family wage earners. The WCA's first boarding home opened on Longworth Street in 1869 and provided working women with room and board, a library, daily worship services, and an employment bureau.

The WCA became the Young Women's Christian Association in 1894 and occupied a building on East Eighth Street near Vine until moving here.

Over the years, fewer and fewer young working women needed the type of housing that the YWCA offered, and this facility closed in 1972. Federally-subsidized housing for the elderly was developed on floors 5-12; the YWCA's administrative offices, as well as its career counseling service for women and fitness program for men and women, occupy the first four floors.

Now occupying the entire block bounded by Eighth, Ninth, Vine, and Walnut Streets, the **47 Main Branch of the Public Library of Cincinnati and Hamilton County,** 800 Vine Street, has always been located in the Frame. Its history begins

*The expanded Main Branch of the Public Library of Cincinnati and Hamilton County fills an entire block on Eighth Street between Vine and Sycamore Streets.*

with legislation passed by the Ohio General Assembly in 1853 that aimed at reorganizing the public schools. The act also allotted property tax money to furnish each district school with a library to be administered by the local board of education. Because all the school libraries were to be alike, the Cincinnati Board of Education decided to create a single facility for the entire school district.

In 1855, the first year of operations, 1,500 volumes were purchased for the Ohio School and Family Library, which was located briefly at Central High School in the West End, then transferred to the Ohio Mechanics Institute at Vine and Sixth Streets. The librarian's report for 1857 noted that of the 20,179 books circulated

that year, 8,220 were novels — "the excessive propensity...for such reading has given us much pain...."

Cincinnati's library was essentially dependent on public donations until 1867 when further legislation allowed boards of education to authorize a property tax for libraries. The following year, the Cincinnati Board of Education's library committee purchased Truman Bishop Handy's partially completed opera house near the southwest corner of Vine and Seventh Streets and commissioned architect James W. McLaughlin to prepare plans for a new library that would consist of the opera house and two other buildings.

The walls of the main library hall in the rear building had five tiers of open alcoves with shelving, accessible by narrow catwalks, that would hold 200,000 books. The Cincinnati Public Library opened in the old opera house on December 6, 1870, and the main hall was dedicated February 25, 1874.

In just sixteen years, the head librarian was urging a new building, citing lack of usable space and the fact that "...the attendants must necessarily ascend and descend [five stories of circular] iron stairs a number of times each day...in search of books...."

State legislation in 1898 extended library privileges to all residents of Hamilton County and authorized library trustees to manage the institution and to certify a county-wide property tax for its support. The trustees undertook a series of much-needed improvements, and six village libraries became public library branches. A gift of $250,000 from steel tycoon Andrew Carnegie, enabled the construction of seven more branches. The Walnut Hills' branch opened first, on April 9, 1906.

Although the main library building grew increasingly inadequate, Hamilton County voters defeated bond issues to erect a new one until 1944. With the end of World War II, property at the northeast corner of Eighth and Vine Streets was acquired. The library board accepted a design by Woodie Garber for the architectural firms of Frederick W. Garber and Samuel Hannaford & Sons in June 1950.

The library's 1.25 million volumes were moved in early January 1955, and the new Public Library of Cincinnati and Hamilton County was dedicated January 31. With additions in 1985, the Main Library building covered an entire city block that had once been filled with small, closely built nineteenth-century homes, shops, and a church that later became the Gayety Burlesk [*sic*] Theater.

By the mid-1980s, the collection of the Main Library and its forty branches included more than three million books, recordings, films, and other materials.

**Turn right (west) on Eighth Street.**

Greenspace is one of the more important land uses in the Frame encouraged by city planners. Downtown Cincinnati would seem cold and unappealing if it were not for Lytle Park, the Central Parkway median strip, P&G's formal gardens, and the

*This thin strip of park on Eighth Street between Vine and Elm was one of the few spaces of greenery in the densely built up downtown of late nineteenth-century Cincinnati.*

oldest of the city's parks, **48 Piatt Park,** on Garfield Place (Eighth Street between Elm and Vine Streets). On April 9, 1817, John H. (1781-1822) and Benjamin M. (1799-1863) Piatt gave this land to the city for a marketplace.

Benjamin served as a judge in the Hamilton County Court of Common Pleas and as a member of the Ohio legislature. John was an early Cincinnati entrepreneur involved in steamboat construction, insurance, banking, and real estate speculation.

Because other markets were nearby, the Piatts' gift was developed as a park, valued by those who lived in the residential district that developed between Seventh and Ninth Streets. On June 18, 1868, Eighth Street Park was formally dedicated. In 1882, a year after the death of President James A. Garfield (1831-1881), the park was renamed Garfield Park for the assassinated Ohioan. On October 20, 1940, it was rededicated in honor of the Piatts.

In the mid-1980s, the city put together a $200 million plan to develop 1,200 units of moderate and upper-income housing along Garfield Place,

hoping to bring night life back to the downtown. A $3 million proposal for the renovation of Piatt Park featured new walks, lighting, fountains, plantings, and benches.

Piatt Park is the setting for some of downtown Cincinnati's earliest civic art. On December 1, 1887, five years after this spot became Garfield Park, a bronze **49 Statue of President James Garfield** was unveiled in the middle of the intersection of Eighth and Race Streets. The figure, the work of Cincinnati-born sculptor Charles A. Niehaus, had arrived in the city from his studio in Rome in 1885, then was stored until the money was raised to by a granite pedestal for it.

By the early twentieth century, the statue had become a nuisance for downtown traffic and was moved to the Elm Street end of the park on January 14, 1915. The Garfield statue was renovated in 1978, and during the renovation of Piatt Park ten years later, both it and the nearby statue of William Henry Harrison were shifted to their present locations.

During the mid-nineteenth century, wealthier Cincinnatians who wanted homes farther away from the commercial center on Third and Fourth Streets looked to the vicinity of Eighth Street Park. One of the finest houses in this area, that of wholesale clothier Marcus Fechheimer (1818-1881), has been preserved as the **50 Willa K. Butterfield Senior Center,** 22 Garfield Place. The sandstone Renaissance Revival style dwelling was built around 1861-1862 and is the oldest surviving building designed by Samuel Hannaford. The elegant home was divided into offices, then was purchased by the Cuvier Press Club in 1937.

The all-male club was formed by the 1911 merger of the Cuvier Club (1871), gentleman hunters and naturalists, and the Pen and Pencil Club, morning edition newspapermen who wanted to get around a midnight closing rule for saloons. The club fell on hard times during the Depression but was able to purchase these quarters with the profits from slot machines installed in the clubhouse. The club left the Fechheimer house in 1973 and moved into rooms in the Fourth and Race Tower, then disbanded in 1984.

Aided by a federal HUD grant, the city acquired the former clubhouse in 1976 and undertook a $1.2 million remodeling and expansion project planned by Cincinnati architects David Lee Smith and Donald Stevens. The Willa K. Butterfield Senior Center, named for the woman who helped create the city's first senior center, offers lunch, recreational facilities, craft and music programs, trips, dances, and lectures.

By the early twentieth century, the area around Garfield Park was becoming a location for offices, clubs, and stores. Although many existing structures, like the Fechheimer house, were converted to fill these functions, new buildings of a much larger scale were also erected.

In 1913, a group of investors headed by Cincinnati businessmen Howard Wurlitzer and William Cooper Procter envisioned the development of a row of Gothic Revival style shops and offices along Garfield Place. Completed in 1923, the **51 Doctors' Building,** 19 Garfield Place, was the only element of this plan to be realized. It was designed to be Cincinnati's

modern medical center for doctors and dentists, and many still occupy some of the offices.

Over the years, the facilities became outdated, and a number of the offices were empty in 1984 when Atlanta-based Ameritas, Inc., bought the property, renovated it, and restored the storefronts' original appearance.

Smaller, older buildings on the north side of Eighth Street were also replaced by the **52 Cincinnati Club Building,** 30 Garfield Place, a 10-story brick and limestone structure erected in 1924. The private all-male Cincinnati Club was founded in 1892 as the Young Business Men's Club; it became the Business-men's Club seven years later, and adopted its current name after moving into this Garfield Place clubhouse designed by Garber & Woodward.

The first three floors of the building and the adjoining annex, the old Phoenix Club Building to which it is connected by an enclosed bridge and underground tunnel, contained a richly decorated meeting and dining rooms, a gymnasium, bowling alleys, a pool, a library, and a women's lounge. The floors above offered lodging rooms for members and guests.

By 1984, only a handful of those rooms were occupied, and the Cincinnati Club was financially troubled. Ameritas, purchased the club's properties for $4.6 million and from 1984 to 1986, carried out an $18 million renovation. The Cincinnati Club retained the second and third floors, while the residential rooms were turned into office space. Some athletic facilities were maintained and managed as a part of the office development.

> **Turn left (south) on Race Street, left (east) on Seventh Street, and left (north) on Vine Street.**

In the 1960s, city planners decided that the Garfield Park area should once again be a residential district, but with the exception of Frank Messer & Sons' 165-unit Garfield Tower, completed at the corner of Race and Garfield Place in 1969, little new housing construction took place. By 1980, when a group of investors proposed erecting a 17-story

apartment tower, the **53 Garfield House,** 2 Garfield Place at Vine Street, many city officials had come to believe that housing projects of this type were not viable without some kind of public support.

By temporarily reducing the tax load that a building's owners would bear, city planners, development officials, and most City Council members hoped that developers would be able to charge less rent for each unit and thereby attract middle-income tenants. In a vote on October 1, 1980, City Council approved a tax abatement for the Garfield House, which was completed in 1982.

Architect Perry Hall, of the New York City firm of Prentis, Chan & Ohlhausen, sought "to keep the project in tune with the scale of the city." The 153-unit structure's appearance was made less overpowering and monolithic than conventional brick or concrete apartment blocks by the use of pre-cast concrete panels in graduated colors on the upper floors, divided by strips of inset balconies with bright red railings. The lower level, occupied by offices and restaurants, had glass canopies and large windows alternating with shiny gray or red enamel wall panels.

> **Turn left (west) on Ninth Street.**

A 175-seat restaurant with an adjacent wine shop, bakery, and meat market—all planned for the lower level of the Cincinnati Club Building—is one element of the project aimed at turning the 4-story **54 Phoenix Club Building,** 27 West Ninth Street, into what a newspaper article described as a "culinary mecca and hospitality center."

This Renaissance Revival style brick and stone building, designed by Samuel Hannaford, opened on October 1, 1894, as the clubhouse of the city's first private Jewish men's club. The Phoenix Club, "A German Club of Jewish Men" was founded May 1, 1856, by prominent Cincinnati Jews who were excluded from other private men's clubs.

The Businessmen's Club bought the building in 1911, sharing it with the original owners. After the new clubhouse was completed, the Phoenix was used to house the Cincinnati Club's athletic and recreational facilities; the ballroom was converted into a gymnasium. When the Phoenix Club was dissolved in 1942, the remaining eighteen members became members of the Cincinnati Club.

The renovated and refurbished Phoenix Club Building opened in the summer of 1988, offering meeting and party rooms, and a ballroom, making it a deluxe location for conferences and gala events.

**Turn left (south) on Race Street, right (west) on Garfield Place/ Eighth Street.**

The equestrian **55 Statue of William Henry Harrison** at the western end of Piatt Park depicts the uniformed general riding with no saddle but his feet in the stirrups. The horse's upraised foreleg signifies that Harrison (1773-1841) was wounded in battle—during campaigns against the Indians when he served as General Anthony Wayne's aide-de-camp.

Harrison, a Virginian, married the daughter of John Cleves Symmes in 1795 and set up a home in North Bend, where he became a successful land speculator and developer. He was appointed governor of the Indian Territory in 1800 and in 1811, defeated the Shawnee tribes near the mouth of Tippecanoe Creek. During the War of 1812, Harrison commanded the Army of the Northwest and emerged a national hero.

Harrison had a long career in the State Legislature and the House of Representatives. In 1840, Harrison, a Whig, became ninth President of the United States and the first elected from Ohio.

Italian-born sculptor Louis T. Rebisso (c.1836-1899) executed this bronze statue, which was dedicated June 25, 1895.

**Turn right (north) on Elm Street.**

Another active though dwindling nineteenth-century congregation remaining in the Frame is that of **56 Covenant-First Presbyterian Church,** 717 Elm Street, the product of the twentieth-century unions of six downtown churches.

The oldest of the six and the oldest congregation in Cincinnati was First Presbyterian Church, established October 16, 1790. The church that members erected in 1792 on Fourth Street between Main and Walnut stood on land that pioneer surveyor Israel Ludlow (1765-1804) had given to the city in part "for the use of a Presbyterian Church."

The members of Second Presbyterian Church (1816) dedicated this stone English Gothic style house of worship on April 11, 1875. The Reverend Lyman Beecher (1775-1863) served Second Presbyterian from 1833 to 1843, as a memorial tablet in the entryway records. Another tablet outside the entrance commemorates Israel Ludlow. A bell in the tower is stamped "Revere, Boston" and is presumed to have been cast by Paul Revere. The pulpit furniture was the work of Cincinnati woodcarvers William and Henry Fry.

In the twentieth century as the basin church became more commercial, downtown congregations declined, leading churches to consolidate. The Church of the Covenant was created in 1907 with the union of Second, Fifth (1831), and Central Presbyterian (1844). First Reformed Presbyterian Church (1829) and West Liberty Presbyterian Church (1857) merged with First Presbyterian in 1914 and 1928, respectively. On October 1, 1933, First Presbyterian and Covenant merged.

By 1987, Convenant-First Presbyterian was a congregation of 253 mostly elderly members. It offered a weekly lunch and service, evening meetings and dinners for women who worked downtown, and a class in Christian education for lay leadership.

Several decades before preservation and "adaptive reuse" were common concepts, the Crosley Company converted a former fraternal lodge into television studios—a facility that became known as **57 Crosley Square,** 140 West Ninth Street. Live programs that in no small way influenced television in the Midwest were broadcast live from WLWT-TV studios here.

The 6-story brick and stone structure had been designed by Cincinnati architect Harry Hake and erected in 1923-1924 as an Elks Temple. Between 1942 and 1944, the Crosley Broadcasting Company bought the hall, converted it into office and studio space, and renamed it for Powel Crosley, Jr.

(1886-1961), inventor, businessman, and radio and television broadcasting pioneer.

Crosley started experimenting with television broadcasting in 1939, obtained an experimental license and the call letters W8XC7 in the mid-1940s, and by 1947 was broadcasting twenty hours of programing each week. He received a commercial license in 1948, and on February 9, WLWT became the first federally licensed Ohio station on the air; its transmission tower was on top of the Carew Tower.

In April 1948, WLWT became the first station to broadcast a Reds game and began feeding network programming to Cincinnati on September 26. WLWT became NBC's first color affiliate with the broadcast of the 1954 Tournament of Roses Parade and became the first Cincinnati station to originate color programming with the broadcast of Ruth Lyon's *50-50 Club* on August 9, 1957.

At one time, WLWT also occupied the building across the street that now houses the offices of the Legal Aid Society.

On June 9, 1975, AVCO, which had purchased the broadcasting concern in 1945, announced the sale of WLWT to Multimedia Corporation, beginning the breakup of the old Crosley broadcasting empire. The new owner, a communications conglomerate with radio, television, newspaper, and productions divisions, took over operations on March 1, 1976, and located its corporate offices here, close to the activity and amenities of the Central Business District.

**Continue on to Central Parkway where tour ends.**

# Over-the-Rhine

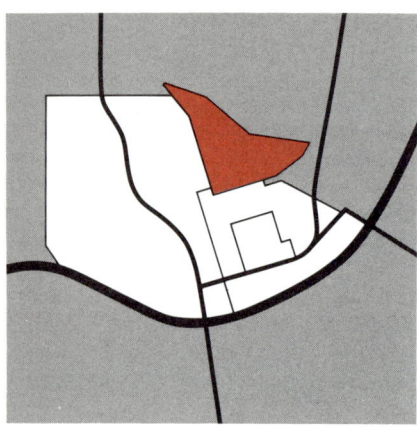

Bounded on the south and west by Central Parkway, on the east by Reading Road and Liberty Street, and on the north by McMicken Avenue, the Over-the-Rhine neighborhood offers sharp contradictions. Other historic areas have been lost to time and urban renewal, but Over-the-Rhine has hundreds of nineteenth-century buildings that tie the city to its past. At the same time, this is Cincinnati's most visible slum and the neighborhood with the second-highest percentage of residents living below the poverty level—about 58% compared to 20% for the city as a whole in the mid-1980s. Revitalization of the area has been held up by lack of public funding and an inability to decide whether low-cost housing, architectural preservation, and private residential and commercial renewal are mutually exclusive goals.

While about half of the district later known as Over-the-Rhine was included in the 1802 Town of Cincinnati, it lay far away from the commercial center on Third and Fourth Streets. Industry was attracted to this less expensive land, particularly after the Miami & Erie Canal was opened between Court and Twelfth Streets in the late 1820s. The property also drew an economically diverse population, including large numbers of immigrants, and the district acquired a reputation as the "foreign" part of the city.

*In the nineteenth century, the Miami & Erie Canal formed the western and southern boundaries of Over-the-Rhine.*

Germans were the most numerous immigrant group to settle here, giving the area a distinct identity. One historian has estimated that although German-born Cincinnatians constituted only about 7% of the city's population in 1840, nearly half of the residents north of the canal were from the various German states such as Prussia, Bavaria, or Saxony. It seemed to many that crossing the Miami & Erie Canal was like crossing the Rhine River into Germany—thus, "Over-the-Rhine." If the name was originally something of a deprecatory comment, by the mid-nineteenth century it was widely used even among German Americans, who took

*Henry Wielert operated one of the best-known of the many saloons, restaurants, and concert halls that lined Vine Street in the late nineteenth century.*

considerable pride in calling attention to the special character of their neighborhood.

The German immigrants also became a significant presence in the area just outside the city limits to the north of Liberty Street. Because the "Northern Liberties" wasn't subject to municipal laws, this district had a concentration of saloons, gambling houses, and brothels. After the city annexed the area in 1849, Cincinnatians regarded Over-the-Rhine as extending up to the foot of the hills at the north end of the basin.

This large and predominantly German-born community worried some native-born Cincinnatians who, in the mid-1800s, came to blame the immigrants for causing every misfortune that befell the city, from epidemics to unemployment. In 1855, a nativist mob attempted to invade Over-the-Rhine, only to be met by the gunfire of the well-armed and highly organized German American militia units and rifle clubs. For two days, five hundred German Americans manned a barricade across Vine Street.

By the turn of the century, German Americans in Cincinnati had established a German language theater, over thirty periodicals, forty-eight churches and synagogues, two orphanages, a home for old men and another for widows, six cemeteries, and numerous clubs, building and loan associations, and singing societies.

While German Americans settled in every part of Cincinnati, most of their cultural institutions and businesses were concentrated in Over-the-Rhine. The largest cluster of saloons, beer gardens, and concert halls—integral parts of German American culture—was along Vine Street and at its peak included more than fifty saloons and five theaters between the canal and McMicken Street. By the 1870s, the Vine Street entertainment district was a major tourist attraction with a national, as well as a local, reputation.

Workshops, homes, and businesses stood side by side. Small and medium-sized plants producing a variety of goods from furniture to fire engines were distributed throughout Over-the-Rhine. The largest factories were concentrated on major transportation routes. As early as the 1850s, Miles Greenwood's ironworks, a stove plant, and lumber and stoneyards were near the Miami & Erie Canal. As more industries moved into the area, many, including a large number of wagon and carriage factories, established themselves on McMicken Street, the road to Hamilton. Breweries were set up along both the canal and McMicken.

Almost every block included housing, some industry, and shops. By the latter decades of the nineteenth century, this mix began to diminish the area's appeal as a residential district. The suburban ideal—single-family homes with yards, isolated from industrial activity—was gaining popularity among middle-income families who began moving to new subdivisions in the surrounding hills. Over-the-Rhine became increasingly a working-class district. At the same time, its German character had to be consciously maintained as immigration decreased and Cincinnati's German Americans became part of the mainstream.

Although feeling against German Americans had largely evaporated by the early twentieth century, it was revived by World War I. There were some signs of anti-German feeling in Cincinnati, but the *Volksblatt*, a German-language daily, could mock spy fever:

*In Over-the-Rhine, homes, workshops, and small businesses stood side by side with larger plants such as Christian Morelein's Elm Street brewery.*

*Quite probably the furnace man*
  *who seems devoid of wits*
*Is now collecting dynamite*
  *to blow you into bits.*
*And we have heard the Kaiser's son*
  *himself, in strange disguise,*
*Is acting as your garbage man,*
  *and leading all the spies!*

After the United States entered the war, reason and humor in Cincinnati and across the country gave way to hysteria and bigotry in the guise of patriotism. Individuals, businesses, and clubs changed their names: the German National Bank, for example, became the Lincoln National Bank. On February 2, 1918, the Cincinnati Board of Education voted to ban the teaching of German in public elementary schools. Thirteen streets lost their German names. German Street became English Street, and Bremen Street, named after the port from which so many had sailed for America, became Republic Street. Schiller and Goethe

Streets remained. On May 9, 1918, the public library withdrew all German books, periodicals, and newspapers from the shelves.

Prohibition and the changes forced on Cincinnati's institutions diminished what remained of Over-the-Rhine's unique character. Vine Street became a dull and tawdry remnant of its former self, and the breweries became warehouses or switched to manufacturing other products. The canal was drained, filled with subway tunnels that were never used, and finally covered by Central Parkway. Over-the-Rhine became essentially an aging district of industry and working-class housing.

By mid-century, however, Over-the-Rhine began to undergo another major change. The low rents for its old housing attracted low-income residents from Appalachia, and the area became the city's "port of entry" for yet another group of newcomers. At the same time, population decreased, falling from around 30,000 in the late 1940s to approximately 25,000 in the mid-1950s.

Later in that decade, blacks displaced by urban renewal projects in the West End began to move into Over-the-Rhine where they found low-rent housing because the area did not experience widespread clearance. City planners did not think of it as a "rock-bottom slum" like the West End, nor was it in the path of a new expressway. Further, the "deterioration" in Over-the-Rhine did not threaten any nearby communities. So the city's limited renewal funds were consigned, instead, to Corryville and Avondale where "blight" might affect adjoining, undeteriorated neighborhoods.

The influx of new black residents from inside the city and of low-income whites from the South caused Over-the-Rhine's population to increase to about 30,000 in 1960. During the 1960s, the neighborhood had the fastest growing crime rate, the highest population density, and the second-lowest average income level of any part of the city. When city officials tried to improve conditions for residents by forcing landlords to conform to building codes, some owners responded by vacating their properties rather than making the needed repairs. The number of available units declined; people generally tried to move out as soon as they could, and little sense of community or common purpose existed. By the late 1960s, Over-the-Rhine's population had fallen back to approximately 20,000.

City government tried to improve conditions in Over-the-Rhine first by creating a unified social service center in 1966, and then by including the area as a target neighborhood in the Model Cities Program. The city adopted a strategy of concentrating renewal funds on projects that seemed to have the greatest potential for stimulating private investment and development. Officials created a plan for Over-the-Rhine that emphasized the "town center" concept—improving a centrally located business area to provide an economic anchor around which housing and other commercial rehabilitation would take place. Such projects were supposed to build residents' confidence and "improve the community's viability," while preserving the area's residential character. No widespread demolition would take place, and only scattered public housing would be built.

The Findlay Market area was chosen for the town center redevelopment. Beginning in 1973, the historic market building was renovated, parking and street fixtures were improved, and a playground created. A neighborhood center and a Boys' Club were established, and housing was rehabilitated with public funds. The Findlay Market Town Center, intended as a "prototype for development" for all of Over-the-Rhine, was only a limited success. The number of adequate housing units in the area continued to fall, as did the number of businesses for which survival was increasingly difficult in the high-crime, low-income neighborhood. By 1980, the population had dropped to approximately 12,000 and was 64% black.

Private initiative, however, had some impact on this neighborhood as individuals unwilling to lose this part of Cincinnati's history began to renovate and occupy old residences in Over-the-Rhine, particularly those near Music Hall and on Sycamore and Broadway between Twelfth and Thirteenth Streets. City officials also began to view historic preservation and individual investment as a means of improving Over-the-Rhine's future. In 1983, the city's Historic Conservation Board recommended the entry of Over-the-Rhine as an historic district on the National Register of Historic Places.

The proposal drew protest from some community organizers who argued that the investment and development that might follow historic designation would produce higher rents and drive out low-income residents. Proponents of the listing and of incentives to encourage home ownership and privately financed redevelopment countered that developers, attracted by an investment tax credit, would create low-income housing. Moreover, because public redevelopment funds were simply not available, the decline of the neighborhood and the loss of housing units would continue without private investment.

Over-the-Rhine seems to offer potential for the development of an economically mixed residential community coexisting with commercial light industry. But questions as to how the neighborhood will be reclaimed remain unsettled.

North

6

5

McMicken Ave.

Findlay St.

7

4

3

Liberty St.

**End**

23  22

2

8

9

13

14

Orchard St.

12

21

14th St.

15

E. 14th St.

20

30       29

24   19
         18

13th St.

12th St.

Reading Rd.

Sycamore St.

Liberty St.

E. 13th St.

11

16

1   27

26       28

25

E. 12th St.

10

17

Central Pkwy.

Pendleton St.

Broadway

Sycamore St.

Main St.

Clay St.

Walnut St.

Vine St.

Race St.

Elm St.

Central Pkwy.

**Start**

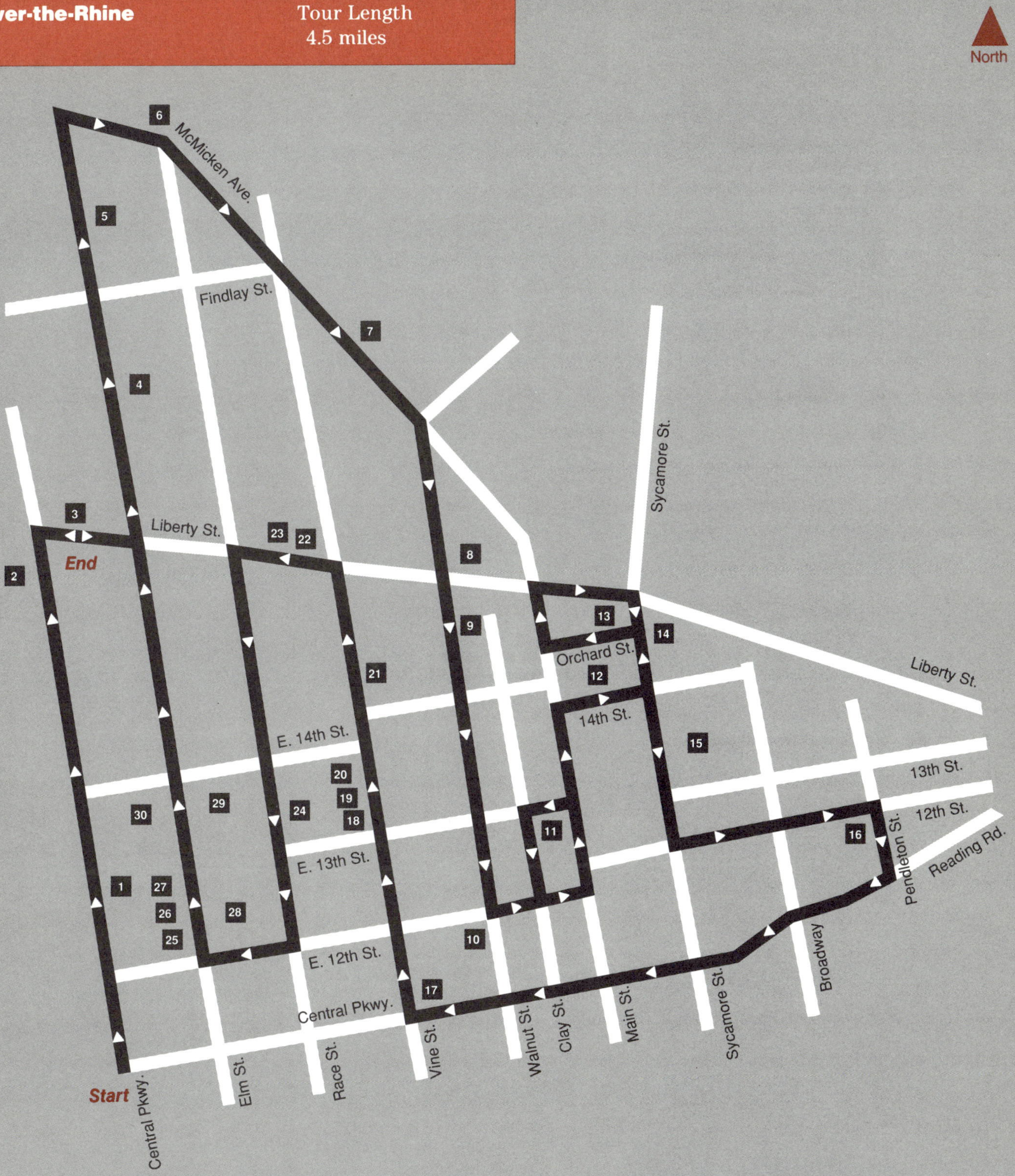

# Tour 4

# Over-the-Rhine

▶ ▶ ▶ ▶ ▶ ▶

**Tour begins at the bend of Central Parkway. Head north.**

Stone relief busts of composers decorate the frame and eight faience cherubs carrying musical instruments stand above the door of **1 Odeon Hall,** 1228 Central Parkway, once part of the old College Conservatory of Music. The college was founded in 1878 by Colonel George Ward Nichols (1837-1886), husband of Maria Long-worth and one of the sponsors of the May Festival and the construction of Music Hall.

When Music Hall was completed, Nichols turned his attention to establishing a college of music as a source of talent; Reuben R. Springer backed the venture with donations totaling nearly $200,000. On October 14, 1878, one hundred students began classes on the third floor of Music Hall; 500 were enrolled by the end of the year. Theodore Thomas, who had conducted May Festival performances, served as the school's music director until 1880.

This 4-story buff brick building was erected in 1882 and contained an auditorium, practice rooms, and offices. The college once included three other buildings—the Lyceum, Schmidlapp dormitory (1902), and Alms Hall (1921)—built around Odeon Hall and later razed for parking lots.

In 1955, because of economic difficulties and the need for more space and a better location, the college merged with the Cincinnati Conservatory of Music (est. 1867) in Mt. Auburn. In 1962, the College Conservatory of Music joined the University of Cincinnati as its fourteenth college.

Odeon Hall has subsequently housed a lodge, various businesses, and union offices.

The 4-story red brick structure at the southwest corner of West Liberty Street and Central Parkway was built in 1866 along the Miami & Erie Canal as the main building of the Windisch-Muhlhauser Brewing Company's **2 Lion Brewery**. Once, two huge stone lions, crouched on the peaks at each end of the building. The warehouse and wagonshed stood across the canal, with workshops and support buildings to the south.

Gottlieb and Henry Muhlhauser,

*The former Lion Brewery, part of a complex that once straddled the boundary between Over-the-Rhine and the West End, was used by the Burger Brewing Company after the repeal of Prohibition.*

German immigrants, came to Cincinnati in the 1840s. In 1866, Gottlieb left the Christian Moerlein Brewing Company to establish a new brewery with his brother-in-law, Conrad Windisch. By 1892, Windisch-Muhlhauser was producing 175,000 barrels annually and was Moerlein's strongest local rival. Approximately 200 men worked in the 2-block complex that included a malting house, cooperage, ice houses, main brew house, and, under the building, two 60-foot-long storage cellars.

The company continued to prosper, producing a variety of beers like Lion Brew and Lion Export. Windisch-Muhlhauser tried to survive Prohibition by switching to the production of root beer and malt extract but closed in 1922.

The complex was leased in 1934 by the Burger Brewing Company, begun in 1880 when Louis Burger and his brother, Charles, set up a malting and brewers' supply business. The firm reorganized as a brewing company in 1934. Burger bought the Lion Brewery complex in 1943, enlarged and modernized the facilities, and eventually removed the old trademark lions. An office addition was completed in 1951.

Burger expanded in the mid-1960s with the purchase of several PepsiCo soft drink bottling companies. It closed on March 16, 1973, driven out of business by competition from larger companies and falling profits. The Hudepohl Brewing Company, another Cincinnati firm, bought Burger and, threatened by these same forces, merged with the Schoenling Brewing Company in 1986.

**Turn right on Liberty Street.**

The 3-story buff brick building now occupied by a manufacturer of automatic temperature controls was originally the **3 Grade School of St. Joseph of Nazareth Roman Catholic Church,** 220 West Liberty Street. St. Joseph's was the successor to St. Stephen Church in Mt. Adams which had been founded in 1914. St. Stephen's was the first parish for German-speaking Hungarians, the last Catholic church to be organized within the original city limits, and the last of the "national" churches—those created for non-English speaking congregations.

Though a small minority of Cincinnati's Catholics, the German Hungarians persuaded Archbishop Henry Moeller to allow them to form their own church. Their pastor purchased an old convent on Baum Street in Mt. Adams, planning to convert the chapel into a parish church and to remodel the rest of the building into apartments for Hungarian families. But the plan failed. German Hungarian families in the basin generally preferred to attend Mass at nearby German churches.

In 1919, the Cincinnati Archdiocese purchased St. Matthew Evangelical Protestant Church and rectory at the corner of Liberty and Elm, and the following year rededicated it as St. Joseph of Nazareth (Hungarian) Church. The parish recorded 600 member families in 1924 and two years later, built this school. The Hungarian designation for the church was dropped in the late 1930s.

St. Joseph's parish dwindled as members moved out of the basin. The school was closed in May 1963 and the parish discontinued on August 1. The church was razed in 1965, but the Catholic School Board of Education used the old school for its offices until 1980.

**Turn left on Elm Street.**

**4 Findlay Market,** located on an esplanade on Elder Street between Elm and Race Streets, is the last remaining municipal market building in Cincinnati. The market was named after General James Findlay (1770-1836), a veteran of the War of 1812 and a mayor of Cincinnati.

Findlay was also a major land speculator; among his holdings was considerable acreage in the Northern Liberties. He intended to start a farmers' market on Elder Street and establish a store nearby, but died before he could do so. After his wife's death in 1847, the executors of the estate decided to donate this site for a public market to be named after General Findlay.

Construction of the Findlay Market, the city's seventh public market building, began in 1852. The earlier ones were located in the heart of the city, closer to the river, but by then, city officials saw a need to provide convenient shopping facilities for the growing northern and western parts of the basin. While these other markets were of frame or brick construction, City Civil Engineer Alfred West Gilbert (1816-1900) directed one of his draftsmen, probably James Stewart, to design a more durable iron building here.

The use of iron construction, common in Great Britain at that time, was a new idea in Cincinnati. Many believed it wouldn't work, but the support of influential people like Miles Greenwood ensured that Gilbert had the opportunity to try the iron structural work. Although the project was delayed by problems with the quality of the work and materials, Findlay Market was still one of the first iron market buildings in the United States.

When Findlay Market was fully opened in 1855, the use of public market buildings was at its height. By the end of the decade, there were nine in Cincinnati. These markets were the "shopping centers" in an age when most city dwellers lived within walking distance of where they worked and shopped. The markets, which housed butchers' shops in the building and produce stalls around the perimeter, were open on alternate days. Other stores lined the streets nearby.

The markets also became convenient points for other kinds of business and socializing. They were frequently the sites for public meetings, served as polling places, and, during the Civil War, were mustering points for the volunteer militia called out to defend the city and northern Kentucky.

In the late 1860s and early 1870s, as public transportation drew people to suburbs outside the basin, neighborhood business districts developed, replacing the markets as retail and social centers. By the late 1800s, only five public markets remained, but

*Findlay Market's clientele includes shoppers from both the immediate vicinity and other Greater Cincinnati neighborhoods outside the basin.*

those which survived were gradually improved by the city as new ideas about public health and disease led city officials to replace or enclose the old market houses. City engineers enclosed Findlay Market in 1902 and added refrigeration. It was remodeled and further updated in 1915.

As Over-the-Rhine changed during the twentieth century, so did the commercial district that included Findlay Market. Between the 1920s and the 1960s, the population of the area became progressively smaller and poorer. Despite the strong traditions associated with doing business in and around Findlay Market—some families stayed in the same building or leased the same market stall for several generations—the volume of business and the number of merchants gradually declined. The buildings, including the market, deteriorated.

In the late 1960s, when federal funds became available for pilot projects in the Model Cities program, Cincinnati officials picked the Findlay Market district for a "town center" project. Apartment buildings around the area were rehabilitated, parking space was created, and the market itself was closed and renovated in 1973-1974 at a cost of over $900,000.

Further, St. John the Baptist Roman Catholic Church, built in 1845 and closed in 1969, was torn down and replaced by a community center. Easily identified by the spire of the old church that was retained to preserve the neighborhood's skyline, the center offered a variety of services including adult education classes, legal assistance, counseling, and recreation.

Although the town center project was not the success planners envisioned, it did help the Findlay Market

district remain a focal point of the Over-the-Rhine community. The project fostered little improvement on adjoining blocks, but the market area itself stabilized. Some of Over-the-Rhine's most viable businesses are here, and the market draws customers from throughout the city.

Cincinnati's first brewery opened in January 1812, and during the nineteenth century, nearly fifty breweries operated for varying periods in and around the city. From the mid-1800s until Prohibition, the city's most prominent local brewery was the Christian Moerlein Company. The **5 Bottling Plant of the Christian Moerlein Brewing Company,** 1910 Elm Street, a 2-story red brick building with beer barrel-like decorations above the main door, is one of the remaining structures of the original complex that filled three blocks around Ninth and Elm Streets. It is now occupied by a lamp company.

Around the corner at 111 West McMicken Avenue, a furniture manufacturing business is housed in the old ice house where vats of fermenting beer were once stored in the massive basement forty-five feet below the street. The rusted, peeling sign on the company's office building, 2019 Elm Street, is barely legible. The French Second Empire style residence next door, 2017 Elm, was the home of Jacob Moerlein, son of the company's founder and its treasurer. Christian Moerlein's home is also still standing at 2407 Ohio Avenue, one block east of Moerlein Avenue, in Fairview.

Christian Moerlein (1818-1897) came to America from Bavaria in 1841 and settled in Cincinnati the following year. He began a brewing company with Adam Dillman in 1853, producing 1,000 barrels of beer that year. When Dillman died, Moerlein took Conrad Windisch into partnership. By 1866, when Windisch left to establish the Lion Brewery, annual production of the Moerlein Brewing Company totaled 26,500 barrels.

Three-fifths of the beer brewed in Cincinnati was consumed locally. Around 1900, when the national per capita average was just over sixteen gallons, Cincinnatians imbibed fifty-eight gallons per capita.

The Christian Moerlein Company distributed its products nationally and was the only Cincinnati brewery to move into the international market.

Particularly successful was Old Jug Lager Krug-Bier, sold in pottery bottles and advertised extensively before its introduction June 1, 1891, as "exhilarating, stimulating, rejuvenating, wholesome, delicious, and pure."

With the advent of Prohibition, the Elm Street Brewery closed. By 1921, most of the Moerlein company's nineteen buildings had been sold and were later either razed or filled by light industry that moved into Over-the-Rhine. In September 1981, the Hudepohl Brewing Company resurrected the Christian Moerlein name for its premium beer.

**Turn right on McMicken Street.**

*Many members of Philippus Church continued to attend services here even after they had moved out of Over-the-Rhine to suburbs like Fairview and Westwood.*

The tall spire of **6 Philippus United Church of Christ,** 106 West McMicken Avenue, is topped by a gilded hand whose index finger points heavenward.

Philippus Kirche, as the congregation was first known, traces its origins to St. John's German Protestant Church, organized in 1814. By 1881, one segment of the congregation had broken away and was flourishing as St. Matthew United Evangelical German Church at Liberty and Elm Streets. Then St. Matthew's pastor introduced Sunday School material to which the church board objected. On

April 27, 1890, the pastor and 170 members formed Philippus German Evangelical Protestant Church and met in the College of Music's Odeon Hall.

Later that year, Philippus bought this lot on the side of Clifton Hill, and the Gothic Revival style red brick church was dedicated on December 6, 1891. The sanctuary was on the second floor, typical of German Protestant churches of the time. Each of the stained glass windows, added later, tells a story relevant to the congregation. The window depicting the story of the Prodigal Son, for example, shows a mother welcoming the returning youth; the woman who donated the panel had a son for whose return she hoped.

An adjacent parsonage was completed in 1895, and a war memorial, a World War I U.S. Army helmet set on a cross above the main entrance, was dedicated in 1968.

Anti-German sentiment during World War I and the increasing number of native-born members forced Philippus to confront the issue of continuing services in German. In 1921, the congregation decided to use English in worship and all organizations, but to hold a monthly German service. This service was discontinued in 1983, when the 93-year-old minister no longer felt up to the task.

Philippus' membership peaked at over 1,000 in the 1920s and 1930s. In 1926, a parsonage was purchased in Westwood, the suburb to which many members had moved, and the original minister's residence was torn down for the construction of a parish house. The interior of the church was rebuilt and remodeled in 1936 after the ceiling collapsed.

Philippus acquired its current name after a series of denominational mergers. This church, too, has been affected by changes in Over-the-Rhine. By 1986, Philippus had only 315 members, many of whom lived in Westwood-Cheviot.

Nevertheless, the church plays an important role in the neighborhood. A significant number of young people participate in its programs. The vacation church school provides a free lunch and is scheduled for the last week of the month when food stamps have frequently run out. Philippus holds an annual Christmas party for 500-600 area children, opens its gym to community groups, operates a youth guidance program, and distributes food baskets at Thanksgiving and Christmas.

In September 1986, Philippus began a year-long survey of area residents' needs so that the church could better serve the inner city neighborhood where it has chosen to remain.

As the carved pediment of the 4-story brick building at 40 East McMicken Avenue indicates, this structure was erected in 1911 as the **7 Main Office and Bottling Works of the Hudepohl Brewing Company**. On the floor of the entryway is a tile mosaic of the company's emblem. Hudepohl is the only surviving Cincinnati brewery that pre-dates Prohibition.

Louis Hudepohl (1842-1902) worked as a maker of surgical instruments until 1886 when he and George H. Kotte (1837-1893) became wholesalers of wine and liquor. In 1885, the two purchased the old Koehler Brewery on East Clifton Avenue. Five years later, their Buckeye Brewery employed nearly one hundred men and produced 40,000 barrels of beer annually.

Kotte's widow died in 1899. Louis Hudepohl bought her share of the business, and the Hudepohl Brewing Company incorporated on February 20, 1900. Like other nineteenth-century businessmen, Louis Hudepohl both lived and worked in Over-the-Rhine. His home at 162 Spring Street is still standing.

The company survived Prohibition by manufacturing soft drinks and near beer (.5% alcohol) and acting as a distributor for other near beers. In 1934, Hudepohl purchased a second plant, the old Lackman Brewery on West Sixth Street, and began producing beer in cans. By the late 1930s, Hudepohl had the largest production capacity of any local concern.

Hudepohl was one of the largest breweries in Ohio by the mid-1950s and began consolidating and modernizing production at the West End plant. The Buckeye Brewery buildings were closed in 1958 and torn down five years later. The main office remained here until 1967 when all operations were moved to Gest Street in the West End. An electrical contracting firm has most recently occupied the old office and bottling works.

**Turn right on Walnut Street.**

In the late nineteenth century, skilled and semi-skilled workers, predominantly German-born, and their families filled most of the buildings that once lined Moore and Walnut Streets. Narrow 2½ to 4-story residential structures and buildings with stores at street level and flats on the floors above mixed with a few commercial enterprises. Francis Thren's Sons, brewery supplies, occupied several buildings on the east side of Walnut and sold bungs and wooden faucets. The Queen City Bottling Works stood on Walnut at Corwine, and a sausage factory operated in a 2-story structure behind the building at 1615.

At 1610 is the Walnut Street Baptist Church; the Gothic lettered nameplate above the main door records that this was originally a *Baptisten Kirche*, **8 First German Baptist Church,** dedicated in 1866.

Two stories about the founding of the church agree that the first congregants were originally members of the Ninth Street Baptist Church. One story holds that in 1854, "Prince Von Puttkammer, a German of royal birth," gathered together the German members of Ninth Street Baptist Church. The other recounts that the Ninth Street congregation brought Reverend Philip W. Bickel to town, and he established First German in 1857.

Apparently Baptist theology was not attractive to German Americans, or perhaps the ban on drinking was too much at odds with German culture, for First German Baptist was the only German Baptist church in the city by World War I. After the United States entered the war, the church became Walnut Street Baptist. It now has a black congregation.

By the early decades of the twentieth century, this area was home for second-generation German Americans, for the most part, as well as Hungarian Germans, "Holland" Germans, and older first-generation German Americans. For example, 1608 Walnut housed baker Bernhard Kollman, his wife, and their five children; Kathryn Schumann, a 69-year old widow who had immigrated from Germany in 1848, and her three adult children; and Otto Vogt, a furniture factory worker, and his wife

and son. Commercial enterprises in the area had changed. An undertaker had opened at the corner of Walnut and Liberty; the sausage factory had become the Giardino di Italia Macaroni Company with three of the partners, all Italian-born, living nearby.

Although small groceries and restaurants remained for many years, they have gradually been replaced by businesses, like a laboratory packaging company, that do not serve the neighborhood.

**9 Grammer's Restaurant,** 1440 Walnut Street, is the last of the old German saloon-and-cafe businesses in the city. Anton Grammer (1832-1911), a German-born baker, opened a saloon on Fifteenth Street between Vine and Republic Streets in 1872. By 1887, Grammer's business had moved to 1446 Walnut; that building was later demolished. The present building, dated 1911 in the pediment, features a striking leaded glass entryway imported from Germany, a stamped tin ceiling, and a copper-covered wooden bar.

After Anton's death, the restaurant passed to his son, Frank Grammer (1872-1950), who managed it until his death. Subsequently, the restaurant was remodeled by various owners, but these changes were not enough to attract patrons to the deteriorating Over-the-Rhine neighborhood, especially as entertainment facilities had relocated elsewhere.

In 1984, Grammer's Restaurant was purchased by Jim Tarbell, a Cincinnati restaurateur and urban conservationist, who has restored the interior, added memorabilia from Cincinnati's breweries, and updated the menu, hoping to preserve this unique Cincinnati institution.

Heinrich A. Rattermann (1832-1923), a German immigrant, erected the 3-story, Renaissance Revival style **10 Germania Building,** 1129 Walnut Street, in 1877 for his German Mutual Insurance Company of Cincinnati. The fourth story was added later. A painted sign reading *Deutsche gegenseitige Versicherungs-Gesellschaft von Cincinnati* is above the first floor of the company's previous offices at Thirteenth and Walnut Streets. Business and culture mixed in the new building as various German American societies met in the hall on the first

*The office building that Heinrich Rattermann built for his German Mutual Insurance Company of Cincinnati was one of the most lavishly decorated commercial structures in Over-the-Rhine.*

floor.

In a niche on the front of the building above the first floor, is a statue of Germania, a figure personifying the German spirit, defending culture, symbolized by a book, a telescope, and an artist's palette. Local architect Johann Bast designed the structure; Cincinnatian Leopold Fettweis carved Germania and the relief of Apollo on the Twelfth Street side, and the Schreiber ironworks on Walnut Street produced the store front and cornice.

A self-taught scholar and businessman, Rattermann, who lived at 510 York Street, was an influential local figure and a nationally-known German American author. He wrote forty-four books, hundreds of articles, and several operas, edited the periodicals *Der Deutsche Pionier* and *Deutsche-Amerikanisches Magazin*, was a mainstay of the German Literary Club, and organized German singing societies.

The Germania Building was a victim of the "hate-the-Hun" hysteria ignited by World War I. Before America entered the war, the Cincinnati press asserted the loyalty of the vast majority of the city's German-born residents. But after the United States entered on the side of the Allies, Cincinnati, like the rest of the nation, was swept by feelings of suspicion and animosity.

On April 5, 1918, the *Post* "explained" that Germania with her outstretched hand was signaling "I want the earth," while the symbols of art, science, and literature lay conquered at her feet. On April 8, Germania was covered with a black cloth, then draped with an American flag. "It's nobody's business why we did it," declared the company's president.

Shortly thereafter, the statue and the building were rechristened Columbia. The company's name, carved in German on the pediment of the building, was covered, and the business became the Hamilton County Mutual Fire Insurance Company of Cincinnati. The United States' motto, *E Pluribus Unum*, was carved on the hem of Columbia's robe and, apparently, the eagle breastplate added. There is no evidence, however, to support the popular belief that the figure held a sword which was removed at this time.

The Germania Building subsequently served as the location for a variety of small businesses, including the insurance company. After a fine restoration in the 1970s, the building housed offices, a thrift shop, and an antique shop.

**Turn left on Twelfth Street, left on Main Street, left on Thirteenth Street.**

Most of Cincinnati's nineteenth-century downtown churches have closed, been torn down, or changed hands as their congregations moved to the suburbs, but **11 Old St. Mary's Roman Catholic Church,** 123 East Thirteenth Street, the city's oldest surviving church building, has adapted to the changes in Over-the-Rhine. Originally, St. Mary's served a large group of German American Catholics. Now it ministers to smaller groups of immigrants, as well as a community composed of elderly long-time residents and low-income Appalachians and blacks, few of whom are Catholic.

By 1840, German-speaking Catholics regularly filled Holy Trinity Church on West Fifth Street, the city's first German Catholic church, to overflowing. Father Johann Martin Henni (1805-1881) and a committee from Holy Trinity purchased land between Twelfth, Thirteenth, Clay, and Main Streets from the estate of General Arthur St. Clair, governor of the Northwest Territory and the man who had named the city Cincinnati. Proceeds from the sale of lots in the eastern portion of the block helped pay for the new church.

The painted brick Greek Revival style building was designed by Franz Ignatz Erd, a German immigrant, and built by the men of the parish from bricks that the women had baked in their ovens. Thousands reportedly attended the ceremonies when the cornerstone—inscribed in German, English, and Latin—was laid on March 25, 1841. St. Marien's Kirche was the first Roman Catholic church in Over-the-Rhine and, measuring 66' x 142', was claimed to be the largest church building in the Ohio Valley. The smallest of St. Mary's bells was used as a fire alarm.

The interior is richly decorated with handcarved woodwork and statuary, wall and ceiling murals, and altar oil paintings that are rotated during the year by a system of pulleys.

The stained glass windows are unusual in that the flowers incorporated in the lower panels are not religious symbols but reminders of the German countryside. The relics of an unknown martyr were brought to St. Mary's in 1844. The building was later enlarged and remodeled, and in 1937, a 2,275-pipe organ was installed.

Continuing immigration to Cincinnati swelled this parish, and eventually four filial churches were created: St. John the Baptist (1844), St. Paul (1850), St. Louis (1870), all in the basin, and St. Francis de Sales (1849) in Walnut Hills. St. Mary's erected parish schools in 1843 and 1852. Church membership peaked in the mid-nineteenth century with an average of nearly 400 baptisms each year. But the development of hilltop suburbs drew younger families away, and between 1870-1900, only about 125 children were baptized annually.

The parish continued to dwindle after World War I as Appalachian families and then blacks from the West End moved into the neighborhood. The boys' and girls' schools were combined in 1938, but in 1961, when fewer than one hundred children were enrolled, St. Mary's school closed. The unused boys' school was later demolished for a parking lot. Ten baptisms were recorded in 1965.

St. Mary's was determined to continue its downtown ministry and to serve the largely non-Catholic community. As the archdiocese's official International Church, St. Mary's offered a Mass in French, one in Spanish for Cubans who had fled Castro, and a Hungarian service for refugees who had begun arriving in Cincinnati in 1956 as the Soviet Union crushed the Hungarian revolution. St. Mary's is the only church in the city still offering both a German and a Latin Mass. It is also the Cincinnati Archdiocese's church for the sick.

The former girls' school is open for community meetings and houses the St. John Social Service Center which provides emergency food and clothing, housing aid, referral services, home visitations, and family and job counseling. Old St. Mary's offers a weekly liturgy for the mentally retarded, and its guide training program allows the historic church to be opened to more visitors. The parish listed 250 member families in 1988 and was growing.

Known as Old St. Mary's since the

dedication of St. Mary Church in Hyde Park in 1904, this church was placed on the National Register of Historic Places in 1976. Its restoration was the archdiocese's city bicentennial project.

**Turn left on Clay Street, left on Twelfth Street, left on Main Street, and right on Fourteenth Street.**

Although some large factories and breweries were located in Over-the-Rhine in the nineteenth century, medium and small-sized workshops were far more common. The **12 Ahrens Manufacturing Company,** for example, occupied the buildings at 214-216 East Fourteenth Street, turning out fire apparatus.

The firm was founded by Christopher F. Ahrens (1836-1919) who immigrated to the United States in 1853 and joined two older brothers living in Cincinnati. In Germany, Ahrens had been apprenticed to an ironsmith, and in this country, he became a machinist for the Lane & Bodley Company, working on the construction of fire apparatus. In 1863, Lane & Bodley had taken over the production of Latta steam fire engines from the Buckeye Iron Works of Alexander Latta. Latta, along with

*As the Ahrens Fire Engine Company grew—eventually becoming a part of the American Fire Engine Company—the firm expanded its operations by building or taking over structures that adjoined its original 3-story works.*

Abel Shawk, another Cincinnatian, had built the first successful steam fire engine in North America in 1852.

Lane & Bodley ceased making fire engines around 1868. Ahrens purchased the rights to the design, and by 1869, a new firm, C. Ahrens & Company, was assembling "Improved Latta Style" steam pumpers at a small workshop on Webster (East Fourteenth) Street.

Because the fire apparatus industry was extremely competitive and business was initially slow, Ahrens and many of his employees also served as paid firefighters. Ahrens worked at Engine Company No. 7—directly across the street from his factory—until the fire department adopted regulations in 1873 that prohibited its personnel from having other jobs.

Reorganized in 1875, Ahrens Manufacturing became more aggressive in selling both new engines and its services in rebuilding old models. Ahrens offered rebates and fire equipment accessories, and provided engineers to train purchasers in using new engines. The firm increased its average annual production from seven and one half engines to almost twenty-five machines. By the 1880s, the fire departments of many cities, including Cincinnati, were equipped solely with Ahrens pumpers.

Christopher Ahrens erected two 5-story additions that housed machine shops and the assembly floor. An adjoining 3-story workshop building, now demolished, housed the offices.

At its peak, the Webster Street works employed around one hundred

men, most of whom were of German descent; German was almost universally spoken. The company's officers and foremen, all related to Christopher Ahrens by blood or marriage, included his brother, sons, son-in-law, and brother-in-law, and until the mid-1880s, many of them lived near the factory. Christopher lived with his large family in an Italianate style brick house on Orchard Street, directly behind the works. John Peter Ahrens, while serving both Engine Company 7 and his brother's business, lived across the street in the firehouse. Many employees lived on Woodward and Main Streets.

Fierce competition in the fire apparatus industry led to a number of mergers. In 1891, Ahrens manufacturing combined with three firms to form the American Fire Engine Company. The new company retained one plant in Seneca Falls, New York, and the one in Cincinnati. By 1893, Ahrens family members controlled the combine, and Christopher Ahrens became its president.

In 1902, American Fire Engine joined with La France to form the American La France Company. By 1905, the Ahrens family had withdrawn to start a firm that eventually became known as Ahrens-Fox, a major producer of motorized fire apparatus.

At the same time, American La France stopped making fire engines in Cincinnati. The Fourteenth Street factory was sold. It has continued in use as an industrial site, housing a variety of concerns, including an auto top manufacturer and most recently the Hale X-Ray Company.

> **Turn left on Sycamore Street, left on Orchard Street, right on Main Street, right on Liberty Street, and right on Sycamore Street.**

Another of Cincinnati's surviving nineteenth-century churches is **13 Salem United Church of Christ,** 1419-1425 Sycamore Street, which has broadened the scope and nature of its ministry to serve the changing neighborhood.

The congregation of what was originally Third German Reform Church first met on January 5, 1857. Church records describe the founders, as "poor but honest, God-fearing,

thrifty, and industrious." The group purchased this lot in 1863 and laid the foundation, but the Civil War delayed further work.

The church, dedicated May 24, 1868, has a second-floor sanctuary with carved altar and decorated walls and ceiling. The building's best-known feature is the 9½-foot high figure of the Angel Gabriel atop the steeple, reminding observers of the call to judgment and indicating the direction of the wind.

The statue was made by a local company to replace one knocked down by a storm in the mid-1960s. The original Gabriel was probably the Angle Moroni taken from the Mormon temple in Nauvoo, Illinois, after persecution drove the congregation away in 1846. That figure is now in Salt Lake City.

With German migration to Cincinnati and Over-the-Rhine, Salem's congregation grew to 900 members by 1873. In the 1930s, though the neighborhood was less attractive than it had once been, Salem still drew more than 500 to Sunday services which by then were in English. In the late 1950s, the congregation improved the old building and added new Sunday school rooms.

The church's name changed over the years. From the late 1870s, it was Salem German Evangelical Reformed Church—Deutsche Evangelisch Reformirt, Salem's Kirche, as is inscribed on the tablet above the main door—then, dropping the "German" during World War I, Salem Reformed Church; now, after several denominational unions, Salem United Church of Christ.

The church began Gabriel's Corner Arts Ministry in 1977, hoping to promote harmony among the culturally, racially, and economically diverse community residents. In 1985, approximately 7,000 persons from throughout the city participated in activities including theater and music performances, workshops in grant writing, art and clogging classes, and meetings of arts groups.

Most of Salem's one hundred current members at that time were former residents of Over-the-Rhine and of German descent.

The long, low, brick building across from Salem Church was originally the **14 Car Barn of the Cincinnati Inclined Plane Railway (CIP),** which built and operated the

Mt. Auburn Main Street Incline, the earliest of five such lines in the city. The inclines—Mt. Auburn, Price Hill, Bellevue, Mt. Adams, and Fairview—helped the development of Cincinnati suburbs by making the trip up the steep hillsides possible for those of modest means. Workers eagerly sought homes in cleaner, less crowded neighborhoods.

On the day of the line's grand opening—May 12, 1872—Cincinnatians heading for the annual festival of the German Protestant Orphan Home in Mt. Auburn swelled the expected crowd of curiosity seekers. An estimated 6,000 people made the trip from the bottom station at Mulberry and Main Streets to the top station at Jackson Hill, a 900-foot trip that took a minute and a half.

George A. Smith (1819-1888), head of the CIP, realized that the magnificent view from the top of the line made it an ideal site for a public garden and "refreshment saloon." His Lookout House was the model for the city's three other "hilltop houses." All offered fresh air, food, drink, and entertainment—and drew passengers to the inclines. In its first year, the Mt. Auburn Incline had an estimated one million riders.

Within the next few years, the incline was integrated into a wider transportation system. In 1873, a horsecar line connected the Main Street station with Fountain Square, and omnibuses ran from the top of the line to Clifton, Walnut Hills, and Avondale. In 1877, the CIP opened a line to the zoo, and in 1878, added platforms to haul horse-drawn streetcars up the hill. After Smith's death in 1888, a Louisville group bought the company and purchased twenty electric cars for the line, making it the city's first sizable electric streetcar line.

After an accident on October 15, 1889, in which six passengers were killed, the company rebuilt the incline. It added an extension to St. Bernard in 1890.

Hard times came to the Cincinnati Inclined Plane Railway Company when the City of Cincinnati brought a lawsuit claiming it had no legal right to operate under its original steam railroad charter. In 1898, after the Cincinnati Street Railway Company of Charles and John Kilgour bought the section of the line that ran to the zoo, the Mt. Auburn Incline was closed. The

Vine Street Incline became the main route to and from town.

The car barn was vacant for a number of years, as it is now, but from the 1930s into the 1980s, the French-Bauer Dairy Company used it as a garage.

Now housing the School for the Creative and Performing Arts, **15 Old Woodward High School,** 1310 Sycamore Street, claims to be the first high school west of the Alleghenies and the oldest, continuously operating, free public high school in the world.

In 1826, William Woodward (1768-1833), a successful farmer and tanner, conveyed land in trust to provide funds to set up Woodward Free Grammar School and pay for the education of poor boys. When the common or public school system was established in Cincinnati in 1829 and filled the need for elementary education, Woodward reconveyed the 7-acre property and an adjacent acre for a building site for a secondary school.

The Woodward High School of Cincinnati opened on October 24, 1831, in a 2-story building on the northeast corner of the present school lot. The curriculum included courses in rhetoric, history, English, political and moral philosophy, languages, and chemistry. From 1843 to 1845, William Holmes McGuffey, famous for compiling the *Eclectic Reader* series, taught languages at Woodward.

A college department offering two years of work was formed in 1836, and the name was changed to the Woodward College of Cincinnati. By the early 1850s, the endowment proved insufficient, and the high school and college were discontinued. Woodward High School then became part of the public school system.

Growing enrollment called for a larger facility, and in 1854-1855, a 3-story Gothic style school designed by English-born architect John R. Hamilton was erected on the southwest corner of the property. Additions were made in 1867 and 1880.

In 1860, Woodward trustees, responding to a petition from the students, reinterred the bodies of William Woodward and his wife, Abigail Cutter (1785-1853), in a grave opposite the school's main entrance where a bronze statue of Woodward was unveiled on October 24, 1878.

The school was razed in 1907 for the construction of the present 5-story brick, stone, and terra cotta building designed by Gustav Drach (1861-1940). William Howard Taft, a member of the graduating class of 1874, laid the cornerstone, and dedication ceremonies were held on October 24, 1910. The new school could accommodate 2,000 students and boasted the most modern facilities of the time, including indoor toilets, central heating, a 1,100-seat auditorium, swimming pool, and two gymnasiums. Woodward became a junior and senior high school in 1928.

The population shift out of the basin and to the suburbs called for a new high school for the northern section of the city. In 1953, the school opened on Reading Road in Bond Hill; the Woodward name was transferred there, as was the Woodward statue. The Woodward Memorial stained glass window stayed, as did the remains of Woodward and his wife, relocated on the south side of the school, which became Abigail Cutter Junior High.

The School for the Creative and Performing Arts opened in 1973 in the Mt. Adams Elementary School building with eighty-seven students in grades 4-6. It moved to the Jewish Community Center in Roselawn in 1975, then to Cutter Junior High in 1976. By putting the most attractive of the public school system's more than forty alternative programs here, the Board of Education successfully created a racially-balanced school. Today, about 1,100 students, grades 4-12, are enrolled in SCPA which offers academic work in combination with study in drama, dance, vocal and instrumental music, technical theater production, and visual arts.

This inner city school draws students from throughout the city, Kentucky, Indiana, and other parts of Ohio. Of the approximately 1,000 youngsters who audition each year, about one-third are accepted. SCPA's students put on over one hundred performances each year, and they have appeared in productions of community groups, the Playhouse in the Park, Cincinnati Symphony Orchestra, Cincinnati Ballet Company, and Cincinnati Opera; in the national touring companies of Broadway musicals and Hollywood films, as well as with the Dance Theater of Harlem and the New York City Ballet Company.

The old building has become crowded and lacks many of the facilities that an art school needs. In 1986, after learning that the auditorium did not meet city codes and could no longer be used for its productions, the school successfully undertook a fund drive to rebuild the theater.

**Turn left on Twelfth Street.**

As Over-the-Rhine changed and its population declined, one of its most splendid churches, **16 St. Paul Roman Catholic Church,** 1117 Pendleton Street, was threatened with demolition. In 1981, however, the I.V. Verdin company bought the building and converted it into St. Paul's Church Mart, a unique display and sales center for church goods which draws manufacturers and customers from across the nation.

As nineteenth-century German Catholic immigrants continued to settle in Over-the-Rhine, they created the need for another parish. In 1848, Father Joseph Ferneding (1802-1872), pastor at St. Mary's, and a committee of parishioners chose this site for a new church. They bought four blocks of land between Broadway, Pendleton, Woodward, and Hunt (Twelfth) Streets, subdivided the tract into building lots, sold the lots, and used the profits to pay for the construction of St. Paul Church.

St. Paulus Kirche was the ninth Catholic church in the city and the seventh erected by German Catholics. The cornerstone was laid on June 24, 1848, and a huge parade through the muddy streets of Cincinnati celebrated the dedication of St. Paul's on January 20, 1850.

The rectory was the former home of Nathaniel Greene Pendleton (1793-1861) who had sold the land for the church. The house had been moved from its original location at Broadway and Reading Road, then linked to the church by a covered, second-story level walkway.

By the mid-1890s, the "Ferneding subdivision" had grown dramatically, and St. Paul's, with more than 1,000 member families, was one of the largest congregations in the diocese. St. Paul's added a boys' school in 1887, a Sisters' residence in 1904, and a girls' school in 1908.

From the first, the congregation included a number of independent small businessmen who gave generous support. In 1893, one of these men donated a magnificent stained glass window entitled "The Marriage Feast of Cana," designed by F.X. Zettler of Munich. The piece had won a prize at the Chicago World's Fair. A second Zettler window, "The Ascension of Our Lord," was installed in 1895.

On August 19, 1899, as St. Paul's prepared for its fiftieth anniversary, a fire gutted the church. Rebuilding began at once, and on October 7, 1900, St. Paul's was rededicated. Cincinnati architect Samuel Hannaford redesigned the facade and designed the new steeple that was topped with a clock tower, a gilded "pope's mitre" cupola, and a cross.

However, the congregation shrank as people moved out of the basin, and by the late 1930s, St. Paul's had only 165 member families. The two schools were combined into one which closed in 1964, and by the late 1970s, there were only seventy parishioners. St. Paul's parish was discontinued on January 1, 1974, and the church closed. The buildings were entered on the National Register of Historic Places.

A group of young people organized to try to maintain the complex to serve the neighborhood. Community council offices, a hot lunch program, and recreational activities were set up in the girls' school, but the effort was generally unsuccessful.

The city bought the property, hoping to stimulate a revival in the decaying Over-the-Rhine, and then sold the church for ten dollars to the Verdin Company, a manufacturer of tower clocks, church bells, and carillons. The city guaranteed low interest loans for rehabilitation on the condition that the church be restored to some use beneficial to Cincinnati.

Deciding that St. Paul's Church was too fine for a storeroom, Verdin undertook a spectacular one million dollar renovation and restoration, creating the church mart. The adjacent boys' school, 1118 Pendleton Street, became the Pendleton Design Center, offering home furnishings to architects, designers, and their clients; the girls' school showcases business interiors. The convent, 1110 Pendleton, is occupied by Sisters of St. Francis of the Poor who do social work in the area.

Visitors, by prior arrangement, can see St. Paul's exquisitely restored stained glass windows, mosaic floors, and ceiling "frescos" and "mosaics" that are painted on canvas.

> **Turn right on Pendleton Street, right on Reading Road, bear left on Central Parkway, and turn right on Vine Street.**

**17** **Vine Street** has a long-standing reputation for its many bars, but there always have been many different of activities taking place along the two miles of Vine Street between the Ohio River and McMicken Avenue. An entertainment district grew up here after the Civil War with more than one hundred drinking places, as well as concert halls, burlesque houses, theaters, and shooting galleries. Entrepreneurs along Vine, particularly from the canal to McMicken, worked hard to create the atmosphere of cosmopolitan gaiety that made the area one of Cincinnati's major tourist attractions in the second half of the nineteenth century.

Hubert Heuck (1834-1909) operated two of the most famous Vine Street theaters— **18** **People's Theater,** northwest corner of Vine and

*In the 1880s and 1890s, People's Theater featured nationally known musical, theatrical, and vaudeville acts.*

Thirteenth Streets, and Heuck's Opera House, once at 1221 Vine Street. Heuck opened the former establishment around 1876, calling it Heuck's Opera House. In 1882, when Heuck took over the Coliseum Theater—built by another entrepreneur only the year before—he designated it Heuck's Opera House and renamed his first theater People's.

The new Heuck's Opera House, a combination playhouse and saloon, had a reputation as the best auditorium west of New York City. It attracted nationally-known circus, musical, theatrical, and vaudeville acts like Buffalo Bill's Wild West Show. Heuck boasted that his was the first showhouse in America equipped with electric footlights and a revolving door. The two theaters continued operating until 1921. Heuck's Opera House Company finally dissolved in 1946.

The Opera House was razed around 1959, while People's Theater was converted into a men's clothing store in the 1920s. Today the structure is abandoned and deteriorating.

**19** **Cosmopolitan Hall,** 1313 Vine Street, was a popular meeting place for those who lived in Over-the-Rhine and for former residents who returned to socialize. The 4-story stone building, erected in 1885 in the popular Italian Renaissance style, was

a site for events ranging from athletic contests to weddings and concerts.

As Vine Street declined in popularity during the early twentieth century, however, institutions such as the Cosmopolitan were affected. Like Heuck's theater, it was converted into a store which is now vacant.

Yet Vine Street was more than a strip of saloons and playhouses. Shops scattered between the entertainment halls served the daily needs of residents, selling everything from dry goods to grave stones; families lived in the apartments over the stores. In the 1880s and 1890s, larger buildings of flats, such as **20 The Kirby,** 1321-1325 Vine Street, were erected. The Kirby was built as an investment in 1885. While shops occupied the first floor, the upper stories housed middle-income residents. The Kirby has recently been renovated and is known as the Community Apartments.

Another Vine Street institution that drew patrons from throughout Cincinnati was **21 Wielert's Pavilion Saloon, Concert Hall and Beer Garden,** 1408-1410 Vine Street. The 2-story Italian Renaissance style building was completed in 1873; this date and the initials of the proprietor, Heinrich Wielert (c.1836-1892), are carved in stone tablets set in the facade of the building.

Henry Wielert, a German immigrant and Civil War veteran, was an active Republican, and his saloon became an unofficial political center for Cincinnati's Republican machine headed by "Boss" George B. Cox (1853-1916). Cox held court in Wielert's at a table that was permanently reserved for him.

After Wielert's death, the business continued under other proprietors. With the advent of Prohibition, the saloon became a cafe offering nightly entertainment, then a funeral home, and then a Christian drug rehabilitation center.

Today, there is still considerable variety on Vine Street, although the businesses now have names like the Silver Dollar Cafe and Nick's Pool Room rather than Wielert's or Heuck's. Stores remain, although there are fewer of them and many are only marginally viable; used furniture or clothing stores are common. Some buildings closer to Central Parkway have been or are in the process of being renovated for office space, but these do not yet predominate. And Vine Street is still a place of residence for many people, most on low or fixed incomes, who live over storefronts or in buildings like The Kirby.

**Turn left on Liberty Street.**

The city's first Catholic church, Christ Church, a small frame building, was erected in 1819 when, a later account noted, out of Cincinnati's over 10,000 inhabitants, there were "about one hundred poor Irish Catholics." **22 St. Francis Seraph Roman Catholic Church,** Liberty and Vine Streets, stands on the site of that church and a later Catholic cemetery.

There is no truth to the popular notion that an ordinance prohibited the building of a Catholic church within city limits; property there was simply too expensive. James Findlay, anxious to promote development of property he owned, offered the small group two lots for $1,200. Christ Church was able to execute a first mortgage for $750.

Some years later, Bishop Edward Fenwick (1768-1832) decided that Christ Church should be nearer the center of the city and his Third Street residence. The church collapsed during the move, but was rebuilt near the site of present-day St. Xavier Church on Sycamore Street. It served until the first diocesan cathedral, St. Peter the Apostle, was completed beside it in 1826. The Liberty Street site became a Catholic cemetery.

In 1844, Bishop John B. Purcell, in need of German-speaking priests to serve Cincinnati's most recent arrivals, welcomed some Franciscans from Austria. The Brothers took charge of parishes in Kentucky, Indiana, Cincinnati, and elsewhere in Ohio. But in 1857, the Tyrolese Provincial authorities ordered the friars home.

The Franciscans then determined to found an independent Cincinnati province and to support themselves by founding a "college"—a high school seminary—for German Catholic boys. Archbishop Purcell transferred the land at Vine and Liberty as a site for a friary, college, and church. Classes at St. Francis College began in October 1858 in a rented house on Vine Street, and subsequently were held in the parish school and several later college buildings on Republic Street.

A fund-raising drive produced funds for erecting the present church, designed by local architect James W. McLaughlin (1834-1923). Remains in the cemetery were reinterred in a crypt below the church; tombstones—mostly with Irish names—paved the floor. Some 20,000 persons reportedly observed the cornerstone-laying ceremonies on November 7, 1858, and the church, dedicated to St. Francis of Assisi, was consecrated December 18, 1859.

The Romanesque style building with its two 140-foot towers has been remodeled and redecorated over the years. Stained glass windows and paintings were added; the statue of St. Francis, from the Royal Bavarian Foundries in Munich where the Tyler Davidson Fountain was cast, was set in the niche above the main door in the 1860s. In 1925, a glazed brick shell was put on the church to preserve it. The interior was simplified for more economical maintenance during a renovation in the 1970s.

The first friary, on Republic Street, was completed in 1860; a boys' school was dedicated in 1861. Girls went to St. John's school until 1891 when St. Francis parish purchased a nearby building for a temporary girls' school and residence for the Sisters of St. Francis of Oldenberg, Indiana, who staffed the schools.

St. Francis recorded some 900 families around the turn of the century. After the parish erected the present school and convent, 14 East Liberty Street, in 1906-1908, the old school became a community house and the Friars Gym and Athletic Club, providing men in the basin with recreational opportunities. (In 1931, the Order opened another club in Fairview.) The current headquarters of the Cincinnati Province and the St. Francis Friary, 1615 Vine Street, was dedicated in 1907 and stands on the site of the original friary.

This parish, too, dwindled in the twentieth century with membership falling to 500 families by 1921. St. Francis Seminary was moved to Mt. Airy in 1924, then closed in 1980. By 1988, St. Francis had 200 active parishioners, an increase over the past few years. Of the 160 children enrolled in the school, only about twenty were Catholic.

The Franciscans have maintained their commitment to the neighborhood and were instrumental in the founding of Tender Mercies, a nonprofit ecumenical group which manages four buildings near Washington Park that provide secure housing for deinstitutionalized mental patients. The Order continues its Roger Bacon High School in St. Bernard and has opened the St. Anthony Shrine and Novitiate, dedicated in Mt. Airy in 1889, for use by other church groups.

The Order has also continued publishing. The **23 Offices of the St. Anthony Messenger** (the magazine and the press) have been located next door at 1615 Republic Street since 1961. The Franciscans founded the magazine, now the most widely circulated Catholic publication in the nation, in 1893. The *Messenger* was originally designed to promote knowledge of the Franciscan movement, but over the years has developed into a family-oriented and general interest publication.

The monthly magazine is only one of the Order's many publications and has been put out from several locations including St. Bonaventure Church in Fairmount and St. George Church in Corryville. The press, begun in 1970s, has published a number of religious books.

**Turn left on Race Street.**

**24 Nast Memorial Methodist Episcopal Church,** 1310 Race Street, was named to honor Wilhelm Nast, the founder of both German Methodism and of this congregation. The dates inscribed on the facade of this stone church—1835, 1842, and 1880—trace the group's history.

Wilhelm Nast (1807-1899) arrived in America in 1828. While a professor of languages at Kenyon College, Nast joined the Methodist Episcopal Church. In 1835, he offered to preach to German immigrants in their language and was sent to Cincinnati, where he preached in the Sunday school room of Wesley Chapel, in tenements, private homes, and saloons and beer gardens. Nast met with considerable opposition, both on the street and in the German press, and by the end of the first year could report only three converts.

He was sent elsewhere but returned to Cincinnati in 1838 and organized the first German Methodist Society. Nast's 26-member congregation rented a chapel on Vine near Fourth Street, then dedicated its own building here in 1842. First German Methodist Episcopal Church was the first congregation of this denomination in the world.

The present building, designed by Samuel Hannaford's architectural firm, was erected in 1880. The name of the congregation was changed in 1938, the congregation's one hundredth anniversary. German Methodists began what is now Bethesda Hospital and Bethesda Scarlet Oaks Retirement Community.

In the late nineteenth and early twentieth centuries, church school attendance at Nast Memorial averaged 300 weekly, but membership fell as German immigrants and their descendants moved away from the neighborhood and the Southern Appalachian families who moved in were not attracted to the denomination. Nast's congregation, however, decided to continue to serve the community. The adjacent Emmanuel Community Center, dedicated in 1924, provided a day care center, housing for working women and young men, and room for a variety of clubs and athletic activities.

On June 1, 1958, Nast merged with Trinity Methodist Episcopal Church on West Ninth Street, which had been founded in 1837. Trinity had also experienced a drop in membership. The combined Nast-Trinity congregation of 465 hoped to make better use of its resources. But membership continued to fall, and by the mid-1980s, the congregation had only 140 members, a mix of area residents and loyal former residents.

Nast-Trinity provides space for time-release Christian education classes, evening craft classes, a senior citizens' luncheon, meetings of United Methodist women's and men's groups, and emergency food and clothing services. Its monthly free community dinner draws approximately 300 people.

**Turn right on Twelfth Street, right on Elm Street.**

The red brick German Gothic style building that is now Bethlehem Temple was originally, as the inscription above the main door records, Deutsche Protestaniche St. Johannes Kirche — **25 St. John German Protestant Church,** 1205 Elm Street. St. John's was Cincinnati's first German congregation, organized in 1814 by Joseph Zaeslin who gathered both German Protestants and Catholics as the German Evangelical Lutheran and Reformed Church. The group was "independent" or "free," that is, not affiliated with any established denomination.

In 1824, the congregation of about sixty members moved into its first building, a schoolhouse near Third Street and Broadway. Catholic members left later that year when a priest who could preach in German arrived in the city.

When the original congregation incorporated as St. John German Protestant Church in 1829, its constitution stipulated that services and records were to be in German; an additional resolution declared that the paragraph on language usage could never be repealed. Debates over language—whether High or Low German should be used—and theology—whether an orthodox Lutheran or a more liberal service should be observed—split St. John's congregation in 1832 and 1838. Worship services in English were begun in the early 1900s, and the exclusive use of English became the rule in 1918, though an annual German service was held for years.

Under the leadership of Reverend Augustus Kroell (1806-1874), pastor for thirty-three years, St. John's became Cincinnati's leading German Protestant congregation. The group finally outgrew the old Third Street building and moved to Over-the-Rhine, dedicating this church in October 1868. The structure's Gothic spire was damaged by a storm in 1916 and replaced with a Crown steeple.

St. John's joined the American Unitarian Association in 1924, reincorporating as First Protestant St. John's Unitarian Church. Its members began leaving the basin, and after the last service here was held on February 24, 1946, the congregation moved to Clifton. In 1973, this church was entered on the National Register of Historic Places.

Next door, the group of **26**

**Nineteenth-Century Residences,** 1207-1217 Elm Street, is one of a number of solid, mixed style streetscapes that have helped establish Over-the-Rhine's unique character.

According to the 1880 census, the residents of the six homes that stood here were small businessmen, predominantly German-born. At 1207 lived Herman Eggers, 57, a street sprinkler, his wife, three sons, and a servant, and Karl Pallat, 42, a music teacher with two daughters. Julius Esselborn, 44, a millinery wholesaler, resided at 1211 with his wife, three daughters, a son, a servant, two brothers-in-law, and a sister-in-law. John Galvagni kept a saloon on the first floor of the frame building that was then at 1213 and occupied the rooms above with his wife and four

*Homes in Over-the-Rhine were typically built close to the street and to each other in order to get as much use as possible from the limited amount of space available.*

children. German-born Philip Weber, a cutlery manufacturer and dealer, lived with his family at 1217.

By 1900, the residents of these houses were still a mix of professionals and middle-income workers. At 1207 were four households including those of Catherine Allsup, 58, a widow and her two children who had immigrated from England in 1880; French-born Louis Belmont, a contractor and carpenter, and his wife, daughter, and a servant; and Fannie Fullerton, a thirty-one year old widow who supported herself and two young sons by working as a trimmer at a Vine Street

millinery.

Noteworthy for its carved stone facade, 1209 was the office and home of Dr. R. H. Reemelin. Renting 1211 was German-born John Lederer, the proprietor of the Atlantic Garden concert hall at 615 Vine Street. Reverend Hugo Eisenlohr of St. John's Church and his family lived at 1213, another recently built structure. Caroline Weber, Philip's widow, lived at 1217 with a stepdaughter and her four children.

The use of these row houses had changed dramatically by the late 1920s: 1211-1217 were all renting furnished rooms. Schaffenberger & Son, undertakers, and the Sulmagfo medicine company occupied parts of 1207 and 1209, respectively, while the rooms above were rented.

These row houses continued as rooming houses and private residences. Dr. James Miller had his office at 1209 into the mid-1970s. Number 1207 was the headquarters of the Cincinnati Council of the Boy Scouts of America during 1930-1940, then the offices of a credit management bureau, and from the 1960s until the early 1970s, the Wee Sang Hong curio company. The rehabilitation and renovation of these dwellings took place, for the most part, in the 1980s; 1211-1217 are all owner-occupied.

Many Cincinnatians are unfamiliar with the **27 Hamilton County Memorial Building,** 1225 Elm Street, dedicated June 13, 1908, as a memorial to the county's "soldiers, sailors, marines, and pioneers."

The construction of Memorial Hall

was the result of years of lobbying by various Grand Army of the Republic—Union army veterans—posts, of which Cincinnati alone had thirteen. In 1903, a bond issue was passed to finance the construction of this monument. Supporters of the Memorial Building had first hoped to erect it in Washington Park, near Music Hall, but the city needed park space. This site was purchased, four buildings razed, and ground broken March 25, 1905.

Samuel Hannaford & Sons designed the stone 2½-story Neo-Classical style hall. Six figures wearing uniforms from the Revolutionary through Spanish-American Wars stand along the cornice.

Inside are a kitchen and meeting rooms for veterans' groups. Marble stairs curve up to a marble-tiled lobby where one bronze plaque lists the names of Revolutionary War veterans buried in Hamilton County, another commemorates Cincinnati's first mayor, German-born David Ziegler (c.1748-1811), and a third honors the members of the Cincinnati *Turngemeinde* (Turner Society) who died in the Civil War.

The small second-story auditorium has crystal chandeliers, bas relief plaster scrollwork, and a ceiling mural depicting a daytime sky. Rows of electric bulbs, a novelty in 1908, are set in golden rosettes on the stage's proscenium arch, illuminating words painted there as a guide to right living: Martyrdom, Integrity, Philanthropy, Patriotism, Manliness, Wisdom, Will. The stage ceiling is decorated with a painting of an eagle holding the American flag.

Veterans' groups and their auxiliaries met regularly at Memorial Hall, and later, the theater was used for performances by touring musical companies, theater groups, and the Cincinnati College of Music, and for Chase Law School graduations. But as Cincinnatians moved to the suburbs and various institutions found quarters of their own, major events here became sporadic.

The unused and neglected building was entered on the National Register of Historic Places in 1979. Significant renovation and renewal began in 1981 when the Cincinnati Commission on the Arts gained management control (though the Board of County Commissioners still owns Memorial Hall) and began restoring both the structure and its status as a meeting place and theater. It then became headquarters for the Miami Purchase Association, a local preservation group.

Across the street is **28 Washington Park,** bounded by Twelfth, Elm, and Race Streets, and Washington Park School, and made up of land that was originally Presbyterian, German Protestant, and Episcopal burying grounds.

Mid-nineteenth century public health officials worried that "miasmas"—vapors that were believed to rise from corpses—might be responsible for urban health problems. A new park would provide city dwellers with shaded lawns where they could relax and socialize in the fresh air. The city purchased the Presbyterian cemetery in 1855, reinterred the bodies in Spring Grove Cemetery, and bought the remaining land in 1860.

An 1869 account praised the park's "noble trees, beautiful lawns, fountain, and other beauties" which were "much enjoyed by the multitudes who frequent it." The 1888 Centennial Exposition of the Ohio Valley and Central States set up some buildings in Washington Park, and Cincinnati's German Americans held musical and social events here well into the 1920s.

Among the park's furnishings are a 10-ton boulder (held by popular lore to be the largest meteorite to have fallen in North America) commemorating the Park Board, a covered octagonal bandstand, memorials to Friedrich Hecker and Colonel Robert L. McCook, and a cannon from the fleet of Civil War admiral David G. Farragut.

Hecker (1811-1881), a refugee from the unsuccessful democratic German revolution of 1848, was a writer and philosopher. The Cincinnati *Turngemeinde*, a social, cultural, educational, and athletic organization which he founded, was the first Turner society in the country and is now the oldest. The large Central *Turnhalle*—Turner Hall—stood at 1409-1413 Walnut Street. Hecker served as a brigadier general in the Union army. The German inscription on the monument's base honors his fight for freedom "in the old and new Fatherlands."

Robert McCook (1827-1862) commanded the 9th Ohio Volunteer Infantry Regiment, Cincinnati's all-German unit. He was killed when Confederate

troops captured the hospital train on which he was riding. These memorials were erected in 1883 and 1878, respectively.

The deterioration of Washington Park mirrored that of the neighborhood. By the 1960s, it was widely regarded as unsafe. The Park Board has been able to do little more than provide routine maintenance.

The 1948 *Master Plan* called for a school to be built north of Washington Park, even though the report predicted a 30% drop in the population of Over-the-Rhine by 1970. Voters approved a bond issue in 1954, and the following year, the city acquired and razed eleven buildings to clear a site for **29 Washington Park Elementary School,** 115 West Fourteenth Street.

When the new school opened in 1958, it was heralded as "the school of tomorrow." The contemporary style building boasted modern equipment, classrooms for slow learners, and a dental clinic complete with an X-ray room. Though many spoke of Washington Park School as "a shining promise for the future," its principal noted that the school faced the highest mobility rate of any in the city as students' families, mainly low-income, were constantly moving.

In the 1970s, Washington Park school's enrollment was about two-thirds of its 960-pupil capacity and remained at this level. It was one of seven predominantly black (82%), low-achieving schools targeted in 1984 for special funding to boost achievement.

Washington Park Elementary has continued to struggle with the difficulties that accompany low family income levels and a 59% student mobility rate—41% of the students who are enrolled at the beginning of the year are there at the end. One of its most exciting efforts came in 1986, when a Partners in Education program was established with the Kroger Company. A "Super Kids" scholarship fund was set up for each child, and Kroger pays $300 into each account for every term the child receives all A's and B's in his or her academic classes.

**30 Cincinnati Music Hall,** 1241-1243 Elm Street, remains the city's center for performing arts and is one of its best-known landmarks. Architect Samuel Hannaford (1834-

1911) won the competition to design the Music Hall with plans for a structure that has been labeled High Victorian Gothic, Romanesque, or "Sauerbraten Byzantine."

The 3½-story cherry red pressed brick building with gables, towers, parapets, and insets, has an acoustically excellent concert hall. But the gray sandstone trim carved with flowers, birds, and symbols of crafts, arts, and sciences, indicates the variety of uses for which Music Hall—actually three detached buildings under one roof—was originally intended when it was dedicated on April 8, 1878.

The Cincinnati Orphan Asylum was first erected here around 1818, on city-owned land. The 4-story building became a public infirmary after 1837, and in 1869, temporary quarters for the Commercial Hospital and Lunatic Asylum.

By 1870, the infirmary and asylum had been relocated to present-day Hartwell and Bond Hill, and the building became an exposition hall. A frame *Saenger Halle* was erected beside it for the summer convention of the *Nord Amerikanisher Saengerbund*, a national German American choral society with headquarters in Cincinnati. The *Saengerfests* drew singing societies from across the country to Cincinnati for days of pageantry, popular songs, competitions, socializing, and beer.

But a 1909 publication recollected: "It occurred to those [Cincinnatians] of the English-speaking element that grand concerts might be given without the lavish resort to stimulants which was an offense to the religiously-inclined people." Local German Americans were largely excluded from the Music Festival Association that planned the first May Festival for the performance of classical music.

In 1870, the city bought the Saenger Halle, and on May 6, 1873, the first 4-day long May Festival began. Theodore Thomas (1835-1905), nationally-known conductor of the New York Philharmonic, directed the 800-voice chorus and the 108-piece orchestra. Though some selections were delayed by the torrential rains that pelted the hall's metal roof, the Festival was acclaimed a great success, and the *New York Tribune* declared the chorus unequaled in the nation.

*By the 1930s and 1940s, many Cincinnatians regarded Music Hall as old-fashioned and obsolete. Fortunately, the building survived, was eventually renovated, and became the permanent home of several of the city's cultural organizations.*

Cincinnati wanted a more permanent, more worthy structure. The Music Hall Association, headed by Colonel George W. Nichols (1837-1886), began the task of erecting such a building with a gift of land from the city and $125,000 from dry goods merchant and philanthropist Reuben R. Springer (1800-1884). The rest of the money—about $300,000—was raised by public subscription.

Planners intended that the general public would be exposed to the elevating influence of music at the new hall and, so, become better citizens. More, the hall would attract conventions and exhibitions, boosting the city's economy and national reputation. When bitter debate between the industrial and musical factions over the primary function of the proposed building almost ended the project,

Springer offered $50,000 more for the construction of two wings—the Art and Industry Halls (1879).

On May 1, 1877, the old exhibition building and the Saenger Halle were torn down and excavations begun. Music Hall was dedicated the following April, and the third May Festival opened on May 14, 1878. A public drive had raised the money for a 6,287-pipe organ, the largest in America and for years among the five largest in the world. Benn Pitman (1822-1910) and William and Henry Fry, all noted woodcarvers, had supervised the crafting of the elaborate wild cherry organ screen by female volunteers.

Music Hall hosted the 1880 Democratic National Convention whose nominee, Major General Winfield Scott Hancock, was defeated by Ohioan James A. Garfield. At the Eleventh Industrial Exposition held in Music Hall in 1883, Thomas Edison won a gold medal for the best incandescent light. When a Carnival of Venice was staged for the 1888 Centennial Exposition of the Ohio Valley and Central States, the Miami & Erie Canal (now

Central Parkway) was roofed over between Twelfth and Fourteenth Streets, and gondolas sailed the "Grand Canal."

From 1882 to 1886, Music Hall was the home of the Art Museum, and from 1886 to 1901, of the Technical School of Cincinnati (later the College of Engineering of the University of Cincinnati). It became the home of the Cincinnati Symphony Orchestra in 1896 (though the musicians performed in Emery Auditorium at the Ohio Mechanics' Institute from 1912 to 1936), and later of the city's opera and ballet companies. Billy Sunday's revival meetings, ice and auto shows, and wrestling and tennis matches have been staged in the wings.

The building has undergone numerous changes: electrical lights replaced gas; the proscenium arch, stage, and gallery were added; plaster walls replaced wood paneling, and Arthur Thomas painted an allegorical mural of the arts on the domed ceiling of the 3,600-seat auditorium. The city bought back Music Hall in 1941 when the Association, which had sold bonds to pay for a restoration of the facade and wings, went bankrupt.

The Corbett Foundation spearheaded a major remodeling effort in 1969-1975 when the old organ, beyond repair, was dismantled and replaced, air conditioning and escalators were installed, a garage with a connecting second-story walkway was built, the stage was enlarged and improved, and other modern improvements were made. Mr. and Mrs. J. Ralph Corbett, generous patrons of the arts in Cincinnati, gave the massive Czechoslovakian crystal chandelier in the grand auditorium and the five smaller ones in the foyer where there are several sculptures, including one of Reuben Springer.

Music Hall is today the home of the Cincinnati Symphony Orchestra, May Festival, Cincinnati Opera, and Cincinnati Ballet. It was entered into the National Register of Historic Places in 1975 and featured in 1978 on a United States Postal Service postcard commemorating historic preservation.

**Turn left on Liberty Street to Central Parkway where tour ends.**

# Tour 5

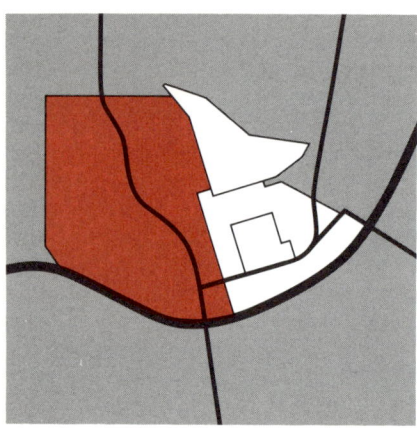

# West End

The West End, bounded by Central Avenue on the east, the Mill Creek to the west, Bank Street to the north, and the Ohio River at the south, interested land speculators from the time of the founding of Cincinnati. One of the area's earliest residents was William Betts, Sr. (1763-1815), a brickmaker and developer, who got eleven acres of land in what is now the Queensgate II district from Joel Williams as part of a debt settlement. After Betts' death, part of this land passed to his children, who were among the first subdividers of the West End.

In 1809, William Barr (d.1837) bought sixty acres of land between Fifth and Eighth Streets west of Western Row (Central Avenue) from the Israel Ludlow estate. Barr was the first of the city's banker-speculators to move to the West End. He built his own home here in 1816, and around the same time, subdivided another fifteen lots and erected houses on several of them.

After Barr died, his son-in-law, William J. Van Horne, further subdivided the Barr estate. By the 1820s, there were several developed residential blocks west of Western Row, a large, unimproved subdivision between Fifth Street and the river, some factories and worker housing, and a ropewalk at Seventh and Western where hemp was woven into rope.

In 1841, Charles Cist, one of the city's early chroniclers, noted that, in addition to the homes of the wealthy, "many frame cottages surrounded by trees and shrubbery make this an attractive residence quarter for people of moderate means." The West End's population was also increasingly diverse, ethnically as well as economically. This area was a port of entry for newcomers. As Cincinnati's black population rose from a few hundred in the 1820s, to more than 3,000 by 1850, many of these people concentrated in a part of the West End near the river. By the 1840s, the West End's black community had its own churches, businesses, and a hotel, The Dumas.

Jews, too, were drawn to the West End. In 1821, Nicholas Longworth sold a small plot of land near Chestnut Street and Central Avenue to the small Jewish community in Cincinnati for use as a cemetery. There were probably no more than 2,500 Jews in the city in 1845, but over the next fifteen years, this figure increased fourfold. As the first residents of the West End moved away to hilltop suburbs, growing numbers of immigrant Jews moved in.

Although Cincinnati's first Jewish congregations were located downtown, the Jewish Hospital was on Central Avenue, the first site of the Hebrew Union College was in the West End, and in 1868, Bene Israel, one of the oldest and largest Jewish congregations in Cincinnati, moved there. By 1900, nine of the city's eleven Jewish congregations were in the West End.

The ongoing movement of industry and population into the West End reduced the attractiveness of the area for more affluent Cincinnatians. In the last half of the nineteenth century, this part of the basin came to be characterized by factories and aging and overcrowded houses built too closely together. Population density increased as absentee landlords converted single-family houses into flats and built huge tenements like Trinity Court which covered the entire block on Smith Street between Fourth and Fifth Streets. By the turn of the century, most middle-income families were leaving, and although

*By the early twentieth century, parts of the West End were showing signs of decline and deterioration.*

a few working-class families remained, the West End was quickly becoming the city's largest and poorest slum.

In the late nineteenth and early twentieth centuries, new immigrants, often impoverished and from backgrounds that left them poorly prepared for life in a crowded urban setting, further contributed to congestion in the West End. Around the turn of the century, the area saw an influx of East European Jews. Then, during World War I, the black community in the West End grew considerably.

The wartime shortage of labor and increasingly bad social and economic conditions in the South encouraged blacks to move to Northern cities to take factory jobs. The West End, with plenty of cheap housing, became home to large numbers of these migrants. By 1925, almost 80% of the city's 38,000 blacks lived there, while most residents of other ethnic backgrounds, including East European Jews, had moved out.

As population density increased and housing deteriorated, conditions in the area worsened. A 1933 survey of 13,000 apartments and 26,000 rooms in the West End found that fewer than one in five had adequate sanitation. Shared privies served 60% of the population. Furthermore, the mortality rates in this area were two to five times higher than in the rest of the city. Population density, at 136 people per acre, was more than five times the city average.

Buildings were crowded onto lots as narrow as sixteen feet; many homes were literally falling down. By one account, some single-family dwellings housed as many as a dozen families. In most places 80% of the land was built over. Often the only open spaces were the streets where children played in competition with wagons and trucks going to and from the area's factories.

Nevertheless, the black community in the West End had a strong sense of identity that was often developed and expressed through its institutions. There was a multitude of churches, some located in the ornate buildings of earlier, more affluent Christian and Jewish congregations, and some in storefronts. Nor were all the residents of the West End poor. The neighborhood was home to numerous black tradesmen, entrepreneurs, and professionals. The Cotton Club, modeled

103

on its Harlem namesake, brought jazz greats and other celebrities to Cincinnati in the 1920s and 1930s.

At the turn of the century when the West End was first generally recognized as a slum, philanthropists attempted to deal with its problems through benevolent institutions such as settlement houses and milk funds. By the late 1920s, however, changing political philosophies led to abandonment of such efforts. Correlating population density with poor health and sanitation and high crime rates, city officials looked to projects that would clear out the tenements and old factories. For the next forty years, the city would practice urban renewal by bulldozer. The construction of Union Terminal from 1929 to 1933 and the creation of the West End Playground at Gest and Dalton Streets were the first such ventures.

In 1933, Franklin Roosevelt's administration established the Public Works Administration to provide work for the unemployed. Among its projects was construction of subsidized housing. Largely because of the West End, Cincinnati was an early target. Using federal funds, the city began to buy property and raze the slums just east of Union Terminal, and in 1938, the Laurel Homes, with 1,039 apartments mostly for whites, was completed. Two years later, another 264 units exclusively for blacks were added. In 1942, the slightly smaller Lincoln Court, also for blacks, was finished.

*Much of the public housing built in the West End was originally intended for white families, like this group moving out of Laurel Homes in 1944.*

Though these large apartment blocks were more modern and comfortable than the slums they replaced, only 10% of 1,600 West End families displaced by the projects were able to meet income and employment qualifications necessary to move into the new units. Although officials defended the construction of public housing in the West End, the city's 1948 *Metropolitan Master Plan* considered industrial development more appropriate for the neighborhood.

In the early 1950s, city officials started to plan what later became Queensgate. Their goal was to replace the old factories and tenements with industrial "superblocks" and a limited amount of housing. Over the next thirty years, Queensgate I and II, the Mill Creek Expressway

*Conditions in the West End varied from street to street even before urban renewal. Many blocks, such as this section of Richmond Street shown in the 1950s, were characterized by well-kept older homes and active institutions and businesses.*

(I-75), and residential projects including Park Town, Richmond Village, and Stanley Rowe Towers all reshaped the West End.

Later that decade, redevelopment focused on the Kenyon-Barr district just south of what is now Ezzard Charles Drive between the railyards and Central Avenue. There Cincinnati embarked on the nation's second largest slum clearance up to that time. Nearly 3,700 buildings on 450 acres were razed. Ninety-eight hundred families, 27,000 people—97% of whom were black—were displaced. At the same time, the Laurel-Richmond housing project, later to become Park Town and Richmond Village, became stalled. At issue was whether private developers were to put up low-cost housing or be allowed to develop the area as they chose. Adding to the delay was uncertainty about the planned route for the expressway. Kenyon-Barr residents were evicted from their homes with nowhere to go.

It was suggested that these Cincinnatians be moved temporarily into houses the city had purchased along the route of the proposed Northeast Expressway (I-71). There, it was said, they would shed the habits of the ghetto and prepare themselves for middle-class lives. Instead, the city's relocation and zoning policies, combined with the restrictive nature of local real estate practices at that time, directed displaced blacks to Walnut Hills, Mt. Auburn, Evanston, and Avondale where there were already black communities. Landlords were encouraged, or at least were not hindered, in subdividing large older homes into many small apartments. Handling relocation in this manner created new ghettos as well as a considerable degree of anger, frustration, and tension among black Cincinnatians.

In 1962, two private housing projects, Park Town and Richmond Village, opened with approximately 550 units to house 2,000 people.

Park Town was a cooperative where residents needed down payments of $250 to $650 to move in, and Richmond Village was a private apartment complex that rented units at market price. In contrast to the federally-subsidized Laurel Homes and Lincoln Court, Park Town and Richmond Village were not fully tenanted for several years.

By that time, West End redevelopment had taken yet another direction. In 1964, three blocks of notable nineteenth century houses along Dayton Street were declared a local historic district in order to protect them from demolition. The Miami Purchase Association, a local preservation group, bought a number of these dwellings, rehabilitating some and selling others to those who wished to do the same. The city, too, now promised to help promote small-scale renovation. Queensgate II was to include carefully managed rehabilitation of older housing to attract a mix of families.

Economic uncertainty in the 1970s and federal spending cuts slowed these projects, and several buildings, including row houses along Ezzard Charles Drive, remained empty and deteriorating. In late 1985, over the objections of many community residents, the city sold a number of houses in the Betts-Longworth Historic District to Chicago developers who promised to work with the community in redeveloping them.

Cutbacks in federal spending had another impact on the West End. After forty years of hard use, both Laurel Homes and Lincoln Court needed repair and renovation. In 1979, the Cincinnati Metropolitan Housing Authority began that work, but two years, later federal money dried up.

The results of the redevelopment projects in the West End were mixed. The Queensgate I area generally was successful as a commercial/industrial park with relatively few vacant or deteriorated buildings. But in other parts of the neighborhood, many structures, particularly houses and small stores, stood empty and crumbling, years after they had been scheduled for rehabilitation.

Both population and neighborhood-oriented businesses left the West End, and between 1960 and 1980, the number of people living in the area decreased from 42,000 to 12,000. Provident Bank closed its branch office there in 1971, and the Kroger Company left two years later. Families that remained in the West End were forced to do their banking and much of their shopping outside the community—often a hardship for those who had to rely on public transportation.

At the same time, it was evident that the West End had made progress. Businesses continued to seek and utilize sites throughout the area. A West End building—Union Terminal—was selected in 1985 to house the city's new museum center, and older structures throughout the West End were slowly being renovated or removed. Even with all its problems, the neighborhood was no longer the "city's worst slum," and its residents continued to maintain a strong sense of community identity. Their concern for and pride in their neighborhood remains an important element in the city's hopes to further improve the West End as a place to live and do business.

# West End

Tour Length
7.5 miles

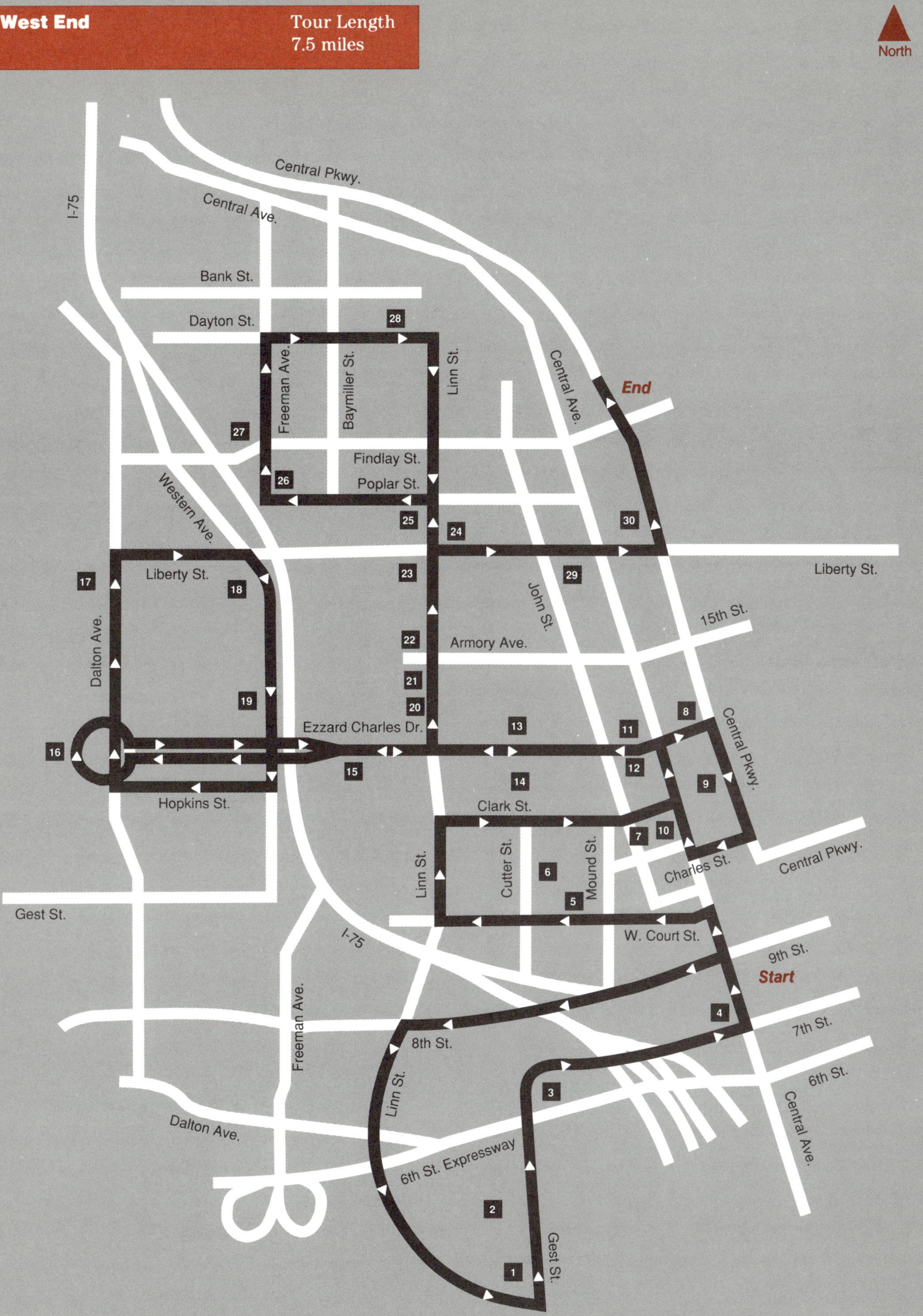
North
Central Pkwy.
Central Ave.
I-75
Bank St.
Dayton St.
28
Freeman Ave.
Baymiller St.
Linn St.
Central Ave.
End
27
Findlay St.
26
Poplar St.
Western Ave.
25
24
30
Liberty St.
17
18
23
29
John St.
Dalton Ave.
15th St.
22
Armory Ave.
21
19
20
Ezzard Charles Dr.
13
11
8
Central Pkwy.
16
15
12
9
14
Hopkins St.
Clark St.
Cutter St.
Mound St.
7
10
Linn St.
6
Charles St.
Central Pkwy.
5
Gest St.
W. Court St.
I-75
9th St.
Start
Freeman Ave.
4
8th St.
7th St.
6th St.
3
Linn St.
Dalton Ave.
Central Ave.
6th St. Expressway
2
1
Gest St.

# Tour 5

▶ ▶ ▶ ▶ ▶ ▶ ▶

**Tour begins at Central Avenue and Ninth Street. Proceed west on Eighth Street, turn left on Linn Street.**

Although the southern half of the West End is now taken up by industrial and commercial development, in the late nineteenth century, the blocks north of Third Street and east of Baymiller and Hoadley Streets were largely residential. The streets were lined with houses and tenements, churches, synagogues, public and private schools, and public service facilities such as firehouses and the **1 Fourth District Police Station,** 754 West Fifth Street, one of the few remaining artifacts of that community.

The southern part of the West End was already heavily developed when, in 1867, the city built a police station at Third and Mill Streets for the Fourth District. This district included all of the riverfront between Vine Street and the Mill Creek, and the West End south of Seventh Street.

Fourth District personnel patrolled a varied community. North of Third Street were the homes of middle-income families and a few scattered factories, such as the Ohio Saw Works and Lackman's United States Brewery. Near the Mill Creek and the river, working-class residents' homes were tucked between rolling mills, lumberyards, and freight depots.

The Fourth District also included some of the "toughest" parts of the city—the Mill Creek bottoms, where poor blacks lived, and "Shantytown," a collection of shacks and crude houseboats along the river's edge. According to one newspaperman who was familiar with police affairs in the 1880s and 1890s, this area was populated by "river gypsies" who spent all their available time either "stealing or preparing to steal."

By the late nineteenth century, the Fourth District was one of the busiest of the city's police districts. Its three lieutenants, two sergeants and forty-one patrolmen dealt with approximately 200 crimes a year, mostly larcenies. The policemen also helped rescue people from fires, stopped runaway horse teams, and aided accident victims. Because of the many factories and railyards within the Fourth Street District, serious,

# West End

often fatal, industrial accidents took place almost daily, and the District's horse-drawn patrol wagon frequently served as an ambulance.

In 1893, the Board of Police Commissioners built a new station on Fifth Street that was supposed to serve for "one hundred years hence." The brick and stone Romanesque Revival style structure with its arched doorway for vehicles was "light and airy, with good ventilation." The holding cell included the "latest improvements in sanitation for prison use."

Despite the redrawing of district boundaries in 1931, the station house continued to serve as the Fourth District headquarters. It was abandoned in 1955 when police districts were consolidated and operations were moved into new centralized stations. By the early 1960s, industry had replaced most of the homes in the vicinity, and the former police station was incorporated into the expanding Butternut Bread company facilities. The building, painted to blend in with the adjoining plant, sits at the southwest corner of Butternut's complex.

**Turn left—a sharp left—on Gest Street.**

In 1885, Louis Hudepohl (1842-1902) and George Kotte bought the Koehler Brewery on McMicken Street in Over-the-Rhine. In 1893, Hudepohl bought out Kotte's widow, and from that time until the 1980s, his descendants have run the **2 Hudepohl Brewery,** 505 Gest Street.

Cincinnati had twenty-six breweries at the turn of the century; Hudepohl, unlike many of these, survived Prohibition by producing soft drinks and near beer (.5% alcohol), and by distributing beverages made by others. In 1933, the brewery reopened and the next year, bought the Gest Street complex of the Lackman Brewing Company that had been constructed in the 1850s and expanded in 1880.

Over the years, Hudepohl transferred all its operations to the former Lackman site. When Hudepohl's annual production reached 700,000 barrels in the late 1940s, the plant was enlarged. By 1960, only offices and storage remained in Over-the-Rhine. With the development of Queensgate

I, which Hudepohl helped promote, the brewery moved all its facilities here. In the early 1980s, the firm sought $7 million in tax-free industrial revenue bonds to modernize this plant.

The years after Prohibition proved difficult ones for independent brewers. As a result of the large "national" brands' mass media advertising and widespread distribution, the industry is now dominated by five giants that account for 90% of the beer produced in this country. In 1985, with 300 employees and production just under 300,000 barrels a year, Hudepohl ranked thirteenth nationwide.

Despite the production of low alcohol beers, as well as a premium brand, Christian Moerlein beer, Hudepohl had not expanded its work force since World War II. While Hudepohl had a leading market share in Cincinnati, it was not widely sold elsewhere. Hudepohl became a local distributor of other beers, and in 1986, it merged with Cincinnati's other surviving independent brewer, Schoenling. The combined firm, known as Hudepohl-Shoenling, ceased brewing operations at the Gest Street plant the following year.

The 4-story, tile roofed Citi Center office building at 635 West Seventh Street was originally the **3 Harriet Beecher Stowe School,** opened in 1923 as an all-black junior high school. Its first principal, Jennie Davis Porter (1875-1936), was the first black woman to hold such a position in Cincinnati.

Public schools built specifically for black children were not new to Cincinnati. From 1856 to 1874, the Cincinnati Independent Colored School System was administered by an all-black board elected by black male voters. The system was abolished because whites began to fear the strength of the black vote, and management of the black schools then passed to the white Cincinnati Board of Education.

State legislation abolished segregation in public schools in 1887 but did not promote integration. In Cincinnati, the mostly-black schools, became "Branch" schools, and the majority of black children attended these. Black teachers, not permitted to teach white children, were phased out of the public school system except

*Unlike many West End buildings along the route of I-75, the former Harriet Beecher Stowe School was out of the path of road improvement projects and so escaped demolition.*

at the all-black Douglass School in Walnut Hills. By 1901, only 1,855 of 3,730 school-age black children were still attending Cincinnati's public schools.

Jennie Porter, daughter of a former slave, aided by white philanthropist Annie Laws, began a kindergarten for black children in the West End in 1911. Soon afterwards, the program was transferred to the old Hughes High School building on West Fifth at Mound Street. In September 1914, this venture became the independent Jackson Colony School with nineteen teachers and 350 students. The following year, the institution was renamed the Harriet Beecher Stowe School to honor the author of the antislavery novel *Uncle Tom's Cabin.*

Porter, a follower of Booker T. Washington, believed in self-help and that separate black schools should be places where black teachers could teach children the vocational and cultural skills necessary for survival in a society that sharply limited their opportunities. From the start, she faced opposition from local black leaders, most notably newspaper publisher Wendell Phillips Dabney (1865-1952) and the Cincinnati branch of the NAACP, organized in 1915. While allowing that separate schools did offer the only employment for black teachers, Dabney and others argued that Porter was accommodating racism and limiting the aspirations of black youth.

The Board of Education, however, supported Porter's efforts. In 1916, as the migration of blacks into the West End strengthened the argument that a school for blacks was needed there, the board approved the construction of a new Stowe School, but war

delayed the work.

This brick school building, dedicated in 1923, had a pipe organ, branch library, gym, swimming pool, and penny lunchroom. There was vocational training in household arts, catering, and housekeeping for girls, and in printing, cement work, and bricklaying for boys. But Stowe School provided more than vocational training. Graduates received awards for excellence in scholarship. Theodore Berry (b.1906), Cincinnati's first black mayor, is a Stowe alumnus.

Stowe opened as an undistricted junior high for blacks from all over the city; it later became an elementary school. By the 1940s, 1,300 pupils attended the school. In 1953, Stowe was made a district school for the entire West End and thus, remained an all-black school.

Urban renewal soon tore down the homes of many potential students. Only 592 children attended in 1961-1962, and Stowe was closed. It reopened that fall as the Hamilton County School for Mentally Retarded Children and a federally-funded adult education center.

The programs for low-income or unemployed adults were canceled in 1980, and the building was put up for sale. A West End group, the Harriet Beecher Stowe Historical-Cultural Society, tried to buy the property, hoping to turn it into a black museum, social center, and historical archive, but the city turned down requests for funding assistance. The school was sold in 1982 and renovated for office space.

**Turn right on West Seventh Street.**

**4 Union Baptist Church,** 405 West Seventh Street, the second oldest black congregation in the city, was

founded July 21, 1831, by fourteen members of Enon Baptist Church who had withdrawn after white members insisted that blacks sit at the back of the church. The new congregation met as the First African Baptist Church in a residence on Third Street between Plum and Elm Streets.

In 1835, the group built its own house of worship, a small brick building on Western Row near Second Street. This was the first black church in Cincinnati and likely a station on the "Underground Railroad." The church was a center for anti-slavery activity, hosting mass meetings where abolitionists William Lloyd Garrison, Frederick Douglass, and Henry Ward Beecher spoke.

First African became Union Baptist in 1845 and in 1864 bought the Enon Baptist building. From 1876 to 1879, George Washington Williams (1849-1891) served as pastor. Williams later became the first black elected to the Ohio legislature (1880-1882) and wrote *History of the Negro Race in America* (1883), the first study of its kind.

In 1895, Union Baptist Church completed a brick Gothic Revival style church at the southwest corner of Richmond and Mound Streets. The Reverend Wilbur Page (1895-1985) took charge of the congregation of about 200 in 1919, beginning seventy-six years of community service. In 1979, Page led a congregation of 1,600 and was honored as a Great Living Cincinnatian.

On February 17, 1960, the city notified Union Baptist that its buildings were scheduled for demolition as part of Queensgate II. The group was offered old churches in Walnut Hills, Avondale, Over-the-Rhine, and Kennedy Heights, but members felt that their roots were downtown and that the church still had much to offer the neighborhood. Thus, Union Baptist became the only church displaced by West End clearance to buy new property nearby.

The congregation encountered difficulties with the Planning Commission, which claimed its design looked "too suburban." However, some contended that planners were trying to keep blacks out of the redevelopment area. The present church, which opened June 15, 1971, was designed by Glaser & Myers & Associates to have "urban character"—the box-like structure had recessed windows and hard-surfaced brick that would not show dirt. The building also incorporated memorial plaques, pictures, and a stained glass window from the old church.

The role of Union Baptist expanded when it sponsored a government-built, 14-story apartment building for low-income persons. The adjacent high-rise, known as Page Tower, is the most prominent example of black enterprise in the Queensgate-West End redevelopment. Union Baptist, with approximately 900 members in 1988, will become full owner of the building in 2013.

**Turn left on Central Avenue, left on West Court Street.**

The congregation of **5** **Jerriel Baptist Church,** 1018 Wesley Avenue, occupies one of the structures that survived the clearance of this area for Hays and Porter schools. The stone-faced church was erected in the late nineteenth century by the white, middle-income congregation of the First Baptist Church. Around 1915, the church became the synagogue of Beth Hamedrash Hagodol; at the end of the 1920s, it was sold to the Shiloh Seventh Day Adventist Church. In 1955, Jerriel Baptist moved here.

Jerriel Baptist Church was founded in 1925. Members met briefly in a storefront on Cutter, then in their own building at Armory and Baymiller Streets. At one time an integrated group, the all-black congregation had about 600 members drawn from throughout the city by the mid-1980s.

After World War II, the Cincinnati Board of Education undertook a $28 million building and rehabilitation program. Two schools resulting from that effort were **6** **Jennie D. Porter Middle School,** 1030 Cutter Street, and **George W. Hays Elementary School,** 1035 Mound Street. Both opened in 1953, and both were named after prominent black Cincinnatians. Porter was a local leader in black education, and Hays (1847-1933), a former slave, served for sixty-one years as crier for the U.S. District Court at Cincinnati and for three terms as a member of the Ohio Legislature.

When, in 1950, the city cleared the block bounded by Clark, Cutter, West Court, and Mound Streets, more than one hundred structures were leveled including several churches, scores of homes and residential-commercial buildings, and the Elizabeth Gamble Deaconess Home and Cincinnati Missionary Training School.

Due to slum clearance and declining birth rates, Porter and Hays schools were soon nearly 99% black and enrolled at half capacity. In 1978, the Board of Education, responding to an NAACP suit charging discrimination in the system, changed the attendance boundaries for Porter. The move unleashed what a contemporary observer called an "avalanche" of opposition from white parents in Lower Price Hill, Riverside, and Sedamsville as students from those communities were transferred here.

Hays remained predominantly black, with about 430 enrolled during 1987-1988. Preschool classes, geared to enhancing children's chances for later academic success, taught basics like the alphabet, colors, and organizing from left to right. Porter's Alternative College Readiness Program offered an academic curriculum for those who do not qualify for Walnut Hills. Of its approximately 430 students in 1988, 40% were white.

**Turn right on Linn Street, right on Clark Street.**

**7** **Clark Street,** in the heart of the Betts-Longworth Historic District, was named after Elizabeth Clark Betts, mother of William Betts, Sr. (1763-1815), who settled here around 1804 and constructed the 2-story brick farmhouse at 416. The street's history reflects the development of much of the West End.

In the 1830s, following the settlement of Betts' estate, one hundred acres of his property were sold at auction and the remaining eleven acres parceled out among his family. Betts' widow, Phebe, divided the properties on the south side of the street among her daughters and a son, who sold a number of lots.

Isaac Betts (1809-1891) controlled the family property on the north side of the street and began leasing out lots and houses a decade later. Several members of the Betts family also built on the eastern end of the street. In 1848, Isaac built a 3-

story brick house at 412, which was altered with major additions after the turn of the century.

William Betts' house passed to his daughter and her husband. In the late 1870s, they leased a side lot to physician Frederick C. Schmuck, who built a 3-story stone-faced brick dwelling there, 414 Clark, in 1878. Isaac's older brother, Oliver, lived across the street at 419, a 2-story Greek Revival style home built around 1825. Next door at 421 Clark, the 3-story Italianate style house with the carved sandstone doorway was built in 1873 by William F. Doepke, the department store magnate, on land bought from Oliver Bett's daughter.

Across the street, 422 was first rented to James Gamble, who then bought it in 1889. Gamble's daughters lived there until 1921, when the house was sold to the Anshe Shalom Romanian Jewish congregation which added a new facade to the building three years later. After Anshe Shalom moved in 1934, the house was divided into apartments. A brick double home that once stood at 428-430 was designed at mid-century by William Walter, whose father drew plans for St. Peter in Chains Cathedral on Eighth Street. Walter sold the eastern half of the house to downtown jeweler

*Despite their fine architectural character, proximity to downtown, and significant history, many of the houses on Clark Street were, in the late 1980s, in danger of decaying beyond repair while awaiting renovation.*

Frank Herschede in 1883. Sausage maker George Schwein erected 437, another Greek Revival style brick dwelling, in the 1860s.

As the West End became densely built up, the area grew increasingly less attractive to wealthy householders, such as the Betts, the Doepkes, and the Gambles; many sold out to more modest professionals in the 1870s and 1880s. Within a short time they, too, left and were replaced by working-class tenants and owners.

The character of Clark Street changed more slowly than that of the surrounding area. But by the 1920s, Isaac Bett's house at 412 had become a tenement, as had other houses on the street. Even so, a few homes, remained in the hands of owner-occupants and were not as badly abused. As a result, Clark Street looked to be a prime candidate for rehabilitation when the city created the Betts-Longworth Historic District.

By 1988, however, the chances for revitalization appeared bleak. Redevelopment costs had risen steadily, federal funds had dried up, dozens of vacant buildings awaiting renovation had deteriorated so badly that they had to be torn down, and there was a general uncertainty as to whether the city or a Chicago developer would complete projects that had been begun in Betts-Longworth.

On Clark Street, three homes had been restored and were occupied. Isaac Betts' house and the one that William Walter had designed had been torn down. The remaining structures on the street were vacant, windows gaping, steps fallen away, yards overgrown, bricks crumbling. William Betts' house, the oldest house in Cincinnati on its original site seemed beyond repair.

**Turn left on Central Avenue, right on Ezzard Charles Drive.**

The **8 District One Police Station,** 310 Ezzard Charles Drive, was built in 1955 when Cincinnati Police districts were redrawn to reflect the postwar growth of the city. District One, which previously included the northern part of the West End and downtown, was expanded to include the West End from Eighth Street to the river. In addition to serving as a station house, the building was headquarters for administration as well as the traffic, youth, and missing persons bureaus. In 1969, a third story was added to the building to house communications.

A year later, the Police Department consolidated Districts One and Two, making the building not just a neighborhood station house but a centrally located administrative and communications center. The new district included the entire basin, most of Mohawk-Brighton, Eden Park, Mt. Adams, and Over-the-Rhine, another low-income, high crime area. In addition, the downtown area draws great numbers of people by day and during special events, and has many businesses to protect at night. District One is thus one of the two busiest police districts in the city.

**Turn right on Central Parkway.**

The **9 Crosley Telecommunications Center,** 1223 Central Parkway, houses Cincinnati's public television and radio stations, WCET-TV and WGUC-FM, and the Gray History of the Wireless Museum. With its adjoining parking garage and covered walkways to Music Hall and the Queen City Vocational Center, Crosley Center is one element of the ambitious Queensgate II Town Center plan that has been realized.

The Queensgate II Town Center, as originally conceived, was a $20 million project that called for business, educational, cultural, and residential facilities in the 2-block area bounded by Central Parkway, Ezzard Charles Drive, Twelfth Street, and a line midway to John Street. The development was part of the city's plan to attract and serve a culturally diverse West End community.

Eighty-three local foundations provided funds for the development of the studio complex designed by Roth & Associates that opened in 1976. However, the anticipated residential and commercial renaissance did not materialize, except for the rehabilitation of a few homes on the surrounding blocks.

**WCET, Channel 48,** noncommercial educational television, began UHF broadcasting July 16, 1954. WCET was Ohio's first educational television station, the seventh such station in the nation, and the first officially licensed by the FCC. The new station rented a spot for its transmitter on the WLW tower for a dollar a year and broadcast fifteen hours weekly from the studios of the Cincinnati College of Music on the third floor of Music Hall.

During the 1950s, WCET produced more than one hundred programs for national distribution and high school and university-level telecourses, as well as high school football games. In 1959, the station moved to the home of WLW-TV on Chickasaw Avenue, renting quarters for a dollar a year.

In the 1960s, the defeat of several school levies left the station in a desperate financial position. Until 1967, public school subscriptions to WCET had provided the major portion of the station's budget. Cutbacks resulted in suspensions of programing, but the community rallied to the station's support.

WCET has constantly increased the size of its audience and the quality, range, and hours of its programing. Support comes from members, an annual televised auction, corporate underwriters, and private and government grants. Recently, WCET created a commercial subsidiary to sell telecommunications products and services.

Here, too, are the studios of **WGUC, 90.9 FM,** noncommercial fine arts public radio, which began broadcasting at 4:00 p.m. on September 21, 1960 in a converted cafeteria on the University of Cincinnati campus. At that time, WGUC was the only educational radio station in the Greater Cincinnati area and was financed by donations and an annual grant from the university.

WGUC moved to the College Conservatory of Music complex in 1968, and during the 1970s expanded its broadcast time to twenty-four hours a day. It recorded performances by the Cincinnati Symphony Orchestra, LaSalle Quartet, and the May Festival chorus for national distribution.

The station began broadcasting from the Corbett Studio in the Crosley Center on September 21, 1980, at 4:00, exactly twenty years after its first transmission. Today, only National Public Radio headquarters supplies more network programing than does WGUC.

On the first floor of the building is the **Gray History of the Wireless**

**Museum**. This replica of the studio of broadcast pioneer Powel Crosley, Jr. (1886-1961), is equipped with electronic devices used in the 1920s and displays of other vintage equipment. The collection was gathered by Jack Gray, an amateur radio operator and a long-time employee of the Crosley Broadcasting Company.

**Turn right on Charles Street.**

Behind the former Rosen's dry goods store is the **10 Chestnut Street Jewish Cemetery,** the oldest Jewish cemetery west of the Alleghenies. It was established at the deathbed request of Benjamin Leib, or Lape, who had married a Christian woman and raised his children as Christians but wanted to be buried in a Jewish cemetery with Jewish rites.

*The West End's once-significant Jewish population left behind a number of reminders of its presence here, including the small Chestnut Street Cemetery.*

At that time, Cincinnati's 10,000 citizens included six practicing Jews: Jacob and Abraham Jonas, Moses and Solomon Morris, David Johnson, and Moses Nathanson. On November 6, 1821, these men paid Nicholas Longworth $75 for a 25' x 60' piece of land. Longworth donated an adjacent parcel, and later purchases completed acquisition of the present lot.

While many downtown cemeteries were later relocated to the suburbs, this tiny graveyard has remained, though sometimes subject to neglect and vandalism. There are about one hundred graves here, many of which still have stones inscribed in English or Hebrew.

**Turn right on Central Avenue, left on Ezzard Charles Drive.**

Until **11 Robert A. Taft High School,** 420 Ezzard Charles Drive, opened in 1955, Old Woodward—now the School for the Creative and Performing Arts at Thirteenth and Sycamore Streets—served all downtown area high school students. By 1925, 1,650 students filled that building to capacity. The *Official Plan of the City* proposed that a second high school be built "somewhere between Ludlow and Colerain Avenues and near the proposed Central Parkway," so that it would be easily accessible from northern and northeastern suburbs, including Bond Hill and Camp Washington.

The Depression and World War II stalled new construction, but in December 1946, this site was approved for Basin Senior High School.

The Cincinnati firm of Tietig & Lee designed the modern 3-story brick building with a capacity of 1,400. The Board of Education planned to name it in honor of former President William Howard Taft (1857-1930), but because there was already a William Howard Taft School in Mt. Auburn, the President's son, Senator Robert A. Taft (1889-1953) was commemorated instead. Vice-president Richard M. Nixon spoke at the cornerstone laying ceremonies on April 20, 1954. Taft opened with 1,213 students, 74% of them black.

Taft, with both academic and vocational curricula, was the only school in the system to have just grades 10-12. Its student body was drawn principally from the West End, and despite the completion of a vocational annex in 1966, enrollment declined as surrounding residential neighborhoods were razed.

In 1973, the West End Task Force, a neighborhood organization concerned about the quality of redevelopment, pressed the Board of Education to make Taft a "total community" high school. A joint effort of the Board and the Cincinnati Recreation Commission produced a sports complex and community center north of the school and a new vocational facility. By 1987-1988, approximately 1,050 students were enrolled at Taft.

The **12 Queen City Vocational Center,** 425 Ezzard Charles Drive, connected to Taft High School by a covered second-level walkway, opened in 1978. By then, the CRC had pulled out of the recreation center project, and the development plan was restructured to meet the school's needs. A lighted stadium, two tennis courts, a running track, outdoor basketball courts, and locker rooms were completed in 1986.

That year, the Board of Education recommended that Taft, because of an enrollment of only 634, become a 4-year program. Vocational programs at Taft include health and child care, food service, building maintenance, occupational work experience, and animal care.

In 1933, government concern with the housing problems of the poor led to the creation of the federal Public Works Administration that made money available for construction of new housing. By year's end, the Cincinnati Metropolitan Housing Authority (CMHA) was established.

In 1934, the Housing Authority began acquiring property for the first federally-funded housing project in Cincinnati. Some 1,600 families living in the 16-block area bounded by Armory and Freeman Avenues, Clark and John Streets were moved out, and demolition began early in 1936. By June 1938, the 1,039-unit **13 Laurel Homes** apartment complex was opened for public inspection.

On August 22, the first tenants moved into Laurel Homes, which was owned by the Federal Housing Administration and leased to CMHA. Within six months, 95% of Laurel Homes had been rented, primarily to low-income white families. Critics of the project charged that many families living there could afford adequate housing elsewhere and that only 10% of those dispossessed by the complex were able to move in. Also, while 50% of the residents of the old apartments and tenements had been black, only 321 new units were opened to black families. By mid-1939, plans had been approved for an additional 264 units for blacks.

A year later, work began on a second complex of 1,015 apartments, **14 Lincoln Court,** exclusively for blacks. Through the prosperous 1950s and early 1960s, Laurel Homes and

*In the 1930s, hundreds of densely-packed nineteenth-century structures were torn down and replaced with the green spaces and modern housing blocks of Laurel Homes and Lincoln Court.*

Lincoln Court, then owned solely by CMHA, continued to be a stepping stone to private home ownership for low-income families of both races. But when the entire housing development became integrated in the late 1960s, whites moved out, and these projects became exclusively black and increasingly elderly.

By the late 1980s, 81% of the families who lived here were unemployed and 83% were headed by women. In the 1950s, a typical stay at CMHA housing was slightly more than two years, but the average 1982 resident remained for just over seven years.

Laurel Homes and Lincoln Court aimed to provide sanitary, basic housing at the lowest possible cost. In this they succeeded. But over the years, they encountered many problems, some of which reflected broader social ills, while others were caused by the way the projects were built and run.

When Laurel Homes and Lincoln Court were planned, they were meant to house families who were only temporarily impoverished. Many blacks, however, did not share in postwar prosperity and did not quickly move out. Later, the block-like appearance of these projects encouraged

critics of public housing projects to call them warehouses for the poor.

CMHA began to remodel Lincoln Court in order to give it a less institutional appearance and to provide additional privacy for tenants. Between 1979 and 1981, five buildings—fewer than 10% of the total—were renovated by local architects Glaser & Myers. Then, under the Reagan administration, federal money for further renovation dried up, and there remained little immediate prospect for additional repairs.

Laurel Homes, the second largest public housing project funded by the Public Works Administration, was placed on the National Register of Historic Places in May 1987.

At one time, there were at least a half-dozen Catholic churches in the West End. By the 1980s, only **15** **St. Joseph Roman Catholic Church and School,** 735-745 Ezzard Charles Drive, remained.

St. Joseph parish was organized in 1846 for German immigrants who swelled the congregations of the two other Catholic churches in the area. The archdiocese purchased a lot on the corner of Linn and Laurel Streets in March and had completed a combination church and school by September. A congregation of approximately 400 families dedicated a permanent church on December 10, 1848.

St. Joseph's was a vigorous parish

with 800 families by 1895. Members furnished their church with four large bells in the tower, oak pews, a hand-carved altar and Stations of the Cross, stained glass windows from Germany, and wall and ceiling murals by William Lamprecht, a German immigrant. A highly regarded church painter, Lamprecht also created murals for St. Peter in Chains Cathedral and the chapel of Mount St. Joseph.

Between 1908 and 1910 a convent, rectory, and school were added. Above the school entrance is carved the inscription: *Lasset Die Kinder Zu Mir Kommen*—Suffer the children to come unto me.

With the transformation of the West End, St. Joseph became a predominantly black parish in the 1940s, but it always retained some white members. The church building itself was also affected by the changes in the West End. As plans moved forward for the Laurel-Richmond development, the building stood on land needed for the widening of Linn Street. The last Mass was held on November 13, 1960, and the building was razed in March. During St. Joseph's 112-year history, 18,683 people had been baptized there.

The present brown brick church was dedicated on March 28, 1965. Its modern design fits the "redevelopment look" of the West End, and incorporates the windows, Stations of the Cross, bells, and some of the murals from the original church.

In 1988, St. Joseph's congregation of approximately 500 was 99% black. That year 145 students—about 15% of them Catholic—were enrolled in the school, paying tuition at a rate based on family income.

Out of concern for decent housing and neighborhood stability, St. Joseph joined the Community Land Cooperative, which purchases and renovates properties in the West End and resells them to those who could not otherwise afford homes. New homeowners must promise either to pass the property along to their children or resell it to the cooperative.

As **16** **The Cincinnati Union Terminal,** 1301 Freeman Avenue, was being constructed between 1931 and 1933, civic officials worried that the depressed national economy and new forms of transportation had already made it obsolete. Many claimed that the Terminal was too

113

large and was being built too late. Nevertheless, the station was completed, and it stands as a monument to the city and to the Art Deco style, as well as to the importance of the railroads themselves.

As early as 1905, city planners sought a single terminal to replace the five stations that served Cincinnati. In 1910, the Cincinnati Union Depot and Terminal Company proposed a complex of offices, warehouses, and a passenger depot be constructed on the north side of Third Street between Walnut and Main.

In 1923, the Cincinnati Railroad Development Company hired C. A. Wilson (d.1935) to design a terminal. Four years later, the Cincinnati Union Terminal Company commissioned a New York architectural firm specializing in railway stations, Fellheimer & Wagner (Alfred Fellheimer, 1875-1959, Steward Wagner, 1886-1958), to design a terminal. When the Terminal Company rejected the Neo-Classical structure proposed by architect Roland A. Wank (1898-1970), Fellheimer & Wagner called in Paul Cret (1876-1945) of Philadelphia.

Cret's final design was largely Art Deco, a style that aimed at uniting art and industry by using sweeping, graceful lines, new materials, and elaborate decoration. The large arch and half-dome of Union Terminal were to be a metaphorical gateway to the city. The facade was highlighted by two figures representing Transportation and Commerce, carved in relief by sculptor Maxwell Keck.

Inside, the giant rotunda, 180 feet across and 106 feet high, provided a large open area where passengers could mill about, and housed a wide range of services: barber and beauty shops, toy stores, a central newsstand, and three restaurants, including a tea room finished with Rookwood tiles.

In addition to its distinctive design, the Terminal was noted for its decoration. Spectacular concourse and rotunda murals designed by Winold Reiss (1886-1953), a German-born artist, depicted the settlement and the development of commerce and industry in southwestern Ohio, and a map of the United States flanked by the two hemispheres. The Ravenna Mosaic Company of New York prepared the murals with highlights in small glass tiles and a background of tinted stucco.

Linoleum etchings by Pierre Bour-

*Lincoln Park, an oasis of greenery, light, and fresh air for West End residents, was cleared away for the construction of the approach to Union Terminal.*

delle, runner-up to Reiss in the mural competition, decorated smaller areas such as lounges and waiting rooms. Pillars and walls featured marble and exotic wood parquetry.

A portion of the property on which the Terminal was built had been owned by the city since 1837. In 1858, the land was redeveloped as a park. By the turn of the century, Lincoln Park was one of the most heavily used in the city. In winter, as many as 5,000 people skated on the frozen pond, and during the summer, an estimated 1,500 tenement dwellers slept there each night to escape the hot, stagnant air of their homes. But by the late 1920s, the West End had become a vast slum, and to clear the park and nearby buildings seemed a civic improvement.

By then, the city needed a single terminal located away from the riverfront and the danger of flooding. For years, Cincinnati had been a railroad bottleneck. But civic conservatism, World War I, and the recession of 1918-1921 had delayed a new terminal until the late 1920s and early 1930s, the years of the Great Depression. Such a project required considerable space, and the city bought and razed more than one hundred residential and commercial structures in the West End to clear the acreage it then sold to the Union Terminal Company.

The Terminal Company then used fill dirt to raise the level of an area one and a half miles long and almost a quarter of a mile wide by as much as fifty-eight feet in some places. Huge steam shovels scraped 5.5 million cubic yards of dirt from Bald Knob Hill in Fairmount, and pilings

sixty feet long were driven into the ground to support the massive building. The first piling—gold tipped—for Union Terminal was driven on May 5, 1931, and the cornerstone was laid November 20.

Most Cincinnatians viewed the $41 million project with pride. On March 19, 1933, spring floodwaters that inundated older rail facilities closer to the river pressed the Terminal into early service. Within a few days after its dedication on March 31, more than 100,000 people had visited the Terminal, and in June, *Fortune* magazine praised it as a beautiful and efficient "child of the century."

Union Terminal—a complex that included twenty-two buildings on 287 acres of land—served seven major railroads with sixteen tracks, and could accommodate 17,000 travelers and 216 trains daily. The station's most active years were during World War II when it was not uncommon for the Terminal to handle more than 18,000-20,000 travelers and 200 trains each day, many of them special troop trains.

By the 1950s, however, the number of trains passing through each day had declined to around sixty. The railroad age was ending. The Union Terminal came to be regarded as a white elephant, and the Terminal Company began its long search for some alternative use for the massive facility.

By 1962, Cincinnati Union Terminal had only twenty-four trains scheduled daily, and the Terminal Company, trying to relieve itself of high operating costs and taxes, offered it to the city. During the mid-1960s, the Terminal was losing $6 million annually.

The federal government assumed control of rail passenger traffic in the early 1970s, and Amtrak consolidated and cut back service—only four trains ran through Cincinnati each day. At 11:30 on October 28, 1972, the last train left Union Terminal; Amtrak moved to a small utilitarian station along River Road.

The Terminal Company put the station up for sale for $10 million. The Southern Railway bought the railyards, planning to take down the concourse so that new piggy-back freight cars (flatcars carrying truck trailers) could come through.

A citizen's group formed the first of several "Save the Terminal" committees. Architecture critic Ada Louis Huxtable, writing in the *New York Times*, declared the building an "extravagant monument to the past" that should be preserved. Still, there was the problem of finding an appropriate use for a structure so massive and costly to maintain. Union Terminal briefly housed a museum of science and industry, but that project ended because of inadequate funding.

In early 1973, Southern applied for a permit to begin tearing down the Terminal concourse, promising to help preserve the murals. The city refused the demolition permit as numerous groups scrambled to raise money to save the murals, if nothing else. In August and September, the fourteen industrial murals were removed to the Greater Cincinnati International Airport. Only the mosaic maps were lost when the concourse was demolished.

Over the next few years, a range of plans for the reuse of the Terminal was proposed, including a bus terminal and a site for the School for the Creative and Performing Arts. In August 1975, the city finally bought the Terminal for two dollars, plus $1 million for the land, and subsequently offered it for lease.

A long-term lease agreement with an option to buy was reached with Joseph Skilken & Company of Columbus. Skilken proposed a shopping center to be called Oz, with stores, restaurants, and roller skate and ice rinks, and between 1978 and 1980, invested $8 million in careful renovation.

By the time the mall opened in 1980, however, the nation was in its worst recession in forty years, and a number of prospective tenants withdrew. Within a few months, shop owners complained of too few customers and a lack of adequate promotion. The developer's plan was never com-

pletely carried out, and the retail tenants gradually left. As activity at the mall continued to decrease, the city and the developer each charged the other with failure to live up to agreements made about operation and ownership of the Terminal property. By 1984, the argument had gone to court in a series of suits and countersuits.

During the same period, both the Cincinnati Historical Society and the Cincinnati Museum of Natural History were searching for more space. On May 6, 1986, voters of Hamilton County approved a $33 million bond issue that, with $8 million in state funds, would allow the renovation of Union Terminal.

Plans called for the Terminal to house an enlarged natural history museum, a new historical museum, the Historical Society's library, the Children's Discovery Center, and an Omnimax theater. The Center was scheduled to begin opening in late 1990. An agreement was worked out between the Skilken company and city officials by which the City of Cincinnati bought back complete control of the building for $3 million in 1987 so the museum project could proceed.

The Discovery Center plans feature exhibits aimed at helping young people understand the world around them. The Museum of Natural History Museum planned to install an enlarged version of its limestone cavern exhibit and to recreate a glacial ice cave and outwash plain based on Sharon Woods Gorge. The new Cincinnati Historical Society Museum will include a walk-through representation of the Public Landing in the 1850s and Vine Street in the 1880s. There will also be participatory exhibits on local and neighborhood history, Cincinnati industries, and popular culture.

**Return to Western Avenue. Turn right on Western Avenue, right on Hopkins Street, right on Dalton Avenue.**

In the early 1930s, the City Planning Commission and the federal government sought an appropriate site for a new post office annex. Many hoped to locate it near a proposed civic center, but because mail traveled by railroad, the planned facility had

to be easily accessible to the new Union Terminal in the West End. The city purchased and cleared the property bounded by McLean, Dalton, and Sherman Avenues, and Liberty Street.

The Cincinnati firm of Samuel Hannaford & Sons designed the annex, now the **17 U.S. Postal Service Main Office,** 1591 Dalton Avenue, which was finished October 8, 1933. Because of unstable ground, 2,762 piles, forty feet long, were driven to support the reinforced concrete superstructure. The walls of the new facility were faced with Ohio sandstone, the base with granite. The building featured an American eagle carved in lintels over the entrances, bronze doors, and marble floor and wainscoting in the foyer. Special gates were installed in the basement to protect the structure and its contents from floods.

This complex, originally known as the Dalton Street Annex, was connected to Union Terminal's mail handling building by a covered truck ramp and a conveyor bridge that carried sacks of mail. In the late 1930s, more than one million pieces of mail passed through the Annex each day. By the early 1960s, space was inadequate, and the adjoining buff brick tower and truck terminal building were added. Within a few years, however, the Postal Service began to move all mail by air; the last mail shipment by rail arrived November 17, 1967.

The Annex became the Cincinnati Main Post Office in the 1980s, and all administrative offices moved here. At that time, 2,200 employees and several automated code reading systems handled the processing and distribution of incoming and outgoing mail at a rate of five to seven million pieces daily.

**Turn right on Liberty Street, right on Western Avenue.**

In the late 1950s, city planners began to create what ultimately became **18 Queensgate I**. The idea of a large modern industrial park in the West End began with the Cincinnati *Metropolitan Master Plan* of 1948 that pointed out the lack of industrial sites close to the city. It noted as well that much of the West End was unsuitable for residential use.

Parts of the West End had been cleared for Union Terminal, the Postal Annex, and federal housing projects, but some of the oldest and most overbuilt areas remained untouched. The dense mix of housing and industry made the Kenyon-Barr district, stretching from Clark Street and Lincoln Park Drive south to Fourth Street, too expensive to clear. But when federal funds for slum clearance became available, the city decided to tackle this area.

In 1956, the Highway Act allowed the city to acquire land for the Mill Creek Expressway (I-75) which was to divide the industrial and residential areas of the new West End. Voters approved a $9 million urban redevelopment bond issue and clearance of the West End began in earnest.

City planners hailed a new era, envisioning thirteen "superblocks"— industrial complexes dedicated to light industry, warehousing, and service businesses. But for residents, redevelopment meant the end of the community as they had known it. Many people wondered where the

*Before highway construction and renewal projects like Queensgate I took place, the West End was a large and heavily developed industrial and residential neighborhood.*

8,600 families who had lost their homes would live By 1960, despite these concerns, only a few sites, such as United Parcel Service and Interstate Bakeries, which fit with industrial redevelopment, had not been leveled.

City Redevelopment Director Charles H. Stamm hired an advertising agency that made Kenyon-Barr into Queensgate I, the gateway to the Queen City. The magazine *Architectural Forum* applauded the Queensgate concept but warned the city to keep the development in local hands to assure that it would retain distinctive Cincinnati character. The first superblock, Number 10, along the Sixth Street Expressway near Gest, was sold to a local realty consortium, but most went to outside concerns whose construction left Queensgate looking like thousands of other industrial parks across the nation.

Nevertheless, Queensgate developed largely as planned: an area of service industries, light manufacturing, transportation facilities, and warehouses. There are also hotels, restaurants, automobile dealerships, and some older industries. Although it has not developed as quickly as civic leaders had hoped, Queensgate represents the most economically

successful redevelopment effort in the West End.

The Cincinnati Job Corps Center occupies the 5-story buff brick and stone building with a bell tower and cross-topped steeple that was originally the **19 Convent and School of the Sisters of Mercy,** 1409 Western Avenue. Designed by Samuel Hannaford & Sons, the structure served as the motherhouse of Cincinnati's Mercy community (1905-1929), Provincial house (1929-1937), Our Lady of Mercy Academy High School (1898-1957), and Provincial novitiate (1957-1969).

Nine Sisters of Mercy arrived in Cincinnati from Ireland on August 8, 1858. The group established the Convent of the Divine Will on Sycamore Street, and two years later, moved to a former boys' orphanage on West Fourth Street. The Sisters set up a House of Mercy on West Third Street to care for destitute women and children, and offered sewing classes to help women support themselves. During the Civil War, the House of Mercy became a military hospital, and immediately after the war, a children's hospital.

The Sisters of Mercy also taught at various schools in the basin. Concluding that children from middle-class families were the most likely candidates for the religious life, they decided to establish a private girls' school.

In 1884, the Order purchased property on Freeman Avenue on which stood a plain brick home and the Victorian Italianate mansion that was home first of Enoch Carson (1822-1899), collector of the Port of Cincinnati, and later of Joseph and Anna Longworth. Our Lady of Mercy Academy and a branch house for the nuns opened there in 1885.

A new school, the portion of the present building north of the bell tower, was dedicated September 12, 1898. The convent section of the building along Kenner Road was not completed until 1905. The Carson mansion then became the Mt. Carmel Home for employed and retired women. In 1908, the Sisters, celebrating fifty years in Cincinnati, broke ground for a new chapel that was dedicated November 1, 1909.

Over the next twenty-five years, the Mercy Sisters took charge of more suburban parish schools and estab-

lished hospitals, homes for the aged and for older children, and schools of their own. The Order founded Our Lady of Cincinnati College (later Edgecliff College) in Walnut Hills in 1935 and currently occupies a number of buildings on Grandview Avenue in that neighborhood.

Our Lady of Mercy Academy became a diocesan high school in 1929, but by 1957, enrollment had dropped from around 300 to one hundred, and the school was closed. The building then became the Provincial novitiate—a residence and training center. In the late 1960s, it, too, was closed; furnishings and some of the art works were sold at auction. Though the Salvation Army offered one million dollars for the property, Archbishop Karl Alter would not approve the sale. On January 14, 1970, the U.S. Department of Labor bought the land and buildings for $208,000.

The Job Corps Center opened in May, offering academic and vocational training to men and women sixteen through twenty-one years old, from low-income homes. The program provides housing, health and dental care, counseling, meals, pay and clothing allowances, recreational programs, and job placement. The Cincinnati Center offers training in business skills, health occupations, automotive mechanics, building maintenance, welding, carpentry, and culinary arts.

**Turn left on Ezzard Charles Drive, left on Linn Street.**

In the early twentieth century, the West End teemed with apartments, tenements, and small businesses. Today, most of the area has been cleared, and only a few blocks of the **20 Linn Street Business District** remain.

Through the 1920s and 1930s, Linn Street between Gest and Liberty Streets was crowded with stores offering a range of goods and services to residents, many of whom lived in rooms and apartments on the floors above. These small-scale commercial enterprises were little affected by the Depression, although some businesses gave way to larger chain stores.

Most West End shops also survived federal housing construction which lowered population density and pushed many Linn Street businesses northward. Only in the late 1950s did this pattern of living and doing business change as slum clearance began on a massive scale. As the number of residents decreased significantly, small businesses had to struggle to survive.

By the early 1960s, commerce in the West End was centered around the remaining population, mostly in Laurel Homes, Lincoln Court, Park Town, Richmond Village and the Stanley Rowe Towers. Along Linn Street were a handful of local services: convenience stores, cleaners, beauty and barber shops, a pawnbroker, a loan company, groceries, a branch bank, and a movie house—the metal-domed Regal Theater, 1201 Linn, built in 1908 as the Casino Theater.

This diminished business district was further hurt in the 1970s by Queensgate II. Hoping to promote renovation of the remaining nineteenth century houses in the Betts-Longworth district just south of Ezzard Charles Drive, the city bought up property and moved residents out, anticipating the sale of these houses. When rehabilitation slowed and the population of the West End continued to decline, even major chain stores had difficulties. After losing money for several years, Kroger abandoned its store at 1515 Linn Street, turning the lease over to the community's Arts Consortium.

Established in 1972, the Consortium is a nonprofit organization offering instruction in art, music, dance, and drama. It also sponsors cultural events including a recreation of the West End Cotton Club of the 1930s. The former supermarket building is decorated with the "Wall of Progress" mural, completed in 1975, which depicts black culture in the West End.

In addition to offices and classrooms, the Arts Consortium's building houses galleries that exhibit the work of local black artists. When the Museum Center at Union Terminal opens, the Consortium will also maintain an exhibit facility there.

Although business activity along Linn Street has suffered in recent decades, the street remains a focal point for the surrounding community. It offers a good central location for local institutions including a YMCA branch, a health clinic, and one of the remaining links to the old West End, **21 Washburn School,** 1425 Linn Street.

Constructed in 1910 as the Eleventh District School, the 4-story buff brick building was designed by E. H. Dornette and is trimmed in terra cotta with plaques honoring American writers and thinkers such as Louis Agassiz, Washington Irving, Edgar Allan Poe, and Henry Wadsworth Longfellow. Washburn's 1987-1988 student body of 629, all black and 97% from homes on public assistance, consistently achieved top scores in city testing. According to Principal Jennifer Cottingham, hard work on the part of students, staff, and faculty made this one of the best elementary schools in Cincinnati.

Not all of the housing built over the last fifty years in the West End was publicly sponsored. In the 1950s, as part of Queensgate II, the city planned for private developers to construct low to moderate-income housing for Laurel-Richmond. After several false starts, partly because out-of-town developers were unsure of city plans and requirements, ground was broken for **22 Park Town,** 858 Wade Walk, in 1960.

Like other public housing in the area, Park Town was built in part with federal funds, but it was developed privately. The 323 units in the complex were laid out in smaller blocks with apartments ranging in size from studios to four bedrooms. Most significantly, Park Town is a cooperative, and the project's goal is to have all units owner-occupied.

The Park Town complex is controlled by a board of nine resident directors and two consultants, and is wholly self-governed. Although the complex is intended for low-income families, the costs, particularly the downpayments, are higher than public housing. Thus, when Park Town opened in 1962, it filled up slowly. Nevertheless, more than twenty years later, almost one-quarter of Park Town's residents had lived here since the units opened, and 85% looked toward eventual ownership of their apartments.

**23 Richmond Village,** 871 Ezzard Charles Drive, is another private housing complex and was built at the same time as Park Town. Richmond Village is privately owned and managed, and although many of its residents qualify for housing aid, they pay full market rents.

The quarters of **24 Engine Company No. 29 and Ladder Company No. 2,** at the northeast corner of Liberty and Linn Streets, is now the only firehouse in the West End. But when this engine house was erected in 1939, there were four firehouses with six engine and ladder companies located in this part of the city.

At that time, the West End had approximately 43,000 inhabitants living and working in more than 10,000 densely-packed structures, most of which dated from the nineteenth century. In an area so susceptible to major fires, the fire department had to maintain large numbers of men and machines.

Before this firehouse was built, West End fire companies were located at 604 West Fifth Street, Ninth and Freeman, 434 Bank Street, and Wade and Freeman. After Laurel Homes was completed in 1938, the city decided to move one engine and ladder company closer to the complex. The new buff brick and concrete Art Moderne style firehouse also provided space for a fire department training facility.

Until 1916, firefighters had been trained on the job. Then drill schools were established in each fire district. By the late 1930s, these gave way to one centralized school designed to train new men before they were assigned to companies. The new facility had a 7-story drill tower that gave recruits practical experience using ladders, rescue gear, and hose lines in a multi-story situation. The tower also helped the department weed out recruits who had difficulty with heights.

The West End's fire companies were among the busiest in the city until slum clearance and freeway construction reduced the number of people and structures in this vicinity. Most of the companies in the West End were gradually disbanded or moved. Only Engine 29 and Ladder 2 were retained, along with their centrally-located house, newer and larger than any of the others in the area, and the Fire College (as the drill school became known in the 1940s).

**Turn left on Poplar Street.**

Named for the first director of CMHA, **25 Stanley Rowe Towers,** 1621 Linn Street and 835 Poplar Street, houses 685 people in 436 units. Built in 1964 at a cost of more than $4 million, these two structures were constructed when the popularity of high-rise apartments was at its peak. Rowe Towers was to house families in one 13-story block and the elderly and handicapped in the other 14-story block.

In time, CMHA realized that high-rises were not good homes for families with children. Parents were unable to supervise children easily, even in the playground that was part of the complex. Children kept indoors frequently played in the hallways and elevators, creating hazards and maintenance problems. Therefore, as families moved out of Rowe Towers, the 2-bedroom apartments were adapted to the needs of the elderly and handicapped.

Today, **26 Sands Montessori School,** 940 Poplar Street, once a neighborhood elementary school, is one of Cincinnati's alternative schools.

Cincinnati architects Tietig & Lee designed this attractive brick and stone building that opened in 1912. The present structure replaced the old Fourteenth District School that had been erected here in 1862. The 27-room school had a capacity of 1,400 students, K-8. It was named for George F. Sands, principal of Third Intermediate School (located on the site of present-day Bloom Junior High) and president of the National Base Ball Association, 1867-1868. In 1931, the first year for which statistics are available, Sands enrolled 1,074 West End youngsters, 78% of them white.

Changes in the West End brought changes to the school. While the total enrollment remained constant into the 1950s, the percentage of black students rose to 45% in 1940-1941, then to 71% in 1945-1946. By 1965-1966, all of the school's 913 students were black. Subsequently, the number of students declined, reaching 312 in 1978-1979, the last year Sands served as a neighborhood school.

Faced with court-ordered desegregation, the Cincinnati Board of Education merged its three Montessori programs, and Sands became a Montessori school, grades K-6, in 1979. Sands Montessori School maintained equal numbers of black and

white students, and in 1987-1988, enrollment was 681.

While academically oriented, Sands' Montessori program addresses the "whole child"—intellectually, socially, physically, and emotionally—to create independent, self-motivated and self-disciplined learners. The school offers Suzuki violin, band, computer lab, Great Books, and Young Authors, a creative writing program.

**Turn right on Freeman Avenue.**

Beginning in 1912, Redland Field, later named **27 Crosley Field,** 1200 Findlay Street at Western Avenue, was the home of the Cincinnati Reds. As early as 1860, Cincinnati had a baseball club, but the team known as the Red Stockings was founded on July 23, 1866. Imbued with a desire not only to play but also to win, amateur clubs began to recruit and pay talented players. In 1868, the Cincinnati Base Ball Club, as it was officially known, hired four professionals.

After the 1868 season, the club decided to field an all-professional team. Although such a move had been discussed elsewhere, the Cincinnati club was the first to act. The 1869 Red Stockings, with talent gathered from across the nation, was unbeaten in all sixty-nine games and won another sixty-one the next year.

This streak was broken when the team lost to the Brooklyn Atlantics on June 14, 1870. After this, the club disintegrated. The next year, when the National Association of Professional Base-Ball Clubs was formed, largely as a result of the popularity brought to the game by the winning Reds, the Cincinnati club was not in it. The team was a founding member of the National League in 1876, but was thrown out four years later for allowing beer in the stands and for renting the field to amateur teams on Sundays.

The Cincinnati team played at several fields throughout the city before settling on a site at Western Avenue and Findlay in 1884.

In 1902, a consortium including "Boss" George B. Cox, Julius and Max Fleischmann, and August "Garry" Herrmann, who was to run the club until 1927, purchased the team and built the first concrete grandstands in baseball. The Palace of Fans, an ornate structure adorned with Classical style columns and pillars, was home to the Reds for another ten years.

As baseball became increasingly popular, the Reds outgrew the Palace, and in 1912, the club built Redland Field, its stadium for more than half a century. The stadium was renamed Crosley Field in 1934 when the Reds were owned by Cincinnati business-man and inventor Powel Crosley, Jr.

In the opinion of baseball afici-onados, the first night game was one of the most notable events to take place in this ball park. As early as 1909, Garry Herrmann had experimented with night games, but professional baseball's first official night game was not played until 1935 when Crosley convinced the league to permit the Reds to play under the lights.

By the late 1930s, both the city and the club were dissatisfied with the old stadium. The West End was by then a slum, and driving and parking there were difficult. The 1948 Cincin-nati *Metropolitan Master Plan* called for a multi-sports stadium to be built on the riverfront just east of the Suspension Bridge.

This plan languished for another decade until Crosley threatened to move the team or sell it if the city did not improve conditions at the old stadium. In response, the city pro-vided more parking space, and the club remodeled and expanded seating to almost 30,000.

After Crosley's death in 1961, the

*Crosley Field provided a more distinctive and intimate setting for ballgames than its successor, Riverfront Stadium, but by the 1960s, its size and location had made it less attractive and profitable.*

Reds were sold to William DeWitt (1902-1982), past general manager and owner of several other teams, who opposed a downtown stadium loca-tion. Nevertheless, the team and the city eventually settled on a riverfront site east of the Suspension Bridge, and in 1968, ground was broken for the new stadium.

On June 24, 1970, the last game, a victory against the San Francisco Giants, was played at Crosley Field. The Reds had played 4,523 games there, winning National League pen-nants in 1939 and 1961, and World Championships in 1919 and 1940.

Although Crosley Field has been torn down, it is preserved in the memories of Cincinnati baseball fans, in a ballfield in Blue Ash that combines some features and fragments from the old stadium, and by Phillips Supply Company, 1 Crosley Field Lane, which occupies a building on the site of the field and has put down a home plate where the old home plate was located and set up a block of grandstand seats.

**Turn right on Dayton Street.**

**28** **Dayton Street,** between Linn and Baymiller Streets, was first developed in the 1860s. The eastern portion of the street was a subdivision of Charles S. Clarkson, real estate speculator in both Clifton and the West End.

Among the earliest houses on the street is the 2-story Italian Renais-sance style brick and painted sand-stone residence at 830. It was built by George Hatch, a Mt. Adams devel-oper, soap and candle manufacturer,

and Southern sympathizer who became mayor of Cincinnati in 1861 and left town immediately after his term ended.

Another early resident of Dayton Street was Silas Snodgrass, a carpen-ter, builder, and contractor who moved his family to 817, a 3-story brick home with a facade identical to that of 815, during the Civil War. Toward the end of the war, tanner Henry Martin moved into 809, and for the next sixty years, members of his family occupied that house. Joseph Earnshaw, an English-born surveyor and landscape engineer who was involved with the landscaping of Spring Grove Cemetery, lived at 846.

In the 1880s, Dayton Street acquired its reputation as "Million-aires Row." Many of the early houses had been given highly ornamented facades, and several new ones were built in the richly embellished Italian Renaissance Revival style.

Part of Dayton Street's attractive-ness for some residents was its prox-imity to businesses in the basin. The Hauck Brewery, for example, was only a block away. By 1880, the 2-story brick house with stone facade at 812, as well as the homes at 816 and 842, were owned by Hauck family members. Those at 808, 835, and 847, belonged to the Windisch and Wet-terer brewing families who also had large plants not far away.

Other residents of Dayton Street included Andrew Hickenlooper, a Civil War brevet brigadier general and later head of Cincinnati Gas-Light & Coke Company on Fourth Street, who lived at 838. Hickenlooper's house is notable for its elaborately ornamented stone facade including a decorative swag above the second-story center win-dow. Alice and Annie Laws, who established the city's first free kinder-garten and the nursing and teacher's training schools that were later affil-iated with the University of Cincinnati, lived in the 2-story stone and brick house at 818 Dayton Street. Large carriage houses are still standing behind both of these homes.

By the early decades of the twen-tieth century, however, most well-to-do Cincinnatians had left the West End and had been replaced first by middle-income families, then by lower-income people, including many Euro-pean immigrants and blacks.

By the early 1920s, Dayton Street had roughly thirty houses which were

home to seventy-two adults, many of whom were single people living in flats and rooms carved out of the older houses. There were only seven single-family homes on the street.

A decade later, at the worst point in the Depression, there were just three single-family dwellings left here, and eighty-two people called Dayton Street home. Post-World War II prosperity reversed the trend; the number of single-family owner-occupied residences gradually increased. Nevertheless, in 1948, eighty people still lived on the block.

By 1956, thirteen houses were owner-occupied and sixteen were single-family dwellings. A number of homes, such as those at 813 and 825, went from multiple to single residences. That year, city government began using federal funds to raze much of the West End, creating a housing shortage. By 1963, there were only seven single-family houses on the block, although fourteen owners lived on the street. The population of the street declined, partly because of some demolition but also because few people wanted to live in the West End.

Nevertheless, a number of Cincinnatians were committed to the rehabilitation of the West End. In the mid-1960s, the Miami Purchase Association (MPA), a local preservation group, made Dayton Street both its headquarters and its particular project, buying a number of the houses and renovating them or selling them to persons interested in restoration. The John Hauck House at 812 served as a museum and the Association's office until the organization moved to Memorial Hall on Elm Street next to Music Hall in 1988.

Despite MPA's efforts, the number of single-family homes and resident owners has remained relatively constant. As of 1987, twelve of the twenty-eight structures on the street were single family, and nine or ten property owners lived here. Four houses were vacant, and approximately sixty-five adults lived on the block.

**Turn right on Linn Street, left on Liberty Street.**

Since August 1928, the congregation of **29 Revelation Baptist Church,** 1556 John Street, has occupied what was originally the syna-gogue of Ahabeth Achim (Brethren in Love), erected in 1866.

Ahabeth Achim, a congregation of Polish Jews, was organized in 1848 in Over-the-Rhine. In 1891, it merged with another downtown Orthodox group, Sh'ereth Israel (Remnant of Israel), founded in 1855. The group followed the early twentieth-century movement of Jews out of the West End, completed a synagogue on Reading Road in 1906, and finally merged with Wise Temple in 1931.

In 1904, the German Evangelical Lutheran Emmaus Church bought the synagogue; it sold the building to Revelation Baptist in 1928.

Revelation Baptist Church, an important black institution in the community, was founded on November 20, 1921, when twelve members met in a small room on George Street. The congregation grew and moved to quarters on West Fifth Street before settling here. From 1960 to 1966, Revelation's pastor was the Reverend Fred L. Shuttlesworth, a nationally recognized civil rights activist and secretary to Martin Luther King, Jr.'s Southern Christian Leadership Conference. The church was renovated and rededicated April 24, 1977. Ten years later, Revelation Baptist Church had some 750 members and was active in community outreach work.

**Turn left on Central Parkway.**

The area of the West End that is north of Liberty Street and between Central Parkway and Linn Street was always a mix of housing and industry. Nineteenth-century businessmen located their factories and warehouses here to take advantage of the nearby canal, and even in the twentieth century, numerous workshops and medium-size plants continued to operate in both old and new structures scattered throughout this district. One of the largest concerns was the **30 Schoenling Brewing Company,** 1625 Central Parkway, now a part of the Hudepohl-Schoenling Brewing Company.

Originally this site was occupied by the Schoenling Coal & Ice Company, which the Schoenling and Lichtendahl families had started in the mid-nineteenth century. Edward A. Schoenling (1889-1982), son of the firm's founder, decided to enter the brewing business immediately after the repeal of Prohibition when, the story goes, he went to the Bruckmann Brewery for a case of beer and had to wait in a line two blocks long.

The brewery grew from a small local operation to a modest regional business selling in sixteen states. By the 1980s, the company occupied an 11-building complex that included a number of older structures which the company adapted to brewing operations. Among these are an ice house, the first brewhouse, a cooperage or barrel-making shop, a 3-story former apartment building, and a bakery. A bottle house stands on the site of the old coalyard.

The main bottling plant, built in 1947, has tiled interior walls, stainless steel doors, and terrazzo floors. Portions of the below-ground walls were designed in such a way that one day the brewery could knock out these sections and have access to a proposed subway that was to run below the parkway.

Schoenling constructed additional cellars, warehouses, and other buildings in the 1960s and 1970s, and took over two former film distribution offices on either side of the bottling plant. A warehouse that had been occupied by the nationally-known Ahrens-Fox Fire Engine Company, was razed for expansion.

In 1985, Schoenling employed 160 workers in a computerized operation that produced 350,000 barrels or one million gallons of Little Kings Cream Ale, Top Hat, and Big Jug beer annually. The ale, a specialty brew, was largely responsible for Schoenling's continued survival during a period when many other small breweries went out of business or were purchased by larger firms.

The following year, the company merged with the Hudepohl Brewing Company, and all brewing operations were combined at the Central Avenue plant. In 1988, under the leadership of President Ken Lichtendahl, Hudepohl-Schoenling had 120 employees and an annual production of 500,000 barrels. The company distributed its products in forty-four states, Canada, and Taiwan, making it the ninth largest brewery by volume in the United States.

**Tour ends.**

# Older Suburbs

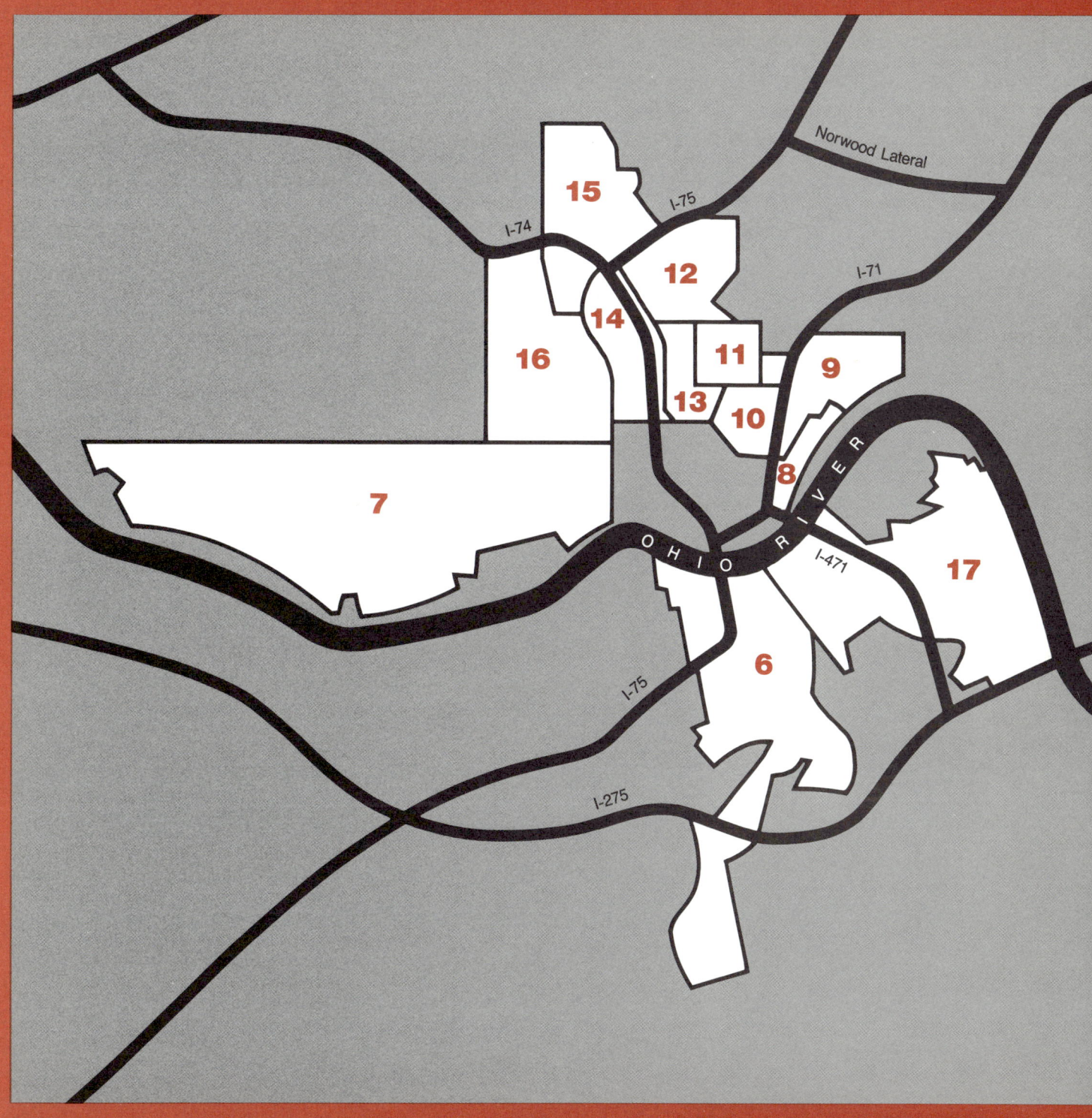

6
**Covington**

7
**Price Hill-Delhi**

8
**Mt. Adams-Eden Park**

9
**Walnut Hills**

10
**Mt. Auburn**

11
**Corryville**

12
**Clifton**

13
**Fairview-Clifton Heights**

14
**Mohawk-Brighton-
Camp Washington**

15
**Cumminsville-Northside-
South Cumminsville**

16
**Fairmount**

17
**Newport-Ft. Thomas**

# Tour 6

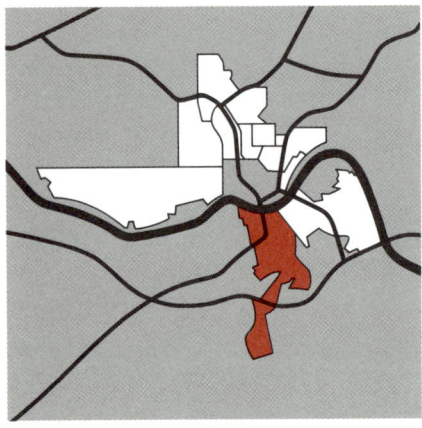

# Covington

Covington, Kentucky's fourth largest city, is located across the Ohio River from Cincinnati. The original plat of August 31, 1815, ran from the Licking River to just west of present-day Madison Avenue and from the Ohio River to south of Fifth Street. During the nineteenth and early twentieth centuries, Covington grew considerably and now extends west to Devou Park, I-71, Kenton Vale, and the L&N Railroad tracks, south beyond I-275, and east along Taylor Mill Road to the Licking River.

Covington's first permanent white resident was Thomas Kennedy, a Pennsylvanian who came to the area around 1790. After staying briefly in Cincinnati, he bought 200 acres from James Welch and began operating a ferryboat across the Ohio to Cincinnati. Around 1795, Kennedy also opened a tavern. At that time, there were fewer than seventy residents in the area, which was called either the Point, from its location at the mouth—or point—of the Licking River, or Kennedy's Ferry.

In 1814, Kennedy sold 150 acres to John S. Gano (1766-1822), Richard M. Gano (1774-1815), and Thomas D. Carneal (1786-1860), speculators who set up a number of towns throughout the vicinity. The Ganos, veterans of the War of 1812, named the town after their commander, General Leonard Covington (b. 1768), who died at the Battle of Chrysler Field in 1813.

The first sale of property in Covington took place in March 1815 when almost one hundred lots were sold at prices ranging from $8 to $12 per front foot, and 200 more were scheduled for sale in May. By then, Carneal had sold most of his holdings to Bakewell, Page & Bakewell of Philadelphia. John Gano and his son, David, continued to sell land until the Panic of 1819 when, unable to keep up payments, they were forced to return part of Kennedy's property to him.

Over the next few years, Covington established a 4-man town patrol and built a small log schoolhouse that also served as church and courthouse. Residents formed the first volunteer fire company in 1821, an important service at a time when fewer than eleven of the town's buildings were made of brick. By then, Alexander Connelly had set up a "house of public entertainment" on Garrard Street north of Second Street, and Benjamin W. Leathers built a brick store and bank at the northwest corner of Greenup Street and present-day Park Place.

In 1824, the Covington Company, which had founded the town, was dissolved. A settlement between Gano's heirs and Bakewell, Page & Bakewell split the company's assets, including 181 unsold lots. Two years later, the first trustees, headed by Connelly, were elected, and they immediately conducted a census, which found 404 residents.

A year later, Carneal sold seven lots on the riverfront between Greenup and Scott to a group of investors who wanted to build a cotton factory. They were led by two Cincinnati businessmen, Charles MacAlester, Jr., a grocer and produce merchant, and Robert Buchanan (1797-1879), a merchant and commission agent who was later a director of the Western Insurance Company and president of Spring Grove Cemetery Association. The next year, Buchanan also helped to establish the McNickle Rolling Mill, which processed steel, just west of the cotton factory.

By 1836, Covington could boast of a nail factory, a sawmill, five tobacco and five cigar factories, two distilleries, a brewery, a ropewalk, and a second cotton manufacturer, all of which helped boost the town's

*Nineteenth-century Covington was an important manufacturing center with many plants concentrated near the Licking River as well as along the Ohio riverfront and the railroad lines.*

population ahead of its neighbor to the east, Newport.

Covington's population exceeded 1,500 by 1834 when it was chartered as a city. Its first newspaper, *The Farmer's Record and Covington Literary Journal*, was published in 1831, and in 1833, the town got its first firehouse, on the public square between Court and Greenup Streets. Three years later the town's trustees provided Fire Company No. 1 with a hand-drawn engine. In 1835, Major John Tilford became president of the newly-founded Northern Bank of Kentucky, with an office in Covington and headquarters in Lexington.

Until 1834, the only regular religious meetings in Covington were held by the Methodist Society, founded in 1827 with ten members. As Covington grew in the 1830s and 1840s, two Catholic and four Protestant congregations were founded, and in 1835, the Western Baptist Educational Society purchased 370 acres southwest of town.

In 1840, after subdividing and selling lots, the Society hired Seneca Palmer, who also planned the Lane Seminary in Cincinnati, to design a theological institute. The school opened five years later, but over the next decade, it was torn by conflicts over slavery, and in the mid-1850s, it was dissolved. During the Civil War, the seminary building was used as a federal hospital and afterward was sold to the Sisters of the Poor of St. Francis who established St. Elizabeth Hospital.

Covington's population jumped from 2,026 in 1840 to 9,408 a decade later, and was nearly 16,500 before the Civil War. The city also expanded geographically, as major annexations quadrupled its size and extended its boundaries from Twelfth Street in 1840 to the Wallace farm, south of Twentieth Street, in 1850.

With growth came political tensions. As in Cincinnati, a large number of those who came to Covington were from Germany. By 1854, approximately one-third of Covington's residents were foreign-born; this sparked a nativist backlash. In 1855, candidates belonging to the American Party captured the entire municipal ticket. For several years, local government passed back and forth between Democrats, who often represented the foreign-born, and a group called "The Opposition," composed of Unionists, Freesoilers, and Know-Nothings, who, in a slave state, dared not call themselves Republicans.

Pride in German culture, as well as nativism, caused Covington's German community to draw more closely together, and in 1855, the Covington *Turnverein*, or Turners Society, an organization committed to physical training as well as the preservation of German culture in America, was formed.

These social and political tensions did not hamper Covington's economy, which grew steadily in the 1850s. Among the city's major businessmen were Amos and Vincent Shinkle, who invested in coal and riverboats, and Robert Hemingray, whose glass manufacturing company made electrical insulators for telegraph wires. The packing house of Milward & Oldershaw on the Licking River sent its products as far as Europe. During these years, Covington constructed a city hall, hired a chief engineer for the fire volunteers, and directed improvement of wharf facilities. The completion of the Covington & Lexington Railroad in the early 1850s sparked a building boom and pulled the business district away from the courthouse and marketplace toward its terminal at Pike and Washington Streets.

In 1841, a Board of School Visitors was established, and that fall, a public school was opened for 150 students. Over the next decade, enrollments in the three city schools grew to 650, and the board established Kentucky's first public high school. In 1852, a fourth district school opened and the city gave J. Southgate an 18-year franchise to provide gas light to city residents.

The Civil War disrupted some of Covington's business, but it also sparked new industry and redirected the city's commerce, tying it more closely to Cincinnati. Recognizing this, many Cincinnati businessmen who had earlier opposed building a bridge over the Ohio River, now saw it as a means of more closely linking the economies of the two cities. On New Year's Day 1867, the Covington & Cincinnati Suspension Bridge, long sought by Amos Shinkle, was dedicated and later that year, the 3-year-old Cincinnati, Newport & Covington Company ran the first mule-drawn streetcars across it.

As early as 1854, Covington had been tied to Lexington by the Covington & Lexington Railroad. Through several changes of ownership, this railway became the Kentucky Central Railroad, part of the Chesapeake & Ohio in the late 1870s and the Louisville & Nashville in 1890. By the 1880s, railroads connected Covington to the East Coast and to the South, which was trying to rebuild its industries. Covington's rail connections to the north also improved with opening of the C&O Bridge to Cincinnati in 1888.

The improvement of transportation made it possible for manufacturers to locate plants in Covington while doing business in Cincinnati, and for workers to live on either side of the river. During these years, Covington, then Kentucky's second largest city, entered its period of greatest growth.

Covington's prosperity was most clearly reflected in the expansion of business from the 1880s through the turn of the century. The Covington Machine Works began operation in 1880, and in 1885, the New

England Distilling Company opened on Pike Street between Washington and Russell. By 1886, the city had three iron rolling mills, five banks with a combined capital in excess of $2.25 million, and four breweries, including the Bavarian Brewing Company.

The Kelley-Koett Company, which pioneered in the manufacturing of X-ray equipment, was founded in 1903, a year after the Stewart Iron Works moved from across the river. The same year, Haehne Provision Company created the Blue Grass Brand Meats & Lard Company. Among the city's other major industries were the Sebastian Lathe Company, the Licking Valley Iron Works, and the Star Foundry.

*The consolidation and electrification of streetcar lines contributed to the growth of commuter traffic between Covington and Cincinnati in the late nineteenth and early twentieth centuries.*

City services were also extended and professionalized in these years. In 1892, the Covington, Newport & Cincinnati Railway was formed out of several horsecar lines, and in 1901, the Union Heat, Light & Power Company replaced several earlier gas and electric companies. The volunteer fire companies were replaced by a professional fire department which, by 1873, had four engine houses and a hook and ladder company. Covington's telephone exchange began operating in 1879, and in 1882, the marshal's office was abolished in favor of a police department. In 1888, J. D. Hearne founded Covington's YMCA, and in 1901, the Covington Public Library opened as successor to several earlier libraries including one run by the volunteer fire companies. At its centennial in 1915, Covington boasted a police force of sixty-five, eight fire companies, twelve public school buildings, and the 635-acre Devou Park, as well as three smaller parks and two playgrounds.

In 1900, Covington's population stood at 42,938, and the city began another round of annexations, adding Central Covington (1906), Latonia (1909), Devou Park (1911), Latonia Terrace (1913), Rosedale (1916), and West Covington (1916). In the process, the city's population rose to almost 57,000.

Between 1920 and 1930, the city continued to grow, but outlying Kenton County grew faster. Suburban growth was slowed by the Great Depression and World War II, but after the war, the exodus of Americans from older cities to newer communities took its toll. Between 1950 and 1960, Covington's population declined by 6.3%; a 1984 estimate put it at 46,422, down more than 3,000 from the 1980 census.

In the late 1960s, responding to suburban growth, Covington embarked on a program of urban renewal designed to remove areas of blight while protecting the city's nineteenth-century architectural heritage. By 1987, the city had created thirteen national historic districts covering more than 3,800 buildings. Covington also sponsored another half-dozen local historic districts in order to encourage the rehabilitation of older housing for both commercial and residential purposes, and has passed historic preservation ordinances and created an Urban Design Review Board.

Covington has also tried to redevelop its riverfront and upper west end. Since the 1970s, the regional Internal Revenue Center, a new justice center, a new library and a number of hotels, restaurants, condominiums and businesses have all been built here, and Rivercenter, a complex of offices and hotels, is planned for the 1990s.

## Covington

Tour Length
9 miles

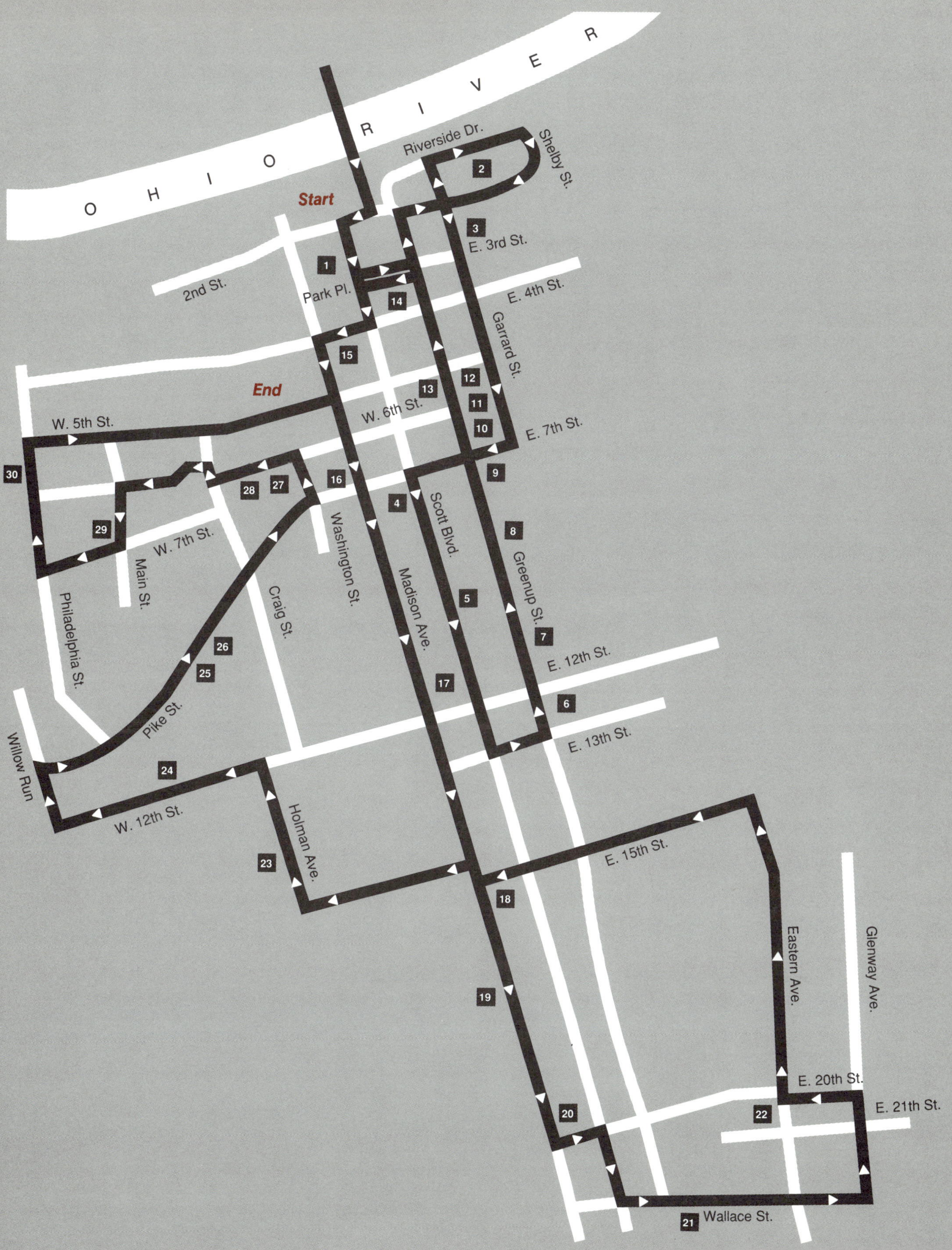
North
OHIO RIVER
Start
End
Riverside Dr.
Shelby St.
E. 3rd St.
2nd St.
Park Pl.
E. 4th St.
Garrard St.
W. 5th St.
W. 6th St.
E. 7th St.
W. 7th St.
Main St.
Philadelphia St.
Craig St.
Washington St.
Madison Ave.
Scott Blvd.
Greenup St.
E. 12th St.
E. 13th St.
Pike St.
Willow Run
W. 12th St.
Holman Ave.
E. 15th St.
Eastern Ave.
Glenway Ave.
E. 20th St.
E. 21th St.
Wallace St.
1
2
3
4
5
6
7
8
9
10
11
12
13
14
15
16
17
18
19
20
21
22
23
24
25
26
27
28
29
30

# Tour 6

# Covington

▶ ▶ ▶ ▶ ▶ ▶

**Tour begins in Cincinnati at the John R. Roebling Suspension Bridge. Cross the Ohio River. Turn right on Second Street and left on Scott Boulevard.**

The Covington branch of **1 The Northern Bank of Kentucky,** was located at East Third Street and Scott Boulevard in what was then the heart of Covington's commercial district. The 2-story Greek Revival style structure was built around 1836 and is probably Covington's oldest commercial building. The bank also had offices in Lexington and Paris, and by the 1870s, it was, in terms of deposits, the largest bank in the state.

*The former Northern Bank of Kentucky building is located a few blocks from the Ohio River in what was once the commercial center of Covington.*

Among the presidents of the Covington branch were Colonel James Taylor, son of the founder of Newport, and William and John P. Ernst. William Ernst, whose family lived in apartments behind the bank, served as president of the bank from 1867 to 1888. He was succeeded by his son, John. In 1895, John P. Ernst resigned the presidency of the bank in order to turn his attention to the family's other Covington bank, the more profitable German National, which was located closer to the center of Covington's business district on Madison Avenue.

In 1896, under the direction of a new president, the bank moved to newly remodeled offices at Sixth Street and Madison Avenue, near the city's five other banks. This move helped revive the bank, but after Kentucky passed tighter banking laws, the directors of the Northern Bank decided to liquidate its assets.

Until the passage of Prohibition, the old bank building was used by Myers & Company, distillers and wholesalers of liquors, who probably added the third story. The next occupant was the Mosler Safe Company, located here until 1958. After that, the Wadsworth Electric Company used it for storage until 1970. The structure continued to be a warehouse through the late 1980s, when the City of Covington targeted it for renewal.

**Turn left on East Third Street, left on Greenup Street, right on Second Street, left on Garrard Street, and right on Riverside Drive. Follow Riverside Drive right to Shelby Street and turn right on Second Street.**

The history of Covington begins at "The Point," where the Ohio and Licking rivers come together. Legend has it that Indian hunting and war parties rendezvoused at this site. In 1782, General George Rogers Clark gathered his forces here on the way to fight the Shawnees in Ohio. Much of Covington's earliest settlement took place in what is now designated as **2 The Ohio Riverside Historic District.**

In the early 1790s, Thomas Kennedy set up his ferry and built a large stone house and tavern here. Since then, many noted Covington residents have lived in this area. Riverside House, 321 Riverside Drive, was built in 1916 by the artist Charles McLaughlin, who tried to model the structure after antebellum Southern mansions. The McLaughlin family owned the house until 1965, when it was sold and restored.

The Fallis-Lovell House, 412 East Second Street, dates from the late 1850s and was erected by Thomas Porter, a real estate developer. Daniel J. Fallis, a Cincinnati banker and founder of Merchant's National Bank, purchased the residence in the early 1860s, and it remained in his family until 1950. The Greek Revival pillars were added around the turn of the century, when the house was moved to face Second Street.

At 405 East Second Street is the Gano-Southgate House, often called the Carneal House after Thomas Carneal, one of the founders of Covington, though he apparently had nothing to do with the dwelling. The house was built around 1820-1821 for Aaron G. Gano, son of Carneal's partner, John S. Gano. Aaron's brother, Daniel, sold the house in 1825 to William W. Southgate (1800-1845), a prominent lawyer and Whig politician, and a slaveowner.

Because of its age and glamour, the house is the subject of several myths. According to legend, the house was the scene of a grand ball for the Marquis de Lafayette in 1825, and later served as a station in the Underground Railroad. The house is also alleged to have a ghost, the Lady in Gray, Sallie Carneal (1821-1850), who supposedly killed herself for love of Lafayette. In fact, Lafayette was in Covington only long enough to stop for a drink at a tavern, and Sallie Carneal was four years old at the time and lived another twenty-five years. Nor were the proslavery Southgates likely to have harbored runaways.

Apart from legend and history, the Federal style house is distinguished by its architecture, which follows the principles of Andrea Palladio, the noted sixteenth-century Italian theorist. An 1835 addition to the back of the house is in the Greek Revival style.

Across from the Gano-Southgate House is the Laidley House, 404 East Second Street. Built after the Civil War, it was first occupied by W. J. Lowry, a commission merchant. By the mid-1880s, the house belonged to Frederick A. Laidley, a Cincinnati businessman involved in river trade, commission sales, and porkpacking. The house remained in the family for almost a hundred years.

The Lovell-Graziani House, 326 East Second Street, a French Second Empire style mansion, was built for Howell L. Lovell, Sr. (1824-1900), one of the owners of the Rich, Lovell & Buffington Tobacco Company. In 1873, Lovell moved his factory from Cincinnati to Scott Street, and this house was probably built in the late 1870s. Benjamin F. Graziani, a lawyer and reform politician, later occupied it.

Across from the Lovell-Graziani House is Governor's Point, 323 East Second Street, an apartment and condominium complex. The 5-story building, constructed in 1926 as the William Booth Memorial Hospital, was on the site of The Castle, the extravagant home of Amos Shinkle (1818-1892). In 1914, the Shinkle family gave the house to the Salvation Army, which used it as a hospital for several years before building a larger facility. In 1979, the Booth Memorial Hospital moved to Florence, Kentucky, and sold the site to the Riverside Development Company, which converted the building to luxury apartments.

At 230-242 East Second Street is Shinkle's Row, a series of seven townhouses probably built in the 1860s by Amos Shinkle. Shinkle was one of Covington's wealthiest and most prominent citizens. He began his career shipping coal, and later owned a fleet of riverboats. As early as 1849, Shinkle began investing in Covington real estate, and when he died, he owned more than twenty lots and had built and sold thirty to forty houses. Aside from The Castle, this row of Renaissance Revival townhouses was Shinkle's largest residential building project. It was restored in the mid 1970s.

**Turn left on Garrard Street.**

Before putting up The Castle, Amos Shinkle lived on **3 Garrard Street,** as did a number of Covington's most prominent citizens.

Among the street's most notable residents were Jonathan D. Hearne (1829-1905) and William Ernst (1813-1895). Hearne, who built the house at 500 in 1874, was a Covington manufacturer, banker, and philanthropist, who, in 1882, became president of Cincinnati's Third National Bank, later a part of the Fifth-Third Bank.

Ernst, a Pennsylvanian, came to Covington in 1838 as a teller for the Northern Bank of Kentucky and became its president in 1867. He erected the Queen Anne style mansion at 401 Garrard Street in the late 1880s. His son Richard (1858-1934), a Republican senator from Kentucky in the 1920s, lived at 405, also built in the 1880s.

The part of Garrard Street south of Fifth was developed later and was often used for multiple-family dwellings. Two luxury apartment buildings, the Burton (now demolished) and the Carlisle were built in 1903 and 1913, respectively.

The Home for Aged and Indigent Women, since 1981 the Covington Ladies Home, 702 Garrard, was founded in 1886. In 1892, the Home

purchased a lot on Garrard Street from Amos Shinkle, and on July 14, 1894, the new facility opened. The Home is governed by an all-female board of managers. The facility is the only privately run non-sectarian residence home in Kenton County and operates on an endowment, without state or federal funding. In 1987, twenty-one women lived here.

**Turn right on East Seventh Street, left on Scott Boulevard.**

Beginning in the 1870s, **4 Scott Boulevard** south of Seventh Street developed as a residential area convenient to downtown Covington. Many of the Italianate and Queen Anne style houses here are larger and more ornate than those built on side streets, and several have been adapted for commercial use.

Emery Row, 810-828, is the most impressive structure along this part of Scott. These 3-story townhouses were built around 1880 by Thomas J. Emery's Sons, since 1850 one of Cincinnati's leading real estate developers.

The design for the houses has been attributed to Samuel Hannaford and is in the Kensington Queen Anne style. Despite the diversity among the units, the north and south halves of the row are mirror images of one another.

From the outset, these townhouses were put to mixed use. Some were subdivided for working-class tenants, while others were owned by affluent residents, a pattern that continued into the 1970s. In 1984, a fire partially destroyed 814 and 816. Three years later, the City of Covington signed an agreement with a local partnership to redevelop Emery Row as ten units for middle to upper-income residents.

The **5 Carnegie Arts Center,** 1028 Scott Boulevard, was built in 1902-1904 and was one of the first public libraries built by the Carnegie Foundation.

Designed in the Beaux Arts style by architects John H. Boll and Charles C. Taylor, the building, which includes a 700-seat auditorium, served as Covington's library until the 1970s, when it was replaced by a new complex at Fifth and Scott Streets. In

1975, the City of Covington leased the building to the Northern Kentucky Arts Council, which sponsors exhibitions, lectures, a gift shop, and public events.

**Turn left on East Thirteenth Street, left on Greenup Street.**

Frank Duveneck (1848-1919) was born in Covington of German immigrant parents, Bernard Decker, who died of cholera in 1849, and Katherine Siemers, a maid in the home of the noted portraitist, James Beard. By the time he was fifteen, Duveneck, who took the name of his stepfather, "Squire" Joseph Duveneck, a local magistrate and justice of the peace, was apprenticed to Covington's Institute of Catholic Art.

Frank Duveneck was raised in **6 The Duveneck Home,** 1226 Greenup Street, and lived here the last twenty years of his life. In 1869, he went to study in Munich at the Royal Academy of Fine Arts, where he shed the conservative idealist style of a church painter to become a realist, conscious of light, technique, and the use of bold, unfinished brushwork. According to all accounts, Duveneck excelled in his studies, but in 1874, he came home, having failed to produce a major work.

Duveneck returned to church painting and executed a few portrait commissions as well as studies of his parents. But Cincinnati did not give him a warm welcome. He taught briefly at the Ohio Mechanics Institute, but held only one show, in a store window. In 1875, he left for Boston, and then Munich, where he became the center of a growing colony of young American artists. John Singer Sargent, one of the United States' most notable painters, later said, "After all's said, Frank Duveneck is the greatest talent of the brush of this generation."

From 1879 to 1881, Duveneck set up his own studio and school in Florence. In the mid-1880s, his use of color lightened and his brushwork softened, allegedly under the influence of Elizabeth Boott, whom he married in 1886. He also turned to nature, painting outdoor scenes and giving up his technique of painting wet-on-wet. According to one art historian, in doing so, "he gave up more than he gained . . . [and] became only a good painter . . . whereas he had been a great one before."

After his wife's death in 1888, Duveneck returned to the United States, living first in Boston and then in his family's Covington home. Duveneck taught at the Art Academy of Cincinnati in the early 1890s, before returning once more to Europe. In 1900, he accepted a permanent appointment to the Art Academy of Cincinnati.

Between 1904 and 1909, he painted a large mural for Covington's Cathedral Basilica, a gift in memory of his mother. Although he was mostly forgotten as a painter in his later years, Duveneck trained a generation of painters at the Art Academy and lived to see an exhibition of his work at the Panama-Pacific Exposition in 1915. He died in Cincinnati four years later and was buried in Mother of God Cemetery in Covington.

In the late 1960s, Duveneck's artistic stock began to rise, and he is now considered a minor American master. His work has been collected by the Cincinnati Art Museum, to which he gave many of his works, and by the Kenton County Public Library. In 1987, the Cincinnati Art Museum held a special exhibit of his work.

In 1850, Covington's black population, mostly household slaves and free blacks, numbered 317, or 3.3% of the population. But as the controversy over slavery flared, increasing numbers of slaveowners shipped their human property away from Covington, which was just across the river from freedom. By 1860, blacks, more than a third of whom were free, accounted for only 1.6% of Covington's population. From these beginnings emerged Covington's black community.

One of that community's earliest leaders was the Reverend Jacob Price (1839-1923), a successful lumber dealer, for whom the **7 Jacob Price Homes,** 1044 Greenup Street, were named. Price was one of the seventy-six free blacks living in Covington before the Civil War. After emancipation, Price, who was literate, established the First (Colored) Baptist Church, where he was pastor, and the first Covington school for blacks. Both the school and church originally met in his Bremen (Pershing) Street home.

Initially, Covington's black population was scattered throughout the

*Covington resident Frank Duveneck, one of the most prominent artists born in the Greater Cincinnati area, is shown here with one of his classes at the Cincinnati Art Academy.*

city, but by the turn of the century, most blacks lived in the area between Eighth to Tenth Streets, from Scott to Greenup. In 1937, after federal housing funds became available for slum clearance and construction of low-rent housing, the Covington Municipal Housing Authority (now the Housing Authority of Covington) began two projects, Latonia Terrace, with 235 units for whites, and Jacob Price Homes, with 163 units for blacks.

Since their completion in 1939, the Price Homes have been desegregated. By the late 1980s, roughly 10% of the tenants here were white. Latonia Terrace has about 15% black families. In the 1970s and 1980s, the Jacob Price Homes were renovated, using federal funds.

After the Civil War, Covington blacks set out to educate themselves, first at classes held in Jacob Price's house and later in the First Baptist Church on Third Street. Out of this effort came the **8 Lincoln-Grant School,** 834 Greenup Street.

In the early 1870s, William Grant (1820-1882), a Democrat, supported legislation to establish black public schools. Grant had been a Republican and a staunch Unionist, and his career was marked by a desire to support black education.

An 1872 amendment to the Covington city charter provided for the education of black children, and the Board of Education hired a teacher and opened a black school. By 1875, 138 children were enrolled in two "colored" schools located in black churches on Madison and Robbins Streets. Three years later, when enrollments had reached 229, the Board of Education was spending two dollars on each black student, about one-half the sum spent on each white pupil.

In 1880, the board built a schoolhouse on land donated by Grant, and six years later, opened a high school. The primary and intermediate schools were known as the Seventh Street School, and the high school was named after Grant. That year, three teachers served more than 200 students. By 1893, enrollment had increased to 439, and the school's nine black teachers were, for the first time, paid salaries nearly equal to those of their white counterparts.

In 1909, when Latonia was annexed to Covington, the Seventh Street School was merged with the black school there, taking its name, the Lincoln School. Thereafter, Covington's black schools were known as the Lincoln-Grant School. The present building, opened in 1932, was designed in the Art Deco style by E. Landberg. The school was integrated in 1965 and closed in 1976.

That fall, the Northern Kentucky Community Center took over most of the facility, sharing it with some school board offices, which remained here until 1987. The community center provides family social services.

The privately owned and federally-subsidized La Salette Gardens Apartments, 706 Greenup Street, provide housing for the elderly and handicapped. Until 1977, however, this 3-story brick Georgian style building was the home of the **9 La Salette Academy.**

In 1856, at the request of Bishop George A. Carrell, the Sisters of Charity of Nazareth opened the Our Lady of La Salette Academy, the first girls' school in the Covington Diocese. The academy occupied a small 2-story brick house at the corner of Seventh and Greenup Streets and offered instruction in both fine arts and "useful arts," including sewing, music, and embroidery.

In 1887, the Sisters of La Sallette erected a new 2-story school. Continued increases in enrollments led to the addition of a third story in 1903 and a new building for the high school in 1939. La Salette had approximately 400 pupils in 1959, but by the 1970s, the number of students had declined. The academy also suffered from a lack of funds and a shortage of teaching Sisters, and closed in 1977. Private developers then purchased the academy and converted it to apartments, which opened in December 1980.

The **10 Baker-Hunt Foundation,** 620 Greenup Street, occupies the former home of Cincinnati businessman John W. Baker. In 1839, he and Henry Von Phul formed Baker & Von Phul, specializing in the sale of "lamps and chandeliers, tallow candles, molds and sperm oil." Although his business was in Cincinnati, Baker purchased the house on Greenup Street in 1854. During the 1860s, he remodeled the interior and added Italianate elements to the exterior.

In 1872 Baker's daughter, Margaretta, married Dr. William Hunt, a physician. She continued to live here after the deaths of her husband and father. In 1922, Hunt and her niece, Kate Scudder, established the Baker-Hunt Foundation to "promote in Covington and the vicinity the study of art, education, and science, and to encourage religious and spiritual life."

The Baker home became the center for the foundation's activities and served as a family museum where some of Hunt's jewelry, family furniture, and paintings by noted local artists Robert Duncanson and Frank Duveneck are on display.

In 1929, the foundation built the Baker-Hunt Natural History Museum behind the old house. The single-story Georgian style building, designed by Frederic Garber, was erected to house the collection of Archie J. Williams, a naturalist and local Boy Scout leader. The museum closed in 1957, and the building is presently used for art classes.

The Baker-Hunt Foundation has provided a variety of programs including a religious school for children, courses in drama, and a crafts shop. The foundation is best known for its program of art education developed by Betty Shenkel, executive director from 1969 to 1984, who shifted the program's emphasis to the fine arts.

The **11 Covington Art Club,** 604 Greenup Street, was established in 1877 as the Young Ladies Art Union for women interested in painting, embroidery, woodworking, and china painting.

Around the turn of the century, the Art Club expanded its interests into municipal reform, supporting Covington's smoke abatement movement and the establishment of city playgrounds. The civic activities and artistic interests of the Covington Art Club helped persuade Kate Scudder that it would be an appropriate neighbor for the Baker-Hunt Foundation, and in 1926, she sold this building to the club.

At present, the Covington Art Club offers programs for book lovers and those interested in drama, arts and crafts, needlework, and spiritual values. The club is also active in civic affairs, administering eyesight tests to pre-school children in Kenton and Campbell counties.

From 1859 to 1873, Jesse and Hannah Grant, the parents of President Ulysses S. Grant, lived in the Greek Revival style **12 Grant House,** 518-520 Greenup Street, which was built in stages from the late 1840s to the 1880s.

Born in Westmoreland, Pennsylvania, Jesse Grant (1794-1873) served as postmaster of Covington from 1866 until 1872. After Grant's death, the house had numerous owners. In the early 1960s, it was divided into apartments, but has since been renovated.

The **13 First United Methodist Church,** 501 Greenup Street, traces its origins to the first Methodist Society in Covington. By 1832, society membership was 195 and the church school served 172 students. That year, the congregation built a new house of worship on Garrard Street. Membership reached 350 by 1843, when the Methodists built yet another church on Scott Boulevard.

After intense debates over slavery at its 1844 General Conference, the Methodist Episcopal Church voted to allow Southerners to form the Methodist Episcopal Church South. Two years later, the Methodist Society in Covington decided to align itself with the Southern branch and formed the Scott Street Methodist Episcopal Church South.

Twenty-seven members remained within the Methodist Episcopal Church, and in 1848, they built a small wooden structure, Wesley Chapel, at the southeast corner of Third and Scott Streets, largely because a city ordinance blocked this "abolitionist church" from meeting in public buildings. Increased membership led Wesley Chapel to construct a Greenup Street Station in 1855.

With substantial financial assistance from wealthy members, most notably Amos Shinkle, the congregation erected the present building in 1867. This High Victorian Gothic style structure, designed by the Cincinnati architectural firm of William Walter & William Stewart, became Union Methodist Episcopal Church. While the group had black members it restricted them to seats in the balcony.

By the early 1930s, financial difficulties had forced the Scott Street Church to attend evening services at Union Methodist. The flooding of the Scott Street Church in 1937 led to increased cooperation between the two congregations. Finally, in 1939, the two churches merged to form the First United Methodist Church.

After reunification, church membership grew from 716 in 1940 to a peak of 901 in 1959. In 1947, the church was damaged by fire and subsequently restored. A March 1986 tornado struck the spire of the church, which was rebuilt. In 1988, the church had about 500 members.

**Turn left on Park Place.**

131

Designed by architect Carl C. Bankemper & Associates and completed in 1969, the **14 Covington-Kenton County Municipal Building,** 303 Court Street, was built to serve both the city and county governments. It replaced the 1902 city building and courthouse at 224 Court Street, which was razed to provide parking. City offices have since been moved out of this building.

The Covington Master Plan of 1967 envisioned the Covington-Kenton County Municipal Building as a major component of a new government center that included a main library, fire station, state offices, and other public buildings. That center never materialized, in part because it was inconvenient to downtown Covington.

In 1974, a city plan committed Covington to rehabilitate rather than replace historic structures, and the just-completed municipal building was condemned to isolation. The building was expanded and received a post-modern restyling in 1986.

*From the 1840s until 1902, this building, located about a block to the north of the present Municipal Building, served as the Kenton County Courthouse.*

*Turn left on Scott Boulevard, right on East Fourth Street, and left on Madison Avenue.*

**15 The Odd Fellows Hall,** 434-440 Madison Avenue, has been a Covington landmark since it was dedicated in 1857. Designed by Gedge & Brothers, the 3-story Greek Revival style building originally consisted of five storefronts, a second floor auditorium, and third floor lodge rooms. Iron rods and walls two feet thick support the second and third floors, which have no pillars. Amos Shinkle, a member of the Odd Fellows, was partly responsible for construction of the lodge building, and because of his connection to John Roebling, it has long been rumored that the suspension of the upper floors was the work of the famed bridge builder.

After the building opened, its auditorium became a community meeting place. At the eve of the Civil War, Kentucky's Union Party met at the hall, and after the war, General Ulysses S. Grant was fêted here. During the war, the building was used to house Confederate prisoners. The hall was also the scene of a duel between State Senator William Goebel and Thomas L. Sanford, second president of the First National Bank. Goebel was later assassinated after a contested gubernatorial election, and his body lay in state here.

The Odd Fellows hall has been the scene of many civic and social events. In the late 1860s, the Covington Theater used the auditorium, and the Tusculan Literary Society met here. Toward the end of the nineteenth century, the auditorium was also used for Chautauqua lectures. In 1906, the New Covington Theater opened, offering "High Class Vaudeville [and the] Latest Moving Picture Between Acts." At various times, religious congregations have met in the hall, and in 1913, the City of Covington sponsored a municipal dance in it.

In the 1920s and 1930s, the hall was used to stage boxing matches and as a nightclub. From the 1940s until the late 1950s, the second floor auditorium was a roller skating rink. Since then, the upper stories have been empty. The building is structurally sound, and its owners have sought funds to rehabilitate it.

The **16 Madison Avenue Business District,** between Third and Robbins Streets, is both a neighborhood and a central business district. It flourished in the late nineteenth century after the construction of the Kentucky Central Railroad and continued to grow during the first half of the twentieth century.

Between 1940 and 1955, about 225 businesses operated here. By 1961, however, that number had decreased to about 195, and by 1988, to approximately 120.

This decline reflects not only the drop in Covington's population, but the growth of suburban shopping centers, especially the Florence Mall, which opened in 1976. As a result, a number of old Covington businesses closed between 1965 and 1985. H. Eilerman & Sons, a men's and boys' clothing store was established in Newport in 1882. Fourteen years later, Henry Eilerman opened a Covington store at the northeast corner of Madison Avenue and Pike Street that remained here until it went out of business in 1973. Constructed in the 1890s, the 4-story Victorian style Eilerman building is now owned and occupied by the Peoples Liberty Bank.

Another Madison Avenue institution, Coppin's Department Store, closed in 1977. Its founder, John R. Coppin, began with a modest dry goods store on Madison Avenue in 1873. His success enabled him to construct the 7-story building at 636 Madison Avenue in 1909. In 1966, Coppin's was acquired by the Chicago-based Gamble's department stores. A decade later, citing a decline in business due to Florence Mall, Coppin's closed. In 1988, the City of Covington purchased the building with plans to renovate it for city offices.

Ostrow's furniture store, 717-719, a fixture in Covington since the early 1940s, went out of business in 1981. The structure was originally used as a stable by undertakers Henry Linneman and Edward Moore and still has a sculpture of a horse's head over the entrance. Since 1983, the building has been home to Storer Communications, which provides cable television service for Boone, Campbell, and Kenton counties.

In addition to independent stores, major chains including Sears, J. C. Penney, and Montgomery Ward also closed their Covington outlets during these years. Ward's opened in Covington about 1930 and closed in 1967. The building it occupied at 727 Madison Avenue features a tiled upper face with medallions depicting Diana the huntress and, inexplicably, what appear to be meat cleavers. This structure is now a furniture store. When it opened in Florence Mall, Sears closed its Covington store. J.C. Penney, Covington's last major department store, closed in 1984.

In response to the attraction of the suburban malls, the City of Covington tried to revitalize downtown business. The Old Town Plaza, opened on Pike Street between Madison and Washington Avenue in 1977, was part of this effort. But the concept of locating small specialty shops in an urban mall has not been a success, largely because of the lack of pedestrian traffic and readily accessible off-street parking. Ten years after the opening of the plaza, many of its storefronts were empty.

Despite these problems, a few businesses continue to do well on Madison Avenue. Peoples Liberty Bank, created by the 1928 merger of two older banks, now has nine branches, and Motch Jewelers, 613 Madison Avenue, established in 1857 by M. C. Motch, has also remained prosperous. In addition, Kentucky National Bank and Covington Trust, now Huntington Bank, are located here, as are a number of retail stores, service businesses, and restaurants.

The **17 Cathedral Basilica of the Assumption,** Madison Avenue between Eleventh and Twelfth Streets, has been described as one of the most impressive church buildings in the Midwest. The imposing medieval French Gothic style structure is 190 feet long and has a 128-foot high facade modeled after Notre Dame Cathedral in Paris. Flying buttresses and high pinnacles dominate the rear and the sides of the building, and gargoyles look out from the towers. The cathedral has eighty-two stained glass windows, including one measuring 24' x 67', reportedly among the largest in the United States.

Artists and craftsmen from Europe and the United States worked on the cathedral. Mayer & Company of Munich, Germany, made the stained glass windows on the lower and clerestory levels. Ellrich Studios of Venice constructed the fourteen mosaic Stations of the Cross. Artist Frank Duveneck, a Covingtonian who enjoyed a national reputation, contributed four murals for the chapel and a triptych on the east wall. Clement J. Barnhorn, a renowned Cincinnati sculptor, made the statue of the Madonna and the carving of the Assumption of Mary above the front door of the cathedral.

The Basilica replaced a much more modest cathedral on Eighth Street that had been erected in 1853 to serve the newly created Covington diocese. By 1885, however, the diocese served 38,000 Catholics, and the old cathedral no longer met the needs of the community.

Between 1890 and 1893, Bishop Camillus Paul Maes acquired property along Madison Avenue and hired Leon Coquard, a Detroit architect, to design the cathedral. Construction began in 1894. Building costs for the cathedral, which Maes intended to be "the leading feature of the city," greatly exceeded expectations. Although wealthy Catholics gave generously—distiller James Walsh contributed $50,000—the diocese had only enough money to build the apse, nave, and foundation. The faceless cathedral was dedicated on January 27, 1901.

Four years later, James Walsh's son, Nicholas, gave the diocese $100,000, enabling construction of the facade. Cincinnati architect David Davis was hired to direct the work, which began in 1908. The facade was dedicated in 1910.

*Among the features that the designers of the facade of the Basilica of the Assumption copied from the Cathedral of Notre Dame in Paris was the immense central rose window.*

The **18 Madison Avenue Christian Church,** 1530 Madison Avenue, was founded in 1874 when approximately sixty members left the Fifth Street Christian Church to form a new congregation. A year later, the group erected its own building at 115 Fourth Street and became the Fourth Street Christian Church.

In the early 1890s, the Fourth Street Christian Church, which included some of Covington's most prominent families, began considering a move. The March 11, 1893, *Kentucky Post* observed the "tendency [of] church property to drift southward," reflecting a shift in residential patterns as well-to-do Covingtonians moved to the suburbs.

In 1912, the Fourth Street church merged with the Central Christian Church, established in 1909, to form the Madison Avenue Christian Church. The following year, the 400-member congregation erected this Italian Renaissance style church building. Prominent members, such as Owen W. Carpenter of the Old Dexter Distilling Company, Richard C. Stewart of Stewart Iron Works Company, and tobacco merchants William G. Walker and J. B. Heizer, all lived in suburbs near the church.

Suburbanization continued to affect the Madison Avenue Christian

Church, and during the 1960s and 1970s, the church lost members to newer and more distant suburbs. The congregation considered relocating but decided to stay in what is now an inner city neighborhood where members feel the church has an important mission. In the late 1980s, the church had about 360 active members.

In 1906, the L&N Railroad, successor to the Kentucky Central, donated a site and $7,000 for the construction of a new **19 YMCA Railroad Department Building,** 1629 Madison Avenue, for railroad workers. Throughout the nation, the YMCA Railroad Department operated boarding houses for railroad men. Designed, in part, to keep the men out of saloons, these establishments provided affordable sleeping rooms and educational and recreational facilities. Earlier, the Railroad Department constructed a 10-room, 2-story structure on Fifteenth Street, but by the turn of the century, it no longer met the needs of the increasing number of railroad workers.

The new building opened in 1910. The 3-story Spanish Mission style structure, designed by Covington architects Schofield & Walker, featured a large classroom, reading room, billiard room, nine double bedrooms, and seven single bedrooms. Members of the YMCA Railroad Department paid ten cents per night for a room; non-members were charged a quarter. At its dedication, H. O. Williams, a member of the international committee of the railroad YMCA, asserted that the new building would "make better citizens" out of the railroad men and become an asset to the "life of the entire community."

Today, the railroad hotel and the freight terminal and roundhouse of the Kentucky Central, at Fourteenth Street and Madison Avenue, are the sole remnants of railroad days in Covington. The roundhouse, the only one still standing in the area, was built in the late 1870s. It became the home of the Triangle Paper Bag Manufacturing Company in the 1930s, and since 1965, the Duro Bag Company. The YMCA Railway Department closed in 1958-1959, and since 1980, the Y building has been occupied by a drapery shop.

The **20 Covington Police Department Headquarters,** 1929 Madison Avenue, was completed in 1981. Formerly located on the second floor of the Covington-Kenton County Municipal Building, the department outgrew its facilities and sought a new, centrally located building.

The Covington Police Department was established in 1882 and by 1906 included five officers, four detectives, and thirty-eight patrolmen. As Covington expanded over the next decade, its police department grew, but when the city's population and tax base began to decline, it had to manage with fewer men. In 1978, when Covington annexed the suburb of Oakridge, the police department maintained a force of approximately one hundred officers. By 1988, the force had about eighty-five members.

> *Turn left on East Twentieth Street, right on Scott Boulevard, and left on Wallace Street.*

The historic homes along Wallace Avenue are part of the **21 Wallace Woods** subdivision, developed around the turn of the century. The subdivision occupies land that once belonged to Robert Wallace, a Cincinnati merchant and steamboat captain, who purchased the property in 1833 and began living here shortly thereafter. The 1850 census listed Wallace and his family as the only residents of the area, but they were soon joined by the Levassor and Holmes families.

Eugene Levassor, a Cincinnati merchant of French descent, purchased land south of Wallace's property in 1831 but did not make his home here until the early 1850s. Another prominent merchant, Daniel H. Holmes, who founded the New Orleans department store chain of the same name, bought land adjacent to the Levassor property in 1855.

The area began to lose its rural character when a new city charter, approved March 2, 1850, moved Covington's southern corporation line to the northern edge of Wallace's property. In 1867, the completion of a street railway to Madison Avenue and Eighteenth Street made the southern part of town more accessible, and by 1891, housing developments completely surrounded what was left of the Wallace, Levassor, and Holmes farms. After the death of

Robert Wallace's son, Charles G. Wallace, in 1893, the family estate was platted to create the Wallace Woods subdivision.

As the size of the homes on Wallace Avenue indicate, this property was developed for people of considerable wealth. Tobacco merchant Joseph B. Heizer built the Colonial Revival style house with Corinthian columns, 103 Wallace Avenue, in 1908. W. A. Stewart, vice president of the Stewart Iron Works, occupied the massive 3-story house at 117 Wallace Avenue. Designed by the prominent Cincinnati architect Harry Hake and built in 1909, this Colonial Revival style structure featured a third floor ballroom and a walk-in icebox in the kitchen.

The three 2½-story Victorian houses known as Morton's Row, 229-233 Wallace Avenue, were a speculative venture of Elizabeth Morton, the granddaughter of Robert Wallace. Covington attorney Alexander G. Simrall built the Victorian home located at 400 Wallace Avenue in 1891. Around 1920 James T. Hatfield of the Hatfield Coal Company expanded the structure.

In the 500 block of Wallace Avenue, the character of the neighborhood shifts from large, single-family homes to more modest houses and apartments, many of which were built as investments by local residents. Although Wallace Woods is no longer a rural community, it has remained an affluent suburb, and most of its current residents are middle-income professionals.

> *Turn left on Glenway Avenue, left on East Twentieth Street.*

In 1860, Henrietta E. Cleveland approached Covington's Roman Catholic bishop, George A. Carrell, with the idea of establishing a hospital for the poor. At Carrell's request, two Sisters of the Poor of St. Francis came from Cincinnati to Covington in November 1860 and established what later became **22 St. Elizabeth Medical Center—North Unit,** 410 East Twentieth Street.

The Sisters started their work in a small brick house on Seventh Street. The new hospital, dependent on donations, struggled during its early years, and the Sisters often faced shortages of food and coal. During the Civil War, the Sisters cared for ill soldiers and took in war orphans.

When, in 1867, the City of Covington decided to establish a market place on the hospital site, the diocese purchased a building on Eleventh Street that had been part of the Western Baptist Theological Institute. The Sisters opened a new 110-bed facility in the spring of 1868.

In its first year at this site, St. Elizabeth Hospital served 151 patients, a number that reached 1,123 by 1910. The growing patient load and a desire to escape the noise and smoke of nearby railyards led hospital officials to seek a new location. The diocese bought a tract of land along Eastern Avenue and broke ground in 1911. The 4-story, 270-bed facility,

*In 1868, the Sisters of the Poor of St. Francis moved their hospital to a former Baptist seminary building.*

which remains at the center of the hospital complex, was completed in 1914. Between 1915 and 1955, the number of patients served each year rose from 1,835 to 14,499, and the hospital built additions in 1953, 1954, and 1959.

In 1978, St. Elizabeth Hospital opened a new branch, the St. Elizabeth Medical Center-South Unit, in suburban Edgewood. In 1985 and 1986, St. Elizabeth's relocated the pediatrics and obstetrics departments to the hospital's Edgewood branch.

*Turn right on Eastern Avenue, left on East Fifteenth Street. Cross Madison Avenue, and follow Fifteenth Street as it jogs to the right. Turn right on Holman Avenue.*

The **23 Linden Grove Cemetery,** at Holman Avenue and East Fourteenth Street, was laid out by the Western Baptist Theological Institute in the 1840s. After the Institute was dissolved, Samuel J. Walker of Covington purchased Linden Grove as an investment in 1857 and put it into a trusteeship three years later.

Walker realized little profit from the cemetery, and by the mid-1880s, financial difficulties prevented the trustees from maintaining the grounds properly. In 1929, public spirited citizens attempted a fundraising campaign to clean up the cemetery. Their efforts did not provide for upkeep, however, and the deterioration of Linden Grove continued. After the cemetery went into receivership in 1948, no services were provided to lot owners. Undertakers had to dig graves and install tombstones themselves, and groundskeeping and security were neglected.

In 1960, the Kentucky legislature passed a law that permitted cities to take over abandoned cemeteries, but the City of Covington chose not to acquire Linden Grove. A decade later, the death of the receiver again raised the question of improving Linden Grove. Covington officials considered converting the cemetery into a park. Others, most notably the Linden Grove Society, hoped to preserve it as a historic cemetery, arguing that it provided a resting place for some of Covington's most prominent citizens.

In November 1971, the courts named a new receiver for Linden Grove, and the cemetery's articles of incorporation were amended to give it non-profit status. With financial support from the city, county and state, Linden Grove has been cleaned up and maintained.

A number of prominent Northern Kentuckians are interred here, including James Kennedy, a general in the War of 1812, and John G. Carlisle, a prominent figure in the state and national Democratic party in the late nineteenth century.

*Turn left on West Twelfth Street.*

The **24 Bavarian Brewing Company,** 528 West Twelfth Street, began in 1866 as the Deglow Brewing Company. The firm became the Bavarian Brewery Company in 1870 and, under the direction of William Riedlin, grew to be one of the most successful breweries in Covington.

Born in Baden, Germany, Riedlin emigrated to the United States in 1870. After a short stay in Baltimore, he came to Cincinnati and began working as a blacksmith. By 1877, Riedlin had saved enough money to open a grocery and saloon at the corner of Green and Elm Streets. He sold this business in 1879 and bought the Tivoli Hall, a popular Cincinnati "amusement house," which he operated until he became a partner in the Bavarian Brewery in 1884.

Under Riedlin's management, the company increased its output of beer from 7,000 barrels in 1882 to 32,000 barrels in 1896. Bavarian enjoyed continued prosperity until Prohibition forced it to close.

Bavarian reopened in 1934, but like many small local breweries, it was threatened by larger concerns. The brewery went into receivership in 1937 and was purchased by four members of the Schott family, who were grandsons of William Riedlin. In

1959, they sold the company to International Breweries Incorporated, of Buffalo, New York. Seven years later, International sold Bavarian to the Detroit-based Associated Brewing Company, which closed the plant, putting 200 employees out of work. Associated continued to use the label at another facility.

For a time, the building was used as a taproom, and the rear portion is used by Shipman Industries, a manufacturer of industrial fans.

*William Riedlin's Bavarian Brewing Company operated Covington's largest brewery.*

**Turn right on Willow Run, east of the I-75 underpass, and right on Pike Street.**

Built in 1877, the **25 Turner Hall,** 447 Pike Street, still serves as the headquarters of the Covington Turner Society. German immigrants who settled in Covington during the mid-nineteenth century established the Covington *Turngemeinde,* a social and physical fitness club, in 1855. The society also worked to preserve German culture and pride in old world traditions, often in the face of nativist hostility.

On Whitmonday, May 12, 1856, the Turners gathered for a picnic on Forrest, or Botany Hill, just west of town. Members exchanged insults with nativist youths, and a fight broke out. Partly in defense and partly as a show of force, the Turners then paraded through Covington. The march ended in violence. The Turners retreated to their hall in Newport and were forced to give up several members accused of assaulting city marshals. After a long trial, all were acquitted.

It is rare now to hear German spoken at Turner Hall, and German ancestry has long since ceased to be a requirement for membership in the society. The Turners remain involved in athletics, but younger members prefer softball, basketball, and volleyball to the more traditional gymnastics. The Covington Turner Society sponsors boys' and girls' teams in a variety of Covington area sports leagues and in regional and national Turner competitions.

**26 John G. Carlisle Elementary School,** at Robbins Street and Holman Avenue, was named after Carlisle (1835-1910), a Covingtonian who served as lieutenant governor of Kentucky, speaker of the United States House of Representatives, United States senator, and secretary of the treasury in the first administration of Grover Cleveland.

The Art Deco style school was built in 1938 with the aid of the WPA and originally served as both a grade school and junior high. In 1974, the junior high school was relocated when the system was reorganized.

The Covington school system began in the 1830s when the city established two common schools. Before 1850, families who could afford to pay tuition were required to do so, while the children from poor families attended free of charge. Covington's schools grew rapidly during its first twenty years, and between 1837 and 1851, enrollments jumped from 45 to 716. By 1851, the system had five school buildings, and in 1853, the first public high school was opened.

During the first quarter of the twentieth century, the Covington school system expanded as the city grew. Two new elementary schools were constructed in 1904 and 1906. In 1918, Covington High School moved to its present location and was named after Daniel Holmes. A new junior high school was built in 1926.

Between 1904 and 1929, enrollment in the Covington public schools increased from 4,292 to 7,340. By then, the district operated a high school, two junior high schools, and eleven elementary schools for whites, and one high school and one elementary school for blacks. Enrollments peaked in the late 1950s, when more than 8,500 students attended the Covington public schools. In 1988, that figure was 5,800.

**Turn left on Washington Street, left on West Sixth Street.**

Designed by Daniel Segar, the 2-story stone building at 100 West Sixth Street served as the **27 Headquarters of the Covington Fire Department** from 1898 until 1975, when the fire department moved into a new building at 100 East Robbins Street. Restaurateur Mick Noll then purchased the old firehouse from the city and converted it into the Covington Haus restaurant, which closed in 1988.

The Covington Fire Department was established in 1833 when the City Council set aside $225 for the construction of a firehouse on Third Street near Court Avenue. In 1838, a city ordinance provided for the election of fire wardens to inspect buildings, stoves, and flues, and to direct the work of the volunteer firemen. The city established its first paid fire department in 1864, and by 1893 had installed 279 fire hydrants, forty-two cisterns, and fifty alarm boxes. As early as 1870, this site housed Covington's Fire Company No. 1.

The fire department began to provide ambulance service in July 1934, using a converted 7-passenger Packard sedan. In 1988, the fire department operated three life squad units that answered almost 5,000 calls per year.

Faced with suburban growth, the Covington Fire Department has had to expand its services with little additional manpower. In 1978, when the city annexed Oakridge, the fire department closed two of its inner city stations and opened a new one at Taylor Mill Road near Hands Pike in order to provide that area with fire protection.

The parish that erected **28 Mother of God Roman Catholic Church,** 119 West Sixth Street, was formed in 1841 for German families. The new congregation began worshiping in a hall on Scott Street between Fourth and Fifth Streets. Using funds donated by the Leopoldine Mission Society of Vienna, the parish was able to purchase land along Sixth Street between Russell and Washington Streets and erected a church in 1842. But by the late 1860s, the congregation needed a larger house of worship.

Designed by Walter & Stewart and completed in 1871, the present Italian Renaissance Revival style church features two 200-foot-tall bell towers. In 1890, to commemorate its golden jubilee, the parish commissioned Johann Schmitt, a local artist who trained Frank Duveneck, to paint five murals, depicting the Five Joyful Mysteries, on the sanctuary walls. In addition, well-known Cincinnati sculptors Frederick and Henry Schroeder were hired to carve wooden altars for the church.

Throughout most of its history, Mother of God parish operated a grade school. The first classes were reportedly conducted in a rented building on Pike Street. When the congregation erected its first church in 1842, the school moved to the sacristy, which soon proved inadequate. In 1847, the parish built a one-story brick school at the rear of the church lot. Increasing enrollments required the addition of a second floor in 1855 and, seven years later, the construction of a new 3-story school building, located opposite the church.

The parish erected a still larger school in 1906. Designed by Samuel Hannaford & Sons, this structure consisted of ten classrooms, a 900-seat auditorium, and a teachers' lounge. During the 1950s, enrollments began to decline. Mother of God School closed in 1962, and the building was razed in the early 1970s.

Unlike many inner city parishes that have lost members to the suburbs, Mother of God has not been diminished by this migration. Over the last fifteen years, membership has increased because the church is permitted to accept people who live outside the parish into the congregation and because the parish has become involved in the community.

The church suffered extensive water damage after the dome caught fire in September 1986. Subsequent renovations took more than a year and a half.

**Turn right on Craig Street, left on West Sixth Street, and left on Main Street.**

The small specialty shops along the 600 block of Main Street are part of the **29 Main Strasse** development project, dedicated in September 1979.

In 1972, the Northern Kentucky Area Planning Commission published a housing survey which indicated that 1,102 of the 1,574 dwellings located in the lower west side were in poor condition. Three years later, the city designated the area for renovation. At the same time, the Northern Kentucky Convention and Visitors Bureau argued that the lower west side was ripe for redevelopment as a "village"—Main Strasse—using a "Rhineland in America" theme.

Despite the German theme of Main Strasse, the Main Street area historically has been heterogeneous. North of Sixth Street, the neighborhood was Irish, and to the south lived Germans, as well as a few blacks, including the Reverend Jacob Price.

The Main Strasse concept was incorporated into the 1976 Main Street Development Plan, which sought to improve the area bounded by the C&O Railroad on the east, Fourth Street on the north, I-75 on the west, and Pike Street on the south. The plan recommended a "public/private effort" to restore housing and establish an active business district composed of specialty shops. A year later, the Northern Kentucky Convention and Visitors Bureau received a $2.5 million State Tourist and Visitors Development Grant to help finance these improvements.

Main Strasse at first received mixed reviews. In 1982, the *Kentucky Post* complained that some buildings in the district were run-down and "out of character with the area's German village theme." Nevertheless, the appearance of the area has been greatly improved, and Main Strasse has become an important site for local festivals, and many small crafts, antiques and specialty shops, and

*The Main Strasse district is Covington's best-known example of older buildings being saved and used as an integral part of a redevelopment project.*

restaurants are located here.

**Turn right at West Seventh Street, right at Philadelphia Street.**

Bounded by Philadelphia Street on the east, Ninth Street on the south, I-75 on the west, and Fifth Street on the north, **30 Goebel Park** was established in 1909. The City of Covington initially leased the site from Arthur Goebel, a Cincinnati merchant and brother of William Goebel, for whom the park is named. After his victory in a hotly contested 1899 Kentucky gubernatorial election, William Goebel was shot on the day of his inauguration and was sworn into office on his deathbed.

Goebel Park, particularly its Carroll Bell Tower, is an important part of Main Strasse. The 1976 development plan called for expanding the park as a focal point for the neighborhood. Financed with state and federal funds, the park was redeveloped in three phases.

The first step was to build a shelterhouse and the Carroll Bell Tower. Named for Kentucky Governor Julian M. Carroll, a staunch supporter of the project, the tower was designed by the I. T. Verdin Company of Cincinnati and stands one hundred feet tall with a forty-three bell carillon and clock dials on four sides of the turret. Based on medieval European designs, the clocks in the bell tower are activated by animated jacquemarts—mechanical figures—that act out the tale of the Pied Piper of Hamlin.

In the second phase of the project, the city extended the park from Seventh to Ninth Street and built a swimming pool at Eighth and Dalton Streets. During the third phase, the city constructed bicycle and jogging paths and moved the basketball courts to a location near Ninth Street.

**Tour ends. Return to downtown Covington on West Fifth Street.**

# Tour 7

# Price Hill - Delhi

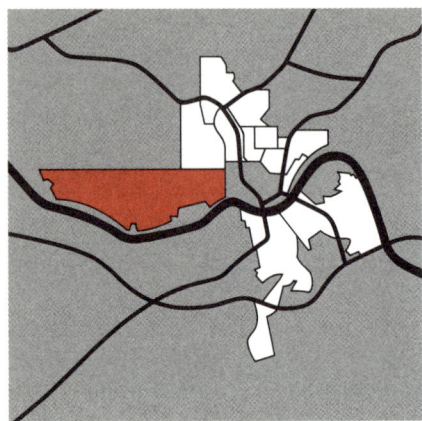

Price Hill and Delhi Township lie to the west of downtown Cincinnati. Each is comprised of a series of communities settled in progressively westward steps over almost two centuries as successive groups of city dwellers sought to escape the crowded basin and find newer housing.

Initially, the area now occupied by these communities was all part of Delhi Township, and the greater part of the land was used for farming. But at a very early stage, speculators began to see opportunities for non-agricultural development. During the first two decades of the nineteenth century, Evans Price (d.1821), a successful merchant who came to Cincinnati in 1807, began investing in land between the Mill Creek and the steep slope called Bold Face Hill, supposedly named after an Indian who once lived there.

Around the time of Evans Price's death, his son, Rees Price (1795-1875), laid out a subdivision in the vicinity of what is now Eighth Street and State Avenue. To encourage development, he established a sawmill and brickyard, and by the 1830s, a small community existed at the foot of the hill.

At this time, the only village on the western hilltops was Warsaw, established in the mid-1820s along what is now Glenway Avenue between Rosemont Street and Rapid Run Pike. Delhi Township west of Bold Face Hill remained agricultural. The farmland was used primarily for dairies or growing fruit and vegetables. Viticulture was common around Warsaw where a number of vineyards, including some started by Nicholas Longworth, were located. By the mid-1830s, the village was a thriving community with several shops and a winery. Around the middle of the nineteenth century, a second village, Cedar Grove, was laid out immediately to the east of Warsaw, but little development took place there until almost fifty years later.

Population grew slowly but steadily in Delhi Township, particularly in the eastern quarter where about half of the inhabitants lived. In 1835, a separate township called Storrs was carved out of this more heavily populated eastern portion of Delhi Township.

Storrs Township extended from the Mill Creek to a line that ran along what is now Academy Avenue and through the Seton High School grounds. When it was annexed by Cincinnati in 1870, Storrs Township had a population of approximately 4,000. That part of the new township near the Mill Creek continued to develop as a lower middle-income community which by the 1840s was named Neave, after one of its developers. At the same time, the property on the hilltop immediately above began to attract a number of wealthy residents who built suburban estates.

New development in Neave, particularly industrial development, was facilitated by the construction of the Cincinnati, Hamilton & Dayton Railroad in 1851. By the 1860s, the vicinity had more than 250 structures including houses, stores, small factories, two large distilleries, and a major rolling mill. Although the nearby hilltop was less accessible, upper-income Cincinnatians such as merchants Peter and William Neff, porkpacker Steven Wilder, and members of the Price family built estates there. The area's isolation was an attraction in some cases; the Archdiocese of Cincinnati built its seminary on the hill.

The hill was desirable for both residential and commercial development. It was above the basin's soot and smoke, and the prevailing winds usually blew pollution away. The hilltop also offered a splendid view. In 1874, Rees Price's son, William (c.1840-c.1888), built an inclined plane railway on the eastern slope of Bold Face Hill. At its upper terminus, he opened an amusement complex where the primary attractions were the view of the Cincinnati and the Price Hill House, one of the city's popular hilltop entertainment halls.

The incline and the resort caused the area to become known as Price's Hill, commonly shortened to Price Hill. Although Price started the incline and entertainment complex as a profit-making venture rather than to encourage residential development, it fostered interest in the area. The incline made the hilltop more accessible, and transportation to Price Hill was further improved in the late 1870s with the extension of a horsecar line from downtown Cincinnati along Eighth Street to State Avenue. Around 1885, tracks were laid on the hill itself, running from the head of the incline along Warsaw Avenue to the city's western boundary.

These improvements increased the potential for development. Price Hill landowners subdivided their property, and a wave of housing construction began. By the mid 1880s, Lower Price Hill was becoming more heavily industrialized with stockyards, a stoneworks, ink and varnish plants, an ironworks adjoining the rolling mill, distilleries, and wheel, spring, and carriage factories. The newer parts of Price Hill, however, were completely residential.

*Lower Price Hill was a bustling manufacturing district by the mid-1800s, but railroads encouraged even more industrial development there in the second half of the century.*

Some of the new housing, such as that in the Elberon Land Company Subdivision around Purcell Avenue, was intended for upper-income buyers, but most homes were designed for the middle-income market. In the 1890s, the addition of two electric streetcar lines at Elberon and Warsaw Avenues made Price Hill even more accessible to families of modest means. Development moved progressively westward along Eighth Street, Warsaw, and Glenway.

Around the turn of the century, the residents of the section of Delhi Township just beyond Price Hill sought annexation to the city to obtain adequate public services. Annexation took place in 1902, and this area, which included the village of Warsaw, became known as West Price Hill, while the older part of the hilltop suburb located around the upper terminus of the incline was called East Price Hill.

During the early twentieth century, as residential construction continued to fill in the remaining space, Price Hill took on its own identity as a distinct and somewhat insular community. By the 1920s, approximately 60% of the area's 25,000 residents were Catholics of Irish or German descent. The majority were middle-income families; most of those commuted to jobs in other parts of the city. Although opportunities for employment were relatively limited in East and West Price Hill, a thriving business district developed along Warsaw and Glenway Avenues to supply the residents' daily needs. Large churches dominated the various neighborhoods, providing social as well as spiritual focal points.

Despite the number of streetcar lines serving the area and the construction of the Eighth Street Viaduct in 1928, Cincinnatians continued to perceive Price Hill as an isolated community. The sense of separation was reinforced by the tendency of residents to remain in or near Price Hill. Adult children moving away from their families and people seeking larger or more modern homes often moved only a short distance, to the next street or perhaps to the next subdivision.

Each decade brought new development farther and farther west. Covedale, on the border of Delhi and Green Townships, was established in the 1920s. Cincinnati annexed a significant portion of this area in 1930. A major subdivision called Wynnburn Park was begun northwest of Price Hill in the 1930s, and in the late 1940s, developers laid out large subdivisions in Delhi Township just outside the city limits.

Older areas to the east, however, began to decline as many middle-income people left them for newer suburban environments. Lower Price Hill became increasingly poor; the authors of the 1948 *Metropolitan Master Plan* believed industry would replace housing and the residential neighborhood would gradually disappear.

The planners held that residential development would continue to move westward into rural Delhi Township. While the eastern portions of the township were becoming relatively urbanized, truck farms, nurseries, and orchards were still common in the western section. During the mid-1950s, there was considerable sentiment for incorporation or annexation by Cincinnati among many Delhi residents, but the majority of township voters refused to approve either proposal.

While Delhi's growth continued into the 1960s, parts of the neighborhoods that made up Price Hill faced increasing problems. East and West Price Hill, with a combined population of about 40,000,

*Dehli Township was a quiet agricultural district well into the twentieth century.*

reached the saturation point for housing construction. New development required reuse of existing sites. Residents' average income levels continued to drop. Lower Price Hill— contrary to expectations—survived as a community, but it became a community of predominantly poor whites from the Appalachian South. By the 1970s, "poverty pockets" had also spread into older parts of East Price Hill.

Most of Price Hill, however, remained a stable, middle-income community with a remarkably strong neighborhood business district. In problem areas, community groups and social service organizations like the Santa Maria Community Services made efforts to better conditions. Deteriorating housing was improved with federal rehabilitation funds and by people interested in renovating some of the reasonably-priced older homes which had great character and fine architectural details. Individuals were also attracted by hillside properties with good views. It was the view from East Price Hill that led developers to erect a number of new apartment buildings there.

At the same time, Delhi experienced a residential construction boom. The new homes, particularly those farther to the west, were generally for higher-income buyers than those built closer to Price Hill. The boom finally slowed in the 1980s as the township began to reach its saturation point, a population of approximately 30,000.

Today, residents and officials are increasingly concerned about maintaining public services while continuing to remain independent from the city. Delhi is an essentially urban area with a rural governmental structure. To deal with the need to maintain services, township trustees hired a full-time administrator in 1979. Yet in spite of the problems brought on by development, Delhi Township has remained an extremely popular bedroom suburb.

141

North

see insert

Guerley Rd.

Glenway Ave.

Rapid Run Pike

21

22

23

Sunset Ave.

W. Liberty St.

20

1st Ave.

19

18

Manss Ave.

17

Seton Ave.

W. 8th St.

Quebec Rd.

15

Enright Ave.

16

McPherson Ave.

Glenway Ave.

Fairbanks Ave.

14

Lehman Rd.

Delhi Pike

Elberon Ave.

Purcell Ave.

10

9

Grand Ave.

Fairbanks Ave.

Delhi Pike

11

Bassett Ave.

Considine Ave.

Price Ave.

Warsaw Ave.

13

Mt. Echo Dr.

Phillips Ave.

6

River Rd.

Mt. Hope Ave.

8

12

Matson Pl.

7

Maryland Ave.

5

Seminary Ave.

2

1

3

4

State Ave.

Burns St.

Saint Michael St.

Hatmaker St.

**Start / End**

8th St. Viaduct

Bender Rd.

25

Neeb Rd.

24

Cleves-Warsaw Pike

Anderson Ferry Rd.

Rapid Run Pike

Glenway Ave.

26

Delhi Pike

Delhi Pike

▶ ▶ ▶ ▶ ▶ ▶

**Tour begins downtown on Eighth Street. Drive west, crossing the Eighth Street Viaduct.**

Since the 1870s, daily life in Lower Price Hill has centered around the **1 Eighth Street and State Avenue Business District**. The area has long been an important industrial district with concerns such as Sayers & Scovill hearses, Globe Rolling Mills, Ahrens-Fox/LeBlond-Schacht trucks, Hutchinson sporting goods, and Manischewitz matzos. Eventually it also included a busy commercial cluster at the foot of Price Hill. The entire neighborhood is often known as "Eighth and State."

Eighth Street and State Avenue developed later than much of the surrounding community. Most early residential development was in the vicinity of St. Michael's Church, while industry was concentrated to the east between the CH&D tracks and the Mill Creek. In the 1870s, however, construction of the incline and the beginning of horsecar service along Eighth Street encouraged many bus-

*The vicinity of Eighth and State was occupied primarily by industry until the incline and streetcar lines attracted retail businesses to this intersection.*

inessmen to locate in this area.

Eighth Street, from Burns to the foot of Price Hill, quickly became the commercial center of Lower Price Hill. The district included both businesses that served local residents and beer halls that catered in large part to commuters and funeral parties going on their way to Price Hill, which was largely "dry" until the early 1880s.

By the early twentieth century, Eighth and State had become an active retail district with fifty to sixty businesses serving the surrounding community. The wide variety of offices, shops, and stores included grocers, druggists, butchers, doctors, hardware stores, a fish market, clothier, theater, and a bank. In addition, a public library branch and a post office were near the intersection. Most of the buildings were 3 or 4-story structures in the Greek Revival, Italianate, or Queen Anne styles, dating from 1875 to 1900. One notable exception was the Neo-Classical style West End Bank, 2155 Eighth Street, built in 1914.

This district remained essentially unchanged into the early 1950s. Later in that decade, however, many of Lower Price Hill's middle-income families began to move out, generally to East or West Price Hill. Population and the average income level fell, and crime became more common. As older

businessmen died, retired, or moved away, few new merchants replaced them. By 1960, the number of stores at Eighth and State had decreased by 20%.

Within the next twenty years, this commercial district shrank 50% more. Of the fifteen to twenty businesses that remained, about one-third were operations that did not serve local residents' daily needs: printers, plumbing and heating contractors, and remodelers. Restaurants and retail shops disappeared. In 1985, the Fifth-Third Bank branch that occupied the former West End Bank building closed.

By 1987, there were only about a dozen businesses left. Many stores were vacant and boarded up. Even so, the area around Eighth and State remained the focal point of the community. A few small groceries continued to serve residents, local social agencies used former shop space in the area, and the city had torn down a number of empty and deteriorating buildings for new development, including a health center.

**Turn left on State Avenue, left on St. Michael Street.**

Early in 1847, forty-five German Catholics who lived in Storrs Township organized to build a church and schoolhouse. The group bought land between Storrs and West Sixth Street and laid it out into lots that were sold to pay for construction of the parish complex.

A 1-room schoolhouse was finished first, and worship services were held there until the spring of 1848 when **2 St. Michael Roman Catholic Church,** 2110 St. Michael Street, was completed. A statue of the congregation's patron, St. Michael the Archangel, and a tablet inscribed with the church's German name are above the main door.

The parishioners added a parsonage, two wings, and three school buildings, one of which also served as a Sisters' residence. The church was furnished with stained glass memorial windows, carved plaster and woodwork, and ceilings and walls decorated with paintings. When the church was remodeled in 1947 for its centennial celebration, the steeple, four bells, and much of the interior woodwork were

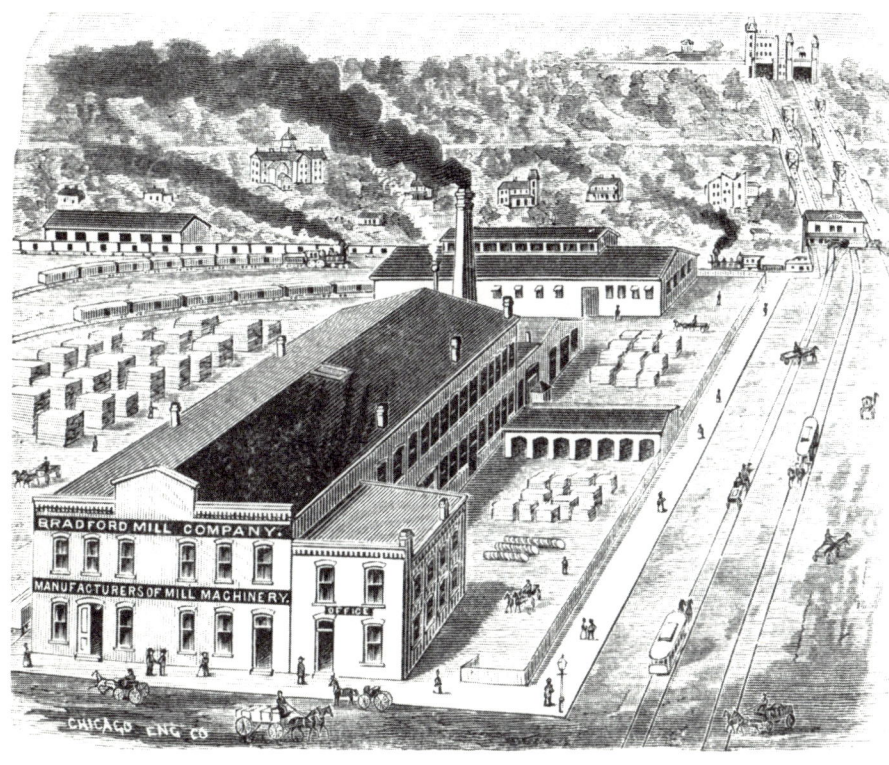

removed.

In the mid-1890s, St. Michael's recorded 450 member families. But in the twentieth century, this neighborhood underwent major changes. The parish lost members as the construction of the Sixth Street Viaduct in the 1930s cleared the small business district along River Road, as jobs disappeared with the decline of the railroads and nearby industry, and as suburban development offered more attractive modern housing.

The elementary school closed in the early 1960s, and in 1964-1965, the Comboni Missionaries, who traditionally work in the poorest parishes, took charge of St. Michael's. In the late 1980s, the parish's approximately 150 households included Appalachian newcomers, long-time residents, former residents who returned for services, and members of Blessed Sacrament Church, an English-language parish established nearby in 1874 and discontinued in 1974.

Comboni seminarians attending local universities stay in the school and convent buildings, which also contain offices and a chapel. The basement of the priest's home is used for the Food Pantry, a free food and clothing service.

The ground-level cafeteria in the newer St. Michael School building, 2104 St. Michael Street, serves as a community meeting hall and location for Santa Maria Community Services and the Lower Price Hill Community School.

**3  Santa Maria Community Services** dates back to the Italian Educational and Industrial Institute founded on Third Street in 1897 by two Sisters of Charity, Blandine and Justine Seagle, themselves Italian immigrants. By the 1920s, the Institute's program had included Italian language classes, an orphanage, clinic, employment bureau, sewing and child care classes, boys' night school, prison and tenement visits, and distribution of food, clothing, and money.

As Italian Americans prospered, acculturated, and moved from the basin, the Institute turned its attention to Cincinnati's newer "immigrants," blacks and Appalachians. In 1966, Santa Maria moved to Lower Price Hill. It has become a neighborhood organization, working with residents and city social service agencies to develop local leadership and improve the community. The Institute incorporated as the Santa Maria Community Services in 1972, though some Sisters remained on the staff.

Santa Maria, a United Appeal agency, operates two day care centers, a Youth Project, and two multi-service neighborhood houses in Price Hill. It offers counseling, advocacy, support for local organizations, programs for youth and the elderly, and employment and housing search assistance.

This building is shared by the **Lower Price Hill Community School,** an independent, nonprofit corporation founded by neighborhood residents and now run by its graduates. About 250 students each year attend adult education classes in preparation for the high school equivalency exam. Freshman and sophomore-level college classes, offered in conjunction with Xavier University, aim at encouraging further education and easing the cultural adjustments that Lower Price Hill residents make if they choose to pursue college degrees.

> **Turn left on Burns Street, left on Hatmaker Street.**

Dedicated on December 19, 1931, **4 Oyler School,** 2121 Hatmaker Street, was the second school built on this site. The first schoolhouse, the Storrs Township or Twenty-first District School, was erected in 1872 and consolidated several area schools. Renamed the George W. Oyler Public School in 1901 to honor its retiring principal, the school offered academic courses, but emphasized practical skills.

The present buff brick building, designed by Samuel Hannaford & Sons for 1,200 students, grades K-9, was strikingly ornate. Elaborate terra cotta trim included griffins and the figures of a boy and a girl, one on each side of the main entrance.

The school had an auditorium, lunchroom, two gyms, classrooms, and offices, as well as metal, electrical, woodworking, printing, and mechanical shops, and cooking and sewing rooms. Oyler also had two rooftop playgrounds because ground level space in this densely built neighborhood was too expensive.

By the 1940s, city planners referred to the neighborhood between Price Hill and the Mill Creek as Oyler and predicted it would eventually be cleared for industrial expansion. However, much of the industry closed or moved away. Lower Price Hill survived as a neighborhood, but Oyler School was affected by the general decline of the area. Enrollment, which held at 1,000 or more throughout the

*The exterior of Oyler School is embellished with decorative tilework and a number of terra cotta sculptures.*

1950s, peaked at 1,355 in 1960-1961. The opening of Roberts Junior High School on Grand Avenue in 1966-1967 took away grades 7-9, though the seventh graders returned during 1969-1979 because of overcrowding at the newer school.

In the 1970s, the Cincinnati Board of Education tried to improve racial balance at essentially all-white Oyler with a Montessori and an Applied Arts alternative programs. The successful Montessori program was later moved to Sands School in the West End. In 1987-1988, Oyler's student population of 650 was still approximately 90% white.

That year, the Board of Education announced a desegregation plan involving this and other Price Hill schools and several predominantly black schools in the West End. Strong protest from Price Hill parents brought about the formation of a committee of residents from both neighborhoods that offered an alternate proposal to the board.

*Turn right on State Avenue, left on Glenway Avenue, right on Grand Avenue, right on Lehman Road, right on Seminary Avenue, and circle through the campus of Cincinnati Bible Seminary.*

Peter Rudolph Neff (1832-1919) and his brother, William Howard Neff (1828-1902), were among the wealthy nineteenth-century businessmen attracted to Price Hill. Sons of a prosperous wholesaler of hardware and boots, Peter and William carried on their father's business. The father and sons were also involved in land speculation, owning both residential and commercial property in Lower Price Hill. Peter was also a founder and later, president of the College of Music.

The former **5 Home of Peter R. Neff,** 2700 Glenway Avenue, a 2½-story mansion called Mistletoe Heights, was erected around 1860 of stone quarried on Neff's 21-acre estate, now the campus of the Cincinnati Bible Seminary. The house serves as the school's administration building.

Around 1901, Peter sold his estate to Dr. Joseph Ratliff for the Grandview Sanitarium, later called Grandview Hospital, which treated patients for nervous and mental disorders, alcoholism, and drug addiction. The facility closed in 1939 in the wake of the Depression, and the old Neff estate was sold. The new owner was the Cincinnati Bible Seminary (CBS), established in 1924. Classes began in Neff's home in September 1940, and CBS has since erected five buildings on this campus.

CBS is a private, nondenominational institution offering associate and baccalaureate degrees, as well as graduate work. It receives support from the Christian Churches and the Churches of Christ in the United States.

**Return to Lehman Road and turn left.**

The 3-story stone house at 2935 Lehman Road was built in the early nineteenth century and served briefly as the **6 Mount St. Vincent Motherhouse and Academy of the Sisters of Charity.** The Order arrived in Cincinnati in 1836, acquired this residence in 1853, and the following year opened its Academy.

Three years later, the Sisters moved to the more substantial Cedar Groves estate, later the site of Seton High School. During the Civil War, the 10th Regiment of Ohio Volunteers was headquartered here because of the house's strategic location above the city. The building lost much of its historic character as later owners divided it into small apartments.

**Turn left on Grand Avenue, left on Price Avenue, right on Matson Place.**

Evans Price (d.1821) is often identified as the founder of Price Hill, but his descendants actually had a much greater impact on the area's development through the commercial enterprises they established. Chief among these was the **7 Price Hill Inclined Plane Railroad** and the entertainment complex on the hilltop, now the site of the Queen's Tower

*The Price Hill Incline had two sets of tracks—one set with passenger cars and the other with platforms to carry freight and vehicles.*

apartments, 810 Matson Place.

The Price family's involvement with the region west of the Mill Creek began in the early nineteenth century when Evans Price purchased land in eastern Delhi Township. In the 1820s, his son, Rees Price (1795-1875), established a lumber mill and brickyard in what is now Lower Price Hill to provide building materials for new homes and stores.

Rees Price was somewhat eccentric. He was a successful entrepreneur and a general in the Ohio militia, but he listed his occupation as "theocrat" in the 1850 census. His religious beliefs led him to oppose slavery, drinking, and the United States' war with Mexico. According to family tradition, he also refused his wife's dowry on the grounds that he had not earned it. Price was, however, an astute businessman, and shortly before his death, he organized a company to erect an inclined plane railroad on the face of Price Hill.

William Price (c.1840-1888), Rees' son, took control of the incline company and opened the passenger tracks of the Price Hill Inclined Plane in 1874. The two passenger cars, the "Highland Mary" and the "Lily of the Valley," were named for William's daughters. Two years later, the company opened a second set of tracks that used open

platforms to carry vehicles and freight.

Unlike most Cincinnati inclines, the Price Hill Incline was never a-dapted for transporting streetcars. A horsecar line brought passengers to the foot of the plane on Eighth Street. Once travelers reached the top of the hill, they had to find their own transportation or transfer to the Warsaw Avenue horsecar line, which opened around 1885.

Within a few years of starting the incline, William Price opened a recreational facility on the hilltop to increase ridership. The Price Hill House complex included a dancing pavilion, music hall, art gallery, observation deck, and picnic grounds.

In contrast to other hilltop resorts of the time, Price's operation served no alcoholic beverages. Some sources suggest that William Price shared his father's anti-drinking sentiments, while others maintain that the ban on liquor was a condition the elder Price demanded in his will. Whatever its origin, the prohibition of alcohol at the Price Hill House was strictly enforced in its early years, earning Price Hill the nickname Buttermilk Hill.

In 1879, William Price's brother, John, and his nephews, George and Rees McDuffie, took over the incline company as William's health failed. They leased the hilltop resort to an independent operator and removed the liquor ban.

The popularity of the Price Hill House increased, and traffic on the incline grew. From 1880 to the mid-1890s, the incline carried several hundred thousand passengers annually. Carriages and wagons sometimes lined up for blocks awaiting their turn on the platform.

The incline and the resort helped attract some residential development, but it was the construction of electric streetcar lines on Elberon and Warsaw Avenues in 1894 that really started a housing boom in Price Hill. Although the Price Hill Incline continued to carry large numbers of passengers, it became more of a tourist attraction than a means of everyday public transportation. The freight plane carried buses up and down the hill, but even that traffic gradually decreased, and the company shut down the freight platform in 1929.

The Price Hill House closed in 1932, and the building became an American Legion Post. People continued to ride the incline, most to enjoy the view. As the incline's machinery aged, city officials became concerned about its safety. In 1943, one of the cars jumped its track, and the city forced the company to close the incline. The incline was eventually dismantled, and the powerhouse was torn down in 1953.

The hilltop location of the powerhouse and the resort held potential for other uses. In 1948, radio station WSAI demolished the Price Hill House and built a transmitter tower on the site. In 1963, a group of local investors erected a high-rise apartment building, the Incline House, on the powerhouse site. The 20-story, 117-unit apartment tower designed by E. A. Glendening opened in 1964. The developers razed many nearby homes, including those where members of the Price family once lived, to provide parking and tennis courts.

Like the Highland House in Mt. Adams, the new building offered luxury apartments with an excellent view of the city. But the Incline House was not immediately successful. After the first year of operation, only thirty of the units were occupied, and the owners defaulted on the mortgages. Connecticut General Life Insurance Company, which held the mortgages, purchased the building at sheriff's auction in 1965 and renamed it the Queen's Tower.

**Turn right on West Eighth Street.**

When residential development of **8 East Price Hill** accelerated in the late nineteenth century, wealthy and middle-income families already lived on this portion of the hill. As the population increased, the middle-income families quickly became a majority, giving East Price Hill a distinct identity and character. Although pockets of upper-income residents remained, most of those who moved to Price Hill in the 1890s and early twentieth century were of more modest means: office workers, clerks, municipal employees, and salesmen who settled in unpretentious single-family or multi-unit dwellings.

In the 1880s and 1890s, enterprising developers built a large number of rowhouses as rental properties. One such venture was the 3-story gray brick Italianate style building at 781-785 Summit Street. Those who lived here were typical of the residents of the area.

Around 1900, 781 Summit was rented by James Scallan, 60, an Irish-born shoe salesman, his wife, and their nine children. His next door neighbor was James Veazy, 23, a traveling salesman with a wife and two young children. On the corner at 785 Summit lived Abraham Roseberry, 48, an electrical engineer from New Jersey, his wife, and their three sons.

Many East Price Hill residents were Roman Catholics who attended St. Lawrence Church in Cedar Grove. As new housing rapidly filled the streets near the incline, the people who lived there wanted a church nearer their homes. In 1883, twenty families organized Holy Family parish and in 1884 completed a temporary church on Price Avenue.

By the early 1910s, the parish had expanded to more than 760 families and a new, larger church was erected. The second Holy Family Roman Catholic Church, 814 Hawthorne Avenue, is a Renaissance Revival style structure designed by J. F. Sheblessy. Eventually, the parish complex included a school built in 1925 and a convent erected in 1926.

In the 1930s, Holy Family recorded 830 member families, and to many East Price Hill residents, the parish was the community. The church was a social as well as a religious and educational center, not only because so many of the area's residents were Catholic (more than 60% by the mid-twentieth century) but also because Price Hill was still largely isolated from the rest of the city. East Price Hill families focused their lives on their neighborhood and its institutions. Holy Family Church provided sports programs, festivals, theatrical performances, and a variety of clubs and societies.

After 1950, East Price Hill became less homogeneous. Population decreased as children moved away and a growing number of lower-income, more transient residents—relatively few of whom were Catholic—moved in. Further, in the 1960s and 1970s, well-to-do families returned, filling the expensive apartment buildings erected to take advantage of the view or purchasing and renovating some of the elegant older homes.

Despite these changes, Holy Family retained an important role in the community. The parish grew smaller —from 1,500 families in the 1940s to 650 in the early 1970s—and was no longer automatically the social center it once had been. But parish leaders adapted many of their activities to the neighborhood's changing circumstances, and Holy Family became a principal agency for helping the area's poorer families obtain adequate food, clothing, and furniture.

Lay people also became more important in parish functions. Holy Family responded to the dwindling number of Catholics in the vicinity by pooling resources with other parishes, starting with a school merger in the early 1970s.

**Turn left on Considine Avenue, right on Phillips Avenue.**

One of Cincinnati's architecturally unique ecclesiastical buildings is the former **9 Price Hill Methodist Episcopal Church,** Phillips and Considine Avenues. The congregation that erected this Shingle style structure first met on September 21, 1884, in the Price Hill House. The original nineteen members—middle-income families and well-to-do businessmen newly arrived in the western suburbs—included Zera Gretchell, head of a roofing and concrete company on State Street, and J. R. Stewart, president of the Bradford Mill Company on Evans Street.

Price Hill Methodist Episcopal purchased this lot in 1884; construction began in 1889, and the church was dedicated February 1, 1891. The octagon shape of the sanctuary is repeated in the tower that dominates the exterior of the building.

By 1931, membership had increased to nearly 400 and continued to grow. The congregation began to look for a newer, larger building. In February 1959, Price Hill Methodist Episcopal Church purchased the nineteenth-century mansion at 704 Elberon Avenue that had belonged to Charles R. Bishop, partner in the third largest butcher supply company in the nation. It was remodeled for religious education and office use.

A new fellowship hall-sanctuary was erected next to the "mansion church" in 1965, and two years later, the old church was sold to another

congregation. In 1978, after the furnishings, woodwork, and other artifacts were sold at auction, the mansion was razed. Three carved mantels were saved and installed in the present modern sanctuary which was completed in December 1979.

Membership remained around 450 throughout the 1960s but gradually declined as older residents died and families moved to newer suburbs. By the late 1980s, Price Hill United Methodist Church listed around 150 members. New residents in the area, chiefly less prosperous Appalachian families, have not been drawn to "main line" denominations.

The church continues to serve the community, opening its Fellowship Hall to mental health, Alcoholics Anonymous, and Weight Watchers meetings, aerobics classes, square dances, and other social events. Price Hill United Methodist has also worked with other community churches to build Senior Chateau on the Hill, a residence for senior citizens, which opened at Eighth Street and Grand Avenue in 1979.

**Turn left on Purcell Avenue.**

While most of Price Hill developed as a primarily lower and middle-income community, the **10 Purcell Avenue Homes,** 583-501 Purcell Avenue, were built between 1890 and 1920 for the well-to-do. They remain some of the area's most attractive and desirable housing. These large 2½-story homes, in a variety of styles and materials, are set back from the street on good-sized lots (50-100' x 175'). Features such as stained glass windows, large porches, and tower rooms suggest that the original owners were families of means.

The Elberon Land Company, which developed thirty-five acres east of Elberon Avenue and south of Price Avenue, proclaimed that there were "no choicer building sites on the Hill than these." The Elberon electric streetcar line ran through the property, making "every foot readily accessible to the business portions of the city." To encourage the sale of lots, the company built three model homes of eight to ten rooms each, with laundry facilities, bathrooms, hot and cold water, gas, and "all modern conveniences."

By 1895, residents of Purcell Avenue near Phillips included Edwin H. Murdock, president of the Ebony Lamp Black Company on Evans Street; Charles R. Resor, partner in the stove manufacturing business of William Resor & Company on State Street, and E. F. Rychen of The Queen City Printing Ink Company on South Street, all in Lower Price Hill. The noted architectural firm of Samuel Hannaford & Sons designed the home of George Scott, at 565.

The houses further south on the street are less substantial and impressive. But one block to the north, at the intersection of Elberon and Phillips, there were residences that could rightly be called mansions, such as the home of carriage manufacturer Alfred Klausmeyer, now the Price Hill Nursing Home.

**Turn right on Bassett Avenue, left on Elberon Avenue, right into Mt. Echo Park. Continue on Mt. Echo Drive.**

From the 1880s to the early 1900s, most of eastern Price Hill was developed for residential use, but the rugged, hilly area called Mt. Echo remained unused. In 1908, the Cincinnati Park Commission, acting under the recently adopted Kessler plan, purchased approximately forty-six acres of this undeveloped property and created **11 Mt. Echo Park,** 375 Elberon Avenue.

Within four years, voters approved bond issues that provided $1.75 million to the Park Board for improvement and purchase of additional park land. Park Commissioners added four acres to Mt. Echo Park, and city workers planted several hundred trees and constructed a roadway from the Elberon Avenue entrance to the top of the hill, bringing the park within a five minute walk from the Elberon streetcars. Further road improvements came in the 1920s, and the commissioners purchased adjacent land.

During the Depression, Mt. Echo and other city parks provided work as well as recreation for the unemployed. The Works Progress Administration funded construction of a shelterhouse, comfort station, and other buildings, relocation and reconstruction of the roadway, and extensive landscaping in the park.

Park attendance rose in the 1940s as wartime rationing of gasoline and tires limited long distance travel and encouraged Cincinnatians to use nearby recreational sites. The number of visitors continued to increase after the war, largely because of the greater amount of leisure time that came with a shorter work week. In 1949, the Park Board added a small tract that brought the park to its present size, nearly eighty-eight acres.

Recently, Mt. Echo, like other city parks, has faced problems due to budget cuts. In January 1984, the Board of Park Commissioners temporarily closed the park, except for Overview Drive, the shelter building, and the play area in the western end. After the park reopened, $300,000 in federal grants aided the renovation of several park structures.

Community groups actively participated in efforts to improve and care for the park. These endeavors were, in part, supported by the installation of a United Dairy Farmers' snack bar in the shelterhouse.

Mt. Echo Park, with its spectacular view of the Ohio River and downtown Cincinnati, still fulfills the goals set forth in the Kessler plan: to provide "open places, the opportunity for recreation out of doors, as well as for enjoyment of natural surroundings."

**Return to Elberon Avenue and turn right. Turn left on Mt. Hope Avenue.**

The old **12** **Kuerze House,** 919 Mt. Hope Avenue, is a remnant of the era when Price Hill was a popular location for suburban residences of prosperous Cincinnati businessmen. Robert M. Kuerze (1847-1903) was an officer of the Gerke Brewing Company on Plum Street when he built this Chateauesque style mansion around 1885.

Kuerze, Swiss-born, arrived in Cincinnati in 1864. In 1873, he married Elizabeth Gerke whose father was co-founder of the Eagle Brewery. Eight years later, Kuerze became secretary-treasurer of the concern, which had reincorporated as the Gerke Brewery, and then became president in 1889. He also served as Switzerland's consul for Ohio and Indiana, 1887-1889, and

*The Roman Catholic Archdiocese of Cincinnati once trained young men for the priesthood at Mount. St. Mary's Seminary in Price Hill.*

as a director of the Western German Bank and the German Mutual Insurance Company.

Edward J. Kuerze (c.1876-1965) succeeded his father as president of the brewery, which survived until about 1912-1913, and lived in the family home until his death. The Kuerze home stood vacant for nearly a decade; Price Hill no longer attracted the wealthy who could afford to maintain the large older homes. After going through the hands of a number of different owners and uses, the house was bought in 1982 by the Franciscan Fathers of the Sacred Heart and used for a few years as their residence.

**Turn left on Maryland Avenue, right on Grand Avenue, left on Warsaw Avenue.**

Rural Price Hill was the location of **13** **Mount St. Mary Seminary of the West** and later **Mount St. Mary Convent of the Good Shepherd and Training School for Girls,** Warsaw and Grand Avenues. Today, the Horizon Hills Apartments occupy the grounds, and the only remaining evidence of the old institutions is the arched gateway with the name of the school carved in the pillar.

Cincinnati's first Roman Catholic seminary opened in 1828 in a frame building on Sycamore Street. During the next decade, students were transferred to several locations until

Patrick Considine, a successful, Irish-born merchant, donated this land. The Mount St. Mary Seminary of the West was dedicated here on October 2, 1851. (The seminary is presently located on Beechmont Avenue in Mt. Washington.)

The Sisters of the Good Shepherd bought the property in 1904, moving their school and two convents out of the increasingly crowded basin to Price Hill. Mount St. Mary Training School's St. Aloysius Class educated children, age three to sixteen, who were brought by their parents or sent by the Catholic Charities. The Senior Department was composed of "problem" girls assigned by social service agencies or Juvenile Court.

The Sisters also maintained the Community of Magdalenes for women drawn to the religious life but lacking the qualities required to join the Order: legitimate birth, good morals, and an irreproachable life.

The Good Shepherd Sisters received support from the Community Chest, donations, and agencies or individuals who placed girls with them. But the bulk of their income came from the operation of workshops—commercial laundries, sewing rooms where shirts were produced, and knitting rooms—staffed by convent residents.

Anti-Catholicism motivated many of the charges that the girls were exploited, but Archbishops Elder and Moeller did receive complaints from some of the Sisters themselves that, in several instances, confirmed rumors of long hours and mistreatment. The archdiocese intervened in several instances to improve conditions in the workshops.

In 1937, Mount St. Mary Training School was housing and educating 200 girls, but by 1954, with changes in the welfare and justice systems, that number had fallen to eighty. In June 1949, the school announced a merger with Girls' Town, another temporary shelter for "problem" girls. That facility on North Bend Road in Finneytown was remodeled to accommodate the 112 girls both agencies were then serving.

In the early 1960s, a private developer purchased the Mount St. Mary property, razed the old buildings, and used the site to erect much-needed multi-family housing.

**Turn left on McPherson Avenue.**

In 1885, a group of German American residents of Price Hill, tired of having to travel into the basin for worship, met at the Price Hill House and formed the **14** **First German Protestant Church of Price Hill,** now Price Hill United Church of Christ, 927 McPherson Avenue. The congregation heard its first sermon on October 18.

The thirty-six charter members were, for the most part, artisans and their families, including stonemason Ernest Budke, tailor Henry Detert, varnisher Louis Hottewitz, and carpenter G. L. Kuhlman. The congregation was incorporated in December, and the church designed by architect Emil Bode was dedicated November 18, 1888.

In 1912, "staunch German families [were] the backbone of the church," and records were kept in German and English. But during the war, the Price Hill congregation adopted English as its official language. This change occurred in many German-language churches in response to anti-German feeling and because increasing numbers of younger, American-born members spoke English and felt no attachment to German.

First German Protestant Church became Price Hill Evangelical Church after joining the Evangelical Synod and, with the 1965 union of the Evangelical and Reformed Church and the Congregational Christian Church, gained its current designation.

As post-World War II suburban development drew away many families, Price Hill United found itself in a mixed neighborhood of older, long-time residents and more recently arrived blacks and Appalachians. In 1988, it had 193 members. The church serves its members and the community by providing meeting space for a writers' club, a summertime youth sports program, Girl Scout troops, Alcoholics Anonymous, and adult leadership groups.

**Turn right on West Eighth Street.**

Cincinnati's first cemeteries were located in the downtown basin; the first Catholic cemetery was at Liberty and Vine Streets. By the 1840s, however, rural settings for cemeteries were becoming more common. On August 2, 1842, Archbishop John B. Purcell bought nineteen acres in Price Hill for another, much-needed burial ground in what was then an undeveloped area. Purcell's burial ground is now **15** **St. Joseph Old Cemetery,** 3823 West Eighth Street.

The cultural, economic, and ethnic differences that had produced often antagonistic German-speaking and English-speaking parishes were carried to the grave. On January 14, 1843, Father Edward Purcell deeded half of the Price Hill cemetery property to the German Catholic Cemetery Association, and two St. Joseph cemeteries were consecrated on May 7.

The extension of West Eighth Street in the 1870s clearly defined the separation. The land on the northwest corner of Eighth and Enright Avenue became known as St. Joseph Irish Cemetery and that on the southwest corner as St. Joseph German Cemetery, both now a part of St. Joseph Old. Irish graves that had been in the way of the street were removed to another burial ground that Purcell had started in 1854. This cemetery, today called St. Joseph New Cemetery, Pedretti Avenue and Foley Road, includes 186 acres. According to a later account, the suggestion that the reinterments be made in the nearby German cemetery "caused an uproar because such integration seemed unthinkable."

Black newspaper publisher Wendell Phillips Dabney noted in the early 1900s that St. Joseph New Cemetery had been one of the few white burial grounds to accept blacks. However, blacks were buried in sections that were largely segregated.

After the Purcells' bank failed in 1878, the Cincinnati Archdiocese transferred management of the two cemeteries for English-speaking Catholics to the St. Joseph's Cemetery Association. The small plot at Eighth and Enright suffered over the years from neglect and vandalism. A fire in the late 1920s or early 1930s destroyed the sexton's house and all the records there. General deterioration and complaints from neighbors prompted a refurbishing in the 1960s.

St. Joseph Old Cemetery now encompasses 110 acres; the mausoleum and chapel building was erected in 1970. The Cincinnati Catholic Cemetery Association administers this and two other properties.

**Turn right on Enright Avenue, bear left on Warsaw Avenue.**

Unlike St. Michael Church in Lower Price Hill, which is almost hidden by the nearby buildings, the imposing **16** **St. Lawrence Roman Catholic Church,** 3680 Warsaw Avenue, dominates its surroundings.

Catholics on the hilltop attended services at the chapel of Mount St. Mary Seminary until 1868 when an English-language parish was organized. A lot on the south side of Wabash at Rapid Run Pike (now Warsaw and St. Lawrence Avenues) was purchased, and a 2-story brick church and school building was dedicated June 12, 1870. Archbishop Purcell worried that the new church would be "profaned by the close proximity of a drinking and dancing saloon, which should never be set up at the gate of a graveyard." (Saloonkeepers found ready customers among members of funeral processions who had made the long trip from downtown.)

With the extension of horsecar lines in this area in the 1870s and 1880s, St. Lawrence parish, extending from the brow of the hill to St. Joseph New Cemetery, grew to 150 families by 1883. Even though Holy Family parish, created in 1884, took the families in the area east of Elberon Avenue, St. Lawrence soon needed a new, larger church.

Construction began in 1885 on a lot across from the old church school. But parishioners had badly miscalculated building costs, and funds ran out. The basement was roofed over and used for services. Work on the superstructure began in April 1893, and the present stone building was dedicated September 30, 1894. St. Lawrence's rich interior features stained glass windows imported from Germany, the original ornate main altar, and frescos painted behind the altar in the 1950s.

*The area known as St. Lawrence Corner took its name from this imposing church on Warsaw Avenue.*

The parish grew more rapidly in the 1890s with the coming of electric streetcar lines, and by 1895, the Cincinnati Archdiocese judged St. Lawrence, with 475 families, to be the most flourishing Catholic parish in the city. In 1914, the parish recorded 1,400 member families. St. Lawrence was Price Hill's "mother parish" as four other parishes were carved from its territory: Holy Family (1884), St. William (1909), St. Teresa (1916), and Resurrection (1919).

The 3½-story school behind the church was dedicated June 21, 1905; Elder High School was founded here. A priests' residence, connected to the church by a covered walkway, was completed in 1912. A half-timbered convent for the Sisters of Charity who staffed the school was built in 1927 at Laclede and Carson Avenues. In 1987-1988, 416 children, grades K-8,

were enrolled in the school, and the parish recorded some 800 member families.

> **Turn left on Glenway Avenue, right on Manss Avenue.**

About 1906, a new Jewish settlement was started in Price Hill when the United Jewish Charities moved a number of families here so that members with tuberculosis could receive treatment at the sanatorium. By 1920, the area's population, though predominantly Catholic, included a significant number of Jews, most of whom had moved out of the declining West End.

The Orthodox congregation of Beth Jacob worshipped at its synagogue at 3770 St. Lawrence Street until the 1970s when it sold the building. The **17** **Synagogue of Sephardic Beth Shalom,** 1262 Manss Avenue, was dedicated March 19, 1934, by the eighty to ninety member families of the Spanish Hebrew Society.

Sephardic Judaism traces its roots to Jews who were expelled from Catholic Spain during the Inquisition. Sephardim have their own rituals and customs and speak Ladino, a mixture of Hebrew and Spanish. Cincinnati's Sephardic Jews arrived in the early 1900s, and by 1913, according to one study, their tightly-knit community in the West End numbered 219. The Spanish Sephardic Congregation begun that year soon broke up, as many members gradually moved to New York City and as men were called to fight in World War I.

Cincinnati's other Jewish congregations were reluctant to bury Sephardim in their cemeteries, so a burial society, The Spanish Hebrew Society, was chartered in 1919. By 1920, the Society had bought its own cemetery within the Ohav Shalom Cemetery on Sunset Avenue. The congregation met in private homes until 1934 when it opened Beth Shalom.

Although some new members, Greek Jews who had survived the Holocaust, arrived in Price Hill after World War II, the synagogue was increasingly inconvenient as most of Cincinnati's Jews were moving to Avondale, Bond Hill, and Roselawn. Members of Beth Shalom followed, often joining other congregations and

assimilating into the Ashkenazic Jewish mainstream.

In the 1980s, The Spanish Hebrew Society had forty member families, but only four members of Beth Shalom lived in Price Hill. In use until 1987, this synagogue was the only one of its kind in Ohio.

> **Turn left on West Liberty Street, left on First Avenue, right on Glenway Avenue.**

Although Catholics were concerned about maintaining their own school system at an early date, Catholic secondary education did not become widely available until the early twentieth century. Some parish elementary schools added courses for older children; some religious orders opened secondary schools, but these were often too expensive for many families.

**18** **Seton High School,** Glenway and Beech Avenues, originated as an academy for girls run by the Sisters of Charity and was one of those earlier institutions that initially served a limited number of families. But along with neighboring Elder High School, the city's first interparochial high school, both institutions were important in the expansion of Catholic secondary education.

Seton High School's history begins in 1853 when the Sisters of Charity opened Mount St. Vincent Academy at their first motherhouse on Lehman Road. Four years later, the Order purchased this property, an estate named The Cedars, built a new motherhouse, and opened classes in the old home here on November 14, 1858.

In 1870, day students were sent to St. Lawrence School, but in 1884, Cedar Grove Academy again accepted day students and added a kindergarten for boys. The motherhouse and boarding students were eventually transferred to the Mount St. Joseph College campus in Delhi.

The Order bought land surrounding the academy until its holdings stretched from Glenway Avenue to West Eighth Street, and from St. Lawrence Church to Iliff Avenue. Some twenty acres were later sold for a subdivision for which the Sisters chose several street names: Seton for the founder of the Order; Vincent for its patron saint; Regina for the mother superior who had purchased the land for Mount St. Joseph College, and Academy for the school itself. Another portion of the grounds was sold for the construction of Elder High School.

In 1927, at the request of Archbishop John McNicholas, Cedar Grove Academy became Seton High School, receiving female students from fourteen western parishes. The school added a science lab and auditorium building in 1932. Three nineteenth-century buildings, including a chapel, were torn down for the present school, dedicated in 1957 as part of the Sisters' celebration of one hundred years of work in this location. Enrollment at Seton peaked at 1,500 in 1972-1973; by 1987-1988, the number of students was 723, about 85% of whom were white.

Named for the Cincinnati Archdiocese's second archbishop, the adjacent **19 Elder High School,** 3900 Vincent Avenue, was a product of Archbishop Henry Moeller's desire to prevent the proliferation of mediocre parish schools. Moeller hoped to found modern, well-equipped secondary institutions by having parishes pool their resources.

An all-boys school since 1927, Elder began with a few secondary classes that St. Lawrence School instituted in 1912. The program developed into a two-year commercial course, then in 1920, a regular four-year high school for both boys and girls. That year, Archbishop Moeller declared, "High schools are to be erected as soon as possible; and in the larger cities, a central high school for several parishes should be provided."

Pastors representing eleven western parishes met in November 1921 to establish such an institution. One

*Elder High School began as a coeducational facility in the early 1920s but changed to an all-male institution in 1927.*

month later, clergymen of eastern parishes launched a similar effort that led to the establishment of Purcell (now Purcell Marion) High School in Walnut Hills.

The archdiocese issued bonds to finance the Price Hill school; Kunz & Beck designed the Tudor Gothic style building, which was dedicated on September 9, 1923. Classes had begun in 1922 and were held in St. Lawrence School and a nearby Knights of Columbus hall. For the first time in Cincinnati, members of different religious orders taught at the same school.

The growth of the student population at coeducational Elder High School soon required that a second school be built. In 1927, Seton took all the female students, and Elder became an all-male school.

Expansion at Elder began in 1938 with the football stadium. Two Elder students drew blueprints, and the art instructor supervised students who built forms and mixed and poured the concrete. Enlarged in 1947 to seat 10,000, the structure became the largest high school stadium in the city. Elder is known for its athletic successes. In 1972-1973, the school's fiftieth anniversary, its basketball, baseball, and cross-country teams won state championships, and its football team went undefeated.

Two temporary classroom buildings were razed to make way for a new wing, completed in 1959. The north wing was built four years later and the fieldhouse finished in 1981.

Elder's enrollment peaked at 1,915 in 1969-1970, then declined steadily until by 1987-1988, it was 1,040 and nearly 99% white. At that time, 60% of living alumni resided within a five-mile radius of the school and more than half the faculty were Elder graduates, suggesting the stability of the neighborhood and the degree of loyalty the school has inspired.

The **20 Warsaw-Glenway Business District,** now an almost continuous strip of commercial structures through East and West Price Hill, began in the 1880s as small clusters of businesses scattered along the route of a newly built streetcar line. A grocery, a drugstore, lumberyards, a harnessmaker, and several saloons operated along the Pike and in the villages, but further to the east in Price Hill itself, there was almost no commercial activity.

Before streetcar service began in this area, most of Warsaw Pike was lined with undeveloped property and the large and elegant residences of wealthy suburbanites who did not have to rely on public transportation to commute to their jobs. In 1883, George McDuffie, a member of the Price family, obtained a franchise for a horsecar line along this route which he sold to the Consolidated Streetcar Company in 1885. Shortly thereafter, the company opened the horsecar line, and the residential development of Price Hill and northeastern Delhi Township began in earnest.

As large numbers of middle-income families moved into the area, businesses appeared along the streetcar route to serve them. By the mid-1890s, when electric trolleys replaced the horsecars, more than sixty businesses operated along Warsaw Pike from Grand Avenue west to the city line. The largest cluster was near the intersection of Warsaw, St. Lawrence Street, and Terry Street where over twenty concerns, including a marbleworks, two paint stores, a carpenter's shop, grocer, druggist, beer garden, feed store, and concert hall were located.

Although the villages of Cedar Grove and Warsaw were just beyond the end of the streetcar line, the number of businesses there also grew in the mid-1890s to include a dozen shops and a bowling alley. In other parts of Price Hill, however, there were only a few scattered businesses, mostly along the streetcar route on Elberon Avenue and the upper terminus of the incline. Warsaw Pike was definitely Price Hill's primary shopping district.

In 1902, Cincinnati annexed the northeast corner of Delhi Township, including Cedar Grove and Warsaw. Residential development soon extended further west, and the shopping areas also expanded westward along

Warsaw Pike (renamed Glenway Avenue) from the intersection of Quebec Avenue to the new city limits.

As the area's population increased in the early twentieth century, new commercial operations appeared all along the Warsaw-Glenway strip. By the mid-1930s, almost 160 businesses lined the road from Considine and Warsaw to Glenway and Cleves-Warsaw Pike. Among these enterprises were at least two movie houses, a dance hall, and three bowling alleys. The half-dozen filling stations, car repair shops, and three auto sales lots reflected the growing popularity of the automobile.

More than a third of the district's shops were at St. Lawrence corner. All along the strip, however, commercial activity had largely replaced residences. Most of the older homes were either demolished or converted into offices or funeral homes. The Joseph Radel Funeral Home, 4122 Glenway Avenue, for example, occupies the house that hardware dealer Henry Schulte built in the 1880s.

Even after mid-century when many neighborhood business districts were shrinking, the Warsaw-Glenway strip remained healthy. The number of businesses at the eastern end of Warsaw started to decline as the surrounding area became a lower middle-income community, but new commercial enterprises continually appeared to take advantage of the high volume of traffic and low rents. Some of these new businesses became quite successful. Skyline Chili, for example, opened its first outlet in 1949 at 3820 Glenway and now has more than thirty chili parlors throughout Greater Cincinnati.

From the 1960s to the 1970s, the Price Hill business community retained its variety and vitality. In the late 1980s, the Warsaw-Glenway district consisted of more than 170 businesses with a high proportion of them primarily serving the residents of the area.

**One block after Amanda Place, turn right on Rapid Run Pike.**

**21 Rapid Run Park,** at Rapid Run Pike and Glenway Avenue, is one of the few major Cincinnati parks that was not envisioned in the 1907 Kessler plan for a city park and parkway

system. When that plan was created, this land was still undeveloped. By the mid-1920s, however, residential construction was changing the rural character of West Price Hill.

In 1925, city planners recommended that the Park Board acquire land for a park and parkway between Guerley Road and Sunset Avenue in order to preserve an area in which "outstanding scenic possibilities are rapidly being destroyed by new development." The city began purchasing the property for parkland along Guerley Road and Rutledge Avenue in 1928 and built a shelterhouse and a small artificial lake.

This new park, which was originally named Lick Run, preserved some of West Price Hill's undeveloped land and provided a recreational facility for its growing population. Additional acquisitions, including the 1934 addition of the section of Potter's Field Cemetery on the east side of Guerley, expanded the park and connected Rapid Run Pike and Sunset Avenue.

In 1941, the federal Works Progress Administration funded roadwork and improvements designed to make the park more useful throughout the year. When this work was completed in 1942, the park and parkway lands, comprising almost fifty-three acres, were renamed Rapid Run Park.

Today, the park, together with the adjoining cemeteries and the nearby Dunham complex, form a large island of greenspace in an otherwise heavily built-up area.

**Continue on Rapid Run Pike, which bends left into Sunset Avenue.**

The area around Sunset Avenue that city maps often identify simply as Judah Touro Cemetery is, in fact, nine **22 Jewish Cemeteries** that date from the mid-1800s. When in 1855, City Council passed an ordinance prohibiting further interments within city limits, Cincinnati's Jewish community and synagogues were located almost exclusively in the West End, and so Jews looked to nearby rural Price Hill for land for new burial grounds.

The first Jewish cemetery, established in 1821 on Chestnut Street in

the West End, closed in 1849. Bene Israel (Wise Temple) and B'nai Yeshurun (Rockdale Temple) incorporated as United Jewish Cemeteries in 1862 to maintain a cemetery in Walnut Hills.

Not all Jews, however, could afford to pay for membership in either congregation or buy individual burial plots. In November 1855, some German Jews organized the Judah Touro *Verein*, a burial and mutual aid society named in honor of a wealthy New Orleans businessman who had left money for Jewish charities all over the country. The *Verein* opened a cemetery in the Sunset Avenue area in which any Jew could be buried, supported sick members, and set up a fund to help members' widows and children. In 1860, its one hundred members contributed six dollars annually.

Rabbi Isaac Wise of Bene Israel and Rabbi Max Lilienthal of B'nai Yeshurun, attacked the *Verein*, arguing that another Jewish cemetery was not needed. Moreover, they contended, many Jews would not join and support a congregation if free burial was available. Despite such opposition, the Judah Touro Cemetery Association has survived to the present day.

Other congregations and associations located their cemeteries on adjacent land: Adath Israel, the Spanish Hebrew Society, Love Brothers, Chesed Shel Emes, Hirsch Hoffert, Montefiore Mutual Relief Society, Schachnus, and United Jewish Cemetery. A number of other Jewish congregations have cemeteries around Anderson Ferry Road in Price Hill.

**Turn left on Guerley Road where it intersects Sunset Avenue.**

In nineteenth-century America, tuberculosis—the "great white plague" —killed more people each year than either cancer or heart disease. After the bacillus that caused TB was identified in the 1880s, municipalities began creating hospitals and sanatoriums specifically for those with the disease. **23 Dunham Hospital of Hamilton County** was one such facility. Much of the original fourteen-building complex has been demolished, but several of the remaining structures now serve as the Cincinnati

Recreation Commission's Dunham Recreation Complex, 4320 Guerley Road.

Dunham Hospital had its origins in a series of general infectious disease hospitals. An 1816 Cincinnati ordinance called for the establishment of an isolation hospital for those with contagious diseases, primarily smallpox but also cholera, typhoid, and yellow fever. Such a hospital, popularly referred to as the Pest House, was set up during the 1830s on the site now occupied by Music Hall.

The facility was moved across the canal during the 1840s, and then in 1867, to Clifton Heights where it was designated the Rohs Hill Branch of Cincinnati Hospital. In 1879, the Branch Hospital for Contagious Diseases opened on the Guerley farm in Green Township. Tuberculosis victims were still treated in the medical wards of Cincinnati (now University) Hospital until June 8, 1897, when overcrowding and the discovery that TB was an infectious disease brought about the transfer of fifteen patients to the Guerley Road branch.

A bond issue in 1909 funded the construction of additional buildings. The following year was Cincinnati's worst for tuberculosis deaths—1,025. More wards were opened for TB victims, and there was further construction. In 1912, the branch was separated from the hospital and became the Cincinnati Tubercular

*Dunham Hospital's rural location on the western side of Cincinnati ensured that the tuberculosis patients there could enjoy fresh, clean air.*

Hospital.

By the 1920s, city officials felt they could no longer support the sanatorium, which accepted all patients regardless of ability to pay. In 1927, Hamilton County leased the property with an option to buy, and the facility became the Hamilton County Tuberculosis Sanatorium. In 1945, the complex was renamed Dunham Hospital, honoring Dr. Henry Kennon Dunham who had served, without pay, as medical director from 1909 to 1940. The city transferred ownership of the hospital to the county in 1952.

The Hamilton County Tuberculosis Hospital was one of the nation's leading centers for combating the disease. At its peak, it had fourteen buildings spread over one hundred acres, a capacity for nearly 600 patients, and a medical staff of sixteen doctors, 150 nurses, and twelve technicians. Treatment—a year's stay on average—consisted of rest, medication, and possibly surgery to collapse the infected lung so that it could rest and heal. Patients were educated about their illness and provided with vocational training, work therapy, and a variety of recreational opportunities.

Because most patients waited until the tuberculosis was well advanced before seeking diagnosis or treatment, the "San" was seen as a place to go to die rather than to be cured. Among blacks, who were generally poorer and more reluctant to seek diagnosis or enter the institution, the death rate was six times that of whites.

The first "wonder drug," streptomycin, was discovered in 1946, and six years later, a cure for TB was found in isoniazid. By 1967, Dunham Hospital had only 168 patients, and local officials began discussing what to do with the complex. Dunham was not suited for a general hospital or a hospital for the mentally retarded—two suggested options—and on January 21, 1971, trustees voted to close it.

After the operating levy expired at the end of that year, the property reverted to the City of Cincinnati which, in 1973, tore down many of the old structures, including the main hospital building, to make way for playfields that Price Hill badly needed.

The old Occupational Therapy Building is now used for art classes, theater performances, day camps, and other activities. The former nurses' dormitory is a community center for the Dunham Seniors group. The Spanish Colonial style Children's Preventorium Building, where doctors once built up the resistance of children exposed to TB, has become Allen House, a temporary county shelter for abused and neglected children.

*Cross the intersection with Glenway Avenue. Continue on Guerley Road, which becomes Cleves-Warsaw Pike. Turn left on Neeb Road.*

For most of its history, **24 Delhi Township** has been an agricultural area with a small population, but as

153

it was too far from Cincinnati for its inhabitants to use the churches and schools there, township residents established their own institutions. Many of these are clustered along Neeb Road, a north-south road that runs through the middle of the township and is intersected by all the major east-west roads in Delhi.

The first church in the vicinity was the South Bend Baptist Church, founded in 1803. Its members set up a meeting house on the site of the present Delhi Township Administration Building at 934 Neeb Road, almost at what was then the geographic center of the township. The congregation established a burial ground that continued to function as a community cemetery after the church disbanded in 1835. The township still maintains the plot as a memorial its early settlers.

Several churches moved to Neeb Road in the mid-nineteenth century. In 1834, the German Catholics of Delhi started Maria Zum Siege parish in a log church on donated property on Rapid Run Road. Eighteen years later, the parish moved the log building to 810 Neeb. The congregation, which later became Our Lady of Victory, built new church and school buildings on the same site in 1852, 1909, and 1980.

St. John's Evangelical Protestant Church also started in a different part of the township when it was established in 1850, but thirteen years later, members decided to move to Neeb Road. Like the Catholic parish, St. John's congregation reused the same location when it built new churches in 1900 and 1969.

In the nineteenth century, the Delhi Rural School District built most of its schoolhouses either on Rapid Run or Neeb. In the early twentieth century, however, when new residential construction was concentrated in the northern and eastern portions of the Township, the schools were built there. During the 1950s when Delhi's post-World War II building boom began, school officials again chose a site on Neeb Road for a new elementary school because development was shifting to the western and central parts of Delhi. In 1961, the C. O. Harrison School, named for a long-time principal of Delhi Elementary, opened at 585 Neeb Road.

During the 1950s and 1960s, population growth began Delhi's transformation into an "urban town-ship" needing better police, fire, and maintenance services. Before then, public services had been limited; now the township needed facilities to house these newly expanded services. In the late 1960s, officials began moving their public service facilities to Neeb Road and eventually constructed a new administration building next to the cemetery in 1972.

As Delhi became urbanized, some officials felt that township constables and county police could no longer provide adequate protection. The Delhi police began operations in 1964 and moved to Neeb Road in 1969. The expanding maintenance department followed shortly thereafter, and the new administration building housed all of the township offices and activities. Besides the 23-member police force and a 6-man maintenance department, a zoning office created to address the problems of rapid development and, since 1976, a juvenile court were located here.

The Delhi Fire Department has maintained a station on Neeb Road since it was created as an independent volunteer organization in 1935. The township took control of the combined paid and volunteer department in 1986. Although it planned to increase protection by strengthening satellite fire stations, the township retained the firehouse at 697 Neeb Road as the headquarters.

> **Turn right on Delhi Pike, right into the College of Mount St. Joseph. Circle through the old campus to Bender Road.**

The expansion of the city in the decade after the Civil War made land in Price Hill increasingly valuable. The Sisters of Charity sold some of the acreage around their Cedar Grove Academy for residential development. In 1869, the Order purchased the Biggs farm, five miles to the west in Delhi, named the property Mount St. Joseph, and used the farmhouse as a novitiate. Three years later, the Sisters transferred the motherhouse to the new location, and in 1883, established a cemetery nearby.

In July 1884, a fire destroyed most of the buildings, but within two years, reconstruction was complete. Using money from the sale of the Price Hill land, the Sisters constructed a sprawl-ing brick building with a chapel. Twenty years later, the boarding school was moved from Price Hill to the 400-acre Delhi site.

In 1920, the Sisters of Charity opened **25 The College of Mount St. Joseph-on-the-Ohio,** now 5701 Delhi Road, in the boarding school building. Mount St. Joseph was Ohio's first Catholic women's college to offer the baccalaureate degree. Although Catholic in tradition, the college has a faculty, staff, and student body with diverse religious backgrounds; it has been coed since 1969, though the change was formalized only in 1986. The Sisters of Charity promote the institution as a Christian educational community offering liberal arts, nursing, paralegal, and other programs.

In September 1962, the Order moved the college across Delhi Pike into eleven new contemporary style buildings. The complex includes an auditorium with a theater, administrative offices, Archbishop Alter Library, Aquinas Hall, Mater Dei Chapel, Seton Hall, gymnasium, fine arts center, and science building. The old campus houses recreational facilities for the elderly and a preschool. It also serves as the residence for the Sisters and a site for retreats and homecoming activities.

By the early 1970s, the school administrators faced major budgetary deficits. Like many small private colleges, Mount St. Joseph was suffering from inflation and declining enrollment. In 1964, the institution had 1,000 full-time students, and the administrators had projected an enrollment of 1,600 by the early 1970s. By 1975, however, the college had fewer than 900 students and was on the verge of closing.

But in the late 1970s, the institution made a comeback under the administration of Sister Jean Patrice Harrington. She cut the staff, froze salaries, instigated an aggressive fundraising campaign, raised tuition, limited tenured positions, and started a number of non-traditional degree and certificate programs. By the mid-1980s, Mount St. Joseph was prospering at a time when many small colleges had failed.

> **Turn right on Bender Road, left on Delhi Pike.**

*The College of Mount St. Joseph was considerably expanded in the early 1960s.*

Before Delhi Township began its rapid growth in the 1950s, the area that is now the **26 Delhi Pike Business District,** a commercial strip concentrated mostly between Anderson Ferry and Greenwell Roads, was occupied primarily by greenhouses and truck farms. While most Delhi farmers took their produce to the markets in Cincinnati, some of the growers, particularly those along the Pike, sold directly to the public from the greenhouses or farm markets that were established in the early twentieth century.

When interest in the area as a commuter suburb began to grow in the 1930s and 1940s, modest homes also began to appear on this section of Delhi Pike. The residential development of Delhi Township accelerated considerably after World War II. Between 1950 and 1970, Delhi's population grew from 6,347 to more than 25,000, and the new residents needed more shopping facilities. Initially, small stores such as meat markets, carry-outs, and dry cleaners opened in scattered clusters along the Pike. But by the late 1950s, larger businesses also began to operate here.

In 1956, developers purchased a large estate on the south side of the Pike near the western end of Mt. Alverno Road. Two years later, the Delfair Shopping Center opened at 5915 Delhi Pike. Delfair, an early example of a suburban shopping center, had large stores set well back from the road and a spacious common parking lot in front.

The center included a hardware store, a Kresge's 5-and-10-cents store, an Alber's supermarket, a bowling alley, and miscellaneous small shops. The center differed from the earlier shopping clusters because of its size and ample parking lot. It was also unlike most later shopping centers because it had a second floor over the bowling alley with offices for doctors, a dentist, insurance agents, and a loan company.

Though the *Hamilton County Master Plan* of 1964 called for the preservation of some suburban agricultural land to combine with parkland in creating greenspace, residential and commercial development steadily eroded Delhi Township's farm acreage. Gas stations, discount department stores, drugstores, banks, and fast food restaurants steadily replaced the older homes and greenhouses.

In 1974, the Huenefeld family sold the last major farm on this section of Delhi Pike, a 20-acre tract to the east of the Delfair Shopping Center. Despite the opposition of homeowners on Mt. Alverno Road, K-Mart built the Delco Shopping Plaza on the site. By the mid-1980s, the Delhi Garden Center, 5222 Delhi Pike, was one of the few old greenhouse businesses that remained.

Heavy development along the Road brought a number of problems, the worst of which was traffic congestion. Delhi Pike could not accommodate the number of cars attracted by the stores until the Hamilton County Engineering Department widened that section of the road to five lanes in 1986.

The uncontrolled development on Delhi Pike also concerned township officials and residents. After Delhi Township took over local control of its zoning process and appointed a full-time zoning officer in 1974, the township structured the zoning at each end of the business district to prevent further commercial encroachment into residential areas on the Pike.

The new restrictions involved the use of "down-zoning," a system of graduated zones that bracketed a commercial area first with an area for offices, then multi-family units, and finally single-family homes on the outer edge. The regular turnover in store occupancy further limited the need for new business construction; in the 1980s, many of the major structures already housed a second or third-generation tenant. Merchants wishing to enter the area could generally find space, which reduced pressure to expand the district.

*Continue on Delhi Pike, turn right on Fairbanks Avenue, left to River Road, and left on State Avenue, returning to the Eighth Street Viaduct where the tour ends.*

155

# Tour 8

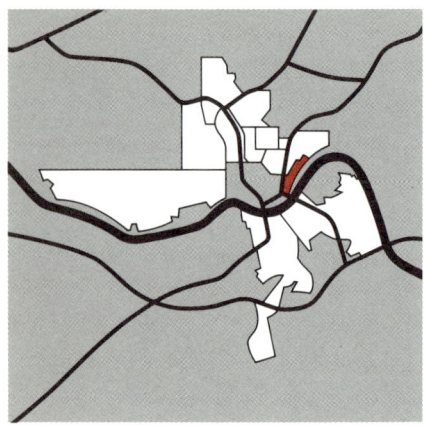

# Mt. Adams - Eden Park

Although today property in the Mt. Adams-Eden Park area is among the most desirable and attractive in the city, Cincinnatians of the early nineteenth century generally regarded the area as largely useless wasteland. From 1800 to 1830, the steep slopes, gullies, and rocky hilltops that lay between the eastern edge of the basin and the Kemper family's Walnut Hill farm—later the southern part of Walnut Hills—were occupied only by stone quarries and a few scattered houses. While much of the area lay within city limits and was not far from the center of town, its rough features and inaccessibility prevented it from being developed.

Most of the property in this eastern area was owned at that time by Martin Baum (1795-1831), Jacob Wheeler, David Kilgour (1767-1830), and William Lytle (1790-1831), all bankers and merchants. Primarily speculators rather than developers, these men only divided some land at the base of the hill into smaller lots for sale. This changed in 1830 when Nicholas Longworth (1782-1863) acquired a great part of the property in this area. Longworth not only speculated with the land but also put it to use.

One of Longworth's pet projects was wine production. During the 1830s and 1840s, Longworth established a number of vineyards around Cincinnati, including one on a large tract south of the Kempers' Walnut Hill farm. This vineyard, which he called the Garden of Eden, produced excellent Catawba grapes. From these, his wineries made a sparkling wine known as Golden Wedding Champagne, which Henry Wadsworth Longfellow praised as:

> . . . the richest and best
> Is the wine of the West
> That grows by the beautiful river . . .
> And this song of the wine
> This greeting of mine
> The winds and the birds shall deliver
> To the Queen of the West
> In her garlands dressed
> By the banks of the beautiful river.

Longworth also donated four acres on the southern section of the hilltop to the Cincinnati Astronomical Society for an observatory site. Critics maintained that he made the gift merely to enhance the value of his adjoining acreage. While Longworth was a frequent and generous supporter of many local cultural, scientific, and charitable organizations, the new observatory did call attention to the area.

When the Cincinnati Observatory's cornerstone was laid in 1843, former President John Quincy Adams spoke at the dedication. City Council named the hill—until then known unofficially as Mt. Ida—Mt. Adams in his honor. From the mid-1840s to the late 1860s, a new generation of speculators and developers including E. and F. Avery, Henry Miller, George Martin, and Timothy Kirby purchased land in Mt. Adams that they subdivided and began selling. These men also laid out and named the area's streets. Martin Street, for example, passed through George Martin's subdivision, and Hatch Street was named after George Hatch, trustee of the Avery estate.

Longworth wanted his Garden of Eden to remain intact, however. In 1842, around the same time he donated land for the observatory,

*Mt. Adams' streets on the hilltop and on the slopes were densely built up with homes for working-class families.*

Longworth offered to sell the vineyard to the city for parkland at a quarter of what he considered its market value. City officials felt that the acreage was not worth the price and rejected the proposition. Longworth periodically repeated his offer, both before and after 1850 when Cincinnati annexed the remainder of this hilltop along with the southern part of Walnut Hills.

Disease destroyed southwestern Ohio's wine industry in the late 1850s and ended the Garden of Eden's use as a vineyard, but Longworth was confident that the land would increase in value as residential development continued. He was angered by the city's view that there was no need for public parks outside the basin where most Cincinnatians lived. By 1860-1861, when council created the Board of Park Trustees to manage city parks, over $100,000 had been spent on parks in Over-the-Rhine and the West End.

Only in the mid-1860s, several years after Longworth's death, did city officials, motivated by concerns about public health, negotiate with Longworth's son, Joseph (1813-1883), for the Garden of Eden. The Board of Health strongly maintained that more parks, which provided city residents a place to relax in the fresh air, were needed. Further, an 1866 Water Works Department report argued that a large, new reservoir on high ground would soon be needed to provide water to the growing hilltop suburbs and would improve the quality of the water supply.

The area north of Mt. Adams was ideal for both of these purposes, and in 1865-1866, the city leased or purchased the Longworth property and several adjoining tracts. This land became Eden Park and was officially opened to the public in 1870-1871.

But Eden Park and Mt. Adams were still difficult to reach. The few roads that went up the hillsides were too steep for horse-drawn streetcars to ascend and descend safely. In 1874, the construction of the Mt. Adams Incline, which ran from the foot of the hill up to Celestial Street, made the area more accessible. The incline consisted of platforms drawn up and down two parallel tracks by a stationary steam engine, and it carried both passengers and freight. At the end of the 1870s, the incline began to carry horsecars, becoming a link in George Kerper's streetcar lines that ran from downtown to Mt. Adams and Walnut Hills.

With its new accessibility, Mt. Adams experienced a building boom between the 1870s and 1890s. Its streets were quickly lined with the modest brick and frame houses of lower middle-income families and a variety of neighborhood institutions, including churches, bakeries, saloons, groceries, a savings and loan association, a firehouse, and a bowling alley. Most of the businesses and institutions clustered on St. Gregory and Pavilion Streets, but individual groceries and saloons were also scattered throughout the community.

Development was largely determined by topography. Mt. Adams was primarily a residential area because the hilltop was not well suited for industry. It did provide an excellent location for the observatory until the 1870s, when pollution forced the facility to be relocated. Because of Mt. Adams' excellent view of the Ohio River, two artillery emplacements were set up here during the Civil War, one at the end of Fort View Place and the other on the site of the playground and overlook near Playhouse in the Park. They were part of the city's defense against Confederate attack.

The views from the hill also attracted entertainment establishments that counted on these panoramas to draw customers. At the Pyrotechnic Garden, H.P. Diehl put on exhibitions of fireworks he manufactured. The Highland House, an extremely popular beer garden and concert hall, was built next to the incline in 1875.

Mt. Adams, however, lacked the space and transportation facilities needed for manufacturing. Aside from a few very specialized small

*The Rookwood Pottery was the best-known of the few industries that were located on Mt. Adams.*

158

workshops such as Diehl's fireworks plant, the Sterling Cut Glass Company works, and the Rookwood Pottery, factories were not established on the hill.

Most of the workers living in Mt. Adams were employed in the nearby Deer Creek Valley and on the riverfront. In the second half of the nineteenth century, railyards, the waterworks, grain and coal elevators, cotton mills, and factories producing galvanized metal, white lead, chemicals, sheet metal, steam engines, and wagons lay within a few blocks of the hill's eastern and southern slopes. During this period, the employees of these firms, even the semi-skilled, tried to move out of the crowded basin just as wealthier citizens were doing. Neighborhoods like Mt. Adams provided an alternative to life in the crowded streets of Over-the-Rhine or downtown for many who could not afford to live in more distant, more expensive suburbs.

At the same time that Mt. Adams became popular as a residential area, Eden Park grew in popularity. The character of the former Garden of Eden was shaped for most of the first decade of its use by Park Superintendent Adolph Strauch (1822-1883). Strauch, a Prussian immigrant and landscape architect, was known for his natural designs for cemeteries, including Spring Grove, and private estates such as Robert Bowler's Mt. Storm in Clifton. Strauch tried to retain the natural features of the parks as much as possible, arguing that people benefited more from visiting a park that preserved and celebrated nature than a landscape cluttered with structures and contrived plantings.

In the 1880s, after Strauch had left the park system, the city stripped the Park Board of its responsibilities. The public parks became a source of land for a variety of projects. Portions of Eden Park on Gilbert Avenue were sold off for industrial development, and property in its heart was designated for the Art Museum and Academy, just as land in Burnet Woods was taken for the University of Cincinnati. Other man-made additions followed, such as a bandstand and eventually, a variety of monuments and memorials.

By the early twentieth century, the remaining usable land in Mt. Adams had been built on, and until the 1940s, the area was a very stable neighborhood. A few new structures periodically replaced old buildings, but land use and the size of the new buildings remained essentially unchanged. Population was also stable, both in size and character—predominantly white, lower middle-income Catholic families. But in the years after World War II, many of the younger residents began leaving Mt. Adams for new suburban communities that offered modern housing, bigger yards, and ample parking space.

By the mid-1950s, residents and public officials perceived the area to be declining. Many of the small neighborhood stores had closed. A growing percentage of the homes were no longer owner-occupied, and some showed signs of neglect and abuse. The industries that once had crowded at the base of the hill were also moving away or closing, often because of road improvements. City planners and some community residents began suggesting that the only way to improve the neighborhood was to tear everything down and start over.

Even as this philosophy was becoming widespread, a new trend was developing. In the early 1950s, upper-income professionals had begun moving to Mt. Adams and remodeling or replacing old houses to take advantage of the fine views and proximity to downtown. The public became increasingly aware of Mt. Adams as a potentially desirable neighborhood. It was within walking distance not only of the central business district but also Eden Park which had become a center of the city's cultural activities with the addition of the Playhouse, Natural History Museum, and Krohn Conservatory.

In the early 1960s, investors began buying and renovating buildings, and in 1962-1963, Marvin L. Warner built a 24-story apartment tower on the southwest brow of the hill. Mt. Adams was undergoing a renaissance, attracting not only upper-income residents but also many young people who wanted to take advantage of that portion of housing stock that was still inexpensive to rent or purchase. A new generation of bars, specialty shops, and restaurants serving a city-wide clientele and growing tourist traffic took the place of the older neighborhood businesses.

For a while, there was considerable tension between the different groups living on and visiting Mt. Adams. Old residents often resented the influx of newcomers, especially the young with their different lifestyles and values. Noise, parking problems, and litter accompanied the growing patronage of the businesses and bars by customers from outside the community. Many longtime residents complained that the "hippies" and "tourists" had ruined Mt. Adams, while the more recent residents and businessmen often felt that the "old timers" were narrow-minded and bigoted. These tensions gradually eased, property values continued to rise, and the new residents, a predominantly middle to upper-income population, adopted a more middle-class lifestyle.

Due to a series of economic recessions and changing shopping patterns, the specialty shops were gone by the 1980s, but a second generation of bars and restaurants appeared that, like the housing, catered to a higher-income clientele.

Mt. Adams has frequently been held up as an example of successful neighborhood renovation without government support. Certain factors—its views, location, and small size—gave it advantages over other old neighborhoods, but even so, the change that Mt. Adams underwent in twenty years was remarkable. In the late 1980s, however, the area still had its problems. Parking was scarce though several new parking lots had been created. Residents also lacked some basic services, such as a bank or a drugstore in their neighborhood.

Landslides were common after heavy rains, particularly where new development had altered the slopes. A serious landslide took place on the southwest side of the hill in the late 1970s because new highway construction had chewed away the bottom of the slope. The instability was corrected only with the demolition of most of the structures on that part of Mt. Adams and the construction of a $25 million retaining wall. Nonetheless, Mt. Adams has remained an extremely popular area and continues to attract and retain new residents.

**Mt. Adams-Eden Park**

Tour Length
5 miles

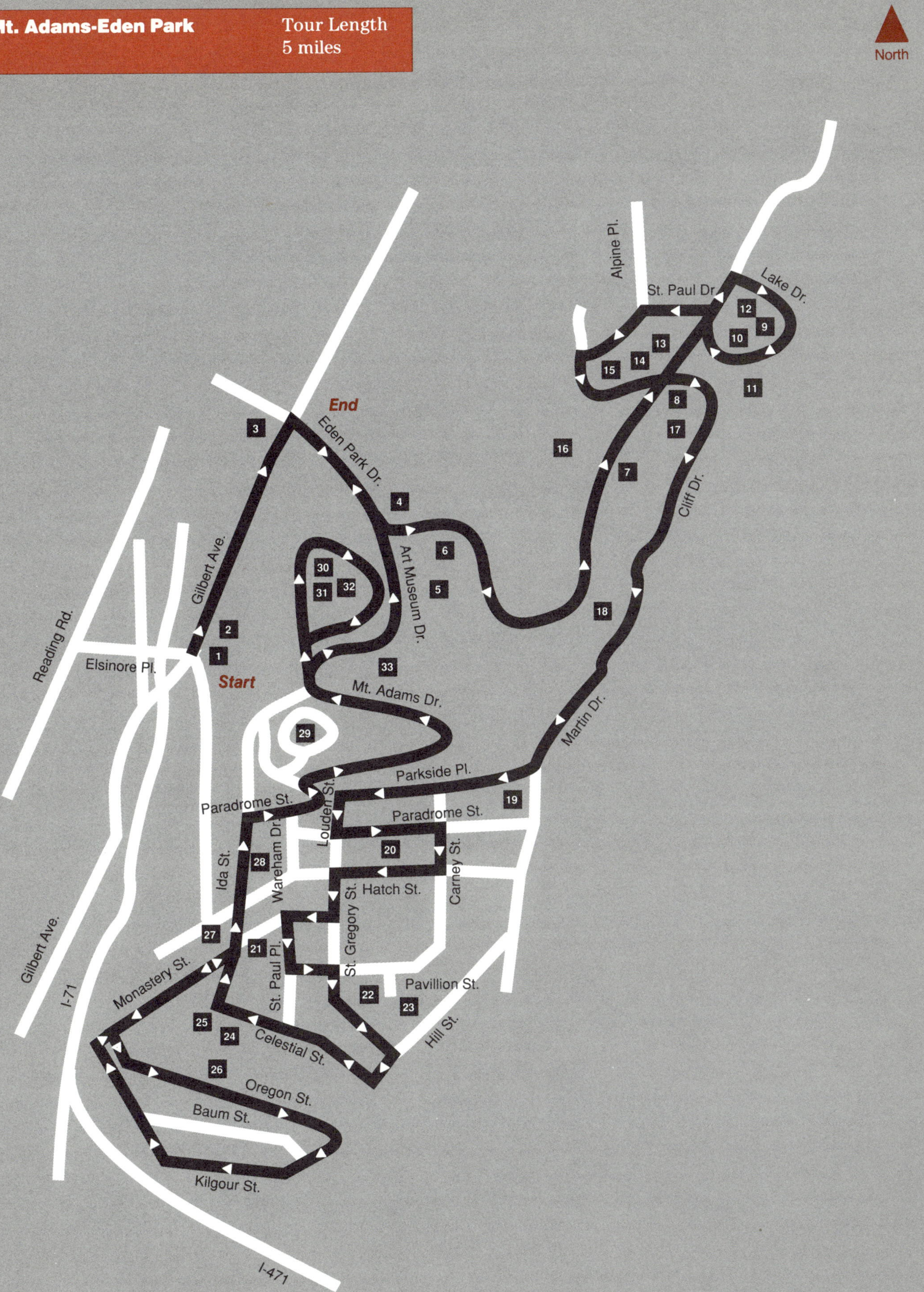

Alpine Pl.

St. Paul Dr

Lake Dr.

12
9
13
10
15 14
11
8
17
16
7
**End**
3
Eden Park Dr.
Gilbert Ave.
4
18
30 32
31
6
5
Art Museum Dr.
2
1
Reading Rd.
Elsinore Pl.
**Start**
33
Mt. Adams Dr.
Martin Dr.
29
Parkside Pl.
Paradrome St.
19
Paradrome St.
Ida St.
Wareham Dr.
Louden St.
20
28
Hatch St.
Carney St.
Gilbert Ave.
I-71
27
St. Gregory St.
Monastery St.
21
St. Paul Pl.
22
Pavillion St.
23
25
Hill St.
24
Celestial St.
26
Oregon St.
Baum St.
Kilgour St.

I-471

# Mt. Adams - Eden Park

**Tour begins on Gilbert Avenue at Elsinore Place. Proceed north on Gilbert Avenue.**

The stone **1 Elsinore Tower,** at Gilbert Avenue and Elsinore Place, was built in 1883 as a valve house for the Eden Park Reservoir. It once also served as an entrance to Eden Park; the stone steps behind the gate are a short cut up the hill to the Art Museum. Because the Water Works Department wanted to enhance the park landscape, a competition for the project was held. Cincinnati architect Samuel Hannaford (1860-1936) won the contest with a design that is presumed to have been inspired by Elsinore Castle in Denmark where Shakespeare set *Hamlet*.

The reservoir valves are now housed in a vault underneath the tower.

The modern limestone-faced building that **2 The Cincinnati Museum of Natural History,** 1720 Gilbert Avenue, dedicated on August 13, 1957, was erected on land that had been deeded to the Art Museum in 1881. The establishment of the museum in Eden Park is an example of the use of parklands for cultural or civic purposes.

The museum traces its history back to the Western Museum—the first museum of natural history west of the Alleghenies—that Daniel Drake (1785-1852) and others interested in science set up in 1818 in the Cincinnati College, using their collections of Indian relics and fossils. For a time, John James Audubon (1785-1851) stuffed birds and animals and painted exhibit cases for the museum.

But Cincinnatians of the economically uncertain 1820s had little interest in scientific education. When Drake, always the most powerful force behind the Western Museum, left Cincinnati for several years, the project was abandoned. The directors tried to sell the collections but, in 1823 gave the materials to the curator, Joseph Dorfeuille, a scientist and entrepreneur who had lectured for the museum.

Dorfeuille quickly changed the museum from the scientific to the sensational. Crowds flocked to Third and Sycamore Streets to see the horrific "Infernal Regions," a depiction of Hell conceived of by British author Frances Trollope. The scene featured wax and mechanical figures created by local sculptor Hiram Powers (1805-1873) and animated by clockmaker Luman Watson (1790-1834). There was also an exhibit portraying local murderers committing their crimes.

In 1835, Dr. Drake and other founders of the old Western Museum made another attempt at promoting the serious study of natural history, setting up the Western Academy of Natural Sciences.

Thirty-five years later, a group of men that included members of the Western Academy founded the Cincinnati Society of Natural History, incorporating the academy's library, collections, and treasury. This venture succeeded. In 1875, the organization received a bequest of $50,000, and two years later bought a building at Broadway near Third Street to house its collections. The Society of Natural History created programs for school children and contributed to Cincinnati's intellectual life by featuring world-famous scientists as speakers.

In 1934, the Ohio Mechanics Institute (OMI) on Walnut at Central Parkway offered the Society the use of its ground floor. This proposal was made, in large measure, due to interest taken in the museum by the Cincinnatus Association, especially Frederick A. Geier, president of the Cincinnati Milling Machine Company.

By the mid-1950s, the Society of Natural History was recording some 100,000 visitors each year and was also involved in important fieldwork, including archaeological excavations at Newtown and Saylor Park. Then in 1957, OMI announced that it needed the floor space; the society and its museum had to move.

The Geier family contributed generously to the building fund, and the city approved use of part of the land in Eden Park that the Art Museum controlled. Once established on Gilbert Avenue, the Cincinnati Museum of Natural History (CMNH) almost immediately began construction of the first of five additions. In 1961, the planetarium—Cincinnati's first—was completed; the 1960s also saw the completion of the Wilderness Trail, an exhibit of native animals, and one of the nation's first walk-through reconstructions of a cave.

The Museum of Natural History has constantly expanded its school and public programing. Its scientists have undertaken research on Fort Ancient Indians, Ohio Valley Ice Age fossils, birds of prey of the tropics, and a number of other subjects. CMNH's Edge of Appalachia Preserve System in Adams County, Ohio, was acquired in 1957 and by 1985 had grown to almost 6,000 acres, making it the largest museum-managed nature preserve in the United States.

After Hamilton County voters passed a bond issue on May 6, 1986, the Museum of Natural History began planning a move to larger quarters in the Union Terminal in the West End.

One of the few remnants of the nearby industries which employed many Mt. Adams workers is the former **3 Baldwin Piano Company Building,** 1801 Gilbert Avenue. The 7-story brick building with distinctive clock-tower originally housed Baldwin's assembly department, administrative offices, and laboratories that provided 800 to 900 jobs. The building was

*Before fire destroyed a major part of the Baldwin Piano Company factory complex in 1964, the plant spread over a considerable part of the Deer Creek Valley opposite Eden Park.*

completed in 1920 and replaced a number of older structures.

Dwight H. Baldwin (1821-1899) came to Cincinnati from Pennsylvania in 1856, taught music, and in 1862, began selling pianos and organs from a shop on Fourth Street. Around 1866, he hired Lucien Wulsin (1845-1912) who oversaw the company's growth for the next forty-six years and whose children and grandchildren later served as Baldwin Company directors. It was Wulsin who gradually made the Baldwin Company the most prominent dealer of pianos and organs in the South and West.

In the mid-1880s, Eastern manufacturers began to react against Baldwin's growth, cutting back its retail territory and even canceling contracts with the company. Baldwin began to manufacture its own pianos and organs in 1890 in a converted planing mill on this Eden Park site, purchased in 1886 after the Park Board had decided that all parkland west of Gilbert Avenue was "no longer necessary for park and municipal purposes."

Baldwin pianos and organs were shipped all over the world and won national and international prizes. Presidents Taft, Coolidge, and Truman have owned Baldwin pianos, as have Leonard Bernstein, Erroll Garner, Burt Bacharach, and Liberace. Pope Pius XI designated the company "Purveyor to the Holy See." But the biggest part of Baldwin's business was the production of instruments that middle-income families could afford and, by the 1930s, piano cases were designed to match various styles of furniture.

In 1925, Baldwin sold 11,000 player pianos alone, but the growing popularity of radio essentially destroyed this market. The Depression added to the company's problems. During the 1940s and 1950s, Baldwin became heavily involved in defense production, making code disks for missile guidance systems and electronic fuses for explosives. This research gave the company an edge in the new electric organ market.

In 1960 and 1961, several portions of the firm's business were moved to plants in the South where labor costs were lower. The one millionth piano was completed on March 22, 1974.

Baldwin began diversification in the late 1960s, moving into banking, finance, and insurance. By 1981, it had merged with United Corporation to become Baldwin-United, a corporate giant. However, the purchase that year of MGIC Corporation, the nation's largest mortgage insurer, marked the downturn of the company's fortunes. Baldwin-United filed for Chapter 11 bankruptcy in 1983; its figures showed a $1.4 billion operating loss and a negative worth of $1 billion.

A group of company executives bought the still profitable Baldwin Piano & Organ Company in 1984 and maintained headquarters here until March 1986, when the business moved to Clermont County. That same year, the largest Chapter 11 reorganization in U.S. Bankruptcy Court history became a reality as Baldwin's remaining subsidiaries were remodeled into a much smaller company engaged in trading stamps, insurance, and travel.

In December 1987, the Baldwin Piano & Organ Company announced the purchase of the piano and electronic keyboard business of the Wurlitzer Company, another historic Cincinnati firm founded by Rudolph Wurlitzer in 1862. The acquisition gave Baldwin a 30% share of the market; the remainder largely belongs to Japanese imports.

Corporex, a real estate development firm, purchased the former piano company building for renovation as the Grand Baldwin, the centerpiece of a proposed $200 million office complex project aimed at extending Cincinnati's business district further north along the Reading Road- I-71 corridor.

**Turn right on Eden Park Drive.**

On the left, near the fork of the road, a bronze plaque marks the oaks of **4 Heroes' Grove,** planted in memory of men and women who died in World War I. The trees both enhance the park and provide patriotic inspiration.

**Bear left at the fork in the road, staying on Eden Park Drive.**

Quite probably Eden Park owes its existence to the Water Works Department which recommended that a reservoir be built on a hill in Mt. Adams where the elevation would provide enough pressure to send water to the newer suburbs. **5 Mirror Lake,** a shallow, three-quarter acre reflecting pool, was constructed in 1965 when the city completed conversion of the double tank, 100 million gallon capacity reservoir built from 1866 to 1878. The massive limestone wall around the reservoir was 1,252 feet long, over forty-eight feet thick at the base, and eighteen feet wide at the top.

The Deer Creek and city sewers emptied raw sewage into the Ohio River near the pumping station on Front Street, and the reservoir there held less than a day's supply of water. Cincinnati needed to insure an adequate supply of uncontaminated water, but there was no money to construct a new waterworks plant further upstream. Facilities were established in Eden Park.

Debris in the water that was pumped directly from the Ohio River was allowed to settle in the open basins of the new reservoir before the water flowed into the downtown main. However, when the basins were cleaned in alternate years, everything from the bodies of suicide victims to wrecked cars was found on the scum-coated bottoms. More pleasant were the summer picnics and dances held in the cleaned basins before they were refilled.

Though chemical purification of city water began in 1907 at the plant upriver at California, Ohio, the Eden Park reservoir remained open. In the 1960s, the present, deeper, 80 million gallon tank was built within the walls of the old upper basin. The stone retaining wall around the lower basin was largely removed and the basin filled in for ballfields.

In 1874, Superintendent of Public Parks Adolph Strauch wrote: *"In regard to the adornments of our Parks I will merely say, that most people visit Parks and Gardens for the purpose of enjoying the productions of nature, and very seldom stone and mortar, and that the greatest admiration is always expressed for free nature when but little embellished by art."*

His vision was gradually modified, and one of the earlier landscape "decorations" was the fanciful bronze and stone **6 Gazebo** completed in 1904 at the junction of Eden Park and

*Eden Park was created both as a recreational area for the city's residents and as a site for important waterworks facilities, including the massive Eden Park Reservoir.*

Fulton Drives. It replaced a thatched roof springhouse built over a spring whose waters were alleged to have medicinal value. The spring was closed when the water was found to be polluted.

During the early 1970s, artists and craftspersons from across the country came annually to the area around the gazebo to exhibit and sell their works at Summerfair, now held at Coney Island. Summerfair, Inc., which organizes the show, headed a fund drive that paid for a much-needed restoration of the gazebo in 1983.

The Board of Park Commissioners report for 1894 judged that the greenhouse completed that year in Eden Park had proven to be "an admirable investment" for growing and preserving plants used in Cincinnati parks and for attracting visitors. The commissioners hoped that a larger greenhouse could be built "to meet all the needs of the various parks, and then there might be established such a small and well-labeled collection of plants as would attract still more interest." The **7** **Irwin M. Krohn Conservatory,** opened April 1, 1933, has far exceeded these aspirations.

Covering 22,000 square feet, the glass and steel Eden Park Greenhouse

was renamed in 1937 to honor Irwin Krohn (c.1869-1948) for his twenty-five years of service on the Park Board. It is not used as a practical laboratory by high school and university instructors as the Park Board's two previous greenhouses had been, but it continues the tradition of seasonal and holiday displays.

The Krohn Conservatory contains the central Palm House with tropical foliage, fishponds, and a 20-foot waterfall, and the Desert Garden, Tropical House, Floral Display, and Orchid House wings. Large stained glass pieces on each side of the entryway depict trees and flowers.

Another 1894 improvement made Eden Park more accessible to visitors. The **8** **Melan Arch Bridge,** crossing above Eden Park Drive to connect Marshall Hill and Cliff Drive, was begun by Austrian Fritz von Empergen of the Melan Arch Construction Company of New York. With this project, the firm pioneered a new technology that used concrete to encase an arch made of steel I-beams. The cold winter forced Von Empergen to abandon his work, and the bridge was finished the following spring by a local contractor, Ludwig Eig.

The four granite eagles atop stone columns on each side of the road were taken from the Chamber of Commerce building downtown which was gutted by fire in 1911. A 1966 marker commemorates the Melan Arch Bridge as the first of its kind in Ohio.

**Turn right on Lakes Drive to one of Eden Park's Ohio River overlooks.**

Spanned by a concrete footbridge, the **9** **Twin Lakes** cover what was once part of a limestone quarry that, along with the many others nearby, provided building materials for numerous Cincinnati houses.

Civic and ethnic pride lay behind the presentation of a bronze replica of **10** **"The Wolf of Rome,"** "Lupa Romana," on September 20, 1931, by the Cincinnati chapter of the Order of the Sons of Italy. The statue is the official symbol of the City of Rome and depicts the legend of its founding: a larger-than-life she-wolf suckles the twins Romulus and Remus.

The piece was a gift of the government of Benito Mussolini in recognition of the fact that Cincinnati was the only American city to bear the name of a Roman hero—Cincinnatus. The monument also recognized the contributions of Italian Americans to the progress of Cincinnati and Ohio.

Several locations for the Capitoline Wolf were suggested before the work was installed in Eden Park: on Central Parkway, at the zoo, on Fountain Square, or on a tall column on one of the terraces around the Art Museum.

The wrong version of the wolf had been shipped from Rome for the dedication ceremonies; the correct copy of the statue was unveiled on June 12, 1932.

Two of the war memorials near the overlook are dedicated to men who served in World War I. Both are stone benches, useful as well as aesthetically appropriate for a park.

The first, the **11 Battery F, 13th Field Artillery Memorial,** to the right of the drive behind the play area, was presented in 1925 by the mothers of the 324 officers and men whose names are listed on a bronze tablet. The **12 Frederick W. Galbraith Memorial,** on the left-hand side of the roadway, was dedicated in 1923 by the American Legion to honor its founder and first national commander.

**Turn left on Eden Park Drive, right on St. Paul Drive.**

Two other war memorials are located in this portion of Eden Park. A fund drive by the local chapter of the Vietnam Veterans paid for the **13 Vietnam Memorial,** dedicated April 8, 1984. It is the work of Cincinnati sculptor Kenneth Bradford. Bronze figures of two American soldiers, one black, one white, stand on a granite block. One man is consoling the other over the loss of a friend.

Behind this statue is the **14 GAR Flagstaff** with its ornamental base, moved here from its original location on the overlook. Presented by the Daughters of the Union Veterans of the Civil War, it was dedicated in 1930 during the sixty-fourth national encampment of the Grand Army of the Republic in Eden Park.

**At intersection with Alpine Place, continue left on St. Paul Drive, and turn left on Cliff Drive.**

The red brick **15 Water Tower** was designed by the Cincinnati firm of Samuel Hannaford & Sons so that, as the Water Works' engineer recommended, it "should in no way detract from the beauty of the park landscape." The tower was used as a pressure tank to move water from the reservoir to the mains and hydrants in Walnut Hills. And for five cents, park visitors could ride an elevator to the top of the tower to enjoy the panoramic view. Many felt that the tower improved the scenery along the Ohio River as castles in Germany enhanced the Rhine River valley.

The tower was closed in 1912, but during World War I, it served as a guardhouse for infantry encamped in the park. Somewhat later, when night flying was still new, a revolving beacon was placed atop the water tower. In 1943, the city turned the tower over to the Park Board for preservation. However, the copper spire that capped the smaller section of the tower was removed during a wartime scrap metal drive.

In 1947, the city abandoned an effort to remodel the landmark for use as a Safety Department communications center when several workers contracted a fever caused by the pigeon droppings that had accumulated there over the years. The tower remains an ornament to Eden Park.

*The Eden Park Water Tower has graced this hilltop in the park since 1894.*

Behind the water tower are four **16 Memorial Groves**. The earliest, just east of the water tower, is a second **Heroes' Grove,** "Planted and Dedicated to the Memory of the Heroes of 1776 and the Patriots who Suffered with Washington at Valley Forge," as a marker there explains. A Cincinnati doctor, A. E. Jones, brought many of these oaks from Revolutionary War battlefields, and the first tree was planted, as he had wished, in 1876.

The other three groves owe their inspiration to a group of Cincinnati German Americans who consulted with the Royal Chief Forester of the German Empire when he visited the city in 1881, about planting trees in public parks.

On April 27, 1882, Arbor Day, school children marched to this hillside. Following a 13-gun salute and considerable oratory, the children and members of the American Forestry Congress, then meeting in Cincinnati, planted the trees that would, the *Cincinnati Enquirer* reported, "forever remind us of our great men in politics, literature, and good works, and their good deeds." Adolph Strauch arranged the plantings.

The largest of the four groves is **Presidents' Grove** where a tree has been planted for every American president. The white oak honoring George Washington was brought from near his tomb. Since 1882, Presidents have selected the sort of tree to honor them. Franklin Roosevelt requested a tulip tree; Richard Nixon, a bald cyprus; Jimmy Carter, a loblolly pine, and Ronald Reagan, an American sycamore. Each tree has a small granite marker.

South of Presidents' Grove is **Pioneers' Grove** where thirty-six deciduous trees were planted in memory of Cincinnati's founders. A stone tablet in the grove lists the pioneers' names.

On April 30, 1882, thirty-five trees were planted in **Authors' Grove** to honor writers of local, national, and international reputation, including Cooper, Poe, Hawthorne, Whittier, Emerson, and German-born American Revolutionary War general Baron von Steuben. In 1980, the Park Board set the granite name markers that were still in good condition in a semicircular brick wall here.

**Continue on Cliff Drive, crossing the Melan Arch Bridge.**

The **17 Navigation Monument,** a 30-foot high, gray granite obelisk, was dedicated on October 23, 1929, by President Herbert C. Hoover during the celebration of the canalization of the Ohio River. A series of forty-nine locks and dams gave the river a depth of nine feet, making it navigable year round.

The obelisk marks the approximate mid-point of the 980 miles of waterway between Pittsburgh and Cairo, Illinois. Bronze tablets on the monument record the names of those who led the canalization effort.

**Follow roadway as it curves right and downhill. Turn left on Martin Drive.**

The red brick building at 1430 Martin Drive was once the **18 Pumping Station** for the reservoir, put into service in 1894 along with the water tower and, like it, designed to enhance the park landscape. The station was abandoned in the early twentieth century, and in 1939 was converted into the central radio communications center for the Cincinnati Safety Department. That facility was dismantled in the mid-1980s.

The remains of the lower reservoir basin can also be seen to the right of the road.

**Turn right on Parkside Place.**

Among the cultural and arts institutions in Eden Park is the **19 Cincinnati Art Club,** 1021 Parkside Place, the second-oldest art club in the United States. The club was founded in 1890 and maintained quarters on East Third Street from 1924 until that house and four others were demolished for the construction of I-71.

Many leading Cincinnati artists have belonged to the club. Past presidents include Henry Farny, Frank Duveneck, Clement Barnhorn, and Herman Wessel. The club works to advance the knowledge and love of art through exhibitions, lectures, demonstrations, sketch groups, and an art library.

**Turn left on Louden Street, left on Paradrome Street, right on Carney Street, and right on Hatch Street.**

Most residential development on the upper part of Mt. Adams, including the former **20 Avery Property,** located between Hatch Street and Eden Park, took place later than that on the lower portions of the hill. In the 1850s and 1860s, considerable construction was underway on the hillsides facing the city, while at the north end of Mt. Adams in the area owned by the Avery family, streets like Hatch, Ida, Paradrome, and Louden had been planned but not yet developed.

In 1859, would-be Arctic explorer Charles Francis Hall (1812-1871) camped on this part of the hill, practicing his cold-weather survival skills. Hall eventually made three trips to the Arctic, wrote a book about his first voyage, and completed mappings of waterways before dying suddenly in Greenland.

Toward the end of the century, home building at the north end of Mt. Adams slowly increased as smaller tracts were sold to developers, and accelerated significantly after the horsecar line began operating along Ida Street in the early 1880s. Most of the older structures here date from the 1880s through the 1910s.

A number of different developers working at different times erected a wide variety of housing. Rowhouses, such as those at 901-947 Paradrome Street, were built in the 1890s. On the north side of Hatch Street, modest brick and frame single-family houses date from 1885-1895, while Paradrome east of Louden was filled in the early twentieth century with a series of 4-family brick structures.

Small neighborhood businesses such as corner groceries intermingled with the housing that was intended for lower middle-income families, often of German and Irish descent. Residents around the turn of the century had occupations such as butcher, policeman, streetcar conductor, distillery foreman, shoemaker, dressmaker, and railroad clerk.

Families like these continued to occupy Mt. Adams homes, which remained in relatively good condition through the mid-twentieth century. By the 1960s, however, the multi-family units had deteriorated somewhat, and their low rents attracted new residents, including young people and some blacks. As the Mt. Adams renaissance took place, this group was in turn gradually displaced. Most of

this housing has now been renovated, either by individuals or companies such as Towne Properties.

**Turn left on St. Gregory Street, right on Monastery Street, left on St. Paul Place.**

On the summit of one of Mt. Adams' hills are the old **21 Holy Cross Roman Catholic Church** and **Monastery,** 1055 St. Paul Place, both closed as religious institutions and now maintained by a private developer. In 1872, Passionist Fathers set up the first monastery in the abandoned Cincinnati Observatory building on this site.

*Most Mt. Adams Catholics of Irish descent worshipped in the church attached to Holy Cross Monastery.*

The astronomical observatory had been built primarily due to the efforts of Professor Ormsby McKnight Mitchel (1809-1862) of Cincinnati College. Mitchel had raised the money to buy a telescope, said to be the second largest in the world, and to house it here on four acres donated by Nicholas Longworth. When smoke and exhaust steam from the growing number of factories in the basin finally made accurate use of the telescope difficult, the observatory moved to property donated by John Kilgour (1834-1914) in Mt. Lookout.

Both German and Irish Catholics attended services at Immaculata Church, but there were economic, cultural, and social tensions between the two groups. The *Cincinnati Daily Gazette* of June 9, 1864, reported a fight between Irish and German Americans "near the Catholic Church [Immaculata] on Mt. Adams" during which one man was killed. The organization of Holy Cross parish in 1873 for English-speaking Catholics not only separated the antagonistic groups but also relieved overcrowding.

Passionist Fathers arrived in Cincinnati in 1871, leased the observatory property for ninety-nine years with an option to purchase, and moved there from the Immaculata rectory. Six thousand attended the ceremonies on June 22, 1873, when Archbishop Purcell dedicated the monastery and the adjacent frame church.

The congregation grew, and by the late 1890s, with approximately 220 families, needed a larger church. After the last service on March 25, 1894, the altars were moved to the school hall and the old building was dismantled. The present brick and stone Romanesque style church with a seating capacity of 700 was dedicated August 25, 1895. The 3-story brick monastery was completed in June 1901.

Holy Cross contained several famous relics: a crucifix supposedly carved from a cedar of Lebanon, the remains of the martyred St. Constance, and a painting of the Madonna and Child said to have been one of two authorized copies of an original by St. Luke. Beneath the church was Our Lady of Lourdes Grotto, a reproduction of the shrine at Lourdes, dedicated in 1898.

Church membership declined as older members died and young people moved from this urban neighborhood to the suburbs, and economic difficulties forced the church to close in 1970. A combined congregation, Holy Cross-Immaculata, was formed.

The monastery closed in late 1977 and was sold the next year to Towne Properties, a local firm long involved in Mt. Adams' revitalization, which turned it into an office building. The grotto and crucifix were moved to Immaculata, while the other relics went to various Passionist centers.

> **Turn left on Pavilion Street, right on St. Gregory Street.**

The largest concentration of **22 Small Businesses in Mt. Adams** has always been located along St. Gregory and Pavilion Streets. These streets pass through two of the earliest subdivisions platted on the hilltop—those of H. Hall and banker Timothy Kirby. By the 1880s, most of the lots were filled. Although a number of saloons and groceries (the two most common types of neighborhood businesses at that time) were scattered throughout Mt. Adams, the largest cluster was around the intersection of Pavilion and Observatory, as St. Gregory was known until 1889.

In the late nineteenth century, these streets were the center of the community. The Catholic school and the Mt. Adams Public School, along with a post office substation, were here. A small bowling alley, still recognizable by the wooden balls and pins carved in its cornice, was at 966 Pavilion opposite Immaculata, and Fire Company No. 15 occupied the building at 1108 St. Gregory.

In the early twentieth century, a small but active business district along these streets served the local residents. There were shoemakers, meat markets, a dressmaker, a plumber, confectioners, soft drink vendors, a fruit store, barber, notions shop, shoe store, and beauty parlor. The number and variety of businesses decreased in the 1940s and 1950s, but those concerns that remained continued to serve the neighborhood. In the 1960s, new enterprises began to replace the old.

The new shops and restaurants served a city-wide clientele, particularly younger people. Stores selling jewelry, art, "mod" clothing, antiques, and miscellaneous counterculture paraphernalia; restaurants with names like The Love Bird and the Red Onion, and bars called Dilly's and The Blind Lemon operated side by side with longtime Mt. Adams establishments such as Roos' Bakery, Glutz's Market, Pia's Sandwich Shop, and Crowley's Highland House Tavern.

Many of these ventures were short-lived but have been replaced by newer enterprises that continue to attract patrons from outside the neighborhood. At the same time, some of the old family businesses such as Glutz's and the Mt. Adams dry cleaners prosper.

In many Cincinnati neighborhoods, two or more Catholic churches stand within blocks of each other. In the nineteenth and early twentieth century, "nationality churches" served congregations of a specific ethnic background—German, Irish, Italian, Hungarian, Polish—that preferred services in their native languages.

One former German-language church is the Church of the Immaculate Conception, now **23 Holy Cross-Immaculata Roman Catholic Church,** 30 Guido Street, a familiar landmark where "praying the steps" on Good Friday has become a local tradition.

The parish of the Immaculate Conception was organized in 1859, and the limestone church, designed by the local firm of Piket & Sons, was dedicated December 9, 1860. One story holds that the building was set on the brow of the hill to recall parishioners' native Germany; another, that Archbishop Purcell, once caught in a violent storm at sea, vowed to build a church on Cincinnati's highest hill if he survived.

The stained glass windows with flower motifs resemble those of Old St. Mary's Church in Over-the-Rhine; German immigrants often preferred reminders of the countryside to religious symbols. Immaculata was extensively refurbished in 1909 when new altars, statuary, and a mosaic floor were added. The Good Friday ritual began around 1860; in 1862, Immaculata was designated a pilgrimage church. Over the years, thousands of people of all religions have climbed the stairs, saying a prayer on each step.

Another local tradition involves

*The Good Friday tradition of "praying the steps" up to Immaculata Church began in the mid-nineteenth century.*

167

*The elaborate "hilltop resort" on Celestial Street encouraged ridership on the Mt. Adams incline and helped make it a popular tourist attraction.*

the statue of St. Patrick, standing on the right side of the nave. Every year, the Ancient Order of Hibernians "steals" the figure for use in Cincinnati's St. Patrick's Day parade.

Immaculata parish, like Holy Cross, declined in the mid-twentieth century. When Holy Cross was closed, the Passionist Fathers took charge of the new combined parish that worshipped here.

**Turn right on Hill Street, right on Celestial Street.**

When the "back-to-the-city" movement began in Cincinnati in the 1950s, Mt. Adams, with its view and its proximity to downtown, was one of the first older neighborhoods to attract middle and upper-income professionals. At the time, some argued that restoration and renovation of the original buildings were the best ways to rejuvenate older urban areas. Others contended that the best course was to tear down outdated structures and build new ones.

Inevitably, both occurred. Thus, the **24 Highland Towers,** 1071 Celestial Street, a 24-story luxury apartment complex, is seen by some as sharply out-of-scale with adjacent structures and by others, as a local newspaper judged at its 1964 opening, as "a fabulous addition to Cincinnati's skyline." Financier Marvin Warner, who renovated the Rookwood Pottery complex, was also behind this project.

A plaque inside the apartment tower notes that it occupies the site of the Highland House, preeminent among Cincinnati's four incline entertainment houses. The 3-story gabled and turreted Highland House opened December 21, 1876, and drew thousands of Cincinnatians with its outdoor concert and dancing pavilion, pool rooms, bowling salon, private party rooms, ballroom, dining room, wine cellar, beer bottling plant, and a beer garden self-proclaimed as "the largest and finest in the world." The Highland House maintained its own light opera company, and Theodore Thomas often conducted the Cincinnati Symphony in summer concerts there.

But the Highland House and the others, as well as the inclines that served them, could not survive population shifts, new modes of transportation, enforcement of Sunday closing laws which prohibited the sale of alcoholic beverages, and an increasingly rough crowd of patrons. After it was seriously damaged by fire, the Highland House was razed in 1895.

The Highland Towers has become a prestigious Cincinnati address. The Celestial Restaurant here offers a panoramic view of the Ohio River Valley.

Offices and a popular restaurant and bar now occupy buildings that were erected for the **25 Rookwood Pottery Company,** 1077 Celestial Street, the best-known art pottery in the United States and one of the few, small, specialized industries that was located in Mt. Adams. The pottery, like the Cincinnati Art Museum, was a product of the late nineteenth-

century desire to unite the beautiful with the useful and to encourage a uniquely American art. Further, china painting was then extremely popular among upper-class women looking for socially acceptable creative occupations.

In 1877, eleven Cincinnati women led by Louise McLaughlin founded the Pottery Club and worked at the local Coultrey Pottery. An invitation to Maria Longworth Nichols (1849-1932), granddaughter of Nicholas Longworth I, apparently went astray, and she set up a pottery of her own, solely, she claimed, for personal gratification.

Maria's father, Joseph Longworth (1813-1883), gave her a schoolhouse on Eastern Avenue near the Little Miami Railroad crossing for her Rookwood Pottery. The name was that of Longworth's Walnut Hills estate and sounded like the prestigious British "Wedgwood." On Thanksgiving Day 1880, the first pieces were taken from the kiln, and the pottery quickly became a tourist attraction.

The following year, Rookwood Pottery hired a full-time decorator to join a staff that included Henry Farny (1847-1916), later a well-known painter of American Indian subjects. Rookwood also began a school to train decorators that attracted students from as far away as Chicago and Pittsburgh.

In 1883, when William Watts Taylor (d.1913) became manager, he reorganized sales methods and hired chemists to develop unique glazes. Taylor also discontinued the school, pointing out that students who could afford the three dollar a week tuition were not likely to work for Rookwood where wages were three to five dollars a week. Women generally received the lesser amount.

After Maria married lawyer Bellamy Storer (1847-1922), her interest in the pottery waned. When the Rookwood Pottery Company incorporated in 1890, Taylor owned 380 of the 490 shares of stock issued.

The Eastern Avenue schoolhouse was a noisy and dirty location, and in 1883 and 1884, it was flooded by the Ohio River. In 1891, the cornerstone was laid for the pottery's new Mt. Adams facility, a half-timbered building designed by Taylor and architect H. Neill Wilson.

At the time, Rookwood employed more than fifty artists, some of whom it sent to Europe and Japan to study. Their one-of-a-kind signed works from cast or thrown pieces won national and international awards. The best known of Rookwood's logos, the reversed capital "R" joined to a capital "P" and surrounded by radiating lines representing flames, was developed during 1886-1900.

Rookwood expanded its Mt. Adams plant and its product line. An architectural department, established in 1902, produced decorative faience used, for example, in the Carew Tower arcade, on Gidding-Jenny's storefront, and in the Union Terminal lunchroom. Manufacture of garden pottery and ornaments began in 1906.

The 1920s were the pottery's most prosperous years. The Rookwood Pottery employed 200 men and women, had 4,000-5,000 visitors annually, and produced unique luxury goods as well as inexpensive mass-produced items.

The Depression hit the company hard. The architectural business was shut down, the market for artistic wares declined, and Rookwood employed artists only on an irregular basis. Although salaries were cut in 1933, figures for 1934 showed a net loss of $47,000. By 1936, the pottery was operating an average of one week a month and at only a fraction of capacity. On April 17, 1941, Rookwood went into receivership.

The pottery was sold to a group of local businessmen headed by automobile dealer Walter Schott. During the previous decade, the struggling company had quietly shipped items from three valuable collections—two of its own and one on "loan" to the Cincinnati Art Museum—to New York City for special sale. Schott continued the liquidation; the *Times-Star* of January 6, 1942, advertised a cut-price sale that included items called in from the company's agents.

Manufacture of pottery continued on a limited scale throughout the war. At last, the decorating staff was discontinued in 1949, and space in the main building was rented out for offices. In the 1950s, two new owners, first local realtor James M. Smith and then the Herschede Hall Clock Company, attempted unsuccessfully to revive Rookwood's prestige and sales in the face of competition from cheap foreign imports. In 1960, Rookwood moved to Starkville, Mississippi, taking some 1,200 original

molds.

Inflation and continued foreign competition finally forced the Rookwood Pottery out of business in 1967. A Michigan dentist bought the molds and the rights to the logo. Working with a kiln in his backyard, he continued manufacturing Rookwood wares, specially marked to distinguish them as "new" Rookwood.

The Mt. Adams building was virtually unused until 1966 when Marvin Warner, who had built the neighboring Highland Towers, bought the property, leased office space, and commissioned a restoration and renovation. The Rookwood Pottery restaurant opened in 1976 with tables set in and around the remaining beehive kilns. Rookwood wares, which continue to increase in value and reputation, are displayed in cases in the restaurant.

Follow Celestial around the bend. Turn left—a sharp left—on Monastery Street, left on Oregon Street.

The first significant residential development of Mt. Adams took place on the lower and middle portions of its hillsides, along streets including 26 **Oregon and Baum Streets**. Today, some of the original mid-nineteenth century housing still stands, scattered among empty lots and a few very recent structures.

The older frame and brick buildings that remain date principally from the 1850s to the 1880s, although most were considerably remodeled in the 1960s and 1970s; a few no longer even resemble nineteenth-century homes. These houses were originally inhabited by workers from the factories, mills, and railyards that lay in the nearby Deer Creek Valley and along the riverfront.

Oregon Street, more intact than Baum, has retained its mid-nineteenth century rowhouses and one of the last of the old neighborhood businesses, the City View Tavern, 403 Oregon. Originally a combination bar and grocery, this business was operated by the Lagemann family from 1909 until the 1980s and is known for the excellent view from its back porch.

The elevated tracks of the Mt. Adams incline were located immediately to the east of the City View, and

the stone pylons that supported the tracks from 1874 to 1952 are still standing on the north side of the street.

Few of the original brick homes remain on Baum Street, which was named for Martin Baum, the early nineteenth-century land speculator who owned most of this hillside property.

Baum Street was also the site of the Convent of the Good Shepherd from 1873 to 1905. The Sisters ran a reform school for girls that was incorporated into the main home, later known as Girls' Town, on North Bend Road in Finneytown. After the Sisters of the Good Shepherd moved out, the chapel was used by the archdiocese in an attempt to establish a Hungarian Catholic parish. This ethnic parish was more successful downtown as St. Joseph of Nazareth church and school on Liberty Street.

Both Oregon and Baum Streets experienced some deterioration in the mid-twentieth century, but in the 1960s and early 1970s, much of the housing was renovated and new middle-income residents moved in. The newcomers included many workers from downtown stores and offices who were attracted to this location by the view and, as the first residents had been, because the central city was within walking distance.

Unfortunately, new highway construction at the foot of the hill undermined its base, and the streets above began to slip. Walls cracked, pipes broke, and people were forced to leave their homes. Despite the efforts of Mt. Adams residents to save the area, the city acquired and demolished all the buildings on Kilgour Street and the west side of Baum in order to construct a 60-foot high retaining wall to prevent further slippage.

This wall, which runs along Kilgour Street, consists of a concrete pile wall anchored to the hillside by steel cables. The $25 million stabilization project—the most expensive in the nation—was completed in 1982 and gradually stopped the hill's slide, although its construction caused more settling that damaged some of the remaining Baum Street buildings and forced their demolition.

The surviving houses on this part of Mt. Adams still hold great appeal, retaining their nineteenth-century charm and affording wonderful views of the city.

**Follow Oregon Street around the bend. At the intersection of Oregon, Baum, and Kilgour Streets, bear left on Kilgour. Return up the hill on Monastery Street. Turn left on Ida Street.**

When the city dedicated the **27 Ida Street Bridge** on September 12, 1931, the *Times-Star* rhapsodized: "That structure is a revelation of what man can accomplish when the desire for beauty is wedded to the need for efficiency." Ceremonies included a parade, concert, speeches, fireworks, and dancing on the bridge until midnight.

The reinforced concrete viaduct designed by J. R. Biedinger replaced a wrought iron and wood span. Both bridges had two streetcar tracks, but the growing popularity of the automobile and the deterioration of the old span called for a new structure.

The modest dimensions of **28 Pilgrim Presbyterian Church,** 1222 Ida Street, suggest that in the mid-1800s, the population of Mt. Adams was predominantly Catholic. The neighborhood's few Presbyterians worshiped in the basin until that downtown congregation moved to Walnut Hills. The pastor then proposed a new church building be erected in Mt. Adams, and Catholics in the neighborhood cooperated in the fundraising efforts of the building committee.

The cornerstone for Pilgrim Chapel was laid in 1889, and the building was finished the following year. The congregation has been served both by regular pastors and a series of guest ministers. The 2-story red brick and stone church is listed on the National Register of Historic Places.

**Turn right on Paradrome Street. Cross Wareham Drive to continue on Mt. Adams Drive.**

The small stone building that now serves as the Thompson Shelterhouse Theater was, as its name implies, a shelterhouse constructed in 1872 to furnish visitors to Eden Park with a spot to rest, rent a chair, and have a drink of water. During World War II, the Red Cross turned it into a club for enlisted men and NCOs, then the structure was essentially abandoned and headed for demolition.

In the late 1950s, it was proposed that the shelterhouse be converted to a theater for a professional repertory company. The Park Board gave unanimous approval, judging the project "ideally suited to the city's cultural tradition." **29 Cincinnati Playhouse in the Park,** 962 Mt. Adams Circle, also fit Eden Park's tradition as a location for cultural institutions.

On October 10, 1960, the Shelterhouse Theater opened, but because of the limited seating capacity, seasons regularly ended with a deficit. Shares of stock in the theater were sold to cover costs of production and renovation, and fund drives and grants helped solve the financial difficulties that plagued the operation.

The larger Robert S. Marx Theater opened next to the Shelterhouse in July 1968; its name honored a financial commitment by the estate of the late Ohio Supreme Court judge. Other donors to the building fund were recognized in the signed, glazed ceramic tiles of the interior Signature Wall (now covered with wood paneling).

The Albert Vontz Theater Center was funded by businessman Albert Vontz, Jr., as a memorial to his father, a German immigrant who founded the Vienna Brewing Company in Cincinnati. The Shelterhouse Theater was renamed in recognition of the support given by Cincinnati businessman Jay Thompson.

The nationally-recognized Playhouse offers quality productions of ten works each season and innovative programs to attract and involve the community.

**Circle the Playhouse. Turn right on Art Museum Drive, left into the Cincinnati Art Museum grounds, and circle the building.**

Despite the theory that public parks ought to be "natural" retreats, culture first invaded Eden Park in 1882 when the city provided the Art Museum Association with almost twenty acres here "to build a museum for the preservation and exhibition of works of art and nature"—the **30 Cincinnati Art Museum (CAM)**.

Cincinnati wanted to leave behind its image as "Porkopolis" and demonstrate that it was a cultural as well as a commercial center. As urban industrialization seemed to threaten the quality of life and the human spirit, many believed that a museum of both fine and decorative arts would also cultivate popular tastes, furnish intellectual enjoyment, and provide craftsmen with examples of artistic creativity that could be incorporated in assembly-line products.

In 1877, a group of local women who had held a highly successful display of their china and other decorative art works at the Centennial Exposition in Philadelphia founded the Women's Art Museum Association. The women sought to encourage "the cultivation of the principles of art, and their application to industrial pursuits"; this was not to be art for art's sake.

The Women's Association envisioned a school of technical art and an accompanying museum. It asked nine prominent Cincinnati businessmen to handle the financial arrangements for the establishment of the museum, a politic and pragmatic decision as most money would come from men either directly or indirectly through their wives, widows, and daughters.

In 1880, Charles W. West (1810-1884), a successful flour mill operator, offered $150,000 for the project if leading Cincinnatians would match the sum. Julius Dexter, J. A. Frazier, Joseph Longworth, David Sinton, and Reuben Springer led the drive that met West's challenge within the month.

The Cincinnati Art Museum Association, incorporated early in 1881, superseded the Women's Art Museum Association. West later gave another $150,000 to the endowment fund. On May 17, 1886, an estimated 5,000 Cincinnatians attended dedication ceremonies for the new art museum, a limestone-faced Romanesque style building designed by James McLaughlin (1834-1925).

Later additions now almost completely surround the original museum, providing the necessary space to show constantly increasing collections and linked it to the building housing the Art Academy, the Museum's sister institution.

As a general museum, the CAM presents an overview of art spanning more than 5,000 years. The internationally-known permanent collection appeals to a variety of interests. Paintings include works by Titian, Gainsborough, Rubens, Botticelli, and El Greco. One of the best known of the American paintings is Grant Wood's "Daughters of the Revolution." Frank Duveneck, the most celebrated of Cincinnati area artists, is represented by a comprehensive collection of his works. The CAM also has a small but good collection of the works of modern artists like Picasso, Modigliani, and Matisse.

In addition to temporary exhibits, the museum's more than one hundred galleries offer Near Eastern material, a series of period rooms that present European and American versions of the good life, musical instruments, fashions of other eras, American Indian and African art, and Cincinnati's art pottery, including Rookwood.

As the women of the Art Museum Association had hoped, a school of art did develop in conjunction with the museum. In 1887, the **31 Art Academy of Cincinnati,** then called the Art School of Cincinnati, moved to this 3-story building also designed by James McLaughlin.

The effort to found an art academy began in 1854 with the Ladies Academy of Fine Arts which raised $5,000 to purchase copies of Old Masters and received $1,000 from Charles McMicken, merchant and real estate speculator, to buy plaster casts of classical statues. The Ladies Academy ran into financial troubles and finally disbanded in 1864, storing its collection.

Charles McMicken, in the meantime, had left approximately one million dollars to the city for the establishment of an institution of higher learning. Trustees, using the academy's collection of art works, opened the McMicken School of Drawing and Design in January 1869 in a rented building at Third and Main Streets. Four years later, classes moved to better quarters in the Cincinnati College.

Many felt, however, that a combined academy and museum would better serve artists and the city. In 1881, Joseph Longworth (1813-1883) offered an endowment of nearly

$370,000 to improve the school and its program if the university would transfer control to the Art Museum Association, of which he had just become president. The university agreed, and the school became the Art School of Cincinnati. Reuben Springer (1800-1884) and David Sinton (1808-1900) paid for the new building in Eden Park. Six years later, in 1887, 410 students paid an annual tuition of $10.

The Art Academy has attracted famous artists both as teachers and students, among them Clement Barnhorn, Solon Borglun, Joseph DeCamp, Benn Pitman, Louis Rebisso, John Twachtman, Russell Wright, and, perhaps best known, Frank Duveneck.

Today the school offers programs in fine and commercial art and in art history. Some of its classrooms, offices, and a computer lab are housed in the old Mt. Adams Public School, 1027 St. Gregory Street.

Located in the Adams-Emery Wing of the Cincinnati Art Museum from 1964 until its move to the Union Terminal in 1991, **32 The Cincinnati Historical Society** is the oldest historical society in the state and yet another Eden Park cultural institution.

Founded in Columbus on February 11, 1831, as the Historical and Philosophical Society of Ohio (HPSO), the Society and its collection of historical materials was regularly shuttled from room to room in the Statehouse. In 1844, HPSO was transferred to Cincinnati, and years later, merged with the more vital Cincinnati Historical Society, founded in 1844, but lacking a charter.

After the Civil War, HPSO occupied rooms in the Cincinnati College Building on Walnut near Fourth Street, and then maintained a library on West Eighth. But it gradually languished as a "gentlemen's club" with membership essentially drawn from the economic, social, and intellectual elite of the city. In 1901, the organization's collections were moved to the University of Cincinnati library; members met in various places throughout Cincinnati.

In the 1940s, the scope of membership was broadened as the organization began to redefine itself as an institution with a role in disseminating information to the public, as well as collecting and preserving historical

materials. This new orientation was more effectively realized after the Cincinnati Historical Society (CHS)—that name adopted in 1963—moved to Eden Park.

The Historical Society maintains an extensive collection of periodicals, books, newspapers, maps, photographs, art work, manuscripts, and architectural drawings related to the history of Cincinnati, the Miami Valley, and the Northwest Territory in reference to Ohio and the Ohio River. The Hauck Room contains an outstanding collection of rare books gathered by Cornelius J. Hauck (1893-1967), Cincinnati businessman, philanthropist, and a member and president of the Park Board for nearly twenty years.

CHS seeks to preserve the history of the area and to help Cincinnatians explore their heritage with lectures, tours, educational programs, and various publications.

**Turn left on Art Museum Drive.**

The **33 Murray Seasongood Pavilion** is the fourth of Eden Park's bandstands. Musical performances in the park began in 1872 with summer concerts every Sunday afternoon. By 1890, the city was having trouble paying for the programs and asked for help. The Schmidlapp family donated $50,000, and the income from that fund paid for the "Schmidlapp concerts" which 78,200 Cincinnatians attended in 1892.

The shelterhouse that served as a bandstand was rebuilt in 1901; then in 1914, a new bandstand was built in this natural amphitheater. The concrete Seasongood Pavilion was dedicated in 1960 and opened with a concert by Les Brown's band. The pavilion was erected with a gift in honor of Murray Seasongood (1878-1983), a Cincinnati attorney and the first Charter Committee member to be elected mayor.

The Seasongood Pavilion is regularly the site of a variety of concerts, including one of the series of summer performances in Cincinnati's parks by the Cincinnati Pops Orchestra.

**Turn left on Eden Park Drive to return to Gilbert Avenue where tour ends.**

# Tour 9

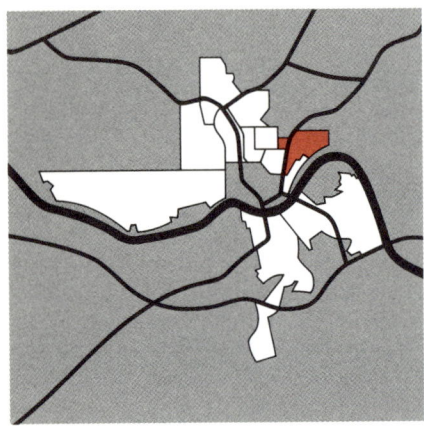

# Walnut Hills

Walnut Hills is a series of neighborhoods stretching from the northern end of Eden Park to the western edge of the Cincinnati Country Club, near Hyde Park. Each of these communities developed separately, had its own district identity, and was annexed by the city at a different time.

The oldest community arose on land that the Reverend James Kemper (1753-1834) bought from John Cleves Symmes in the 1790s. Kemper's property was located between the Deer Creek Valley and the bluffs overlooking the Ohio River, just to the north of the area that later became Eden Park. Here Kemper built a blockhouse which he and his family occupied until the danger from Indian attacks had diminished. The farm was eventually divided between Kemper's children, and some land was sold. The Kemper family called the growing village Walnut Hill, but later the name Walnut Hills came into general use.

Religion was a major factor in the early development of this village. In 1818, James Kemper founded the First Presbyterian Church, and family members provided the property for Lane Theological Seminary, which opened in 1832.

The character of the village was also shaped by the intersection of two main thoroughfares, the road to Lebanon and the upper road to Columbia (now the intersection of Gilbert Avenue and McMillan Streets). This was an ideal site for commercial activity, and by the early 1840s, a variety of small businesses was established at the crossroads, which was known as Kay's Corner after one of the first entrepreneurs.

Walnut Hills, like neighboring Mt. Auburn to the west, attracted wealthy residents from the city. Cincinnati officials saw these suburbs as sources of new tax revenues, and the portion of Walnut Hills south of McMillan Street was annexed to Cincinnati in March 1850, less than a year after Mt. Auburn had been added to the city. The remainder of the village lying north of McMillan Street was annexed in 1870.

Another wealthy residential suburb that inhabitants generally called East Walnut Hills lay between Walnut Hills and Mt. Lookout. Beginning in the late 1830s and 1840s, well-to-do Cincinnatians, including merchant Josiah Lawrence, banker Charles B. Foote, and lawyer Timothy Walker, built elegant estates in East Walnut Hills. Most of these homes were located on lots of five to ten acres, but some occupied more than twenty acres, and a few had as many as 110 acres of grounds. The western half of this area, approximately one square mile in size, was incorporated in 1866 as the Village of Woodburn. The eastern portion was annexed to Cincinnati in 1870 along with Mt. Lookout and a little community called O'Bryonville. Woodburn remained independent until 1873.

The growth of all these areas was facilitated in the 1880s by cable cars running up Gilbert Avenue. In 1898, the cable cars were replaced by faster, more reliable electric streetcars, which made even more of Walnut Hills easily accessible from downtown. While wealthy families continued to build fine homes in East Walnut Hills, developers such as the Emery brothers erected less expensive housing for middle-income residents near the streetcar lines. From the 1890s to the 1920s, rowhouses, apartment buildings, and modest single-family houses multiplied rapidly in Walnut Hills and the western part of Woodburn around DeSales Corner.

The ongoing improvement of the public transportation system also contributed to the rapid development of the increasingly busy commercial district at the intersection of Gilbert Avenue and McMillan Street. In the 1880s, Kay's Corner became known as Peebles' Corner after Joseph Peebles, owner of a grocery store there. Businessmen such as Peebles took advantage of the intersection's role as a major transfer point for streetcar passengers and created the second busiest shopping district in the city.

*Walnut Hills' principal business district was at Peebles' Corner—the intersection of a number of important roads and streetcar lines.*

After the turn of the century, Walnut Hills began to attract new migrants from the downtown basin, including many Jews who were moving out of the West End. While German Jews tended to settle in North Avondale, Walnut Hills and South Avondale became home for many Eastern European Jewish families. Italians also moved to Walnut Hills, and an area on the western side of Gilbert Avenue south of McMillan Street became known as "Little Italy."

In the 1930s, a considerable number of black families, many of whom were displaced from the West End by the construction related to Union Terminal and new public housing projects, moved to this community. Walnut Hills was one of the few neighborhoods open to them, as some blacks had been living here since the 1860s. Up through the mid-twentieth century, black families usually could move only into neighborhoods where members of their race already lived. The largest concentration of blacks in the Walnut Hills area was to the northeast of Peebles' Corner. This was the best neighborhood in which middle-class black families could settle during the pre-World War II era. Slightly less well-to-do blacks settled in O'Bryonville.

*While many of Walnut Hills' historic homes have been preserved and renovated in recent years, there have been some notable exceptions, including the Emery house—shown here in the 1960s— which was demolished in 1987.*

Because of the changing character of Walnut Hills' population and the effects of the Depression on business activity, residents and city officials became concerned that the community was declining. It was not until after World War II, however, that any real deterioration became evident. Like other old Cincinnati neighborhoods, Walnut Hills lost many middle-class white residents to more modern post-war suburbs. They were replaced by less affluent minorities, including many blacks who had lost homes in the basin to urban renewal and freeway construction.

This influx, in turn, accelerated the departure of white residents, and even many of the middle-class blacks moved to "better" neighborhoods that were opening up to them. The social makeup of the community changed rapidly. By 1970, more than 80% of Walnut Hills' approximately 14,000 residents were black, and a significant number had low incomes. A portion of East Walnut Hills retained its prestige, primarily because of the efforts of active neighborhood associations and strict zoning that prevented large houses from being divided into apartments. In the rest of Walnut Hills, the usual pattern of absentee landlords, division of single-family units into multi-family ones, lack of maintenance, declining property values, and increasing crime rates was evident.

The business community also suffered, partly because the area was perceived as increasingly dangerous, but more because of changing shopping patterns. Shoppers came to prefer suburban shopping centers with their extensive parking lots, and old neighborhood business districts such as Peebles' Corner saw much less activity.

The city's plans for revitalization of Walnut Hills centered on the improvement of housing stock and the business districts. In the late 1960s and into the 1970s, some low-income housing was developed, new parking was created, and street improvements were made in key locations. New businesses were induced to move in. It eventually became clear, however, that low-income customers could not give enough support to local commercial establishments to keep them viable. Further, Walnut Hills' population had declined, decreasing by about 4,000 between 1970 and 1980, and thus reducing the number of potential customers.

In the late 1970s and early 1980s, the city and developers placed considerable hopes for improving the neighborhood on the rehabilitation of homes for well-to-do professionals interested in living close to downtown. A number of buildings have been renovated, especially in the area bordering Eden Park and East Walnut Hills, and this has reintroduced a more varied mix of social and economic groups into Walnut Hills.

North

Walnut Hills

Tour Length
7.5 miles

Start

End

# Walnut Hills

In his 1867 annual message, Mayor Charles F. Wilstach (1818-1882) suggested the city fight a possible cholera epidemic by creating parks, building new waterworks, prohibiting overcrowded housing, replacing all the privies in the city with water closets connected to sewers, and constructing broad avenues.

City officials regarded a densely packed population, poor sanitation, and bad water as chief causes of cholera epidemics, and hoped large suburban parks and roads out of the basin would enable Cincinnatians to escape the central city, at least temporarily. One of the most important of these "avenues of exit from the city" was **1 Gilbert Avenue** between downtown and Walnut Hills.

The proposed road was named after Alfred West Gilbert (1816-1900), who had become Cincinnati's first city engineer in 1850. He received considerable abuse from local newspapers, particularly Murat Halstead's *Cincinnati Commercial*, because of the costly construction and maintenance projects he supported.

But Gilbert's interest in public health motivated many of his proposals, including the improvement of the Deer Creek Valley in the late 1860s and the 1870s. The project involved removing the slaughterhouses from that area, filling in the many gullies, building large sewers—among them the great Eggleston Avenue sewer—cleaning up a public dump that stretched from the edge of downtown to the Eden Park entrance, and the construction of Gilbert Avenue, which began in 1868.

The six identical 2½-story **2 Rowhouses,** 2156-2166 Gilbert Avenue, now known as the Emery Row Apartments, are one example of the moderate rent housing that Thomas Emery's Sons built in the basin and in the hilltop suburbs from the 1880s through the early 1900s. The *Cincinnati Daily Gazette* declared in 1882: "The Emery Sons have wealth and they have seen fit to use it in buying ground and building houses and they have built more houses than any men or firm known to our citizens."

Thomas Emery, Sr. (d.1857), came to America from England and arrived in Cincinnati in the late 1830s. He opened a real estate office, offering assistance particularly to immigrants from the British Isles, and then began manufacturing candles. After Emery's death, his three sons, Thomas J. (1830-1906), John J. (d.1908), and J. Howard (d.1886), took over the business. It was Thomas and John J. Emery who made exceptional contributions to, literally, the building of Cincinnati.

While the Carew Tower-Netherland Plaza hotel is the Emerys' most widely recognized construction project, the *Gazette*'s praise for their home building efforts was well founded. The Emerys are credited with erecting the first apartment buildings in the city. The individual apartments, called "French flats," were not simply sleeping rooms, but had private bathrooms and kitchens. The first buildings were given European names: the Lombardy on West Fourth Street, the Brittany and Saxony at Ninth and Race Streets, and the Normandy on Race near Fifth Street.

As streetcars made the hilltops more accessible, the company completed dozens of apartment buildings and rowhouse units in Avondale, Clifton, and Walnut Hills. In Walnut Hills, the Emerys built the Alexandra, Clermont, Verona, and Navarre apartment houses, as well as single-family homes and townhouses that attracted middle-income families.

For example, in the 1900s, residents of these Gilbert Avenue rowhouses included Clement English, retired head of a bellows and forge manufacturing firm, his wife Cordelia, and their two adult children at 2156; salesman Jacob Henger, his wife Lillian, their two young children, one servant, and two boarders at 2158; and city "sanitary officer" Charles P. Tibbles, his wife Elizabeth, and daughters, Emma, a dressmaker, Mary, a library attendant, and Lillian, a stenographer, at 2166.

By 1930, these single-family homes had been subdivided into space for small businesses and two or more apartments rented to working-class families. The properties, vandalized and neglected, had deteriorated by the end of the 1960s. Several were vacant, while a few were rented by lower-income individuals.

A grassroots movement to restore the once-elegant homes and rowhouses began around 1977. City and neighborhood groups developed the Nassau-Eden Plan that envisioned an economically and racially mixed community. Work started as individuals bought and rehabbed the stone rowhouses and a former school on Morris Street, then homes on surrounding streets. The Gilbert Avenue corridor was still an eyesore, however, until a local company, River City Development, purchased these brick rowhouses, as well as the frame homes just to the north, also built by the Emerys.

Committed to historic preservation and bringing back the neighborhood, as well as to making a profit, River City faced a formidable task in the rehabilitation of the seven Emery Row Apartments. Five had been damaged by fire; all were partially demolished inside, and the recent bulldozing of storefronts added in the 1930s had not only torn off the stairways and porches, but had also pulled the facades away from the buildings.

The $2 million renovation of the two complexes—Emery Row and Emery Village—was a significant contribution to restoring Gilbert Avenue as an attractive residential and commercial strip.

Although Gilbert Avenue provided fine access to Eden Park, it had drawbacks as a commuter route. A horsecar line began service on Gilbert Avenue in 1872, but it took thirty minutes for the streetcars to ascend the long, steep hill from Broadway to Peebles' Corner. Even so, the streetcar companies believed the route had great potential.

In 1881, the head of the Mt. Adams and Eden Park Inclined Railway Company, George B. Kerper (1839-1913), acquired Route No. 10 on Gilbert Avenue from his chief competitor, John Kilgour's Cincinnati Street Railway Company. By 1883, the route was carrying thousands of passengers each day, but Kerper felt it could do even better. He engaged Henry Marcus Lane (1851-1929) to design a cable car system.

Lane was an innovative mechanical engineer who had already designed the machinery for Kerper's Mt. Adam's Incline. Son of Lane & Bodley founder P. P. Lane, he was educated in the Cincinnati public

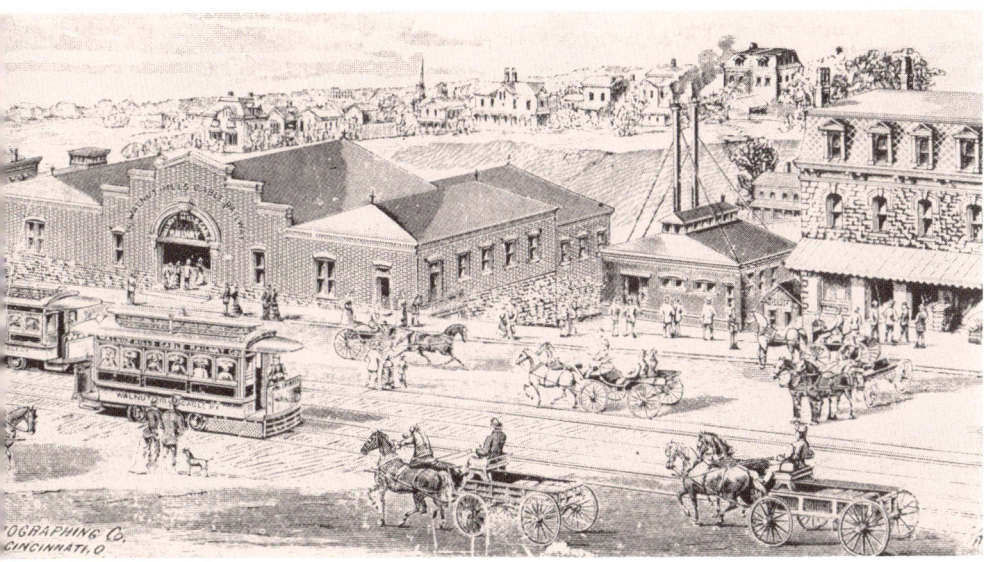

*George Kerper's cable cars significantly reduced the amount of time it took commuters to travel from downtown, up Gilbert Avenue, to Walnut Hills and other nearby suburbs.*

schools and the Massachusetts Institute of Technology. Besides the work he did for Kerper, Lane also designed the machinery for the Bellevue Incline and the Cincinnati Street Railway's Vine Street cable line, and worked on cable car systems throughout the country, including the one in San Francisco.

The Walnut Hills line went into service in 1885 with a combination of horsecar and cable tracks from downtown to Woodburn. The **3 Walnut Hills Cable Line's Machinery and Powerhouse** were located at 2243-2247 Gilbert Avenue. The system was unique in utilizing convertible horsecars. Horses drew the cars to the foot of the hill where the animals were unhitched and a unit that gripped the moving cable was attached to the car. At the top of the hill, the unit was disengaged, and horses were once again hitched on the vehicle.

In addition to starting the Walnut Hills cable road, the first such line in Cincinnati, Kerper introduced the first electric streetcars to operate in Cincinnati in 1888.

Some newspapermen regarded "Kable Kar Kerper" as a folk hero because he offered the only serious competition to John Kilgour's streetcar monopoly, but in 1890, Kilgour forced Kerper out of the Mt. Adams and Eden Park line.

Six years later, the firm, along with its Gilbert Avenue cable division, was merged into the Cincinnati Street Railway Company, which completely electrified the Gilbert Avenue route in 1898. Ridership increased; growing numbers of commuters traveled on the faster, more reliable electric lines to homes in Walnut Hills, stopping to shop when they got off or transferred at Peebles' Corner. Gilbert Avenue remained an important route for public transit even after buses replaced the streetcars in the 1950s.

Some of the former streetcar support buildings have survived, including the cable house, which served a variety of light industrial uses until the mid-1980s when it was renovated for office space.

Until the early twentieth century, Gilbert Avenue south of Peebles' Corner was lined with homes and small stores. Gradually, these structures were replaced by clusters of larger commercial and light industrial buildings.

Among the first commercial structures was the limestone-faced building at 2400 Gilbert Avenue which originally housed the **4 Offices of Harry Hake,** founder of one of the city's most prolific architectural firms. Headed first by Hake, then his son and grandson, the firm carried out more than 1,500 commissions over eighty-two years. Its work shaped the architectural character of Cincinnati, especially downtown, where many Hake buildings remain.

Harry Hake, Sr. (1871-1955), was educated at the Ohio Mechanics' Institute and the Cincinnati Art Academy. He began his career in 1889,

working as a draftsman for established architects, and started his own firm in 1897.

Hake's ardent support of the Hamilton County Republican Party brought his firm important commissions, including remodeling the County Courthouse, more than two dozen jobs for the city fire and police departments, residential work for "machine" politicians Rud Hynicka and Mike Mullen, and designing various buildings for the University of Cincinnati, Cincinnati Bell, CG&E, and the Pennsylvania Railroad.

Hake's firm occupied downtown offices until it moved here in 1924. Hake & Associates designed the structure using Neo-Classical elements typical of its work during this period. Harry Hake & Partners dissolved in 1979. The building was then occupied by other commercial tenants, including an advertising art studio and an air conditioning company.

One of the oldest surviving institutions in this community, **5 Walnut Hills United Presbyterian Church,** 2601 Gilbert Avenue, was begun in late 1817 by a handful of men and women who first met for worship in the home of the Reverend James Kemper. The First Presbyterian Church of Walnut Hills, with eight communicants, dedicated its church at Melrose and McMillan Avenues on July 4, 1819. Kemper was the first minister.

The church grew slowly: twenty-three members in 1850, fifty in 1860, and 120 in 1878 when it joined with Lane Seminary Church. Despite the merger, the professors who filled the Lane Pulpit and the trustees of First Presbyterian were divided—as was the Presbyterian Church in America—by a controversy over theology and the question of slavery.

The united congregation met at each church on alternating Sundays until the Lane chapel ceiling began to collapse. The group then purchased this lot and commissioned Cincinnati architect Samuel Hannaford to design a new building. The present church was dedicated November 8, 1885, when First Presbyterian had 431 members.

The church facilities continued to grow. A chapel was completed in 1891, an office addition by Samuel Hannaford & Sons in 1929. The congregation likewise grew, numbering nearly 900 in 1918. Many prominent Walnut Hills families were associated with this church for generations, as memorial plaques throughout the building attest.

The early twentieth century saw a decline in church membership. Members died, many moved, children ceased to identify with the old church, and conflicts with pastors drove others away. Walnut Hills Presbyterian merged with Walnut Hills Congregational Church in 1941 and First United Church in Avondale in 1958 in an attempt to sustain these declining institutions.

In the late 1980s, Walnut Hills United Presbyterian, with sixty or so members, found itself struggling to survive. The Baldwin Music Education Center was housed in one portion of the under-used church complex.

*A few of the old Lane Presbyterian Theological Seminary buildings survived until the 1950s, then were torn down.*

A Cadillac dealership now occupies part of the grounds of the **6 Lane Theological Seminary** that was headed from 1832 to 1850 by Reverend Lyman Beecher (1775-1863). Lane Seminary, named after two New Orleans businessmen who gave initial support, opened in 1830 on sixty acres of land donated by a son of Reverend James Kemper. Eventually, the campus included over a dozen building on about ten acres on Gilbert Avenue between Yale and Chapel Streets.

Lane Seminary became the center of a national scandal in August 1834, when Lane's board of directors abolished the students' Anti-Slavery Society and prohibited discussion of slavery in any public room of the institution. Cincinnati newspapers and magazines applauded the decision, and Beecher, who favored gradual emancipation, acquiesced. Thirty-four students led by Theodore D. Weld (1803-1895) walked out. By the end of the year, ninety-five of the 103-member student body had left; many eventually went to Oberlin College.

The Presbyterian seminary never quite recovered, though classes continued. To pay the bills, Lane subdivided its grounds and gave perpetual leases to homeowners. Because the seminary did not discriminate, blacks had begun to purchase some of the lots in the mid-1800s. In 1914, the school had twenty-six graduates; in 1931, eleven students and four graduates.

Lane merged with the McCormick Theological Seminary of Chicago in 1932. Shortly afterwards, eleven of the old buildings, including dormitories that had become rooming houses, were torn down for the construction of apartment buildings. The Presbytery of Cincinnati located the offices of the Board of National Missions in one of the remaining structures for about a decade. The seminary hall and library were torn down in 1953 to make way for the car dealership, and demolition of the last structures—dormitories that had been divided into apartments—came in 1956.

**Turn right on Foraker Avenue.**

The **7 Harriet Beecher Stowe House,** 2950 Gilbert Avenue, was built as a residence for Lyman Beecher when he was head of Lane Seminary. Among the members of the family who lived here was Harriet Beecher Stowe, author of the anti-slavery novel *Uncle Tom's Cabin.*

Reverend Beecher's daughter, Harriet Elizabeth Beecher (1811-1896) married Calvin Ellis Stowe (1802-1886), a professor at Lane, in 1836 and moved to a house on the site of the present Church of the Assumption. While in Cincinnati and during a few visits to Kentucky, Harriet gathered impressions of slavery and stories like the one minister John Rankin of Ripley, Ohio, told about helping a slave escape across the frozen Ohio River. Stowe wrote *Uncle Tom's Cabin* after she left Cincinnati.

This most famous of her many novels first appeared as a serial in an anti-slavery newspaper. The story was issued in book form on March 20, 1852, and sold 300,000 copies within a year. There have been innumerable translations of the work, and dramatized versions of *Uncle Tom's Cabin* have been performed more often than any other play in the English language.

After it was no longer occupied by Seminary staff, the Beecher family residence was used for many years as a rooming house. Efforts to convert the 2-story brick structure into a museum and neighborhood center began in the 1920s. On December 21, 1943, the Harriet Beecher Stowe Home Memorial Association received the deed; it renovated and refurbished the house, then turned it over to the Ohio Historical Society in 1946.

But by the 1970s, the building had deteriorated; it was closed to the public and then rented as office space for one dollar a year. A group composed largely of Walnut Hills High School students approached the Citizens Committee on Youth for help in restoring the house. The renovated home officially reopened on October 7, 1979.

Today, the Harriet Beecher Stowe

House serves as a resource center on early Cincinnati history and a public meeting place, offers art exhibits and classes in Afro-American history and computer education, and works to compile the histories of local black families.

**Turn right on Park Avenue, left on Chapel Street, and right on Alms Place.**

**8 Frederick Douglass Reading/Language Arts Demonstration Center,** 2825 Alms Place, is one of the Cincinnati Public School system's alternative or magnet schools, drawing students from all parts of the city in an effort to achieve quality integrated education. It has inherited the name of the old Douglass Elementary School, a black institution which once stood on this lot.

Reverend Dangerfield Early, minister of First Baptist Church, started a school for black children in his home in 1860. When Cincinnati annexed Walnut Hills in 1870, this school became part of the city's Independent Colored School System, and in 1872, was replaced by the new Elm Street School on the corner of Chapel and Elm (Alms) Streets with an enrollment of 185 students.

An 1829 state law excluded blacks from public schools, so schools for black children depended on white philanthropy. Finally, in 1849, legislation called for a proportionate share of taxes to be spent for black schools that were to be managed by a board of trustees composed of blacks and elected by black males.

The City of Cincinnati and the Common School Board fought the act, but in 1856, the Independent Colored School System was established. John I. Gaines (1821-1859), clerk of the system, Peter H. Clark (1829-1926), teacher and principal of Gaines High School, and William H. Parham, superintendent, led the fight for black education.

By 1870-1871, the Colored School Board oversaw five schools with 1,111 students. In 1874, when white political parties determined to control the black vote, the independent board was abolished. The all-white Common School Board would run all of Cincinnati's public schools.

The following year, the Arnett Bill repealed the laws which had allowed for the organization of separate schools for black children. Many Ohioans, black and white, hoped that schools would now be integrated, but *de facto* segregation replaced mandated segregation. Black schools continued as "branch" schools, open to black youngsters living anywhere in the city. Black teachers, not permitted to teach in white schools, were phased out of the system.

Though branch schools were officially open to white children, they were recognized as black institutions and, gradually, all were closed but Elm Street School. The name Frederick Douglass Elementary School was adopted in 1902 to honor the famous black author and abolitionist.

Political pressure from the black community kept Douglass School open and led to the construction of a 5-story building in 1911. The new Douglass Elementary was a showplace with a wealth of modern features, including a 500-seat auditorium, doctor's office, public library branch, open air classrooms, carpenter shop, domestic science department, gym, and a strip of land around the building for children's gardens. Douglass enrolled youngsters from all over the city and attracted the best black teachers.

Even after the city's school system was supposed to become integrated, the student population of Douglass was still predominantly black. By the mid-1970s, enrollment was just over 400—about two-thirds capacity—and 97% black.

The school became a community center and a symbol of black achievement that gained national and international recognition. When Douglass was demolished in April 1981, City Council member Marian Spencer remarked that it both symbolized segregation in Cincinnati and had been "a place where blacks fought to give their people what they couldn't possibly have received anywhere else."

The present Douglass Reading Center, designed by E. A. Glendening and opened in January 1981, serves approximately 700 students, about two-thirds or more black. The school offers reading enrichment and reading intervention programs, and an occupational therapist who works with students who have neurological problems.

**Turn right on Yale Avenue, right on Gilbert Avenue, left on Oak Street, left on Stanton Avenue, and right on Oak Street.**

**9 Bethesda Oak Hospital,** 615 Oak Street, began in 1898, when the German Methodist Deaconess Home Association purchased a private hospital and adjacent house at the corner of Reading Road and Oak Street. Seven German Methodist deaconesses—women who had chosen the religious life and service to Methodist institutions—staffed the hospital. Reverend Christian Golder (1849-1922) served as hospital superintendent, and his sister, Louise (1857-1929), as superintendent of the deaconesses. Bethesda accepted patients of all denominations, whether or not they could pay for their medical care.

In 1914, when Bethesda Hospital had a 215-bed capacity, it initiated a nursing program. Three years later, the women working at the hospital moved into the 4-story Louise Golder Deaconess Home and the Fanny Nast Gamble Memorial Chapel building, 2710 Reading Road, which also contained lecture rooms, a dining room, and gym. A 30-bed hospital for children was opened in 1920 at Reading Road and June Street, and a new hospital building dedicated here in 1926.

Over the years, older buildings were demolished, and a new nurses' dormitory, maternity wing, chapel, office building, and an out-patient surgery center were constructed. A satellite hospital, Bethesda North, opened in suburban Montgomery in 1970.

The Bethesda Oak facility offers special services including cardiac and physical rehabilitation, childbirth education, diabetes care, group health programs, genetic counseling, infertility and sleep disorders clinics, as well as traditional medical and surgical treatment. In 1981, the Cincinnati Hospice, providing a care system for the terminally ill, opened in the Golder-Gamble building.

The Bethesda Oak complex includes one nineteenth-century building, which it uses for office and classroom space. The rough stone Gothic style mansion on the northeast corner of Oak and Reading was erected around 1879 by A. S. Winslow, a vice-president of the First National Bank. Cincinnati woodcarver William Fry (1830-1929) crafted much of the interior woodwork.

The Ursuline Sisters of Brown County purchased the home and operated Ursuline Academy, a private junior and senior high school for girls, from 1906 until 1970 when the school moved from this busy intersection to Blue Ash.

In the mid-nineteenth century, a small community called Vernon developed in the area between present-day Burnet Avenue and Reading Road. Anthony D. Bullock (1824-1890), pioneer railroad builder and one of the founders of the City & Suburban Telegraph Association, built a magnificent stone mansion on nine acres of grounds here in 1868. Today the Bullock estate is the site of the **10 Vernon Manor Hotel,** 400 Oak Street.

Erected at a cost of $1.5 million, the Vernon Manor Apartment Hotel opened in 1924 and is said to have been modeled after Hatfield House, one of England's stately homes. The hotel provided wealthy, retired persons with luxurious apartment suites, though there were also hotel rooms and restaurants open to the public.

*The Vernon Manor opened in 1924 as an "apartment hotel" for well-to-do tenants.*

The Vernon Manor faced bankruptcy in 1934 and was judged "considerably run-down-at-the-heels" in 1945 when it was purchased by car dealer Walter Schott. The surrounding area became less desirable, particularly after the racial violence and unrest in neighboring Avondale and Mt. Auburn during the 1960s and 1970s. When the hotel was sold in 1977

for $650,000, 80% of the occupants were permanent residents.

The Vernon Manor's image changed in the 1980s with a multi-million dollar restoration and a marketing campaign that aimed to attract business customers by offering impressive accommodations for seminars and out-of-town guests.

**11 Gibson-Hauck House,** 425 Oak Street, stands across from the Vernon Manor Hotel. Currently occupied by the University of Cincinnati Foundation, which raises money for the school, this 2-story Federal style dwelling dates from around 1856 and is one of the few remaining summer homes built in Vernon Village. Anthony Bullock lived here before erecting his more splendid mansion.

In 1911, the home was occupied by Louis J. Hauck, son of brewer John Hauck, who brought his family from Dayton Street in the West End to Walnut Hills. Hauck's daughter, Katherine Hauck Gibson, inherited the home; a son, Cornelius (1893-1967), moved into a farmhouse around the corner at 2625 Reading Road in 1924.

Cornelius Hauck's commitment to this urban neighborhood produced the **12 Hauck Botanic Gardens,** 2625 Reading Road (not on the tour). This 8-acre park was his estate, Sooty Acres, given its tongue-in-cheek name because the first trees that Hauck planted died from the soot and grime that poured from the city's coal-burning homes and factories. Hauck bought additional land south of his home and cleared the "shack-ridden slum" that stood there to create an arboretum.

Hauck headed the family's investment firm and was a director of the Little Miami Railroad and the Fifth-Third Union Trust Company, but his passion was gardening. He served on the Park Board for eighteen years, was an officer of the Garden Center of Greater Cincinnati, and belonged to numerous horticultural societies.

By 1960, Hauck had planted 900 varieties of trees, shrubs, and evergreens around his home and had developed and patented a new variety of lilac. He also gathered 12,000 books and other publications relating to botany, horticulture, and landscape design. Hauck gave these and other rare books to the Cincinnati Historical Society and willed Sooty Acres to the

Park Board, along with a trust to maintain it.

Hauck and his wife also donated a portion of their land for the headquarters of the Civic Garden Center, 2715 Reading Road, which opened in 1951. The 2-acre tract was the site of the home of the nineteenth-century Shakespearean actor, James Edward Murdoch (1810-1893).

*Turn left on Highland Avenue, right on William Howard Taft Road, left on Auburn Avenue, and left on McMillan Street.*

Although Walnut Hills was principally a residential neighborhood, in the early twentieth century, a number of light manufacturing concerns moved from the basin to larger and more modern facilities in the vicinity of McMillan and Iowa Streets. The **13 Gruen Watch Company,** and a subsidiary, the Gruen National Watch Case Company, moved from Fifth and Walnut Streets in 1917 to the half-timbered Tudor style building at 401 East McMillan, designed by Guy Burroughs and John Henri Deeken. Swiss-born Dietrich Gruen (1847-1911) had begun the business in Columbus in 1874, assembling timepieces at the rate of ten per day.

In 1878, the firm pioneered stem-wound pocket watches, and in the 1880s, Gruen developed the popular size-16 watch that became standard for railroad use. The company moved to Cincinnati in 1896.

Dietrich Gruen's sons, Fred (1872-1945) and George (1878-1952), joined the firm and led D. Gruen & Sons during the decades when it produced the first octagon watch (1912), stylish women's wrist watches, the first rectangular watch (1925), and the Curvex (1935), the only watch with curved movements.

The Gruen company became one of the nation's largest producers of watches—1,500 to 2,000 a day by 1940—with plants on both sides of the Atlantic. At "Time Hill" on McMillan, Gruen manufactured watch cases and assembled and serviced watches. The watch movements were made in a Swiss plant that Dietrich Gruen had established, and in a New York factory. The firm also maintained its own watch making school in Cincinnati.

However, by 1935, when Benjamin

*The architects of the Gruen Watch Company building designed an attractive plant to fit into the suburban, residential neighborhood.*

S. Katz, founder of a New York City watch case manufacturing firm, took over Gruen, the company had accumulated a $1.8 million debt. Under Katz's direction, the firm entered the fine watch market, reaching record sales volume and profits in fiscal 1953. After Katz retired, the company suffered as his successors struggled for control of the firm and ill-advised diversification caused nearly $10 million in losses. In 1958, the company reorganized as Gruen Industries, Inc., and left Cincinnati for its New York facility.

In 1976, Gruen Industries filed a Chapter 11 bankruptcy petition to reorganize. The firm was dissolved three years later. Time Hill was renovated in the mid-1970s as an office building.

Across the street, the Tudor style, half-timbered, stone and brick structure is best known as the former home of **14 Beau Brummel Ties, Inc.,** 440 East McMillan Street. Erected in 1921, the building was designed by Elzner & Anderson for the Procter & Collins printing and advertising agency; the tower held water for a sprinkler system.

The Weisbaum Brothers Brower Company, which moved into the building around 1936, was founded by necktie salesmen Harry and Edward Weisbaum and Sam A. Brower. Around 1940, the tie company adopted the name Beau Brummell, a reference to the British dandy who epitomized male elegance.

At this plant, neckties were cut, lined, assembled, sewn (mostly by women who were judged more dexterous than men at operating the power machines), pressed, and packed for shipping. Beau Brummell became a multi-million dollar business, selling ties all over the world.

The business declined in the 1970s, and in 1982, a New York conglomerate which then owned Beau Brummell closed the plant. The building has been acquired by a jewelry manufacturing firm.

For years, a number of custom tailoring companies have occupied the 2-story concrete building, 490 East McMillan Street, that the **15 Herschede Hall Clock Company** built in 1912-1915. Established in 1892, the Hall Clock Company was the second successful business founded by Frank Herschede, who began his career with a jewelry store in 1877.

Herschede's internationally-recognized grandfather clocks offered customers the choice of three chime tunes, including one written expressly for the company. Herschede was America's oldest maker of chiming floor clocks and the only one still manufacturing the movements when the company moved from Walnut Hills to Starkeville, Mississippi, in 1960.

In the mid-1930s, the Storrs-Schaefer custom tailoring company, became the first of many such firms to locate in the Herschede plant. One of the best known was the Hamilton Tailoring Company which, in the 1960s, employed 800 men and women, and produced 100,000 suits a year, including uniforms for 90% of the nation's commercial airlines, the United States Air Force Academy, and police and railway lines around the country.

Hamilton, along with the Globe Company and a half dozen associated firms that by then filled the building, made up what a contemporary newspaper account claimed was the nation's largest custom tailoring company.

For most of its history, the **16 Sattler Building,** 608 East McMillan Street, has served educational purposes rather than the industrial uses for which it was intended. Kruckemeyer & Strong designed this 3-story limestone building for the Randolph Sattler Company, steel engraved printers and publishers. (Note the "S" in the oval above the door.) In 1927, the Sattler Company moved here from Third and Vine Streets; its woodworking and machine shops and foundry were located in an adjacent structure.

By about 1930, the company maintained only an office downtown, and the Printing Trades School had been moved here. Four temporary buildings were erected, and an adjoining garage was remodeled as a machine shop for the Mechanical Trades School.

After World War II, the Sattler building housed the Veterans Vocational Training Center and two vocational high schools, but in 1953, Cincinnati's vocational high school programs were transferred to the new Central High School on Central Parkway.

The administrative offices of the Board of Education were here until 1967, and in September 1969, the McMillan Adult Center for junior and senior high students failing in their regular schools opened. In 1987, the McMillan Center enrolled about 850 students in four programs: academic help, vocational training, Adult Basic Education, and Graduate Equivalency Diploma preparation classes.

That year, however, a study concluded the school was not having a significant impact on the system's drop-out problem, nor helping enough of its students—teenage parents, drug abusers, chronic truants, and convicted criminals—return to their regular schools. The Board of Education voted to close the school and seek

*Peebles' Corner was still one of the city's most active business districts in the 1940s.*

funding for another program for high-risk youngsters.

Once Cincinnati's second largest shopping district, **17 Peebles Corner** is at the intersection of Gilbert and McMillan Avenues. William S. Peebles (1816-1861), whose Walnut Hills "grocery house" occupied the northeast corner of the intersection, allegedly used gifts of cigars and groceries to induce streetcar motormen to call out "Peebles' Corner!" at this stop.

Peebles' grocery business was founded on December 24, 1840, when William and his brother, Joseph R. (1818-1866), opened a small store on Fifth Street. The Joseph R. Peebles' Sons Company, "Dealers in Staple and Fancy Groceries, and Importers of Wine, Cigars &c.," moved to West Fourth Street in 1879, established the Walnut Hills store in 1883, and by the turn of the century, had yet another store located on Fifth Street. The company also operated in Hyde Park, Wyoming, and Bond Hill before going out of business in 1935.

The "fancy groceries" for which Peebles was especially noted became luxuries that few could afford during the Depression, and competition from

the growing Kroger and A&P chains helped settle the business's fate.

In the 1920s, the Peebles' Corner business district consisted of more than 215 businesses, including stores selling clothing, groceries, meat, flowers, auto parts, hardware, furniture, and paint. In addition, there were banks, theaters, doctors' offices, a public comfort station, a library, and a post office within a few blocks of the intersection, making it a community focal point.

Among the public buildings in this vicinity was the firehouse of Engine Company No. 16, built at 773 East McMillan Street in 1870. Nine years later, Engine 16's men were among the first firefighters in the country to use a metal sliding pole to get from the second to the first floor of their firehouse. The company continued to occupy this small brick engine house until 1976.

The empty building has been vandalized, but the city hopes that a private developer will renovate the firehouse.

Since 1931, Peebles' Corner has been dominated by the striking Art Deco style Paramount Building, 900 East McMillan Avenue, a 2-story limestone office and retail structure with a 3-story metal-capped tower. Erected on the former site of Peebles' store, the building was originally attached to the 1,100-seat Paramount

Theater to the east, which was closed in 1961 and subsequently razed.

Its architect, Edward J. Schulte (1890-1975), achieved national recognition for his church commissions, including St. Cecilia's in Oakley, St. Monica's in Fairview, and the renovations of St. Peter in Chains Cathedral. Schulte had his offices at Peebles' Corner.

By the mid-1950s, business activity at Peebles' Corner began to fall off, and thirty years later, many of the storefronts, as well as the firehouse, stood vacant. Nevertheless, Peebles' Corner, with encouragement from city government, has retained a certain degree of vitality and variety. Unlike some neighborhood business districts that have become the site of specialty shops or service-type operations, this district has several stores—a variety store, hardware, pharmacy, and supermarket—that supply everyday needs of area residents.

**Turn right on Victory Parkway.**

The 6-story Victory Parkway Executive Building, 2368 Victory Parkway, was originally the **18 L. B. Harrison Club Hotel,** a low-cost residence for young men.

Learner Blackman Harrison (1815-1902), in whose memory his seven children created the hotel, rose from grocery clerk to be a founder and later, president of the First National Bank of Cincinnati. Harrison acquired a large estate on Grandin Road in East Walnut Hills by the late 1860s and was a leading figure in the establishment of the Cincinnati Observatory, Art Academy, Art Museum, and zoo.

The first L. B. Harrison Hotel for Young Men, a 5-story building on West Seventh Street in the West End, opened on April 14, 1914. Young working men paid from $3.50 to $7.00 a week for one of the 225 rooms, three meals a day, and use of the library, billiard room, and showers. Rent was on the honor system. Each paid what he could afford and reported every raise so his rent could be increased appropriately.

The L. B. Harrison aimed to provide a "home away from home" with companionship and leisure time activities. An annex with a pool and gym was erected in 1915, and eventually the LBH had amateur and semipro sports teams.

The LBH's managers fostered a "booster spirit." Determined to build strength of character, they took personal interest in each of "the boys" and enforced an 11:00 p.m. curfew and such rules as: "Have your gym suit washed once in a while" and "Do not associate with any young man or woman who would not be good company to take home to meet your own mother or sister."

During the 1920s, the basin became more crowded and a less desirable place to live, and LBH trustees chose Walnut Hills for a new club-hotel building. This lot was purchased in 1929, and several adjacent homes were razed. The new LBH was completed on April 20, 1930. The Seventh Street building was taken over by Union Bethel until 1942, when it was sold again to become a hotel and club for blacks.

After World War II, the men who filled the hotel's rooms were more mature, more sophisticated—over half attended college or had served in the military—and wanted less guidance. Despite changes in styles of living, a more rapid turnover, and the growing popularity of the automobile that expanded social and recreational opportunities, the LBH community spirit endured, as did its low rents—$18.00 a week in 1964.

Nonetheless, increased maintenance costs made balancing expenses with income more difficult. In addition, the residential club had become an outdated institution. Vacancies increased, and finally, the L.B. Harrison Club Hotel closed.

In 1973, neighboring Edgecliff College purchased the building, which became a dormitory, Harrison Hall. In 1981, the Walnut Hills Development Foundation bought the property in a joint venture with two private investors. A 1983 remodeling produced an office building with a pool, sauna, and exercise facilities for the tenants.

**Turn left on Cyprus Street, right on Ashland Avenue.**

In June 1935, Archbishop John T. McNicholas (1877-1950) announced that the College of the Sacred Heart in Clifton was closing and that the Sisters of Mercy would open a liberal arts college for women to replace it.

**19 Our Lady of Cincinnati College,** later Edgecliff College, and briefly the Edgecliff Campus of Xavier University, 2220 Victory Parkway, opened that September in two nineteenth-century mansions that the Sisters first leased and then purchased.

Edgecliff, the 1881 3-story stone residence of real estate developer Thomas J. (1830-1906) and Mary M. (1844-1927) Emery had been designed by Samuel Hannaford. Its location offered a spectacular view of the Ohio River. Though most of the Emerys' art collection had been removed to the Art Museum, Our Lady Hall, the college's main building, contained much of the original furniture carved by Benn Pitman (1821-1910) and William Fry (1830-1929).

Maxwelton, the former home of Judge Lawrence Maxwell (1853-1927), was renamed McAuley Hall and used for a social hall, home economics classes, and boarders' rooms.

In the next two years, the Mercy Sisters purchased two other houses, and began a new administration building. The curriculum of Our Lady of Cincinnati was expanded regularly, as was the physical plant of the college with construction of library, dormitory, classroom, and office buildings in the 1950s and 1960s. The institution formally adopted the name Edgecliff College in 1969.

Edgecliff admitted full-time male students in 1970, and with the acquisition of the neighboring L. B. Harrison Club Hotel, gained athletic facilities and much-needed housing for out-of-town male students.

*In recent decades, the elegant homes on streets such as Upland Place, with their architectural character and convenient location, have attracted middle and upper-income homebuyers.*

However, by the late 1970s, enrollment at Edgecliff College was falling. Xavier University in Avondale assumed operation of the campus in 1980, combining programs and sharing facilities. Xavier purchased the 8-building campus three years later, but in March 1986, administrators announced that the joint operation had proven financially unsound. The property was sold in early 1987 to private developers who planned luxury condominiums for part of the grounds.

All programs and students on the Edgecliff campus were moved to Xavier University's main campus, and the new owners quickly razed the Emery home, to public dismay. Maxwelton was spared. Shortly thereafter, the University of Cincinnati disclosed plans to relocate its OMI College of Applied Science from Central Parkway to several of the remaining buildings on this campus.

**Turn left on Upland Place.**

The **20 Homes on Upland Place** date from the late nineteenth and early twentieth centuries, and reflect their original owners' considerable wealth. The 2- and 2½-story residences were built on large lots and with a variety of materials and in a variety of styles; many have special features like towers, fancy woodwork, and stained glass windows. Some even had "auto houses"—garages for the automobiles that only a few could then afford.

Alfred Day Fisher, a grain commission merchant, built the Swiss chalet style house at 2214 in 1892. Lucien F. Plympton was the architect for the structure with its colorfully-decorated facade hewn and finished

in Switzerland. Lawrence B. Cahill, of the Cahill-Holters shoe manufacturing firm at Denman and Kenner Streets, built 2326 around 1900. Family history recounts that while the stone for the dwelling was being shipped from Spain, one vessel was lost at sea, delaying completion of the home by two years. Joseph T. Carew, co-founder of the Mabley & Carew department stores, bought the 2-story brick house at the northwest corner of Upland and McMillan.

Well-to-do businessmen and professionals continued to live here into the early decades of the twentieth century, but as many parts of Walnut Hills became less desirable residential neighborhoods, families who could afford to maintain these large homes moved away. Some of the houses were divided into apartments; others became rest homes, and the Carew residence was converted into a funeral home.

In 1952, Jackson Grey Storey (1902-1978), a nationally-known painter of Western scenes, moved his Central Academy of Commercial Art to 2326, the former Cahill home. Classrooms were erected behind the house in 1962.

Evidence of years of neglect and hard use is still visible, though determined rehabilitation efforts in recent years have restored much of the former elegance of these old homes, now a mix of private residences and institutional and apartment buildings.

> **Turn right on East McMillan Street.**

Sisters of St. Ursula first arrived in Cincinnati from France in 1845. In April 1910, twenty members of the Brown County, Ohio, community organized an independent community that established **21 St. Ursula Convent** and **Academy,** 1339 East McMillan Street.

On September 17, seventy-three students began classes in a house at the corner of McMillan and Ingleside Avenues while renovations were made in the two homes where the school and convent are now located. The red brick dwelling at the corner of McMillan and Upland Place was erected in the early 1870s by Joseph W. Cotteral, a contractor and builder. The convent and school opened here in 1911 and,

the following year, expanded to the adjacent home. The similarity of the two structures suggests that Cotteral built both.

A third building connecting the two nineteenth-century residences and containing a chapel, sacristy, classrooms, and guest rooms, was begun in 1915, aided by the generous support of Maria Longworth Storer (1849-1932), founder of the Rookwood Pottery, and her husband, Ambassador Bellamy Storer (1847-1922). The Storers had private rooms in an addition built at the Upland Place end of the convent, a private entrance, and their own kitchen and laundry (later the chemistry and home economics labs, respectively).

St. Ursula Academy enrolled 200 students by 1935. In the post-war years, enrollment grew to nearly 400 students, K-12. The Ursulines purchased two smaller 2½-story brick boarding houses on Upland in 1954, and completed a new gym-auditorium building in 1955.

To meet the increased need for classroom space, the school stopped taking boarders in 1957. Three years later, when 525 pupils crowded the school, the Sisters bought the Richard K. LeBlond estate in Mt. Lookout where they opened St. Ursula Villa School, preschool through eighth grade. A high school wing was added to the Cotteral home in 1967.

St. Ursula Academy enrolled 430 high school students in 1986-1987. The convent and school continue as Walnut Hills landmarks and integral parts of the community. The buildings are opened to conferences and community groups, and Jesuit volunteers housed in one of the Upland Place houses do social work in the area.

> **Turn left on Woodburn Avenue.**

Much of the village of Woodburn was characterized by the large estates established there in the 1840s and 1850s. But by the 1860s, there were also more modest houses and several stores clustered along Madison Road near Hackberry Street. There, the village's principle business, Boedker's Grocery & Feed Store, was located. Eventually, this cluster of buildings became part of the neighborhood business district known as **22 De Sales Corner,** after its most notable

landmark, St. Francis De Sales Church.

After horsecar service into this vicinity began during the 1870s, new homes were erected near the Madison and Hackberry intersection. As the area's population grew and its business district became more important, the city, which had annexed the village in 1873, had to provide Woodburn with better public services such as fire protection. Engine Company No. 23 and Ladder Company No. 9 went into service in the firehouse at 1700 Madison Road in 1885.

Further development followed after George Kerper's Walnut Hills Cable Railway improved transportation to the area in 1885-1886. The inexpensive and reliable cable cars drew large numbers of middle-income families to many homes and multi-family dwellings in western Woodburn, like the 6-story San Marco Flats, constructed around 1893 at 1601 Madison Road.

The majority of new growth was located close to the streetcar line that was further improved in 1898 when electric cars replaced the cable cars. This development shifted the center of Woodburn's business district from Madison and Hackberry to the Madison and Woodburn intersection. By the 1920s, more than half of the area's approximately eighty businesses were located on Woodburn Avenue.

De Sales Corner changed in the mid-twentieth century as middle-income families moved out; many buildings, such as the San Marco, showed signs of age and neglect. By the late 1960s, De Sales Corner had become a lower-income neighborhood. Although the number of businesses there did not decline, fewer were retail operations that served the surrounding community.

In the 1970s, both city government and private developers initiated rehabilitation projects in and around De Sales Corner. Some projects failed, including a 1972-1973 attempt to renovate the San Marco. But in 1977, the Cincinnati Metropolitan Housing Authority began a second renovation effort; in 1982, thirty modernized apartments for elderly or handicapped lower-income tenants opened there.

The city also razed abandoned buildings in the vicinity and carried out some new construction, including modern quarters for Engine 23 at 1623

*The village of Woodburn was not just large estates and mansions; middle-income housing and numerous businesses clustered in the vicinity of St. Francis de Sales Church.*

Madison and a vest-pocket park with a gazebo next to the San Marco.

The limestone, Gothic style **23 St. Francis De Sales Roman Catholic Church,** 1600 Madison Road, with its soaring 230-foot tower, is the second church erected by this parish. In 1849, Marianist Brothers arrived in Cincinnati from France and established St. Francis de Sales parish for German Catholics living in Walnut Hills. Some fifty families began worshipping in a barn located near McMillan Street and Moorman Avenue.

Archbishop Purcell laid the cornerstone for the first church on May 12, 1850, on a lot at the corner of Hackberry Street and Forest Avenue (William Howard Taft Road). The original priests' residence is still standing at 2563 Hackberry Street.

The growing parish built a new, larger complex at Woodburn Avenue and Madison Pike, completing a school, rectory, and sacristy in 1877; the present church was dedicated in 1879.

The most famous feature of St. Francis de Sales Church is "Joseph" or "Big Joe," a bell named after the donor, Joseph Buddeke, partner in a wholesale dry goods and notions concern on Pearl Street. Cast by the E. W. Van Duzen Company on Second Street, the bell weighs 35,000 pounds and is seven feet high and nine feet in diameter, and is said to be the largest free swinging bell in the world. Fourteen horses were required to haul the bell up the hills from the basin to the church. When "Big Joe" was rung for the first time in early January 1896, its E-flat peal rattled nearby buildings and shattered windows.

In the late 1930s, the parish recorded more than 3,000 members, but later decades saw membership decline to 300 families by the late 1980s. Enrollment in the school changed, reflecting changes in the neighborhood: 95% of the 200 children enrolled in 1987 were black.

St. Francis de Sales parish sold one acre of land behind the church for the construction of an archdiocesan high school for boys. **24 Purcell Marian High School,** 2935 Hackberry Street, named for Archbishop John Purcell (1800-1883), opened in 1928 in a red brick and stone building designed by Crowe & Schulte. Movie actor Tyrone Power and former football quarterback Roger Staubach are Purcell alumni.

Purcell's enrollment peaked in the late 1950s at 1,200 boys, but the opening of Moeller High in Kenwood in 1961 relieved the crowding. Then declining enrollment—564 in 1980—and increasing costs brought about a merger with Marian High School in 1981. The girls' school had opened on Madison Road in Hyde Park in 1963.

The merger proved successful. The Marianist Brothers and Sisters of Charity jointly manage the school that enrolls about 1,000 each year and has forged new traditions with strong academic and athletic programs.

**Turn right on Madison Road.**

Cincinnati's oldest nondenominational private school, **25 Seven Hills Doherty School** and **Middle School,** 2726-2735 Johnstone Place, was begun in 1906. Mary Harlan Doherty (1862-1948) organized the College Preparatory School for Girls here in the former home of George Hoadley (1826-1902), a mayor of Woodburn and governor of Ohio. Doherty gained national prominence as an educator and for her advocacy of college education for women.

The College Preparatory School (CPS) became an accredited high school in 1959. Previously, administrators had felt that an independent school ought to be truly independent of the system.

The following year, boys were admitted to the first through sixth grades, and in 1961, when the student body numbered 281, the school bought and remodeled the red brick home that had once belonged to another Cincinnati mayor, Russell Wilson (1876-1946). Also in the 1960s, the old Hoadley residence was razed and a new classroom building erected.

In 1974, CPS was facing financial difficulties and merged with Hillsdale-Lotspeich Schools to form the Seven Hills Schools. In 1987-1988, about 390 children, preschool-8, were enrolled here.

Large and elegant homes were still being erected in this vicinity in the early twentieth century. Two such mansions are now occupied by the **26 St. Thomas Institute,** 1840-1842 Madison Road. The St. Thomas Institute, formerly the Institum Divi Thomae, was founded in 1935 by Archbishop John T. McNicholas (1877-1950) who wanted not only to encourage the advancement of scientific knowledge but to demonstrate that there was no inherent conflict between science and religion.

The Institum, first located at St. Gregory Seminary in Mt. Washington, served as the graduate school of scientific research and education of the Athenaeum of Ohio, the institution that included all of the Cincinnati Archdiocese's institutions of higher learning. Dr. George Speri Sperti (b.1900), co-founder and director of the University of Cincinnati's Basic Science Laboratory, directed the new school.

The Institum's purposes were broad and included investigation of fundamental problems in the various fields of science, the establishment of cooperative research laboratories at affiliated institutions, and the consideration of science in relation to philosophy. The faculty, composed of chemists, biologists, biochemists, biophysicists, botanists, geneticists, and mathematicians, has focused on cancer research but has also investigated infectious diseases, growth and metabolism, and "borderline" problems where the biological and physical sciences overlap.

Dr. Sperti, a member of the Pontifical Academy of Sciences since 1936, was given the University of Cincinnati's William Howard Taft medal in 1970. His Sperti Sun Lamp, Bio Dyne ointment for burns, and Preparation-H hemorrhoid treatment are all well known.

The Institum Divi Thomae became independent from the archdiocese in 1953 and incorporated as a nonprofit research and educational center in 1955. The St. Thomas Institute (the official name since 1970) offers 2-year masters and 4-year doctoral programs.

The two Jacobethan Revival style homes that house the Institute were erected on lots carved from the 40-acre estate of W. W. Scarborough, lawyer and president of the Cincinnati Gas-Light & Coke Company. After Scarborough's death, his trustees subdivided the property and sold residential lots to wealthy Cincinnatians.

William M. Greene, manager of the Big Four Railroad and vice-president of the Baltimore & Ohio Southwestern Railway Company, erected the brick dwelling in 1903. Louis P. Ficks, founder and president of the National Carriage & Reed Company, completed the adjacent stone mansion in 1907. The archdiocese bought the Greene house in 1940, and the Institum Divi Thomae Foundation bought the Ficks home in 1945.

**Turn right on Keys Crescent Avenue.**

East Walnut Hills' long history as a prestigious residential area is evidenced by the mansions and large homes, dating from the mid-nineteenth to the early twentieth century, many of which remain single-family residences.

The magnificent rough sandstone **27 Holabird-Ludeking Castle,** 1833 Keys Crescent, was built in 1929 for Otto Ludeking, one of Cincinnati's leading haberdashers, and his wife, Catherine Holabird, granddaughter of a pioneer in the machine tool business. A contemporary account declared the German-born Ludeking had "made his name synonymous with all that is fashionable and up-to-date in gentle-

men's furnishings . . . In his six stores can be found the finest products . . . of the great metropolises of this country and the Old World."

Bloodgood Tuttle, a Cleveland architect, designed this French Renaissance style residence, which was an adaptation of three chateaux of King Francis I of France. Les Tours—The Towers—had marble floors and a fountain. The east tower was lined with circular bookshelves and ornamented with frescos and stained glass windows. The sunken drawing room had 20-foot high leaded glass windows and a fireplace large enough to walk into.

One of Walnut Hill's earliest wealthy residents, John Baker, built the 2-story painted brick house at 1831 Keys Crescent for his daughter, Julia, and her husband, Samuel Keys, around 1853. This street was named for the couple. The residence is best known, however, as the **28 Home of John Baker Hollister,** Baker's great-grandson.

Hollister (1890-1979), Robert A. Taft (1889-1953), and John Longworth Stettinius (1832-1904) organized the Cincinnati law firm of Taft, Stettinius & Hollister in 1924. Hollister was also president of the Covington & Cincinnati Suspension Bridge Company and a member of the board of directors for the Pennsylvania and Little Miami railroads, Emery Industries, and Fifth-Third Union Trust, and also served as a congressman.

**Turn right on Madison Road, right on Baker Place.**

On the right is Woodburn, 1887 Madison Road, the **29 Home of John Baker**. Baker (1792-1857), after whom the street is named, came to Cincinnati from New Jersey in 1814 and, according to family tradition, traded a white horse for "a piece of Fourth and Walnut" Streets. He later bought a large tract in East Walnut Hills.

In 1853, Baker engaged James Keyes Wilson (1828-1894), Cincinnati's most prominent architect, to design this asymmetrical 2-story brick home. With its square tower and elegant tracery, Woodburn is one of the city's few residential examples of the Gothic Revival style. Baker's son,

Nathan, brought much of the home's furniture from Europe. The house later underwent some modernization, including the addition of a wing in 1910.

In 1979, the sixth generation of Baker's descendants decided to sell the home and its furnishings, setting off a battle between preservationists who wanted to convert the structure to a museum with all of the contents intact and neighbors who wanted to maintain the "fragile, but stable" residential character of the area. The home was sold to a private owner and listed on the National Register of Historic Places.

**Return to Madison Road and turn right.**

The 10½-acre **30 Owl's Nest Park,** north side of Madison Road opposite Elmhurst Street, takes its name from the farm of James Handasyd Perkins (1810-1849) who settled here in 1845.

Perkins arrived in Cincinnati in 1832. He studied law and was admitted to the bar. He then edited a local newspaper, was briefly involved with a mining and milling venture, and next became minister for the First Congregational Church on Eighth Street. Perkins also wrote a popular history of the Northwest Territory, *Annals of the West* (1846).

On December 14, 1849, Perkins left his wallet and watch in his mailbox and disappeared. Friends traced his footsteps to a barge on the river where his hat and coat were found. He was presumed to have drowned, though a local gardener contended that the minister was living in a Trappist monastery in Kentucky.

In July 1905, two of Perkins' sons, Charles and Edward, donated the 5-acre farm to the city with the stipulation that it be kept as an open playground and not be used for ornamental plantings or "fancy park work." The homestead and a schoolhouse on the property were razed; a boulder with a bronze plaque marks the site of the farmhouse. A granddaughter later donated a drinking fountain, ornamental bronze gate, and wrought iron fence. The fence was taken down in 1942 for a wartime scrap metal drive, the gate in 1975.

Improvements were not made

until 1931, when the shelterhouse building was erected. Additional lots to the north were later acquired and leased to the Cincinnati Recreation Commission which built and maintains playfields, equipment, and a swimming pool.

While Woodburn was an upper-income suburb with elegant homes and spacious grounds, **31 O'Bry- onville** was characterized by modest lots and houses for less well-to-do families. The village was named for the O'Bryon family, Irish immigrants who, sometime before the Civil War, purchased land that lay north of present-day Madison Road, between Owl's Nest Park and Easthill Avenue.

Around 1865, some of the O'Bryon land near the intersection of Torrence Parkway, and Madison and Grandin Roads was subdivided. Businessmen, including a carpenter, blacksmith,

*The hamlet known as O'Bryonville was small but had several businesses, among them this blacksmith's shop that is now a restaurant.*

liquor dealer, and stonemason established shops along Madison Road. Gradually, other portions of the estate were sold for subdivisions that offered simple brick and frame homes for lower and middle-income families. Laura O'Bryon's Subdivision consisted of 25' x 100' building lots on O'Bryon Street.

Many of the residents of the houses on such streets as Cinnamon,

Pogue, and Cohoon were Irish, German, and English immigrants, and many were employees of the large landowners in nearby Woodburn and East Walnut Hills. In the late nineteenth century, the area also housed a small black community. The number of black residents increased during the 1930s and again after World War II.

Unlike other nineteenth-century subdivisions such as Vernon Village, which lost its separate identity as it was absorbed into the Walnut Hills community, O'Bryonville did not disappear as an identifiable area. Its housing was clearly different from that of Woodburn or East Walnut Hills, its population had become predominantly black, and the small business district made it easy to distinguish where O'Bryonville began and ended.

In the 1970s and 1980s, the O'Bryonville business district acquired new businesses, specialty shops and restaurants that catered to a middle and upper-income clientele from throughout the city, rather than residents of O'Bryonville itself. The residential streets to the north of Madison Road, however, remained largely unchanged.

**Turn left on O'Bryon Street, right on Pogue Avenue.**

The Associated Charities of Cin-

cinnati first advanced plans for **32 Beechwood Home,** 2140 Pogue Avenue, in 1888. Although Cincinnati had a number of public hospitals at that time, there was no facility for the care of persons suffering from chronic diseases.

By the spring of 1890, a nurse had been hired and a house rented in Mt. Auburn where the Beechwood Home for Incurables opened on October 1. In 1893, the Home moved to a larger building on Kemper Lane in Walnut Hills, a location more convenient for the wealthy women who staffed the board and regularly visited patients.

Over the years, bequests, pageants, carnivals, charity balls, lawn fetes, and outdoor suppers helped raise funds to operate, furnish, and expand Beechwood. In January 1902, the board purchased five acres of land on Beechwood (Pogue) Avenue. Helped by generous donations, including sums from Thomas J. Emery and Charles Kilgour, the Home built a new structure with a children's ward.

A wing was added in 1911, a nurses wing in 1937. That complex was razed for the construction of Beechwood's present 70-bed building, completed in 1970.

In its early years, the Home admitted anyone with an incurable disease, except tuberculosis, who could testify to his or her respectable character. But as institutions developed to treat cancer, heart disease, and other illnesses, persons needing specialized care were referred there. Today's residents of the Home are chiefly victims of multiple sclerosis, cerebral palsy, Parkinson's disease, arthritis, stroke, and birth defects.

**Turn right on East Hill Avenue to return to Madison Road where tour ends.**

# Tour 10

# Mt. Auburn

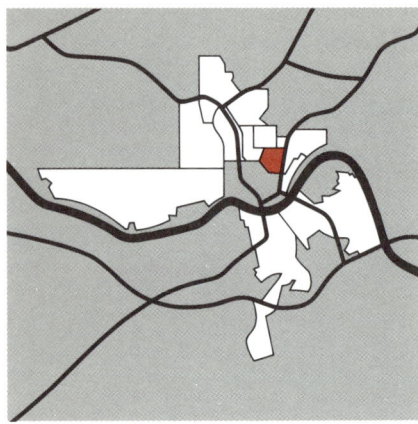

Mt. Auburn was Cincinnati's original hilltop suburb—the first area outside the basin to which the city's wealthy migrated. Mt. Auburn consisted of the property lying between McMillan Street on the north, McMicken Avenue and Liberty Street on the south, Reading Road on the east, and Vine Street on the west. These boundaries were not always clear, and residents or developers who desired the prestige associated with this neighborhood often included parts of Corryville, Walnut Hills, and Avondale in Mt. Auburn. Conversely, in the mid-twentieth century when the area had deteriorated, nearby properties were renamed so they would not have "undesirable" associations.

The land that was to become Mt. Auburn passed quickly through the hands of a series of speculators during the 1790s and early 1800s. The first landowners to build homes on the hilltop were James Keys, a director of the Cincinnati branch of the Bank of the United States, and Gorham A. Worth, cashier of the bank. They erected their houses between 1818 and 1819. Because Keys lived here and owned considerable adjoining property, the area became known as Keys' Hill.

Despite the hill's steep slopes, the appeal of its rural beauty drew more of the merchant class from the downtown basin. Although many houses were originally built as summer residences, a growing number of the city's elite soon began living on the hill year-round, and an elegant suburb developed. In the late 1820s and early 1830s, subdivisions were platted on the crest of the hill, and by 1835, this area of large lots and fine houses was called Mt. Auburn. The name, a testament to the new suburb's attractiveness, was supposed to have been invented by an Englishwoman who took it either from a line in a poem by Oliver Goldsmith or from a garden-like cemetery near Boston. Whatever its

*During the nineteenth century, well-to-do Cincinnatians built substantial homes in a wide variety of styles atop Mt. Auburn.*

source, the name Mt. Auburn was adopted and became synonymous with the concept of an elite suburban way of life.

Mt. Auburn was annexed to the City of Cincinnati in 1849 as a part of the Special Road District of Millcreek Township. Annexation brought Mt. Auburn's residents access to public services such as water, police and fire protection, and street improvements. The move also enabled Cincinnati to "recapture" a portion of the population that had slipped beyond its boundaries to suburbs where people could enjoy the advantages of proximity to the city without paying city taxes.

Mt. Auburn continued to attract members of the city's elite even after other upper-income suburbs such as Clifton developed. It was the home of many influential individuals: Judge Alphonso Taft, Lafayette Bank president Joseph Butler, iron and steel tycoon Matthew Addy, legislator George H. Pendleton, and Civil War general Edward Noyes. Mt. Auburn was also the site of several institutions, including the Mt. Auburn Young Ladies Institute and the Cincinnati Orphan Asylum.

At the same time that Cincinnati's wealthy citizens were moving to the top of Mt. Auburn, middle-income families were working their way up the sides of the hill. Although the steep hillsides were not ideal building sites, residents from crowded basin neighborhoods like Over-the-Rhine erected modest homes along the narrow streets carved on the face of the hill. These new neighborhoods, parts of which could be reached only by walking or climbing steep steps, were culturally and functionally more related to Over-the-Rhine than to Mt. Auburn.

During the latter part of the nineteenth century, new public transportation lines began bringing more modest-income people into Mt. Auburn itself. The Main Street Incline (1872) and the Mt. Auburn Cable Railway (1887) reduced the time it took to ascend the hill and opened the suburb to renters and less affluent home buyers. Soon, multi-family dwellings and smaller houses were interspersed with the mansions.

As the older wealthy families died or moved on to newer suburbs, the neighborhood became increasingly middle-income, and by the early twentieth century, most of the buildings had passed into the hands of absentee landlords. However, the introduction of medical facilities in the area had the most serious impact on the character of Mt. Auburn. Christ Hospital, which had moved to Mt. Auburn in 1893, drew doctors' offices and related businesses here. Throughout the first half of the twentieth century, housing was gradually replaced by offices, nurses' residences, and parking space. According to neighborhood leaders, community spirit was fragmented and disrupted, contributing to Mt. Auburn's general problems of deteriorating housing stock and widespread juvenile delinquency.

In the late 1950s and 1960s, black families displaced by urban renewal in the West End moved into Mt. Auburn, and the neighborhood's weakened sense of community proved unable to deal with the change. Many white residents fled, while absentee landlords further subdivided the large houses and often neglected even basic maintenance.

The Mt. Auburn medical community claimed that the development of medical facilities helped the neighborhood, but conditions off the main streets continued to worsen. Finally, the residents themselves responded by creating groups such as the Mt. Auburn Good Housing

*In the 1970s and 1980s, many of Mt. Auburn's older buildings were saved from decay and put to new uses; a portion of Taft Elementary School was renovated as a health clinic.*

Foundation (1967) and the Mt. Auburn Development Corporation (1971). Led by black neighborhood activists, of whom Carl Westmoreland was the most prominent, these groups initiated projects to renovate abandoned buildings for quality low-income housing. The projects benefited from the residents' sense of commitment, association with the early stages of the historic preservation movement, and a concerted effort to drive drug traffic from the community.

By 1975, these successes had attracted white, middle-income speculators to Mt. Auburn. As the "back to the city" movement of the 1970s grew and property in areas like Mt. Adams became more expensive, speculators renovated inexpensive structures, mostly on the southern face of Mt. Auburn—known in the real estate market as Liberty Hill and Prospect Hill—where there were views of the city. Soon neighborhood groups and speculators were competing for Mt. Auburn housing, and displacement of low-income residents became a problem.

This competition became less intense in the 1980s as a new generation of middle-income professionals showed less interest in urban life. The Mt. Auburn real estate market slowed, as did redevelopment and rehabilitation, but in 1987, a portion of Auburn Avenue was designated a local historic district to the gratification of neighborhood groups who had worked to preserve the character and improve the quality of life in Mt. Auburn.

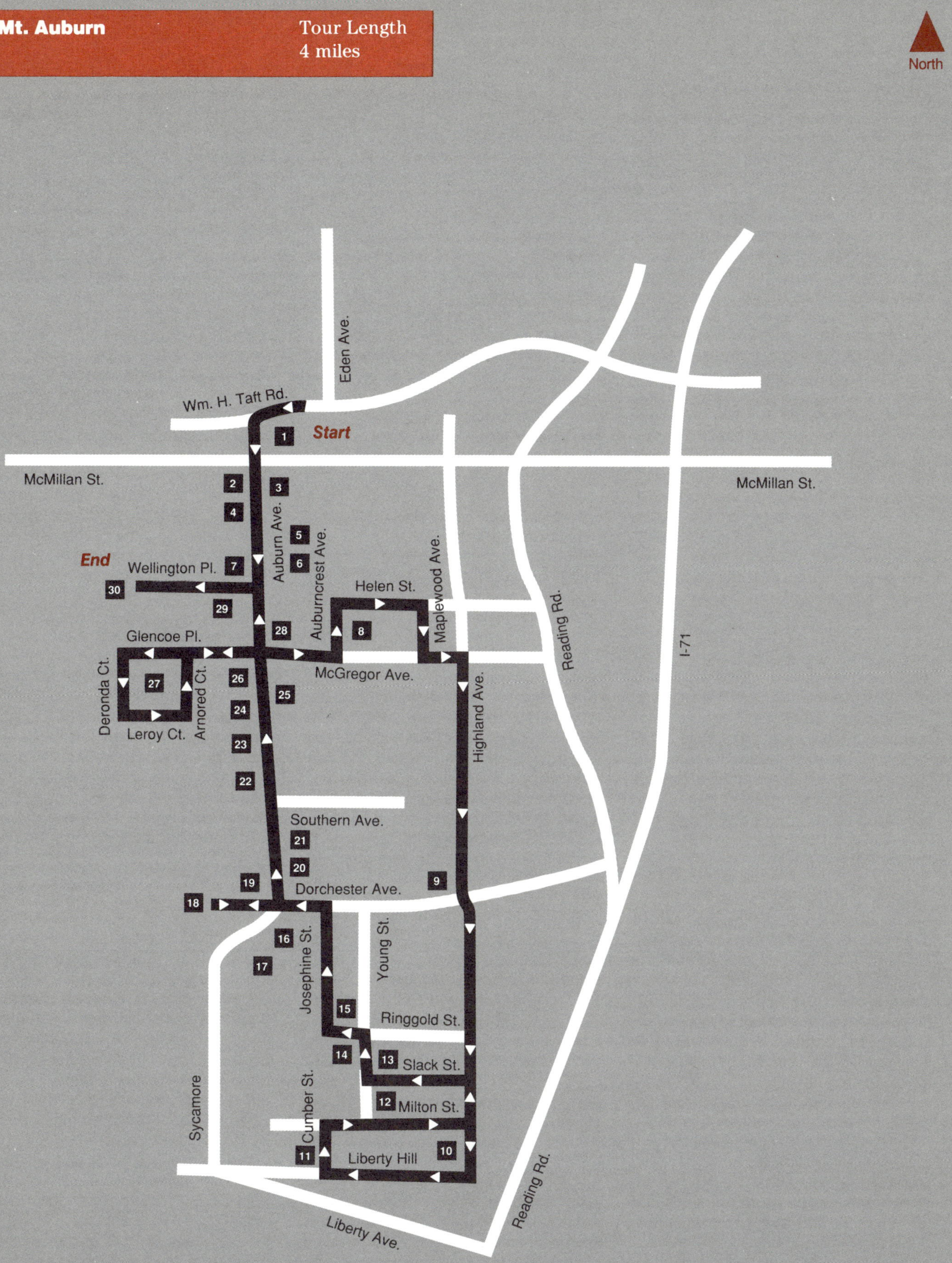

Eden Ave.

Wm. H. Taft Rd.

**1** *Start*

McMillan St.

**2**

**3**

**4**

**5**

Auburn Ave.

**6**

Auburncrest Ave.

Wellington Pl. **7**

*End*

**30**

**29**

Helen St.

Maplewood Ave.

**8**

Glencoe Pl.

**28**

McGregor Ave.

Deronda Ct.

**27**

**26**

**25**

Arnored Ct.

**24**

Highland Ave.

Leroy Ct.

**23**

**22**

Southern Ave.

**21**

**20**

Dorchester Ave.

**19**

**9**

**18**

**16**

Josephine St.

Young St.

**17**

**15**

Ringgold St.

**14**

**13** Slack St.

Cumber St.

**12** Milton St.

**11**

Liberty Hill

**10**

Sycamore

Reading Rd.

Liberty Ave.

Reading Rd.

I-71

McMillan St.

# Tour 10

# Mt. Auburn

▶ ▶ ▶ ▶ ▶ ▶

**Tour begins on William Howard Taft Road at Eden Avenue. Drive west on Taft.**

**1 Mt. Auburn Presbyterian Church** and **Center**, 103 William Howard Taft Road, began in 1866 when five downtown Presbyterian churches resolved to erect a house of worship in this suburb. Twelve Mt. Auburn residents met in January 1867 to discuss forming a congregation, and in May, public meetings for those interested in this project were held in the basement of the Mt. Auburn Methodist Church.

Sixty-nine men and women, meeting in the chapel of the Cincinnati Orphan Asylum on Wellington Place, formally established the new congregation on October 13, 1868. James W. McLaughlin was selected to design a 2-story frame church that was dedicated January 1869.

In the early 1880s, as public transportation opened this hilltop suburb, the congregation grew. Mt. Auburn Presbyterian decided that a new house of worship was needed, but on October 10, 1888, before any definite plans could be made, fire destroyed the roof and badly damaged the walls and spire of their building. Members moved quickly to begin construction of a new stone church, chosing Cincinnatian Henry E. Siter as the architect.

For a time, services were held in the Turner Hall on Vine Street in Corryville. Then Mrs. Matthew Addy, a member of the congregation, donated a lot at Vine Street in Corryville where a temporary house of worship, Clifford Chapel (later Clifford Presbyterian Church), was completed in January 1890. The chapel was named for the Addys' son who had died in an accident.

The rough stone Victorian Gothic style church that Siter designed features carved stone decoration including two gargoyles on the square tower, extensive oak paneling and woodwork, stained glass windows, and an oil painting over the organ loft depicting Christ blessing the children. Though the first service was held in the new building in March 1890, the church was not dedicated until it was free of debt in May 1896.

The congregation grew rapidly in the early twentieth century and listed nearly 900 members by 1936. A gradual decline came in the post-war years as the neighborhood changed and young families moved away, but the congregation remained strong, dedicating a chapel commemorating members' wartime service in 1946 and a 3-story education building in 1958. Only in the late 1960s and early 1970s did membership drop precipitously as Mt. Auburn became a predominantly black, lower-income community.

With the arrival of a new pastor, rejuvenation of the area, and a determination of the congregation to minister to the whole city rather than just to the immediate area, this downward trend was reversed. In 1988, Mt. Auburn Presbyterian had 260 active members and was racially and economically integrated.

Mt. Auburn Presbyterian Church has traditionally sought to meet the needs of its diverse community. As the "home church" for many university students and nurses, it has developed special programs for them. During the 1930s, the church and the National Youth Administration co-sponsored a center for black youth. Today, it sponsors a day care center and opens its facilities to groups including the League of Women Voters, United Christian Ministries, Center for Peace Education, Physicians for Social Responsibility, and the Woman's City Club.

The Woman's City Club was established in 1915 and has defined itself as a civic activist organization. WCC members felt that women had a right to play an active role in every aspect of community life. Club members worked for a range of civic improvements including international good will, city planning, child welfare, housing, health, education, safety, utilities, recreation, race relations, and legislation.

**Turn left on Auburn Avenue.**

**2 Mt. Auburn United Methodist Church**, 2439 Auburn Avenue, the first church in this neighborhood, was organized in 1851 as a community church for Protestants of various denominations. Reverend John Flavel Wright, a prominent Methodist and, from 1832 to 1844, the head of a Methodist publishing concern at Eighth and Main Streets, owned a considerable tract of land on McMillan Avenue from Auburn Avenue to Vine Street. He donated this lot with the stipulation that "a suitable house of worship be built thereon."

Perhaps because of this connection, the early ministers were Methodist, and a frame building erected in 1852 eventually became a Methodist church. The City of Cincinnati paid for part of the cost of the church bell on the condition that it could be used for fire alarms and other civic purposes. Thirty years later, the present brick building with its stenciled stained glass windows was completed.

In 1893, the Mt. Auburn Methodist congregation moved to a quieter location on Maplewood Avenue. A German Methodist congregation that had been holding services in a store on Vine Street bought this building, which then became the Auburn Avenue Methodist Episcopal Church.

After fire destroyed the Maplewood Avenue church in 1957, the two congregations merged, and this building again became Mt. Auburn Methodist Church. The 3-story brick addition was completed in 1962, when membership was near its peak. To make best use of its facilities, Mt. Auburn United Methodist has opened the addition to a Head Start Program, offices of the Community Action Commission and the Council of Christian Communions of Greater Cincinnati, and Womonways, a women's center.

During the last decades of the nineteenth century, the incline and the cable railway made Mt. Auburn accessible to middle-income families, many of whom were Catholic. **3 Holy Name Roman Catholic Church**, 2448 Auburn Avenue, was built by members of a parish created in 1904. The archdiocese gave the new parish the former home of Eugene Zimmerman, which was used as a school, church, and rectory until a 2-story brick church and school building was completed on East McMillan Street in 1906. It was replaced by a larger buff brick structure in the 1920s.

As Holy Name parish grew, it needed a larger church and more classroom space, so two adjacent Mt. Auburn mansions were torn down for the present stone church, dedicated in 1951. Holy Name Church features Stations of the Cross imported from

Germany and a baptismal font and main altar of Italian marble.

The 3-story painted brick rectory was built as a home in the mid-1860s by Elimore W. Cunningham (1812-1901), a successful meatpacker. In 1880, Eugene Zimmerman (1845-1914), an oil and railroad tycoon, purchased the residence. Zimmerman later sold his oil businesss to the Standard Oil Company and turned to railroad building. He became vice-president of the Cincinnati, Hamilton & Dayton Railroad (the CH&D, popularly known in its early years as "Charge High and Damn Rough Ride") and was a major stockholder in the Cincinnati Southern line.

One of the old houses razed for the church was the parish school, formerly the home of Matthew Addy. Addy (1835-1896) had acquired the Cincinnati & Newport Iron and Pipe Company; in 1899, his Addyston Pipe & Steel Company established a large plant west of Cincinnati in a river town that took its name from the company. Addyston Pipe & Steel once supplied most of the pipe used for water and gas mains in this section of the country, including the Norwood water mains, laid in the 1890s.

Holy Name's membership peaked at around 1,000 in the 1950s and then began to decline. At the end of the 1976-1977 academic year, the school was closed, and children were sent to Corryville Catholic School, formerly St. George School. The Holy Name school was remodeled for a dental clinic. In 1987, the parish recorded approximately 500 members.

One of the earliest structures in Auburn is the Greek Revival style **4 John C. Wright House**, 2411 Auburn Avenue. The metal stars above the entrance are the end pieces of iron tie rods used to strengthen the building. The oval plaque with a design of an early fire engine and the date 1839 over the door indicates that the homeowners had paid for fire insurance.

John Wright (1763-1861) served in the Ohio House of Representatives and was a justice of the state Supreme Court. He moved to Cincinnati where, with his law partner Timothy Walker, he founded the Cincinnati Law School in 1833. He was editor of the *Cincinnati Gazette* and a director of the Cincinnati, Hamilton & Dayton Railroad.

Mt. Auburn's historic role in medicine, and public health is represented by the two red brick Georgian Revival style houses at 2406 and 2404 Auburn Avenue.

The residence at 2404, with Ionic columns and an elliptical fanlight above the door, was for many years the **5 Home of Dr. Elizabeth Campbell**, a nationally-recognized pioneer in social hygiene and public health. Campbell (1862-1945) graduated from the Medical College of the University of Cincinnati in 1896. Six years later, she became the first female staff member at Christ Hospital and, in 1910, became the first woman to be elected vice-president of the Cincinnati Academy of Medicine.

In 1917, Campbell organized the Cincinnati Social Hygiene Society, credited with closing down the city's "red light" district and setting up a venereal disease screening and testing program. Twelve years later, she challenged the prevailing restrictions against making available birth control information, a prohibition which she felt especially hurt poor families. She established the Committee on Maternal Health, which held a weekly clinic at General Hospital. The Committee changed its name to the Planned Parenthood Association of Cincinnati

*Affluent Mt. Auburn residents occupied some elegant multi-unit buildings such as Philip Hinkle's townhouses, as well as single-family homes.*

in 1947.

Campbell willed her home to Planned Parenthood, which sold it to purchase the house next door, 2406, where the association's administrative offices were located from 1964 to 1987.

In 1876, Philip Hinkle (1811-1880), who lived just down the street, built the four stylish **6 Townhouses**, 2356-2362 Auburn Avenue, for well-to-do families. His promotional material lavishly praised the 3-story brick residences, citing walnut woodwork, marble mantels, niches for statuary, bronze and gilt gas chandeliers, silver-plated water fixtures, and dumb waiters, as well as modern heating and plumbing systems.

However, "the most ornate description of their finish, appointments, and excellencies could not be equivalent to ocular demonstration." The Mt. Auburn location offered a magnificent view of the city, healthful air, and access to services and parks. Finally: *"A tasteful and well-arranged home exerts a valuable influence upon every member of the family. It teaches order, neatness, and self-control . . . . The moral influence of these surroundings is not entirely unworthy of regard, and their social value is inestimable."*

Among the first residents of these dwellings were Daniel Ray, a lawyer, who lived at 2362 with his wife, four

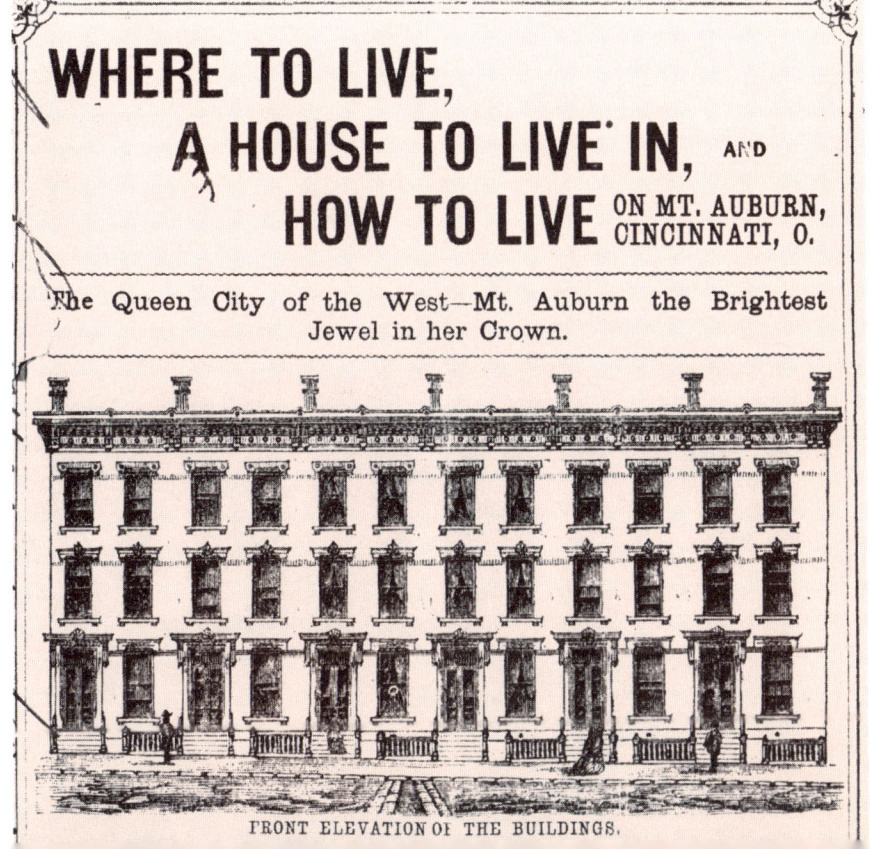

WHERE TO LIVE, A HOUSE TO LIVE IN, AND HOW TO LIVE ON MT. AUBURN, CINCINNATI, O.

The Queen City of the West—Mt. Auburn the Brightest Jewel in her Crown.

FRONT ELEVATION OF THE BUILDINGS.

sons, a daughter, and three servants, and Patrick Mallen, also a lawyer, whose household at 2356 included his wife, daughter, three sons, and two servants.

As Mt. Auburn and styles of living changed, the sort of upper-income families who once chose Hinkle's townhouses moved to newer communities with more modern housing. By the 1920s, each of these four units had been divided into four or five flats that were occupied by middle-income professionals and business people. Forty years later, almost half of these units were vacant; the others were occupied by students, low-income workers, and elderly people with limited incomes.

Renovation of these townhouses in the mid-1970s brought back some of their original elegance and desirability.

One of the most impressive of the nineteenth-century residences on this street is the **7 Mordecai Morris White Home**, 2343 Auburn Avenue, an elaborately trimmed, 2-story red brick Italian Villa style structure with a 3-story tower built in the early 1870s.

Mordecai White (1829-1913), a Quaker, inherited a fortune and a North Carolina plantation with slaves from his grandfather. White came to Cincinnati in 1853 and established a wholesale grocery business. Four years later, he began bringing his slaves north, freeing them, and providing them with homes in Indiana.

In 1862, White entered the banking business. He was involved with several banks, and a biographer claimed that White "probably owns more bank stock than any other individual in Cincinnati."

After White's widow died, the Mt. Auburn house served first as offices for the Red Cross, later as a social service agency, and most recently as business office space.

**Turn left on McGregor Avenue, left on Auburncrest Avenue.**

Listed on the National Register of Historic Places in 1973, the **8 Gorham A. Worth House**, 2316 Auburncrest Avenue, was probably the oldest, continuously-occupied private residence in Cincinnati when it was bought for preservation and

restoration by the Miami Purchase Association in 1965. The central portion of the 2-story frame Federal style house was constructed in 1819 and was possibly the work of the same architect who designed Martin Baum's home, now the Taft Museum, which was built the following year. Gorham A. Worth (1783-1856), a New York-born financier, came to Cincinnati in 1817 to serve as the cashier of the branch of the United States Bank.

Robert McGregor, after whom nearby McGregor Avenue is named, was the next owner and is believed to have erected the additions at either end of the house for the 1860 visit of the Prince of Wales. McGregor's heirs divided the estate into building lots in 1868.

In 1905, the Worth house became the residence of Guy Ward Mallon (1864-1933), a lawyer and state legislator who was one of the four authors of Cincinnati's first city charter. For a few years in the 1970s, this was Talbert House, a drug rehabilitation facility. Then it became a private residence again.

**Turn right on Helen Street, right on Maplewood Avenue, left on McGregor Avenue, and right on Highland Avenue.**

*Access to Mt. Auburn was facilitated in the 1880s and 1890s by the Mt. Auburn Cable Railway.*

The brick building with arched entrances and windows was originally the **9 Powerhouse and Car Barns of the Mt. Auburn Cable Railway**, 2001 Highland Avenue. Henry Martin, a Mt. Auburn resident, headed the company.

The Mt. Auburn line ran up Sycamore Street from Fourth Street, across the canal to Dorchester Avenue, and on to the intersection of Reading Road and Rockdale Avenue in Avondale. The 8.7 mile round trip took sixty-five minutes. Vises on the grip car which pulled passenger cars clutched a wire cable that moved in a slotted, cast iron tunnel in the street; the cars moved on iron rails.

The original brick and frame powerhouse and twenty-four cars were destroyed in 1892 by a fire that was believed to have been started by the friction of the drive wheels. Martin rebuilt immediately, erecting this building which housed the power machinery in the basement and offices and car repair shops on the first floor. Two years later, the company was running nine to eleven cars and carrying approximately 5,000 passengers each day. The consolidation of the city's streetcar lines brought the cable railway under the control of John Kilgour's Cincinnati Street Railway Company in 1896.

The Mt. Auburn Cable Railway was the last of Cincinnati's cable lines to close, ending operations on June 9, 1902.

The 3-story brick structure with Mansard roof and dormer windows was the **10 Home of George Hunt Pendleton**, 559 Liberty Hill, the residence of the man known as the "Father of the Civil Service System." Pendleton (1825-1889) attended Woodward High School and Cincinnati College. He married Alice Key, daughter of composer Francis Scott Key, in 1846, and practiced law in Cincinnati before being elected to the state senate in 1853.

From 1856 to 1865, Pendleton served in Congress and was a leader of the "Peace Democrats" who opposed many of the military policies of the Lincoln administration. His political career included unsuccessful bids for the vice-presidency, for the presidential nomination, and for governor of Ohio. In 1878, the Ohio legislature elected Pendleton to the United States Senate.

The 1881 assassination of President James Garfield by a disgruntled federal job seeker spurred reform of the spoils system whereby political parties had rewarded supporters with job appointments. Pendleton was chairman of the Senate Committee on Civil Service Reform. Tradition holds that either the first draft or the final version of the bill known as the Pendleton Act (though it was authored by Dorman B. Eaton, the first head of the Civil Service Commission) was written in this house. The act provided for the establishment of a civil service commission and competitive examinations for federal jobs.

During Pendleton's lifetime, his home was a center for political and cultural activity, but time and change reduced it to a neglected boarding house. In 1964, the structure was designated a National Historic Landmark, and a realty company succeeded in getting the City Planning Commission to rezone the house for restoration as office space.

The 4-story brick and stone building at 412 Liberty Street was originally the **11 First District Elementary School** (1867), designed by William Walter, who had assisted his father, Henry Walter, with the plans for St. Peter in Chains Cathedral. The 21-classroom building had a capacity of 1,134 students, grades 1-8, and drew youngsters from Over-the-Rhine and Mt. Auburn. However, new schools with better facilities and playground space were completed, and this building was closed in 1914.

When federal legislation in 1917 provided aid for vocational education, the Cincinnati Board of Education planned to enroll 50% of the city's high school age students in such programs, and First District Elementary was reopened as the Building and Trades Vocational High School. In the 1930s, the programs of the Tailoring Vocational High School were also located here.

*In the 1970s, buildings on the part of Mt. Auburn that offered a view of downtown, like the former First District School, were renovated for occupancy by middle and upper middle-income tenants.*

Reorganization and consolidation of vocational programs during 1942-1945 ended the building's use as a school. It was divided into apartments, and had become a deteriorating tenement before a local firm purchased the school in the 1970s and restored and remodeled it for condominiums.

The **12 Great American Broadcasting Company**, 1718 Young Street, formerly Taft Broadcasting Company, might trace its long history in communications to April 25, 1840, when the first edition of Cincinnati's first daily newspaper, the *Spirit of the Times*, was issued. This paper was the forerunner of Charles P. Taft I's *Cincinnati Times-Star* whose twentieth-century offspring, Radio Cincinnati, Inc., eventually grew into the Taft entertainment empire.

Taft Broadcasting Company's immediate beginning was on August 17, 1939, when the *Times-Star*, headed by Hulbert Taft, Sr. (1877-1959), purchased CBS-affiliated WKRC-Radio with studios in the Alms Hotel on East Fifth Street. After CBS changed its affiliation, WKRC struggled, and the newspaper covered its losses. The station recoverd, however, and WKRC personalities became household names: Ruth Lyons was program director before starting her own radio program, and Waite Hoyt announced Reds games.

A separate corporation, Radio Cincinnati, was formed in 1948 with Hulbert Taft, Jr. (1906-1967), as its president. The following year, the company bought land in Mt. Auburn on Highland Avenue, built new studios, and began television broadcasting. The five hours of daily programming included live local shows and kinescope recordings of network productions. On September 25, 1949, Cincinnati got its first live network telecast: a football game between the Pittsburgh Steelers and the New York Giants.

During the 1950s, Radio Cincinnati purchased other radio and television stations. Local television personalities Glen "Skipper" Ryle and Nick Clooney began their careers here. In 1954, when WKRC boosted its television signal to 316,000 watts, the federal limit, it became the most powerful station in the city and began to underwrite the losses of the *Times-Star*. The newspaper was sold to the *Cincinnati Post* in 1959 and on July 2, the Taft Broadcasting Company was incorporated. The company moved to a new facility on Highland Avenue in 1960, and WKRC-TV became the first station in the country to broadcast using remote-controlled cameras.

Taft Broadcasting continued to expand. The 1966 acquisition of Hanna-Barbera, the world's largest animator for television, began developments that later mushroomed into the Taft Entertainment Group. Taft's entertainment holdings included the licensing and merchandising of

Hanna-Barbera characters and products, studios on the West Coast, and, at one time, ownership of fifteen radio stations and twelve major market television stations—more than any other operator in the industry. Taft's Worldvision Enterprises sold and distributed the company's television programs internationally, and the company entered the cable broadcast market.

Taft opened this brick and glass facility in 1980, staying in Mt. Auburn where it enjoyed the advantages for broadcasting of a hilltop location near the downtown business center.

Taft operated Coney Island amusement park and, in partnership with the Kroger Company, opened King's Island. Taft sold King's Island and three other parks in late 1983, though it retained the adjoining College Football Hall of Fame and the Jack Nicklaus Sports Center.

In 1987, a limited partnership headed by Cincinnati entrepreneur Carl Lindner purchased Taft Broadcasting, ending a struggle for control of the firm begun two years earlier by a Texas-based group of investors. Lindner's action kept the company in the city, and Taft became Great American Broadcasting.

**Turn right on Young Street.**

An excellent example of adaptive reuse of old buildings is Taft Broadcasting's renovation of the **13 Firehouse of Engine Company No. 30**, 1726 Young Street.

When Mt. Auburn was annexed to Cincinnati in 1849, volunteer companies equipped with hand-powered apparatus provided fire protection. Mt. Auburn was served by Mohawk Engine Company No. 12, located some distance away on Hamilton Road (McMicken Avenue) opposite Vine Street. Even after the city took over the fire department in 1853 and provided horses to pull engines, Mt. Auburn was a difficult neighborhood to protect. The fire companies in the basin could be summoned quickly by a ringing church bell or, later, by the fire alarm telegraph, but the men and equipment still had to make the slow and exhausting trip up the steep hillside.

In 1871, fire protection on the hilltops was considerably improved

with the creation of Engine Company No. 19 in Corryville. Equipped with a horse-drawn steam pumper and accompanied by Ladder Company No. 4 which was housed in the same building, Engine 19 could handle most problems in Mt. Auburn.

By the late 1880s, however, the inclines and streetcars had spawned so much growth in the hilltop suburbs that the Cincinnati Fire Department built a series of smaller firehouses to support the existing suburban companies. Engine Company No. 30 was organized and assigned to a Mt. Auburn engine house constructed at Young and Slack Streets.

The 30's house was a small 1-bay brick structure. The company was equipped with horse-drawn reels that were later replaced by a hose wagon. Because their company had no pumper, the members had to work with hoses directly from hydrants until an engine company could arrive. In 1896, the Mt. Auburn company was provided with a horse-drawn chemical engine—large soda acid extinguisher tanks mounted on a wheeled carriage—that could be used on fires in areas that had poor water service or hydrants with low pressure.

Engine Company 30 was disbanded in 1920. Like many of the smaller houses created in the 1880s and 1890s, it became superfluous after the introduction of motorized pumpers. The firehouse was sold, and over a period of years, it housed a variety of businesses including an auto painting shop and a roofing company. In the early 1980s, the building was remodeled for offices. The few external alterations complimented the original design, and the characteristics of the firehouse remained intact.

The 2-acre **14 Filson Overlook Playground**, southwest corner of Young and Slack Streets, is said to be the spot from which John Filson, Kentucky historian and surveyor, conceived the plan for the city he envisioned in the basin below.

Filson, a partner of John Cleves Symmes, had explored much of the Kentucky wilderness and written a biography of Daniel Boone (1772) and the first history of Kentucky (1774). He came to Ohio in 1788 and is given credit for naming the settlement on the banks of the Ohio River opposite the Licking River: Losantiville. Filson wandered off from the surveying party

and was never seen again. Most probably, he was killed by Indians.

The Cincinnati Park Board purchased this piece of land in 1909. A swimming pool was soon opened, and a new pool, bathhouse, playground equipment, and a baseball field were added later.

The Reverend Martin Wells Knapp (1853-1901) founded **15 God's Bible School, College, and Missionary Training Home**, 1810 Young Street, in a Mt. Auburn residence in 1900. The school is an interdenominational, independently operated, conservative evangelical institution that offers an accredited high school curriculum and 4- and 5-year programs in music, nursing, theology, Christian education, and missions. It also was involved in the longest-running case in Hamilton County Common Pleas Court.

In his will, Knapp left the school "to God." When the courts decided that God could not legally own property in Hamilton County, a fight began over whether the school and grounds were Knapp's personal property or a public charitable institution. In 1907, the school was declared a public institution to be administered by the courts.

Three years later, Reverend Meredith G. Standley, Knapp's son-in-law, officially took over operations, and one of Knapp's daughters was made a trustee. The campus grew from a $20,000 concern to one valued at $1.9 million with thirteen acres, fourteen buildings—new structures and older houses—and a $1 million debt. In 1949, the court appointed five independent trustees to run the institution.

Dr. Samuel E. Deets, a God's Bible School graduate, took over as president in 1965 and soon paid off the remaining debt. The school was turned over to its alumni on July 1, 1975. Receivership was terminated and the case was closed on April 27, 1982.

In the 1987-1988 academic year, 360 students from thirty states and six foreign countries were enrolled here. The thirty buildings on the campus include men's and women's dormitories, student center, music studio, classroom and administration buildings, chapel, and housing for staff, faculty, and married students. God's Bible School is "faith operated," that is, while tuition payments cover

*The campus of God's Bible School consists of a cluster of buildings in the vicinity of Young Street.*

a small portion of its annual budget, most of the operating costs come from its supporters. In addition, gifts allow the Donated Student Fund to offer on-campus jobs whereby students can earn their tuition fees.

The Revivalist Press, which Knapp founded in 1888, continues to print *God's Revivalist*, a bi-weekly religious publication. God's Bible School students operate missions in poorer neighborhoods in the area, and 80% of its graduates enter the Christian ministry.

**Turn left on Ringgold Street, right on Josephine Street, left on Dorchester Avenue, and continue across Auburn Avenue.**

The 2½-story Second Empire style **16 Henry Martin House**, 1947 Auburn Avenue, was erected about 1870. Martin, a dry goods merchant, built and operated the Mt. Auburn Cable Railway. The story is told that Martin was a pious man who tried to observe the Sabbath as a day of rest. But Cincinnatians needed public transportation on Sundays, and Martin, a practical businessman, could not shut down his lucrative line. So every Saturday evening, he transferred the title of the railway to one of his employees and resumed ownership himself each Monday morning.

Martin's mansion, like so many others in Mt. Auburn, was divided into flats in the early twentieth century. In the late 1940s, its nine units were occupied by a employee of the Cincinnati Gas & Electric Company, a shipping clerk for the Manischewitz matzos bakery, a bookkeeper, a secretary, a sculptor, a salesman, an office clerk, a waiter, and an assembler. Twenty years later, there was a delicatessen in one part of the old house, and the deli's owner and his wife lived in one apartment. Three units were occupied by retired persons, and four were vacant.

The house's reclamation for use as a community health center was another achievement of the Mt. Auburn Good Housing Foundation, as was the rehabilitation of the stone-faced brick dwellings that stand behind the Martin House on Park Place.

Dating from the 1880s, the **17 Park Place Rowhouses** were subdivided in the 1920s into thirty-two apartments for moderate-income workers. By the late 1960s, only three units were occupied. Renovation created sixteen apartments for low-income families.

*Even those who could not afford to live on Mt. Auburn in the 1870s and 1880s could enjoy the view and hilltop breezes by visiting the Lookout House at the upper terminus of the Main Street Incline.*

The 8-acre **18 Jackson Hill Park**, end of Dorchester Avenue, features a fine view of downtown and is the site of some spectacular episodes in the city's history.

In the mid-nineteenth century, Cincinnati's continued growth seemed doomed by the steep hills that blocked expansion out of the basin. However, the inclined plane railway offered a means of scaling the hillsides and began the development of hilltop suburbs. George Smith (c.1818-1888) organized the Cincinnati Inclined Plane Railway and on May 12, 1872, opened the city's first incline up Mt. Auburn. The Mt. Auburn incline line ran from a station at Mulberry and Main Streets, up Main Street to Jackson Park. Later, lines were extended to the zoo and to St. Bernard.

Smith had quickly recognized the attractions offered by cool breezes and the view from Mt. Auburn and opened the Lookout House, the first of Cincinnati's four hilltop "resorts" that offered music, beer, and entertainment, including fireworks displays and hot air balloon ascensions. One of the Lookout House's proprietors, Frank Harff, devised a phenomenal attraction. A white whale was installed in a salt water tank. Unfortunately, the animal lived only a month, and Harff's attempt to salvage his investment by having the whale embalmed was a disaster. The beast began to decay in a matter of days—not six months, as the embalmer had promised. The body was taken to a

local factory and rendered into soap, and the Lookout House was fumigated.

In 1889, six people were killed in an accident on this line when a clutch failed and the car plunged down the hill. Although the company rebuilt the incline, riders chose the nearby cable railway to get to the northern suburbs, and the incline was closed in 1898. Automobiles and streetcars soon made both inclines and cable railways obsolete.

The Lookout House survived the debacle of the whale exhibit, but an 1888 state law prohibiting liquor sales on Sunday—the best business day—finally drove it out of business. By 1900, all four of the city's incline houses were closed. The city acquired this hilltop land in 1930 and developed it into a park.

**Return to Auburn Avenue and turn left.**

The Italian Villa style **19 Adam N. Riddle Home**, 2021 Auburn Avenue, was built about 1857 for a prominent Cincinnati lawyer and state legislator. After Riddle died in 1870, his widow sold the house to Mrs. Thomas Phillips, the widow of an iron manufacturer and head of the American Bolt & Nut Works on Second Street. Thomas Phillips is said to have gained fame—or notoriety—when he bought a Tennessee ironworks, freed the slaves who ran the operation, and rehired them as free men.

This 2-story brick house with a 3-story tower served for several decades in the twentieth century as the Adult Deaf Welfare Center, then as a Catholic mission for the deaf and a chapel. In the 1950s and the 1960s, the old residence was used for a nursing home.

Riddle's mansion stood vacant and deteriorating during much of the 1970s, until it was renovated for law offices.

Hamilton County Juvenile Court refers delinquent youths to the **20 County Juvenile Court Youth Center and Detention Home**, 2020 Auburn Avenue, for up to ninety days. The brick and reinforced concrete building has a reception room, clinic, probation department, dormitories, classrooms, cafeteria, and gymnasium. Original plans proposed that such a facility be erected downtown near the courthouse, but the center was built in less crowded, more residential Mt. Auburn on the site of the estates of the Bodmann and Burckhardt families.

Ferdinand Bodmann (1801-1874) is credited with having founded the leaf tobacco trade in Cincinnati. His son, Charles (1827-1875), took over the business, and Ferdinand's daughter, Loretta Louisa Bodmann, augmented the family's fortune with marriages to wholesale druggist Joseph Reakirt and then John B. Gibson, one of the founders of the Gibson House, later the Gibson Hotel. Leopold Burckhardt (1818-1911), whose mansion stood next door, was a coal oil commission merchant and manufacturer of the oils used in soap and candles.

The Hamilton County Board of Commissioners bought these properties in 1950, razed the old mansions, and completed the Detention Home five years later.

The **21 William Howard Taft Birthplace**, 2038 Auburn Avenue, was the boyhood home of the only man to serve as President of the United States and Chief Justice of the Supreme Court. William Howard Taft (1857-1930) was born here and lived in this house until he left Cincinnati to attend Yale University.

Alphonso Taft (1810-1891) bought the 2-story brick house in 1851 and added the rear portion. He was president of the Mt. Auburn Street Railway Company, a judge on the Superior Court of Cincinnati, and the first member of the family to achieve national prominence, serving as secretary of war, attorney general, and ambassador to Austria-Hungary and Russia.

Alphonso Taft had two sons from his first marriage, Charles Phelps (1843-1929), publisher of the *Cincinnati Times-Star*, and Peter, a lawyer and author.

William Howard Taft, a son of Alphonso's second marriage, attended Mt. Auburn Public School, Woodward High School, Yale, and Cincinnati Law School. He practiced law, then served on the bench of the Superior Court of Ohio and the Sixth Circuit Court. His career in national politics began when President Harrison appointed him solicitor general. Taft was the first governor general of the Philippines and went on to become Theodore Roosevelt's secretary of war. In 1908, at Roosevelt's urging, the reluctant Taft ran for and was elected President of the United States. From 1921 until one month before his death, he served more happily and effectively as Chief Justice of the United States Supreme Court.

William Howard Taft had two sons who also carved important political niches for themselves: Senator Robert Alphonso Taft (1889-1953)—"Mr. Republican"—and Charles Phelps Taft II (1897-1983)—"Mr. Cincinnati"—who served for many years on City Council and as a leader of the Charter Committee.

The Taft home was usually rented out after Alphonso Taft became secretary of war in 1876, and was divided into apartments by the 1920s. Over the years it suffered from hard use, age, and neglect. The William Howard Taft Memorial Association finally acquired the property in 1960. The National Park Service, which assumed curatorial duties in 1972, is completing preservation and restoration work on the Taft Birthplace, a National Historic Landmark and a National Historic Site.

**22 The Christ Hospital**, 2139 Auburn Avenue, dominates the street and has made Mt. Auburn one of Cincinnati's "Pill Hills." The institution began in 1889 due to the efforts of Isabella Thoburn. Thoburn had been brought to the city the year before by James Gamble (1803-1891), cofounder of the Procter & Gamble Company, to establish a home for deaconesses—Methodist women who had chosen to devote their lives to church work. The Elizabeth Gamble Deaconess Home, a residence and training center, opened in December 1888 on York Street in the West End.

It is said that the following year, Thoburn met a woman whom the Cincinnati Hospital had refused to admit because she was from another state. This event convinced Thoburn there was a need for additional medical facilities in the city; on September 23, The Christ Hospital opened next to the deaconesses' center.

The deaconesses' hospital was soon overcrowded. In 1893, a 20-bed hospital opened on this site where the Mt. Auburn Young Ladies Institute

*William Howard Taft spent his boyhood years in this simple but elegant home on Auburn Avenue.*

(1856), a college, had been located. The Christ Hospital underwent renovation, expansion, and additions in the succeeding years. In 1930, the 10-story brick center structure with a tower and two wings was completed. The School of Nursing, which graduated its first class of eight in 1903, stands nearby on Eleanor Place. The hospital's James N. Gamble Institute of Medical Research, founded in 1927, conducts clinical research in virology and immunology. In the 1940s, it fought tuberculosis; today, flu.

The 660-bed Christ Hospital recorded 24,296 admissions in 1987. It boasts facilities for patients with serious and specialized illnesses and has units of obstetrics, orthopedic surgery, and behavioral medicine. The Christ Hospital plans to develop "centers of excellence" offering care and treatment for cancer, heart, and stroke patients.

Informal outdoor Sunday School classes for neighborhood children led to the establishment of **23 Mt. Auburn Baptist Church**, 2147 Auburn Avenue. On January 29, 1856, nineteen members of Ninth Street Baptist Church who lived in this suburb met and adopted a covenant and articles of faith for a new congregation.

The first church, a frame building, was dedicated on November 28, 1861. Some twenty years later, members decided that the congregation's growth called for a larger church. The present stone-faced Late Gothic Revival style structure was begun in 1884 (the date carved on the facade above the central stained glass window) and dedicated on February 1, 1886. The 3-story brick Education Building behind the church was completed in 1937.

As Mt. Auburn changed from a well-to-do white suburb to a predominantly black neighborhood, former members organized "daughter" churches in other communities. By the early 1970s, Mt. Auburn Baptist's integrated congregation consisted of only about one hundred members. In 1971, the church created the Missioners Program by which it sought to revitalize current programs and extend its outreach by "borrowing" a family from one of the stronger suburban "daughter" churches to work as members here.

The former **24 Home of Henry Powell**, 2209 Auburn Avenue, a 3-story brick structure with pressed metal trim, was built around 1858. Henry Powell (d.1888) came from England with his family in 1835. His father, William Powell (b.1790), had founded a lace factory in Belgium. In Cincinnati, William established the Union Brass Works, later the William Powell Company, and is sometimes credited as the founder of the brass industry in the West. The company expanded to several plants in Camp Washington and became the nation's leading manufacturer of industrial valves.

Henry Powell was a partner in the business from 1854 to 1886 and, as a successful industrialist, moved to the new and prestigious suburb of Mt. Auburn.

Now divided into apartments, the 3-story Second Empire style brick houses at 2210 and 2214 Auburn Avenue were once the **25 Homes of Philip and Thornton M. Hinkle**, respectively.

Philip Hinkle (1811-1880) was born in Pennsylvania and came to Cincinnati by way of New Orleans in 1832. He worked as a carpenter and in 1840, erected his own planing mill. The growing business soon moved to Front Street where Hinkle & Company produced window sashes, doors, blinds, and "portable homes"—kits of precut lumber which, shipped west, "carried Mr. Hinkle's name to the frontier pioneer settlements." By 1880, Hinkle had retired and lived in this house with his wife, a friend, and two servants.

Thornton Mills Hinkle (1840-1920), Philip's son, was a prominent Cincinnati attorney. His household included his wife, daughter, two sons, and two servants.

The **26 William Howard Doane Home**, 2223 Auburn Avenue, an Italian Villa style brick house with a 4-story tower, was built around 1850 by Jethro Mitchell, president of a lumber company on Third Street. In 1879, he sold the house to William and Fannie Doane. The initials WHD are carved on one post in front of the

*Despite the expansion of medical facilities and offices along Auburn Avenue in recent decades, a number of historic houses have survived, including the William Howard Doane home, which dates from the 1850s.*

house, and the property's name, Sunny Side, is on the other.

William Doane (1832-1915) came from Connecticut in 1861 to head the Cincinnati general offices of the J.A. Fay Company, manufacturers of woodworking machinery, and became president of the firm in 1866. Doane patented seventy inventions and helped Fay equipment win the Grand Prix at the Paris Exposition of 1889; Doane himself was awarded the Legion of Honor by the French government. Fay machinery was sold worldwide.

Doane was an active member of the Mt. Auburn Baptist Church and wrote hundreds hymns that were translated and sung all over the world. His study and music room housed an extensive collection of antique and unusual musical instruments, given to the Cincinnati Art Museum on his death, and manuscripts and autographs of famous composers.

Later, nurses working at Christ Hospital lived here. Today, the hospital owns this and the Henry Powell house.

> **Turn left on Glencoe Place, left on Deronda Court, left on Leroy Court, and left on Adnored Court.**

An impressive success of the Mt. Auburn Good Housing Foundation is the **27 Glencoe Place Redevelopment Project**, ninety-nine low-cost housing units developed from several blocks of nearly deserted tenement buildings known to area residents as "the Hole."

The castle-like office building of the Glencoe Hotel Apartment House is a part of a complex allegedly built by Cincinnati builder and contractor Truman Bishop Handy after his plans to build a residential hotel on Auburn Avenue were thwarted by the wealthy families who lived there. It is said that, seeking revenge, he vowed to build 1,000 apartments in Mt. Auburn. The Glencoe Hotel and the 5-story structure later known as Standish Apartments were built beginning in 1899. Handy, however, died in 1884, so it is more likely that his son-in-law, Jethro Mitchell, who owned this 4-acre site, was the builder.

In August 1964, the Standish Apartments were the scene of Cincinnati's first rent strike; tenants complained of rats, roaches, and improper wiring. The issue was resolved in court, with most of the protestors getting evicted. These tenements were incorporated into the city's redevelopment plan, and demolition of unsound buildings began in 1973. From the remaining 500 old units, the Good Housing Foundation created attractive homes and used the open space for playgrounds, parking, and parks. Prospecitve tenants went through credit and police checks and an interview by a screening committee of residents.

By 1977, the Housing Foundation controlled $9 million worth of property. By 1979, it had overseen the renewal of some 2,000 homes and neighborhood stores. The Glencoe Place Redevelopment has been honored by local, state, and national urban development organizations.

> **Turn right on Glencoe Place, left on Auburn Avenue.**

In 1974, Planned Parenthood opened the Margaret Sanger Center in the former home of porkpacker Jason Evans, which stood on the site of the present **28 Elizabeth Campbell Center**, 2314 Auburn Avenue. The 2-story Second Empire style house

with an observatory had been built around 1865 when Evans moved from Eighth Street to cleaner, quieter Mt. Auburn. By 1880, the home belonged to Melville Ingalls, president of the Cincinnati, Indianapolis & St. Louis Railroad, who lived here with his wife, daughter, three sons, nurse, gardener, and three servants.

The Center, named for Margaret Sanger, a pioneer in family planning education, provided birth control information and pregnancy diagnosis and counseling. It was badly damaged by a firebombing on December 30, 1985. Though preservationists opposed demolition of the mansion, renovation would have cost at least $200,000. Planned Parenthood designed a larger, more comprehensive reproductive health center; the old residence was razed, and the Campbell Center was dedicated in November 1987.

**Turn left on Wellington Place.**

Doctor's offices now occupy the brick and stone building that was originally the **29 Children's Convalescent Home of the Cincinnati Orphan Asylum**, 111 Wellington Place, built in 1930 to replace the Cincinnati Orphan Asylum that had been on the site since 1861. The stone gate posts of the old orphanage still stand on Auburn Avenue.

The Orphan Asylum was begun after the cholera epidemic of 1832 when, during one two-month period, about 500 people died. The Female Auxiliary Bible Society began the Asylum, which was incorporated in 1833. Until then, orphaned or neglected children had been placed in the Commercial Hospital, "mixed in among the senile or the insane in the cellars," as one account explains. The women began their work in rooms in the Pest House—the isolation hospital on Elm Street for those with contagious diseases—where children had to sleep three to a bed or on the floor.

The first orphan asylum was on Elm Street, on part of the land now occupied by Music Hall; operations were supported by public tax money, private subscription, and donations. In 1861, the children were moved out of the crowded basin to Auburn Avenue and a new, larger, 3-story brick building with 4-story towers on each end. The hall was decorated with the motto: "When my father and mother forsake me, then the Lord will take me in."

The asylum usually received one hundred youngsters each year, and up to 150 or 200 in hard times. Children were fed, washed, clothed, and given schooling as well as "moral and religious training." Eventually, they were placed in adoptive homes, temporary homes, or in apprenticeships; some were returned to their families.

The Orphan Asylum required that "No child is to be taken out of the asylum until it [sic] has remained there at least one year, so that vicious habits may be corrected. . . ." Parents wishing to reclaim their children or those looking to take in a child were rigorously scrutinized. No child was "to be placed out with any person who keeps a hotel, tavern, or coffee-house; nor with any one who does not regularly attend religious worship."

During the 1920s, the increased use of family homes for permanent and temporary placement of children caused the asylum's board (all women until 1965) to consider turning the facility into a convalescent hospital. In 1922, the institution lost its right to place children for adoption, and the move to change was accelerated.

The Cincinnati Orphan Asylum closed on February 18, 1930, and the old building was razed. The new Jacobethan style structure, designed by the firm of Samuel Hannaford & Sons, was dedicated as the Children's Convalescent Home in January 1931. The Home, later the Children's Convalescent Hospital, was accredited as a pediatric rehabilitation hospital in 1955 and became affiliated with Children's Hospital. In 1973, the Children's Convalescent Hospital was closed and its services moved to the Children's Hospital Medical Center in Corryville. The building remained vacant for several years before it was remodeled for its present use.

The land that comprises **30 Inwood Park**, at the end of Wellington Place, originally belonged to Clifton millionaire George K. Schoenberger who had his summer home here in "Schoenberger's Woods." The stone used for the foundations of many Cincinnati homes was later quarried on this hillside. After the quarry was abandoned, the site became a dump. The city acquired the

To honor the founder of the Turner movement in the United States, Cincinnati German Americans erected this monument in Inwood Park near Corryville and Fairview, two distinctly German neighborhoods adjacent to Mt. Auburn.

land around 1904 and completed a park that had been started by local volunteers.

Perhaps Inwood Park's most remarkable feature is the 10-foot tall, rough granite monument honoring Friedrich Ludwig Jahn (1778-1852), *Turnvater* or founder of the Turner Society in Germany. Local Turner societies, which promoted gymnastics and education, regularly paraded up Vine Street from their hall at Fourteenth and Walnut Streets to hold picnics and other events here. On October 22, 1911, they unveiled this monument with the carving of an oak tree and a marble relief portrait of Jahn.

Today, the 20-acre park has baseball fields, play equipment, picnic tables, a recreation building-dance pavilion, pool, and artificial lake (once a natural pond) for ice skating.

**Tour ends.**

# Tour 11

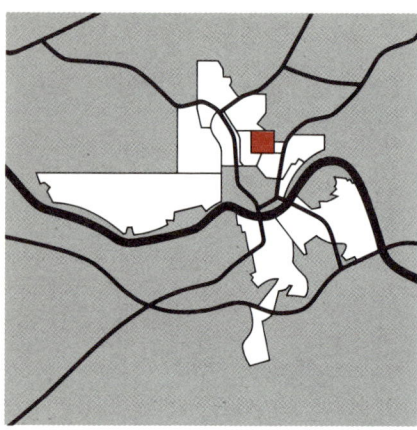

# Corryville

The community of Corryville is bounded by Clifton Avenue on the west, McMillan Avenue on the south, Burnet Avenue on the east, and a line running along the edge of present-day Burnet Woods on the north. This hilltop area north of the basin was first an agricultural and then a residential community. Today Corryville encompasses Burnet Woods, the University of Cincinnati, the Environmental Protection Agency, and several hospitals.

William McMillan (1761-1804) built the first house on the hilltop in 1797. When McMillan died, his nephew, William Corry (1778-1833), acquired the house and most of the land. Corry's heirs subdivided the property in 1843, laying out a plan for a village which they referred to as Corryville. Isolated from the city by the steep slopes on the south, Corryville was, at first, inconveniently situated for residential development. But the land here, unlike that in neighboring Fairview and Clifton Heights, could be used for farming. Mid-nineteenth century Corryville became a center of suburban agriculture; its dairies, hothouses, and truck farms marketed their products in Cincinnati.

Although Corryville was annexed to Cincinnati in 1870, its physical isolation ended only in 1876 with the construction of the Bellevue Inclined Plane Railway from the end of Elm Street up the hillside to Ohio Avenue in Fairview. Streetcar lines were soon extended through the center of Corryville along Vine Street. What had previously been a trickle of basin dwellers moving to the hilltop suddenly became a flood.

The majority of these people were of German descent: Corryville had an even greater proportion of German American residents—at least two-thirds—than Over-the-Rhine. A large number of these new residents commuted to downtown jobs on the incline and streetcars. The German families who migrated to Corryville were mostly middle or upper middle-income and included many businessmen and manufacturers. A thriving local business district grew up along the streetcar lines, providing a variety of services to the community. Among these businesses were saloons and beer gardens which were key elements in the cultural life of Cincinnati's German Americans.

Corryville was preeminently a residential neighborhood and developed differently than adjoining areas. It began to grow later than Clifton, and its smaller lots attracted less affluent people who constructed more modest houses. However, Corryville was built up earlier than Clifton Heights and most of Fairview because its more level terrain was easier to build on. Furthermore, the migration from the downtown basin tended to follow the streetcar lines which went through Corryville at an earlier date.

This stable, middle-income neighborhood did not change much until the mid-twentieth century. Community-oriented businesses remained in family hands, as did residential property. But eventually the descendents of the original residents died or moved away. In addition, the streets of Corryville, which had not been laid out to accommodate the automobile, were often clogged by traffic, and the small but pleasant backyards and gardens of its houses were replaced by narrow driveways and cramped garages.

In the 1940s and 1950s, the character of Corryville's population began to include a greater proportion of rental tenants, more students,

*The impact of recent institutional expansion in Corryville is evident in area to the north of St. George's Church, where a once heavily-populated residential area is now occupied by Sander Hall dormitory and other University of Cincinnati buildings.*

and poorer people. New migrations from the basin included Appalachians and then blacks. By the mid-1950s, the City of Cincinnati's Avondale/Corryville Urban Renewal Project targeted Corryville as a part of an area that required "renewal." City officials identified the rapid turnover in residents and the increasing number of multiple family dwellings as symptoms of deterioration. In order to "preserve a residential area from active pressures of deterioration and blight," they called for clearance of "blighted" structures, road improvements, construction of "vest pocket" parks and playgrounds, and ordinances to slow the growth of "cheap, substandard rental units."

Urban renewal did not take place, however, until 1963-1964, and then it was limited only to the widening of Martin Luther King, Jr., Drive (formerly St. Clair Street) and the creation of some off-street parking.

The real changes in Corryville were brought about by redevelopment which seriously altered the residential nature of the neighborhood. First, in the 1960s, the University of Cincinnati reduced the area's housing stock by tearing down buildings in western Corryville that were home to approximately 200 families in order to construct new parking areas and student dormitories. Next, more housing, this time in the northern portion of Corryville, was lost to the expanding hospital and parking facilities. Finally, the construction of the Environmental Protection Agency building had the greatest impact on the community, displacing 250 families.

One positive result of the university's expansion was the shifting of a large part of its student population to a location where the students could patronize Corryville merchants. As the university grew, new people were introduced into the Corryville community who took an interest in its improvement. Starting in 1964, investors began restoring buildings along Vine Street in the business district and then in other parts of the area. New businesses—record stores, specialty shops, a concert hall—opened to serve the student market, accompanied by adaptive reuse of various old structures—a firehouse reopened as a restaurant, a meeting hall became a dance theater and boutique.

Yet the area retained basic neighborhood services, such as a library, laundromat, post office, banks, and grocery stores. These factors plus growing interest among speculators in Corryville properties slowed deterioration. However, Corryville's population continues to be a largely transient one, and expansion of both the university and the hospitals threatens the remaining housing stock.

## Corryville

Tour Length
5 miles

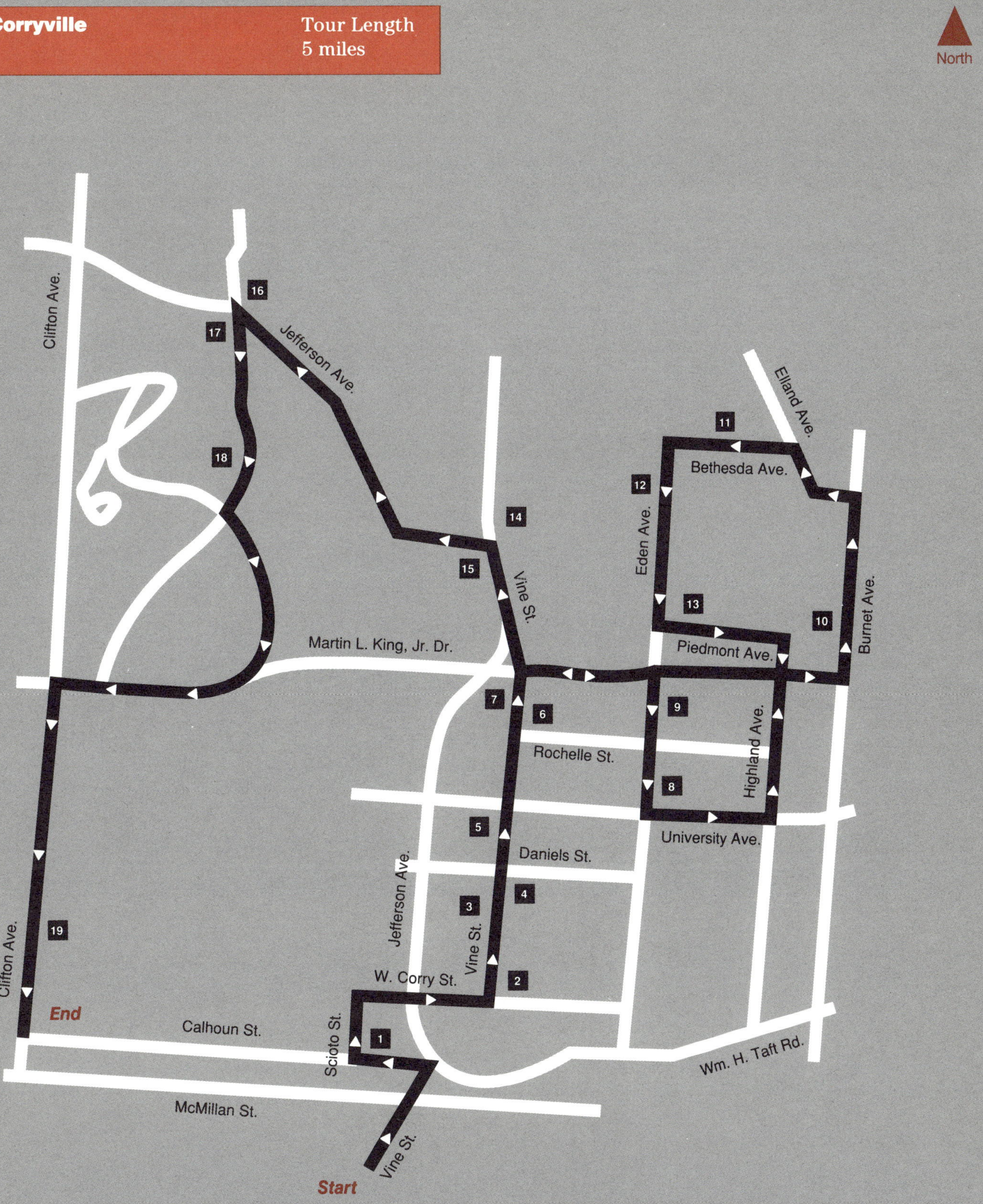

North
Clifton Ave.
Jefferson Ave.
Elland Ave.
Bethesda Ave.
Eden Ave.
Vine St.
Burnet Ave.
Martin L. King, Jr. Dr.
Piedmont Ave.
Rochelle St.
Highland Ave.
University Ave.
Daniels St.
Jefferson Ave.
Vine St.
Clifton Ave.
W. Corry St.
End
Calhoun St.
Sciotto St.
Wm. H. Taft Rd.
McMillan St.
Vine St.
Start
1
2
3
4
5
6
7
8
9
10
11
12
13
14
15
16
17
18
19

# Corryville

**Tour begins on Vine Street; drive north. Turn left on Calhoun Street.**

Franciscan fathers organized **1** **St. George's Parish,** 42 Calhoun Street, in 1868 to serve Catholics in this strongly German American community. A 2-story brick building with a chapel on the first floor and schoolrooms on the second was dedicated on November 15, on the site of the present church parking lot.

To accommodate the increasing number of German Catholics moving from Over-the-Rhine to Corryville, the parish purchased adjacent lots in 1872. A large Romanesque Revival church, designed by Samuel Hannaford, was dedicated June 28, 1874, and the old building became the parish school.

St. George's was an active church. By 1895, it served more than 700 families and had added high school classes to its school program. But at the same time, archdiocesan officials had become concerned that the Franciscans were more interested in church politics than in the welfare of their parishioners. The Franciscans, in turn, regarded any attempt to establish new churches in nearby communities as an assault on one of their most important parishes.

Following the creation of Holy Name parish in Mt. Auburn in 1904 and St. Monica's in Fairview in 1911, St. George's did lose some old parishioners, but they were replaced, to a certain extent, by new middle-income families moving to the hilltops at that time. In 1914, St. George's built a new Jacobethan style school to accommodate the children of this growing suburb. By 1928, the Franciscans and the archdiocese had settled their differences, so that when St. George's completed a new Romanesque style monastery and rectory addition to the church, the archdiocese moved its teachers' college into the original parish building.

St. George's parish experienced the same decline that its neighborhood went through in the mid-twentieth century as the population became poorer and more transient. The teachers' college moved out in 1947, and the building was demolished to provide a parking lot.

The number of parishioners con-

tinued to drop as university and hospital expansion depleted Corryville's housing stock. By the early 1970s, only sixty resident member families remained. On the other hand, the university population has proven crucial to the revitalization of St. George's as students and others connected with the university gradually became a majority of the active parishioners. In 1974, the archdiocese and the Franciscans combined the parish and the university's Newman Center, a cooperative effort that sharply contrasted with their earlier antagonism.

The Franciscans and the archdiocese worked together again in 1977 when declining enrollment led to the combination of six parish schools—those of St. George's, St. Monica's, Holy Name, Assumption in Walnut Hills, Sacred Heart in Camp Washington, and St. Andrew's in Avondale—into a single school called Corryville Catholic. The elementary school was located at St. George's because of the size and good condition of its school building, and its central location.

In 1987-1988, Corryville Catholic enrolled 206 youngsters, 60% black, preschool-grade 8. Its classes for gifted children and for children with reading difficulties, as well as an environment which some parents felt

*As the types of businesses along Vine Street in Corryville became more specialized, that business district attracted customers from all over the city as well as the immediate neighborhood.*

to be better than that in the public schools, had drawn a significant number of non-Catholic children—nearly one-third of the student body.

**Turn right on Scioto Street, right on West Corry Street, left on Vine Street.**

Originally, Vine Street ran uninterrupted from downtown, up the hill, and through the center of Corryville, and the four blocks of Vine between Corry and Rochelle Streets have comprised a major portion of the **2** **Corryville Business District** since the mid-nineteenth century. Approximately 40% of the area's businesses—groceries, saloons, a bakery, barber, apothecary, confectioner, and some notions shops—were here. Further, most of the neighborhood institutions were located within these blocks, making this the geographical, social, and commercial center of the community.

Throughout the first half of the twentieth century, the shops and stores along Vine Street retained this neighborhood orientation. Even the major additions to the district during the 1910s and 1920s, the Nordland theater and a Piggly-Wiggly store that was Cincinnati's first "supermarket," were still intended primarily to serve the community. The convenient combination of streetcar lines that ran along Vine Street, public institutions,

and businesses in one central strip contributed to the success and longevity of the shopping district.

By the mid-twentieth century, however, older neighborhood commercial districts such as Corryville's had declined as the population changed and as shoppers switched from patronizing the local districts to the new, larger retail strips and centers designed to accommodate automobiles.

In the 1960s and 1970s, city government pursued a program of renewal in Corryville which was intended, in part, to revitalize the business district. Streets were widened, new lighting installed, and more off-street parking and on-street spaces created. In the late 1960s, a modern shopping plaza replaced two blocks of residential buildings and a section of Vine Street itself. This new complex, University Plaza, offered considerable parking.

The center strengthened the Corryville business community as it housed a major supermarket and drugstore, as well as a bank, nightclub, and miscellaneous specialty shops. It also changed the traffic pattern in the area, reducing congestion in the old business district.

The district experienced a further "renaissance" as businessmen themselves began the renovation and reuse of buildings along Vine Street. The first of these projects was Cincinnati architect Bruce Goetzman's 1964 renovation of a residence at 2602 Vine Street for office space. Then Bogart's nightclub opened in the former Nordland theater, Zino's restaurant in the old firehouse, and the Rags-2-Riches clothing store in the Turner Hall.

The new generation of shops and restaurants cater mainly to university students, and employees of the surrounding hospitals, schools, and research facilities, as well as a city-wide market. That the district is now called University Village reflects its new orientation.

The former **3** **Headquarters of Engine Company No. 19,** 2701 Vine Street, is tangible evidence of Cincinnati's concern for the residents of its hilltop suburbs. After Corryville was annexed to Cincinnati in 1870, the city provided fire protection.

As the horse-drawn apparatus from downtown took too long to respond to fires in this neighborhood,

Samuel Hannaford designed this 2-story brick Queen Anne style firehouse which opened in June 1871 as the home of Corryville Steam Company No. 19. The company included six men equipped with a Cincinnati-made Ahrens steam fire engine, a hose reel, three horses, and a cat. In August, a new ladder company, the Northern Hook and Ladder Company No. 4, which consisted of two men and a horse-drawn ladder wagon built by I. B. Bruce of Cincinnati, was added.

The engine house was one of the first firehouses built in what was to become the standard configuration of a rectilinear 2-story flat-roofed structure with square doorways. The apparatus was located on the main floor, stables at the rear; the dormitory and hayloft were on the second floor. Engine 19 became a central distribution point for horses for the hilltop fire district when a stable was constructed behind the firehouse for animals used by other companies.

Unlike most of the neighborhood's residents, the first firefighters assigned here were not generally of German descent. But later, more Germans were appointed to Engine 19 and Ladder 4.

Corryville's fire companies were motorized in 1917 with new Ahrens-Fox apparatus. While motorization enabled the city to disband almost one-third of its fire companies, Engine 19 and Ladder 4 survived because their fire house was large enough to accommodate the new machines and was centrally located. Only in the late 1960s did larger apparatus made larger quarters necessary. In 1968, Engine 19 and Ladder 4 moved to a new building at 2814 Vine Street. The former engine house was vacant only briefly before it was purchased and converted into a restaurant, Zino's Firehouse.

Architect Tom Hefley's renovation of Engine 19's house was a major element in the reconstruction and reorientation of the Corryville business district. Like most of the other new businesses in University Village, Zino's drew customers from the University of Cincinnati and from outside the immediate area. The renovation of the Corryville firehouse also stimulated interest in abandoned municipal buildings, making other empty firehouses, schools, and police stations more desirable as commercial properties.

For many Cincinnatians of German ancestry, meeting halls and gymnasiums like those at the former **4** **North Cincinnati Turner Hall,** 2728 Vine Street, were an important part of their daily lives. The Turner movement, founded in Germany in 1811 by Friedrich Ludwig Jahn, was dedicated to improving society through physical education. German immigrants had brought this idea to the United States, but it was not seriously promoted until the political upheavals and unrest in Europe during the late 1840s sent large numbers of reform-minded Germans to North America.

Cincinnati's first *Turnverein*, or Turner Society, was organized in 1848, with the Central *Turnhalle* located on Walnut Street in Over-the-Rhine. In addition to its athletic programs of calisthenics, wrestling, gymnastics, and fencing, the Turners functioned as a social organization for German families. The *Turnverein* was an institution around which Cincinnati German American culture developed.

The Turners supported liberal political causes—abolition, the secret ballot, direct election of senators, and proportional representation. One of the few major nineteenth-century reforms not supported by Turners was Prohibition, which they viewed as a direct attack on their cultural and social life.

German Americans who moved to Corryville transplanted or re-created many of the organizations that they had in the basin. The North Cincinnati *Turnverein* was founded around 1884, and a building was erected at the southeast corner of Vine and Boone (Daniels) Streets to serve as its meeting hall and gymnasium. It offered athletic classes and social activities for women, children, young men, and older men, who also debated political and social questions. The older men, known as the "Bears," were especially active in opposing temperance issues.

The hall was expanded in 1894 to include a swimming pool and bowling alley. Rooms at the hall were available for weddings, parties, or meetings of community groups.

German American life in Corryville was disrupted during World War I by the vehement reaction against all things German. The Turner Hall was renamed the North Cincinnati Gymnasium, and the Turner Society, which

*The German Americans who settled Corryville in the nineteenth century established their own institutions, including the North Cincinnati Turnverein, which built a Turnhalle at the corner of Vine and Daniels Streets.*

had already been declining in membership, quickly faded in importance. The gym closed in 1934.

A restaurant opened in the gym, which became the United Automobile Workers local union hall in 1945. By the mid-1950s, another restaurant had replaced the union; some community groups continued to meet here. In 1977, the Turner Hall was renovated as commercial space, and a clothing store opened on the main floor. The building also became the home of the Contemporary Dance Theater, which offers performances as well as dance and exercise classes.

The present **5 Louis M. Schiel Public School,** 2821 Vine Street, replaced earlier neighborhood schools on the same site. Corryville's first school was built here in the early 1860s and improved in 1866. When the village was annexed in 1870, 300 children attended classes in the 2-story, 5-room structure that became the Twenty-third District School under the direction of the Cincinnati Board of Education.

Because the city had annexed such a large area in 1870 (Corryville, part of Walnut Hills, Camp Washington, Lick Run, Price Hill, and a portion of the East End), it had difficulty in

providing services to all its new citizens. The Corryville school was deemed adequate, and city officials left it in service.

The building was expanded in 1878 and in 1885 to accommodate the growing number of families that moved to Corryville after completion of the Bellevue Incline. The board purchased additional land adjoining the school in 1895 for future expansion and for use as playground space, an idea that was then gaining popularity.

In 1904-1905, the Board of Education began a program to "modernize" its buildings. New structures were erected and old ones were remodeled or enlarged. In 1911, a major addition designed by J. Gilmore replaced much of the original structure of the Twenty-third District School. Like most of the public school architecture at that time, the new building had Jacobethan touches, including a cut-stone entrance, but the exterior detailing was not as elaborate as that of buildings remodeled earlier because the Board of Education had become more cost-conscious.

The interior also had many of the pleasant features common to Cincinnati schools of the period—elaborate plasterwork ceilings, decorative cast-metal railings and light fixtures, oak woodwork, and built-in glass-front bookcases. Most of these decorative elements, plus a Rookwood fountain and a bronze plaque by Clement Barnhorn in memory of Principal

Louis Schiel (c.1857-1941), have survived several generations of students and subsequent renovations.

The new addition doubled the capacity of the building to more than 900; in 1929-1930, another addition designed by the firm of Samuel Hannaford & Sons obliterated the remaining vestiges of the old building.

In 1942, the school was renamed for Schiel in recognition of his forty-two years of service to the school and to the community. Though Corryville changed in the 1950s and 1960s with the arrival of black and Appalachian families, Schiel School was enrolled close to capacity and continued as a focal point of the neighborhood.

All this changed abruptly in the early 1970s when construction began on the new Environmental Protection Agency building. Large blocks of Corryville housing were demolished, and the school population fell by more than half. In 1974, the school took on a new role in the public school system when German-language programs were established at Schiel and nearby Fairview Elementary, making them two of Cincinnati's alternative or magnet schools, a venture designed to provide quality integrated education. Instruction in French was added later.

Schiel next housed the German Bilingual Academy, a middle school, and then two alternative programs. One, the Academy for World Languages, offered fourth graders classes in Arabic, Chinese, Japanese, and Russian; it was soon moved to Sawyer School in Evanston. The other, the School for Arts Enrichment, has continued here, offering art, music, dance, drama, and Suzuki cello, piano, and violin instruction for children, grades K-3, drawn from throughout the city.

The original occupants of the former **6 Home of Christopher Ahrens,** 3010 Vine Street, were typical of many of Corryville's nineteenth-century residents. As public transportation and the incline transformed this rural area, the east side of Vine Street was soon lined with single-family dwellings that housed predominantly middle and upper middle-income families of German descent. Among this group was fire apparatus manufacturer Christopher F. Ahrens (1836-1919). Born in Germany, Ahrens immigrated to the United States in 1853 and created a company that provided a comfortable living for himself and a number of relatives.

Originally his family lived near the factory on Webster (East Fourteenth) Street in Over-the-Rhine, but in the early 1880s, Ahrens took advantage of the incline and streetcars and moved to Corryville. He built this relatively modest Italianate style home on Vine Street around 1884. Other businessmen of similar status erected dwellings in the area in the 1880s and 1890s. While these residences were certainly not comparable in size and elegance to the mansions then being built in Clifton, they were definitely larger than the houses, apartments, and tenements left behind in the basin.

The character of the buildings on this block is varied, including as it does the Romanesque Revival style Clifford Presbyterian Church at 3028 Vine, built in 1888-1890, and the apartment building at the northeast corner of Vine and Rochelle which Ahrens erected as an investment in the 1890s. The block has remained predominantly residential, but the type of residents has changed considerably.

By the 1920s and 1930s, most of the original occupants, including the Ahrens family, were gone. The houses were gradually divided into apartments, and by 1960, many of the residents were lower-income blacks and Appalachians. By the early 1970s, the Clifford Presbyterian Church building had been acquired by the Truth Missionary Baptist Church, a black congregation that worshipped here for about fifteen years, and a beauty parlor operated on the first floor of the former Ahrens residence.

While much of Corryville experienced rehabilitation and rebuilding in the 1970s, this end of Vine Street was relatively unaffected.

The west side of Vine Street between Rochelle and Martin Luther King, Jr., Drive is dominated by a large brick structure that was originally the **7 Vine-Clifton Car Barn of the Cincinnati Street Railway Company**. Built in 1907, the building was used to store the streetcar equipment used on the central hilltop routes.

The hilltop streetcar lines, laid during the 1870s and 1880s, were expanded and improved following the annexation of Clifton and Avondale in 1896. This barn, located on the main line to the outlying suburbs, became even more important for the entire

transit network when the main storage facilities in the Mill Creek Valley were flooded. At those times, streetcars from various parts of the city were stored in satellite barns such as this one until the flood waters receded.

When the streetcars were finally replaced by buses in 1951, the Street Railway Company no longer needed the Vine Street barn, and it was converted into warehouse space. Different sections of the building served various purposes, including a coffee warehouse, paint warehouse, and, in the 1960s, offices. In 1970, the University of Cincinnati acquired the former car barn for use as its central storehouse. In the 1980s, the university converted part of it into studios for graduate architecture students.

**Turn right on Martin Luther King, Jr., Drive, right on Eden Avenue, left on University Avenue, left on Highland Avenue.**

*With its vine-shaded garden and outspoken waiters, Mecklenburg's was the last of Cincinnati's traditional beer gardens.*

The vacant building at 302 East University Avenue was at one time **8 Mecklenburg's Garden,** the last of Cincinnati's original beer gardens. The earliest part of the Italianate structure was built about 1865, probably as a residence; around 1870, it became the Mt. Auburn Garden, Restaurant, and Billiard Saloon, operated by John Neeb.

Neeb's bartender, Louis Mecklenburg, who began working and boarding at the saloon in 1882, acquired the business in 1886, and the name was eventually changed to Mecklenburg's Garden. Over the years, the building was expanded. Its most popular feature was its garden, consisting of the adjoining lot walled in by latticework trellises and shaded by grape vines.

Under Mecklenburg's management, the saloon became a favorite institution among German Americans in Corryville. Beer gardens such as this were not simply bars, but functioned also as social centers for their neighborhoods, bringing people together in an environment that reinforced their sense of community.

In the early twentieth century, this sense of community was almost

a caricature of itself at Mecklenburg's, as the establishment became the unofficial "town hall" of the fictional town of "Kloppenburg," a name derived from the noise made by patrons rapping empty beer steins on their tables to call for refills. Mock elections were held for imaginary positions with nonsensical names, and participation in these campaigns became obligatory for politicians and businessmen who wished to parade their association with what survived of the old German American community.

Prohibition drove many of the old neighborhood beer gardens out of business, but Mecklenburg's survived by selling illegal liquor to its regular customers and providing good German food. Louis Mecklenburg's son, Carl, succeeded him, and though the business passed out of the family's hands following Carl's death in 1938, the name and tradition remained. In the 1940s and 1950s, Mecklenburg's Garden was well-known for its opinionated waiters who felt free to argue with the patrons over the wisdom of their selections from the menu.

As Corryville deteriorated in the 1960s and early 1970s, the restaurant's fortunes also declined. When the area experienced a revival in the mid-1970s, Mecklenburg's was acquired by an ashram and rehabilitated as a fashionable restaurant. But the area did not undergo the expected renaissance, and Mecklenburg's closed in 1983, only to reopen for a short time as a pizza restaurant.

The creation of the **9 Rollman Psychiatric Institute,** 3009 Burnet Avenue, was the culmination of an effort organized in 1948 by Judge Chase M. Davies and retired department store head Justin A. Rollman (1887-1975) to obtain a state-supported mental health care center that would serve "early and incipient" cases as an alternative to Longview State Hospital. Not only was Longview seriously overcrowded, but concerned citizens and mental health professionals believed that a receiving hospital could provide prompt diagnosis and short-term, concentrated treatment to "borderline" and voluntary commitment cases.

Rollman advocated using a building at Burnet and Melish Avenues which had been erected in the mid-nineteenth century as the General Protestant Orphans' Home. That in-

stitution had been organized by various German Protestant denominations in 1849 following a cholera epidemic. When the orphanage moved to its present location on Beechmont Avenue in Mt. Washington, the old property became available.

The site was purchased in 1949, and the building was renovated by the state Division of Mental Hygiene. In August 1954, the Rollman Receiving Hospital was dedicated and named after Justin Rollman in recognition of his key role in its establishment. Wings were added in 1960 and 1973 to provide a more modern facility and a more homelike environment for patients. The original structure, built in 1850 with additions in 1867 and 1885, was demolished in 1977.

Patients stay at Rollman Hospital for an average of seven weeks before being released or sent to other institutions if longer care is necessary.

> **Turn right on Martin Luther King, Jr., Drive, left on Burnet Avenue.**

The **10 University of Cincinnati Medical Center** and **Hospital,** Eden and Bethesda Avenues, have their origins in the early nineteenth century when Dr. Daniel Drake (1785-1852) sought to establish a public hospital that would include teaching as a part of its operation. Drake believed such a facility would improve the health of Cincinnati's poor, thereby making them more productive. This, in turn, would contribute to the prosperity of Cincinnati and enhance its status as a regional metropolis.

In 1821, state legislation provided funds to set up public hospitals for those who could not afford care in private institutions. Cincinnati's first public hospital, the Commercial Hospital and Lunatic Asylum, opened in 1823 in a 3-story brick building at Twelfth Street and Western Row (Central Avenue). It had four departments—medical, surgical, obstetrical, and an asylum for the mentally-ill; a section of the building was set aside as a Poor House.

In 1861, the hospital was reorganized and renamed the Commercial Hospital. To relieve overcrowding, a temporary annex was established on Elm Street near Twelfth in 1865. Municipal funding was obtained for

construction of an ornate modern structure completed on the site of the Commercial Hospital in January 1869.

When this building, in turn, became overcrowded and obsolete, the city bought a large tract in Corryville. Despite the objections of several prominent physicians who wanted the hospital to remain in the basin, a new facility (the current administration building) designed by Samuel Hannaford was erected on this site between 1911 and 1915. The new Cincinnati General Hospital was placed under the direct control of the City of Cincinnati.

Dr. Christian R. Holmes, hospital trustee and chairman of the City Hospital building committee, intended that Cincinnati General would function as a teaching hospital. One of his reasons for bringing the new hospital to Corryville was to place it close to the University of Cincinnati, and cooperation between the university's medical college and the hospital began as soon as the new complex opened. In 1920, the working relationship became official as Cincinnati General Hospital acquired status as a university hospital.

Cincinnati General Hospital's ability to provided medical care was expanded in 1928 by the construction of the Christian R. Holmes Hospital on Bethesda Avenue. This infirmary for private patients was funded as a memorial by the doctor's widow and was directly affiliated with the University of Cincinnati Medical College. Wings were added to General Hospital in 1931 and 1944, but by 1960, the medical complex needed renovation, reorganization, and expansion. Cincinnati voters approved a $17 million bond issue for this work and sanctioned transfer of administration of the complex to the university. Major new facilities were erected during the 1960s.

In 1979, Holmes and Cincinnati General hospitals became University Hospital. Holmes, which had been expanded in 1959 and 1966, received another addition.

By 1987, University Hospital was the city's largest, with a 754-bed capacity, more than fifty out-patient departments, a staff of nearly 4,000, approximately 24,000 admissions, and about 122,000 emergency and out-patient cases recorded that year. The staff of the Medical Center, which included the Colleges of Medicine,

Nursing, and Pharmacy, and the Kettering Environmental Health Laboratory, added another 4,000 persons to the complex's total.

The goal of University Hospital is to provide complete health care for patients who can pay and those who cannot; however, its particular strengths are its cardiovascular, geriatrics, neurosciences, oncology, prenatal, preventative medicine, and trauma service programs. Further, all heart, liver, and pancreas transplants on adults in the Cincinnati area are performed here.

**Turn left on Elland Avenue, left on Bethesda Avenue.**

The idea behind the **11 Children's Hospital Medical Center,** Bethesda and Elland Avenues, originated among a group of influential Episcopal women who were concerned about the lack of a local medical facility specifically for children. The result was the Hospital of the Protestant Episcopal Church, which opened in March 1884, was to provide free medical care to poor children "without regard to creed, color or country."

The first hospital was set up in a house at the corner of Park Avenue and Kemper (Yale) Street in Walnut Hills. In this small, "home-like" institution, a volunteer medical staff, housemother, teacher, and nursing volunteers sought to provide both spiritual and physical care for the children. This 12-bed facility soon proved too small. In 1887, Thomas and John J. Emery donated land for a new facility in Mt. Auburn. The new hospital, closer to downtown neighborhoods where many needy children lived, could accommodate up to forty-five patients.

As the demand for the hospital's services increased, the staff grew, taking on paid practitioners, professional nursing personnel, and specialists in areas such as dentistry. Expenses also grew, and in 1889, the hospital began admitting private patients. A new wing added in 1903 again increased capacity and required a larger nursing staff. The hospital's own nursing school was created in 1906. The board was reorganized in 1921, and the institution's name was changed to The Children's Hospital.

Continued expansion of services and staff and the growing number of patients, especially non-charity cases, brought the move to Bethesda and Elland Avenues in 1926. This site could accommodate future additions and was close to General Hospital, around which a distinct hospital district was beginning to develop. A fund drive led by William C. Procter enabled the hospital to build a 5-story Gothic style building designed by architects A.O. Elzner and Stanley Matthews.

In Corryville, Children's Hospital

*Children's Hospital was an important institution for Cincinnati families because it accepted young patients of all races long before such a policy was common.*

became a center of pediatric research, a development encouraged by its relationship with the University of Cincinnati Medical College. As pediatrics became more concerned with prevention, a number of the hospital's medical staff became well known, including immunologist Dr. Albert Sabin (b.1906), inventor of an oral polio vaccine, and Dr. Josef Warkany, a specialist in mental retardation and hereditary malformations.

Additions to the hospital were built in 1930, 1950, 1966, 1974, 1980, and 1983. Planning for the most significant improvement, the Children's Hospital Medical Center, began in 1966, construction got underway in 1971, and the center opened in 1974.

Children's Hospital became an integral part of the complex of medical facilities that occupies a large portion of northeastern Corryville. In some ways, however, it had less of an impact on the local community than other institutions. This site was purchased when the area was fairly undeveloped, and expansion took relatively little housing. Rather, another institution, the Cincinnati *Altenheim* or Home for Aged Men, which had stood nearby since 1891, was razed.

In June 1976, Children's Hospital became a partially tax supported institution for the first time in its history. Over a decade later, with 344 beds, more than 14,000 admissions, and 168,000 emergency and outpatient cases, a staff of approximately 2,500, and a budget of more than $65 million, the Children's Hospital Medical Center claims to be the largest facility of its kind in the nation.

**Turn left on Eden Avenue.**

The **12 University of Cincinnati College of Medicine,** 210 Bethesda Avenue, a part of the University Medical Center, traces its origins to the beginning of medical history in Cincinnati. Hoping to replace the more usual apprenticeship system, Dr. Daniel Drake (1785-1852) established the Medical College of Ohio in 1819. However, because of bitter disagreements with his colleagues, Drake was able to teach there only periodically.

Frequent changes in location, reorganizations, and faculty dissension at the Medical College of Ohio caused several disgruntled staff to leave the school and attempt to found rival institutions. One of the more successful of these ventures was the Miami Medical College, organized in 1852 by Dr. Reuben D. Mussey, a professor of surgery who had become disgusted by the problems at the Medical College of Ohio.

The University of Cincinnati was created in 1870-1871, and in 1886, both medical colleges had established a trial affiliation with the new school. Ten years later, the Medical College of Ohio formally merged with the university, and its classes were moved to the old McMicken Hall on Clifton Avenue near Vine Street. The Miami Medical College merged with UC in 1909, becoming a part of the Ohio-Miami Medical College of the University of Cincinnati.

The university medical school moved to new buildings adjacent to the recently constructed Cincinnati Hospital in 1916-1917. This location provided the medical school with larger, more modern facilities and helped bring together the university medical college and the hospital to create a teaching hospital. This relationship became official in 1920 when the name of the school was changed to the College of Medicine of the University of Cincinnati.

In 1948, the university established the Kettering Laboratory of Applied Physiology to study industrial health problems and in 1959, erected the William B. Wherry Medical Research Building. These research facilities improved the status and recruiting ability of the College of Medicine. A new 10-story Medical Sciences Building was constructed between 1970 and 1974 to train more doctors.

The University Medical Center includes these research and training facilities and University Hospital—the City Hospital which became General Hospital before adopting its present, more prestigious sounding name. Here, too, were the School of Nursing and the College of Pharmacy, both descended from institutions that had originally been independent of the university.

Two schools of nursing, the Cincinnati Training School for Nurses (1889) and the Cincinnati Hospital Training School (1891), were merged in 1916 as the School of Nursing and Health of the University of Cincinnati. The nursing school, located at the university medical complex since then, is now housed in William Cooper Procter Hall, built 1965-1967.

The College of Pharmacy, founded in 1850 as the Cincinnati College of Pharmacy, merged with the university in 1954 and was then located in a building on the Burnet Woods campus. It moved to this complex in 1976.

**Turn left on Piedmont Avenue.**

The **13** **Shriners' Burns Institute,** 202 Goodman Street, was established by the Ancient Arabic Order of the Nobles of the Mystic Shrine, a national fraternal and philanthropic society known popularly as the Shriners, that became interested in supporting medical facilities for burned children. Regarding serious burns as the major unmet medical problem of the time, the organization appropriated funds in 1962 to build and operate a group of hospitals specifically designed to care for burns cases.

The Shriners required that these special hospital facilities be adjacent to and associated with major medical schools and easily reached from airports so emergency cases could be moved quickly. Twenty-one cities applied. In 1963, three sites were chosen: Boston, Galveston, and Cincinnati.

Cincinnati was selected for a number of reasons. The University of Cincinnati Medical College had a fine reputation and was already engaged in research on burns treatment. The city also had Greater Cincinnati and Lunken airports. Finally, its central geographic location meant cases could be brought here from throughout the Midwest and South.

Construction began in 1964 on property provided by the University of Cincinnati. The 30-bed hospital opened in 1967 with the specific purpose of providing specialized care, without cost to the parents of the victims.

The success and importance of the Shriners' Burns Institute led to development of plans in 1982 for a major renovation and expansion, but it was determined that a completely new building would be needed to accommodate the intended improvements. The University of Cincinnati donated another piece of property for this new structure in the University Hospital complex, thereby maintaining the relationship between it and the Shriners' Burns hospital.

**Turn right on Highland Avenue, right on Martin Luther King, Jr., Drive, right on Vine Street.**

A full-range medical, surgical, and psychiatric hospital, the **14** **VA Medical Center,** 3200 Vine Street, was built between 1948 and 1954. After World War II, the Veterans' Administration was created to provide assistance in a variety of areas for the massive number of former United States military personnel. A Cincinnati regional office was set up in 1946. Medical assistance was a key element in the program, and planning for a Veterans' Administration Hospital in Cincinnati began in 1947. The City of Cincinnati provided a 15-acre site adjoining the UC Medical College-Cincinnati General Hospital complex, and the firm of Samuel Hannaford & Sons designed the hospital building.

The new Veterans' Hospital, with a capacity of 500 beds, opened in May 1954. In 1958, all in-patient and out-patient care for eligible veterans in the region (some of which had previously been handled at the VA nursing home in Ft. Thomas, Kentucky) was consolidated at the hospital in Corryville.

As time went on, the VA hospital increasingly emphasized research and out-patient care, and the relationship between medical staff and the University of Cincinnati Medical College and University Hospital doctors became more important. The building was remodeled and expanded, reflecting this shift. A 1982 addition was specifically designed for out-patient care, and although two more floors were added in 1984, capacity was reduced by almost 150 beds because research and improved technology required more space. The remaining in-patient facilities were redesigned to provide greater patient privacy.

The VA Hospital sought to meet the growing needs of the veterans of World War II and the Korean War as they aged. It has also recognized the special health problems of the Vietnam veterans with treatment and research. In the mid-1980s, this 342-bed institution recorded more than 140,000 out-patient visits and treatment of some 11,000 admissions. Staff members carried on medical research in a variety of areas, and a 206-bed unit in Fort Thomas, Kentucky, provided long-term care.

**Turn left on Jefferson Avenue.**

The **15 Environmental Protection Agency Building,** 26 Martin Luther King, Jr., Drive West, resulted from the creation in 1970 of a single government bureau to consolidate the environmental activities carried out by fifteen components of five executive agencies and federal departments. Some of the most important of this work, related primarily to water pollution, was underway in Cincinnati at several different facilities. Andrew A. Breidenbach, director of the National Environmental Research Laboratories in the Robert A. Taft Center on Columbia Parkway in Linwood, led the effort to bring the research activities in Cincinnati together at one site.

One of Breidenbach's major concerns was to improve interaction between the University of Cincinnati and the government's environmental labs. Thus, he was interested in seeing a new facility erected near the university. The city, eager to have the large federal facility built in Cincinnati, purchased twenty-two acres of residential property in Corryville between UC and the University Hospital complex and donated it as the site for the new building.

Funds were appropriated for the project in 1971, the building was occupied in 1976, and following Breidenbach's death in 1980, it was rededicated as the Andrew A. Breidenbach Environmental Research Center. The 10-story structure, designed by the architectural firm of A.M. Kinney Associates, had 200,000 square feet of usable space. It included a 300-seat auditorium, a library, and cafeteria, along with specialized facilities for animal quarantine and care, computers, electron microscopy, media preparation, and a microbiological infections suite.

When the building was ready, the Water Engineering Research Lab, the Environmental Monitoring and Support Lab, the Toxicology and Microbiology Division of the Health Effects Research Lab, and the Hazardous Waste Engineering Research Lab, all elements of the EPA's Office of Research and Development (ORD), were moved in. Other ORD components also relocated to the Corryville building, including the Center for Environmental Research Information, the Environmental Criteria and Assessment Office, and the Support Services/Public Affairs Office. Some 600 workers in the center were engaged in research and disseminating the information generated in the labs to the public, other branches of the EPA, government agencies, contractors, industry, and the academic community.

The placement of the Breidenbach Center in Corryville has been of significant importance to UC researchers; departments such as engineering, chemistry, biology, and health sciences frequently use the center's library. But the surrounding community was also affected in a less positive way. A large portion of the area's housing stock was eliminated, and 225 families were displaced, forcing neighborhood businesses to reorient themselves.

**Bear right on Jefferson Avenue.**

In the second half of the nineteenth century, Corryville was an attractive suburb for middle-income residents of the basin, some of whom were attracted by a new type of building typified by the **16 Parkside Flats,** 3315-3317 Jefferson Avenue. Many of those who wished to move out of the crowded downtown could not afford to buy or build even a fairly modest home and were, therefore, prospective tenants for large buildings of apartments or "flats."

These structures, common in Europe in the mid-nineteenth century, began appearing in the United States in the 1860s and 1870s. They were generally known as "French flats" and were considerably different from boarding houses or tenements. The apartment buildings were designed for middle-class family living and were on residential streets, rather than next to factories; they had private kitchens and baths, and many even had a shady courtyard and individual porches.

One of the earliest apartment buildings of this kind erected in Corryville was the Parkside Flats, built around 1895. Its appeal derived from both the growing popularity of apartment living, its design, and its location. The structure itself is a very large, frame Shingle style building with an irregular shape intended to make it resemble single-family dwellings of the period. Its proximity to the streetcar line which ran along Jefferson Avenue was crucial, as potential tenants relied on public transportation. And, as the building's name pointed out, Burnet Woods lay just behind it.

Over the years, the Parkside Flats suffered from neglect and hard use from a transient population that included students. But a refurbishing in the 1970s made it, like many of Corryville's older structures, an appealing residence once again.

The large, stone Chateauesque style **17 Home of George B. Cox,** 3400 Brookline Avenue, looks as though it belongs among the "baronial" mansions of Clifton, rather than in Corryville. The house, known as Parkview, was designed by Samuel Hannaford and built in 1894-1895 for Republican political boss George Cox (1853-1916).

Both Cox and his wife came from humble origins. That they erected their magnificent new home as close as possible to the prestigious suburb of Clifton was an expression of their desire to be accepted into the upper levels of Cincinnati society. This acceptance, which the Coxes sought for both social and political reasons, never took place. Cox was always regarded by the elite as a rather coarse and questionable individual, so most of the guests who were entertained at Parkview tended to be from political circles, rather than from Clifton society. Many, however, were major figures in the Republican party at the turn of the century.

George Cox died in 1916, and his wife, Caroline, continued to live in the house until her death in 1938. The estate was left to a variety of charities. The house became the property of the Cincinnati Union Bethel which operated it as a dormitory for young women, similar to the Anna Louise Inn downtown. Known as Cox Hall, it was especially popular with female students at the University of Cincinnati.

213

In 1948, Cox Hall was sold to the university's Pi Kappa Alpha fraternity. Many of the home's original interior features, such as light fixtures, mantels, and plaster work, remained intact, and the house was placed on the National Register of Historic Places in 1977.

> **Turn left on Burnet Woods Drive, which bends to the left.**

**18** **Burnet Woods Park,** along Clifton Avenue between Ludlow Avenue and Martin Luther King, Jr., Drive, came into existence because many Cincinnati civic leaders believed public parks were needed to improve the quality of life in the city. In the late 1860s and early 1870s, city government acquired land for its first parks.

One of the most appealing potential sites was a tract in Corryville known as Burnet Woods. This piece of land, which extended from Ludlow Avenue almost to Calhoun Street, had been willed by Judge Jacob Burnet (1770-1853) to two of his children, Robert and Elizabeth. Robert Burnet and Elizabeth's husband, William S. Groesbeck, originally planned to subdivide the property for residential development. Instead, in 1871, they offered the land to the city for a park.

There was considerable opposition to accepting the offer. The nation's economy was weak at the time, and some officials argued that although "a city of any pretensions cannot do without parks," Cincinnati had enough parkland and could not afford more. Those who favored the offer, chiefly the Board of Park Commissioners led by Joseph Longworth and Park Superintendent Adolph Strauch, argued that such lands would be needed at a later date, when they would be more expensive. Further, by making improvements in its parks, the city would create some badly-needed jobs.

The Park Commissioners won the argument, and the city entered into a lease agreement with Burnet and the Groesbecks in 1872. Because Superintendent Strauch believed that "most people visit the parks for the purpose of enjoying the productions of nature and very seldom stone and mortar," the only major improvements to Burnet Woods were roadways and a lake.

Burnet Woods Park opened on August 26, 1874, and became tre-mendously popular with the public. Its popularity was no doubt increased by Groesbeck's endowment of a fund to provide free public concerts in the park. In 1881, the city purchased the approximately 165 acres of parkland.

As the years went by, Strauch's ideas on maintaining the rustic nature of the park were increasingly ignored, especially after park management passed to the Board of Public Works between 1876 and 1891. A bandshell and shelterhouse were built in Burnet Woods, and a large part of the park was appropriated as the site for the new University of Cincinnati. Although the first university structure was not erected until 1895, a city ordinance of 1889 had set aside forty-three acres of parkland for the institution's use.

The natural character of Burnet Woods was repeatedly altered in the twentieth century by a variety of projects which were not directly related to property's original function as a park. Among these were the Trailside Museum, built by the WPA and opened in 1942 (later closed due to lack of funds), and the Lone Star Pavilion, erected in 1974 by the Sons of the Republic of Texas as a memorial to Cincinnati's support of the Texas Revolution of 1836. The pavilion features replicas of Cincinnati's gift, two cannons called the "Twin Sisters," which Sam Houston's army used to defeat Santa Anna's forces in the 20-minute Battle of San Jacinto on April 21.

Perhaps the most unusual artifact introduced into the park is the Richardson memorial, consisting of granite blocks salvaged from the old Chamber of Commerce Building that was designed in 1884 by architect H.H. Richardson and destroyed by fire in 1911. In 1972, University of Cincinnati students used the surviving fragments of the structure to create an artificial "ruin" as a monument to Richardson, one of America's foremost architects.

The park has continued to shrink as the University of Cincinnati took over more parkland in 1914, and again in 1950, despite a vigorous Save Burnet Woods campaign. Now approximately half its original size, Burnet Woods remains an extremely popular park.

> **Turn right on Martin Luther King, Jr., Drive, left on Clifton Avenue.**

Today, the **19** **University of Cincinnati** occupies land that was once half of Burnet Woods Park and several blocks of middle-income housing. UC claims 1819 as its founding date, for it was then that the Cincinnati College was created with Jacob Burnet as president of the board of directors. This college closed in 1825 due to financial problems. It reopened in 1835, largely through the efforts of Dr. Daniel Drake, and merged with the Cincinnati Law School, which had been founded in 1833.

The law department became the strongest element in the college, holding classes even when the academic departments were inactive. The law departments of the municipal University of Cincinnati and Cincinnati College entered into a trial merger from 1897 to 1911. In 1918, the college formally merged with the university, enabling UC to place the date 1819 on its seal.

The university itself originated with a bequest by Charles McMicken (1782-1858). McMicken, having made a fortune in real estate, bequeathed approximately one million dollars to the City of Cincinnati to establish a university. A Board of Trustees of McMicken University was created, but due to legal and financial problems, the city was never able to obtain McMicken's entire bequest. In January 1869, the McMicken School of Drawing and Design was opened as a partial means of complying with McMicken's intentions.

In 1870, the state legislature authorized Cincinnati to establish a municipal university and to support it through taxation. McMicken University was chartered in December 1870, and in January 1871, the name was changed to the University of Cincinnati. Within several months, the McMicken fund was turned over to the new university.

In late 1872, voters authorized the city to issue bonds to fund construction of the school. While work began on the site of the former McMicken homestead at Clifton Avenue near Vine Street, classes were held at Woodward High School (now the School for the Creative and Performing Arts) downtown on Sycamore Street. The new building, completed in 1875, was not adequate for long. The Bellevue Incline ran next to it, and by the late 1880s, the structure was overcrowded, dirty, and noisy. In 1889,

*When the University of Cincinnati moved to a site in Burnet Woods, the first buildings, including the original McMicken Hall, were on the hill facing Clifton Avenue.*

City Council appropriated forty-three acres of Burnet Woods Park for a new university site, but legal problems delayed construction until 1893.

The first building, McMicken Hall, was completed in 1895, and a series of additions followed rapidly. Two of these, the Basic Sciences and Old Commons buildings, were still standing in the late 1980s. The main building, however, was demolished in the late 1940s and replaced by the present Georgian Revival style McMicken, Cunningham, and Hanna Halls—all a single structure designed by the Cincinnati firm Hake & Hake.

Two other early structures were the Neo-Classical style Van Wormer Library (now the Administration Building), designed by Samuel Hannaford and built in 1899-1900, and the Technical Building, a utilitarian structure erected around 1902. A major wave of construction took place during the administration of president Charles W. Dabney, which began in 1904. The Geology addition to "Old Tech" was built in 1910, the old gym and central boiler house in 1911, the Baldwin Engineering Building in 1911-1915, the Women's Building (Beecher Hall) in 1916, and the original wing of the Chemistry Building in 1915-1916.

Dabney was also responsible for reorganizing UC so that it functioned as a university in fact, as well as in name. Key elements in this reorganization included the creation of the Teachers' College in 1905 and the opening of the Graduate School of the College of Arts and Sciences in 1906.

Also during this period, Dean Herman Schneider of the College of Engineering instituted a cooperative technical training program for his students, one of the first such programs in the country.

Another period of expansion during the 1920s and 1930s added new service, classroom, and laboratory buildings, and Memorial Hall, a men's dormitory completed in 1924. New buildings included Tanners' Hall (1924), the National Research Laboratory established by the Tanners' Council of America to study problems of the leather industry; Alphonso Taft Hall (1925), the law school building, now hidden by a modern renovation; Nippert Stadium (1924), a memorial to UC student James Gamble Nippert who died from injuries sustained in a football game; Swift Hall (1926), to house the geography department; the Carl Blegen Library erected in 1930; the Teachers' College, Botany, Zoology, and Physics buildings, all completed in 1931; Wilson Memorial Auditorium (1932), and the Student Union Building, constructed, along with an addition to the Chemistry Building, in 1936-1937 with WPA assistance.

Following World War II, the emphasis shifted to residential construction as the university sought to accommodate the influx of students on the GI Bill and later, those of the baby boom. These factors and a new trend to on-campus living were responsible for French Hall (1952-1953), Dabney Hall (1959), three high-rise residence halls on Jefferson Avenue (1964), Daniels, Calhoun, and Charlton Halls (1967), and Sander Hall (1971).

This new construction, plus that of the Alms Applied Arts Building (now DAAP), the Armory Field House, and the parking lots and garages needed to serve commuters, dormitory residents, and the sports facilities, forced the university to take over more of the surrounding area. Another large section of Burnet Woods was acquired and several blocks of housing were demolished in the mid-1960s, displacing more than 200 families. However, the hundreds of dormitory residents supported and thereby contributed to the revitalization of Corryville businesses and institutions.

As the baby boom generation grew up and enrollment began to recede, the university again concentrated on projects serving specific educational or research functions. Among these were the massive Brodie Science and Engineering complex (1966-1970), Corbett Center, home of the College Conservatory of Music (1967), Patricia Corbett Pavilion's five performing arts facilities (1972), the Walter C. Langsam Library (1979), and Lindner Hall for the College of Business Administration (1986).

These were expensive projects, and although much of the work was funded by private donors such as J. Ralph and Patricia Corbett and Carl Lindner, other support was also needed. Such funds came primarily from the State of Ohio, as by the mid-1960s, the city could no longer adequately maintain and improve the university. In 1967, the University of Cincinnati became affiliated with the state university system, thus ending its status as one of the oldest and largest municipal universities in the country.

On July 1, 1977, the University of Cincinnati acquired full state university status and with that development, received building and improvement funds that enabled it to undertake eight major construction projects on the campus during the subsequent decade.

**Tour ends.**

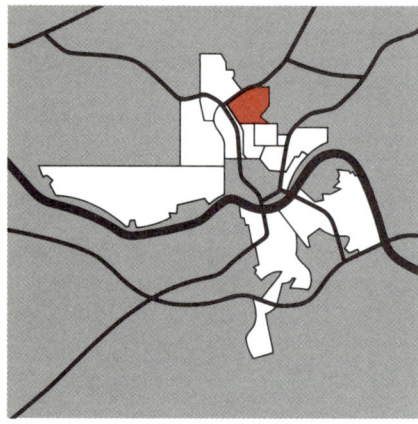

# Clifton

Before 1830, the area that would become Clifton was 1,200 acres of rough, wooded hillside in Millcreek Township, with poor soil on the hilltops. The Clifton area included the land between the Miami & Erie Canal (Central Parkway) on the west and north, Vine Street on the east, and a line along what later became Howell Avenue on the south. This property repeatedly changed hands among a number of land speculators who rented parts of their holdings to tenant farmers who generally worked the western and northern slopes of the hills. When the canal was opened in 1829, the small farmers and the few manufacturing enterprises at the base of the hills were able to transport their goods more easily. The hilltops of Clifton, however, remained mostly isolated and undeveloped.

In the 1830s, the deaths and bankruptcies of some of the speculators placed 500 acres—almost half of the total Clifton area—on the real estate market. Charles Clarkson bought the land and named his property Clifton Farm, from which the suburb eventually took its name. Clarkson's purchase was financed largely by the Lafayette Bank whose chief cashier, William G. T. Gano, also acquired land in that vicinity between 1838 and 1844.

Gano encouraged his friends and business associates to make similar purchases. Unlike earlier speculators, these men bought property with the intention of living on it, at least during the summer months when wealthy Cincinnatians tried to escape the heat, noise, dirt, disease, and crowding of the central city. Because of the limited agricultural and commercial value of the land atop the hills of Clifton, these businessmen were able to accumulate large "parks" and estates there.

*The Clifton area was isolated and largely undeveloped until wealthy Cincinnati businessmen established country estates like Batterberry, which stove manufacturer Reuben Resor built.*

Gano was one of the first of this group to begin living in Clifton year-round. During the 1840s and 1850s, a contingent of other bankers and merchants, interrelated by marriage and economic interests, also moved their families to the area. Some of them built new homes, while others expanded or improved their summer houses.

The area, which by that time had come to be called Clifton, rapidly gained acceptance among Cincinnati's elite as a desirable place to live; property values increased dramatically. More land became available following the Lafayette Bank's foreclosure on Clarkson in 1842, and many large impressive homes were constructed on the spacious lots created by the subdivision of his Clifton Farm. A distinct, new "suburban" style of architecture and landscaping developed for these estates. Clifton mansions were designed specifically for their suburban setting and emphasized their owners' status as men who were "of the city, but not in it."

By 1850, the suburb was populous enough to require certain services, and Clifton was incorporated as a village. Village government was organized and dominated by representatives of the elite residents. In addition to enabling the community to establish a school and to provide police and fire protection, incorporation also allowed property owners to pass ordinances designed to keep Clifton the sort of neighborhood they wanted it to be.

The City of Cincinnati posed a major threat to local control of Clifton. During the late 1860s, City Council discussed the possibility of annexing this and several other suburbs. Council realized that the migration of people and businesses beyond the city's borders reduced its tax base and altered its population statistics, making Cincinnati appear less dynamic and economically competitive than it actually was. People living in unincorporated areas adjacent to Cincinnati were generally receptive to annexation and the promise of improved public services that annexation offered. But the residents of incorporated villages such as Clifton felt that they had nothing to gain and much to lose by such a union.

In 1870, the Ohio General Assembly amended a law to make annexation contingent upon a majority vote in favor of the move by the combined electorate of all the territory that Cincinnati was attempting to annex. In an election held that spring, the votes from communities that did not desire annexation were counted together with votes from those that did. The annexation measure was approved by a small margin, and it appeared that a large area including Clifton, Avondale, and Cumminsville was about to become part of the city. However, opponents of annexation from these and other communities initiated a legal battle that resulted in the Supreme Court of Ohio declaring the 1870 annexation law unconstitutional.

Yet even with lawsuits and ordinances, Clifton could not prevent change. Gradually, the type of people drawn to the neighborhood changed, and this affected the character of the village. Most of the first group of wealthy residents were merchants or bankers. But the second wave of Cincinnati's elite that arrived between the late 1850s and the 1870s were primarily manufacturers, and many were foreign born. Some of these men built the monumental houses for which Clifton is noted. George Schoenberger, Robert Bowler, Henry Probasco, and William Neff,

*By the early twentieth century, the community focal point of Clifton had shifted to the Ludlow Avenue business district where the streetcar line was located.*

builders of the "castles" on Lafayette Avenue, were known as the "barons of Mt. Storm."

With the development of public transportation and the division of some of the large estates into smaller lots, yet another type of resident, somewhat less affluent, came to Clifton. Many were salaried people who worked in businesses downtown, and they relied on the streetcar lines that gradually pushed into Clifton during the late 1880s and 1890s. Large apartment buildings began to appear along the routes where a business strip also began to evolve, particularly on Ludlow Avenue. By the time annexation to Cincinnati finally took place in 1896 and more streetcar lines were laid into Clifton, the area's isolation completely ended.

Cincinnati's acquisition of Clifton had been made possible by the passage of a new state law in 1893. This legislation, known as the Lillard Law, allowed annexation to be determined by a combined vote of the annexing municipality and the area being annexed. This gave the advantage to the larger of the two communities. Cincinnati again sought to add Clifton to its territory, and despite residents' continued opposition, the village lost its independent status. In 1896, an annexation agreement was reached under which Cincinnati took responsibility for the village's debts and agreed to maintain certain services and amenities for Clifton residents.

Although some members of the social elite remained in Clifton, by the early twentieth century, they were no longer the dominant force in shaping the character of the community. More of the huge estates were subdivided, some of the large homes were torn down, and others were converted to different uses. The orientation of the neighborhood shifted south, away from the big houses north of McAlpin Street to the Ludlow Avenue business district.

The first two decades of the twentieth century saw a boom in the creation of smaller lots and the construction of multi-unit housing that attracted an increasingly diverse group of residents, including many Catholics and people associated with the university and nearby hospitals. But Clifton continued to attract some middle and upper middle-income people as well. These individuals were generally a more socially and politically liberal group than their nineteenth century predecessors, but like them, they worked to maintain the "village" character of the neighborhood.

By the mid-twentieth century, preservation of the suburb's unique identity and appearance increasingly became a concern for many of the people who lived there. Some residents felt that Clifton's special character was threatened in the 1950s and 1960s by the city's plans to install better lighting and make street improvements. Unlike adjacent neighborhoods such as Corryville, where the expansion of public institutions and widening of streets brought about the demolition of local landmarks and hundreds of homes, Clifton was able to lessen the impact of these changes through the efforts of a strong civic group formed in 1961, the Clifton Town Meeting.

In addition to its concerned and well-organized residents, Clifton had advantages over other neighborhoods that helped it maintain its character. The automobile and large institutions had less of a physical effect upon Clifton than they did in neighboring Clifton Heights and Corryville. Clifton's larger building lots and the wider, more level streets were better suited to cars and parking facilities, so relatively little housing had to be sacrificed.

Clifton also avoided the destruction of residential blocks that afflicted other nearby communities because of its greater distance from the large institutions and the fact that the institutions that did settle in the immediate vicinity were generally small or medium-sized. In some cases, organizations that bought Clifton property were able to adapt the large old mansions for their use, rather than demolishing them.

Fueled by a sense of nostalgia and the appeal of what survives of the neighborhood's nineteenth-century character, area residents have continued to foster that sense of separate community identity and to preserve many of the physical elements that help make Clifton's identity visible and unique.

*Turn-of-the-century apartment buildings like the Roanoke displayed architectural detail commonly found on private homes of the period.*

Clifton

Tour Length
7 miles

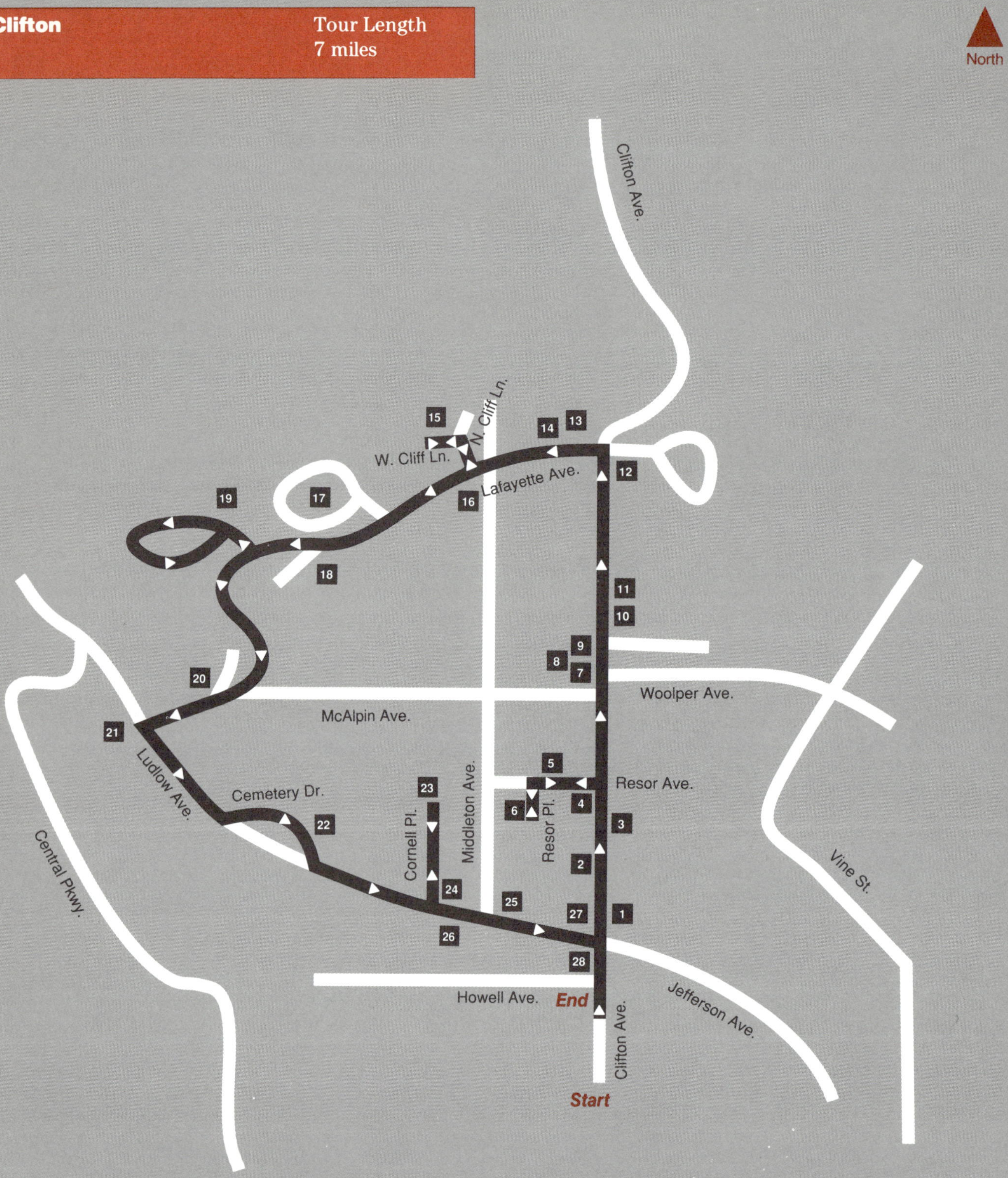

North
Clifton Ave.
N. Cliff Ln.
W. Cliff Ln.
Lafayette Ave.
Woolper Ave.
McAlpin Ave.
Resor Ave.
Ludlow Ave.
Cemetery Dr.
Cornell Pl.
Middleton Ave.
Resor Pl.
Central Pkwy.
Vine St.
Howell Ave.
End
Jefferson Ave.
Clifton Ave.
Start
1
2
3
4
5
6
7
8
9
10
11
12
13
14
15
16
17
18
19
20
21
22
23
24
25
26
27
28

# Tour 12

▶ ▶ ▶ ▶ ▶ ▶

# Clifton

**Tour begins on Clifton Avenue at Ludlow and Jefferson Avenues. Drive north on Clifton Avenue.**

The few Methodists who lived in Clifton in the mid-nineteenth century had to travel downtown to attend services. Later, circuit ministers led worship in the homes of various families. The congregation that would build the Gothic style **1 Clifton United Methodist Church,** 3416 Clifton Avenue, was organized on March 7, 1890.

One member, Dr. William B. Davis, donated the lot where the new church was to stand, and publisher Obed J. Wilson and his wife, also members, gave funds to cover half the construction costs. Ground was broken on November 15, 1891, and the thirty-seven founding members met for the first service in the completed building on November 20, 1892.

The Wilson family continued its support of the church with gifts of the first organ and the windows on the west wall. The Good Samaritan memorial window on the east wall of the sanctuary came from the studios of Louis Tiffany.

Adult membership grew slowly, but enough high school and university students were attracted to prompt the formation of an Epworth League. The university students formed their own group, the Wesley Foundation Unit, in 1929.

The church underwent periodic remodeling and refurbishing, and an educational wing was added in 1961.

Clifton United Methodist has continued its service to the increasingly diverse community. In the 1970s, it hosted a Korean congregation—now in its own building on West McMillan—and in the 1980s, held Sunday School classes for Cambodian immigrants. During 1985-1987, stone buttresses with an iron framework were constructed to support the front wall of the church.

**2 Immanuel Presbyterian Church,** 3445 Clifton Avenue, was also founded by residents of the new suburb who wanted to worship in their neighborhood and not have to travel to Mt. Auburn or downtown.

Presbyterian Sunday school classes for children were organized in

*The Resor Academy building served not only as a school, town hall, and firehouse, but also as a meeting place for the Immanuel Presbyterian congregation until they erected a church of their own.*

1879 and held in the Town Council chamber in the Resor Academy building. As more and more adults joined the children, Lane Seminary in Walnut Hills sent a student to lead Bible classes. Subsequently, the lot at the southwest corner of Clifton and Bryant Avenues was purchased.

The first church building, a Gothic style stone structure, was dedicated Easter Sunday, April 5, 1885. The original chancel and sanctuary were about half their present size, and the bell tower was topped with a steeple.

The outbreak of World War I caused a temporary split between those who held to the traditional gospel of peace and those who supported the war effort. After the war, the division was healed, and plans were drawn to enlarge the church. The first service in the completed building with additional memorial windows, new organ, and tower chimes, was held January 16, 1927. Thirty years later, the congregation broke ground for a modern classroom addition that was completed in 1959.

Inside the church are fourteen stained glass memorial windows, including three given by the family of George Washington McAlpin (1827-1890), founder of the local department store chain. In the front of the sanctuary is a glass mosaic depicting the Resurrection, also given in memory of McAlpin.

The former **3 Home of Sir Alfred T. Goshorn,** 3540 Clifton Avenue, was the residence of Cincinnati's only genuine knight. This 3-story Romanesque style mansion with a tiled gambrel roof was built in 1888 and designed by Cincinnati architect James McLaughlin. It featured a sky-lit art gallery and gold-plated chandelier.

Alfred Trabor Goshorn (1833-1902), president of a paint manufacturing company, became known as the "father" of the Cincinnati Industrial Expositions, which were held almost every year from 1870 to 1888 to encourage invention and trade. The Expositions enlightened the public with examples of the progress of art and technology, and demonstrated that Cincinnati was a national center of music, art, and industry.

The Expositions also drew exhibitors from other states. Visitors could see thousands of items including steam-powered machinery, furniture, fossils, clothing, medical preparations, wine, paintings, and, beginning in the 1880s, colossal historical pageants that were afterwards purchased and taken on tour by circuses. Music Hall and its several wings were built, in part, to give the Industrial Expositions a permanent site.

In 1873, Goshorn became the Ohio Commissioner to the International Centennial Exposition of the United States of America that was to be held in Philadelphia in 1876. Because of his experience in Cincinnati, Goshorn was elected director-general of the international event.

For his work at the Centennial Exposition, Goshorn was knighted by Queen Victoria (an honor he was able to accept by a special act of Congress). In addition, he was honored by numerous states, and decorated by several countries including Belgium, France, Japan, Norway, Russia, Spain, and Turkey.

A civic booster par excellence, Goshorn was also vice-president of the College of Music, first director of the Cincinnati Art Museum, mayor of Clifton, and a city councilman.

Goshorn's home was entered in the National Register of Historic Places in May 1972.

While most of Clifton's earlier and more affluent residents tended to worship in Protestant congregations, many of the families that moved to the neighborhood in the late nineteenth and early twentieth centuries were Roman Catholics. The **4 Church of the Annunciation of the Blessed Virgin Mary,** 3547 Clifton Avenue, was built by the parish created in 1910 for Clifton families who, until then, had to attend one or another of six nearby Catholic churches.

Services were held in the Martin Building on Ludlow Avenue until the following year when the Theodore Cook estate was purchased from the Sisters of Charity. The nuns had been using the Cook home for a temporary hospital during the construction of the first Good Samaritan Hospital buildings.

Theodore Cook (1833-1894) had been a partner in a business that sold steamboat equipment and supplies, and eventually Cook acquired considerable holdings in shipping companies. Later, he became the first president of the Cincinnati Southern Railroad and, after retiring, purchased and developed land in Clifton.

Cook's home was razed, and the present limestone Greek Revival style church, designed by Boston architect Edward T. P. Graham, was dedicated on October 18, 1931. The church facade is dominated by the portico with six fluted Ionic columns. Columns also line the walls of the church's interior, which features stained glass windows and a brightly painted domed ceiling above the main altar. There is an adjacent elementary school and rectory.

**Turn left on Resor Avenue.**

The modern style **5 St. John's Unitarian Church,** 320 Resor Avenue, traces its history to 1814 when a Moravian missionary organized many of the city's German Protestants and Catholics into a single German-language congregation, the German Evangelical Lutheran and Reformed Church. This was the first German congregation in the city and was not affiliated with any denomination until joining the American Unitarian Association in 1924.

In 1946, the congregation voted to sell its building at Twelfth and Elm Streets, where it had met since 1867, and moved out of the deteriorating Over-the-Rhine neighborhood to Clifton. For the next several years, worship services and Sunday school classes were held in the Hanselmann Masonic Temple on Clifton Avenue.

The building lot, donated by a member of St. John's, was the site of the home of Captain Robert Hosea (1811-1906). Hosea was a steamboat builder and pilot, and later a wholesale grocer.

Dedication ceremonies for the first part of the new church were held November 23, 1952. The sanctuary was begun in 1959. Architect John Garber called its design "heliocentric" because the changing patterns of sunlight were to be an integral part of the room. Garber also designed the organ to be perfectly sized for the sanctuary. Other rooms in the building are named to honor Mahatma Gandhi, Susan B. Anthony, and past ministers.

During recent years, St. John's has become known for its annual Renaissance Festival where costumed participants celebrate that period's music and cuisine, and for opening its doors to a variety of social and cultural groups.

**Turn left on Resor Place.**

Wealthy stove manufacturer Reuben Resor built Hosea's house and another home on the Clifton street named for him. **6 Batterberry,** 3553 Resor Place, a 2-story frame house with a 3-story tower, was constructed completely around the original 3-room cottage Resor had erected for his mother. Resor's grandest effort was the Italianate style Manor House on Cornell Place, atop the hill to the west. Resor Avenue was once the private drive to that estate.

Batterberry has been subdivided into apartments and is surrounded by houses of more modest size built in the 1920s.

**Return to Clifton Avenue and turn left.**

**7 Clifton Multi-Age Intermediate School,** 3711 Clifton Avenue, became part of the Cincinnati public school system after annexation in 1896. One of the conditions Clifton residents asked for was that the Clifton Public School be maintained exclusively for the children of Clifton. The City of Cincinnati refused and was upheld by the courts on this matter, as it was in its rejection of the village's demand for night policemen.

The first Clifton school is said to have been a log cabin located at the northeast corner of Clifton and Lafayette Avenues. Ten years later, William Resor, Reuben Resor's brother and business partner, offered to finance the construction of a new school if the village could obtain an appropriate lot. This site was purchased, and the 2-story Resor School of Clifton was built. The school, which included a public hall, became the center for the community. Outside was a pen where the village marshal incarcerated wandering hogs and other stray livestock.

By 1868, Resor School was inadequate for the community's needs. A group of residents incorporated as the Resor Academy and Literary Institute of Clifton and erected the brick Italianate style Resor Academy, opened in October 1870. The corporation leased rooms in the building to the Village of Clifton for a public hall and council offices, and the Village sublet classrooms to the Clifton Board of Education.

Resor Academy was demolished for the Clifton Public School, a 3-story buff brick building with a clock tower, which opened in 1906. It was designed by E. H. Dornette, the architect for a number of Cincinnati schools.

The newer Clifton Primary School,

3645 Clifton Avenue, stands on the site of another of the area's palatial homes, a 3-story stone mansion that Alexander McDonald (1833-1910), a Scottish immigrant and partner of John D. Rockefeller, built around 1870. McDonald, who began his career as a starch manufacturer and commission merchant, rose to become president of Standard Oil of Kentucky, a director of two railroads and the Third National Bank, and a trustee of the Cincinnati College of Music and the Children's Home. His 35-room home featured handcarved cherry woodwork, a wine cellar, and pool; the ballroom wing, added in 1895, included a built-in pipe organ. The McDonald carriage house still stands behind the school.

In 1920, George R. Balch (1862-1932), president of the Cincinnati Realty Company and treasurer of the Cincinnati, Hamilton & Dayton Railroad, bought McDonald's home. His initial, "B", can be seen in the wrought iron gates on the rear drive. Balch's widow willed the home to the Episcopal Diocese of Southern Ohio, which sold it in 1958 to the Cincinnati Board of Education for use as a school for the handicapped. This plan was not realized, and the mansion was torn down in 1961 to make way for the present building.

Renovation of the old school and the addition of the Clifton Community Recreation Center buildings behind it were completed in 1977. A Rookwood drinking fountain and other elements of the old structure were preserved and incorporated into the new scheme. The grand stairway was removed, however, and the area filled with the cafeteria, library, and auditorium. Architects Richard Tweddell

*When Clifton mayor Henry Probasco donated this fountain to the village in 1887, it was placed near the Resor Academy at what was then the center of the village.*

& Associates' work here won the 1977 Miami Purchase Association Award for Historic Preservation.

In 1987, Clifton schools enrolled approximately 631 students, grades K-6, grouped in classes according to ability. It has a computer lab, a program for hearing-impaired youngsters, and an English as a Second Language program that served primarily the children of Asian immigrants.

Another of the annexation provisions that Clifton demanded was that the city should take over and maintain the **8 Probasco Fountain,** which stands in front of the school. Cincinnati architect Samuel Hannaford designed the 10-foot tall granite and bronze piece which Henry Probasco, successful hardware merchant and then-mayor of Clifton, formally presented on July 9, 1887.

As the inscription on the bronze tablet suggests, the fountain was intended to be a drinking fountain. Passers-by used a dipper that hung here, horses drank from the lower basin, and side bowls at ground level provided water for thirsty dogs. The dome of the fountain is decorated with a chrysanthemum motif.

The Probasco Fountain was renovated and cleaned in 1974, and lights and new plumbing were installed.

That two historic houses on Clifton Avenue are both referred to as the **9 Rawson Home** suggests the extent of the family fortune amassed by Joseph Rawson (1808-1891) after he arrived in Cincinnati from Massachusetts in 1831. Rawson began work as a clerk and then became a member of a meatpacking firm on Sycamore Street in 1836. When the founding partners retired twenty years later, the business became Joseph Rawson & Company.

The 3-story painted brick Italian

Villa style house, 3767 Clifton Avenue, had been built in the late 1860s for John L. Wayne, Jr., who, like Henry Probasco, had made his money in hardware and cutlery. Rawson bought the estate around 1876 and acquired fifty acres of land to the west. The house was entered in the National Register of Historic Places in August 1973.

Rawson's three sons—Warren, Edward, and Joseph, Jr.,—entered their father's business and expanded into banking, real estate, insurance, and the manufacture of chemicals. In 1886, Edward moved from Mt. Auburn into the 2½-story stucco farmhouse, one door to the south of his father's home at 3737 Clifton Avenue. That residence had been built around 1865.

Edward's daughters, Marion (1899-1980) and Dorothy (c.1892-1977), both known throughout the city for their support of cultural institutions, resided here. Marion Rawson participated in the University of Cincinnati-sponsored expedition headed by Dr. Carl W. Blegen (1887-1971) that uncovered the palace of Nestor in Greece and in another UC dig at Troy. Long after Clifton was a settled suburb, the six acres surrounding this Rawson house were still cultivated as a truck farm.

In 1925 and 1928, the Rawson family donated ten and one-half acres of the old farm for the Rawson Woods Bird Preserve, Middleton Avenue at McAlpin Avenue, a bird sanctuary maintained by the city. Another part of the old farm is now a subdivision; its streets are named after the original landowners.

In the mid-1840s, stove manufacturer William Resor (1810- 1974) erected his home, the 3-story **10 Greendale,** 254 Greendale Avenue, on twelve acres of his holdings which originally ran north of Woolper Avenue from Clifton Avenue to Carthage Pike (Vine Street). The estate was subdivided in 1893, and Greendale Avenue—taking its name from the estate—was extended to Vine Street.

Resor, who essentially financed the construction of the Resor Academy (1854), also helped found the Cincinnati Art Museum and the zoo.

Completed in 1867, the limestone Gothic Revival **11 Calvary Episcopal Church,** 3766 Clifton Avenue, was quite different from the frame school-

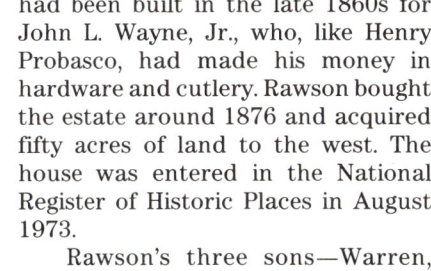

223

*Many of the village's most prominent nineteenth-century residents belonged to Calvary Episcopal Church.*

house where the Right Reverend Charles Pettit McIlvaine (1799-1873), the second Episcopal Bishop of Ohio, had held services in 1847.

In 1848, the 2-story frame Clifton Chapel was built on the northwestern corner of Clifton and Lafayette Avenues. Because the area was still only sparsely settled, the chapel was nondenominational; ministers from various churches led afternoon services. When the state granted a charter to the Incorporated Town of Clifton on March 23, 1850, the notice was reportedly posted here. Eighteen men cast votes in the basement of the chapel in the first election.

In 1856, seventeen communicants signed an agreement to form the Parish of Calvary Church. A lot was purchased from William Resor in 1866, and Henry Probasco, George K. Schoenberger, and Seth C. Foster were elected to the building committee. William Tinsley, who had designed Probasco's home, was the architect for the new church; Francis Pedretti, Probasco's artist-in-residence, frescoed the sanctuary. Probasco and his wife donated the tower and bell in memory of Tyler Davidson, Probasco's brother-in-law and business partner. Bishop McIlvaine consecrated the church on May 5, 1868.

Calvary bought the adjoining lot in 1881, and the brick house there served as a rectory until 1913 when the present stone pastor's residence was completed. The attached chapel was built in 1888 and enlarged five

years later according to plans by Samuel Hannaford. The marble floor installed in 1911 came from the Robert Bowler residence, which had stood on the land that is now Mt. Storm Park.

Calvary Church's parish hall was completed in 1926, and the Children's Chapel in 1937. Two sets of electronic bells were dedicated in 1948. Eleven of Calvary's memorial stained glass windows are from Louis Tiffany's studios. The church was listed on the National Register of Historic Places in January 1976.

When Calvary chose its new rector in 1980, Reverend Mary Chotard Doll became the first woman in the Diocese of Southern Ohio to hold that position.

The 2-story frame house at 3874 Clifton Avenue was built in 1843 and served briefly as the **12 Home of Robert Buchanan,** a cousin of President James Buchanan. Robert Buchanan (1797-1879) was among Clifton's pioneers who, like Gano, Reuben, and Resor, built summer homes in Clifton to escape the heat and the terrifying cholera epidemics of the basin. Buchanan made several additions to this structure; then, around 1848, he built a permanent home, Greenhills, at 230 Lafayette Circle.

Buchanan's business career and civic commitment were wide ranging. Before coming to Cincinnati in 1823, he was a partner in a grocery business and then captain of a steamboat that ran between Cincinnati and New Orleans. Buchanan set up a wholesale grocery business in this city and was also involved in porkpacking.

Robert Buchanan headed or served on the boards of several insurance companies and charitable institutions, and three cotton factories. He had substantial interests in several steamboats and, in partnership, operated the first factory in Cincinnati for making steam engines and sugar mills for Southern plantations.

For some years in the early twentieth century, the 2½-story stone Romanesque style mansion at 3901 Clifton Avenue was the **13 Home of John Uri Lloyd,** pharmacist, author, educator, and drug manufacturer. The house was designed by Cincinnatian James McLaughlin and built around 1885 for Solomon P. Kineon,

president of the Kineon Coal Company.

Lloyd (1849-1936) came from Kentucky at age fifteen to begin apprenticeships with a series of Cincinnati pharmacists. He became an adherent of eclectic medicine, which advocated the use of plant extracts rather than synthetic drugs for the treatment of illnesses. Around 1871, Lloyd took a position as laboratory manager with H. M. Merrell & Company, a Cincinnati pharmaceutical manufacturing firm. His two brothers, Nelson Ashley (1851-1925) and Curtis Gates (1859-1928), soon joined him there, and the business became their property in 1885. The Lloyd Brothers' plant at Court and Plum Streets at first produced drugs exclusively for the eclectics.

Lloyd wrote over 5,000 scientific works and a number of popular novels, including *Stringtown on the Pike, A Tale of Northern-most Kentucky* (1900). He and his brother Curtis began a collection of pharmaceutical and botanical books that evolved into the internationally-recognized Lloyd Library, 917 Plum Street. The library's holdings include a 1493 volume that is the first pharmaceutical book ever set in type.

Lloyd taught chemistry at the Eclectic Medical College and pharmacology at the Cincinnati College of Pharmacy (later affiliated with the University of Cincinnati). His death in 1936 was formally noted as far away as Japan.

**Turn left on Lafayette Avenue.**

In the 1960s, construction of I-71 forced **14 The Cincinnati Woman's Club** to move from its Oak Street clubhouse, opened in 1910, to this 2-level red brick building, 330 Lafayette Avenue. This 1966 clubhouse occupies the site of Sunflower Place, a 3-story red brick mansion decorated with sunflower motifs that was the home of George Washington McAlpin (1826-1890), head of the local department store chain and the man for whom McAlpin Avenue (in Clifton) is named.

The Cincinnati Woman's Club was founded by seven Cincinnati women who, spurred by the success of the Cincinnati Room in the Ohio Building at the Chicago World's Fair of 1893, met to form what its articles of incorporation later defined as "an organized center of thought and action among women for the promotion of social, educational, literary and artistic growth, and whatever relates to the best interests of the city." The first meeting was held on March 26, 1894.

Late nineteenth-century theories held that biology fixed character and ability. Women, therefore, were "natural" mothers; their appropriate role in the life of the community was related to caring for children and the less fortunate, and developing the arts.

The concerns and accomplishments of Cincinnati Woman's Club were and have remained largely traditional. The club began setting up playgrounds in 1897, started a "penny luncheon" program in the schools in 1911, and erected the first community Christmas tree on Government Square in 1913. Club members were involved in the Anti-Tuberculosis League and the Smoke Abatement League (concerned with pollution).

**Turn right on North Cliff Lane, left on West Cliff Lane.**

Preeminent among the mansions of the "barons of Mt. Storm" is Oakwood, the **15 Home of Henry Probasco,** 430 West Cliff Lane, constructed between 1859 and 1865 at a cost of $500,000. This imposing sandstone and limestone castle was designed by William Tinsley (b.1804) in the Norman Romanesque style. No simple retreat, Probasco's home was built to convey the owner's position, wealth, and power.

The 20-acre estate had formal gardens, a rosarium with 4,000 rose bushes, and exotic trees and shrubs from as far away as the Himalayas. The mansion has a ceiling frescoed by the well-known artist Francis Pedretti, an octagonal second floor hall with minstrels' gallery, and carved marble fireplaces. But perhaps foremost is the hand-carved woodwork. The circular staircase that rose to the second floor from the grand hall was carved over a period of three years by William and Henry Fry, though the work is frequently attributed to Benn Pitman. No single design is repeated in these carvings.

Henry Probasco (1820-1902) came to Cincinnati in 1835 and began work as a clerk with Tyler Davidson & Company, a hardware business. Probasco married Davidson's half-sister, Julia Carrington, and became a partner in the flourishing company. In 1866, Davidson died and Probasco sold the firm. He gave the Tyler Davidson Fountain to the city in memory of his brother-in-law in 1871; Tinsley designed the original esplanade.

From 1877 to 1888, Henry Probasco served as mayor of Clifton, opposing annexation which came at last in 1896.

Probasco suffered serious financial losses, and in 1887 sold his collection of rare books and manuscripts, including a Shakespeare First Folio, to the Newberry Library in Chicago. Oakwood was sold for $60,000 in 1899 and then underwent a remodeling during which the Frys returned to carve additional woodwork. Until his death in 1902, Probasco lived in a smaller house in Clifton and earned a modest salary as superintendent of Spring Grove Cemetery, which he had helped found.

This mansion has been a private residence except for the period 1923 to 1934 when, as Oakwood Institute,

*In the 1870s and 1880s, some property owners in Clifton called upon local architects to draw plans for increasingly elaborate houses; James McLaughlin designed Bishop's Place.*

it was a training school for women church workers. The grounds have been divided into building lots and are now reduced to approximately one and one-half acres.

**Return to Lafayette Avenue and turn right.**

In the 1840s, Bishop Charles McIlvaine of Calvary Episcopal Church built what a contemporary account described as a "comfortable mansion, free from ostentation" on the fourteen acres he owned in Clifton. After McIlvaine's death in 1873, Truman Bishop Handy (1829-1884), a prominent Cincinnati builder and contractor, bought the property and razed McIlvaine's home for a far less modest residence of his own.

James McLaughlin designed **16 Bishop's Place,** 429 Lafayette Avenue, which was begun about 1881. Handy died in 1884; the house was finished the following year. The 2½-story Chateauesque style stone mansion has a slate covered roof and turret, wrap-around porch, and protruding bay with two gargoyles atop the parapet.

Bishop's Place was the home of Frank L. Perin (1855-1947), who was engaged at various times as a successful maltster, commission merchant, and finally a manufacturer and jobber of flour and corn products. The Perins'

Front Elevation          Residence of Mr. T. B. Handy, Clifton

*Some large Clifton houses went through a variety of uses over the years. William Neff's home, The Windings, became a girls' school and is now being renovated as condominiums.*

daughter and her husband lived in the house until selling it to stove manufacturer Walter E. Huenefeld (1885-1964) in 1928. Huenefeld's widow gave the home to Bethesda-Scarlet Oaks Community to be used as housing for the elderly, but Bethesda chose to sell the property.

A realty company bought the mansion in late 1966, subdivided the grounds, and built four homes; Bishop's Place was put up for sale. A newspaper article noted that eighty tons of coal were required to heat the more than thirty rooms, and that the house had ten baths, a 3-room kitchen tiled even on the ceiling, a built-in refrigerator with nine doors, sterling silver light brackets, and brocade covered walls. Bishop's Place has remained a private, single-family residence.

The centerpiece of the Bethesda-Scarlet Oaks Retirement Community, 440 and 500 Lafayette Avenue, is Scarlet Oaks, the opulent limestone French-German Gothic style mansion that was originally the **17 Home of George K. Schoenberger**. Schoenberger (1809-1892), another of the "barons of Mt. Storm," came to Cincinnati in 1834 to establish a branch of his father's Pittsburgh iron business. He succeeded, made his fortune, and moved to Clifton.

Schoenberger bought forty-seven acres on Clifton's crown and sent architect James Keyes Wilson (1828-1894) to Europe to study the castles along the Rhine River for inspiration. Schoenberger also brought artisans from Europe to execute the carved woodwork and intricately patterned flooring. When criticized for indulging in such extravagance while the country was suffering a post-war recession, Schoenberger reportedly countered: "Think of all the people to whom I'm giving employment!"

Scarlet Oaks, named for the many oak trees that grew on the property, was completed in 1867 and cost $750,000, exclusive of furnishings. Some have suggested that Schoenberger became one of the prime movers in the development and landscaping of Spring Grove Cemetery, where his wife was later buried, in order to improve the view in the valley beneath his home. He is also said to have fed hundreds of crows, adding a romantic touch to the estate, as a sign of his mourning for his first wife.

Ernest H. Huenefeld, a prominent Cincinnati businessman and supporter of the German Methodist Church, bought Scarlet Oaks in 1908 and presented it to the Bethesda Methodist Deaconess Home for use as a hospital for the elderly. Lafayette Hall, a nursing home in the modern sense, was built nearby in 1918-1919.

The adjoining Scarlet Oaks Manor, a 112-room residential building, was dedicated in 1960, the Health Center in 1966, and additional apartments in 1975. The improved and restored Schoenberger mansion, listed on the National Register of Historic Places in 1973, now houses a chapel, library, beauty shop, craft and recreational facilities, drawing room, and a private dining room. The facility is nonsectarian.

In the 1980s, a private developer received permission from the City of Cincinnati to convert the four buildings that once comprised the Academy of the Sacred Heart, 525 Lafayette Avenue, into condominiums. The original and most notable structure on the property is The Windings, the former **18 Home of William Clifford Neff** who earned his fortune in porkpacking.

The Windings, built around 1868, is a massive limestone house of eclectic design with English Gothic elements. Architect Thomas Sargeant supposedly modeled the home after Kenilworth Castle in England. It is said that Swiss artisans spent two years carving the woodwork, mantels, and stairway. But the estate was so costly to maintain that Neff (1829-1890) could not afford to live there, and in 1876, The Windings became home to the Ladies of the Sacred Heart of Jesus and their Academy.

The first Academy of the Sacred Heart, a primary and secondary boarding school for Catholic and Protestant girls, had opened on West Sixth Street in 1869; in 1874, the Academy moved to Grandin Road. In October 1876, the Ladies of the Sacred Heart opened another school in Neff's castle in Clifton.

*The Catholic Telegraph* rhapsodized that the Academy's *"plan of instruction. . . united every advantage which can contribute to a solid and refined education. Particular attention is paid to the formation of Christian and lady-like manners, and to the cultivation of habits of neatness and order."* The annual charge for board and tuition was $200, thirty dollars more for laundry. Harp lessons cost eighty dollars extra, but there was "no charge for the French language which is universally spoken in the Institution."

A library (1882), chapel (1887) designed by Samuel Hannaford, and classroom and dormitory wing (1893) were eventually added. When the Academy acquired the adjacent Edgewood from the estate of Max Fleischmann (1877-1951), the college department, chartered in 1915, moved to that property. St. Madeleine's Hall, a classroom building, was erected in 1928-1929.

By 1933, the institution was feeling the effects of the Depression. Edgewood was closed, and the college program was discontinued in 1935.

The Academy of the Sacred Heart, which had 330 students as its maximum enrollment, graduated its last class in June 1970. Then, because the construction of a needed building could not be justified by the increasing operating deficit, the school was closed.

In 1972, the complex was sold to the Metropolitan Ministry of the United Methodist Church, which hoped to develop it as a facility for the care of the elderly. The nuns had offered the property for development as a park, but the Park Board could not raise the money. The following year, The Windings was entered in the National Register of Historic Places and the estate was sold to a mortgage banking firm. Talk began of developing multi-story apartment units in this area of single-family homes.

In 1974, the city bought the buildings and twenty-five surrounding acres for $500,000. It sold the home and a portion of the grounds to architect-developer John M. Kurak, Jr., who planned a condominium development that showcases the historic architecture.

Circle through Mt. Storm Park.

The Temple of Love in **19 Mt. Storm Park,** 700 Lafayette Avenue, is a remnant of an estate that was begun in 1844 when Robert Bonner Bowler, proprietor of the Kentucky Central Railroad, purchased approximately seventy-three acres of land from the Lafayette Bank. Bowler first built a small frame summer home,

*Mt. Storm Park was once the estate of Robert Bowler, but today the only structures from that estate that survive are the stables and the Temple of Love, seen at the left in this turn-of-the-century photograph.*

then, in 1846, deciding he liked the area, erected a 2-story brick residence that he named Mt. Storm. This permanent dwelling had a glass-roofed conservatory and, later, a square 4-story tower. Edward, Prince of Wales, visited Bowler's home in 1860; tradition holds that Charles Dickens attended one of the many lavish parties given there.

Adolph Strauch (1822-1883), a Prussian landscape gardener, had met Bowler in Europe. In 1852, while traveling in America, Strauch found himself stranded in Cincinnati. He called on Bowler and was persuaded to landscape this estate as well as those of other wealthy Clifton residents including Henry Probasco and George Schoenberger. Strauch also served as the superintendent of Spring Grove Cemetery.

Strauch is credited with designing the Temple of Love, a patterned dome supported by eight fluted iron columns on a stone base. The placement of ornaments on the landscape to create a "vista" was fashionable in the nineteenth century. The Temple, a copy of nothing in particular, reportedly stood over a reservoir that stored water pumped from the Miami & Erie Canal for use in the estate's many gardens and greenhouses.

In 1910, Bowler's heirs sold the estate to the city for a park. The mansion was razed around 1917, and in 1936, the stone shelterhouse designed by the firm of Samuel Hannaford & Sons was erected.

Turn right on Lafayette Avenue.

The Bowler estate's **20 Stables and Servants' Quarters,** 724 Lafayette Avenue, a 2-story U-shaped vernacular style brick building with a typical arched entrance to the stable-yard, is on the slope below the park. It has been remodeled into stylish condominiums.

Turn left on Ludlow Avenue.

**21 Cincinnati Technical College (CTC),** 3520 Central Parkway, is one of seventeen Ohio technical colleges and offers associate and certificate programs in health, business, mathematics, science, and engineering technologies. CTC, with day and evening courses, is one of the top ten cooperative technical colleges in the country and boasts a graduate placement rate of 99%.

The complex of buildings that CTC occupies opened in September 1953 as Central Vocational High School, a single campus where the Cincinnati public school system's five vocational high schools were consolidated. The Cincinnati firm of Harry Hake & Son designed the $10 million, 8-building complex which had a capacity of 3,000 students.

Central offered technical training for students intending to enroll in college engineering programs, intensive vocational training in a single occupational area, and short-term industrial training to prepare students who would leave school early to make a living. Central High graduates obtained the same number of academic credits as students in comprehensive high schools.

A wide range of skills were taught here: metalwork, woodworking, trowel trades, foundry work and heat treating, welding, auto and aircraft service, power sewing, trade embroidery, commercial food preparation, graphic arts, cosmetology, cabinet and pattern making, air conditioning, plumbing, and more. The Central High complex also included a gym, pool, and the Howard C. Trechter Stadium, named for the only Cincinnati teacher to be killed in World War II.

In 1966, the school was renamed Courter Technical High School to honor Dr. Claude V. Courter (1888-1964), superintendent of the public schools from 1937 to 1959, and the Cincinnati Cooperative School of Technology was established in a wing of the complex. CCST was a two-year, cooperative, post-graduate high school program that was founded by the State of Ohio to provide approximately 200 students with additional training and work experience in preparation for finding a job. It also encouraged some to pursue a college education.

The State of Ohio bought Courter Tech in June 1970. The Board of Education planned to use the $8.4 million from the sale, plus matching federal and state money, to erect vocational wings at several Cincinnati high schools, phasing out the facilities here. The system's vocational program was to be decentralized as it had been prior to the construction of Central High.

By 1974, the vocational programs were completely moved out of the Central complex, and the Cincinnati Technical Institute took over the institution. CTI was later renamed the Cincinnati State Technical College, and then given its present name.

**Turn left on Cemetery Drive.**

The history of the origins of the **22 Jewish Cemetery,** 730 Ludlow Avenue, one of five now under the management of the United Jewish Cemetery, sheds considerable light on the sort of community that early Clifton residents wanted to create and maintain.

The story goes that Charles and Rachel Kahn (no relation to the Kahns in the meatpacking business) planned to build a new house on this 3-acre site. But a self-appointed committee from the neighborhood visited Kahn at his home on Western Row (Central Avenue) and advised him that he and

*Many of the markers in the Jewish cemetery on Ludlow Avenue have inscriptions in Hebrew or German.*

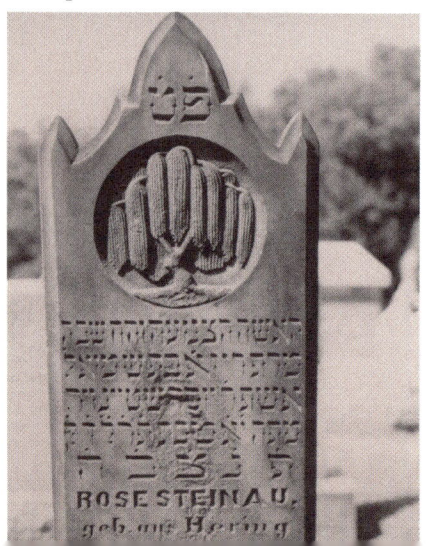

his family would certainly be happier some place other than Clifton. "Very well, gentlemen," Kahn is supposed to have replied, "if you do not care to have Jews living near you, you cannot object to dead Jews, and you shall have many of these for many years, in no condition to offend you."

On May 16, 1848, Kahn sold the property to the West End congregation Ahabeth Achim for a cemetery. The little daughter of Marcus Schoenberg was the first to be buried here, on May 1, 1850. The brick chapel in the cemetery was built in 1906.

In 1931, Ahabeth Achim merged with Wise Temple. Wise had co-founded the United Jewish Cemetery in 1850. This property was transferred to the United Jewish Cemetery on May 1, 1949.

Many of the markers on the approximately 1,850 graves record, in Hebrew or German, European birthplaces for those buried here.

**Turn left on Ludlow Avenue, left on Cornell Place.**

One of the most unusual residences in Clifton is Manor House, 3517-3519 Cornell Place. The former **23 Home of Reuben P. Resor** is a 2-story stucco building with Gothic-Italianate influences and a 3-story octagonal tower. Resor (d.1853), who inherited a stove manufacturing company his father had founded, built several homes in Clifton before erecting this mansion around 1846.

David Gibson (1813-1897), a commission merchant, owned the home next, then Seth Evans (1817-1890), a meatpacker and the man for whom Evanswood Street is named. In 1896, the Resor home became Miss E. Antoinette Ely's Clifton School for Young Ladies. Miss Ely's school was well known for its high academic standards; its College Preparatory Course fit students "for admission into any of the colleges open to women."

In 1900, this school was consolidated with Dr. George K. Bartholomew's equally swank English and Classical School for Young Ladies and Children, at Third and Lawrence Streets. Then suddenly, in 1920, the Clifton School closed without explanation. Since then, there have been persistent accounts of a ghost that inhabits the first floor of the old

mansion. Metaphysicists from the University of Cincinnati have been unable to explain the knocks, cries, footsteps, and unlocking doors.

Resor's 40-acre estate was divided into building lots in the 1850s, but only a few houses were built along Resor Avenue, once the private approach to Manor House from Clifton Avenue. Steps from Hedgerow Lane at the end of Resor Avenue lead up to the house, which has been subdivided into apartments.

**Return to Ludlow Avenue and turn left.**

The population of Clifton increased as streetcars and then automobiles opened this once distant and exclusive suburb. Builders tried to design apartment buildings that offered less expensive housing but still fit Clifton's image as a special residential area and had something of the appearance of a single-family dwelling. To accomplish this, architects borrowed forms and features from the nearby mansions and incorporated special details to suggest the structures were not public buildings.

The **24 Tudor Court Apartments,** 404-420 Ludlow Avenue and 3405-3419 Middleton Avenue, were built in the 1920s after multi-family dwellings had become more acceptable, so this structure needed less "disguising." The 4-story brick and stone building offers residents a tree-shaded courtyard that is lit by the same sort of round-globed boulevard lights that line Clifton Avenue.

The older **25 Roslyn Apartments,** 3404-3420 Middleton Avenue, are more elegantly detailed. Built around 1902, the massive 4-story painted brick and stone structure strongly resembles the imposing houses of Clifton's millionaires. The decorative brick work and porch columns with carved capitals suggest that the Roslyn was a fine residence.

Across the street, the **26 Roanoke Apartments** (circa 1900), 359 Ludlow Avenue, also reveals the architect's desire to make it look like a comfortable home. The U-shaped 3½-story brick and wood building has a central courtyard and wood-floored porches—a common setting for nineteenth-century socializing. A small entrance suggests a private home; there are protruding bays at the interior corners, individual porches, and porch columns that are different on each floor.

"*Clifton*," wrote Chamber of Commerce president Sidney D. Maxwell in 1870, "*is a purely suburban place. There is nothing of the town about it. There is neither store, grocery, mechanic's shop, nor saloon, and the whole place is so completely under the control of those who desire to keep it for country residence, that it must be many years before the general character of the place can change. Of course it will become more thickly settled . . . . until it will become less retired; but it will be among the last places about Cincinnati that will suffer from the encroachments of business.*"

Despite Maxwell's prediction, by the 1880s, the **27 Ludlow Avenue Business District,** which runs several blocks on either side of Clifton Avenue, was beginning to develop. In 1888, the Cincinnati Street Railway ran tracks along Ludlow, connecting Clifton with Fountain Square, and businesses opened along the streetcar routes. By 1896, a saloon, two groceries, drugstore, bakery, and candy manufacturer were established near the intersection of Clifton and Ludlow Avenues.

The number of businesses serving Clifton residents, the students and faculty from the nearby universities and hospitals, and those who traveled through the area on their way to and from work, continued to grow. By the mid-1920s, there were nearly forty establishments on Ludlow between Ormond and Brookline Avenues, including five groceries, four pharmacies, four dry cleaners, a beauty parlor, barber shop, library, fruit market, tailor's shop, confectionery, hardware, real estate office, and cigar store. The Ludlow Garage, 342-346, was built in 1924; it held 125 cars and had an "auto laundry."

Yet Maxwell's belief that Clifton's residential character would not be lost to commercial development has proven accurate to a certain degree. Over the years, the number of businesses has remained at or below forty, though the type of enterprise has changed. A movie theater, wine and cheese shop, organic foods store, Indian foods market, gift shops, and video tape rental store have operated here alongside the hardware, restaurants, and dry cleaners.

Several businesses are long-time residents of the street: Stier's Pharmacy, Adrian's Flower shop, and the Virginia Bakery. Adrian's, at 302, occupies the building that was originally Adolph Meyer's general store—the initials "AM" are carved on a shield on the corner of the building. The Smith-Andrews stables once occupied part of the northeast corner of the intersection where Clifton Cab and Virginia Bakery now stand.

The Ludlow Avenue district has remained an active and attractive location, although there is little prospect of further expansion. The business district is bounded by Burnet Woods and valuable residential properties, and the stores on Vine Street in nearby Corryville provide many of the services not available here. Further, parking in this area is quite limited; while one parking lot has been created, demolition of old houses to create additional lots is unlikely. Finally, Clifton residents are determined to preserve the character of this portion of their community, to prevent it from expanding further or taking on the appearance of a "strip" development.

The **28 Firehouse of Engine Company No. 34,** 301 Ludlow Avenue, is one of the city's oldest fire department buildings still in active service, but it was not the first firehouse to be located in Clifton. When Clifton was an independent village, its volunteer fire company was housed in a bay at the Resor Academy at Clifton and McAlpin Avenues. After Cincinnati annexed Clifton in 1896, it took control of the fire company's quarters and equipment and made two of the former village firefighters paid employees of the city fire department.

This process followed the usual pattern for providing public services in annexed areas. City government generally could not afford to make many immediate improvements but usually were able to maintain existing services. Engine Company 34, set up in 1896, provided Clifton with the protection of a two-man company with one hose wagon, and a firehouse with no living quarters. This complement, however adequate for a rural village, could not provide sufficient protection for the suburban community that Clifton was becoming.

Nevertheless, Engine 34 did not change until 1906. In that year, revenues from a major bond issue enabled the city to upgrade fire protection for a number of the communities that had been annexed over the previous decade. The Clifton fire company was expanded to eight men and equipped with an Ahrens steam fire engine. Together with Ladder Company No. 11, Engine 34 was moved to a new building designed by architect Harry Hake. Because of Hake's support of the local Republican party, this was one of many such commissions he received from the city around that time.

Like many of the early twentieth-century firehouses in Cincinnati, the new Clifton firehouse was designed to be consistent with the architecture of the surrounding neighborhood. The elegance of the Clifton area was reflected in the elaborate detailing of the station, which otherwise was a conventional city firehouse.

The location of the new firehouse reflected the changing orientation of the community. The old house in Resor Academy had been situated to serve the Clifton of the later nineteenth century which centered around the large homes in the northern and central portions of the village. Placing the new firehouse at Clifton and Ludlow was an acknowledgment that the focal point of the community had shifted south to the Ludlow Avenue business district with its apartment houses and stores. The site was also closer to the growing University of Cincinnati.

The company has survived primarily because of the university. While other old suburban companies have been disbanded or moved, especially after motorization, Engine Company 34, which was motorized around 1920, was kept in place to insure prompt and adequate response to emergencies at UC.

**Tour ends.**

229

# Tour 13

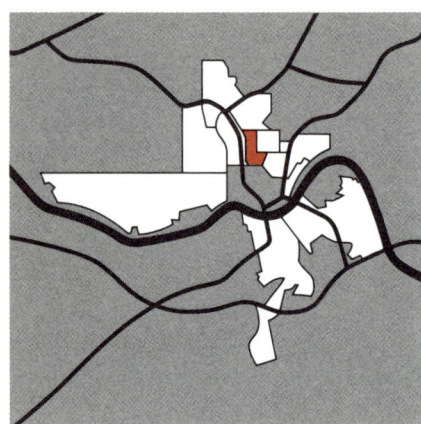

# Fairview - Clifton Heights

Historically, the neighborhoods of Fairview and Clifton Heights have had vague and shifting boundaries and today are often identified as part of Clifton. In fact, these two areas were originally distinct suburban communities which developed in different ways and at different times than the adjoining villages of Clifton and Corryville. Furthermore, since the early twentieth century, their residents have maintained and sought to foster separate community identities.

Situated on the southwestern portion of the steep hills immediately north of Over-the-Rhine, Fairview and Clifton Heights were unincorporated areas of Millcreek Township in the first half of the nineteenth century. Before the 1860s, Colonel John Riddle (1760-1847), a veteran of the Indian wars and the War of 1812, was the largest single landowner here. This land was organized into large "farms," even though the terrain was relatively unsuitable for agriculture. And because the steep hillsides made the area difficult to reach from the basin, the Clifton Heights and Fairview areas were very thinly populated. The only significant commercial activity was some small-scale truck farming and a stone quarry on the hillside below what is now Fairview Park.

This southwestern portion of the hills came to be regarded as two separate areas primarily because it was not all annexed to the City of Cincinnati at the same time. The land that was to become Fairview was included in the Special Road District of Millcreek Township which Cincinnati annexed in 1849. Clifton Heights was annexed along with Camp Washington on May 9, 1870.

Bounded by Vine Street on the east, McMillan and Straight Streets on the north, the Miami & Erie Canal (Central Parkway) on the west, and Emming Street and Clifton Avenue on the south, Fairview was originally called Riddle's Hill. In the late 1860s, Fairview came into use. The name was taken from Fairview Avenue, built around 1856, and named because the hilltop did provide a fine view of the basin and the lower Mill Creek Valley.

Clifton Heights consisted of the property lying between the Miami & Erie Canal on the west, Straight Street on the south, Clifton Avenue on the east, and Howell Avenue on the north. In the early 1850s, the land was subdivided for residential development. It was referred to as Clifton Heights to create a positive association in the minds of potential buyers with the Village of Clifton immediately to the north and already one of Cincinnati's most desirable suburbs. However, the smaller and cheaper lots in Clifton Heights were designed to attract the less affluent.

This area remained largely undeveloped until the early twentieth century. While Clifton residents could rely on streetcars, lines were not extended into Clifton Heights until 1894. In addition, Clifton Heights lacked the basic services that were available in other parts of the city or incorporated villages such as Clifton. Even though Clifton Heights was annexed in 1870, most of the area remained without services such as water and gas lines, sewers, and improved streets until the late 1890s.

Fairview developed more quickly than Clifton Heights because its public services were put in place sooner. The Bellevue Incline, scaling the hillside from Clifton Avenue to Ohio Avenue, opened in 1876 and made the eastern portion of Fairview accessible from the basin. Homes went up along those streets close to the incline and to the streetcar line that ran from the upper terminus. But the larger part of Fairview

*Visitors to the "resort" at the upper terminus of the Bellevue incline could enjoy the view and products from the brewery, shown in the foreground, that was owned by Fairview resident Christian Moerlein.*

which lay to the west remained unpopulated.

Because of the excellent view and the fact that Fairview offered the cheapest undeveloped land close to the basin, a group of speculators related by marriage, business, and political ties, began purchasing large tracts here in the 1870s and 1880s as the estates of the original owners were broken up. The largest sections, including much of the former Riddle farm, were acquired by lawyer and politician Isaac J. Miller (1833-1910) who had moved to Fairview around 1866. Besides Miller, brewer Christian Moerlein and his son-in-law, John Goetz, Jr., law partners Gustav Tafel and Francis Lampe, Dr. Massilon Cassat, and hat manufacturer Phillip Volkert built homes and invested in land in western Fairview and the extreme southern portion of Clifton Heights.

This property became more desirable after the Cincinnati Street Railway Company built the Fairview Incline in 1892-1894 on land obtained from Isaac Miller. The incline, which ran from McMicken Avenue to Fairview Avenue, opened the western part of Fairview. At the same time, the major landowners began using their positions in city government and their family and political connections to bring public services to "Fairview Heights"— those portions of Fairview and southern Clifton Heights which included their subdivisions.

From the late 1880s to the mid-1890s, the Moerlein family, ardent Republicans, had considerable influence in Cincinnati politics. Tafel was a member of the city Board of Administration, Goetz was president of the Board of Fire Commissioners, and Miller was president of the Board of Police Commissioners. During this time, a firehouse, public school, police station, water and gas lines, sewers, and street improvements were all put in place in the still thinly populated Fairview Heights. In most neighborhoods, development and population growth were well underway before such improvements were made. Here, public services were provided before there were really enough residents to justify them.

*The police protection afforded by the Eighth District Patrol Station was one of the amenities that Fairview Heights developers offered to draw potential homebuyers to the area.*

The landowners used the availability of these services to promote sale of their properties. Thus, the western part of Fairview and a few streets in the southern part of Clifton Heights developed differently from other areas of the city.

Most of the available land in Fairview was filled by the late 1920s. However, Clifton Heights property sold more slowly; in the early years of the twentieth century, there was still space for large institutions to settle along Clifton Avenue, among them, Deaconess and Good Samaritan hospitals, Hughes High School, and Hebrew Union College. These institutions and the University of Cincinnati (located in adjoining Corryville) eventually shaped the character of Clifton Heights as students occupied more and more of its housing. But in the first half of the twentieth century, both Fairview and Clifton Heights were middle-class residential neighborhoods with their own neighborhood organizations and institutions.

By the 1950s, Fairview and parts of Clifton Heights began showing symptoms of decline. As the original families died or moved away, many single-family dwellings were converted to rental units, and housing stock deteriorated. New residents were an increasingly transient population of poorer families and students. Neighborhood businesses, such as "mom and pop" grocery stores, began to disappear, and community organizations became weaker.

The increasing popularity of automobile ownership further reduced the attractiveness of the area. The subdivision had been laid out for a population that walked or relied on public transportation; cars created a shortage of parking and congestion on the steep, narrow streets.

In the 1960s, the growing university began to influence Fairview as well as Clifton Heights. As students and staff moved into the area, new businesses oriented to serving them followed. By the 1970s, interest in Fairview-Clifton Heights had resurfaced among speculators who purchased long-neglected houses in the Klotter Street area for renovation. Some developers considered construction of new buildings on the hillside, but concern over the loss of the greenspace on the slopes and potential landslide problems limited such projects.

The first major renovation took place in the early 1980s in a section known as the Hollister Triangle, a block of forty-seven structures between McMillan, Vine, and Hollister Streets. Community Development grants aided renovation of neglected buildings and the creation of additional parking space. Some new structures replaced those buildings that could not be effectively reused.

Through all these changes, the middle-income residents whose families originally populated the area sought to maintain their sense of community and to address the problems of the neighborhood as they perceived them. Since 1910, residents had set up various community organizations to seek improvements from city government, to foster pride in the community, and to encourage rehabilitation of deteriorated areas. Gradually, a new sense of community that included the remaining old residents, the university population, and new homeowners began to develop.

North

**End**

Dixmyth Ave.

Martin Luther King, Jr., Dr.

`19`

Martin Luther King, Jr., Dr.

`18`   `17`

`16`

Clifton Ave.

`15`

Calhoun St.   Wm. H. Taft Rd.

`6`

`7`   W. McMillan St.   `5`

`8`   E. McMillan St.

`14`

Hartshorn Ave.

McMillan St.

Fairview Ave.

`9`

Ada St.

`10`

Victor St.

Stratford Ave.

Chickasaw

Wheeler St.

Warner St.

`2`

Ohio Ave.

Vine St.

`4`

`1`

Fairview Pl.

`12`   `13`

Ravine St.

`11`

Emming

`3`

**Start**

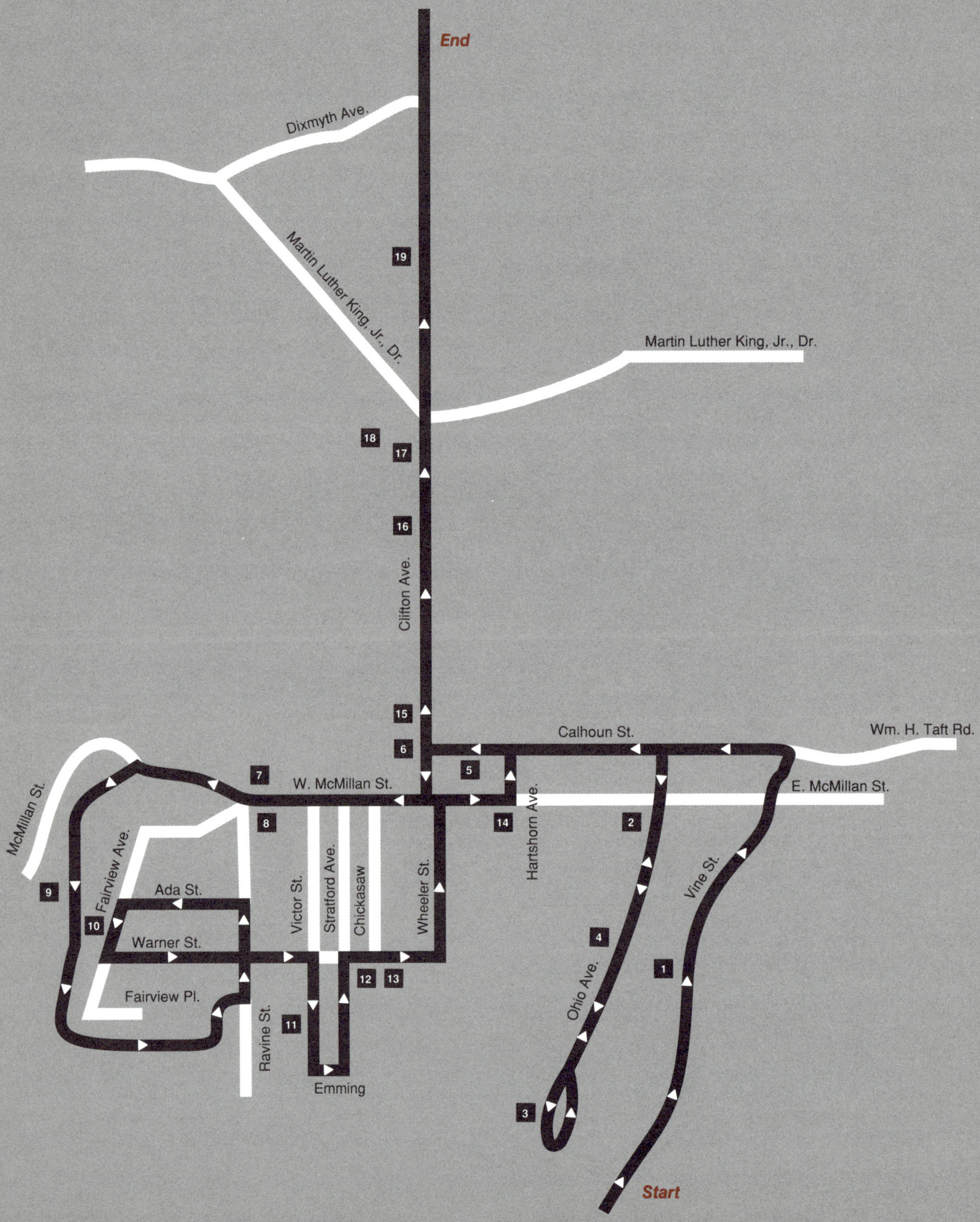

▶ ▶ ▶ ▶ ▶ ▶

**Tour begins on Vine Street going north.**

The 2 ½-story Renaissance Revival style building at 2347 Vine Street was built in 1912-1913 as the **1 Headquarters of the International Union of the United Brewery Workmen of America,** one of the oldest industrial unions in the United States. Founded in 1886 in Baltimore, Maryland, it brought together several local unions including one in Cincinnati, the *Brauer Gesellen Union,* which had been created in 1879. Around 1902, the union moved its headquarters to Cincinnati, a city both geographically central and with many breweries. The union offices were temporarily located first in the Odd Fellows Temple at Sixth and Elm Streets, then in a building on the southwest corner of Vine and Calhoun Streets. By 1913, the union had completed this new office building on Vine Street across from Inwood Park.

The headquarters was on a main streetcar line and accessible from Over-the-Rhine, Corryville, and Fairview, three neighborhoods where many brewery workers lived and which, like the union, had a large percentage of German Americans. The union was headed by men with names such as Zorn, Obergfell, Proelestle, Roder, and Huebner, and its weekly publication, the *Brauer Zeitung (Brewery Workers Journal),* was printed in both German and English until the anti-German hysteria of World War I.

The original goals of the Brewery Workmen's union were to improve conditions and pay. The Cincinnati union called two strikes in the 1880s but met adamant and successful opposition from brewery owners like Christian Moerlein. At last, owners signed an agreement in October 1892, which contained clauses that gave preference in hiring to union men, allowed workers to have free beer on the job, established a 10-hour work day, paid extra for the three hours maximum worked on Sunday, and declared that men would be discharged only for good reason. In the twentieth century, the union became increasingly concerned with opposing Prohibition.

The union broadened its base in 1918 by adding soft drink workers to

*The International Brewery Workers' Union used this Vine Street building as its headquarters from 1913 to 1973.*

its membership, and by 1920, it also included flour and cereal workers. Nonetheless, when Prohibition did come in 1920, thousands of brewers were thrown out of work and the union was severely hurt. Franklin Roosevelt became a hero to brewery workers in 1933 when the Eighteenth Amendment was repealed.

While Prohibition had posed one threat to the union's existence, its survival as an independent entity was also threatened by other unions. As early as 1904, the Teamsters Union had tried to incorporate the brewery workers into its membership. The brewery union successfully held off the takeover attempts and strengthened itself in 1940 by including distillery workers in its membership. The union's resistance to Teamster overtures led to its suspension from the AFL in 1941. The union remained unaffiliated for five years until it joined the Congress of Industrial Organizations (CIO), which, in turn, merged with the AFL in 1955.

Eventually, as the Teamsters became a less controversial organization and the older, more obstinate leaders of the brewery workers died, resistance to incorporation weakened. In 1973, the members of the International Union of Brewery, Flour, Cereal, Soft Drink, and Distillery Workers of American joined the Teamsters and the eighty-seven year old brewery union ceased to exist. The headquar-

ters building was closed and now houses a counseling service.

**Turn left on Calhoun Street, left on Ohio Avenue (one block past Scioto Street).**

The **2 Friars Club,** 65 West McMillan Street, is a nineteenth-century German American institution that originated in Over-the-Rhine and followed the community it served to the hilltop suburbs. The club had its beginnings in 1880 when the pastor of St. Francis Seraph Roman Catholic Church on Liberty Street founded the Sodality of St. Francis to provide guidance and activities for boys from single-parent families or those whose parents both worked. In 1908, an offshoot of the sodality was created, the Friars Gym and Athletic Club, which eventually separated from the parish organization. The Friars Athletic Club was more secular than the sodality. Laymen as well as clergy worked as coaches, counselors, and group leaders, and were the majority on the board of trustees.

The Friars Club went bankrupt in the early years of the Depression, but the Franciscan Fathers, seeking a steady source of money to fund their social programs, decided that a new athletic club could pay off the old debt and provide needed income. This McMillan Street property was originally intended as the site for the Franciscans' Roger Bacon High School, but was too small. Instead, this brick modified Jacobethan style club building was completed in 1931. The Fathers still own and operate it.

The Friars Club is primarily a social service agency. It provides meeting rooms for community groups, a hall for social activities, and eighty low-cost residential rooms for men. In the 1980s, the club has also offered mental health counseling services, served as a foster group home for teenage boys, tutored and counseled emotionally disturbed children, operated recreation programs throughout the city, and organized sports teams for youngsters.

To support this work, the Friars Club sells "senior" memberships in its athletic club (co-ed since 1979) which offers aerobics classes, a pool, sauna, whirlpool, gym, weight room, racquetball court, and fitness center.

> **Turn right at Graham Street into Bellevue Park.**

**3 Bellevue Park,** Ohio Avenue and Parker Street, is on the edge of a hill in southeastern Fairview that overlooks downtown Cincinnati. This land was largely undeveloped until the Cincinnati & Clifton Incline Railway Company built an inclined plane on the site in 1876. The incline carried its platform from the end of Elm Street up to the level area on the hilltop where the power house, boiler room, machine shop, and unloading platform were located.

Within a year, the Bellevue House—an amusement house, beer garden, and dance hall—opened next to the upper terminus. This famous hilltop "resort" reportedly dealt almost exclusively in the products of Christian Moerlein's brewery, which was hardly surprising since his brewery stood on Elm Street and Moerlein himself lived just up the street. The site of the incline and the resort was sometimes called Bellevue Park, but it was more like an amusement park than a park like Burnet Woods.

The Bellevue Incline, also referred to as the Clifton or the Elm Street Incline, connected the streetcar lines of the basin and new lines being established on the hilltops, opening up eastern Fairview, western Mt. Auburn, and Corryville for residential development. Many residents of the basin took

advantage of this new transportation to move into larger houses on lots more spacious than those available downtown. The Cincinnati Street Railroad Company, which took over the Clifton & Cincinnati Incline Company in 1880, rebuilt the incline in 1890 to accommodate streetcars. Passengers could then travel from downtown to the suburbs without having to transfer.

This improvement may have contributed to the demise of the Bellevue House. As streetcar passengers traveled straight through without waiting for transfers, patronage declined, and by 1895, the resort had gone out of business.

The incline itself became less important in the early twentieth century as other forms of transportation provided better access to the suburbs. The Bellevue Incline was closed in 1927. The site remained unused until 1936 when a portion of the land was purchased by the Cincinnati Park Board. Bellevue Park was dedicated that June. The park was expanded in 1954-1955 with land obtained from the Cincinnati Street Railroad Company and the University of Cincinnati. A modernistic style recreation building designed by Carl Freund was erected at that time.

> **Return to Ohio Avenue and turn left.**

After the Bellevue Incline was completed in 1876, the eastern portion of Fairview became easily accessible, and construction began to take place along streetcar lines that ran from the upper end of the incline. One of the earliest buildings to go up along the Ohio Avenue line was the **4 Home of Christian Moerlein,** 2407 Ohio Avenue.

Moerlein (1818-1897) was born in Truppack, Bavaria, and came to Cincinnati in 1842. By the 1860s, he headed a very successful brewery on Elm Street in Over-the-Rhine. The Moerlein family also became prominent in local politics. Moerlein's son, George, controlled a faction of the Hamilton County Republican Party in the late 1880s, and Moerlein himself was a trustee of the Cincinnati Water Works.

Like many German immigrants, Moerlein originally settled and worked

in Over-the-Rhine and later moved out of the basin to a new home above the congestion, noise, and dirt of the central city. This house, which he erected in 1882, is a substantial 3-story brick building in the transitional style. A 2-story addition in the rear housed the family's servants.

As Fairview became an urban rather than a suburban neighborhood, families who could afford to purchase and maintain large homes such as Moerlein's preferred more modern residences in newer suburbs. This house was eventually divided into several apartments.

> **Turn left on Calhoun Street.**

The building occupied by DuBois Bookstore, 321 Calhoun Street, was constructed by the City of Cincinnati in 1889 as quarters for **5 Engine Company No. 27**. The company was organized while John Goetz, Jr., a resident of Fairview, was serving on the Board of Fire Commissioners, and was part of the campaign to provide complete public services to the "Fairview Heights" area. The structure is a standard late-nineteenth century rectilinear firehouse, built in Victorian Italianate style.

Engine Company 27 was initially equipped with a chemical engine suitable for suburban neighborhoods with poor water supplies. After water lines were laid in this area, the company changed to a horse-drawn steam pumper in 1893.

When in service as an engine house, the building had large doors—now bricked up—facing Clifton Avenue for the fire apparatus, and a tower at the western end which served as both a bell tower and hose drying closet. The main floor held the equipment and stables; the dormitory, sitting room, and hayloft were on the second floor. In the late 1800s, one or two unmarried members of the company generally lived upstairs. The rest of the men, when not on duty, lived with their families within a block or two of the firehouse.

After the city's fire department was motorized, Engine Company 27 became superfluous. It was disbanded in 1920, and in 1923, the building was sold to a Masonic lodge. The Masons, political clubs, civic groups, and a church all met in the former firehouse, making it a focal point for the community until 1945 when it was sold and became a photographic studio. In 1958, DuBois Bookstore acquired the property and has served the university population ever since, selling books, sportswear, stationery, and school and office supplies.

*This 1895 photograph of the Fairview Heights firehouse shows its original configuration before it was converted into a Masonic lodge and later, a bookstore.*

**6** **Hughes High School,** 2515 Clifton Avenue, the second oldest high school in the Cincinnati public school system, was established with the bequest of a cobbler, Thomas Hughes (d.1824). Hughes came from England to Cincinnati in the early nineteenth century, acquired some farmland, and set up a shop on Liberty Street between Main and Sycamore, next to tanner William Woodward. Both men bequeathed property to start schools for boys whose parents could not afford to pay for their education.

The trustees of the Hughes bequest allowed the estate to accumulate until 1851 when the Woodward and Hughes funds were united and, as the Union Board of High Schools, became a part of the Cincinnati public school system. Students who lived east of Race Street attended classes at Woodward High School, built in 1831 in Over-the-Rhine. Those who lived west of Race went to Central High School until Hughes High School was completed in 1853 on the corner of Fifth and Mound Streets in the West End.

In the late nineteenth and early twentieth centuries, as the city's population moved out of the basin, so did its institutions. Between 1908 and 1911, the present Hughes High School building, designed by Walter Stevens, was erected in Fairview. The school's Jacobethan style was common for early twentieth century academic buildings, but Hughes also has some interesting Gothic features, such as gargoyles. After the new school opened, the former Hughes became Jackson Elementary School, a "colony" school that enrolled only black children.

During the first several decades of the twentieth century, about half of Hughes' graduates continued their education. Attending the school carried a certain amount of prestige, and among its alumni were a number of Cincinnati businessmen and professionals. Enrollment was near capacity, and additions, designed by Tietig & Lee, were completed in 1954.

The character of Hughes' student population changed in the 1950s and 1960s as redistricting redrew attendance area boundaries, and as Fairview and the other basin and older communities from which the school drew its students also changed. Increasing numbers of poorer Appalachian and then black youngsters attended Hughes, which had previously been predominantly white. The percentage of its graduates going on to college declined, and absenteeism increased. Many of the older faculty members were less able to meet the needs of these students and post-World War II education. In addition, the school lacked adequate athletic facilities.

While this physical problem was addressed in the mid-1960s with the construction of an addition for athletic activities, other problems continued to worsen. By the late 1960s, the school's population had become predominantly black (over 85%). Special programs and vocational courses failed to improve low achievement scores or to prevent increasing apathy, absenteeism, and student crime.

Since then, Hughes has been largely turned around by a new generation of young, highly motivated, and mostly black school administrators, teachers, and staff working with community groups. By the mid-1970s, most of the discipline problems had been reduced to a manageable level, and by the early 1980s, the percentage of graduates continuing their education had returned to about what it had been at mid-century.

In 1984, an alternative or "magnet" program, Computers Unlimited, was set up as part of the Cincinnati system's attempt to improve racial balance and boost enrollment. Further, a day care center opened here providing child care so that teenage mothers could stay in school, as well as offering after school care for the children of working parents.

**Turn left on Clifton Avenue, right on West McMillan Street.**

Catholics who lived in Fairview-Clifton Heights were originally included in St. George's parish in Corryville, but today many attend **7** **St. Monica Roman Catholic Church,** 328 West McMillan Street.

As this hilltop suburb developed in the late 1890s, the Archdiocese of Cincinnati became interested in establishing a new parish here. The Franciscan fathers at St. George's resisted the plan, believing that there was no real need for another Catholic church in the area and that the large landowners simply wanted a parish to help attract working-class Catholics from Over-the-Rhine to their new subdivision.

Because of this opposition, St. Monica's was not established until 1911, by which time the area had undergone considerable development and population growth. A series of compromises on parish territory was worked out between the Franciscans and the archdiocese: St. Monica's would serve the Catholics of Fairview and Clifton Heights, while St. George's was limited primarily to Corryville.

St. Monica's began as a mission church in a small temporary structure put up in 1912. When the building that is now the rectory was completed, services were held there. Eventually, parishioners financed a new, more elaborate building which was erected in 1926-1927.

The Italian Romanesque style church, designed by architects Robert Crowe and Edward J. Schulte, was built from gray limestone. Noteworthy features include a bas-relief crucifixion scene at the entrance and a bronze statue of St. Monica by sculptor Clement J. Barnhorn, and a mural on the dome interior by Carl Zimmerman. The generous support of the pari-

*St. Monica's Church served as a neighborhood parish and, for a time, as the archdiocesan cathedral.*

shioners covered the full cost of the building with enough money left over for a small endowment fund.

The new building's reputation as the most attractive church in the archdiocese may have influenced Archbishop John McNicholas to select it as the new cathedral when he judged that St. Peter in Chains at Eighth and Plum Streets and its surrounding neighborhood had deteriorated too much to continue as the seat of the archdiocese. In 1938, McNicholas received permission from the Vatican to designate St. Monica's the new cathedral.

McNicholas' successor, Archbishop Karl Alter, decided in 1951 that St. Peter in Chains was more appropriate for the cathedral. After an expansion and total renovation, St. Peter in Chains was redesignated as the cathedral of the Archdiocese of Cincinnati in November 1957, and St. Monica's again became a parish church.

As Catholic families moved out of Fairview and Clifton Heights, St. Monica's membership declined; the school closed in the late 1970s, and students were transferred to St. George's school which became Corryville Catholic.

In the early 1890s, the owners of land in Fairview and southern Clifton Heights used their political influence to establish public services here long before most of the lots were occupied. One of the most important facilities

was the **8 Eighth District Patrol Station,** 355 West McMillan Street. Before this patrol house was built, the Eighth District Station House on Vine Street in Corryville provided police protection for this area.

In 1895, Samuel Hannaford was hired to design the small Romanesque Revival style structure which was completed the following year. The new station was initially manned by two watchmen and two patrolmen equipped with a horse-drawn patrol wagon. The stables were located on the first floor, the second floor contained a hayloft.

Although the station's complement of men was small and it was the second least active police station in Cincinnati, there was room for expansion if needed; three more officers were eventually added. Even so, activity at the station remained low, partly because it was too far from the center of the district. When the police force was motorized in 1913-1914 and the neighborhood could be easily covered from other station houses, this facility was downgraded to a substation and stable for the Eighth District.

In 1927, police district boundaries were redrawn, and the station became the Seventh District Patrol House. By 1957, the building was no longer needed and was turned over to the Cincinnati Recreation Commission for renovation as a community center.

Extensive remodeling was completed in 1958, and the new community center became a neighborhood focal point. As the community organizations and the accompanying sense of community identity weakened, the Recreation Commission changed the facility into an Arts Center around 1970. The Fairview Arts Center closed due to lack of funds in 1984, and the city sold the building. The new owner remodeled the former patrol station for offices and graphic arts studios.

**Continue on West McMillan Street. Turn left into Fairview Park.**

**9 Fairview Park** was opened in 1936 as a "double-purpose" park, intended to provide vantage points for viewing the city below and to serve as a "greenbelt" on the hillside. Situated on a narrow strip of land

obtained from several owners, including Isaac Miller's descendants and the Cincinnati Street Railway Company, the park runs from McMillan Street just below Fairview Avenue to Ravine Street below Warner Street. Several overlooks provide views, and the Fairview Playground near Ravine Street has a shelterhouse, playfields, playground equipment, and a pool.

Most of the land in the park was considered unsuitable for commercial or residential use. There were once a few scattered houses here, but only the stone entrance to a springhouse on Isaac Miller's property survives. Until the mid-nineteenth century, a stone quarry operated on the southwestern face of the hill, and there was a truck farm where the playground now is.

This was also probably the site to which local followers of self-proclaimed prophet William Miller (1782-1849) climbed on October 10, 1843, to await the Second Coming of Christ. When the world did not end that day, Miller sent word that he had miscalculated. The faithful climbed the hill again on October 22, 1844, perhaps not so much to be nearer heaven but, instead, to be further away from the crowds of curious spectators and hecklers that surrounded their tabernacle at Seventh and John Streets. When the Second Coming still did not take place, the disillusioned Millerites broke up, some of them joining other sects such as the Shakers, while others eventually formed the Seventh Day Adventists, of which Miller was nominally the head.

The major structure to be erected on this land was the Fairview Inclined Plane which ran from McMicken Avenue up to Fairview Avenue. The incline was built with second-hand machinery in 1894 to make the hilltop lots of Western Fairview-Clifton Heights more accessible to the basin and the hilltop lots more attractive. The incline was erected on land obtained from Isaac  Miller who stood to gain the most from its operation.

In 1921, the incline was deteriorating, and the Street Railway decided that running a car line up McMillan Street would be more profitable. The Fairview Incline was closed to streetcar traffic but continued to carry walk-on passengers until 1923 when it was finally closed and dismantled.

The hillside land remained unused until the Park Board decided to create Fairview Park. As early as 1907, the board had been interested in the property as part of a plan that called for connecting all of the city's parks with parkways and strips of greenbelt. While the plan was never completely carried out, Fairview Park itself was considerably more elaborate than originally intended, as the 1907 plan had no provisions for a playground or activity fields.

Although Fairview Park's distance from the center of the neighborhood limits its usefulness to the immediate community, the park does provide some of the best views of downtown Cincinnati and the Mill Creek Valley.

**Turn left on Ravine Street, left on Ada Street, left on Fairview Avenue.**

Fairview, the modified Italian villa style **10 Home of Isaac J. Miller,** 2367 Fairview Avenue, was built in 1866. Miller (1833-1913) was a successful Cincinnati attorney and politician and one of the first persons to make his home in this undeveloped area while continuing to carry on business in the basin.

Miller married into the landowning Klotter family whose property included Klotter's Sons brewery at the base of the hill in the Mohawk district. He also purchased large tracts of land on the hillside from the heirs of John Riddle.

Miller bought this land as an investment, and over the years, sold part of his holdings to other investors with whom he had business or political connections. Miller paid for some street improvements in the area himself, but most of the public services were introduced because of political influence. Ironically, Miller headed the Committee of One Hundred which investigated corruption in government, and was considered a "reform" politician. Such use of influence evidently was not regarded as graft, but simply an acceptable use of position and connections.

The Miller house is larger than the majority of homes in the area; in fact, the lots on Fairview Avenue tended to be larger and more expensive than most in the subdivision. The frame structure was stuccoed in 1913, a change that was popular at that time. After Miller's death, his family continued to live in the area, although the lot on which the Miller house was located was eventually subdivided and two fairly large houses built here in the 1920s.

The area around Fairview Avenue did not deteriorate as most of the neighborhood did in the mid-twentieth century. Because of the larger lots, it adapted more readily to automobile traffic. Today, the vicinity of the Miller house is still the most desirable part of Fairview.

**Turn left on Warner Street, right on Victor Street.**

The **11 Houses on Flora and Victor Streets,** 2205-2254 Flora Street and 2205-2245 Victor Street, make up a homogeneous residential district of more than sixty buildings which are typical of the houses built in Fairview-Clifton Heights around the turn of the century. The modest 2-story transitional style structures with Mansard roofs were erected between 1890 and 1910 on small inexpensive lots that were attractive to working-class families who wanted to leave the increasingly crowded basin. The well-to-do had already fled the central city, and it was natural for others to join the migration up the hillsides.

Fairview was also attractive because it was near the University of Cincinnati and Burnet Woods Park, had a clean environment, and had public services already in place. The last factor was particularly important because in the 1890s and 1910s, Cincinnati annexed so much territory that it often could not afford to carry out all the improvement projects that residents needed.

The lots in the Flora and Victor Street area were, for the most part, purchased from Dr. Massilon Cassat's Mohawk Land Company for around $1,000-$2,000. The small homes, built using every bit of available space, were quite different from the large homes and lots of the families who created the subdivision. The owners of these dwellings relied on streetcars and inclines, or walked to work, school, shops, and social events, and had no need for driveways or garages.

An early promotional brochure also promised "desirable neighbors" in Fairview. The people who moved to this area were lower middle-income families, predominantly of German descent, and included small businessmen, lower-level city employees, and skilled workmen or shop foremen from the shoe factories, machine shops, breweries, meatpacking plants, and printing firms of the nearby basin and Mill Creek Valley.

They left downtown neighborhoods that had begun to change and, in Fairview, sought to reestablish that sense of tightly-knit community that they believed had once existed. Fairview residents created local organizations which held social events and worked to maintain the community by petitioning the city to repair damaged streets or sewers. In the 1920s and 1930s, residents also tried to prevent changes in the social character of their neighborhood, seeking to keep out "inappropriate" businesses or people. For instance, in 1931, a civic group successfully opposed the establishment of a home for "delinquent colored girls" in the old McMicken University building and dissuaded a Lyon Street homeowner from selling his house to a black family.

Change, however, could not be prevented. The Depression, World War II, and the gradual dispersal of original residents weakened community groups and eroded the homogeneity of the neighborhood. New residents tended to be more transient and poorer than the older families; Appalachians, blacks, and students became a larger part of the area's population. Many of the houses, now rental properties, deteriorated from lack of care and the wear of frequently changing tenants. Parking problems and the disappearance of most of the old neighborhood shops altered the physical character of the area as well.

Since the 1970s, renovation of some older houses has improved the appearance of a few of Fairview's residential streets, but most are still in a state of transition.

**Turn left on Emming Street, left on Stratford Avenue, and right on Warner Street.**

The **12 Fairview German Bilingual School,** 2232 Stratford Avenue, now occupies the old Fairview

Public School. Built in 1888-1889, the school, like the firehouse on Calhoun Street which was erected around the same time, was part of developers' efforts to make the area attractive to potential residents. H. E. Siter designed this large Romanesque Revival style structure as well as a number of other Cincinnati public schools. A modern style addition by Edward J. Schulte was completed in 1959 and contains general purpose rooms, offices, classrooms, a kitchen, and a gym.

The original student body of Fairview Public School was predominantly of German descent. By the 1960s and 1970s, the student population, reflecting changes in the neighborhood and in the school's attendance district, included mostly youngsters from lower-income families, many of Appalachian background. In 1973-1974, only 10% of Fairview school's students was black.

The following year, in response to suit filed by the NAACP, the Cincinnati Board of Education established a German-English bilingual program for grades 1-2 at Fairview and at Schiel school in Corryville. These alternative or "magnet" programs were designed to improve racial balance. The board located some of the more popular programs in what were regarded as the less desirable neighborhoods, hoping to draw children from a wide variety of backgrounds from throughout the system. Fairview began offering both bilingual and standard elementary curricula. This was the first time German had been taught in Cincinnati's elementary public schools since, under the influence of World War I anti-German sentiment, the board had voted a ban on February 2, 1918.

By the end of the decade, the German-English program had fulfilled all expectations. A bilingual middle school, grades 6-8, was established at Schiel, and Fairview became an entirely alternative school in 1980. Since then, its students have scored highest or a close second on standard achievement tests in Cincinnati's elementary schools. In 1987, the racial composition of the student body was 47% black, 49% white, and 4% other. Fairview regularly has a waiting list for enrollment in its kindergarten and first grade classes.

In addition to a strong academic program that continues through the eighth grade at the Cincinnati Bilingual Academy, the German-English schools have an exchange program that offers seventh and eighth graders a chance to spend one month living with a German family and going to school there. An active parents' group sponsors activities to raise money to help pay the way for those children who would not otherwise be able to afford the trip.

Today, the most distinctive structures on Fairview Hill are the former **13 WLW Transmitter Tower and Buildings,** off the route at 2208-2222 Chickasaw Street.

The site was chosen by Powel Crosley, Jr., in the early 1930s for a new transmitter station because its high elevation reduced interference from other hills or tall buildings. Crosley had begun radio broadcasting in his College Hill home in 1921, using equipment he had built himself and playing phonograph records. Quickly seeing the commercial possibilities of radio, he started radio station WLW in 1922 and acquired another station, WSAI, in 1923. Originally, the studios and transmitters were in his factories in South Cumminsville-Northside and Camp Washington. This Art Moderne style structure designed by Samuel Hannaford & Sons was completed in 1936. Additions were built in 1937-1938 to accommodate WLW's transmission facilities which were moved here.

Between 1920 and 1940, WLW increased its transmitting power to 50,000, then 500,000 watts, a signal stronger than any in the world. It became "the Nation's Station" and "the Cradle of the Stars." Among the entertainers who worked for this Cincinnati giant were Doris Day, Ruth Lyons, Rod Serling, Red Skelton, Virginia Payne as "Ma Perkins," and Thomas "Fats" Waller.

During World War II, Camp Washington factory space was needed for defense work, and the radio studios were moved to a former Elks Lodge at Ninth and Elm Streets. Crosley sold WSAI in 1944, and only WLW Radio remained in the Warner and Chickasaw Street building.

In 1947-1948, Aviation Corporation (AVCO), which had pur- chased Crosley Radio Corporation, decided to take advantage of the available space here to construct a TV studio and tower. WLW-TV began broadcasting on February 10, 1948, the first television station in Ohio. WLW-TV moved its studios to Ninth Street in 1951, leaving the building on Fairview Hill to serve once again solely as a transmission facility.

Multimedia, Inc., purchased the radio station in 1975, and the former WLW facility became Production Plaza, housing the offices of Multimedia syndication and Young Peoples' Specials programs, plus facilities for video and film production and post-production work.

**Turn left on Wheeler Street, right on West McMillan Street.**

The Queen Anne style building, erected in 1891, that is now Lenhardt's Restaurant, 151 West McMillan Street, was originally the **14 Home of John Goetz, Jr.** Goetz (1855-1899) was an attorney who, in 1881, married Lizzie Moerlein, daughter of brewery owner Christian Moerlein. The couple began married life next door to Moerlein on Ohio Avenue; Goetz became secretary of the Christian Moerlein Brewing Company and was eventually made vice-president.

*Most homes in Fairview Heights were quite modest, but there were some exceptions, among them the home of John Goetz, Jr.*

Moerlein and Goetz purchased a considerable amount of what was then inexpensive, undeveloped land in Fairview and the southern part of Clifton Heights. Both men used their political influence to secure improvements for the area. Goetz, a member of the Board of Fire Commissioners from the late 1880s through the mid-1890s, also served on a city government committee which established the police patrol station at West McMillan and Ravine Streets.

Goetz' house is typical of the spacious, well-built mansions that speculators built on large, level lots in or near their subdivisions. It stands in contrast to the more modest structures crowded onto the narrow lots which make up the larger part of the neighborhood.

The house remained a private residence until around 1955, but changes in the neighborhood made Fairview less attractive for the families who could afford large residences such as these. The Goetz home became a fraternity house for about ten years until Hungarian immigrants Anton and Emmy Lenhardt converted it into a restaurant.

Despite the modern addition to the front, the Goetz house is a visible remnant of the period when Fairview was home to some very wealthy families, as well middle, and lower-middle income people.

**Turn left on Hartshorn Street, left on Calhoun Street, right on Clifton Avenue.**

**15 Deaconess Hospital,** 311 Straight Street, had its origins in 1888, when the ministers of several German American Protestant denominations created the Deaconess Society. That organization opened a 27-bed hospital on East Liberty Street under the direction of two deaconesses—women who had chosen a life of service to the church and its institutions—who had received medical training in Germany.

In 1896, the Deaconess Society took over the management of the Ohio Maternity Hospital on West Liberty Street, maintaining both facilities, which cared for charity and full-payment patients. When more space was needed, the society looked at reasonably priced land on the Clifton Heights hilltop, which was considered a more healthful and pleasant location than the basin.

In 1901, work began on a 70-bed hospital at Clifton Avenue and Straight Street, and the new Deaconess Hospital opened in 1903. Prop-

erty just behind the hospital was purchased, and between 1916 and 1919, quarters for nurses were built. As the nursing program grew, homes on Stratford and Straight Streets were acquired and converted for use as classrooms and housing. A 5-story wing built in 1925-1926 is the oldest surviving part of the hospital.

Over the years, the hospital has undergone a series of remodelings and additions. When construction for a new nursing school started in 1965, the old residences and classroom buildings came down. Space for the new buildings was limited, and in 1975-1976, the original frame hospital was razed for the construction of a 12-story wing.

By 1987, Deaconess was a 276-bed hospital offering general, out-patient, and emergency care, as well as specialized programs in cardiovascular surgery and rehabilitation, sports medicine, asthma and allergy treatment, home health care, a chest pain center, and Elderlife, a health and wellness program.

Isaac M. Wise (1819-1900), the founder of Reform Judaism in America, also founded the **16 Hebrew Union College-Jewish Institute of Religion, (HUC-JIR),** 2849 Clifton Avenue. Wise, who had come to the United States in 1846, believed in "molding Judaism to the times." He was interested in starting a seminary to train Jewish teachers and in 1855 opened a college, the Zion Collegiate Institution. This institution, located at Ninth and Walnut Streets, closed two years later.

In 1873, Wise helped establish the Union of American Hebrew Congregations, one of whose purposes was to support the formation of a theological seminary. Hebrew Union College opened on October 4, 1875; the first classes were held in the vestry rooms of the Plum Street and Mound Street Temples. In 1881, the college moved to a former residence at Sixth and Cutter Streets.

As enrollment at Hebrew Union College increased and Cincinnati's population moved from older downtown neighborhoods to new suburbs, college officials decided to relocate the school. Sizable tracts of land were still available in Clifton Heights. In 1905, land opposite Burnet Woods Park was purchased and construction began. The administration building and the

Bernheim Library, a gift of Isaac W. Bernheim of Louisville, Kentucky, opened in 1913.

Architects A. Lincoln Fechheimer and Benjamin Ihorst designed the buildings in academic Jacobethan style which has been maintained in most additions to the campus. Later structures included dormitories (1923, 1960) and two library buildings (1931, 1965). Hebrew Union College was chartered by the State of Ohio in 1927.

HUC is essentially a graduate school, providing theological training to men and women who have completed undergraduate degrees; the first woman rabbi in the United States was ordained here in 1972. HUC's key resources, its library and archives, have grown consistently over the years. Since 1939, the college has also maintained a museum of Hebraica that is now the largest collection of Jewish ceremonial objects in the United States. Following the Nazis' destruction of Jewish cultural and religious artifacts, this collection has become one of the most important of its kind in the world.

In 1950, HUC merged with the Jewish Institute of Religion in New York City. By the early 1970s, Reform Judaism was being studied in Cincinnati, New York City, and related centers in Jerusalem and Los Angeles. In 1973-1974, consideration was given to closing the Cincinnati school to save money and because the area did not have as large a Jewish population as the other cities. However, the Cincinnati campus was maintained, partly because of its historical status as the home of Reform Judaism in America and also because of its geographically central location.

The Clifton Heights campus, the intellectual center of a branch of one of the world's major religions, was pictured on a 1986 stamp issued by Israel.

Two internationally-recognized scholars have been associated with HUC-JIR. Dr. Jacob Rader Marcus (b.1896), who came to study at HUC when he was fifteen, became a professor of history here in the 1920s. He essentially created the field of American Jewish history, producing dozens of articles and books about the history of American Jews. Marcus also founded the American Jewish Archives at Hebrew Union College. In 1987, the intersection at which he lived—McAlpin and Middleton Streets in Clifton—was named Dr. Jacob Rader Marcus Square in honor of his achievements.

Nelson Glueck (1900-1971) was ordained at HUC in 1923, became a faculty member six years later and president in 1947. Glueck was a Biblical archaeologist who relied on stories in the Old Testament to direct his digs. Working in the Negev Desert, he excavated hundreds of settlements, temples, fortresses, and irrigation and hydraulic systems, some dating back to 4000 BC. Glueck's best known discoveries were King Solomon's copper mines and his major port city on the Gulf of Aqaba. From 1942 to 1947, Glueck used his archaeological excavations as cover to gather intelligence information as a field agent for the Office of Strategic Services in Transjordan.

**17** **Good Samaritan Hospital,** 3217 Clifton Avenue, developed from the 20-bed St. John's Hospital for Invalids that the Sisters of Charity opened in 1852 in a former school building at Broadway and Woodward Streets. Increasing need for their services led the Sisters to move to a

*The availability of building sites in Clifton Heights attracted a number of institutions that were originally located in the basin, including Hebrew Union College.*

larger building, an old house at Third and Plum Streets, which they called St. John's Hospital.

In 1866, two non-Catholic Cincinnatians who admired the work of the Charity Sisters donated money for the purchase of the old Marine Hospital at Locke and Sixth Streets, which the federal government had built during the Civil War. The gift stipulated that the facility be renamed The Hospital of the Good Samaritan.

In the late nineteenth century, Good Samaritan—commonly known as "Good Sam"—became an important element in the practice of medicine in Cincinnati. Most of the city's better-known doctors worked here, and in the 1870s, the hospital provided a lecture hall and teaching clinical amphitheater for the students of the Ohio Medical College and Miami College. A school of nursing directly associated with the hospital was established in 1897.

In order to increase the services offered by the hospital, the Sisters of Charity began looking for a large, relatively inexpensive piece of property where a new facility could be built. The present Clifton Heights site was purchased in 1907. Work on the initial structures, designed by Gustave Drach, was completed in 1915. Later additions included new wings in 1926 and 1945, nurses' residences in 1927 and 1947, and an underground park-

ing garage opened in 1967.

In 1926, the nursing school became the nursing department of the College of Mount St. Joseph.

An administrative reorganization in the late 1970s brought the hospital into the nationwide Sisters of Charity Health Care Corporation which involved more laymen in the management of the facility. During the same period, programs were established to treat special problems including spinal deformation and black lung disease. In 1982, the old wings were replaced by new ones. This work reduced the number of beds in the hospital to 772, but increased special facilities for services such as cardiology, psychiatry, eye and cataract surgery, rehabilitation, spinal disorders, a foot and ankle center, dialysis unit, and helicopter landing pad on the roof.

Behind Good Samaritan Hospital and off the route are the buildings of the **18** **Cincinnati Cremation Company,** 525 Martin Luther King, Jr., Drive. The company was organized in 1884 by a group of businessmen and professionals who were "activated by the serious conviction that the burial of the dead as is in vogue with modern civilized people has been and is a source of innumerable injuries and deadly dangers to the living . . . ." That is, "epidemics of many forms are liable

*When Good Samaritan Hospital relocated to Clifton Heights in 1915, the area was still relatively undeveloped.*

to form and spread their dark wings over homestead, pasture, stream and spring" when the dead, particularly those victims of cholera or yellow fever, were simply buried in the ground. At a meeting in the Turner Hall on October 8, forty Cincinnatians formed an association for the "practical return to the ancient and more rational method . . . of reducing the dead to ashes by fire."

Among those who served on the company's board and held stock in the project were House of Refuge superintendent Henry Oliver, artist Benn Pitman, his daughter Agnes Pitman, clothier A.E. Burkhardt, distillery owner Charles Fleischmann, brewer Christian Moerlein, and assistant United States attorney Harry R. Probasco.

At the time, cremation was by no means widely accepted, but its supporters believed that it was the way to deal with the dead in a "rational," "scientific," and "sanitary" manner. Cremation also forestalled potential graverobbers.

By 1885, a crematorium site was selected in Clifton Heights. The price of the land was reasonable, and the isolated, peaceful setting seemed an appropriate location for the facility. At the same time, the spot was easily reached from the city. The small

Romanesque style crematory building was formally dedicated on November 4, 1888, with speeches by a Baptist clergyman, a lawyer, a doctor, and Benn Pitman.

Improved furnaces were installed in 1893 and the building was altered in 1941 by the addition of a Georgian style chapel and columbaria with niches for permanent placement of the urns. This addition has totally obscured the original structure.

The United Dairy Farmers store at the southwest corner of Clifton and Howell Avenues was originally a **19 Standard Oil of Ohio Filling Station,** 3325 Clifton Avenue. The site was first rented by Sohio in 1914, when the automobile was becoming a popular form of transportation.

Clifton Heights offered space for what was at that time a fairly large auto service outlet. The location was close to the thriving Ludlow Avenue business district without actually being in Clifton where property was more expensive and residents were concerned about maintaining the neighborhood's "village" character. At the same time, the gas station was centrally located to serve Clifton, Clifton Heights, Fairview, Corryville, and the university. The Sohio outlet at Clifton and Howell was not only one of the first service stations in the area, it also became one of the most successful.

The present building was put up by Sohio around 1930. Designed by architect Roy Heaton in the Tudor Revival style then popular for residential construction, the station is characterized by its half-timbered and stucco walls and bell-cast roof. During the 1920s and 1930s, this style was frequently used in service stations in residential areas so they would not contrast too sharply with surrounding homes.

The station survived the Depression, wartime gas rationing, the energy crisis of the 1970s, and several recessions, only to fall victim to a change in gasoline marketing strategies. In the early 1980s, oil companies decided that neighborhood stations were no longer viable, and the Clifton Avenue Sohio was phased out. In 1985, the building was converted into a United Dairy Farmers store as part of that company's vigorous expansion program. The adaptive reuse was sympathetic, and the old station's character remained intact. It is one of the area's few surviving examples of early twentieth-century service station vernacular architecture.

**Tour ends.**

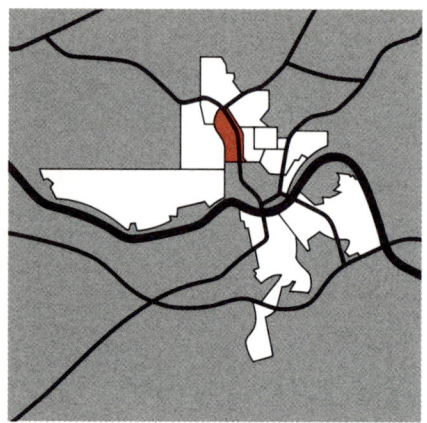

# Mohawk - Brighton - Camp Washington

Mohawk, Brighton, and Camp Washington are three older Cincinnati neighborhoods with a mixture of industry and low-income housing. These communities are located on the eastern side of the Mill Creek Valley between the West End and Cumminsville-Northside.

Brighton, on the west side of Central Parkway, extends roughly from Bank Street on the south to Alfred Street on the north. Mohawk lies across the parkway and includes the homes and businesses at the foot of Fairview Hill and those as far up the hillside as Emming Street. The boundaries of these two neighborhoods have always been indistinct, as neither Mohawk nor Brighton was ever incorporated. For most of the twentieth century, they have generally been regarded as a single district, Mohawk-Brighton, but as the area's population declined in the 1970s and 1980s, city planners generally treated Mohawk and Brighton as parts of Over-the-Rhine and the West End.

Camp Washington, on the other hand, has had more definite boundaries—the canal on the east, the Mill Creek on the west, Alfred Street on the south, and the intersection of Spring Grove Avenue and the railroad tracks on the north. This has given the area a more distinct identity.

The land on which Mohawk, Brighton, and Camp Washington are located was purchased from John Cleves Symmes by a number of individuals, some as speculators, others as settlers. By 1792-1793, the latter had established a small community with a blockhouse. One of the largest landholders there was John Riddle, and the semi-fortified hamlet was commonly known as Riddle's Station. It was located on the east side of the military road (present-day Colerain Avenue) leading out of Cincinnati on a site that is now occupied by I-75, just north of the Western Hills Viaduct.

After the danger of Indian attacks subsided in the early nineteenth century, farms and country homes dotted the land to the north of Riddle's Station. Riddle himself lived in this vicinity until his death in 1847. To the south of the station, a village began to grow up around the point at which Harrison Turnpike branched off the road to Hamilton (now the intersection of Central and Colerain Avenues).

The Mill Creek Valley was already an important transportation corridor for roads out of the Cincinnati basin. The Miami & Erie Canal was constructed in 1825-1827 on level ground on the east side of the creek, making the valley even more accessible.

A typical crossroads business district with taverns, an inn, and hotel grew up at the intersection of Central and Harrison Avenues in a village that became known as Brighton. Although at this time most of the city's slaughtering operations were in the Deer Creek Valley at the foot of Mt. Adams, Brighton had a smaller cluster of these businesses because it was on Colerain Pike, a popular route for drovers bringing livestock to Cincinnati. By the 1830s, slaughterhouses were established near Clearwater Creek, a stream running along Clearwater and Bank Streets and emptying into the Mill Creek.

Across the canal at the foot of the rugged hillside, a small residential community known as Mohawk developed. In the 1840s, speculators started subdividing property in this vicinity, which was within fairly easy walking distance of Cincinnati.

In 1849, the city annexed Mohawk and Brighton as part of the special Road District of Mill Creek Township, and development accelerated. Small factories, breweries, and meatpacking houses were set up, particularly near the canal.

While new homes and commercial buildings were being erected in Mohawk and Brighton, that part of the valley immediately to the north remained largely undeveloped. The availability of large tracts of land in this area attracted activities that required substantial space. During the Mexican War, an army camp was set up about midway between Brighton and Cumminsville. Known as Camp Washington, this site was

*Before Prohibition, many Mohawk-Brighton residents worked for breweries in the vicinity, among them, George Weber's brewery on Mohawk Street.*

245

the muster and drill grounds of the First and Second Regiments of Ohio Volunteer Infantry. The camp was broken up in 1848, but the name remained in use.

Camp Washington was also the site of the first Ohio State Fair in 1850. When the City of Cincinnati needed construction sites for two very large facilities—the House of Refuge (1850) and the Workhouse (1866)—it chose Camp Washington, even though the area was not annexed until 1870.

During the second half of the nineteenth century, new transportation routes were run through the Mill Creek Valley. The Cincinnati, Hamilton & Dayton Railroad (CH&D) was built in the early 1850s, and a horsecar line between Brighton and downtown began service in 1859. In 1861, a new road, Spring Grove Avenue, was built from Brighton to the large cemetery beyond Cumminsville; six years later, the Cincinnati & Marietta rail line was laid directly through Brighton and Camp Washington.

The combination of railroads and available land brought the livestock and packing businesses to Camp Washington. As the land around the slaughterhouses of Brighton and the Deer Creek Valley became more developed, these plants, with their offensive sights and smells, were unpopular neighbors. At the same time, owners of firms engaged in stockhandling, slaughtering, meatpacking, and by-product processing saw a need to consolidate their operations.

Until this time, the slaughterhouses and their related stockyards were in Brighton and the Deer Creek Valley. The packing houses—which in almost all cases were separate from slaughterhouses—were grouped along the canal and on some parts of the riverfront. The by-product processors—soap and candlemakers, tanners, gluemakers, and rendering works—were scattered throughout the city.

In 1871, the Union Stockyard Company was organized to set up a more efficient centralized stockyard complex. By 1873, this organization had set up a large stockhandling facility in Camp Washington. By the 1880s, almost all of Cincinnati's slaughterhouses and many of the packing and processing companies had relocated near the Union Stockyards.

A number of manufacturing firms also began locating there. Some of these plants were new establishments, but many were older firms that left the riverfront or the West End to build larger or more modern facilities. Among these new arrivals were foundries, metalworking shops, machine tool factories, and plants making a variety of products including elevators, iron mantels, fire engines, and valves. This growing industrial activity attracted working-class residents, many of them recent immigrants from eastern Europe. By 1910, Camp Washington was a predominantly lower middle-income community with 10,000 to 11,000 inhabitants.

At this same time, Mohawk-Brighton also had a variety of industries: packing houses, metalworking shops, breweries, and pattern-makers, but most were smaller than those in Camp Washington. This community was also predominantly lower middle-income. However, some of the streets bordering on the West End became increasingly run-down, and the bad housing conditions there led to the inclusion of parts of Mohawk-Brighton in the area served by the Cincinnati Social Service Unit Or-

*At the turn of the century when nearby Fairview Heights was still relatively undeveloped, Mohawk and Brighton were already heavily built up.*

ganization.

This experimental project (generally known as the Mohawk-Brighton Social Unit Organization, although its headquarters and most of its clients were actually in the West End) worked from 1917 to 1919 to provide child health care and health education. After the Social Unit was shut down because some city officials regarded it as dangerously socialistic, the Better Housing League took over the effort to clean up the physical environment of the area.

By 1930, Camp Washington had more than 11,800 residents, and Mohawk-Brighton had several thousand. The people and industries in the Mill Creek Valley suffered during the Depression and were hit hard by the flood of 1937. In the 1940s, the number of companies and the population declined.

Although defense work during World War II and the Korean War revitalized some companies, many of the meatpackers closed or reduced their operations. Other plants moved out of the valley, seeking more up-to-date or spacious quarters. At the same time, many of the residents began moving to newer suburbs, particularly those in the Western Hills area.

Mohawk, Brighton, and Camp Washington were affected by the construction of the I-75 expressway during the late 1950s and early 1960s. Housing and factories were demolished as the road was built. Although the highway did not cut directly through either the Camp

Washington or Brighton business districts, enterprises in both areas increasingly suffered from the competition of new shopping centers, lack of parking, restricted access, and population decline. In 1970, Camp Washington had only 3,147 residents, and by 1980, the number had fallen to 2,198. Mohawk-Brighton had but a few hundred inhabitants left.

The area's population was not only smaller, it was also increasingly poor. The majority of Mohawk-Brighton's residents were low-income blacks, while low-income white families—mostly from Appalachian backgrounds—filled Camp Washington. Cultural differences and misunderstandings between Appalachian families and the Asian refugees who located here occasionally produced troubling conflicts, though community organizations worked to improve relations. Rising crime rates proved the final straw for many local businessmen who gave up and closed after being robbed repeatedly.

City government's primary hope for improving conditions in Mohawk, Brighton, and Camp Washington was industrial development. As early as 1948, the *Metropolitan Master Plan* had described these areas as "deteriorated" and predicted that they would change from mixed residential-industrial districts into a region of warehouses and factories. It was not until 1984, however, that the City Planning Department created a detailed industrial development plan for any of this area, and then it covered only Camp Washington.

Mohawk and Brighton had, by that time, lost their separate identities. City planners, and in fact many area residents, had come to identify most of Mohawk as part of Over-the-Rhine, and Brighton as part of the West End.

Some private investors and smaller companies did move into or expand facilities in Mohawk, Brighton, and Camp Washington. The former Central Trust bank in Brighton was renovated as office space. Other old buildings, such as a former firehouse and livestock exchange, were converted for business. As of the late 1980s, the hoped-for major development projects still had not begun, but this section of the Mill Creek Valley, while a troubled residential area, remained an important industrial district with approximately 200 different firms employing more than 7,000 workers.

## Mohawk-Brighton-Camp Washington

Tour Length
7.5 miles

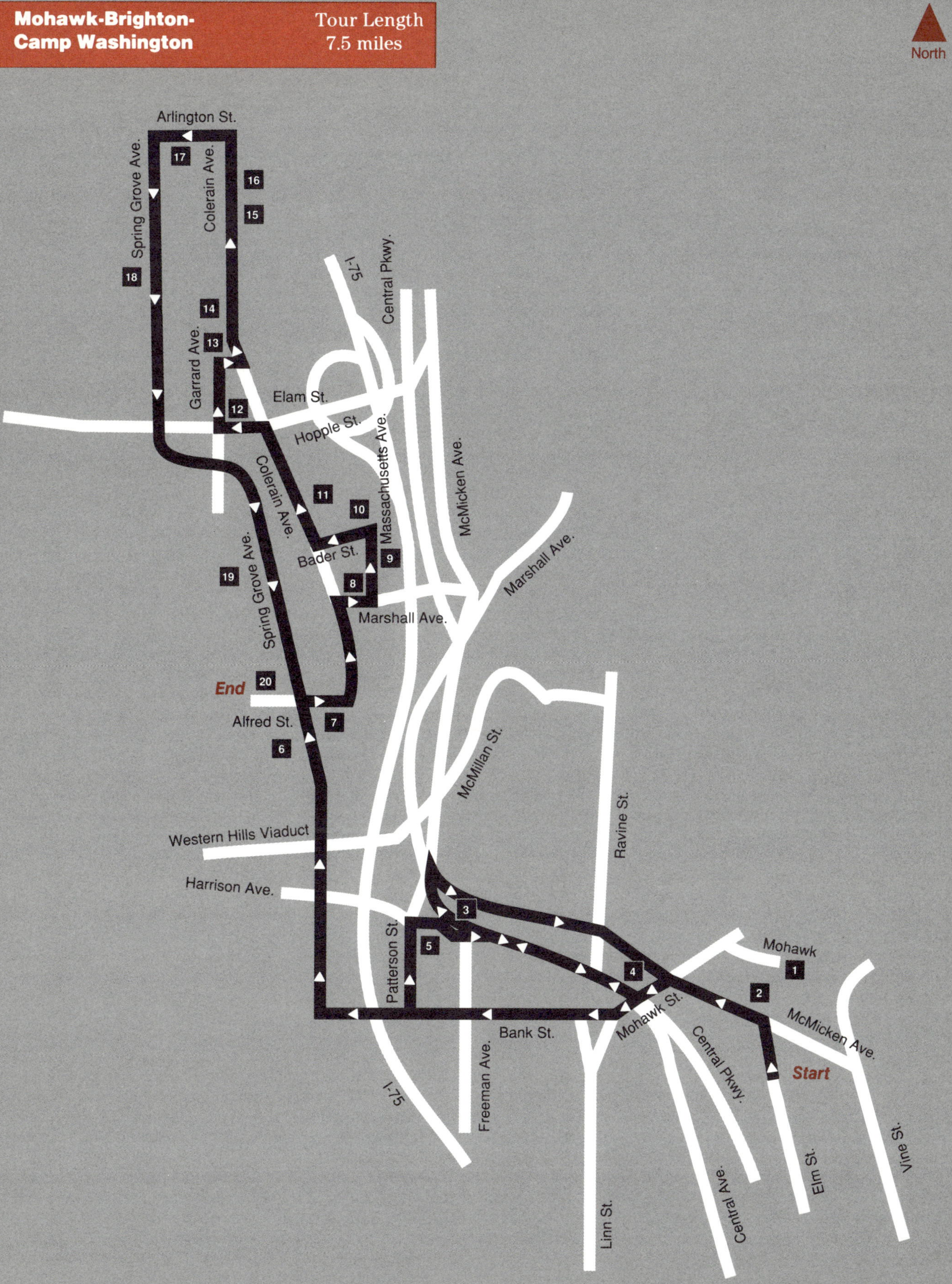

North
Arlington St.
Spring Grove Ave.
Colerain Ave.
I-75
Central Pkwy.
Garrard Ave.
Elam St.
Hopple St.
Massachusetts Ave.
McMicken Ave.
Colerain Ave.
Bader St.
Marshall Ave.
Spring Grove Ave.
Marshall Ave.
End
Alfred St.
McMillan St.
Ravine St.
Western Hills Viaduct
Harrison Ave.
Patterson St.
Mohawk
Mohawk St.
Bank St.
Central Pkwy.
McMicken Ave.
Start
Freeman Ave.
I-75
Linn St.
Central Ave.
Elm St.
Vine St.
1
2
3
4
5
6
7
8
9
10
11
12
13
14
15
16
17
18
19
20

▶ ▶ ▶ ▶ ▶ ▶

**Tour begins at Elm Street and McMicken Avenue. Turn left on McMicken.**

Breweries were among Mohawk-Brighton's earliest industries, and the **1 Brew House of the Jackson Brewing Company,** 202 Mohawk Street, one of the first breweries in the area, is still standing.

In 1853, Meinrad (1823-1872) and Fridolin (d.1870) Kleiner, who had come to America after the failure of the 1848 democratic revolutions in Germany, formed Kleiner & Brother and set up a brewery on the hill above Hamilton Road (McMicken Avenue). Twenty years later, George Weber (1826-1893) bought the brewery. However, due to Weber's unwise speculations in real estate, the George Weber Brewing Company went bankrupt in 1887.

The business was purchased in 1889. Reincorporated as the Jackson Brewing Company, it became profitable again with the production of Pure Old Lager which, "for quality, purity, and flavor challenges the world," according to advertisements.

The large 4-story red brick brew house contained a malt mill, wash tubs, fermenting tanks, malt and hop storage rooms, and eventually, an ice machine. Smaller brick buildings on Elm Street housed the carpenter's shop, office, bottling works, pitch house, and ice storage. Beer was stored in basements and two huge cooling tunnels dug into the hillside.

During Prohibition, the Jackson brewery manufactured ginger beer, root beer, and "medicinal waters," but closed in 1929. The plant reopened in 1933 as Squibb-Pattison Breweries, Inc. Troubled by financial difficulties, the firm was put under new management and again operated as the Jackson brewery. The new owners built a structure at 218 McMicken; above the door was a carved stone relief of bottling equipment, covered by a later tenant.

In 1941, Gibson Wine Company bought the facility and opened a bottling works here. Gibson had started as a retail wine store on East Sixth Street and then entered into the production of wine. The company relocated its main offices and champagne department to McMicken Avenue and later used the plant for aging and warehousing wine.

Around 1961, Cincinnati Metal Blast acquired the property, operating its machine shops in the brew house until going out of business in the mid-1980s. And for some years in the 1960s, the city stocked the cooling tunnels for fallout shelters. Running twenty and forty feet underground, these 200-foot long, 35-foot wide tunnels had 3-foot thick masonry walls and were equipped with air shafts, water and sewer lines, and electricity. The tunnels are now unused.

The **2 Sohn Brewery,** 242 West McMicken, had its origins in the Hamilton Brewery that George Klotter (b.1805) established on this site in the 1840s. John G. Sohn, who worked here as a cooper, became a partner in the late 1850s and took over the brewery the following decade.

J. G. Sohn & Company's brewery complex included the main brew house, the 4-story red brick building at 242 with a terra cotta relief of beer barrel and malt shovels above the door. Fermenting rooms, cellars, and bottling works were in another large building behind the brew house on Mohawk. A frame wagon shed and a warehouse stood at 253 West McMicken. The Sohn family home stood next to the plant until it was torn down for expansion.

In 1910, when there were some thirty breweries in the city, the Mohawk Brewing Company bought Sohn and produced lager beer—even after the enactment of Prohibition. Federal agents raided the Mohawk brewery in 1925 and confiscated truckloads of beer that were reportedly being sent out of Cincinnati. This, however, was an unusual case. While home brewing was widespread, the city was relatively free of large-scale, organized violations of the Volstead Act.

After the repeal of Prohibition, the Clyffside Brewing Company reopened and improved the old Sohn plant and leased the John Hauck Brewing Company's facilities on Dayton Street at Central Avenue. Clyffside was known for its Felsenbrau beer, and that name is spelled out in brick on the front of the building on Mohawk.

In 1945, Clyffside sold out to the Red Top Brewing Company, one of Cincinnati's three big breweries, along

*The former Sohn brewery reopened in the 1930s under the management of the Clyffside Brewing Company.*

with Hudepohl and Burger. By 1947, Red Top was producing a million barrels of beer and ale a year. However, post-war expansion—thirty-two buildings spread over eighteen acres—was poorly timed. Sales declined, and the company faced mounting financial losses. A new product, Wunderbrau beer, only temporarily revived sales.

Red Top sold out to a Chicago Miller High Life beer distributorship in 1955, which in turn sold the business to a Michigan firm in 1957. That concern closed Red Top, laying off its 150 employees, and used the brewery's over $1.3 million losses to reduce its own taxes.

The buildings were sold in 1961 and used for some light manufacturing and storage.

**Turn left on Mohawk Place, right on Central Parkway, right on West McMillan Street, and right on McMicken Avenue.**

Around 1868, shortly after George Klotter left the Hamilton Brewery, Louis Klotter and George Klotter, Jr., formed Klotter's Sons and founded the **3 Bellevue Brewing Company,** 601-615 West McMicken Avenue. Louis lived just across Browne (McMicken) Avenue. The brewery benefited from its proximity to the Miami & Erie Canal and the Brighton House hotel, popular with livestock raisers who brought their animals to Mill Creek Valley slaughterhouses.

By the late 1870s, the Klotters called their business the Bellevue brewery, perhaps choosing the name to suggest a relationship between it and the Bellevue House resort located at the top of the Bellevue Incline in Clifton Heights. (That establishment, however, sold primarily Christian Moerlein's beer.)

The Bellevue complex included the 3-story brick brew house, 603 West McMicken, with beer cellars built partly into the steep hillside, and an office and boiler room building, at 601, that was erected in 1895.

After Prohibition closed the Bellevue brewery, the Brighton Transfer Company—later the Brighton Fireproof Storage Company— purchased the cellar buildings, 607-615. Other sections of the old Bellevue property were later used for auto repair and storage, light manufacturing, and a butchers' supply distribution business. For a few years in the 1970s, a winery and nightclub operated in the old cellar. Recently, the aging brewery buildings have stood vacant.

**Turn right on Mohawk Place, cross Central Parkway to Linn Street, and turn right on Bank Street.**

One of the most common industries in Mohawk-Brighton during the late nineteenth century was meat processing. While the majority of packing houses were small operations, the **4 H. H. Meyer Packing Company,** located at the intersection of Linn and Bank Streets, eventually became one of the largest meat processing firms in Cincinnati.

The company was founded by Henry Meyer (1839-1919) and George Huschart. Meyer's involvement with meatpacking had begun in 1869 when he became a bookkeeper in his father-in-law's firm, Anderegg & Roth, on Front Street. Andregg & Roth had started in 1863 as a commission merchants operation, and then expanded into meatpacking. Like many of the city's meat processing concerns, this company relocated to the Mill Creek Valley near the Union Stockyards, moving to a site in the West End near Freeman Avenue and

Gest Street in 1873.

After John Anderegg died in 1882, Henry Meyer moved up in the company, now Roth-Meyer, eventually becoming its vice president. At the same time he worked in one meatpacking firm, Meyer and his cousin, George Huschart, tried to start a company of their own. Their first attempts in the 1870s were unsuccessful. But in 1888, he and Huschart purchased the former Adam Metz packing house on Clarkson Street in Brighton.

Four years later, Meyer left Roth-Meyer to run the operation, known as Meyer & Huschart. The following year, he bought out his partner, and the firm became the H. H. Meyer Packing Company, one of eight small processing and slaughtering concerns in that vicinity.

Meyer's company flourished. The popularity of its Partridge brand meats and Meyer's interest in innovation—he was one of the first packers in Cincinnati to use mechanical refrigeration— helped make H. H. Meyer the city's leading porkpacker in the early twentieth century.

After Meyer's death, his son and later his grandson, headed the company. Between 1926 and 1957, they oversaw a series of plant improvements. Neighboring factories, as well as numerous stores and homes, were demolished or incorporated into the Meyer plant. The facility eventually expanded into a 3.9-acre complex of twenty-six buildings in which about 550 people were employed.

In 1964, the John Morrell Company of Chicago purchased Meyer meatpacking, retaining the Partridge brand name and the existing management. H. Harold Meyer (1888-1984), who had taken over as president of the firm in 1932, continued to direct the operation until retiring in 1975.

Morrell built a modern 2-story concrete plant here in 1974. But some older parts of the complex survived, including the main processing building (erected in 1936, with a 1957 addition) on Central Avenue and several brick and stone structures dating from the nineteenth and early twentieth centuries along Clearwater Avenue.

Morrell gradually transferred processing activities out of the Brighton facility, and meatpacking ceased at this location in 1982. Some of the buildings were used as a

distribution center, but most of the former Meyer plant either stood vacant or was occupied by other light industrial or warehousing tenants.

In the late 1980s, operations at the old Meyer plant again came under the direction of Cincinnatians. Over the course of a decade, Carl Lindner's American Financial Corporation acquired shares in United Brands, the conglomerate of which Morrell had become a part in 1970. By 1984, AFC was the controlling stockholder of United Brands, and in 1987, Lindner recruited Milton Schloss, the retired head of Kahn's, to take over as the chairman of John Morrell & Company.

**Turn right on Patterson Street, right on Harrison Avenue.**

The **5 Brighton Business District,** once a vibrant mixture of light industry, housing, and retail stores, extended as far west as Harrison Avenue and Winchell Street, and as far east as Central Avenue and Whiteman Street. The heart of the Brighton business district was the intersection of Central, Colerain, and Harrison Avenues, known as Brighton Corner.

In the 1840s, when small factories, breweries, and slaughterhouses were beginning to open up in this vicinity, the Zenith House hotel was set up at the northwest corner of Harrison and Colerain. This establishment was replaced in the early 1850s by the larger Brighton House.

The intersection was also the terminus of one of Cincinnati's first horsecar lines, Route No. 1 of the City Passenger Railway Company, which began service in 1859 from Fourth and Walnut Streets. A second line owned by the Cincinnati Street Railroad Company also traveled between the Brighton area and downtown.

As the transit companies extended their tracks further into the Mill Creek Valley, Brighton Corner became an important transfer point, attracting businesses to the vicinity. Saloons, groceries, and a hardware store served both commuters and area residents. Frederick Lender relocated his hardware company (est. 1839) from Main Street to Brighton in 1860. The Brighton Hardware was purchased by the Hartke family in 1892. Renamed the Hartke Hardware Company, the business moved to 2139

Central Avenue in 1897, where it has remained.

By the turn of the century, the Brighton business district included some forty to fifty concerns. Among these was a bank, organized around 1899 by safe manufacturer Max Mosler (1842-1914), whose factory was nearby. Mosler's Brighton German Bank Company occupied an impressive 3-story stone building completed on the former site of the Brighton House around 1905. This structure was enlarged in 1915 to house a variety of offices, as well as the bank.

Many of the buildings at Brighton Corner had shops or offices on the ground floor and apartments and flats on the upper stories. Until the mid-twentieth century, most of the residents of these buildings were lower middle-income families predominantly of German extraction. But by the early 1900s, a large number were recent immigrants from eastern Europe.

Small factories and workshops were scattered among the stores and apartments. In the late nineteenth century, there were several blacksmiths, a coalyard, two machine tool works, an ice company, wagon painter, tannery, and a malthouse and brewery.

John Wetterer's brewery was a particularly substantial operation. The concern began as a malthouse in 1864. In 1879, Wetterer moved the malthouse from Colerain Avenue to 2117-2125 Central Avenue. The malt company expanded into brewing in 1888, becoming the Germania Brewery. The firm, renamed the Wetterer Brewing Company in 1902, prospered until closed by Prohibition in 1922. The buildings were eventually taken over by a belting manufacturer and an auto repair company.

In the first half of the twentieth century, business activity in this area was still quite varied. Some operations changed hands or closed over time, but other firms took their places. In 1930, the Brighton Bank—the "German" had been dropped during World War I—was closed briefly by the Depression but reopened almost immediately as a Central Trust branch office.

The blacksmiths and ice houses closed, but warehouses, garages, and small workshops took their places, and the brewery was occupied by an ice cream manufacturer. All along

Central and Harrison, groceries, clothing shops, shoe stores, restaurants, tailors, chiropractors, a theater, a post office, confectioners, and a public bathhouse continued to serve local residents and commuters transferring at the intersection.

In the 1950s, however, Brighton merchants faced growing problems. The neighborhood's population decreased. The city closed access ramps from Central Parkway to Brighton Corner. Lack of parking, rising crime, and dwindling numbers of customers drove many businesses away.

By the 1980s, only about twenty companies remained at Brighton Corner. Few retail stores were left, and Hartke's relied on customers seeking special hard-to-find hardware, rather than general "walk-in" trade. The remaining firms included a heating contractor, waterproofer, peanut warehouse, upholsterer, bookbinder, and printer—none of which served a neighborhood market.

Gradually, Brighton Corner stabilized as a light industrial, warehouse, and office district. While a number of Brighton's vacant commercial buildings were demolished to provide brick for new suburban houses, some were

*The Powell Valve Company was one of many major Cincinnati firms to relocate to Camp Washington during the late nineteenth and early twentieth centuries.*

renovated in the 1980s. The bank, which had closed in 1979, was purchased by private investors and converted into offices. An empty store was remodeled as a research lab. But Brighton Corner could no longer be called a neighborhood business district.

> **Cross Colerain Avenue to Central Avenue. Proceed east on Central. Turn right on Linn Street, right on Bank Street, go under the I-75 overpass, and turn right on Spring Grove Avenue.**

The **6 William Powell Company,** 2503 Spring Grove Avenue, produces precision valves for a variety of industrial purposes. It was already a major manufacturing concern in 1893 when it moved from downtown into larger, more modern facilities on this site. For much of the twentieth century, it was one of the largest employers in the Camp Washington area. As late as 1959, the company employed 1,700 workers in Cincinnati, but because of automation and foreign competition, the local payroll fell below 500 by 1987.

The firm was established by an Englishman, William Powell (1790-1867), who arrived in Cincinnati in

1836. Powell, an inventor of tools, a skilled mechanic, and a good businessman, is credited with founding the brass trade in the West.

His original foundry, set up in 1846 on Fifth Street between Plum and Elm Streets, produced brass fittings for plumbers and for the Cincinnati Gas-Light & Coke Company. A few years later, Powell's sons, James (1832-1908) and Henry (1821-1888), joined the firm which was then known as William Powell & Company.

During the Civil War, the company produced sword belt hardware and spurs for the U.S. Cavalry. Afterward, it resumed manufacturing general lines of plumbing and engineering brass fittings. Steady growth followed, and in 1882, the firm moved into larger facilities at 52-54 Plum Street.

James Powell assumed sole control of the business in 1886 and reorganized it as a stock company, the William Powell Company. Like his father, James was involved with design as well as management, and many of the tools used in the factory were his inventions. After his death, corporate management passed to career employees, including three generations of the Coombe family. Nonetheless, the company remained a closely held corporation with most of the stock owned by William Powell's descendants.

In 1893, the firm moved to Spring Grove Avenue. Its Union Brass Works boasted a power plant to supply electricity for incandescent lights, an inter-departmental telephone service, and the use of spent steam to heat the building. A second factory was added in 1926 at 3233-3241 Colerain Avenue.

During World War II, Powell received numerous awards for its work in supplying valves used in the munitions, synthetic rubber, drug, and gasoline industries. The company opened two highly automated factories in South Carolina during the 1970s. This contributed to the reduction in employment at the Cincinnati plants but enabled Powell to retain its position as a premier American valve manufacturer.

**Turn right on Alfred Street.**

During the late nineteenth and early twentieth centuries, many manufacturing firms moved from the crowded basin to new facilities in Camp Washington. Among these was the fire apparatus building concern that eventually became the **7 Ahrens-Fox Fire Engine Company,** 1107 Alfred Street.

Chris Ahrens started in the fire engine industry working for Lane & Bodley, and in 1868 set up his own factory in Over-the-Rhine. The Ahrens Manufacturing Company was one of the few successful builders of steam fire engines in the country, but the highly-competitive nature of that industry led Ahrens to merge with three other apparatus builders to form the American Fire Engine Company. Another merger in 1901, created American La France.

The Ahrens family was not happy in the new conglomerate, and between 1903-1905, Chris Ahrens, his sons, and his son-in-law, all left American La France to start a new company, the Cincinnati Engine & Pump Works, on Elm street in Over-the-Rhine. After a legal dispute with American La France over the use of the Ahrens name was settled in 1905, Cincinnati Engine & Pump was renamed the Ahrens Fire Engine Company and moved to Alfred Street.

Initially, Ahrens Fire Engine produced steam pumpers, but some of the younger family members, particularly Ahrens' son-in-law, Charles Fox, were interested in building motorized apparatus. In 1910, Fox became president of the company, subsequently renamed Ahrens-Fox, and within one year, its engineers were experimenting with a gasoline-powered pumper. In December 1911, the firm began delivering its Model A piston pumper.

Ahrens-Fox quickly became one of the leading builders of this type of machine, and its product line expanded to include salvage cars and aerial ladder trucks. Although Ahrens-Fox machines were expensive—the "Rolls Royce of fire engines"—it became a matter of great pride for a community to own a 'Fox. During the 1920s and for much of the 1930s, the Cincinnati Fire Department used Ahrens-Fox apparatus almost exclusively.

During the Depression, selling these expensive machines grew increasingly difficult. The company was deeply in debt to its chassis supplier, LeBlond-Schacht Trucks. In 1936, stockholders agreed to a merger of Ahrens-Fox and LeBlond-Schacht. The Camp Washington facility was phased out, and fire engine production was moved, first to the LeBlond-Schacht factory on Evans Street in Lower Price Hill, and then to a new plant in Norwood.

Ahrens-Fox experienced a brief resurgence, but World War II brought production to a halt. In 1951, the company was again sold and moved to 1638 Central Avenue in the West End. In 1953, Ahrens-Fox was bankrupt. Standing orders for apparatus were subcontracted to the Beck Bus Company of Sidney, Ohio, and Ahrens-Fox itself was purchased by Curt Nepper, an employee of the firm since 1928.

The last Beck-built 'Fox was delivered in 1958, and Curt Nepper's one-man operation became all that was left of Ahrens-Fox. Nepper continued to provide service and parts for the Ahrens-Fox engines still in service and for a growing number of machines that were used only for parades, collectors' musters, and museum displays. He assembled one last engine, by himself, for a northern Kentucky fire department, during 1969-1977.

In 1980, the Schoenling Brewing Company purchased the Central Avenue building, and Nepper returned with his huge collection of tools, spare parts, and plans, to a part of the original Ahrens-Fox factory complex in Camp Washington.

**Turn left on Colerain Avenue, right on Marshall Avenue.**

Sacred Heart of Jesus parish was created to serve Camp Washington's Catholic families who had to travel to the West End or Northside to attend German-language services. The present **8 Sacred Heart Roman Catholic Church,** 1041 Marshall Avenue with the parsonage at 2733 Massachusetts Avenue, is the second church erected by this parish.

The parish was organized with forty families in August 1870, and completed a small combination church and school in December. The congregation soon needed more room and purchased a lot to the east of the first structure. The dedication of the brick Gothic Revival style church took place in June 1880.

In 1894, Sacred Heart parish, then

some 400 families, completed the first section of the school building on Heywood Avenue. A Sisters' residence was erected next, and the auditorium and classroom addition built in 1924. Such was the mix of residential and industrial development in Camp Washington that, for a time, Stephens & Brothers glue manufacturing works stood diagonally across the street from the church.

As the Depression and then the 1937 flood hurt Mill Creek Valley companies, both parish membership and the area's industries declined. By 1961, church membership had fallen to 200 families. The school closed in 1969, and in July 1970, this church was merged with Sacred Heart Italian Church, Fifth and Broadway.

The Italian parish had been established in 1891 when there were about 4,000 Italian Americans in Cincinnati. Though the church claimed 600 member families at the turn of the century, the congregation dwindled as parishioners moved out of the basin. By the early 1950s, there were fewer than one hundred families.

Procter & Gamble razed the downtown church for company expansion, but the marble altar and railing, statues, and Lourdes grotto were installed in the Camp Washington church. Sacred Heart became the archdiocese's official Italian national church, drawing Cincinnatians of Italian descent from throughout the city. It was put in the charge of the Scalabrini Fathers, who had led the downtown parish.

The school was renovated and opened in 1985 as the Italian Center, a meeting place for groups like the United Italian Society, Sons of Italy, and other Italian American associations.

While there were some tensions between the two congregations after the merger, members—approximately equal numbers of Italian and German descent—now work together at the twice-yearly ravioli and spaghetti dinners begun at the Broadway church in 1928. Sacred Heart also offers emergency food, referral services, and home visits for elderly residents of the community.

**Turn left on Massachusetts Avenue.**

Since the late nineteenth century, Camp Washington has been home to large meatpacking firms such as Kahn's and smaller ones including the **9 Kluener Packing Company,** 2842 Massachusetts Avenue, and **10 Gus Juengling & Son, Inc.,** 2869 Massachusetts Avenue.

In 1872, when slaughtering was beginning to take place year round in Cincinnati, William's *Cincinnati Directory* listed one hundred companies engaged in meat processing. These included twenty-two slaughterhouses, seventy-four meatpacking firms, and four companies with combined slaughtering and packing operations. Only three slaughterhouses were in Camp Washington; most animal-processing operations were in the Deer Creek Valley, the West End, or on the riverfront.

Gradually, the location of the city's meatpacking industry began to change. In 1880, Cincinnati had 119 slaughterhouses. Eighteen were in Camp Washington; almost half were in the vicinity of Massachusetts Avenue. But only one of the city's sixty-three meatpackers—the vast majority of which were still separate from the slaughterhouses—was in Camp Washington. This was the Cincinnati Packing Company, north of the stockyards.

Within a decade, however, thirty-one of the seventy-five slaughterhouses in Cincinnati were located in this part of the Mill Creek Valley, as were six of the city's forty-one meatpackers.

In the early twentieth century, the number of Cincinnati businesses involved in the meat industry became smaller, but those that remained processed more animals than before. Between 1880 and 1900 when Cincinnati had more than one hundred packing and slaughterhouses, generally fewer than 600,000 hogs were killed each year. In contrast, by the early 1920s, the thirty-five or so packing and slaughtering firms in the city processed from 700,000 to 900,000 pigs annually.

Camp Washington became home to an increasingly larger proportion of the pork and beef packing activity in Cincinnati. Although most of the increased meat production was at large concerns such as Meyer's and Kahn's, the small companies in the Massachusetts Avenue area also expanded. German immigrant Joseph Kluener started as a meat distributor

around 1900, but he and his sons gradually turned their operation into a packinghouse. In 1947, the Klueners started their own beef slaughtering department, and by the mid-1980s had eighty-five employees processing 400 to 450 animals each week.

Around the same time that Kluener's began, Gustave Juengling opened a small slaughterhouse at 2873 Massachusetts. In 1904, Juengling moved his business to 2871, where it remained, eventually acquiring neighboring slaughterhouses. By the 1980s, Juengling's forty employees were processing around one hundred animals a week.

While companies such as Juengling and Kluener were relatively small compared with Kahn's, which in the mid-1980s employed 700 workers and could slaughter as many as 10,000 animals a week, they were recognized as an important part of Cincinnati's economy. In 1965, special zoning was applied to an area that included parts of Massachusetts and Sidney Avenues between Marshall Avenue and Bader Street. A "meat-packing zone" was created to preserve small livestock slaughtering operations and to discourage other uses of sites there.

The Camp Washington meatpackers themselves generally like this area because it provides a convenient centralized location with good access to transportation, and they expect to remain here.

**Turn left on Bader Street, right on Colerain Avenue.**

As Camp Washington developed as an industrial district, it also became a densely populated residential community. Since the late nineteenth century, the **11 Camp Washington Business District,** Colerain Avenue between Marshall Avenue and Monmouth Street, has served local residents.

Colerain Avenue has always included a mix of industry, housing, and neighborhood-oriented commercial activity. The people drawn to Camp Washington by its packinghouses and factories needed grocers, doctors, butchers, barbers, and clothiers. By the mid-1890s, about seventy-five stores lined Colerain Avenue in Camp Washington.

In the mid-1920s, when Camp

*The Washington School was a focal point for community pride, and it had a role in many neighborhood activities.*

Washington's population peaked at more than 11,000, the district boasted over one hundred businesses—groceries, bakeries, clothing shops, physicians, a midwife, a theater, hardware and paint stores, pharmacies, barber and beauty shops, garages, restaurants, a jeweler, savings and loan associations, and a bank.

When Camp Washington's population began decreasing in the 1930s, the number of businesses likewise declined. By the mid-1950s, there were 25% fewer neighborhood shops than thirty years before. This trend continued; by the mid-1980s, Camp Washington had fewer than 2,200 residents, and its business district had only about thirty concerns.

Yet a variety of businesses remained. Among the vacant and boarded up storefronts were a bank, a hardware store, a small department store, carry-outs, groceries, and a number of restaurants—including a chili parlor prized by Cincinnati chili aficionados. Some of the businesses were new, while others, such as the Bader Cafe, 2838 Colerain Avenue, had been in the same locations for many years. In fact, that building has continuously housed a saloon since its construction in 1898.

Light and medium industrial operations also continued to occupy space along Colerain Avenue, in large part because Camp Washington was easily reached by I-75. Former stores and homes were put to new uses by firms doing sheet metal work, printing and typesetting, catering, and slaughtering.

One example of the reuse of old buildings in this area is the McAndrews Window & Glass Company's 1985 restoration of the old firehouse of Engine Company No. 12, 2940 Colerain Avenue. The firehouse, which

opened in 1877, was closed after one hundred years of service when new quarters for Engine 12 were built on Spring Grove Avenue. McAndrews Glass invested in this site because it was in a good location and because the firm wanted to demonstrate a commitment to the neighborhood.

**Turn left on Hopple Street.**

In the spring of 1982, the Board of Education closed one of the city's oldest schools, **12 Washington School,** 1326 Hopple Street, because of declining enrollment.

The oldest portion of Washington School dates from 1881-1882, but the first schoolhouse on this site was a 2-story, 2-room brick church erected in 1845 where, around 1850, a day school opened in the Sunday school room. An 11-classroom addition to the church-school building was erected in 1869, but the community soon required a more substantial structure.

In 1881, work began on a new Eighteenth District School, a 3½-story building, designed by Samuel Hannaford (1835-1911), that was then the largest public school in the city. Fourteen teachers instructed 638 students in grades 1-8. That 416 of the youngsters studied German indicates both the proportion of German Americans in Camp Washington and the strength of the German language program in the school system.

The community growth produced a dramatic increase in the number of students at Eighteenth District School: 1,006 in 1887-1888 and 1,340 by 1903. A major classroom addition designed by Harry Bevis was built in 1908. In 1916, a boiler plant and more classrooms were added. Enrollment peaked at over 1,500 in the 1930s.

At the end of the 1955-1956 school year, when Washington had

1,493 children, students in grades 7-9 were transferred elsewhere. Enrollment continued at near 1,000 into the early 1970s. The proportion of black students increased to approximately 25% as district boundaries were redrawn and Washington began receiving children from the predominantly black Millvale Primary School.

The number of students declined as the area's population fell, but an Individual Guided Education alternative program begun in 1980-1981 increased enrollment and improved racial balance to 52% white-48% black. However, the old buildings were deteriorating and maintenance costs were high. The school closed at the end of December 1982, and students were sent to North Fairmount Elementary School, a predominantly black school also suffering from low enrollment.

The building was scheduled for demolition to make way for construction of a highway entry ramp.

**Turn right on Garrard Avenue, right on Elam Street.**

Built during the late 1880s and early 1890s, the 2½-story transitional style brick and frame **13 Elam Street Houses,** 1311-1327, were occupied by the families of skilled workers and foremen who could afford these attractive and substantial dwellings. The early residents of the nine buildings on the south side of the street were predominantly of German ancestry. In all but two of the twenty-two families here, the husband or the wife, and sometimes both, was German-born or had at least one German-born parent.

According to the 1900 census, six families lived at 1327 Elam Street. Among them were George Hanover, a machinist, and his wife, Hattie, and the families of Jacob Metzger and Jacob Weninger, both butchers. Weninger's sons were already working. George, 14, was an apprentice machinist, and Frederick, 12, a clerk in a dry goods store.

At 1323 were Theresa Rehg, a widow, and her three children: Theresa, 19, a soap wrapper; William, 17, a machinist, and 13-year-old Clara. Albert Siebenthaler, a foreman, his widowed mother, wife, and three young children also shared this house.

Six families, again headed mostly by skilled workers including a cabinet-maker, carpenter, tinner, and drafts-man, resided at 1317 and 1315. Planing mill foreman Gabriel Mueller, Katie, his wife, their six children, and two other couples and their children lived at 1311.

In the 1930s, the residences on Elam Street continued as homes mostly to skilled workers including two electricians, a steamfitter, brass-worker, salesman, pressman, and assembler. Among the families at 1327 were those headed by a toolmaker, a printer, a truck driver, a laborer, and a stockkeeper. Theresa Rehg, her son, and his family still lived at 1323.

Twenty-five years later, the residents of these buildings remained a mix of skilled and semi-skilled workers—many of whom worked at Camp Washington companies like Crosley, Powell, and Lodge & Shipley—and the widows of men who had probably held such jobs.

By 1975, the decline of Camp Washington and its industries was reflected by the nature of residents' occupations as well as by the number of vacant dwellings on Elam Street. Of the fourteen households listed in the *Cincinnati Directory* for that year, the heads of four households were retired; others included an inspector for the William Powell Company, a foundry worker, maintenance man, name plate maker, laborer, and yardworker.

**Turn left on Colerain Avenue.**

Cincinnati has been an important machine tool center since the mid-nineteenth century, and the **14 Lodge & Shipley Company,** 3055 Colerain Avenue, which specialized in the manufacture of precision lathes and machine tools, was one of the

city's best-known such firms.

William Lodge (1848-1917), an English-born machinist, arrived in Cincinnati in 1872 and went to work at John Steptoe & Company, milling machine manufacturers. By about 1880, Lodge had saved enough money to found Lodge, Barker & Company, a brassworking machinery concern, on West Fifth Street.

In 1892, Lodge and Murray Shipley, another English immigrant, founded the Lodge & Shipley Machine Tool Company on Culvert Street between Fifth and Sixth. Around 1898, Lodge & Shipley moved to this site in Camp Washington where there was good access to rail transportation and room for expansion.

Around the time of Lodge's death, Shipley left the company to serve as vice-president of the Trailmobile Company. Lodge's descendants retained an interest in the business, and his grandson and then his great-grandson, served as president.

Lodge & Shipley was known for producing innovative, high quality precision lathes. During World War II and the Korean War, Lodge & Shipley expanded to a 3-building complex and employed around 1,000 workers. In 1953, a new central office building was erected and the company diversified through merger acquisitions.

In later decades, however, Lodge & Shipley, like the rest of the nation's machine tool industry, was crippled by foreign competition, slumps in the oil and farm industries which pro-vided half of their business, and other ills. By 1987, the company had suf-fered five straight years of losses and the workforce had been reduced to 150. In February, the company was sold to Belcan, a Cincinnati engineer-ing concern, which merged it into a subsidiary that emphasized high technology machine tools.

The Cincinnati architectural firm of Edwin Anderson and Samuel Han-naford designed the **15 City Work-house,** 3208 Colerain Avenue, a 5-story Gothic style brick building that replaced the overcrowded city and county prisons in the basin.

The Ohio legislature authorized construction of a new correctional facility in 1853, and three years later, Cincinnati purchased twenty-six acres of land adjoining the House of Refuge in Camp Washington. The City Work House was officially opened on

November 17, 1869. The main building contained five tiers of 4x8-foot cells; the south wing housed 606 cells for men, the north, 240 cells for women. Various support buildings were located behind.

Nineteenth-century prison re-formers placed great emphasis on regular labor as part of the reform process and as a way to defray jail costs. Before the Work House opened, prisoners lived in temporary housing on the grounds while helping with construction. In February 1870, the Work House signed its first agreement to provide workers for an outside contractor, and three years later, a workshop building large enough to accommodate all male prisoners was added to the complex.

The system of finding work for the inmates was not abandoned until 1918 when proceeds dropped far below the costs of incarceration.

Over the years, inmates were used on various city projects: crushing rocks for roadbeds, running a large city incinerator, repairing municipal vehicles, and providing assistance during disasters such as the 1937 flood. The Work House earned addi-tional money by charging the county to house its prisoners and by keeping federal detainees awaiting trial.

Cincinnati was proud of the facility, but there were problems. Felons were incarcerated with misde-meanor offenders, those awaiting trial with the convicted, and juveniles with adults. Because there were no toilets and little ventilation, the foul smell of urine, excrement, and vomit pervaded the structure. The only toilet in a cell was a bucket, and for those in solitary confinement, a hole in the floor.

Further, the Work House was built before the days of electric lights, and later installation was too expensive. Solitary confinement cells lacked even a window or a mattress.

The Work House was closed in 1920 when prisoners were transferred to the new Hamilton County Court-house jail. But by 1927, the jail pop-ulation overflowed that facility, and the Work House was reopened. The building was cleaned and partially renovated, but a 1930 report decried living conditions, saying that prisoners were human beings and should be treated as such.

Conditions continued to deterio-rate, but the general public perceived the Work House as a model of efficiency, cleanliness, and reform. Weekly tours were offered as late as the 1940s.

The popular attitude began to change in the late 1950s. In 1962, Superintendent George Studt complained that the structure was utterly outdated and that the mixed prison population made his job "like trying to run a school for criminals." The city manager agreed, but nothing was done.

Because most prisoners were jailed relatively briefly—three to four weeks on average—Workhouse (no longer "Work House") staff could not hope to teach a trade, provide counseling, or combat illiteracy. And there was not enough work to keep inmates occupied. By the 1960s, only about one-third were used to do maintenance work in city parks, playgrounds, streets, and so on. Even fewer were needed to keep the Workhouse running. For the rest, there was nothing constructive to do by day and no way to read in the unlit cells by night. Fights, riots, and escapes became common.

The Workhouse—now the City

*At several points in its long history, the City Workhouse was declared obsolete, but remained in use nonetheless.*

Correctional Institution (CCI)—was investigated and castigated; reports were issued and signed. But nothing changed because Cincinnatians refused to approve funding for another jail. Finally in 1972, the Legal Aid Society filed a class action suit charging that conditions of imprisonment violated the Constitution, the laws of Ohio, and city and county building codes.

While the case was pending, City Council passed a resolution agreeing that CCI should be closed in the future and that the city should participate in the construction of a new city-county jail. In 1976, Judge Gilbert Bettman ordered seventy-nine improvements and closing within two years.

Conditions worsened, fights and escapes increased, yet in 1978, voters rejected a bond issue for a new jail. Another judge allowed the institution to remain open until a new county jail could be built. City Council got out of the jail business in 1977-1978 by repealing almost all city criminal offense ordinances in order to force the county and state to house prisoners. Cincinnati police now charged offenders under state criminal laws.

Finally in 1985, a new Hamilton

County Justice Center opened, housing 848 people in two buildings—one for those awaiting trial, the other for those convicted. On September 16, 1985, CCI closed except for a renovated women's section and the infirmary, which were used for weekend and minimum security prisoners.

Because the former Workhouse is listed on the National Register of Historic Places, a federal hearing is required for demolition and federal funds would not be available for any project that would replace it. The unpleasant odor remains, so there are few possible commercial uses.

In 1987, the Workhouse was reopened to handle the overflow of prisoners from the Hamilton County Justice Center. Light offenders, those convicted of DUI, and men in a work release program were held here.

In the 1840s, municipal governments began to take responsibility for the public welfare, particularly for those groups of individuals, like children, who were seen as helpless victims of their environments. On March 12, 1845, the City of Cincinnati authorized construction of a House of Correction and a "House of Reformation, or Refuge" for the "reclamation

257

and improvement of those young offenders, who might yet be snatched from destruction and saved to the community."

The **16 Cincinnati House of Refuge** was dedicated on October 7, 1850. The site, now occupied by the Highway Maintenance Division building of the Department of Public Works, 3300 Colerain Avenue, was "in the country, one mile from the city, healthful, convenient of access by the turnpike, the canal, or the railroad." The 4-story stone building designed by Henry Walter (1788-1849) could house up to 350 youngsters and sat on ten acres that were surrounded by a high stone wall.

Before the House of Refuge opened, children arrested and convicted of crimes were sent to the county prison. There, wrote the House's superintendent, they *"associated with hardened criminals of every degree in crime . . . and [were] faithfully instructed in every species of vice . . . we were training multitudes for infamy and a life of wretchedness. . . . Our mission is, to take the youth, degraded by poverty and crime, and to lead them by kindness and judicious advice to a life of virtue and usefulness."*

Boys and girls from six to nineteen years became inmates of the House of Refuge if committed by parents, guardians, the masters to whom they had been apprenticed, or the courts. A few without homes sought admission on their own. In the first decades, the most frequent offenses for which children were sent to the institution were vagrancy, petty larceny, and what was called incorrigibility—truancy, running away, or "total want of obedience to proper control." The average age of inmates was around thirteen; about half the children lacked one or both parents. Black children were excluded until 1870.

Children committed to the House of Refuge were placed in one of several divisions or "families" according to age and severity of offense. During their stay, they worked, slept, played, and studied with that group. Black children were eventually segregated into a single division.

While children were committed to the House for an indefinite time for the reformation of bad habits, a system of merits earned through good conduct won most of them release on

*The House of Refuge admitted delinquent youngsters as well as children and infants whose parents could not provide adequate care for them.*

parole in about eighteen months. Many of the boys were apprenticed to learn one of a number of trades, including farming, shoemaking, printing, hatmaking, carpentry, tailoring, bookbinding, and carriage trimming. Girls were placed with families to learn housekeeping.

Six days a week, the schedule for youngsters consisted of about three hours of schoolwork, two hours for play, and six to seven hours learning vocational skills in the workshops. The children's work was intended not only to teach them skills and good work habits, it also helped defray the expenses of operating the institution.

Girls did laundry, sewing, and knitting for the residents of the House, while the boys helped with the upkeep of the building and other expenses by working in the tailor and shoe shops, bakery and greenhouse, doing carpentry and masonry, helping run the power plant, printing the institution's stationery and annual reports, and making brooms for sale. A Colored Waiters class was established in 1895 so that black boys *only* could acquire "superior qualifications for like employment outside."

Daily Scripture readings and Sunday services provided religious education. House administrators claimed that 80 to 90% of the children went on to lead honest lives.

By the 1880s, Cincinnatians were becoming increasingly dissatisfied with the House of Refuge, which had also begun to receive more children who had committed no crime but were simply homeless or without adequate homes. In 1888, half of the 306 admitted fell into these two categories, and many were as young as one year old. A separate kindergarten building erected in 1890 was subsequently adapted for infants.

In 1904, Superintendent James Allison wrote glowingly of the House of Refuge's school work, manual training classes, program of calisthenics and military drill, and the general deportment of the children. The buildings themselves, however, were "not up to modern requirements;" fire protection was "totally inadequate," and the facility itself, now surrounded by housing and factories and in the shadow of the Workhouse, was "an environment totally unfit for young children."

An investigation of the House of Refuge got underway in 1912 during the administration of reform mayor Henry T. Hunt (1878-1956). On February 18, a new head for the House of Refuge was appointed. On April 29, the Bureau of Municipal Research issued a report harshly critical of the House and its policies.

Superintendent Edward N. Clopper (1879-1953), wrote in his annual report at the end of that year: *". . . the old House of Refuge is one of the worst examples in the country of the congregate institution for children. . . . The buildings are old and obsolete; most of them were erected in 1850 as a prison . . . the windows are barred, and the pitiably small playgrounds in the rear are overshadowed by a high and sinister prison wall . . . ."*

The city quickly instituted changes including reducing the percentage of dependent children at the House, hiring parole officers, transferring control of the school to the Board of Education, discarding the military style uniforms that made boys so conspicuous outside the House, opening the 5-acre front lawns for individual gardens, and constructing a playground and wading pool.

A determined campaign to replace the House got underway, and in December, City Council authorized a bond issue for the purchase of Glenview, a farm for delinquent boys in Glendale which opened in spring of 1913, and Hillcrest, for delinquent girls, in Wyoming.

The House of Refuge buildings were vacant by 1916 and were demolished during the 1920s. The site was developed as a park with tennis courts and ballfields. But as the neighborhood became more industrial and less residential, the city decided the property was underused and valuable for other development. The park was closed, and the maintenance building was completed in 1961.

**Turn left on Arlington Street.**

The **17** **Crosley Building,** 1329 Arlington Street, an 8-story concrete building with "C" emblems above the door and on the 9-story tower, was originally headquarters of the Crosley Radio Corporation, at one time the nation's largest manufacturer of low-cost table-top radios. Powel Crosley, Jr. (1886-1961), who headed the company, built his first radio in early 1921.

The story goes that, upon discovering that one of the new crystal sets that his young son wanted cost over one hundred dollars, Crosley used a twenty-five-cent booklet titled *The ABCs of Radio* to assemble his own crystal receiver. He then decided to undertake mass production of the sets; work got underway at Crosley Manufacturing Company plants in Northside and Camp Washington.

Crosley's Harko radio was a huge Christmas success, and the following year, the company was the largest manufacturer of radio sets in the United States.

Crosley determined that he could sell more radios if there was worthwhile programing to listen to. He installed a 20-watt transmitter in his College Hill home and in July 1921, began broadcasting using his own collection of phonograph records. In March 1922, the federal government licensed him to conduct a regular broadcasting station, and WLW went on the air with an unprecedented 50-watt signal.

The strength of the signal was increased to 500 watts in 1923 to improve the quality and range of reception. A contest awarding a box of candy to the first listener from each state to send a telegram to the station drew entries from forty-two states and three Canadian provinces. The signal was boosted to 5,000 watts in 1925, and in 1927, WLW gained sole control of the 700 kilocycle frequency, becoming the first "clear channel" station.

The company manufactured 2,000 radios a day at its peak, though by 1930, it had slipped from first place to fifth. But the Crosley Corporation, employing more than 3,000 workers during its best years, expanded to the production of refrigerators, washing machines, stoves, baby strollers, and the X-ER-VAC, a mechanical scalp massager that reputedly stimulated hair growth.

In 1923, Powel Crosley, along with his brother, Lewis, had established the Crosley Radio Corporation and bought a small brick building at this site. An addition was erected in 1926, and the large Crosley Building in 1929. WLW's studios moved to the eighth floor and became the country's first 50,000-watt commercial station.

Perhaps WLW's most spectacular "first and only" came at 9:03 p.m. on May 2, 1934, when President Franklin D. Roosevelt pressed a gold-plated telegraph key on his White House desk and cut in WLW's 500,000-watt transmitter. The signal was more powerful than any in the world.

WLW's studios were the largest outside New York City, and the station had a 19½-hour daily broadcast schedule. In 1942, as war work required more of the factory space, the radio studios were moved from Camp Washington to a new center downtown.

WLW-Radio was the "Cradle of the Stars." Among the entertainers who worked for this Cincinnati giant were Eddie Albert, sisters Rosemary and Betty Clooney and their brother Nick, Doris Day, the Ink Spots, Ruth Lyons, the Mills Brothers, Rod Serling, Red Skelton, "Fats" Waller, and Andy Williams.

Crosley Radio Corporation also operated a short wave station that supplied owners of its Reado model with sports and new broadcasts delivered on tickertape, and another that provided ten hours of daily Spanish-language programing to Argentina. On September 23, 1944, a massive 20,000-watt short wave transmitter facility at Bethany, Ohio, was dedicated and designated for Voice of America broadcasts. Every day, twenty hours of programs developed by the federal government to offset German propaganda were sent out in twenty-six languages and eleven dialects to Europe, South America, and North Africa.

In 1945, Aviation Corporation (AVCO) bought Crosley's radio broad-

*The Crosley Building housed not only radio manufacturing operations but, for a time, radio studios as well.*

casting and manufacturing interests, and the inventor turned his attention to making small cars, the Crosley, one business venture that failed.

AVCO closed this plant in 1960, dropped the Crosley name, and phased out the product line. The factory was subsequently sold and used for storage and by light manufacturing, direct mail, and small printing companies. Multimedia, Inc., purchased the radio station in 1975.

**Turn left on Spring Grove Avenue.**

The largest Cincinnati meat processing firm operating in the 1980s, **18 Kahn's & Company,** 3241 Spring Grove Avenue, began as a retail meat market. In 1882, Elias Kahn (1835-1899) opened a store at 1433 Central Avenue in the West End and soon started a small slaughtering and processing operation in rooms behind the shop.

After Kahn's death, his children continued to run the business which grew to include five stores in the West End and Avondale. In 1903, the firm opened a separate slaughtering facility on Stark Street, moving it the next year to Livingston Street.

Under the name E. Kahn's Sons, the company continued to expand. Its Livingston Street processing facility handled only cattle, so in 1919, Kahn's purchased the Butcher's Packing Company plant on Poplar Street that was set up to handle pigs and lambs. More processing space was added in 1922, when the firm occupied the former John Hauck brewery on Linn Street.

In 1926, in order to consolidate its operations, Kahn's bought a failing slaughtering company, Cincinnati Abattoir, on Spring Grove Avenue next to the Union Stockyards. Most of the old Abattoir buildings were demolished to make room for the new headquarters that E. Kahn's Sons opened on the site in 1928.

This location, adjacent to the stockyards and rail sidings, increased Kahn's efficiency, but it was the company's aggressive marketing and promotion activities that made it the twelfth largest meatpacker in the United States. Although Kahn's phased out retail outlets in the 1920s, its management remained consumer-oriented. As early as 1883, Kahn's had begun using the American Beauty Rose trademark and advertising that products with this trademark were of the highest, purest quality. By the mid-1930s, Kahn's had surpassed H. H. Meyer as Cincinnati's leading meatpacker.

In the mid-twentieth century, Kahn's made further improvements in its facilities and products. In 1949, the plant was expanded. The company's research and development department introduced products such as hams without the bone, sliced luncheon meat in vacuum-sealed packages, and mildly-spiced all-meat wieners.

Product improvements and coordinated advertising, merchandising, and sales promotions sustained Kahn's success at a time when many packing firms were cutting back or closing. Kahn's provided retailers with advertising plans and ready-made promotional materials. Its marketing people created catchy slogans such as "The Wiener the World Awaited" and a variety of promotions like enclosing recipes or baseball cards in product packages.

But large independent firms became increasingly rare; Kahn's was the last major independent packer in Cincinnati by 1965, and was itself facing a sharp decline in profits. The following year, it became part of the Consolidated Foods Corporation, a Chicago conglomerate.

As part of Consolidated Foods— renamed Sara Lee Corporation in the 1980s—Kahn's was able to hold a major share of a regional market. The company was also able to update and expand its 7-acre complex. In 1974, it acquired about one-third of the Union Stockyards, enabling Kahn's to purchase animals directly from stockmen. Kahn's became the last major meatpacker in the city to continue slaughtering hogs.

By the mid 1980s, Kahn's was by far the largest meatpacking operation in Cincinnati, employing about 600 workers and slaughtering an average of 10,000 hogs each week. Most of the remaining processing companies in the area had fewer that one hundred workers and handled 400 to 600 animals weekly.

When Cincinnati's first railroads entered service in the 1840s and 1850s, the railyards and freight depots were located near the river in the southernmost portions of the Mill Creek and Deer Creek Valleys. In the late nineteenth and early twentieth centuries, however, many of the city's rail facilities followed industry and moved farther up the Mill Creek Valley. Eventually, most of the area's rail equipment maintenance and freight car classification operations were concentrated in a single facility, the **19 CSX Transportation System's Queensgate Yard,** with offices at 2815 Spring Grove Avenue.

It was not until the late 1880s, when the Cincinnati Southern Railroad started expanding its operations, that an important marshalling yard— a facility where cars could be "classified" or assigned destinations and assembled into trains—was built away from the river.

The Cincinnati Southern was a relatively new line, organized in 1869 by Cincinnati business and government leaders to reestablish a profitable economic relationship with the South. This railroad was unique in that it was municipally owned and leased to the Cincinnati, New Orleans & Texas Pacific line. Construction of the line began in 1873 and was completed in 1880. Later that decade, the Southern began building its own series of classification tracks along McLean from Gest to West Liberty Street.

As the Mill Creek Valley developed into a manufacturing center, other rail facilities were built to the north of the Cincinnati Southern railyards. The most significant of these were the Baltimore & Ohio marshalling yards and maintenance shops which were set up around the turn of the century.

B&O classification tracks and freight depots were clustered in Brighton near Harrison Avenue. The roundhouse, workshops, and another group of sidings were in northern Camp Washington where there not only was plenty of level, undeveloped land available, but the noise and dirt of heavy rail traffic, not acceptable in more affluent neighborhoods, were tolerated.

After the 1920s, few major changes were made in the Mill Creek Valley's railyard network, except when Cincinnati Union Terminal was built. The Union Terminal Company's addition of new track and a large roundhouse in Brighton necessitated some rearrangement of freight facilities. For example, between 1930 and 1933, new freight depots for the Big Four line, Cincinnati Southern, and the B&O were erected at 2801-2815 Spring Grove Avenue to replace older depots in the West End and Brighton.

In the mid-twentieth century, ownership of many railroads changed through purchases and mergers. When the Chesapeake & Ohio absorbed the B&O in 1963, most of the railyards in the Mill Creek Valley came under the control of the Chessie System, as the combined railroads

*The railroad facilities that had stretched along the length of Brighton and Camp Washington since the late nineteenth century once included a large roundhouse built as a part of the Union Terminal project.*

were called.

In the 1970s, Chessie officials decided to improve the efficiency of their Cincinnati facilities by consolidation and modernization. Between 1977 and 1981, Chessie spent $72 million to combine five existing railyards from the riverfront to Camp Washington into a single 250-acre yard.

The new complex, known as the Queensgate Yard, had a capacity of 3,200 cars per day, and its computerized operation was vastly more efficient that the previous arrangements. The 140 tracks in the valley system were reduced to fifty, and a computerized control center made it possible to move more cars through the yard more quickly. The yard also utilized a "hump" system in which cars were pushed to the top of a ramp, released, and propelled by gravity into the proper track selected through the controller's computer.

Construction of the new rail complex eliminated most of the earlier yard structures, such as the old B&O roundhouse, but some of the older buildings remained. The Union Terminal roundhouse survived as a warehouse, and the B&O freight depot on Spring Grove became the administrative center for the complex. In the 1980s, the Chessie System was reorganized as CSX Transportation.

**20** **The Andrew Jergens Company,** 2535 Spring Grove Avenue, began in 1882 when Andrew Jergens Sr. (1852-1929), Charles F. Geilfus (1856-1914), and W. L. Haworth opened the Andrews Soap Company at 180 Spring Grove Avenue, just west of the Miami & Erie Canal. All three men had been involved in other short-lived soapmaking ventures, but Jergens is said to have provided the $5,000 capital that financed this business, so the company was named after him and he became president. All three men, however, stirred the soap kettles and sold their products door to door.

Brighton was a logical site for the soapworks. It was close to the slaughterhouses that supplied the necessary lard for soap and near transportation facilities—the canal and rail lines. Those workers who did not live within walking distance could ride the streetcar to their jobs.

The Andrews Soap Company moved to a second plant at 228 Spring Grove in 1887. In 1894, under the name Andrew Jergens & Company, the business and its twenty-five employees moved once again and occupied its present location.

Jergens' company was a late arrival on the Cincinnati soap manufacturing scene, long dominated by the Michael Werk Soap Company (1832) and Procter & Gamble (1837). Unlike the other two firms, however, the Andrews Soap Company began as a soapmaker and made its mark with the production of milder French milled soaps and assorted specialty soaps—glycerin transparent soaps, castile soaps, cocoa soaps, tar soaps, and shaving soaps.

In 1901, the Andrew Jergens Company purchased two firms that gave it two of its best selling products: Woodbury soap, later promoted as the soap "For the Skin You Love to Touch," and Jergens Lotion. Few companies have dominated the market the way Jergens did in hand lotion for eighty years.

Andrew Jergens, Jr. (1881-1967), became president in 1929. Under his leadership, sales increased, the workforce at the Cincinnati plant grew to over 1,000, and plants elsewhere were acquired or expanded. Jergens completed a 4-story, 60,000-square foot addition to the Spring Grove plant in 1966.

Jergens was the world's largest producer of hand care products in 1969, and the combination of relatively small corporate size and product success in one line made the firm a tempting target for takeover. In 1970, American Brands purchased Jergens for $100 million, making it a corporate subsidiary. Later that decade, Jergens' sales rose as the company diversified and improved marketing techniques. In 1988, the company announced that it was being taken over by a Japanese conglomerate.

Jergen's Cincinnati plant is composed of a series of buildings, one of which is the former home of the **Warner Elevator Company,** 2613 Spring Grove Avenue, founded in 1860 by Warren Warner (1811-1891). Credited with inventing the hydraulic elevator in 1855, Warner's company became one of the nation's largest independent manufacturers of elevators.

In 1952, Warner Elevator employees bought out management; a year later, Shepherd Elevator purchased the workers' stock and formed the Shepherd-Warner Elevator Company. After the Spring Grove Avenue building was sold to Jergens, the new company moved to Oakley. In 1958, Dover Elevator Company purchased Shepherd-Warner, and the Warner name disappeared from the elevator market.

**Tour ends.**

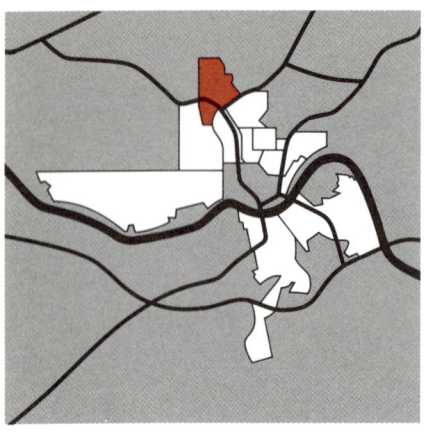

# Cumminsville - Northside - South Cumminsville

The communities of Cumminsville, Northside, and South Cumminsville occupy a 2-square mile area at the widest section of the Mill Creek Valley bordered by Spring Grove Cemetery on the east, Interstate-75 and Camp Washington to the south, Fairmount and Mt. Airy Forest on the west, and College Hill to the north.

When it was first settled at the end of the eighteenth century, this vicinity was known variously as Ludlow's Station and Tan Yard. In 1789, Colonel Israel Ludlow (1765-1804), who had surveyed Cincinnati as United States Surveyor General, acquired 125 acres in partial payment for his work. His tract included parts of present-day Spring Grove Cemetery and Clifton, as well as Northside. A year later, Ludlow erected a fortified station just northeast of the present intersection of Hamilton and Spring Grove Avenues. The blockhouse, built to secure the area from Indian attack, was first known as Mill Creek Station, but then came to be called Ludlow's Station.

In 1805, this territory, approximately five miles from Cincinnati, was occupied only by Robert Badgely, Mathias Roll, Ezekiel Hutchinson, and the heirs of Israel Ludlow. In 1811, Hutchinson built the Hotel of the Golden Lamb at what is now the northwest corner of Blue Rock Street and Hamilton Avenue. By then, Hamilton Pike was already a major route for people and goods traveling between the growing village of Cincinnati and settlements to the north. Six years later, David Cummins purchased four acres of land just south of Hutchinson's and constructed one of the area's first industries, the Grid Iron Tannery.

Hutchinson and Cummins feuded over water rights. Fearing that her livestock would not have enough water in summer, Hutchinson's wife blocked water pipes running from the Mill Creek to the tannery. In retaliation, some tannery workers girdled Hutchinson's fruit trees and hamstrung his stock. By the time their dispute was resolved in court, both men had lost their land because they were unable to pay off mortgages which they had taken to finance litigation against one another.

In the early 1820s, more settlers began arriving. Ephraim Knowlton (1803-1888) came to supervise digging of the Miami & Erie Canal; in 1830, he built a general store on the northwest corner of Spring Grove and Hamilton. This building also served as the area's first post office. When Knowlton was commissioned postmaster in 1838, he named the settlement, then with a population of 200, Cumminsville, after the original owner of his land. At the same time, Jacob Hoffner (1799-1894), a merchant, bought the Hotel of the Golden Lamb and forty-seven acres that had once belonged to Hutchinson.

The Miami & Erie Canal opened in 1829 and spurred some development in Cumminsville. Small industries and a few hotels and taverns were established along its banks. Yet Cumminsville remained essentially rural. Into the 1840s, it consisted of only a single grocery and a few houses.

In 1851, the Cincinnati, Hamilton & Dayton Railroad (CH&D) laid track through the flat flood plain of the Mill Creek Valley, making the area more accessible to commerce and industry. German and Irish workers who came to construct the rail line stayed to work in the factories that were built along the canal and the railroad. In 1845, Knowlton subdivided an area from the Mill Creek to Colerain Avenue for worker housing. Five years later, Hoffner set aside twenty acres for a similar subdivision.

Mule and horse-drawn streetcars linked Cumminsville to the city in the 1860s and spurred additional growth. Later subdividers included the Ludlow family and Timothy Kirby (1797-1876). Kirby, a lawyer and banker who became a major Cincinnati landowner, envisioned his Cumminsville settlement northwest of the CH&D and the early subdivisions and factories as a model village. He hoped to teach workers who lived there the values and responsibilities of middle-class life.

Cumminsville was incorporated in November 1865. Eight years later, in 1873, the community was annexed to Cincinnati. With a population of more than 4,200, nearly half of which was German, Cumminsville wanted the improved public services that the city could provide.

*By the 1880s, area residents and businessmen were identifying the northern part of their community as "North Side," as this advertisement from an 1886 directory indicates.*

From 1880 to 1900, Cumminsville experienced its major period of growth and developed into two distinct communities— Cumminsville and Northside. These changes were tied to the extension of electric streetcar lines along Hamilton Avenue and up Colerain. If Cumminsville had earlier been characterized by factories and worker housing, the new routes along Hamilton Avenue brought in both middle and upper-income families who built houses on streets to the north of the original settlement. To distinguish their enclave from Cumminsville, the residents and developers called this area Northside. By 1910, the combined population of Cumminsville and Northside was approaching 15,000.

The area's expanding population included blacks as well as people of German and Irish descent, who predominated in Northside and the vicinity of Knowlton's Corner. As early as the turn of the century, the blocks around Dreman and Follet Streets became home to a number of black families. This sub-neighborhood, along with much of the rest of the older part of Cumminsville that bordered on Camp Washington, became known as South Cumminsville.

The opening of the Ludlow Avenue Viaduct in 1914 linked Northside and Cumminsville more directly to the city and other Cincinnati neighborhoods and transformed Knowlton's Corner into the third busiest shopping district in the city. By 1930, the population of the

*By the mid-1920s, Northside was fully built up with substantial and attractive middle-income housing.*

area was nearly 22,000.

In the mid-twentieth century, however, a number of factors halted growth in this vicinity. The Depression closed many of the area's factories. In the oldest parts of the community, the housing showed signs of deterioration, and many of those residents who could afford to move away did so. In the 1950s and 1960s, many houses around Knowlton's Corner and in Northside were divided into rental units. As older residents died or moved out, they were often replaced by lower-income white families who saw the area as a step up from Over-the-Rhine. The new residents used the older place names such as Cumminsville and Knowlton's Corner less frequently, and gradually, the entire community, except for South Cumminsville, was identified simply as Northside.

South Cumminsville's future as a community looked even less promising as city planners proposed a route for the construction of the I-74 and I-75 expressways that would cut through South Cumminsville and require the demolition of much "obsolete" housing. The planners also argued that, because of recurrent flooding, South

Cumminsville should be given over entirely to redevelopment for industrial uses.

Instead, the city government chose South Cumminsville as a site for a low-income housing development, the 573-unit Millvale Housing Project, constructed in 1954 expressly for blacks. The black population increased in the 1950s and 1960s until the neighborhood was predominantly black. But little industrial redevelopment took place in the vicinity, and employment opportunities remained limited. Nearly a decade later, the construction of I-74 further isolated South Cumminsville and its black residents from the rest of Cumminsville and Northside.

By the 1970s, the population of South Cumminsville-Northside had declined to what it had been at the beginning of the century. One-sixth of the residents were over 65, 83% had not completed high school, and half earned less than $10,000 per year. In South Cumminsville, 65% of the neighborhood was eligible for some form of federal assistance, and only 31% of the residents owned their own homes. Despite the availability of vacant land and abandoned factories in relatively good condition, manufacturing activity still was not expanding in this area. Small-scale industry predominated in South Cumminsville—twenty-six of the thirty-two firms here had fewer than seventy-five employees.

These neighborhoods, however, were not without hope. Despite a percentage of residents living in poverty that was twice as high as the city average, the number of owner-occupied homes in South Cumminsville increased noticeably in the late 1970s and 1980s. In 1986, a partnership was formed with the City of Cincinnati, Aetna Life & Casualty Company, a local organization called Working in Neighborhoods, and South Cumminsville community groups to rehabilitate old housing and to build new units, all to be sold to low and middle-income homeowners.

Northside faced some of the same problems confronted by other older neighborhoods, but its location made it convenient for commuters. Therefore, many of the neighborhood's single-family homes remained owner-occupied and in moderately good condition.

Recently, Northside has undergone renewal typical of some older neighborhoods that have begun to attract young middle-income families. Its residents have a strong sense of community pride that is expressed through active neighborhood organizations. Group Action in Northside, the Northside Business Club, and the Northside Urban Conservation Corporation have pushed commercial redevelopment in the area, campaigning for better street lighting, more off-street parking, and the repair of buildings.

**Cumminsville - Northside - South Cumminsville**

Tour Length
11.5 miles

North

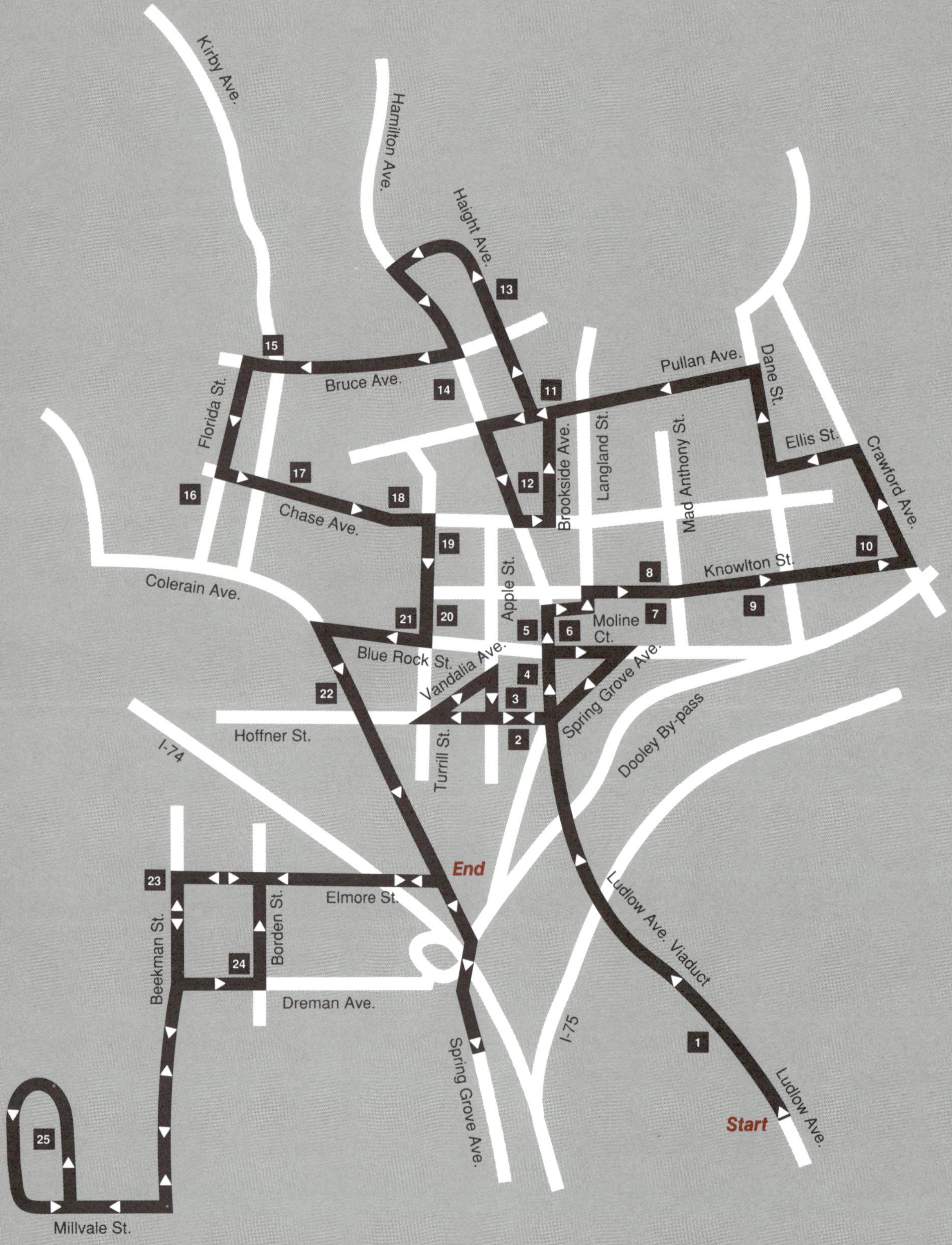

Kirby Ave.
Hamilton Ave.
Haight Ave.
Bruce Ave.
Florida St.
Chase Ave.
Colerain Ave.
Pullan Ave.
Dane St.
Ellis St.
Crawford Ave.
Brookside Ave.
Langland St.
Mad Anthony St.
Knowlton St.
Apple St.
Moline Ct.
Blue Rock St.
Vandalia Ave.
Spring Grove Ave.
Hoffner St.
Turrill St.
Dooley By-pass
I-74
End
Elmore St.
Beekman St.
Borden St.
Dreman Ave.
Ludlow Ave. Viaduct
I-75
Spring Grove Ave.
Ludlow Ave.
Start
Millvale St.
1
2
3
4
5
6
7
8
9
10
11
12
13
14
15
16
17
18
19
20
21
22
23
24
25

# Cumminsville · Northside · South Cumminsville

**Tour begins on Ludlow Avenue at the Ludlow Avenue Viaduct.**

Knowlton's Corner, an intersection of four streetcar lines, was a major business district at the turn of the century. Merchants prospered as people making transfers at the intersection patronized their shops. The streetcars, however, had to cross the B&O-Southwestern railroad tracks on the east side of the Mill Creek, pass over the creek on the Dodsworth Avenue bridge, enter the 5-way intersection of Knowlton's Corner, and then cross another set of B&O tracks at Hamilton Avenue and Blue Rock Street, causing traffic congestion that was both dangerous and inconvenient.

In 1909, city engineers proposed building a viaduct that would carry streetcars over the creek and both sets of railroad tracks and deposit passengers further up Hamilton near Blue Rock. Merchants at the intersection of Spring Grove and Hamilton Avenues objected, fearing a loss of business, so the engineers created a new plan for a shorter viaduct that would terminate at Knowlton's Corner.

Work on this structure began in 1912 and was completed in 1914. The concrete and steel **1 Ludlow Viaduct** was 1,750 feet long and sixty feet wide, with two sets of streetcar tracks down the center and lanes for automobile traffic on each side. While the viaduct was more direct than the old route, it increased congestion by turning Knowlton's Corner into a 6-way intersection and making the area more accessible to cars and trucks. Nonetheless, the viaduct also aided local businesses as the intersection remained a primary public transportation transfer point.

The Ludlow Avenue Viaduct carried streetcars and a growing volume of automobile traffic until the 1937 flood covered its northern end. Had the structure been as long as originally proposed in 1909, it would not have been inundated. Flood damage to the viaduct's foundation required a major rebuilding in 1939.

In 1956, the viaduct was closed again when construction of I-75 made demolition of almost half of its southern end necessary. That section was replaced with a modern highway overpass, but the original concrete arches and pylons at the western end over the Mill Creek remain.

At present, the Ludlow Avenue Viaduct is still a key link between the city and the northwestern suburbs. It carries heavy automobile traffic, as well as the buses that replaced the streetcars in 1951, over the railroad tracks, I-75, and the Mill Creek. The viaduct is still a mixed blessing for the local business district. While it creates traffic congestion that prevents some potential customers from patronizing Northside businesses, it also brings shoppers who otherwise would not come to the area. Its importance to business in Northside was demonstrated in 1986 when land subsidence damaged the structure. While the viaduct was closed, stores along Hamilton Avenue suffered a considerable drop in activity.

**Cross the Ludlow Avenue Viaduct. Turn right on Blue Rock Street, right on Spring Grove Avenue. Cross Hamilton Avenue and bear right to Hoffner Street.**

Above the main entrance of the **2 First United Church of Christ,** 1628 Hoffner Street, the nameplate inscribed *Der Ersten Deutschen Evang. Prot. Gemeinde Kirche in Cumminsville* declares that this was originally the First German Evangelical Protestant Church, one of Cumminsville's several German congregations.

When the original Cumminsville German Evangelical house of worship on Apple Street became too small, the group obtained a lot on one of the suburb's more important streets and erected this Gothic style stone and brick structure. The sanctuary had frescoed walls, a large pipe organ, and rich stained glass windows. The congregation was made up of "substantial citizens who own their homes and have a snug sum put away for a rainy day," according to a contemporary newspaper account. The church was dedicated on April 29, 1894, and the adjacent parsonage completed in 1913.

The flood of 1937 halted work on the auditorium on the east side of the church, but the project was completed in August of that year. By 1945—the year of another flood—First Evangelical Church listed 410 pupils in the Sunday school classes and had recorded a total of 8,005 baptisms, 4,825 funerals, and 2,645 marriages.

This independent Protestant congregation joined the Evangelical and Reformed Church in 1957. In 1955, 1,000 members were listed, but that number declined sharply as new suburbs drew members away from Northside. Today, First United Church of Christ has an aging congregation with fewer than 150 active members. Rummage sales and an annual sauerkraut supper help raise money for the church. Each month, First United serves a free noon meal open to everyone.

**Turn right on Vandalia Avenue, right on Apple Street.**

Today used by the J. C. Steel Food Products Company for production and storage, the 2-story painted brick building at 4014 Apple Street was the first home of the **3 First German Evangelical Church**.

The congregation, organized in September 1855, held its first services in Knowlton's Hall, but bad roads discouraged many from attending. By the end of October, when there were only sixteen members, the congregation decided that a building of its own would help increase attendance. Jacob Hoffner, a Cumminsville landholder and generous supporter of local endeavors, donated the lot.

The cornerstone of this church was laid in October 1856; the structure was enlarged in 1878. However, this building, too, was outgrown, and a new church was dedicated on Hoffner Street in 1894.

In 1895, the Israel Ludlow Post, No. 76, Grand Army of the Republic, purchased the old church to use as a meeting hall. The group of Civil War veterans removed the steeple and mounted a cannon on the cupola. By 1960, the GAR Memorial Hall had served as meeting place for nearly two dozen civic, professional, and fraternal organizations including the Brotherhood of Railway Trainmen, Independent Order of Shepherds, Daughters of Pocahontas, Cincinnati Rabbit Breeders Association, Granite Cutters Union, Knights of Pythias, Spanish American War Veterans, and Veterans of Foreign Wars.

Julius C. Steel bought the structure in 1961 to house his food company but continued to rent out the meeting hall. As the neighborhood became less convenient for social gatherings, the business eventually took over the whole building.

**Turn left on Hoffner Street, left on Hamilton Avenue.**

The two blocks of the **4 Hamilton Avenue Business District,** north and south of Blue Rock Street, began to develop as early as 1811, when Ezekiel Hutchinson built the Hotel of the Golden Lamb at the northwest corner of Hamilton and Blue Rock. In 1825, Ephraim Knowlton opened the general store that later also served as a post office at Hamilton and present day Spring Grove. But it

*Before suburban shopping centers became prevalent, Knowlton's Corner, shown here in the 1940s, was one of the most active business districts in Cincinnati.*

was the construction of the Miami & Erie Canal and then the CH&D railroad that made Hamilton Avenue an important commercial and industrial district.

Through much of the nineteenth century, the Cumminsville business district was oriented toward factories along the canal and railroad and to workers there. Industries such as a wagon and steelworks, as well as groceries and taverns, were established along Hamilton. In 1873, when Cumminsville was annexed to Cincinnati, there were thirty-seven taverns and twenty-two small groceries in this community, as well as an assortment of bakers, barbers, blacksmiths, dry goods merchants, physicians, and a few tailors.

When, during the last two decades of the century, Northside emerged as a community of relatively well-to-do residents, the business district catered to suburban commuters as well as to working-class Cumminsville. In 1881, William Multner opened a modern

store with "a full line of staple and fancy groceries." The founding of the North Side Bank in 1888 reflected the growth and prosperity of the area.

In the first decades of the twentieth century, the Northside Business Club, located at Knowlton's Corner, overlooked a vigorous business district. In 1913, cafe owner Henry Dillmann built the Palm Hotel, and the Park Theater touted as the most modern motion picture theater in the nation, opened at 4163. In addition, Hamilton Avenue businesses included milliners, upholsterers, tailors, and an ice cream shop.

A decade later, the business district was remarkably unchanged. A number of chain stores, such as two Kroger stores, one at Knowlton's Corner and the other at 4124, and an A&P grocery at 4168, joined the older businesses, and a new car dealership, a tire store, and a repair shop heralded the day of the automobile.

By the end of the 1930s, however, the Depression had taken a heavy toll,

particularly among independent businessmen. Nevertheless, a number of the small and medium-sized enterprises survived, and at mid-century, Northside appeared to have a healthy business district with strong ties to the surrounding community.

Hamilton Avenue began to change, however, in the late 1950s and early 1960s. There were a number of vacant stores, and new shops such as the Northside Bargain Center indicated economic decline. By the mid-1960s, the number of cut-rate retail shops in Northside had increased markedly. At the same time, neighborhood stores continued to close and were replaced by service businesses such as office supply stores and collection agencies that did not rely on the immediate area for customers. Vacancies rose and there were more marginal businesses like used and discount clothing and furniture stores, which depended on low rents to survive.

In the 1970s, Northside businessmen seeking ways to attract new commerce turned their attention to the nineteenth-century structures along Hamilton that had not been modernized. In 1982, the City of Cincinnati designated the turn-of-the-century commercial area as a local historic district.

A year later, the Northside Community Council put together a plan to renovate the business district. Several structures in the 4100 block were rehabilitated, including the Park Theatre, which was renovated as the Grote Bakery, and the buildings now occupied by a feminist bookstore and the Northside Urban Conservation League. A number of small shops dealing primarily in crafts and antiques also moved into Northside, but most have not survived.

Presently, the Northside business district is neither a local shopping center, nor is it able to support a broad range of specialty shops. Rather, it continues to mix these functions and to provide a low-rent location for marginal stores selling discount merchandise and for service businesses.

The 2-acre **5 Jacob Hoffner Park,** Hamilton Avenue and Blue Rock Street, was part of the land originally owned by Ezekiel Hutchinson who, in 1811, built a tavern here. Hutchinson went bankrupt in court battles with David Cummins over water rights, and the property was abandoned until 1834 when Jacob Hoffner bought the building and forty-seven acres.

Hoffner (1799-1894) had begun his career in 1815 as an apprentice to a baker on Main Street. Fifteen years later, he erected Cincinnati's largest supply store on that same street. In 1836, Hoffner remodeled Hutchinson's tavern and moved to Cumminsville. He created six acres of gardens that included a greenhouse decorated with bronze griffins, a pool, more than two dozen statues collected during his travels in Europe, and an array of plants ranging from cacti to fruit trees, roses, and petunias.

Hoffner felt a strong commitment to developing Cumminsville as an attractive neighborhood. Around 1850, he subdivided about twenty acres of his farm between present-day Hoffner and Blue Rock Streets. In the deed to each lot was a clause stating that after his death, the estate would be given to the city for a park. Consequently, the adjacent building lots commanded higher prices.

Hoffner also donated lots to the First German Evangelical Church and the Hoffner Masonic Lodge, 4120 Hamilton Avenue, and sold eleven acres at half price for the construction of St. Joseph Orphanage. In 1844, the *Enquirer* noted that Hoffner's "Fortune Founded on a Barrel of Flour" might "now be safely estimated away up in the hundreds of thousands of dollars." "Cumminsville's King" owned both downtown and suburban property.

Jacob Hoffner's plan to give Cumminsville a park failed. Not only did the Park Board refuse the property, but Hoffner's relatives contested his will. The Cincinnati Art Museum received Hoffner's art collection, and the two stone lions that had guarded the entrance of his estate became "Mick" and "Mack," standing in front of McMicken Hall at the University of Cincinnati. The house was razed in 1904 and the remaining land was subdivided.

The City Park Board purchased this corner section for a park in 1916 and constructed a shelterhouse and two swimming pools, one for boys and one for girls, at the Northside Park and Playground. In 1970, when the Cincinnati Recreation commission opened the McKie Recreation Center, a larger and more comprehensive facility on Chase Avenue, the playground here was converted to a park and dedicated on May 7, 1978, as Jacob Hoffner Park.

**Turn right on Moline Court.**

Standing on one of the neighborhood's last brick-paved streets, the six small 2-story Mansard style **6 Moline Court Houses,** 3-11 Moline Court, were built around 1894 by Charles R. Wild, a dealer in coal, lime, plaster, cement, sewer pipe, and tiling. His business was located at the northeast corner of Hamilton and Blue Rock, near the railroad tracks; Wild erected these dwellings so his employees could live near their jobs.

**Turn left on Langland Street, right on Knowlton Street.**

Large-scale manufacture such as the **7 Parks Woodworking Machine Company,** 1501 and 1546 Knowlton Street, came to Cumminsville in the late nineteenth century.

Louis F. Parks (b.1862), a Kentuckian, arrived in Cincinnati in 1884 and began building mortising and tenoning machines in a plant on Colerain Avenue. Parks was an inventor with numerous patents to his name; his foot-powered mortising machine is alleged to be the first of its kind on the market.

The company moved to this location, near the CH&D tracks, around 1900. The 2-story frame shop, 1501 Knowlton Street, where machine parts are made, was erected around 1910, followed by the larger assembly building at 1546, now a warehouse. Parks' company later produced ball bearing band saws for foot and hand power, and various other types of saws and planers.

It is said that Parks was a pacifist, and for that reason was edged out of the business around World War I when Sears, Roebuck & Company bought the firm. Sears catalogues featured Parks' machinery until the 1960s. In 1927, a consortium of local businessmen bought the machine tool company from Sears, but the Depression came, and in 1937, the group was ready to file for bankruptcy. That year, Elizabeth M. Reardon (b.1896), a secretary

*Cumminsville still includes a mix of houses, businesses, and factories such as the Parks Woodworking Machine Company.*

for Parks Woodworking since 1913, bought the concern and ran it with her brothers.

Parks Woodworking Machine Company prospered again after World War II; about seventy-five workers produced fifty machines daily for a worldwide market. However, this old Cumminsville business has been hurt in recent years by competition from foreign imports. It is one of the few woodworking machine manufacturers in the country that has survived, but its workforce and production have dwindled.

The bronze and stone monument standing in the small **8** **DAR Park,** northwest corner of Knowlton and Mad Anthony Streets, marks the approximate location of Ludlow's Station, established in 1790. This site also served as a camp and supply depot for Arthur St. Clair's army in 1791, and Anthony Wayne's forces in 1793.

In 1793, Israel Ludlow built his 2-story home just north of the intersection of present-day Knowlton and Chambers Streets. There, in 1806, General Jared Mansfield, Surveyor General of the United States, set up instruments to determine meridian lines for the survey of the Northwest Territory that President Thomas

Jefferson had ordered.

The limestone columns and the red granite blocks of the marker came from the Hamilton County Courthouse, which was destroyed by fire in the riot of 1884. The Daughters of the American Revolution erected the monument in 1916.

While industry has long played a major role in the communities of South Cumminsville and Northside, **9** **Santo's Florist Shop,** 1409 Knowlton Street, is one remaining piece of evidence that agriculture, too, has had a place in the community. Flowers have been raised on this site for six generations, beginning in the nineteenth century when the Walz family owned the entire block and grew flowers in thirteen greenhouses.

Almost directly to the north is an area once known as Frogtown for the bullfrogs that filled the many ponds and creeks, all of which were drained around 1910. In the mid-1800s, German farmers started market gardens where they raised vegetables in hotbeds until 1912, when George Kissel is said to have built the first greenhouse. By 1957, three families, descendants of the first settlers and all related by marriage, had about five acres under glass and were growing flowers as well as produce. The businesses continue today.

Another Cumminsville industry with origins in the nineteenth century

is **10** **ROTEX, Inc.,** 1230 Knowlton Street. ROTEX has survived and prospered in the twentieth century by developing a new product line of industrial screening machines that are manufactured under license in England, Australia, Belgium, and South Africa, as well as in Cincinnati.

When Isaac Straub founded the company in 1844, it manufactured a portable grist mill, the "Queen of the South," which he had invented. The Straub Mill Company was located at Front and John Streets in the busy riverfront district, and later on West Sixth Street. Straub's mills, also used to grind plaster, drugs, spices, and starch, were sold throughout the country and even exported to Canada and Great Britain. Straub eventually added portable saw mills to his line.

Soon after Robert Simpson came to Cincinnati in 1863 as an insurance agent, he began investing in local enterprises. Simpson, who became president of the Cincinnati Northwestern Railroad and principal stockholder in the Farmers' College in College Hill, was first a partner in Straub & Company and then, around 1870, its president. When steel roller mills began replacing stone grist mills, the company obtained new technology by buying two competitors.

In 1910, the business moved to Cumminsville to a site near a terminal of the College Hill Railroad, which Simpson had helped build. Because the location was regularly flooded, architect Walter L. Rapp (1879-1974) designed the building one story off grade, and a pedestrian bridge was constructed so that workers could cross the spring floodwaters. The plant was expanded in the 1960s and 1970s.

Simpson's son, Orville, and then his grandson, Lowe, joined the firm. In 1912, Lowe designed a sifter to go with the firm's grist mills. The new device—the ROTEX Screener—was used in the processing of food, chemicals, fertilizers, grain, and wood products, allowing the company to enter a new and profitable field.

Today, ROTEX separators are used for liquid/solid separation and wastewater clean up, to size wood chips for the pulp and paper industry, and to screen solids as diverse as rocket fuel, plastics, pet food, and granulated orange drink. The company is now headed by Jeremy Simpson, the fourth generation of the family.

**Turn left on Crawford Avenue, left on Ellis Street, right on Dane Street, left on Pullan Avenue.**

The **11** **Homes on Pullan Avenue** are examples of the middle to upper middle-income housing that was built in Northside from the 1880s through the mid-twentieth century. The oldest, Victorian-style dwellings are closest to Hamilton Avenue; further east are homes of 1930s-1940s Bungalow style, and one later ranch style structure. The narrow lots are typical of a period when commuters traveled by a horse-drawn railway or the Cincinnati, Hamilton & Dayton Railroad, and no one needed garages.

**Turn left on Hamilton Avenue.**

The first preacher to live permanently in Cumminsville was Reverend David Fergus, a Presbyterian minister, who arrived at Ludlow's Station in 1822 with a group of Scottish immigrants. He and his son-in-law, Alexander Langlands, bought 217 acres of land and built a house and barn near where the B&O rail line now crosses Fergus Street. Langlands conducted services in the barn until his death in 1829. In 1832, the records of the Cincinnati Presbytery noted that "a request was presented from several members of that church, residing in the vicinity of Cummings Ville [sic], for the organization of a church in that place."

**12** **North Presbyterian Church,** 4216-4222 Hamilton Avenue, traces its beginnings to 1850 when John Carson and his family arrived from Scotland and started holding worship services in their home. In 1852, Janet Langland, Alexander Langlands' widow (the "s" in the name was dropped by descendants), donated a lot on the southeast corner of present day Lingo and Lakeman Streets, and the First Presbyterian Church of Cumminsville was dedicated on November 13, 1853. The *Presbyterian of the West* recorded that "A large and attentive congregation was present, and the liveliest interest manifested in the prospect of . . . enjoying the means of grace . . . in that destitute and hitherto much neglected place."

First Presbyterian's fifteen charter members included some of Cumminsville's "first families" and largest landowners: Janet Langland, Janet Langland Thomson, Mary Ann Knowlton, Twenty-sixth District School principal Merwin S. Turrill, and industrialist James C. C. Holenshade.

A 2-story parsonage adjacent to the church was completed in 1871; it is now a private home. The original church was razed in 1877.

In the last two decades of the nineteenth century, residential Northside differentiated itself from industrial Cumminsville. At that time, First Presbyterian moved to its present

*Many of Cumminsville and Northside's well-to-do early residents belonged to North Presbyterian Church.*

location, a lot at the corner of the estate of John and Janet Langland Thomson, and dedicated this Victorian Gothic style brick church on July 25, 1886. The congregation adopted its current name in 1891. The Sunday School building was dedicated in 1910, the annex in 1957. Membership reached 1,229 in 1948, then decreased to 207 by 1988.

The church parking lot covers the site of Willowburn, the 2-story mansion belonging to John and Janet Thomson, built around 1840. The estate grounds included the block bounded by Hamilton, Chase, and Brookside. Most of this land was sold and subdivided in the 1880s and 1890s. The church bought the Thomson home in 1923 and used it for classrooms and a parsonage before razing it in 1957.

*Turn left on Chase Avenue, left on Brookside Avenue, left on Pullan Avenue, right on Haight Avenue.*

**13 Parker's Woods,** northeast of Bruce and Haight Avenues, owes its creation to City Council's adoption in 1907 of a plan for a system of parks and connecting parkways. The proposal, prepared by Kansas City landscape architect George E. Kessler, aimed to provide Cincinnati with adequate recreation grounds, improve neglected property, and preserve the many "delightful views" around the city. "North Side Park" was proposed for the Cumminsville area.

The project proceeded slowly until November 1910, when voters approved a $1 million bond issue for the acquisition of lands for parks. The following year, the Board of Park Commissioners purchased or was given over 721 acres of land. Among these new properties was 31.5 acres of the old Langland estate, purchased from Alexander Langland's grandson, Alexander Langland Parker, for whom Parker's Woods was named. Twenty-four and one-half acres bought in 1931 and an acre donated in 1953 brought the total to the present fifty-seven.

The Park Board laid out two blacktopped nature trails, but a baseball diamond created in the late 1930s has not been retained. Parker's Woods is essentially a natural area.

Adjacent to Parker's Woods and off the tour is Buttercup Valley, between Springlawn and Glen Parker Avenues, a 25-acre nature preserve that is one of the oldest, if not the oldest, wooded area within city limits. It is a "climax" forest; that is, though the forest has been selectively harvested, it is much like it would have been when the first pioneers arrived.

The Greater Cincinnati Tree Council, aided by the children of Northside and College Hill, raised enough money to buy eighteen acres that were turned over to the Park Department in the late 1960s. Addition of other parcels came later. Development here has been limited to nature trails, a parking lot, shelterhouse, two foot bridges, and fences. Buttercup Valley is a site for ecological and botanic studies.

*Turn left on Hamilton Avenue, right on Bruce Avenue.*

In the 1880s and 1890s, land on either side of Hamilton Avenue north of Hobart that belonged to Janet Langland Thomson was subdivided into lots. The intersection of Hamilton and Bruce became known as "Millionaires' Corner" for the four wealthy businessmen who built homes here during the 1890s. Jergens Park, 1615 Bruce Avenue, was once the site of the **14 Home of Andrew Jergens**, cofounder of the Andrew Jergens Company.

Jergens (1852-1929) had come from Germany with his family as a child. In 1881, he and two partners founded the Andrews Soap Company; their factory on Spring Grove Avenue was, at one time, the largest toilet soap factory in the world. Andrew Jergens moved into a 3-story Gothic style stone castle in Northside in the early 1890s, his brother moved to the house on the southeast corner of the intersection around 1895, and Charles H. Geilfus, secretary and treasurer of Andrew Jergens & Company, built the residence on the northeast corner two years later. Charles Silverson, president of the Schlueter Cycle Manufacturing Company, lived in a home on the fourth corner.

Andrew Jergens, Jr., headed his

*The influx of new families into Northside around the turn of the century led to the construction of the Kirby Road School in 1910.*

father's company and continued to live in the family home. By 1967 when Jergens died, Northside was no longer an affluent suburb. His will stipulated that the home should be razed within a year of his death if none of his children wanted to live there. The house was torn down in February 1968, and the lot given to the City Park Board. Funds from the Andrew Jergens Foundation paid for the creation of a park and playground—dedicated April 26, 1970—and for maintenance.

An eighteenth-century room that Andrew Jergens, Jr., had shipped—walls, windows, and furnishings—from Syria in 1932 was given to the Art Museum. A set of wrought iron gates from the estate was moved to the Linn Street entrance to Dayton Street as part of that area's beautification program.

**15 Kirby Road Primary School,** 1710 Bruce Avenue, opened in 1910 to serve the population north of Chase Avenue. Cumminsville's first public school, the Union Graded School, had been erected in 1854 on Knowlton Street in the center of the settlement. Before the Union School opened, classes had been held in a log cabin near the intersection of Westmoreland Street and Innes Avenue, then in James C. Ludlow's House of Free Discussion on Spring Grove Avenue, and then in Knowlton's Hall.

The growing community soon needed a second school, and in 1869 erected "old Kirby Road School," a 4-room, 2-story building on Kirby at Hanfield. After four more classrooms

were added in 1878, Kirby School could seat 400 students in grades K-8.

But Cumminsville continued to grow, expanding north as electric streetcar lines extended up Hamilton Avenue, and in 1905, residents called for a larger and better school. There was "quite a contention" among property owners who had lots big enough to accommodate the proposed institution, but at last an elevated plot at the corner of Kirby and Bruce was selected. The Cincinnati firm of Elzner & Anderson designed the sweeping Neo-Classical style building. The first Kirby Road school was closed in 1912 and razed.

In 1985-1986, Kirby Primary enrolled about 635 children, 24% of whom were black. It offered special classes for developmentally and multi-handicapped youngsters and a pre-school program. The student population became more racially balanced in 1986-1987 when Kirby third graders were sent to Chase School and Roll Hill, essentially an all-black school, which was closed and its students in grades K-2 assigned here. The following year, the 650-member student body was approximately 50% black and 50% white.

> **Turn left on Florida Street, left on Chase Avenue.**

Though some lots on **16 Chase Avenue,** once Third Street, have been cleared and rebuilt, the street still retains many residential, commercial, and religious buildings in a mix that was typical of nineteenth-century middle-income neighborhoods. Chase Avenue residents shared their street with small neighborhood enterprises—meat market, doctors' offices, millinery, dress shop, confectionery, drugstore, groceries, bank, and the like.

The homes on the south side of Chase between Gordon and Lakeman Streets are fine examples of late nineteenth-century middle-income housing: 2½-story homes on narrow lots, a mix of architectural styles. The 2½-story stone-faced brick house at 1817 Chase Avenue was designed by Samuel Hannaford & Sons in 1890 for Charles A. Miller, funeral director and political figure.

After Cincinnati annexed Cum-

minsville in 1873, this street was renamed to honor Salmon P. Chase (1808-1873), Cincinnati lawyer, Ohio governor, United States senator, Lincoln's Secretary of the Treasury, and Chief Justice of the Supreme Court. Chase also had presidential aspirations and tried four times to win the nomination. Chase owned land in Cumminsville but lived in Clifton.

**17 St. Boniface Roman Catholic Church,** 1750 Chase Avenue, is evidence of the strength of German Catholic immigration to Cincinnati in the years before the Civil War and the animosity between Irish and German Catholics.

Both German and Irish Catholics settled in Cumminsville. An English-language parish, St. Aloysius, was set up in 1852, and a one-room church was completed the next year on Delaney Street. The Irish Americans living in this neighborhood did not get along with their German co-religionists who were more numerous and were held together by a network of German-language social, cultural, and economic organizations. Moreover, many of the Germans were craftsmen and small businessmen; the Irish were primarily laborers.

Because of these tensions, Archbishop John Purcell (1800-1883) decided to divide the growing parish along ethnic lines. On April 13, 1861, according to tradition, lots were drawn giving the English-speaking portion of the congregation the old property, which was renamed St. Patrick's.

Led by St. Aloysius' priest and with $1,500 from the parish, the German American element completed the first St. Boniface Church and rectory in 1864 on the corner of Blue Rock and Lakeman Streets, now the site of Superior Die & Engineering Company. St. Boniface parish built a school in 1870 and enlarged it in 1885, 1892, and 1903. Four years later, the congregation erected a convent for the Sisters of Charity from Mount St. Joseph who taught at the school. By 1988, St. Boniface recorded 500 member families.

Although two parishes were carved from St. Boniface's territory in 1909 and 1910, the congregation remained strong. In the 1920s, it purchased this lot, Timothy Kirby's estate, and razed the house he had erected in 1843. The present lime-

stone-faced church and rectory were dedicated in July 1927. The imposing Romanesque style church, designed by the Cincinnati architectural firm of Kunz & Beck, featured a ninety-three foot tower with four bells.

Inside were Venetian mosaic Stations of the Cross, a resplendent Italian marble main altar and baldachin, and a domed ceiling covered in gold leaf. The 14-room school was completed in 1933. Despite the hardships of the Depression, all buildings were free of debt when they were put into use. In 1938, when the old parish buildings were demolished, St. Boniface served 525 families, and 480 children were enrolled in the school.

St. Boniface and St. Patrick's schools were athletic rivals for years, reflecting feelings that persisted among the various ethnic groups in the community into the mid-twentieth century. However, when St. Patrick's school closed in 1969, its students were sent to St. Boniface; 150 youngsters were enrolled in 1987-1988.

**18 Northside United Methodist Church,** 1680 Chase Avenue, was established in 1833 when the Methodist Episcopal congregation of Cumminsville erected a small frame church on land donated by developer Timothy Kirby. The lot was on Colerain Pike at the northwestern edge of present-day Wesleyan Cemetery. A brick building, known as Wright Chapel to honor the church's pastor, Reverend John F. Wright, replaced this structure around 1867.

Early members of the Methodist Episcopal Church included Caleb Lingo, proprietor of the Northside Planing Mill; General John McMakin, an attorney and landowner; soap and candle manufacturer Daniel Hunnewell, and Charles Miller, undertaker and politician.

After a fire from an over-stoked furnace destroyed Wright Chapel in 1889, services were held on the second floor of the Hoffner Lodge on Hamilton Avenue. Wishing their church to be more centrally located, trustees bought a lot at Chase Avenue and Delaney Street, and in 1892 began construction of a new church designed by Samuel Hannaford. Work stopped in 1893 due to a lack of funds, but resumed after the old lot was sold. The stone used to face the building was donated by Charles Miller and came from his quarries around Virginia Avenue in Cumminsville.

The present Gothic style church was dedicated October 1, 1894, when there were around 300 members. The building was listed on the National Register of Historic Places in March 1980.

Membership in Northside United Methodist Church has fallen over the years. The aging congregation has only recently begun to attract younger members and to reach children through a weekly time-release class in religion and a Saturday "Sunday school." While the current congregation has only fifty members drawn mostly from Northside, its Food Pantry program and used clothing shop serve as many as 600 each year.

In 1875, 500 pupils were enrolled in Cumminsville's public elementary schools: the Union Graded School at Knowlton and Langland Streets, the old Kirby Road School, and a "colored" school on Dirr Street. But the community was growing rapidly, and in 1882, the Cincinnati Board of Education purchased a 1¼-acre lot for the construction of **19 Salmon P. Chase School,** 1615 Chase Avenue, which served the neighborhood until 1979. Henry E. Siter designed the 3½-story school, which opened in 1888.

By 1914, 2,000 youngsters attended Cumminsville's schools, and the Board of Education talked of replacing Chase School, which lacked facilities like a cafeteria. Students ate lunch on benches in the halls.

The 1925 *Official City Plan* concluded that the elementary school had to be abandoned by 1935 because "a business district will completely surround the present Chase School within a short time." The predicted business development did not occur, but the 1948 *Master Plan* again called for the school to be closed and the site used for a new junior high.

The building was increasingly inadequate and deteriorating by the 1960s when Chase—95% white—was included in the Board of Education's plan to improve facilities and promote integration. Chase Intermediate University Demonstration School opened in 1979 on Turrill Street, two blocks to the west; grades 4-6 went there, while K-3 students were sent to Kirby Road School. The City of Cincinnati then bought this old school and scheduled studies for its redevelopment as commercial office space,

artists' studios, or housing, but Salmon P. Chase Elementary School has remained vacant.

**Turn right on Turrill Street.**

With the construction of the **20 McKie Recreation and Community Center,** 1655 Chase Avenue, and **Chase Elementary University Demonstration School,** 4151 Turrill Street, in the 1970s, the city sought to meet the needs of South Cumminsville and Northside. The facilities, oriented to serving these increasingly crowded and diverse neighborhoods, are located on the **Site of St. Joseph Orphanage,** which opened in 1854 when then-rural Cumminsville offered healthful and spacious surroundings.

St. Joseph Orphanage, held to be the first orphanage established west of the Alleghenies, was begun in October 1829 with the arrival of Sisters of Charity. The women cared for six orphans, first at an orphanage on Sycamore Street near St. Xavier Church, then in a building at Third and Plum Streets. As the city grew, the downtown basin became noisier and more crowded, and the land too expensive for the orphanage to expand.

*The modern style Chase Elementary School building was designed so that it would be relatively unobtrusive in its surroundings.*

In 1852, the archdiocese purchased eleven acres on Blue Rock and Cherry Streets from Jacob Hoffner. When he learned the purpose for which the property was to be used, Hoffner refunded half the $8,200

purchase price. The 4-story St. Joseph Orphanage opened two years later; an average of 200 children lived there at any time.

By the late 1950s, the old building no longer met modern needs. Plans for a new orphanage, St. Joseph Villa in Monfort Heights, were drawn up, and this property was turned over to St. Francis Seminary in Mt. Healthy and served briefly as a branch of its preparatory seminary. By 1964, the city was negotiating for a portion of the land to provide the community with the new school and recreation space it needed. The orphanage was razed, and McKie Community Center and Chase School were erected.

Named to honor Stanley G. McKie, a state legislator and member of the Cincinnati Board of Education and the Recreation Commission, the McKie Center opened in 1970. It offers classes ranging from woodworking to water color, karate to clay sculpture. The Northside Community Council and other groups use the center's meeting rooms. Its athletic programs include basketball, softball, tennis, track, swimming, and gymnastics. The Center shares its gym with Chase School, to which it is connected by a covered walkway.

Chase Elementary University Demonstration School, formerly Chase Intermediate, was built as the result of a 1972 bond issue and a Board of Education plan to end overcrowding, replace obsolete buildings, and promote quality integrated education in the Aiken High School attendance area—the communities of Clifton, College Hill, Mt. Airy, Northside, Winton Place, and Winton Terrace.

For two years after the levy passed, the board debated plans for new construction and for reassigning students from predominantly black Winton Place and Winton Terrace elementary schools and predominantly white Chase and Kirby Road schools. A plan adopted on December 10, 1973, by a "lame duck" liberal board was thrown out the next year by conservative members who had gained dominance in the November 1973 election. Finally, construction of this school was approved in July 1974.

The entire Cincinnati school district had been shut down for three weeks due to a lack of funds when Chase Intermediate opened on December 3, 1979. Nine hundred students grades 4-6, about 57% black and 43% white, entered a facility that was innovative in its architectural design and educational program. The school had one floor below ground, not only to save energy but also because community residents opposed a modern structure that would tower over the older buildings. Chase had both open and traditional classrooms, a greenhouse, a theater, labs for science, art, and music, and a 2½-story, sky-lit library/resource center. It tried to create a "small school atmosphere" with an auditorium and cafeteria that would seat only one-third of its students at a time.

The school's affiliation with the University of Cincinnati's College of Education brings teacher interns here for practical experience, lowers the teacher-to-student ratio, and helps master teachers keep up on new materials and methods. Chase is one of the city's alternative schools, drawing some of its students from throughout Cincinnati. Chase added the third grade and acquired its present name in the 1986-1987 school year.

**Turn right on Blue Rock Street.**

The construction of the CH&D railroad brought many immigrants, including Irish and some German Catholics, to Cumminsville to build the line. St. Aloysius, the community's first parish, was created in 1852 for these laborers and their families. The following year, a small brick church was erected on Delaney Street near St. Joseph Orphanage, which was then under construction.

The parish grew rapidly as more and more German immigrants settled in Cumminsville, and tensions between Irish and German members of the congregation increased. It is generally assumed that when Archbishop Purcell divided the large parish in 1861, all the English-speaking members remained in the old building and became St. Patrick's parish, while all the German members departed to form St. Boniface parish.

In 1870, St. Patrick's congregation had outgrown the original building and purchased a lot at the corner of Blue Rock and Cherry Streets from Jacob Hoffner. On June 21, 1874, the present **21 St. Patrick Roman Catholic Church,** 1662 Blue Rock Street, was dedicated. St. Patrick's priest designed the Gothic Romanesque style brick building with its red tiled steeple. The original church served as a firehouse until 1891 when a new firehouse was completed at Chase and Turrill Avenues.

The small size of the church, relative to St. Boniface, indicates the different sizes and economic strengths of the two parishes. And the stained glass windows that memorialize parishioners with Irish *and* German names suggest that a complete split along ethnic lines might not have occurred and that some German-born members retained an attachment to the original parish.

St. Patrick's parish erected a school at 4115 Cherry Street in 1906 and remodeled the church, facing it with stone, in 1922. By the 1940s, St. Patrick's claimed 3,000 members, but the number dropped as Cumminsville aged and became a less prosperous residential neighborhood. After the school closed in 1969, students were sent to St. Boniface and the gym was converted to a social hall.

St. Patrick Church was entered on the National Register of Historic Places in March 1980.

**Turn left on Colerain Avenue.**

In 1839, four Methodist congregations in the basin purchased land in rural Cumminsville and created **22 Wesleyan Cemetery,** 4003 Colerain Avenue. Urban land had become too expensive to be used for interments, and many believed that the burial of bodies, especially those

of cholera victims, near crowded neighborhoods caused health problems. Rural cemeteries were considered more appropriate sites for the dead and more soothing surroundings for the bereaved. The cemetery was chartered in 1842, making it the oldest continuously-operating cemetery in Hamilton County.

Though a more modest cemetery than nearby Spring Grove, which was chartered in 1845, Wesleyan Cemetery has been the final resting place for many local notables, including Dr. Richard Allison, the first United States Army Surgeon General; William Steinmetz, a recipient of the Congressional Medal of Honor for valor at the Battle of Vicksburg, and Fred Waterman, a member of the 1869 Cincinnati Red Stockings baseball team.

There are German, Greek, and Rumanian Americans here, seven veterans of the Revolutionary War, and many more from the Civil War, including many members of Cincinnati's all-German regiment and one Confederate soldier. Veterans of all subsequent wars are also buried in Wesleyan. At the southern edge of the cemetery along Hoffner Street are several rows of identical white stones that mark the graves of children who died at the House of Refuge, an early juvenile reformatory located next to the Cincinnati Workhouse in Camp Washington. In 1972, remains were moved here from Wesley Chapel on East Fifth Street when the Procter & Gamble Company bought that property for expansion.

The construction of I-74 reduced Wesleyan Cemetery to its present twenty-nine acres.

**Turn right on to Elmore Street.**

**23 Garfield School,** 1905 Elmore Street, now vacant and gutted by vandals, opened in 1896. It was Cumminsville's fourth elementary school, erected during the period of the area's greatest growth.

Henry Siter, architect for at least seven other Cincinnati schools built during 1880-1900, designed this 4-story brick structure that was named to honor Ohio-born President James A. Garfield. The Board of Education's 1897 annual report praised the new facility as "grand and imposing, and an ornament . . . a constant reminder to the citizens there of their duty to the schools . . . . This building will accommodate the children of that vicinity for years and prove a great blessing to the inhabitants of the growing ward."

The City of Cincinnati's 1925 plan found that the nearly 3- acre site was "large and desirable," and because of the growth in the area, an addition would be needed "within twenty-five years at the outside." That building was completed two years later.

But Garfield School was in a neighborhood where some areas were frequently flooded by the Mill Creek and where homes were aging. The city's 1948 *Master Plan* reported that the housing in "most of that part of Cumminsville lying southeast of B&O Railroad . . . is obsolete. . . . Redevelopment for industrial use is proposed for this area . . . ." Nonetheless, Garfield School continued to thrive as an important neighborhood institution with a PTA, men's club, alumni association, and choral club. In 1949-1950, Garfield School had 665 pupils, 77% white and 23% black.

However, the next decades saw great changes in both the school and the community. When slum clearance in the West End displaced hundreds of black families, many of them sought homes in this neighborhood. During the same period, clearance for expressway construction and the completion of I-74 physically isolated South Cumminsville from Northside, which was then also in decline.

By 1977, enrollment at Garfield School was less than half its capacity and predominantly black; the building itself was out-dated. The Board of Education closed the school in June 1979 and sent youngsters to the five other schools in the area. The building, offered unsuccessfully at auction a number of times, remained empty, no longer either an "ornament" or a "great blessing."

**Turn left on Beekman Street, left on Dreman Avenue.**

The parish that built **24** **St. Pius Roman Catholic Church,** 1814 Dreman Avenue, was organized on October 13, 1910, for a low and middle-income, predominantly German, congregation. Today, St. Pius serves a community that is predom-

inantly low-income, black, and largely non-Catholic.

When St. Boniface parish, Cumminsville's first German-language congregation, grew too large, Archbishop Henry Moeller organized St. Pius. The new congregation purchased a lot at the corner of Dreman Avenue and Borden Street, and began construction of a small frame church designed by Cincinnati architect Anthony Kunz, Jr. Nearly 125 families attended weekday services held first in the rectory on Borden.

On April 16, 1911, St. Pius Church was dedicated; 15,000 attended the afternoon ceremony at which the church bell was blessed. St. Pius planned to use a home next to the church for its school, but when 200 children showed up on the first day of classes, plans for a new building were quickly made. Kunz designed the 2-story brick school that was dedicated in 1913 and a new rectory completed in 1922.

His firm, Kunz & Beck, designed the present Romanesque style church with twin towers, dedicated April 24, 1927. Interior features—a white marble altar, mosaic Stations of the Cross, frescoed ceilings, stained glass windows by F. X. Zettler of Munich, and an organ from Stuttgart—reflect the congregation's pride in its church. Kunz & Beck were later the architects for St. Boniface Church.

The old frame church was converted into a hall, and a convent for the Franciscan Sisters of Oldenburg who taught at the school was built in 1941 when St. Pius had 2,000 members. But this area was already becoming a less attractive neighborhood that was hurt further when several streets of housing were demolished for highway ramp construction. St. Pius began its struggle to survive in a community undergoing economic, racial, and religious change.

The Cincinnati Archdiocese, ready to close the failing parish, offered it to the Comboni Missionaries whose service is explicitly to the "poorest and most abandoned." The Combonis, who arrived in Cincinnati in 1939, had taken charge of other dwindling Cincinnati parishes, including Holy Trinity, St. Anne, St. Henry, and St. Anthony (all downtown parishes that are now gone), and St. Michael in Lower Price Hill. In February 1971, the Italian missionary fathers also took over St. Pius and

began regular bingo games that greatly improved the parish's financial security.

Today, St. Pius parish sees itself and the school as a ray of hope in a low-income neighborhood with its share of problems. The church has some 350 members; about half attend services regularly. The Mass now includes gospel music and is longer than the usual service.

In 1979, 84% of St. Pius school's students were eligible for federally-subsidized meals. By 1988, 99% of the 196 students, grades K-8, were black and mostly non-Catholic, drawn from the neighborhood and the several public housing developments in the area. Though most paid the small monthly tuition fee, this charge covered only a part of the costs; the archdiocese met the balance.

**Turn left on Borden Street, left on Elmore Street, left on Beekman Street.**

Among the Cincinnati Metropolitan Housing Authority's (CMHA) subsidized housing developments are the **25** **Millvale North** and **Millvale South Apartments,** 573 units off Beekman Street on Millvale Court and Millvale Circle. The two complexes, completed in 1954 and 1955, are products of an effort to solve a critical shortage of adequate low-rent housing that began in 1933 with the establishment of CMHA.

By 1948, CMHA administered Laurel Homes, Lincoln Court, Winton Terrace, and English Woods, all low-rent federally-funded developments; Valley Homes, a war housing project, and veterans' housing on six sites. The need for public housing continued as much of the West End fell to urban renewal and expressway construction, sending hundreds of displaced families to the city's older suburban neighborhoods.

The City of Cincinnati considered a 36-acre site on Kirby Road for a public housing development, but encountered a "volcano" of community opposition as area homeowners argued that the units, especially as they would be open to blacks, would drive down real estate values. The site on Beekman Street was selected in July 1952 because, the CMHA explained, it was "adjacent to the

*In the 1970s and again in the 1980s, the exteriors of the units in the Millvale housing development were upgraded to provide residents with more attractive homes.*

Millcreek Valley Industrial area, accessible to the center and West End business districts and . . . [thus] suitably located for low wage earners." This subsidized housing was supposed to be temporary, a stepping stone to private homeownership; rent was set relative to income.

But CMHA, in building the Millvale Apartments here, had not forseen the consequences of the clearance of the West End. The Beekman Street location proved increasingly isolated from shopping, employment, and health and welfare services. During the summer of 1968, it was one of several Cincinnati communities that experienced racial disturbances. According to the 1970 census, Millvale residents were predominantly black, a majority had no jobs, and the median family income was below $3,500 a year.

Over the years, city officials,

residents, and others have worked to improve the physical appearance of these buildings and the lives of the residents, as well as to develop a sense of community. From 1966 into the 1980s, the Sisters of Notre Dame operated a Practical Family Living Center here with adult education classes, a day nursery, and arts and crafts programs. In June 1971, the Millvale Community Center was dedicated to provide Millvale, Camp Washington, North Fairmount, South Cumminsville, and English Woods with recreational, health, welfare, library, day care, and other community services.

In 1974, the Millvale Apartments underwent a major facelift designed by Glaser & Myers Associates that won state and local awards for excellence, and in the mid-1980s, the units were refaced with more durable metal siding.

The Millvale Resident and Community Council works to improve the quality of life here. Its activities include a block watch, beautification

projects, and a joint effort with CMHA to get city support for the redevelopment of Garfield School as a job training center or men's shelter. The Cincinnati Union Bethel's Millvale branch offers a range of services including day care, counseling, job training, and crisis intervention.

**Turn right on Millvale Court and circle through the housing development. Return to Beekman Street and turn left. Turn right on Elmore Street and right on Colerain Avenue to Spring Grove Avenue where tour ends.**

277

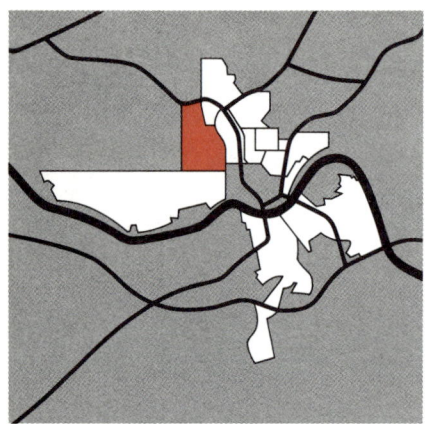

# Fairmount

The neighborhoods that the City of Cincinnati presently identifies as South, North, and Northwest Fairmount occupy approximately two and one-half square miles of hilly land on the western slope of the Mill Creek Valley. This area, known generally as Fairmount, extends from Beekman Street on the east almost to McHenry Avenue on the west. West Liberty Street forms Fairmount's southern boundary, and, if the twentieth-century housing developments of Fay Apartments and English Woods are included, I-74 is the northern boundary. Fairmount's topography, which has contributed to its unique character, features a series of ridges and valleys dominated by two hills, Bald Knob and the *Shuetzenbuckel*, or Shooters' Hill, now the site of St. Clair Heights Park.

The first houses were built in this vicinity after Harrison Pike opened in 1805. Gradually, stone houses and a few businesses, including a brewery, were erected along the Pike. By the 1840s, a small community called Mt. Harrison was laid out on the hills between Quebec and Grand Avenues.

After the Cincinnati, Hamilton & Dayton Railroad (CH&D) began service along the west side of the Mill Creek in 1850, speculators platted other villages and subdivisions in the vicinity of Mt. Harrison. Forbusville and St. Peterstown were on opposite corners at the intersection of Quebec Avenue and Lick Run Pike (Queen City Avenue). Barrsville lay between Westwood and Grand Avenues. Two other communities were adjacent to the railroad line itself: Spring Garden was situated where present-day State and Westwood Avenues meet, and Fairmount lay north of Harrison Pike.

By the late 1860s, Fairmount had become the most significant of these communities. St. Peterstown and Spring Garden each had more than forty structures, but Fairmount had about twice that number. Fairmount was also the largest subdivision, covering most of the property between Harrison and Baltimore Avenues and including 500 lots of various sizes, some as large as 100' x 200'. Joseph A. James, a Cincinnati businessman had started Fairmount in 1853. James' descendants later claimed that he had named the village after Fairmount Park in Philadelphia, but regardless of the source of the name, the developer clearly intended to convey the idea that his property was on attractive high ground. James hoped to draw both middle and upper-income homebuyers.

Although Fairmount, Mt. Harrison, Barrsville, and Spring Garden all offered some large lots, they attracted few upper-income residents, possibly because of the rough terrain. Instead, manufacturing concerns such as the Herancourt brewery and the Fairmount Woolen Mills, settled along the CH&D or the pikes, while workers and middle-income families moved into modest brick and frame houses on the smaller lots.

None of these communities was incorporated before 1870 when they were annexed by Cincinnati. At that time, city officials identified this vicinity as Lick Run, because of the stream that ran through the center of the region to the Mill Creek. But as Fairmount was the largest and most notable subdivision in Lick Run, its name was more widely used and eventually applied to all the land between Price Hill and Cumminsville.

The development of Fairmount as a commuter suburb was initially

*Fairmount started to attract industries such as the Adler & Company Woolen Mills in the mid-nineteenth century.*

somewhat restricted by a lack of affordable public transportation. Regular travel into the city on the CH&D was too expensive for lower and middle-income wage-earners, so Fairmount's population included few commuters. The majority of residents worked in the vicinity, and by the late 1870s, local employers—factories, breweries, and other businesses—supported a population of 7,000 to 8,000.

Fairmount grew even more as public transportation improved. In 1879, a horsecar line was extended from Brighton to the intersection of Harrison and Westwood Avenues, and in the 1880s, the horsecars began service along Beekman Street and Baltimore Avenue to Carll Street. Fairmount thus became more accessible and a more practical place for middle-income commuters to live. Between 1880 and 1890, the area gained approximately 1,400 new residents. Commuting to and from Fairmount became even easier in the 1890s when streetcars were electrified and service became faster and more reliable.

As Fairmount developed in the late nineteenth century, its several sections evolved differently. The older part of the community had a mix of factories and housing, mostly working-class homes. But along the streetcar line and away from the industry, a predominantly residential area, North Fairmount, was established, and the more affluent middle-income families settled here. The only industry in North Fairmount was concentrated along Beekman Street and the railroad.

The industrial character of what became known as South Fairmount, the vicinity around State, Westwood, and Queen City Avenues, was reinforced around the turn of the century as a second generation of manufacturing firms and workshops moved in. Companies began leaving older, smaller sites close to downtown for larger locations further up the Mill Creek Valley. Camp Washington, Cumminsville, and Fairmount were particularly popular. Plants in South Fairmount which were either new or expanded included the Lunkenheimer Valve complex along Beekman Street, P.R. Mitchell's curled hair manufacturing plant on Queen City Avenue, and the Fairmount Brewery at Westwood Avenue and Quebec Road. In addition, smaller concerns—lumber dealers, feed merchants, metal fabricators, foundries, textile mills, box factories, and oil refineries—occupied buildings scattered throughout South Fairmount.

*South Fairmount, shown here in 1913, was a mixture of businesses, factories, and working-class housing.*

Inexpensive housing and the possibility of industrial employment in South Fairmount brought new working-class residents to the area. While the majority of Fairmount's inhabitants were of German descent, the newcomers included many Italian Americans. North Fairmount also continued to develop, particularly after 1916, when the Hopple Street Viaduct made it more accessible. By the 1920s, the population of Fairmount as a whole was about 15,000.

Fairmount residents were served by thriving business districts along its main streets. In the early twentieth century, pharmacies, groceries, theaters, hardware stores, clothing shops, barbers, saloons, and small restaurants lined Queen City, Westwood, Harrison, and Baltimore Avenues. The clusters of small, family-run businesses also served commuters who were traveling in larger and larger numbers over these streets. As early as the mid-nineteenth century, retail shops had set up along the pikes to take advantage of the traffic.

More stores had opened after the Cincinnati & Westwood narrow gauge railroad placed its terminus in South Fairmount in 1876 and streetcar service began. But it was in the early twentieth century, when suburbs like Westwood and Cheviot were growing rapidly and traffic increased substantially, that the business district along Queen City and Harrison Avenues became a shopping center for thousands of west side commuters.

By the 1930s, Fairmount was a stable lower and middle-income community with healthy neighborhood business districts and industries. The Depression caused layoffs and the failure of some smaller businesses, but with the onset of World War II, Fairmount's factories revived. The presence of these plants, as well as other expanding industries in the Mill Creek Valley, was a major factor in the Cincinnati Metropolitan Housing Authority's decision to build a public housing project, English Woods, north of Fairmount in 1940-1942.

Fairmount became less stable after World War II. Many younger families moved to newer suburbs, using veterans' benefits to buy more modern homes in Delhi or Green Townships. With this emigration of middle-income residents, more of the older homes became available to lower-income people seeking inexpensive housing. Large numbers of Appalachians settled in South Fairmount, and in the 1960s, blacks leaving neighborhoods in the basin moved into North Fairmount. By the 1970s, approximately 60% of South Fairmount's residents were of

Appalachian background, while about 75% of North Fairmount's were black.

At the same time, Fairmount's industrial community underwent serious change as aging facilities became obsolete and the general economy shifted away from traditional manufacturing. Starting in the late 1950s with the closing of the Aluminum Industries plant on Beekman Street, many of the once-successful firms in the area went out of business, reduced operations, or moved away. Even the Lunkenheimer Company closed down its Fairmount plant in 1984.

The neighborhood's business districts also suffered. Sales declined as the area's population decreased and average income fell. Businesses closed or moved westward to follow the middle-income population. The South Fairmount district shrank, and retail operations disappeared almost entirely from North Fairmount.

These businesses were hurt further by the city's decision in the early 1970s to make Queen City and Westwood Avenues one-way streets. The change made it more difficult for customers to get to the shops. The one-way system also contributed significantly to the residents' feeling that their community was becoming a place where "people only passed through on their way to somewhere else." Fairmount businesses' difficulties were increased when the Western Hills Viaduct was closed for repairs from 1976 to 1978.

The city carried out economic studies of North and South Fairmount in the early 1980s. Suggestions for helping the businesses there included eliminating the one-way street system and establishing a shopping center in the area between Queen City and Westwood Avenues. When no changes were implemented, many residents felt that city had "written off" these neighborhoods. Residents also believed that their community was being written off by insurance and finance companies. Homeowners and potential homebuyers seeking insurance or loans to improve or buy in Fairmount found that they were victims of "red lining." Financial institutions and insurance companies considered Fairmount property a poor risk, and obtaining mortgages, home improvement loans, or insurance became more difficult.

Residents' own organizations and efforts have provided the only significant source of hope for these neighborhoods. The South Fairmount Development Corporation began rehabbing projects in 1979, though progress has been slow. Local people formed the North Fairmount Community Center in 1980 and the South Fairmount Community Center in 1982. These centers provide senior citizen services, day care, adult education, and food programs, and contribute to community pride. The residents of the predominantly black English Woods and Fay Apartments housing developments have also established organizations to address their concerns.

The hope that the people of North, South, and Northwest Fairmount have for their communities is reinforced through small but encouraging changes. Red lining has been fought successfully in several cases, and some middle-income residents are moving back into the area. Some homes are being renovated by individual owners, and a few new businesses have started. Most of all, residents encourage each other by their own commitment, in the face of considerable obstacles, to making Fairmount's neighborhoods better places to live.

*St. Leo's Church in North Fairmount was one of the focal points for community revitalization in the 1980s.*

Tour Length
10 miles

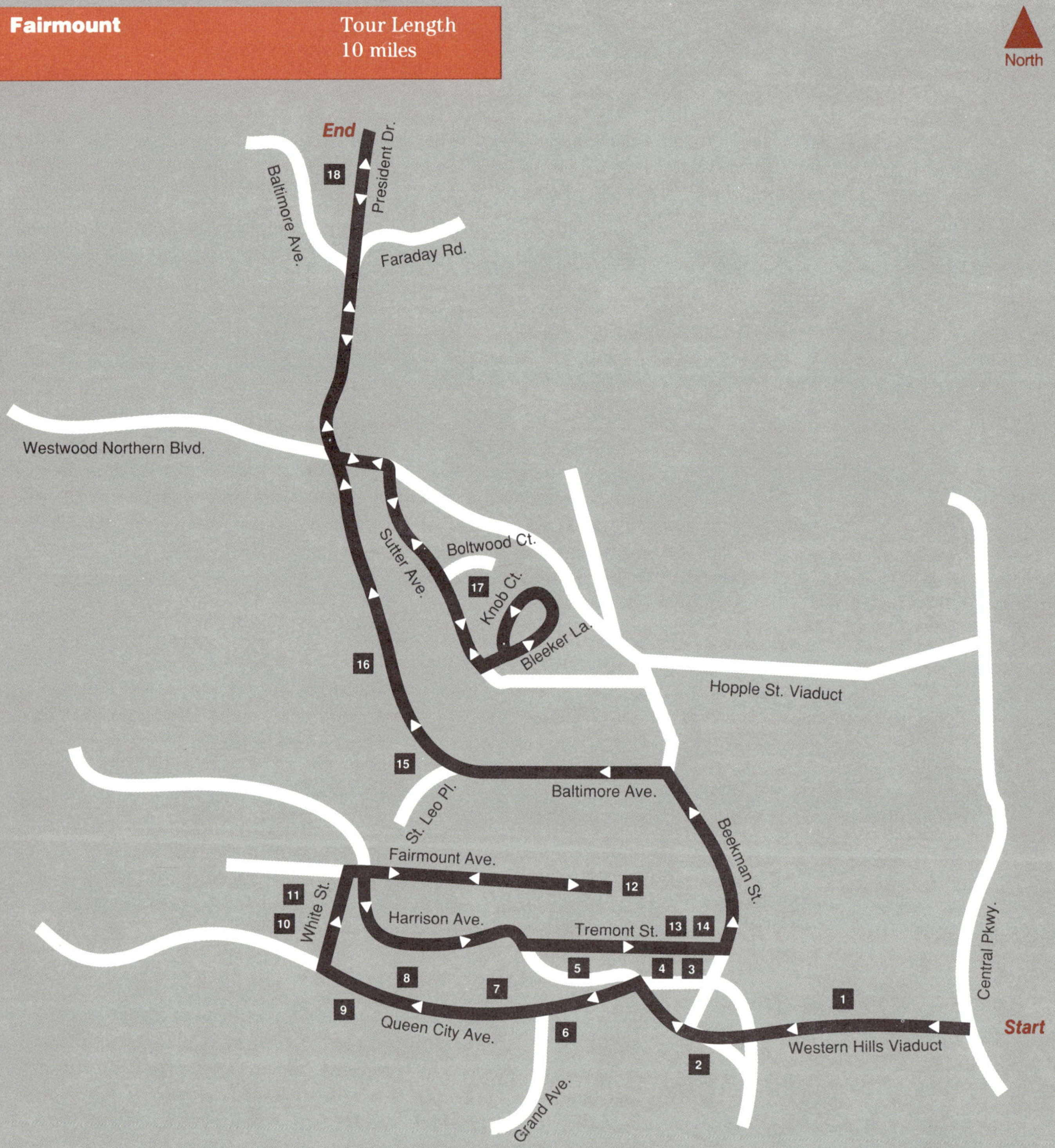
North
End
President Dr.
18
Baltimore Ave.
Faraday Rd.
Westwood Northern Blvd.
Sutter Ave.
Boltwood Ct.
17
Knob Ct.
Bleeker La.
16
Hopple St. Viaduct
15
St. Leo Pl.
Baltimore Ave.
Beekman St.
Fairmount Ave.
12
11
10
White St.
Harrison Ave.
Tremont St.
13
14
5
4
3
8
7
9
Queen City Ave.
6
2
1
Western Hills Viaduct
Start
Central Pkwy.
Grand Ave.

# Tour 16    Fairmount

▶ ▶ ▶ ▶ ▶ ▶

**Tour begins on Central Parkway.
Cross the Western Hills Viaduct.**

The **1 Western Hills Viaduct**
bridges the Mill Creek Valley to connect Central Parkway and Spring
Grove Avenue on the east with Harrison Avenue and Beekman Street on
the west. Built by McDougal Construction and Folwell Engineering under
the supervision of the Union Terminal
Company, this double-decked, Art
Deco style viaduct was completed in
1932. At 3,300 feet in length, it is

*Following the completion of the Western
Hills Viaduct in 1932, growing numbers
of commuters could safely and quickly
cross the Mill Creek Valley and its
railyards.*

Cincinnati's longest viaduct.

As early as the 1890s, west side
residents were advocating the construction of a modern approach to the
western section of the city. Their
efforts helped provide the impetus for
the creation of the Harrison Avenue
Viaduct, completed in 1908. As the
western suburbs grew, however, this
structure could not handle the
increased traffic. The Western Hills
Viaduct helped solve the problem of
providing adequate access to and
from the Western Hills communities.

The massive Western Hills Viaduct

construction project cost $3.5 million;
the city paid $1 million and the Union
Terminal Company, whose new terminal required that the railyards be
elevated to a height not compatible
with the old Harrison Avenue Viaduct,
paid the rest.

Since the 1950s, the Western Hills
Viaduct suffered from deterioration,
poor maintenance, and heavy use. By
the mid-1970s, an estimated 54,000
vehicles passed over it daily. Though
it was repaired and regraded in 1963,
the viaduct had to be closed for major
reconstruction in 1976. The closing,
which lasted almost two years, hurt

small businesses in Fairmount.

South of the viaduct (but not on
the tour route), are several red brick
buildings that were the **2 Engine
House and Beer Cellars of the
Herancourt Brewing Company,**
now occupied by the Cleveland Wrecking Company, 1400 Harrison Avenue.
The brewery plant, which once filled
the area between Harrison Pike and
the Cincinnati, Hamilton & Dayton
Railroad tracks, included a 3-story
stone brew house, a half-dozen smaller
support buildings—wash house,
blacksmith's forge, barrel house, ice
house, and sheds—as well as the
Herancourt family home.

George M. Herancourt (1807-
1880), came from Bavaria to America

in 1830. After several unsuccessful
business ventures, he arrived in
Cincinnati in the late 1840s and
erected a brewery on a 6-acre tract
of land intersected by Harrison Pike.
Production began at fourteen barrels
a day.

Herancourt may have been the
first Cincinnati brewer of lager beer
(1851) and the first to open a large
storage cellar here (1852) in which the
brewery could safely store lager
through the summer. (The use of ice
became common in the 1860s, ice-
making machines in the late 1870s.)

George Herancourt retired in
1864, and his descendants took over
management of the brewery. Over the
years, however, the direction of the
company proved inadequate: relatives
were carelessly appointed to positions
in the company, beer was sold to
customers with poor credit, and
finances were badly managed. In 1901,
unhappy stockholders gained controlling interest, and the company went
into receivership.

Though the Herancourt brewery
developed a regional market, it was
one of Cincinnati's smaller concerns,
producing 35,000 barrels in 1896,
compared to the Christian Moerlein
Company's 225,000 barrels in 1890.
When Prohibition was enacted, Herancourt, the oldest brewery still operating in Cincinnati, was dismantled.

As the first phase of Fairmount's
industrial development ended, a
second generation of light manufacturing and warehousing took over
many of the old buildings. The Cleveland Wrecking Company acquired
part of the Herancourt property,
setting up its subsidiary, Rose Brothers building supply, on the brewery
site and the wrecking company on the
other side of Harrison Avenue. The
American Ice & Cold Storage Company occupied the old beer storage
buildings until closing in the 1950s.
Cleveland Wrecking then took over
those facilities as well.

Established in 1910, the Cleveland
Wrecking Company claims to be the
only chain wrecking company in the
world; it has offices in six U.S. cities.
Through the years, the firm has
demolished a number of Cincinnati
landmarks including the Burnet
House and the Gibson Hotel, the Albee
and Lyric theaters, and much of the
West End in preparation for the
construction of Union Terminal and
the Laurel Homes and Lincoln Court

public housing developments.

Stay in the right lane on the Western Hills Viaduct, which curves to the right, then to the left. Turn left on to Queen City Avenue.

Although one German Evangelical Protestant church, St. Martin (or Martini) Church on Saffin Avenue, had been founded in Fairmount in 1851, the Indiana Home Mission Board and several Cincinnati Evangelical ministers apparently felt that the spiritual needs of the German American families who lived further to the east were not being met.

The history of **3 Immanuel United Church of Christ,** 1520 Queen City Avenue, begins in 1886, when Reverend Frederick Hohmann was assigned to Fairmount. His first service on August 1, drew some forty persons, but interest waned sharply, and only four attended a meeting called on September 9 to organize a congregation. A second attempt ten days later was more successful, and Immanuel German Evangelical Protestant Church was established. Among its eight charter members were stairbuilder Edward Borcherding, laborer Henry Borneman, painter George Dreher, porkpacker Christian Leser, carpenter Frederick Seidenspinner, and stonemason Frederick Voss.

The congregation of twenty-two families purchased a lot on the corner of Tremont and Lawnway Streets, and the first foundation stone of the church was laid on October 10, the birthday of the German reformer Martin Luther. Dedication ceremonies were held July 10, 1887.

Immanuel Evangelical's congregation grew and soon needed a larger building. On January 30, 1927, the approximately 700 members marched from their old church to dedicate the present red brick Gothic style building. After a day of speeches and sermons in English and German, 135 new members were received at evening services. The Lunkenheimer Company later bought and razed the original church for expansion.

In 1935, Immanuel recorded 1,542 members, most from middle-income and working-class families of German descent. The church under-

went several remodelings, including one to repair damage caused by the 1937 flood.

Immanuel Evangelical became Immanuel Evangelical and Reformed Church after the merger of those two denominations and officially adopted its present name in 1962, following the union of the Evangelical and Congregational Christian churches. The Immanuel membership figures reflect Fairmount's decline as a residential community. By 1961, the congregation had only 750 members, many living elsewhere but returning for Sunday services. In 1985, regular worshippers among the 175 members were predominantly elderly and lived outside the neighborhood.

The Immanuel congregation debated a move to a more convenient suburb, but instead, in an effort to reduce costs and preserve older churches, shares a minister with Salem United Church of Christ in Over-the-Rhine. The congregation has opened its building to Immanuel Retirees, a senior citizens' group; Jobs for People, geared to the development of workers' cooperatives; a day care center, and the South Fairmount Youth Group, which works to bridge cultural and racial differences between the area's residents.

Remnants of another old Fairmount manufacturing site now occu-

*The Adler Company and other plants in the community provided employment for many Fairmount residents well into the twentieth century.*

pied by a newer sort of industry are the three connected frame and cement block structures that were formerly the **4 Warehouse and Factory Buildings of the Fairmount Woolen Mills,** now the pigment warehouse, factory, and offices for the Wilson Paint Company, 1616 Harrison Avenue.

The Fairmount Woolen Mills began operations around 1867 when the newly formed partnership of Adler, Karlsruher & Franke purchased and remodeled the old Lick Run Lunatic Asylum in Fairmount. That facility, dating from 1853, had merged with Longview Hospital in 1865. Bernard Adler's sons, Isaac, William, and Morris (all German-born) later joined the business, which produced popular woolen trousers known as Kentucky doeskins.

In the late nineteenth century, Adler & Company abandoned its original line in favor of knitted woolen long underwear and, later, knitted wool socks. The company became the Adler Underwear & Hosiery Manufacturing Company. The former asylum building was replaced by a large 4-story brick factory that was gradually surrounded by additional structures where all the processes from carding, scouring, and spinning the raw wool (and, later, cotton) to knitting, finishing, and packing the completed garments took place. Eventually, the complex spread along Queen City Avenue between Pinetree Street and Harrison Avenue and up the nearby hillside. By the early 1900s, Adler

employed 175 people.

During World War I, the company developed a new specialty, tubular knitted stockinette fabric used in meat packing and under plaster casts. Adler also became the national leader in sales of athletic socks—supplying the 1958 Olympic team—and of bobby socks, riding to success with that fad. Some of its women's brands had lighthearted names like Cable-gams and Snuggle-pups. A line of chlorophyll-treated socks was called Sweet-feet.

But Adler, like many other old Fairmount industries, eventually sought a larger and more modern site. In 1962, still under family management, the company moved its hosiery manufacturing operations to a plant in Tennessee, and three years later, the general offices and stockinette plant on Beekman Avenue followed. Adler, by then a division of Burlington Industries and employing 400 workers, was one of the country's largest branded sock producers.

Part of the complex was demolished in May 1965. The Wilson Paint Company acquired the buildings it now occupies and moved to Fairmount from Reading Road and Broadway, a downtown area no longer suitable for industry.

During the late nineteenth century, the Cincinnati Water Works had relatively little difficulty in supplying water to Mill Creek Valley communities such as South Fairmount, but when the suburbs in Western Hills began growing rapidly in the late 1890s and early 1900s, a new pumping facility became necessary. The first **5** **Western Hills Pumping Station** to occupy the site at 1650 Queen City Avenue was erected in 1907 to provide a reliable supply of water to such communities as Cheviot, Westwood, and Covedale.

The main waterworks on Eastern Avenue pumped water approximately eight miles to this "repumping" station, which then boosted the water up the hill to Westwood and eastern Green Township. Although the steam powered plant could pump five to six million gallons per day, a steadily increasing demand led to the installation of larger pumps in 1910-1911.

As the development of the western suburbs accelerated in the 1920s and 1930s, the need for water grew. By the early 1930s, the Western Hills

pumping station was operating at full capacity. Work on a new facility, however, did not begin until 1936 when a Public Works Administration grant financed the project.

The present Western Hills pumping station was placed in service in November 1937. The limestone Art Deco style building was designed by J. C. Steinkamp & Brothers in association with C. P. Gillespie and Nelson Felsberg. The station's electrically-powered pumps were a considerable improvement over those of its predecessor, which was closed in 1938 and demolished in 1942. The new plant increased the pumping capacity to the Western Hills area by ten million gallons per day.

The pumping station on Queen City Avenue initially sent water to storage tanks on Ferguson Road which, as new development moved farther west, were later replaced by tanks in Westwood, Mack, and Delhi. In the late 1950s, an additional pumping station and reservoir was built at 5666 Glenway Avenue, south of Westwood.

The movement by municipal governments to provide playgrounds for children in urban areas began around the turn of the century. Cincinnati's Board of Park Commissioners, determined to develop "playground sites in the congested portions of the city," bought and improved its first six playgrounds in the basin in 1909. In 1911, using $1 million from a bond issue, the board began a land acquisition program. One of its purchases was the Lick Run Athletic Grounds, now the **6** **South Fairmount Playground and Athletic Field,** approximately four acres bounded by present-day Grand, Westwood, and Queen City Avenues.

This tract, once a part of Joseph James' subdivision, had remained undeveloped except for several temporary classrooms for the Twenty-fifth District School. These frame structures had apparently been razed by the early 1900s, as Park Board reports mention only the need to fill in and grade the area, which was below street level.

While the baseball and football fields offered recreational opportunities for teenagers and adults, Fairmount had no playground for young children until 1930, when the Cincinnati Recreation Commission, which

had received this property in 1927, completed a shallow water pool and bathhouse. The Recreation Commission added a deep water pool and pool house in 1969, play equipment, and basketball and tennis courts.

One version of the history of St. Bonaventure parish recounts that during 1843, some twenty German Catholic families, farmers, and dairymen from the area that became Fairmount sent a delegate to Archbishop Purcell asking him to establish a church in their rural community. Purcell agreed, and in the summer of 1844, a small stone house on Lick Run was dedicated as St. Peter Church. It was the predecessor of **7** **St. Bonaventure Roman Catholic Church,** 1798 Queen City Avenue, which stands approximately a mile east of the site of the old church.

The St. Peterstown subdivision, likely taking its name from the church, grew slowly. By 1869, approximately 150 home lots had been laid out in the area west of Clifford between Harrison and Queen City Avenues, but only a few dozen structures had been erected. Most notable were William Hoffmeister's brewery and St. Martin's German Evangelical Protestant Church.

Because St. Peter's church was at some distance from the more promising Fairmount subdivision, Purcell authorized the construction of a new church and school in this neighborhood in 1862. A church and a rectory were dedicated to St. Bonaventure on November 20, 1869. The stone Roman Basilica style structure could seat about 550 and was later enlarged and remodeled.

The first school opened on this property in 1871, a second in 1892. By the turn of the century, St. Bonaventure listed 450 member families, predominantly working-class. In 1908, a third school replaced the two older buildings; 600 students were enrolled the following year.

The parish prospered by the move to Fairmount; in 1923, it added a 3-story brick Sisters' residence across from the church and the present monastery and school in 1926. The bowling alleys in the basement of the school are typical of the facilities offered by many middle and lower middle-income parishes where the church was a focal point of the community's social life. This period of optimism and growth came to an end with the onset of the Depression; St. Bonaventure's was caught with a $250,000 building debt that festivals and weekly bingo games did not pay off until 1953.

Church membership peaked in 1949-1950 at about 4,000, then declined gradually. The movement of residents to newer suburbs, business closings, and the arrival of large numbers of non-Catholic Appalachian families combined to reduce the congregation from 760 families in 1969 to 365 by 1981. Fewer than 100 children were enrolled in 1979-1980, the school's final year. The Sisters' residence was sold in 1981.

In 1986, 240 families belonged to St. Bonaventure Church; approximately 60% of its members were over sixty-five; half came from outside South Fairmount to attend services, weekly bingo games, and the spring and fall festivals.

Construction of the former **8 St. Francis Hospital,** 1860 Queen City Avenue, a 4½-story red brick and stone complex, began in 1886, twelve years after the Sisters of the Poor of St. Francis had received this 10-acre hillside property from the St. Peter's Cemetery Association. The Sisters wanted to build a new facility for the care of incurably ill and elderly patients.

Financial difficulties probably caused the trustees of the German Catholic Cemetery Association (later St. Peter's), which established a burial ground here in 1843, to sell plots to persons "not in communion with the Church." Archbishop Purcell laid the cemetery under interdict on September 9, 1849, making it no longer consecrated ground; Catholics would not buy plots. After courts ruled that trustees had broken faith with the organization, the association donated the land to the Franciscan Sisters. Graves were moved to St. Joseph Old Cemetery in Price Hill.

A $25,000 bequest from Cincinnati philanthropist Reuben R. Springer (1800-1884) enabled the Sisters to begin construction. The hospital chapel was dedicated December 27, 1888, and St. Francis Hospital admitted its first patient on January 2, 1889. At that time there were only two stories. The upper floors were added in 1893 and 1895, and the wings in 1900. By 1938, St. Francis Hospital had

*After St. Francis Hospital closed in 1981, city officials and area residents sought some means of reusing the attractive historic structure.*

cared for 41,000 patients, 85% of whom had been unable to pay.

St. Francis gained early fame as the only hospital west of the Alleghenies with facilities for treating cancer patients. It was Cincinnati's westernmost hospital and with the growth of the Western Hills communities in the 1930s and 1940s, gradually became a general hospital. In 1941, St Francis began to admit the acutely ill—not just the chronically ill—and five years later, it discontinued the policy of admitting those who were old but not ill. Many such persons had lived at the hospital for decades.

St. Francis established a school for practical nursing in 1955, an intensive care unit ten years later, and in 1972, completed a renovation and updating of the building and equipment that included the opening of a nuclear medicine department. By then, the incurably ill occupied only about forty of the hospital's beds; the remaining 265 beds were devoted to the care of acute illness, cardiac, and intensive care cases. The hospital had changed to meet the area's needs.

Hospital administrators, planning for the future, concluded the facility would soon be obsolete and began negotiations for a merger with St. George Hospital, founded in Westwood in 1944 by the Dominican Sisters of St. Mary of the Springs. St. Francis-St. George Hospital incorporated in 1974; a proposed new hospital was to be operated by the Cincinnati Archdiocese and the Dominican and Franciscan Sisters. St. Francis Hospital closed in 1981, and the $52 million, 290-bed St. Francis-St. George Hospital opened in Westwood in January

1982. In 1987, this institution merged with Providence Hospital, creating one of the largest health care providers in the tri-state area.

The St. Francis Hospital buildings remained vacant; plans were drawn up to turn the complex into a federally-subsidized housing project for the elderly. By 1985, the Council on Aging of the Cincinnati Area had decided to locate its South Fairmount Senior Center here, and the U.S. Department of the Interior had given preliminary approval to tax credits for the renovation of the former hospital. In 1984, the building was added to the National Register of Historic Places.

The 3-story stone building at 1925 Queen City Avenue, now a site for warehousing and light manufacturing, is the only remaining portion of the 10-building complex of the **9 P. R. Mitchell Company,** one of the early manufacturing concerns to establish itself in Fairmount. The company processed feathers, produced feather dusters and bedding goods, and manufactured "curled hair"—hog and cow hair and bristles used for brushes and as stuffing for mattresses, sofas, and cushions.

Perhaps as early as the 1840s, A. D. Bullock & Company, wool dealers and commission merchants, had erected a small curled hair factory on Lick Run Pike. The company took advantage of Cincinnati's status as a porkpacking center, and by 1859 was one of two firms in the city processing the hair and bristles pulled from the 365,000 hogs sold that year. Bullock began processing feathers for bedding and eventually expanded to fill a 3½-acre site at Spring Grove and Harrison Avenues.

In 1893, Pierson R. Mitchell advanced from partner to head the firm, which was reincorporated as the P.R. Mitchell Company. By 1912, the Fairmount portion of the Mitchell Company spread over five acres, employed 125 men, and used 2.5 million pounds of hair a year. One building housed the company offices and cattle tail shearing, picker, spinning, and stock rooms. Other structures contained the bristle shop, washing and dye tanks, and rooms for sorting, drawing, drying, pressing, and storing new and sterilized curled hair.

In the mid-1930s, Joseph F. Bohnert took over the Fairmount facility, which continued under family management, producing curled hair and then upholstery supplies until it closed in the late 1940s.

By that time, Cincinnati's pork-packing and furniture industries, which had provided curled hair manufacturers with materials and a market, respectively, had decreased in importance. Moreover, the furniture industry had found substitutes for curled hair. The stone building stood vacant, then became the Queen City Avenue Industrial Center, quarters for various building contractor and supply firms. The other structures were used for general warehousing until being torn down when Westwood Avenue was extended in 1974.

**Turn right on White Street.**

The growth of industry in South Fairmount in the late nineteenth and early twentieth centuries attracted many working-class families to the community. Italian Americans were among those who followed industry up the Mill Creek Valley, and by the 1920s, there was a sizable "Little Italy" colony here. It was for this group that **10 San Antonio Roman Catholic Church,** 1948 Queen City Avenue, was begun in 1922 by three Sisters of Charity.

Sacred Heart Italian Church at Broadway and Fifth Street was quite a distance from Fairmount. A few Italian families attended Mass at nearby St. Bonaventure Church, but they were uncomfortable in this German parish. Sisters Blandina and Justina Seagle (who had started the Santa Maria Benevolent, Educational and Industrial Home in 1897 to help their fellow countrymen adapt to their new homeland) and Sister Euphrasia

purchased a feed store on Queen City Avenue.

There, on August 6, 1922, they opened St. Anthony Welfare Center and Neighborhood House with a chapel dedicated to St. Anthony of Padua. Two hundred attended the dedication ceremonies on October 8. A church history described the early congregation as being of "modest and meager means"; four of the six officers of the San Antonio's Men's Club, for example, were laborers.

At the time San Antonio Welfare Center opened, small 2-story houses and stores with flats on the floor above lined Queen City Avenue. They were home, primarily, to working-class families of German and Italian ancestry. Pasquale Lucia and Pasquale Marzanna, laborers, lived at 1942. John Hesselbrock ran a grocery at 1946, and Albert Burbage, fireman; Gaetano Cavallo, painter, and John D'Angelo, cook, rented rooms above. Fred Stang's bakery was across the street at 1953; chauffeur Henry Oppelt had a flat there. Joseph Bernhardt, a baker, and dairyman George Geis lived with their families at 1956.

The Welfare Center gradually became a parish of which the Franciscan Fathers took charge in 1928. The old building was remodeled in 1933. In 1936, Italian-language sermons were briefly reinstituted, and the choir gave a spaghetti supper that became an annual tradition.

As the suburbs of Cheviot and Westwood grew, increased traffic required widening of Queen City Avenue. In 1938, the city notified San Antonio that the church would be razed for the new highway construction. The last High Mass was held on November 12, 1939, and the structure was demolished the next day. Parishioners met in a vacant building until the present red brick church was dedicated on December 1, 1940. The sanctuary and office were added in 1953, the bell tower in 1954. The current congregation of around 300 is of Irish and German as well as Italian descent, and most members come from the suburbs for services.

The South Fairmount Improvement Association (SFIA), chartered July 21, 1927, and the earliest of this area's several residents' organizations, meets monthly in the basement of San Antonio Church. SFIA lists among its accomplishments participation in getting a deep water swimming pool

for the community and the construction of the Dunham Recreation complex in Price Hill.

The rapid growth of Fairmount in the 1880s and 1890s crowded the community's only school, the Twenty-fifth District School on Tremont Street, and prompted the construction of new schools. North Fairmount Grammar School (later Carll School) opened in 1892, and **11 Central Fairmount School,** 2475 White Street, in 1909. The 3-story Jacobethan style brick building with castle-like towers was the work of E. H. Dornette, also the architect for Hyde Park, Clifton, and other Cincinnati schools.

*As Fairmount's population grew in the late nineteenth and early twentieth centuries, neighborhood school facilities were expanded to include Central Fairmount School, built in 1909.*

Planned for approximately 500 students, grades 1-8, Central Fairmount enrolled 392 children by 1925, while the nearby parochial schools drew 633. Thus, the 1925 city plan concluded that the facility would be adequate for the next forty-five years. However, as Catholic residents moved away in the decades following World War II, they were replaced by families who sent their children to public schools. In 1970, an addition to Central Fairmount School increased its capacity to about 650.

Throughout the decade, Central Fairmount was enrolled at slightly under capacity and, reflecting the makeup of the neighborhood, had an almost completely white student population—99% in 1973-1974. Though Central Fairmount remained essentially a neighborhood school, an open enrollment policy to improve racial balance and the closing of nearby Roll Hill School produced, by 1986-1987, a student population of 625 pre-school through sixth graders of whom about 70% were white and 30% black.

Central Fairmount center offers computer work for students in grades 4-6 and is supported by an active PTA.

**Turn right on Fairmount Avenue.**

**12** **St. Clair Heights Park,** Fairmount Avenue at Iroquois Street, occupies land originally developed by the Western Baptist Education Society for the Fairmount Theological Seminary. The Baptist organization purchased the land in 1849 and two years later completed the seminary building, a 4-story brick structure topped by an observatory and containing a chapel, library, dormitories, classrooms, and dining hall. The seminary closed in 1858.

In 1866, the building became the home of the *Schuetzen Verein,* or Shooting Society, among whose founders and stockholders were many of Cincinnati's most prominent German American residents including brewers John Hauck, Christian Moerlein, Christian Boss, George Koehler, George Herancourt, Conrad Windisch, Gottlieb Muhlhauser, and Joseph

*In 1866, a former Baptist seminary building became the home of one of Cincinnati's German American organizations, the Schuetzen Verein, or Shooting Society.*

Schaller; candle and soap manufacturer Michael Werk, and newspaper editor, General August Willich. Many Civil War veterans, members of the Ninth Regiment, Cincinnati's German unit, also belonged to the *Verein.* The hill became commonly known as the *Schuetzenbuckel,* or Shooter's Hill.

The Shooting Society reorganized in 1868 as the *Schuetzen* Park Company, transformed the Fairmount property into a beer garden and picnic grounds, as well as a shooting club, and added a bowling alley to the building. The American Sharpshooters Society, with national headquarters in the Central Turner Hall on Vine Street in Over-the-Rhine, held its 1870 shooting festival on the *Schuetzenbuckel.* Legend holds that it was here Annie Oakley, brought to Cincinnati for a shooting contest, met and defeated her future husband, Frank Butler, noted marksman and vaudeville performer.

The *Schuetenplatz* was driven out of business by the construction of similar hilltop recreational complexes like the Bellevue, Price Hill, Lookout and Highland Houses, which were more accessible because they stood next to inclines.

In 1912, two stockholders and sons of founders of the Schuetzen Park Company, Louis J. Hauck, president of the Lincoln National Bank and former president of the Hauck Brewing Company, and George F. Dieterle, treasurer and general manager of the

Union Distilling Company, donated nineteen acres of the property to the Cincinnati Park Board.

The city graded a ballfield, and neighborhood residents constructed a tennis court. Play equipment has been added to the now-17½-acre park. On September 2, 1915, the park received its current name, which honors General Arthur St. Clair (17341818). However, many still refer to this hill as the *Schuetzenbuckel.*

**Return on Fairmount Avenue. Turn left on Harrison Avenue, left on Tremont Street.**

**13** **Roosevelt School,** 1550 Tremont Street, stands on the site previously occupied by Fairmount's Twenty-fifth District School, erected in 1876 to serve children in the area from Liberty Street to North Fairmount. Children first attended classes in a 2-room log cabin, then the 12-room Schotwell School on Harrison Pike. The Twenty-fifth District School was built further east, where more development was taking place.

The continued growth of Fairmount brought about the construction of North Fairmount Grammar School (1892) and Central Fairmount Grammar School (1909), and by the early twentieth century, the Board of Education was promising a larger, more modern building for the approx-

imately 400 children, grades 1-8, attending Twenty-fifth District. Theodore Roosevelt's name was chosen for the attractive brick and stone school completed in 1925. An addition erected in 1964 brought Roosevelt School's capacity to 450.

This South Fairmount school had a predominantly white student population into the early 1970s and, as the community's population decreased, was enrolled almost 25% below capacity by 1977. In 1980, it was merged with nearby Carll School, a predominantly black institution that was also suffering from low enrollment, and the racial balance at Roosevelt improved. In 1986-1987, Roosevelt also began receiving students from Millvale School, giving it approximately equal numbers of black and white youngsters.

With about 380 students in grades K-6, Roosevelt is one of Cincinnati's seven Urban Education Development schools, receiving special funding to meet the additional needs of low-income students.

A second generation of industry developed in Fairmount as, in the late nineteenth and early twentieth centuries, businesses moved from crowded, older parts of the city to newer quarters here. One of these firms was the **14 Lunkenheimer Company,** 1500 Waverly Avenue.

Formerly among the nation's leading manufacturers of pressure valves, Lunkenheimer once occupied a 10-building complex at Beekman Street and Waverly Avenue. The Lunkenheimer Company was founded in 1862 by Frederick Lunkenheimer (1825-1889), a German-born machinist who came to the United States in 1845. He settled in Cincinnati in 1854 and took a job with Miles Greenwood's Eagle Iron Works, a foundry and machine building company on the Miami & Erie Canal. In 1862, Lunkenheimer left Greenwood and established a small shop on Seventh Street where he made riverboat whistles, brass valves, and gas, water, beer, and steam cocks.

In 1867, Lunkenheimer expanded by purchasing an old Jewish synagogue on Lodge Alley, a narrow street between Vine and Walnut Streets. By 1880, that building also proved too small for the growing enterprise which then employed over one hundred workers, and Lunkenheimer's Cincin-

nati Brass Works moved into a 5-story factory on Eighth Street.

In 1889, the company was incorporated as the Lunkenheimer Brass Manufacturing Company. That same year, Frederick Lunkenheimer died, and his son, Edmund (1861-1944), took over the business. The Lunkenheimer Company, as it was renamed in 1893, became a major producer of valves for the national and international markets.

In 1899, Edmund initiated the construction of a 390,000- square foot complex in Fairmount, near the Cincinnati & Westwood Railroad line. From 1900-1920, the Lunkenheimer Company's sales rose from $662,000 to $1.8 million. Continued prosperity, especially during World War I, prompted the company to build a large steel and iron foundry in Carthage in 1923.

In 1919, Edmund Lunken (he dropped the "heimer" in 1892), became chairman of the board of the company and his son, Eshelby (1890-1945), became president. The two men were interested in aviation both for its own sake and for business reasons. The Lunkenheimer Company supplied valves for airplanes; Charles Lindburg used its products in his *Spirit of St. Louis*. In 1930, Edmund gave the city 230 acres of land near Kellog Avenue for the creation of a municipal airport named Lunken Airport in his honor.

During the Depression, the Lunkenheimer Company's sales dropped 77%, and the number of employees fell from 1,372 to 438. Pre-Depression levels were not reached again until 1937, but as a result of the World War II production boom, sales jumped from around $6.6 million to nearly $11 million between 1940 and 1943.

With the deaths of Edmund and Eshelby Lunken in 1944 and 1945, respectively, Frank P. Rhame became president, the first non-family member to run the company. However, Eshelby's son, Demund P. Lunken, became vice-president, and his half-brother, Homer Lunken, became assistant general manager. Homer was also a member of the Mayor's Friendly Relations Committee, which had been organized in 1943 to promote "harmony and tolerance" among the city's racial, ethnic, and religious groups. The Lunkenheimer Company, unlike many other Cincinnati firms, employed blacks during the war years, and Lunken met with area business leaders to try to persuade them to hire

black workers.

The company undertook a $3 million retooling and modernization program from 1947 to 1951. It closed the Carthage plant in 1953 and replaced it with a new, more efficient steel and iron foundry in Fairmount. Lunkenheimer also worked to improve its foreign markets, securing a share of a valve factory in Mexico in

*Before the Lunkenheimer Company experienced severe losses in the early 1980s, the firm was one of Fairmount's major employers.*

1960 and five years later, purchasing a Toronto-based valve company.

During the 1960s, the Lunkenheimer Company changed hands twice, once in the face of stiff opposition from its management and after a number of court battles.

Under the Condec Corporation of Old Greenwich, Connecticut, sales peaked at $60 million in 1979 but fell to $18 million by 1983; monthly losses ran over $1 million. This downturn, the worst since the early 1930s, was accompanied by massive layoffs. The company's problems stemmed from increased foreign competition, a general economic recession, and poor management.

Condec sold the Lunkenheimer Company in 1984. The new owners closed the Fairmount works, sold most of the complex, and transferred valve production to Lunkenheimer plants in Alabama. Until June 1985, some foundry operations were continued by employees who had bought the foundry building and hoped for a loan to buy the equipment.

As part of a plan created to spur business development in the Mill Creek Valley, the city granted Lunkenheimer a tax break in 1985 to keep it from moving to Florence, Kentucky. The Lunkenheimer Company occupies a small office and employs approximately forty people for warehousing and distribution of valves made at other locations. The conspicuously vacant buildings are a bleak reminder of more prosperous days. Fairmount lost a considerable number of jobs with Lunkenheimer's decline, and local businesses that depended on the patronage of company workers have suffered.

**Turn left on Beekman Street, left on Baltimore Avenue.**

More than simply an architectural landmark in North Fairmount, **15 St. Leo Roman Catholic Church,** 2573 St. Leo Place, is a physical and emotional focal point for the community and for residents' determination to improve the quality of their lives.

Archbishop William Elder (1819-1904) organized St. Leo parish in 1886 at the request of German Catholic families who had to travel either to Sacred Heart Church in Camp Washington or St. Bonaventure to attend services. Members selected a building site on New Baltimore Pike and Trade Street, began raising building funds, and rented the second floor of a carpenter shop to hold services. The first St. Leo Church, dedicated April 12, 1888, was a small 2-story brick structure that served as church, rectory, and school for thirty students. By the mid-1890s, this parish listed 150 families, while St. Bonaventure recorded 450.

As North Fairmount developed, the parish grew. By 1904, the congregation had begun a new church adjacent to the old one and worshipped in the roofed-over basement until the present building was completed and dedicated November 26, 1911. The buff brick and stone Romanesque basilica style church had a seating capacity of 800.

The parish also purchased two houses in the neighborhood for a convent and additional classroom space. St. Leo's school was completed in January 1927, and 420 youngsters attended. That year, Trade Street was renamed St. Leo Place in recognition of the parish's importance.

St. Leo's, with about 2,000 members by the end of the 1930s, entered a period of growth in the early 1940s when the federal government opened the English Woods housing development for low-income white families. Nearly half of the units were soon occupied by Catholic families, and St. Leo opened a mission chapel there in 1943. The chapel was replaced six years later by Our Lady of Presentation Mission Church, 2012 Westwood Avenue.

In the 1960s, North Fairmount underwent significant social and economic change. Older residents died; other parishioners moved to newer suburbs. Many small businesses closed. The influx of displaced, low-income black families into English Woods and Fay Apartments spurred "white flight." North Fairmount quickly changed from a predominantly white, middle-income community to one that was largely black and lower-income.

St. Leo's membership fell from 800 families in 1961 to fewer than one hundred parishioners by 1974. The school closed in 1979; children were sent to St. Boniface School in Northside.

But St. Leo parish developed a new thrust for its mission, turning more and more to active community involvement. The North Fairmount Community Council (NFCC) board, formed in 1979, rented the parish school for one dollar, and in 1980, the North Fairmount Community Center opened there, housing day care and Head Start programs, a senior citizens center, adult education classes, and later, a health clinic. NFCC also operates a combination food co-op, thrift shop, and a laundromat. It also plans construction of moderate-rent housing. The Community Center is an independent, nonprofit organization that residents feel is stronger and more successful because they, not a city agency, are responsible for it.

Because of declining memberships, Our Lady of Presentation was closed and its congregation merged with St. Leo's in 1986. The current combined, integrated congregation numbers about 350.

When city planners evaluated Cincinnati's school system in 1925, they concluded that North Fairmount Grammar School, Baltimore Avenue and Trevor Place, "should be retained at its present site" and was "adequate to take care of all future growth." But North Fairmount Grammar, built in 1892, became Carll Primary School which, because of dropping enrollment, was closed in 1980. The red brick building is unused and deteriorating.

Now, area children attend the **16 North Fairmount School,** 2001 Baltimore Avenue, which was designed by Kruckemeyer & Strong and opened in 1954. Its location, northwest of its predecessor, indicates the direction in which North Fairmount's population has shifted.

In the late 1960s and early 1970s, 600 to 700 students, K-6, attended North Fairmount School, but alternative programs have drawn away many youngsters. Annual enrollment at North Fairmount School in the mid-1980s was around 400, 65% black and 35% white. The relatively new, modern style structure is conspicuous among the neighborhood's older buildings.

**Turn right on Westwood Northern Boulevard, right on Sutter Avenue.**

The **17 English Woods Housing Project,** Sutter Avenue and Knob, Boltwood, and Heath Courts, was the third federally-subsidized housing development built by the Cincinnati Metropolitan Housing Authority (CMHA). Named after David English, an early Cincinnati minister, the original 750-apartment complex was finished in May 1942. This North Fairmount hillside site was chosen because of its proximity to public transportation, the newly-paved Westwood-Northern Boulevard, and Mill Creek Valley industries. CMHA intended that most of the white, low-wage, working families for whom this development was planned would find jobs nearby, improve their economic condition, and eventually move from subsidized housing to homes of their own. Older persons with fixed, limited incomes might be permanent residents.

Many Cincinnatians had long been concerned about the shortage of decent, low-rent housing. Both the Better Housing League, formed in 1916, and later, the Citizens' Committee on Slum Clearance and Low-Cost Housing had found that significant improvement in tenement housing could not be produced with the funding that was available at the time.

New possibilities for housing

reform opened up when the National Recovery Act of June 1933 provided federal loans or grants for public corporations that undertook slum clearance and rebuilding or the construction of low-cost housing on undeveloped land. The Cincinnati Metropolitan Housing Authority was established in November, and Laurel Homes, the CMHA's first effort, opened in the West End in 1938.

As the $3.5 million English Woods development neared completion in April 1942, the *Cincinnati Enquirer* noted that if CMHA ever needed tenants, it might advertise: *"Wanted. . . Cincinnati families to move from tenement homes into an attractive residential suburb. Two, three, and five-room apartments available for rents from $12 to $15 a month. Fresh, sootless air guaranteed. One hundred acres of grass, trees, and playground for your children to thrive in."*

The 83-building complex designed by Frederick W. Garber was envisioned as a community with landscaped lawns, wide streets, and ample parking. English Woods homes were a clear improvement over the old, crowded, dilapidated housing in the basin, which were almost the only other choice low-income families had. Prospective residents had to prove that they were living in substandard housing, and that their annual income did not exceed $1,550 or fall below $500.

To foster pride in the homes and keep operating expenses low, CMHA required tenants to care for an allotted portion of the yard and to clean and repair their own apartments; materials were supplied by the Housing Authority. If upkeep costs rose due to individual carelessness, individual rents were increased.

A $2 million, 134-unit, duplex style rowhouse addition by Kruckemeyer & Strong was completed in November 1959. In June 1971, the Marquette Manor high-rise, 1559 Sutter Avenue, named for Bleecker Marquette (c.1892-1980), director of the Better Housing League from 1918 to 1954, opened with low-rent apartments for the elderly. The number of residential units in the development then totaled more than 1,000.

English Woods remained all white into the late 1960s. Black families then began to move in, but this change did not take place without difficulties. In 1973, racial tensions forced the temporary closing of a swimming pool for which residents had helped raise money. By the mid-1980s, 86% of the residents of English Woods were black, and unlike the original population of working families, the majority were primarily elderly or children under seventeen in mostly single-parent, female-headed households. Units in English Woods rent for about 30% of total income, but with 80% of the tenants receiving some form of public assistance, the project served few of them as a stepping stone to private homeownership.

This development, like other public housing projects, has suffered from vandalism, crime, and declining federal support. Some of the newer units have been demolished because of hillside slippage. Residents work to improve their community through a civic association, which secured funding for the Child Development Center that houses a day care center, library, and laundromat.

Turn left on Bleeker Lane, left on Knob Court, right on Bleecker, and return on Sutter Avenue. Turn left on Westwood Northern Boulevard, right on Baltimore Avenue, right on President Drive.

The **18 Fay Apartments,** President Drive, opened during the 1960s housing boom in Cincinnati's western suburbs. Fay's developer, the Hamilton Company, designed the complex as a middle-income white community with, as the *Cincinnati Post* noted, "119 attractive buildings containing a total of 1025 suites, modern in every respect. . . [with] a sweeping view of downtown Cincinnati, the Mill Creek Valley, and wooded Mt. Airy Forest." Fay Apartments' 3,000 residents had ample parking on wide streets, small yards, twenty-two equipped play areas, two security guards, and a 14-member maintenance crew. Rents for the 1 to 4-bedroom units in the 2-story brick and aluminum-sided buildings ranged from $65.50 to $149 a month.

City buses ran from the apartments to both downtown and Western Hills Shopping Center. Roll Hill Elementary opened in 1967 as a neighborhood school. Nonetheless, the development was relatively isolated from shopping, churches, employment, and the variety of community institutions that made Green Township, for example, more attractive to middle-income families. In 1968, the Hamilton Company defaulted on its federally-insured loan, and the Department of Housing and Urban Development (HUD) took control of the property. During this period, many black families were moving into North Fairmount, and by 1980, the population of Fay Apartments was predominantly black.

That year, the City of Cincinnati, anxious not to lose this moderate-income housing to a private developer, bought Fay Apartments for $1 per unit, intending to rehabilitate and convert the complex into cooperative housing; however, the plan proved too costly and was never carried out. More and more of the units were designated subsidized low-income housing; improper construction forced demolition of some units, and, as the city could not meet rising maintenance costs, Fay Apartments deteriorated.

After the federal government cut aid to subsidized housing by 25% in 1982, the city began negotiations to sell this property. In March 1986, a private developer, the Stern-Handy Company, bought the Fay Apartments for $3.6 million and pledged major improvements while maintaining approximately 75% of the units as low-income housing.

In 1986, the Board of Education voted to convert Roll Hill Elementary from a neighborhood school to a reading and language arts alternative school open to students throughout the city. Children from Fay Apartments who did not enroll in the alternative program were reassigned to other schools in the system. This has weakened the role of the school in fostering a sense of community identity, though the special magnet program is a source of neighborhood pride.

Tour ends. Return on President Drive and Baltimore Avenue to Westwood Northern Boulevard.

# Newport - Fort Thomas

Newport, Kentucky, is located on the south bank of the Ohio River, east of the Licking River, and adjoins Fort Thomas, which lies along a bend in the Ohio. Although Fort Thomas is an independent city, it has long functioned as a suburb of both Newport and Cincinnati.

Newport's history began with Hubbard Taylor (b.1760), son of a Virginia planter, who visited Kentucky in 1780 and returned a decade later as a soldier assigned to Fort Washington. On Hubbard's advice, his father, the elder James Taylor, who already owned 2,500 acres in Northern Kentucky, agreed to buy more land and subdivide it. In 1792, Hubbard platted part of his family's holdings.

Although Newport would later be densely built up, the new town was laid out with streets seventy-two feet wide, spacious lots measuring 72'x 214½', and alleyways to separate each range of lots. Those who purchased land here agreed to build houses no smaller than sixteen feet square with stone or brick chimneys within three years, or forfeit their property. The town was named to honor Captain Christopher Newport, who landed the first settlers in Jamestown.

Later, that year Hubbard and his brother, James (1767-1848), enlarged the plat, but sold only nineteen lots over the next three years. In 1794, James began actively to promote the town, seeking to make it the Campbell County seat and applying for a license to operate a ferry between Newport and Cincinnati.

Despite these efforts, Newport remained "a small cluster of cabins" with a population of about one hundred until the Newport Barracks were completed around 1804. Two years later, a dozen Methodists began a class at Jonathan Huling's tavern at Bellevue (Fourth) and Columbia Streets. In 1808, John Brown Lindsey built the first brick house in town, at Front and Columbia Streets. By 1810, Newport had 413 residents.

In 1817, Newport citizens were given the right to elect town trustees, and in 1834, the Commonwealth of Kentucky rechartered Newport as a city, even though it had fewer than 1,000 inhabitants. The 1839-1840 Shaffer's *Directory of Cincinnati, Newport and Covington* noted that Newport's public buildings were "a Court House, one Methodist and one Presbyterian Church, a Cotton Factory, a Bale-rope and Bagging Factory and one Woolen Factory, which when in operation, employ 3-400 hands."

Over the next decade, Newport experienced considerable growth as its population rose to 5,895, largely the result of German immigration. This influx touched off a land boom, and by the mid 1850s, subdivisions equal the size of the original town had been platted.

In 1844, M. T. C. Gould, a Cincinnati land agent, opened a subdivision southwest of Newport. Three years later, James Taylor laid out the Bellevue Subdivision between Fifth and Eighth Streets, east of Monmouth Street. In 1848, J. T. and W. J. Berry, both related by marriage to the Taylors, laid out the General Taylor Buena Vista Addition south of Bellevue Street. In 1850 and 1851, the New Bellevue Subdivision further enlarged the Taylor properties. By 1854, when W. G. Terrell subdivided an area near Seventh and Isabella Streets, Newport's population exceeded 8,300. Three years later, Newport franchised the Covington Gas-Light Company to provide service to the city.

Over the next two decades, Newport's growth slowed, but its services improved, as first a volunteer and then a paid fire company were founded, newspapers were established, and the city's first businesses grew up.

Like the rest of Northern Kentucky, Newport prospered after the Civil War. In 1869, the Louisville, Cincinnati & Lexington Railroad was completed, linking Newport to the rest of the commonwealth and to the South. Two years later, a new railroad bridge connected Newport and Cincinnati.

By then, Newport's German community had become a major social, economic, and political force, controlling three of the city's six city council wards. In addition, German Americans sponsored benevolent and orphan's societies, a Workman's Association, and a Pioneer Association for early German settlers. Of sixteen churches in Newport, no fewer than six were German.

In 1871, Newport had three schools, thirteen cigar and tobacco dealers, four carriagemakers, three hotels, two breweries—one owned by Peter Constans (d.1875), and another by John Butcher (d.1887) and George W. Wiedemann (1833-1890)—but only one heavy industry, the Kenton Iron Works on East Front Street. The city's first waterworks began operating in 1873. Between 1870 and 1880, Newport grew to 20,433 and was one of the nation's one hundred largest municipalities.

Newport had five schools by 1880, including a single-room schoolhouse for blacks, who made up 1% of its population. The city also had ninety-four businesses, the most prominent of which were two banks, a chemical works, a paper factory, a distillery, three steel mills, and three foundries. But most of the city's commerce was made up of small enterprises such as bootmakers, cigarmakers, and carpenter shops.

The 1880s marked Newport's zenith. The city was first settled along the riverfront, and its oldest families continued to live there through most of the nineteenth century. But they had long been plagued by flooding, and the floods of 1883 and 1884 were the final straw. With

*After the floods of the 1880s, many of Newport's affluent residents moved to higher ground, including the area that became known as Mansion Hill.*

*The barracks at Fort Thomas were the peacetime home of several different regular army infantry units during the post's history.*

suburbs opening on high ground to the south and with the prospect of improved transportation, many people left the bottoms for either Mansion Hill, a few blocks to the south, or "the Highlands," as Fort Thomas was then called.

The Highlands was first settled in 1824, when William (1803- 1893) and Alice (d.1838) Taliaferro located their farm on 125 acres of land inherited from her father, Washington Berry. Taliaferro called his estate Mt. Pleasant, and throughout the early nineteenth century, the surrounding area bore that name. In 1832, residents set up a school in Taliaferro's cabin, which was also used for Baptist and Methodist meetings.

For the next two decades, Mt. Pleasant was primarily farm and orchard land. In 1857, Henry Stanberry, soon to be Abraham Lincoln's attorney general and later a defender of Andrew Johnson during his impeachment trial, built a house in Mt. Pleasant.

A quarter of a century later, landowners like Stanberry and Samuel Bigstaff (d.1912), a real estate speculator and a trustee of the James Taylor estate, began to promote the Highlands. In the late 1880s, Bigstaff convinced the federal government to build an army base, Fort Thomas, there. In years to come, the parklike post became both a part of the community and a tourist attraction. Bigstaff also founded the Highland Park Land Company in the 1890s, which promoted the Briarcliff Subdivision, created by the architects E. A. and C. C. Weber and located east of North Fort Thomas Avenue and Memorial Parkway. The company also tried to make the Highlands a resort, building the Inverness Country Club in 1896. Within a few years, the area had three resort hotels, including Bigstaff's Altamont.

Equally important to the future of the Highlands was the development of transportation. In 1882, F. M. Gosney began horse-drawn omnibus service to Newport, making four trips daily. The opening of the Cincinnati, Inverness & Fort Thomas Electric Railroad in the early 1890s reshaped the area. Previously settlement had clustered around the Inverness Subdivision just east of the Newport reservoir, and the military post; now the Highlands became a railway suburb.

By 1914, the population of the Highlands was 4,000, enough for it to incorporate as a city. Some long-time residents wanted the city to take one of its traditional names — Mt. Pleasant or The Highlands. But the city was best known for the military base, and therefore adopted its name.

Fort Thomas's greatest growth came in the first half of the twentieth century. During these years, many of Fort Thomas's civic institutions were established. In 1906, residents organized a volunteer fire department. In 1910, the Fort Thomas Building & Loan Association was formed. From 1920 to 1930, the city's population almost doubled, reaching 10,008, and 35% of the city's present housing was constructed. At the same time, the streets were paved, gas service began, and sewer lines were laid.

As Fort Thomas thrived, Newport's development slowed. Earlier, during Newport's boom, local leaders complained that the city had become complacent and was not doing enough to attract new business. In 1890, one of its largest businesses, the Dueber Watch Case Company, left. Despite this, firms such as the Wadsworth Watch Case Company, founded by a former Dueber employee, and the Wiedemann Brewery continued to prosper.

Nevertheless, by the 1910s, the area along Front Street, once the site of mills and factories, had become a shantytown. In 1916, *The Kentucky Post* observed that Newport had too much unskilled labor, too few skilled workers, and no room to expand.

During the 1920s, Newport solved its lack of space and the loss of its more affluent residents by annexing adjoining communities and undeveloped property. These additions included land along the C&O railroad tracks, the suburb of Cote Brillante, and the area between Alexandria Pike and Grand Avenue. Newport capped its expansion in 1935 by absorbing the City of Clifton. With well established city services, including fire protection and schools, Clifton had long been a target

*Fort Thomas's promoters hoped that guests at resort hotels like Samuel Bigstaff's Altamont would find the area attractive and return to purchase property there.*

for Newport, but its residents had rejected annexation. Only during the Depression were Clifton voters willing to become a part of the larger city, hoping to reduce the tax burden. These annexations more than doubled Newport's size.

At the same time, Newport also gained its reputation as a "sin city," although some traced a tradition of vice back to the days of the Newport Barracks. As early as the 1880s, George M. Dittoe, editor of the *Kentucky State Journal* crusaded against the openly operating gambling houses that were tolerated by city government. With the coming of Prohibition in the 1920s, illegal gambling, alcohol sales, and prostitution flourished in Newport.

The 1930s brought reform, but in the late 1940s, the "Cleveland Syndicate" took over Newport's underground economy and by the end of the 1950s, controlled both local and county government. Reacting to this, Northern Kentucky citizens formed a number of groups, including the Newport Ministerial Association and the Committee of 500, to drive out organized crime.

In 1960, reformers ran a candidate for Campbell County sheriff. The man they chose was George Ratterman, a thirty-four-year-old investment and tax counselor who had been a quarterback for Notre Dame and the Cleveland Browns, and was a football announcer for NBC. After a campaign during which mobsters drugged Ratterman, had him photographed in bed with a stripper, and arrested by Newport police, Ratterman won, and the mob quickly left town.

This victory did little to solve Newport's economic woes. Throughout those years, Newport's population hovered around 30,000, peaking at the beginning of the baby boom before declining to about 20,000 by 1980. In 1949, the median income of Newport residents was nearly 11% below the average for the rest of the Greater Cincinnati area. A decade later, that gap had widened to almost 20%.

As Newport's population became poorer, its housing stock also declined. Fully 90% of the city's housing had been constructed before World War II, and according to regional planners, by 1970, 97% of it was in need of some kind of repair.

In the late 1970s, a newly elected city government took steps to make Newport more attractive, encouraging rehabilitation of older houses and commercial buildings and cracking down on the vice that remained. A decade later, the city and county started work on a new justice center near Sixth and Columbia Streets.

Fort Thomas did not face the same problems as Newport, but it too confronted change in the 1980s. In the immediate postwar era, Fort Thomas became a desirable suburb and grew to about 16,000. By the 1980s, a number of condominiums were built here over the protests of some residents who feared that the city's character would be lost if it were overdeveloped. Others saw new residential and commercial growth as a way to broaden the city's tax base and enable it to provide superior services to those who live here.

**Newport-Fort Thomas**

Tour Length
14.5

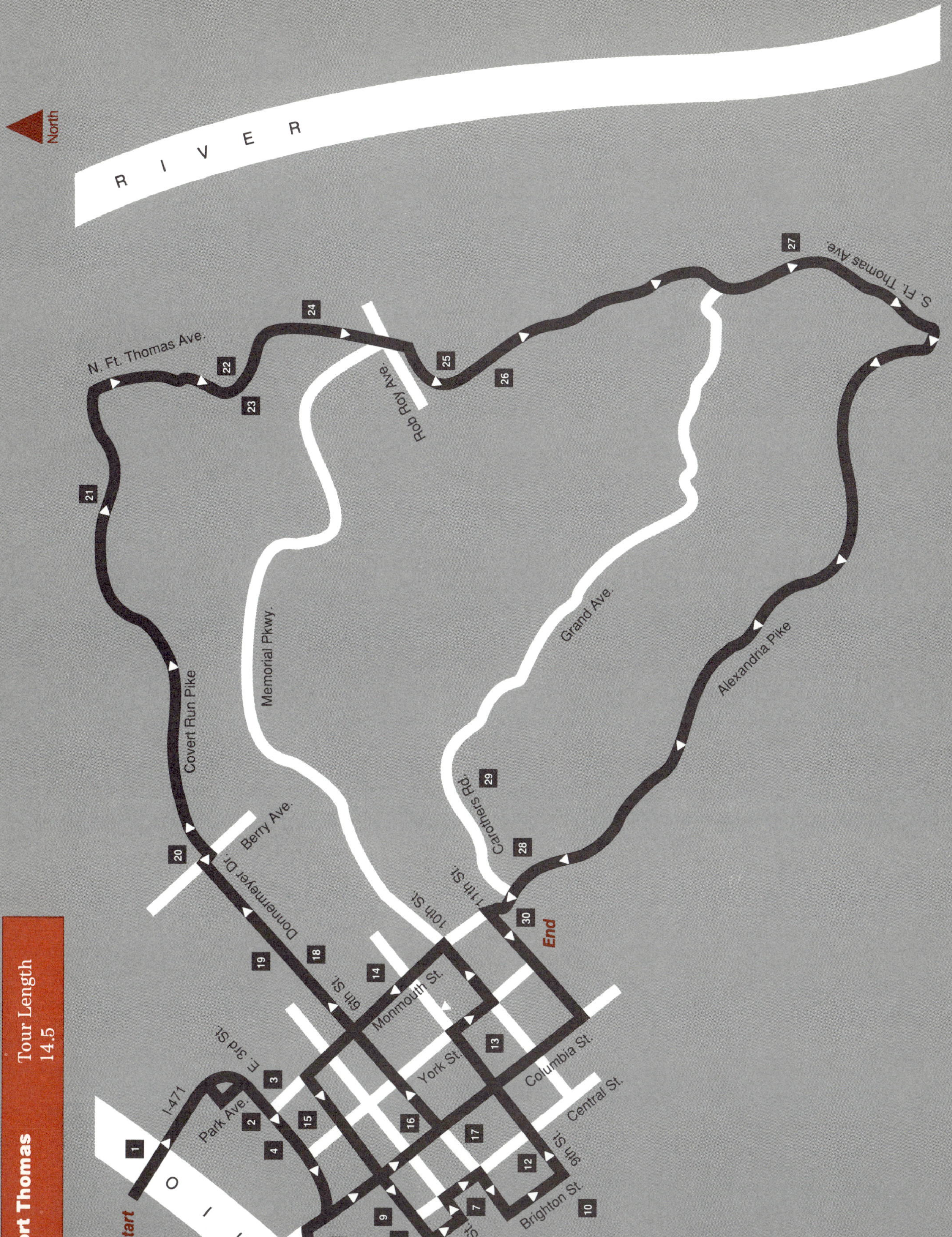

North
RIVER
OHIO
Start
End
I-471
Park Ave.
E. 3rd St.
Riverboat Row
4th St.
5th St.
6th St.
9th St.
10th St.
11th St.
Monmouth St.
York St.
Columbia St.
Central St.
Brighton St.
Donnermeyer Dr.
Berry Ave.
Covert Run Pike
Memorial Pkwy.
N. Ft. Thomas Ave.
Rob Roy Ave.
S. Ft. Thomas Ave.
Grand Ave.
Carothers Rd.
Alexandria Pike
1
2
3
4
5
6
7
8
9
10
11
12
13
14
15
16
17
18
19
20
21
22
23
24
25
26
27
28
29
30

# Tour 17

# Newport - Fort Thomas

▶ ▶ ▶ ▶ ▶ ▶

From Cincinnati, take I-471 south and get off at the first Newport exit. Continue straight on East Third Street.

Constructed in the mid-1970s, the **1 Daniel Carter Beard Bridge** provides easy access from Cincinnati to Newport and Fort Thomas and, along with I-275, has tied Northern Kentucky and Southwestern Ohio more closely together. The bridge is named after Beard (1850-1941), the sixth son of James H. Beard, a nationally known artist who painted portraits of Presidents John Quincy Adams, William Henry Harrison, and Zachary Taylor.

When Daniel Beard was eleven years old, his family moved to Covington and remained there until about 1872. In 1905, Beard founded an organization for boys that, recalling his Kentucky boyhood, he named the Sons of Daniel Boone. This was one of the groups that merged five years later to form the Boy Scouts of America.

The **2 Vonderharr-Stetter-Betz Funeral Home,** 335 East Third Street, was once the home of General James Taylor who built the Greek Revival style mansion, Bellevue, in the mid-1840s. His son, Colonel James Taylor, inherited the residence and left it to his son, Barney, who sold it in 1888. The new owners substantially altered the building and reoriented it to face south instead of north. Vonderharr & Stetter bought Bellevue in 1919 and converted it into a funeral home.

In the early 1880s, the Taylor estate was subdivided by Samuel Bigstaff for development of an upper-income neighborhood that was later known as **3 Mansion Hill.**

Between 1880 and 1915, many prominent businessmen and professionals built homes in the area. Cincinnati grocer Barney Kroger lived at 624 Monroe Street, and Thomas McIlvain, a boiler manufacturer, constructed the Queen Anne style house at 301 Overton Street in 1889. Clarence Davidson, a commission merchant and wholesale fruit dealer, erected the Shingle style building at 315 East Third Street about 1891. During these years, the area was so

fashionable that small 30' x 100' lots sold for as much as $8000.

As wealthy Newport residents continued to leave the city, many of the old homes were converted into apartments, transforming the once-stylish neighborhood into a working-class neighborhood. In the 1970s, young professionals began moving into Mansion Hill and restoring its houses. They formed the Mansion Hill Neighborhood Association in the late 1970s and had the area placed on the National Register of Historic Places in 1980.

The **4 Southgate House,** 24 East Third Street, was built between 1814 and 1821 by Richard Southgate (1776-1857), who settled in Newport in 1795. Southgate was appointed commonwealth attorney for Campbell County in 1798 and between 1803 and 1821, served in the Kentucky legislature. Southgate's grandson, William Southgate Shaler (1841-1906), a noted geologist and dean of the School of Natural Resources at Harvard University, lived here as a child. When Southgate died, his daughter, Frances Mary Taliaferro Parker, inherited the house.

In 1869, Parker deeded the house to her daughter Julia, whose son, John Taliaferro Thompson, invented the Thompson submachine gun. Either Julia or Fannie F. Maddux, who purchased the house in 1888, altered the building, adding a third-floor

*Floating restaurants have been an important part of riverfront development in Newport and other Northern Kentucky communities.*

ballroom and a 4-story entrance.

The Campbell County Knights of Columbus purchased the house in 1914 and added an auditorium and a brick front porch. The building was sold in 1976, and the following year, it became a nightclub.

At York Street, follow Third Street to the left. Turn right on Columbia Street, left on Riverboat Row.

After World War II, Newport took advantage of federal legislation to protect communities along the Ohio River and built a levee and floodwall. At the same time, the city redeveloped the bottoms near the Ohio and Licking Rivers.

Dedicated on October 6, 1974, the **5 General James Taylor Park,** at the west end of Riverboat Row, occupies part of the old Newport Barracks site. In 1803, James Taylor was commissioned to establish a United States Army fort. Taylor donated five acres for the project, and in 1804, he erected an arsenal, a magazine, and a barracks.

The Newport Barracks was used as a military prison during the War of 1812 and as a training center for volunteers during the Mexican War. It also served as the headquarters for the Southern District of the United States Army until the Civil War, when it became a recruiting depot for Union forces. When the army moved to Fort Thomas, the secretary of war transferred this land to the City of Newport

to serve as a public park.

Except for building the flood wall, the city did not use the land until it created Taylor Park. The 10-acre park features a monument marking the site of the Newport Barracks, a picnic area, and a river view.

**Turn around at the end of Riverboat Row and turn right on Columbia Street.**

The restaurants along **6 Riverboat Row** are part of Newport's riverfront redevelopment. In 1982, Newport planners completed the Newport Riverfront Development Plan, a project to capture some of the money spent on dining and entertainment in metropolitan Cincinnati.

The Islands, 301 Riverboat Row, opened in 1983, was floated to Louisville in 1987, and a new restaurant, the Newport Beach, opened in 1988. The Islands was followed by two more floating restaurants, Barleycorn's Yacht Club, 201 Riverboat Row, and Crockett's River Cafe, 1 Riverboat Row, which opened in 1985 and 1986, respectively. All three feature views of Cincinnati's skyline and docking facilities for customers who arrive by boat. Newport officials hope to locate four more restaurants on the river east of I-471.

**Turn right on Fourth Street. Past Isabella Street, bear left to return along Fifth Street.**

In 1950, the Housing Authority of Newport was formed, and over the course of the decade, it constructed three housing sites to replace the slums in the river bottoms. The **7 Peter G. Noll Homes,** 401 West Fifth Street, named after an early Housing Authority official, opened in 1953 with 283 units for whites. The **8 Booker T. Washington Homes,** 301 Isabella Street, with forty-two units for blacks, followed. The final project, the 50-unit **9 McDermott-McLane Homes,** 201 West Fourth Street, also named for local housing executives, opened in 1957. In 1963, Newport added the Grand Towers, a high-rise with 198 units for senior citizens. The Housing Authority of Newport also administers 432 pri-

vately owned scattered-site houses, the currently preferred form of subsidized housing.

Newport's public housing has experienced the problems common to high density housing for the poor. In addition, officials concede that the city government administered its housing in a lax manner, so that by the late 1970s, Newport was faced with a loss of federal funds.

Since then, the Housing Authority of Newport has sought to create a better environment by stepping up law enforcement and more carefully screening prospective tenants. In 1984, the Housing Authority began a 4-phase, $5 million plan to renovate all 375 units.

*The Andrews family acquired the Newport Iron & Steel Company in 1890 and, during the first half of the twentieth century, built it into one of the largest employers in the community.*

**Turn right on Central Street, right on Sixth Street, and left on Brighton Street.**

**10 Newport Steel,** Ninth and Lowell Streets, began in 1858 when Alexander Swift incorporated the Swift Iron & Steel Works, which produced armor plates and castings. In 1880, the company was sold to Edward L. Harper, a pig iron merchant

who also helped establish the Fidelity National Bank. Unsuccessful business ventures led to the closing of the bank and landed Harper in the Ohio penitentiary, his assets impounded by the courts, and the mill closed. In 1888, Henry A. Schriver, a local contractor, and Adam Wagner, a wagonmaker, purchased the company but held it only briefly. A year later, new owners incorporated it as the Newport Iron & Steel Company.

In 1890, the factory was sold to Joseph A. Andrews, owner of Globe Iron Roofing & Corrugating Company of Cincinnati, who used it to supply steel to his roofing business. The newly named Newport Rolling Mill expanded, and in 1908, Andrews estab-

lished the Andrews Steel Company. In 1919, the plant was the scene of a prolonged and violent labor strike that, many felt, damaged Newport as an industrial town.

By 1943, when the Andrews family sold its holdings to the Lehman Brothers brokerage firm of New York, the Andrews Steel Company controlled a small industrial empire consisting of Globe Iron Roofing, Newport Steel, and a coal company, and employed more than 3,000 workers. Over the next twenty years, Newport Steel changed hands several times, yet prospered, largely because of defense spending.

In December 1964, Newport was

acquired by the Interlake Iron Corporation. By the late 1970s, the plant began losing money; between 1976 and 1978, profits fell from $37.9 million to $10.8 million. In 1980, the company proposed a wage freeze to its labor unions. When plant workers refused, the company closed the plant, putting about 1,200 people out of work.

With private financing, support from the federal government, and aid from the cities of Wilder, Covington, Newport, and Dayton, a group of former Interlake executives bought the plant and reopened it in 1981 as the Newport Steel Corporation. The new owners streamlined the operation, reduced the size of the workforce, and concentrated on the production of steel pipe.

In 1908, when Joseph Andrews announced his decision to construct a steel plant he also proposed building a "hotel" for single workers and houses for those with families. The predominance of working-class housing in the area, as exemplified by the **11 Homes on Brighton Street,** indicates the extent to which Newport Steel shaped the neighborhood that surrounds it. The majority of these small, single-family dwellings were erected for steelworkers and their families in the late nineteenth and early twentieth centuries.

**Turn left on Ninth Street.**

**12 Corpus Christi Roman Catholic Church,** 844 Isabella Street, was built by the first Catholic parish in Campbell County. In May 1844, Henry Goodman, a non-Catholic from Cincinnati, donated a lot near Sixth and Chestnut Streets as the site for a Catholic church. That year, a small brick building was constructed to serve thirty families. In 1848, Corpus Christi Church rented a nearby building for a parish school and put up a schoolhouse next to the church the following year.

German immigration in the late 1840s swelled the congregation to more than a hundred families, prompting construction of a Gothic style church, completed in 1854 and added to in 1876. As the parish grew, so did the school. In 1863, the church erected a 3-story brick school with four classrooms and a meeting hall.

By the late 1880s, many parishioners began moving away from the flood-prone riverfront, and the church sought to follow them. The congregation purchased property at the northwest corner of Ninth and Isabella Streets in the 1890s, but financial difficulties delayed construction of a new sanctuary. The present church, a Spanish Mission style structure, was dedicated in 1903 and combined a church, school, and rectory under one roof.

Corpus Christi continued to grow through much of the twentieth century, and by 1960 recorded about 500 member families. By the mid-1980s, suburbanization reduced the congregation to about thirty-five families and school enrollments declined. When Newport's Catholic schools were consolidated, Corpus Christi Parochial School was closed. Since 1986, the parish has leased the school building to the Growing and Learning Child Care Center.

The **13 Ninth Street School,** Ninth and Columbia Streets, served Newport's elementary and secondary students from 1936, when it was built with WPA assistance, until 1959. It replaced an earlier school built in 1903 and designed by architects W. E. Bausmith and C. C. Weber.

As early as 1836, Newport purchased a single-room log cabin on Cabot Street to serve as a school. By 1841, the city's common schools, as they were called, enrolled sixty-four students. As Newport's population began to grow in the 1850s, the schools were made tuition-free. Enrollment climbed from 554 in 1850 and to 1,404 in 1858. In 1860, a high school was established and a Board of Education was created.

By 1900, Newport's eight schools enrolled more than 2,800 students. That number climbed to almost 4,000 by the mid-1930s when the Ninth Street School was built. Within a few years, however, Newport had too many schools, partly because annexations brought schools in Clifton and Cote Brillante into the city. In the 1950s, when other districts were scrambling to add new facilities, Newport's school population was less than it had been before World War II, and the Board of Education shut down several older schools.

After the Ninth Street School closed, it was used for Board of Education offices and as an annex for the old high school. The school was also used for a short time as a National Guard armory, but by the late 1980s, it stood empty.

**Turn right on York, left on Tenth Street, and left on Monmouth Street.**

Newport developed first as a river town, with its factories and shops clustered along the Ohio riverfront. But by 1860, as Newport grew southward, its commerce centered on its major north-south arteries, including Monmouth, Saratoga, and York Streets, and the **14 Monmouth Street Business District** was born.

By 1869, the Louisville, Cincinnati & Lexington Railroad ran along Saratoga Street with its depot at Madison (Fifth) Street. The railroad served the Dueber Watch Case factory and the gasworks built by J. C. Dueber to power his plant, as well as the working-class neighborhood on Saratoga and the more affluent areas to the east.

West of Saratoga was Monmouth Street. Through most of the nineteenth century, Monmouth was the city's primary link to the south, and businesses there relied on or served transportation. In 1871, all four of Newport's wagonmakers were on Monmouth, as were most of the city's flour and feed stores.

To the west, York Street marked the eastern boundary of courthouse square. Here were Newport's lawyers, insurance agents and real estate brokers, while the city's retail commerce was divided between York and Monmouth Streets.

In the late 1880s, two of Newport's major business institutions began on Monmouth, shaping the street's character for years to come. In 1886, H. Eilerman opened a clothing store at 810 Monmouth, and two years later, Louis Marx opened a furniture store just a few doors north at 840. The success of these two businesses, both of which later expanded to Covington, contributed to the emergence of Monmouth as Newport's primary shopping street.

Even after the automobile began to change patterns of commerce, Monmouth Street, with its connections to newly developing suburbs such as Fort Thomas, Highland Heights, and Southgate, remained central. In the 1920s, both Woolworth's and Kresge's, the two major chains in Newport, located their stores on Monmouth. At the same time, fifteen of Newport's twenty-seven building and loan societies were located on Monmouth rather than on York Street, where most of the city's banks were located.

During Prohibition, the street gained a new reputation when Peter Schmidt, an associate of Cincinnati bootlegger George Remus, opened the Glenn Hotel, 928 Monmouth Street. In the late 1930s, mobsters from Chicago came to Newport and set up new casinos alongside the old. But despite the Depression and the presence of gambling, Monmouth Street supported the same local businesses that had characterized the street for half a century.

After World War II, the "Cleveland Syndicate" moved in, taking over local vice operations, and by the early 1950s, gangland activity appeared to have taken a toll on Monmouth Street. Although the street continued to house legitimate businesses, the district also had numerous vacant buildings and several marginal, low-profit discount outlets that relied on low rents to survive.

Reformers drove the mob from Newport in 1961, but that did not halt the transformation of Monmouth Street from a prosperous business district to an area of bars and marginal shops. Like other older business districts throughout Greater Cincinnati, this area gradually lost business to new shopping centers and malls.

**Turn left on Fourth Street.**

Hoping to see Newport become the county seat, the town's proprietor, James Taylor, deeded lots 79 to 84 to the city's trustees in 1795. Today, that public square is the site of the **15 Campbell County Courthouse and Newport City Building,** 24 West Fourth Street.

The first county courthouse was erected in 1797 and was replaced by another wooden building in 1805. Newport's first brick courthouse was constructed in 1815, a plain 2-story structure topped with a spire and a bell. After the county seat moved to

Alexandria in 1840, the building was used for city offices and as a circuit court.

The present courthouse was designed by A. C. Nash, a Cincinnati architect, and was completed in 1884. In 1911 and 1912, annexes for additional city offices were added onto the north and south sides of the courthouse. Another city building, housing police headquarters and a jail, was subsequently added behind the courthouse. With the municipal building here and the fire station across Fifth Street, this block is Newport's civic center.

The courthouse has also made the intersection of Fourth and York Streets a focus for Newport business and banking. Across from the courthouse are the Newport Finance Building built in 1927, and the Journal Building constructed in 1885 as the offices and printing plant of the *Kentucky State Journal.* It was later used by the German National Bank.

**Turn left on Columbia Street.**

*The Wiedemann brewery stables, built in the late nineteenth century and demolished in 1988, were embellished with sculptures of the company emblem and horses' heads.*

In 1870, John Butcher and George Wiedemann established the Jefferson Street Brewery. Eight years later, Wiedemann bought out his partner and established the **16 Wiedemann Brewing Company,** Sixth and Columbia Streets. By 1882, when he took over Peter Constans' brewing company, Wiedemann had become Northern Kentucky's largest brewer. In 1898, Wiedemann built a new modified Romanesque style office and bottle house.

During World War I, the federal government shut down brewers and distillers in order to conserve grain. After the war, Prohibition kept most brewers closed, but Wiedemann stayed open, producing denatured industrial alcohol, but in 1928, the company was charged with producing more than 1.5 million gallons of illegal beer. Wiedemann was found guilty of twenty-three violations of the Volstead Act, and Carl Wiedemann, grandson of the founder, was sentenced to four years in jail.

After the repeal of Prohibition, other family members reopened the brewery and spent $1 million to modernize the plant. By 1957, Wiedemann was producing one million bottles per year. In 1967, one of the nation's brewing giants, the G. Heilemann Company, bought Wiedemann.

For several years, Heilemann continued to brew here, then used the plant as a warehouse, and finally closed it in 1983.

The buildings stood empty until 1988, when all but the offices and bottle house were demolished. The fate of the remaining structure is unclear. Its current owners want to develop it as offices and retail space.

Part of the old Wiedemann site west of Sixth and Columbia Streets was redeveloped as a new **17 Campbell County Justice Center**. Construction began in late 1988, and the completed complex included a new county jail, several courthouses and related offices. City and county officials hope that the center will attract new business to downtown Newport.

**Turn left on Sixth Street.**

Most **18 East Newport Housing** was built between the 1870s and the 1920s. The area has a wide variety of houses, from the mansions of the wealthy, to modest detached homes for middle-income families and densely built rows of workers' houses. East Newport retains its nineteenth century residential character and includes several corner groceries and neighborhood churches. Most of its single-family homes are owner-occupied, and only a few larger ones have been subdivided for rental.

The Hannaford Apartments, 803 East Sixth Street, occupies the building that was originally the **19 Academy of Notre Dame de la Providence**.

The school traces its origins to the Academy and Novitiate of Mount St. Martin's, which was established at Grand and Monmouth Avenues in 1889. In 1901, the Sisters of Divine Providence purchased thirty-six town lots on Oak and Linden Streets between Sixth Street and Nelson Place, and hired Cincinnati architect Samuel Hannaford, who designed the school building in the Second Empire style.

The school was dedicated in 1903 and opened with a coeducational primary school, which closed in 1934, and a girls' high school, which became the central Catholic girls' high school for Campbell County in 1929. By the late 1970s, the school was operating at a deficit, and a few years later, diocesan officials decided to merge it with Newport Catholic High School.

In 1984, a group of Cincinnati investors purchased the school from the Sisters of Divine Providence for $425,000. Over the next two years, they spent slightly more than $3.5 million to redesign the interior, although original architectural features were retained wherever possible, as were portions of the Italian terrazzo floors. The old hardware, leaded glass windows, and woodwork were preserved and reinstalled.

The Hannaford Apartments offers luxury housing in an historic setting close to downtown Cincinnati.

**Continue along Sixth Street, which becomes Donnermeyer Drive in Bellevue.**

In the late 1960s, **20 Bellevue Plaza,** along Donnermeyer Drive, developed from five shops to a modest commercial strip. By the mid-1980s, it had more than twenty businesses ranging from a Kroger store, used by residents of the neighborhood and those who lived in downtown Cincinnati, to a bank, several restaurants and fast food outlets, and gas stations. While not quite a neighborhood business district, many of these shops serve those who live in south Bellevue and Dayton as well as those who pass through.

**Turn right on Berry Avenue, left on Covert Run Pike.**

In the late nineteenth century when the Highlands first opened, the district's main connection to Newport was via the **21 Covert Run Turnpike.** Today, those coming to Fort Thomas from Newport can use not only this scenic, semi-rural route, but also Memorial Parkway, Alexandria Pike, Dayton Pike, or Grand Avenue.

There have long been a few modest houses along the western part of Covert Run Pike in Bellevue. The northeastern sector of the pike closer to Fort Thomas has been built up since the late 1960s.

**Turn right on North Fort Thomas Avenue.**

Founded in 1930, **22 St. Catherine of Siena** Roman Catholic parish reflects Fort Thomas's early growth. The community's first congregation was Highland Methodist founded a century before. Not until after the turn of the century, from 1902 to 1915, were Baptist, Catholic, Episcopal, and Evangelical churches established here. Another wave of church building occurred in the 1920s and 1930s, and St. Catherine's, Fort Thomas' second Roman Catholic parish, was part of this.

The parish began with sixty families. In 1931, the congregation bought and constructed a single-story frame church, using a pre-cut kit ordered from the Sears, Roebuck catalog for $2,000. In 1964, St. Catherine's dedicated a new church, designed by the Covington architectural firm of Carl C. Bankemper & Associates.

St. Catherine's built a school in 1949 and added a second story in 1957. By the mid-1960s, enrollments exceeded 350, but a decade later, the school had only 165 pupils. For the 1987-1988 school year, there were 190 students. The school building includes eight regular classrooms, a library, a computer room, a faculty room, and a resource room.

As the community's major thoroughfare, Fort Thomas Avenue includes a cross section of **23 Fort Thomas Housing**.

At 2103 North Fort Thomas Avenue is one of the community's oldest houses (although the exterior has been completely modernized). It was built sometime around 1845 and later occupied by members of the Southgate family, who had a number of homes along the street. The Colonial style house at 1938 is also reported to have been built before the Civil War. The oldest house on the street, 1810 North Fort Thomas Avenue, is the Taliaferro House. It was begun in 1830 by William R. T. Taliaferro, the first permanent white resident here, and has remained in family hands.

Along the street are several large Victorian houses built around the turn of the century when Fort Thomas became a resort and fashionable residential community. They include the house with a large cornice and quarter-round windows at the corner of North Fort Thomas Avenue and Donnelly Drive; 1620, with a small columned porch surmounted by a balcony; the buff brick house with a large front porch at 1306, and 1230, with a 2-story pillared porch and balcony.

Fort Thomas' first school was started in 1832 near the present-day intersection of Holly and North Fort Thomas Avenues. Forty years later, the District of Highlands formed its own school district, which built three schools in the 1890s, including the Inverness or Mount Pleasant School. When that school was declared unsafe in 1916, the school board decided to build another school for the northern part of the city. In 1923, the **24 Robert D. Johnson School,** Cliffview and North Fort Thomas Avenues, opened with about 150 students. It was named for the school board chairman's brother, who died in World War I.

The growth of the community made additions necessary in 1927 and 1949. The school's enrollments grew from 240 in 1951 to almost 450 in 1967, and stood at 430 in the late 1980s.

The Samuel Woodfill School, Alexandria Pike and South Fort Thomas Avenue, was built on the same plan and named after another World War I hero.

At Rob Roy Avenue, bear right, then immediately turn left on Memorial Parkway.

Fort Thomas' high school began in 1886 and graduated its first class of four in 1891. In 1913, voters approved a $27,500 bond issue to build a new high school. Two years later, **25 Highlands Middle/High School,** 2400 Memorial Parkway, opened with ninety-three students.

The school was enlarged in 1927, 1937, 1955 when a new gym was built, 1960, and 1963 when twenty-five classrooms were added to replace the original school building that had burned down the year before.

Enrollments increased from nearly 450 in 1950 to 962 in 1965. After decreases in the late 1970s and early 1980s, enrollments stood at 989 for the 1987-1988 school year.

In recent years, despite tensions between teachers and administrators, and from salaries that are low compared to other school districts in the metropolitan area, Fort Thomas schools have retained a fine reputation.

Continue on Memorial Parkway, which becomes North Fort Thomas Avenue.

The blocks of North and South Fort Thomas Avenue between Forest Avenue and Chalfonte Place make up the **26 Fort Thomas Business District,** which is home to a variety of neighborhood businesses. Included are two pharmacies, a florist, a jeweler, a number of dentists and physicians, several attorneys, two banks, and three building and loan associations. The district also has a few enterprises that serve a wider area, such as a printer, an educational toy and book store, and various offices. The city building is also here, as are the Fort Thomas Woman's Club, the Masonic Hall, a branch library, and two churches, Christ Church, and St. Andrew's Episcopal.

Despite its vitality, the Fort Thomas business district has suffered from the competition of regional shopping centers. Stegner's Grocery is gone, as is the Kroger store and the A&P. Several local dry goods and department stores have also closed.

Nevertheless, Fort Thomas' business district is larger in the 1980s than in the 1930s. This success is partly due to the prosperous and closely-knit community as well as a conscious effort on the part of the city to maintain the area. In the past twenty years, a new city building, several bank buildings, and a new office building have been constructed here, and the Hiland movie theater has been converted to stores and offices.

Continue on South Fort Thomas Avenue, turning left at the intersection with Grand Avenue.

Although the Fort Thomas military post was turned over the Veterans Administration on October 1, 1946, the **27 VA Nursing Home and Tower Park,** with its officers' housing, armory/drill hall, and mess hall, stand as reminders of the years when the base and town of Fort Thomas were closely linked.

The fort was established in August 1887. It was designed by government architects in the Richardson Romanesque style with elements of Eastlake and Queen Anne styles. The first structure, completed in 1888, was the commanding officer's residence. The first commander was Colonel Melville A. Cochran who moved here from the Newport Barracks. Cochran, who loved horticulture, is widely credited for the parklike atmosphere of the base.

Over the next five years, a water tower, two dozen officers' houses, four barracks for enlisted men, a mess hall, and various support buildings were constructed. The mess hall, built in 1891, was placed on national and state historic registers in 1980 and was renovated in 1988.

Completed in 1892, the water tower, one hundred feet high and holding 100,000 gallons, became a symbol of not only the fort, but the city. Like much of the base, it was constructed by Newport builder Henry A. Schriver.

The base was home to the 6th Infantry when war with Spain broke out in 1898 and the regiment was sent to Cuba. The water tower was dedicated to the twenty-eight officers and enlisted men who died in that war. A bronze tablet designed by Cincinnati sculptor Clement Barnhorn honors them, as do the two "trophy" guns— eighteenth-century Spanish cannon— at the base of the tower.

During the Spanish-American War, the base served as a muster point and convalescent hospital. Built to house only two battalions, the fort was almost abandoned when infantry regiments later grew to three battalions, but political pressure kept it open.

The fort processed approximately 75,000 recruits during World War I. With the return of peace, it once more became a social focus for the community, as it had been since its opening. In 1924, Captain M. A. Gillis described the fort as "a show place to tourists."

With the threat of war in 1940, the 10th Infantry left Fort Thomas, and the WPA renovated it. In 1941, thirteen temporary structures were put up, and during World War II, Fort

Thomas processed 5,000 inductees per day until 1944, when it became an Army Air Force rehabilitation center.

The first Veterans Administration patients arrived in 1947. A decade later, the hospital here was consolidated with the Cincinnati Veterans Hospital. In 1967, the facility was converted to a 206-bed nursing home.

In 1972, the Defense Department parceled out the land on which the army post earlier stood. Eighty-seven acres including the water tower, the

**ter,** Monmouth Street and Parkview Avenue, opened in 1955 after a Cleveland developer decided that Campbell County, then enjoying unprecedented suburban growth, needed a regional shopping center. A decade later, a second center, **29** **Newport Plaza,** Carothers Road and Grand Avenue, was constructed despite opposition from downtown merchants who blamed the first center for declining business. In the 1980s, the same developers erected a K-Mart store, 1301 Monmouth Street, on the site of

to cross the river into Cincinnati with its milk products and Niser brand ice cream, which it acquired in 1968.

By the late 1980s, Trauth Dairy served a 250-mile area around Cincinnati and enjoyed annual growth rates ranging from 10% to 15%. By then, it was one of only three independent dairies in the area and the only one offering a full line of locally made products. In 1985, the dairy spent $4 million to expand its plant and two years later, built new office facilities.

> *Tour ends. Turn right on Columbia Street, right on Second Street, right on York Street, left on Third Street, and left on Park Avenue to return to I-471.*

*Thirty-two of the buildings that housed officers stationed at Fort Thomas have survived and are now owned by the city and the Veterans' Administration.*

mess hall, and the drill hall went to the City of Fort Thomas to become Tower Park. The park includes seventeen houses belonging to the city and another fifteen owned by Veteran's Administration.

Located near the base is Fort Thomas' oldest business district, once called the Midway. It developed first to serve the army post and then the local needs of residents of south Fort Thomas.

> *Turn right at Alexandria Pike, which becomes Monmouth Street.*

**28** **Newport Shopping Cen-**

the Jones Mansion, which had become the Convent of Mount St. Martin in 1889. The convent was established for the Sisters of Divine Providence, who that year began a girls' academy, later Newport's Academy of Notre Dame.

> *Turn left on Eleventh Street.*

**30** **Louis Trauth Dairy, Inc.,** 56 East Eleventh Street, was founded in 1920 in the old house, now considerably expanded, where it remains.

At the time of its founding, Trauth was one of many dairies in the area, most of which delivered to their customers' homes. But the growth of supermarkets changed the dairy business, and direct retailing became a shrinking segment of the market.

In 1972, Trauth Dairy decided to emphasize its wholesale business and